Torkildsen's Sport and Leisure Management

For nearly 40 years, *Torkildsen's Sport and Leisure Management* has been the most comprehensive and engaging introduction to sport and leisure management available to students at all levels. Now in its seventh edition, it is still the only textbook that covers all the key topics taught within contemporary sport and leisure management courses.

This new edition includes expanded coverage of the practical managerial skills that students must develop if aiming for a career in the sport and leisure industry, from planning and managing people to marketing, entrepreneurship, and the law. It includes four completely new chapters on the global sport and leisure economy, historical development, cross-sector collaboration, and management consultancy, reflecting important developments in contemporary sport and leisure. This edition retains the hallmark strengths of previous editions, including in-depth discussion of the social and cultural context of sport and leisure; full analysis of the public, private, and voluntary sectors; and a review of key products and services. Richly illustrated throughout with up-to-date evidence, data, case-studies, and international examples, each chapter also contains a range of useful pedagogical features, such as discussion questions, practical tasks, and structured guides to further reading and resources.

This is an important resource for students working in fields such as sport management, sport business, sport development, leisure management, and events management.

Dedicated online resources offer additional teaching and learning material for students and lecturers.

Rob Wilson is Head of Department in Sheffield Business School's Department of Finance, Accounting, and Business Systems and a member of the Social and Economic Research Institute at Sheffield Hallam University, UK, specialising in the finance and economics of the sport business industry.

Chris Platts is a Senior Lecturer in sport based in the Academy of Sport and Physical Activity at Sheffield Hallam University, UK. He undertook a PhD that explored the education and welfare provisions on offer for young professional footballers who sign as scholars between the ages of 16 and 18.

Daniel Plumley is Principal Lecturer in the Department of Finance, Accounting, and Business Systems in the Sheffield Business School at Sheffield Hallam University, UK. His subject specialism is the finance of sport and leisure.

Torkildsen's Sport and Leisure Management

7th edition

Edited by Rob Wilson, Chris Platts
and Daniel Plumley

Routledge
Taylor & Francis Group

LONDON AND NEW YORK

Cover image: Mary Ann Kulla Owaki

Seventh edition published 2023
by Routledge
4 Park Square, Milton Park, Abingdon, Oxon, OX14 4RN

and by Routledge
605 Third Avenue, New York, NY 10158

Routledge is an imprint of the Taylor & Francis Group, an informa business

First edition published as *Leisure and Recreation Management* by Spon Press 1983
Sixth edition published by Routledge 2011

British Library Cataloguing-in-Publication Data
A catalogue record for this book is available from the British Library

Library of Congress Cataloging-in-Publication Data
Names: Torkildsen, George, Leisure and recreation management. | Wilson, Robert,
   1980– editor. | Platts, Chris, editor. | Plumley, Daniel, editor.
Title: Torkildsen's sport and leisure management / Edited by Rob Wilson, Chris Platts, and
   Daniel Plumley.
Identifiers: LCCN 2022016796 | ISBN 9780367421540 (hardback) | ISBN 9780367423339
   (paperback) | ISBN 9780367823610 (ebook)
Subjects: LCSH: Leisure. | Leisure—Management. | Recreation. | Recreation—Management.
Classification: LCC GV181.5 .T67 2022 | DDC 790.1—dc23/eng/20220422
LC record available at https://lccn.loc.gov/2022016796

ISBN: 978-0-367-42154-0 (hbk)
ISBN: 978-0-367-42333-9 (pbk)
ISBN: 978-0-367-82361-0 (ebk)

DOI: 10.4324/9780367823610

Typeset in Sabon and Frutiger
by Apex CoVantage, LLC

Access the Support Material: www.routledge.com/9780367423339

Contents

Contents

Contents

Contents

Contents

Contents

List of Figures

List of Figures

List of Tables

List of Case Studies

List of Case Studies

Contributors

Rob Bailey is Senior Lecturer in Sport Business Management at Sheffield Hallam University, UK. He is also an active management consultant, and limited company director within the sport and leisure industry.

Matt Beecham is Senior Lecturer in Law and co-programme Leader for Law and Criminology at UWE Bristol, UK. His research interests concern negligence in sport, particularly the duty of care owed by sporting governing bodies towards athletes.

Mathieu Marlier is Associate Professor teaching at LUNEX, the International University of Health, Exercise, and Sports, Luxembourg. His research expertise is cross-sector collaborations in Vital Cities and Social Innovation through sport.

Guy Masterman is a former international racquetball player and has worked in the sports and events industries for over 45 years. He has worked with several UK universities, New York University, Shanghai University of Sport, and the Russian International Olympic University.

Girish Ramchandani is Associate Professor at the Sport Industry Research Centre at Sheffield Hallam University, UK. He is an expert in the economics of sport and leisure and provides research commentary in competitive integrity and home advantage.

Darryl Wilson is Principal Lecturer in the Academy of Sport and Physical Activity at Sheffield Hallam University, UK. His expertise extends to the supply and demand of sport products and services and home advantage in major sport events.

Chris Wolsey is Principal Lecturer within the Carnegie School of Sport at Leeds Beckett University, UK. He has held several senior leadership and management positions within the university, and he specialises in sport business management, with particular reference to issues pertaining to human resource development.

Preface

When George Torkildsen died in 2005, he left a massive hole in the leisure management profession. He was one of the founding fathers of this profession in the UK, and his achievements stretched across facility management, consultancy, service for *World Leisure*, professional presentations, and writing. It is for the last of these that he is perhaps most well-known to countless students wanting an authoritative overview of leisure, leisure industries, and leisure management. The legacy George left is typified by the fifth edition of this book, his last edition, which has remained one of the best-known texts in leisure management. This text was revamped by Professor Peter Taylor in the sixth edition, which formed the platform for this seventh edition. In this latest edition, the legacy of George Torkildsen remains intact, and the historical context of the leisure management profession that George was front and centre of is retained.

Nevertheless, sport and leisure is a dynamic field, and it was necessary in planning this new edition to tread a careful line between preserving the 'essence of George' whilst developing the text to fit the changing sport and leisure scene, a process initiated by Professor Peter Taylor in the sixth edition. The fundamental principles on which to plan and manage sport and leisure are consolidated and expanded in this edition. Although sport and leisure management is interdisciplinary, to structure this seventh edition clearly it retains the same constituent parts as before:

1 Setting the scene with definitions and trends;
2 Reviewing the three major sectors supplying and influencing leisure – commercial, government, and the 'third sector';
3 Examining the major sport and leisure products and services provided;
4 Analysing separately the important management disciplines that coalesce in sport and leisure management.

In this seventh edition titled *Torkilden's Sport and Leisure Management*, we have retained leisure as a binding concept, as it is clear that a major interest of many students and readers of this book in the past has been sport and physical activity. However, whilst leisure remains a focus, sport now moves to become the primary focus of this book. Moreover, we sharpen the focus of this book to be more 'applied management' in nature by:

- Removing much of the content on play and recreation material that were retained in the sixth edition;
- Adding four new chapters on the value of global economies, the rise of management consulting and the importance of collaborating between the traditional sectors of the sport and leisure market;
- Making major revisions to most of the remaining chapters and bringing them up-to-date.

The concept of leisure has been retained from the sixth edition with an updated chapter on leisure in the home, which enables us to signify the importance of modern technologies and connectivity for sport and leisure consumption online.

More international examples have been added to illustrate the globalisation of the sport and leisure industry. And whilst a UK focus is important for UK readers and it provides a coherent core relating to one country, most of the principles in this book are not confined to the UK but extend to other countries, particularly more developed countries. Also, more evidence has been included because knowledge of what the sport and leisure industries consist of is important and because evidence brings principles to life.

The market for this book remains the same – anyone who wants a thorough introduction to the dimensions of sport and leisure markets and industries, and to key disciplines and principles of managing sport and leisure. In the main, this may well mean first year undergraduates in a range of subjects, including not just sport and leisure management but also sports and leisure studies, sports sciences, human movement, physical education, and more generic business and management studies. However, this book will also be useful to sub-degree students and postgraduates first acquainting themselves with the study of sport and leisure management and also to those already in the sport and leisure industries who are looking to develop their knowledge and skills.

Several pedagogical features have been retained and developed in this new edition of this book:

- Chapter summaries provided at the beginning of each chapter;
- Applied case studies included throughout this book;
- Discussion questions embedded at appropriate points throughout the text;
- Practical tasks which will help readers to understand key points;
- Web references for most chapters;
- A comprehensive list of documentary references for each chapter.

It has been an honour and a privilege to bring this seminal text up to date with an editorial team operating at the sharp end of the sport and leisure management market. According to the original agreement, this book should have been completed at the start of 2020, but the onset of the global Coronavirus pandemic provided a unique opportunity to understand the impact that such an event could have on the sport and leisure industry.

The 'Torkildsen Baton' was handed to Professor Peter Taylor for the 6th edition, an architect himself of modern sport management and a mentor to many scholars, including us, working in the field. Peter added to the legacy of George and enabled this seminal text to survive, and thrive, in a market littered with alternative publications. As Peter did before, we can only hope that we have done this book justice, preserving the legacy of these two giants of our field.

The experience of writing this book has been a challenge and, in many ways, a marathon but, more than anything else, a thoroughly rewarding project. We hope you enjoy this book as much as we enjoyed putting it together.

Rob Wilson, Chris Platts, and Dan Plumley
Sheffield Hallam University, UK

Acknowledgements

The task of rewriting such a comprehensive text would not have been possible without several people with specialist knowledge who agreed to take charge of rewriting specific chapters. These contributing authors have done a tremendous job and have been very patient in dealing with suggestions to ensure that their contributions fit the style and purpose of this book. They are:

- Mathieu Marlier, LUNEX International University of Health, Exercise, and Sports, for Chapter 8: 'Cross Sector Collaboration'.
- Girish Ramchandani and Darryl Wilson, Sheffield Hallam University, for Chapter 12: 'Global Economics of Sport and Leisure'.
- Chris Wolsey, Leeds Beckett University, for Chapter 13: 'Managing People in Sport and Leisure'.
- Matt Beecham, University of the West of England, for Chapter 19: 'Law and Leisure Management'.
- Guy Masterman, Russian International Olympic University, for Chapter 20: 'The Importance and Management of Events'.
- Rob Bailey, Sheffield Hallam University, for Chapter 21: 'Management Consulting in the Sport and Leisure Industry'.

Part I

Introducing Sport and Leisure Management

Contents

Chapter 1

Introduction to Sport and Leisure

In This Chapter

- What is the purpose and structure of this book?
- How is management defined, and what is the role of management in sport and leisure?
- How are sport and leisure defined?
- What is George Torkildsen's 'pleisure' principle?

DOI: 10.4324/9780367823610-1

Summary

This chapter sets the scene for the management of sport, leisure, and physical activity by exploring some of the dimensions and meanings of key terms, particularly *sport, leisure,* and *management.* Sport and leisure is big business, particularly in more developed countries. An agreed definition of the subject of this business is, however, elusive – sport and leisure mean different things to different people. Definitions of sport are sometimes confined to competitive sports but are more often wider and include a range of non-competitive physical activities. Definitions of leisure include leisure as time, as activities, and as a state of being. Definitions of management have evolved in line with different theories of management. A clear understanding of these basic concepts provides leisure managers with a clearer focus on their customers and their decision-making.

This chapter also explains how this book is structured and what its underpinning themes are. Part I reviews basic concepts and evidence about the sport and leisure business and how it is changing. Part II examines the main sport and leisure providers, arranged in three sectors: public, private (commercial), and the third sector, which is non-profit (voluntary). Part II also covers cross-sector collaborations and the global economics of sport and leisure in an ever-changing world. Finally, the largest part of this book (Part III) is devoted to different management disciplines, including human resource management, marketing, finance, quality management, enterprise, law, events, and consulting.

Today we have more knowledge, more resources, and more opportunity than before, with which to have a fullness of living undreamed of in times past. Leisure has an increasingly important role to play in modern lifestyles, but the question is: Has leisure achieved its potential in a fulfilling way of life? The extent to which it hasn't is a fundamental reason for improving leisure management. At the heart of sport and leisure management is a concern to provide and manage opportunities for people to get the most out of their sport and leisure experiences, however these are defined.

1.1 Introduction

By taking an interest in leisure management, you are stepping away from your individual leisure consumer's focus on having a good time and beginning to take other people's leisure as a professional interest. Although leisure is enjoyable, it is also a serious business which requires knowledge, analysis, skills, and perceptive decision-making to make it work successfully. Just because it is leisure doesn't mean we can take it for granted or relegate it to an unimportant part of society (Deloitte, 2021). As Auger (2020) notes: 'Leisure is an important part of everyday life. It plays an important role in the health, well-being, and quality of life of individuals and communities' (p. 127). Leisure is also multi-faceted. The health benefits are clear, but it is also an important yardstick for economic prosperity, particularly through service industries. There are, of course, many other important aspects, and this is one of the main reasons for a book like this one.

This book is part of a continuing process, which is now several decades old, of educating students in sport and leisure and its management. Before this process began, managers in sport and leisure were often selected for superficial reasons that were not closely related to their abilities as managers – for example sports managers, because they used to be good at sport, or museum managers, because they were educated in history. However, the modern-day sport and leisure organisation needs managers with not just knowledge of their branch of leisure but also a multitude of applied management skills, including quality management, human resources management, finance, law, and marketing. This book is an introduction to such knowledge and skills.

One reason the management of sport and leisure, and its education, is now taken seriously is because leisure is a large and growing set of industries, particularly in more developed economies. It involves professional management not only in the commercial sector but also by government at the central and local level and in many private, non-profit organisations. A symptom of leisure's importance is spending by consumers. In 2020, the world was rocked by a global health pandemic (COVID-19), and many leisure activities were shut down as social distancing became the norm. However, in 2021, and thanks to effective vaccine roll-outs in some countries, the world of leisure was back in a more positive place. Indeed, analysis for the UK from Deliotte in 2021 cited that there were high levels of pent-up demand (following lockdown periods) and that this boded well for a recovery in the leisure sector. Their data suggested that intentions to spend on eating out at the back end of 2021 had seen a 50 percentage-point jump in Q1 2021 compared to Q4 2020 and a 90 percentage-point increase compared to the same period in the previous year. Large increases were also seen in drinking out in cafés and pubs. Leisure activities, such as attending cultural events and going to the gym, also saw net spending climb. All of these areas highlight the importance of leisure aspects to people in everyday life as noted by Auger (2020) earlier in this chapter.

At the time of writing, as the world is emerging tentatively from the pandemic and economic recession, leisure spending has not disappeared, but as with other forms of spending it has suffered either reduced growth or even reduced levels of economic activity for a while. However, when 'normal service is resumed' in terms of economic growth – and in the long term the trend is for economic growth – leisure industries will continue to play a leading role. In more developed economies, any rise in income is typically spent disproportionately on leisure. This is because after people have attended to the basic needs for housing, food, and transport, leisure provides an endless opportunity for increased enjoyment and fulfilment.

Leisure is not a trivial luxury but an essential part of people's lifestyles. Benjamin Disraeli, a nineteenth-century British prime minister, believed that increased means and increased leisure are the two civilisers of man. Bertrand Russell (1935), English pacifist, philosopher, and mathematician, believed that to be able to fill leisure intelligently is the best product of civilisation. Today, people of all ages demand choice and have higher expectations for healthier lifestyles, quality services, more facilities, and better customer service and management. This applies as much to leisure industries as to any other because leisure is an expression of people's free-time preferences. By taking an interest in how to manage leisure, you are taking an interest in an increasingly important set of activities and industries.

Another reason for taking leisure management seriously in education is that it is complex. It involves two interdisciplinary concepts – leisure and management. Management covers a range of disciplines and skills which are required to run organisations effectively and efficiently. Leisure is a subject that has been analysed by economists, sociologists, geographers, political scientists, philosophers, and management scientists, to name just a few. The management of sport and leisure embraces:

- Planning the products, services, facilities, and other infrastructure that combine to give people leisure;
- Managing the available resources to produce high-quality services;
- Monitoring and improving the resulting outcomes in the form of participation in and enjoyment of leisure activities;

and it stretches to:

- Contributing to possible impacts of sport and leisure on people's health, quality of life, and sense of community.

Therefore, to understand leisure management requires a substantial breadth of considerations.

> ## Discussion Question
>
> If you were studying sport and leisure management and a fellow student who is studying a more traditional subject (e.g. history, maths, or engineering) accused you of studying a 'Mickey Mouse' subject, how would you reply?

Leisure can be perceived in many contexts: individual, community, regional, national, and international. Its delivery is both local and global. Global conditions have a considerable influence on leisure. The world economic climate, for example, has an impact on individuals and nations alike – the 'credit crunch' of 2008–2009 is a stark reminder of this. Environmental issues are arguably a more long-term danger, and they particularly impact on travel and tourism. The terrorist tragedy inflicted on the United States of America on 11 September 2001 continues to have profound effects not only in the military, political, and economic arenas but also on our ways of life, including leisure. The clashes of ideologies of the first half of the twentieth century have been replaced by clashes of cultures in the early twenty-first century which are expressed in both global and local decision-making. In addition to global considerations and contexts, however, it is important to identify the demands of local people in designing and delivering appropriate sport and leisure services. One size does not fit all!

1.2 Why Manage Leisure?

Is there a need to manage people's leisure? Nature provides us, in the natural environment, with abundant resources for leisure and recreation. One could argue that there is no need for expensive additional facilities, services, programmes, and management. Nature has provided fields, woods, rivers, beaches, and sunshine. We have the challenge of the mountains, winter snow, the seas, and the sky. There is beauty to behold, solitude in the country, and peace away from the crowds.

Yet even in natural environments, management of sport and leisure is very important. Access to natural amenities is necessary for a range of sport and leisure visitors – e.g. surfers, hang-gliders, horse riders, walkers, birdwatchers, and sightseers – and this access needs to be provided and maintained in a way that facilitates visiting but without spoiling the attraction. The visitors will want ancillary services such as food and drink and accommodation. The sport and leisure activities of visitors may need to be controlled in the light of environmental issues in specific areas or conflicts between different users. All such functions require planning and managing.

The demand for man-made resources for sport and leisure is greater now than it has ever been because people often have more time and money for leisure and there is a wider choice than ever of what to do. Leisure opportunities must be provided and managed for all ages – from young children wanting to play in safe and exciting environments to old people wanting enjoyable experiences away from their home environment. Planning provision is very important, as is managing facilities to achieve the best effects for individuals and communities.

When the energies of some young people are channelled into acts of violence or vandalism, we see evidence of unsatisfied needs. Can't leisure opportunities surely provide the challenges, experiences, adventure, noise, speed, and independence that young people seek and help meet some of those needs? Opportunities are also needed for adults, for families, for the lonely, the old, the disabled, and the disadvantaged to experience the satisfactions that leisure provides. It is the leisure manager's job to ensure that such experience can happen and that people can get the most out of their leisure.

1.2.1 Defining Management

The meaning of the term *management* has evolved through several phases of theories, all of which contribute to a contemporary understanding of what management is:

- The foundation of **management sciences,** in the early years of the twentieth century, is commonly credited to the work of Frederick Taylor, who emphasised the scientific systems necessary to improve productivity and the efficiency of organisations.
- **Classical management theory** followed, extending the concept of efficiency to the structure and operation of organisations. Leading proponents of classical management theory were Henri Fayol and Max Weber. The theory concentrates on five managerial processes: planning, organising, commanding, coordinating, and controlling. It entails hierarchical chains of command which are now criticised for their formality and bureaucracy but are nevertheless still an important feature of many organisations.
- In the 1950s and 1960s a **human relations movement** in management thinking concentrated more on the motivations and needs of the individuals in organisations, inspired by such writers as Abraham Maslow, Chester Barnard, and Elton Mayo. This movement concentrated on managerial effectiveness, rather than the efficiency of organisations, with concern for interpersonal relationships and the effects of supervision on the morale as well as the productivity of workers.
- The human relations movement led to a more general **behaviourist** view of management, which concentrated on more informal and flexible organisational structures and greater employee involvement. It emphasised the importance of motivators in generating staff satisfaction, such as achievement, recognition, and personal development and the importance of hygiene factors in creating dissatisfaction, such as working conditions, salary, status, and job security.
- Towards the end of the twentieth century, emphasis in management theories switched firmly to **customer orientation,** which is at the heart of not only marketing theory but also quality management. The simple premise behind this approach is that customer needs are

the starting point for the design and delivery of products and the structures and processes in organisations.

● In the early 2020s, with the world moving at a phenomenal pace, the emphasis of management has perhaps shifted again, with the process now being more on 'getting things done' **efficiently** and **effectively**. This also requires an acknowledgment about the important of **process** as a third cog to produce the other two.

1.2.2 The Sport and Leisure Services to be Managed

Leisure and recreation are made possible by means of a range of services and facilities, both indoor and outdoor, in and around the home, in the urban environment, in rural areas and in the countryside – see Table 1.1 for an illustrative rather than exhaustive list. A range of services and programmes are provided by the commercial, public, and third sectors to meet the diverse needs and demands of individuals, families, groups, clubs, societies, and businesses.

Demands are met, however, not just by providing infrastructure and facilities but also by attracting people to use and enjoy them through services, management policy, and effective management action. Problems inevitably occur, e.g. a strike at airports or a political dispute that causes immense hardship for business and leisure passengers, sometimes stranded at locations around the world. A greater number of resources are available for leisure today than before. With them come greater opportunities and greater problems – opportunities which should be seized and problems which leisure managers must help to solve.

Table 1.1 Sport and Leisure Facilities: Examples

In home	Resources and equipment in the home for exercise, relaxation, social recreation, entertainment, hobbies, and pastimes
Out of home	Gardens and open spaces, allotments, play areas, and sports grounds. Facilities for entertainment, the arts, music, drama, literary activities, education, sport and physical activities including halls and meeting rooms, libraries, theatres, museums, sports and leisure centres, swimming pools, community centres, entertainment centres, pubs, clubs, cinemas, concert halls, studios, and art and craft workshops
Countryside infrastructure	Roads and rail networks, maps and signposting, stopping-off points, scenic viewing points, picnic sites, car parking, camping and caravan sites, clean beaches and lakes, water recreation areas, walkways, footpaths, nature reserves and many others
Tourism	Tourist Information Centres, travel agents, visitor attractions, roads, rail and air transport, accommodation and hospitality

> ### Discussion Question
>
> Is there such a thing as sport or leisure that does not need management to help it? Discuss examples such as a walk in the countryside, reading a book, or chatting with friends.

1.3 The Structure of this Book

The purpose of this book is to describe and analyse issues relevant to sport and leisure managers and in doing so help these managers to make better decisions. Sport and leisure planners, providers, and managers are in key positions for using resources and creating opportunities which can help to enhance the quality of life for many people. This book deals with important contextual information for sport and leisure managers and best practice principles for sport and leisure management. It is not, however, a technical textbook dealing with leisure 'hardware' such as facility design and construction, physical maintenance requirements, and catering and bar requirements. Instead, this book is concerned with what might be termed 'soft' skills – namely, knowledge of sport and leisure markets and the nature of demand, the quality of sport and leisure services, facilities and experiences, the principles and techniques for planning provision, and principles underpinning management decision-making.

This book is structured broadly in three parts:

- Part I considers the scope and development of sport and leisure by examining definitions of key terms; looking at sport and leisure from a historical perspective; identifying trends in leisure time, participation, and expenditure, as well as general demographic and socio-economic trends which impact on leisure; and exploring the nature of people's needs and sport and leisure demands.
- Part II is focused on the providers of sport and leisure services, facilities, and activities in the public (government), private (commercial), and non-profit (voluntary) sectors; the relationships between these sectors and opportunity for cross-collaboration; how these interact with trends in sport, physical activity, participation, and leisure in the home; and the wider global economics of sport and leisure.
- Part III examines core disciplines important to the management of leisure, i.e. human resource management, marketing, programming, quality management, financial management, enterprise, law, event management, and consulting.

1.3.1 Part I: Concepts and Trends

Having set the scene and introduced key definitions in this first chapter, a key concept of George Torkildsen's is introduced – the 'pleisure principle'. This illustrates the essence of the leisure experience, a concept which helps leisure managers understand what is needed to satisfy people's needs through leisure.

Chapter 2 provides a historical overview of the sport and leisure industry up to the 1990s, and early 2000s, before the real commodification of sport. This enables an understanding of the historical development of leisure and how it can be useful for a leisure manager today. In that regard, the approach taken is different from a more conventional method seen in historical accounts of leisure. Rather than outlining a set of dates and events that, added together and shown chronologically, make the history of leisure, this chapter examines some of the most important processes that have fostered sets of circumstances within which leisure has developed.

Chapter 3 establishes a statistical overview of leisure by reviewing some major trends in leisure from the 1960s onwards, including leisure time, participation, and expenditure. Leisure is a changing, volatile industry and is affected by changes in legislation, demography, technology, and the economy.

Chapter 4 explores in detail the concepts of human needs and sport and leisure demands – fundamentals of any examination of sport and leisure management in an era when 'the customer is king'. The following questions are raised: What factors influence leisure activity and, importantly, what circumstances constrain them?

1.3.2 Part II: Sport and Leisure Provision

Chapters 5–7 focus on the major providers of leisure services and facilities in the public, commercial, and third sectors. Chapter 5 explores central and local government and the influence that they have on sport and leisure, both through direct provision and through regulation and legislation. Government enables and constrains what sport and leisure providers may and may not do. The influence of lead departments, such as the Department for Culture, Media, and Sport in the UK, is explored, along with their national agencies. Local government plays a significant role in supplying sport and leisure opportunities.

Chapter 6 looks at the commercial sector, which is the largest sector, certainly in relation to money and expenditure. It details the importance of private leisure providers and gives an insight into the top level of sport all the way up to professional sport teams. Whilst many may scoff at the money in the commercial sector and believe that sport and leisure are 'purer' than this, we cannot underestimate the financial support that the commercial sector often provides to other sectors, through grant funding, cross-subsidising, or other means of financial support.

The 'third sector' is covered in Chapter 7, and it includes voluntary organisations, non-profit social enterprises, and sport and leisure provision by companies for their employees. The opportunities offered to people through thousands of voluntary clubs, associations, and organisations represent collectively a massive contribution to sport and leisure. The increasing importance of social enterprises to the management of public sector sport and leisure services and facilities is assessed.

Chapter 8 outlines how cross-sector collaborations are one of the most promising and necessary ways to solve interdisciplinary, complex, often multi-faceted problems. In sport and leisure, cross-sector collaborations show great potential to increase participation in sport and leisure. Using the knowledge, skills, and resources of the social, health, and private sectors is a sure way to reach more people who are not yet engaging in sport and leisure activities. However, in many cases, sport organisations still adopt an isolated approach and do not know how to engage in cross-sector collaborations or how these sectors can cross-collaborate and co-create.

Chapter 9 deals with sport, recreation, and physical activity – increasingly important areas in leisure provision and leisure management at a time when there are multi-national concerns about increasing obesity and related health problems. The leisure opportunities provided by sport are varied – from recreational participation for fun and fitness, through competitive participation for performance, to elite participation for medals and championships. All three main providing sectors have important roles to play in sport and physical activity – the commercial sector is very active in major sports and activities such as football and fitness, as well as in media coverage; governments support, promote, and provide sporting opportunities from local to national sports centres; whilst volunteers are the bedrock of a large majority of sports clubs.

Chapter 10 focuses on leisure in the home, particularly the increasing importance of technology in the form of computers and the internet, games consoles, and audio-visual systems. The supply of such leisure opportunities is largely in the hands of the commercial sector and demonstrates the power of technological change and marketing in driving consumer demands and expenditure. Government policy is also concerned, particularly in such issues as competition, standards, and censorship. Computing and the use of the internet connect strongly with other leisure pursuits, particularly social media, streaming of films, gambling, and esports.

Chapter 11 considers planning from two important perspectives. First, the formal planning process involves government processes, planning policy guidance, planning models, and development plans. Second, planning from an organisational perspective involves such techniques as demand forecasting and public consultation.

Chapter 12 closes Part II of this book with a look at the global economics of sport and leisure – in most developed economies accounting for around 2% of GDP, in some a lot more. The economics of sport used to treat the sport market as a national market, looking at the demand side and the supply side of the market and analysing the main factors affecting each. An increasing and hugely important part of every country's sport market is international or global.

1.3.3 Part III: Management Skills and Techniques

Chapters 13–21 introduce and explore several key management disciplines of which a leisure manager needs to be aware. Management involves a multi-disciplinary set of theories, principles, and skills. Each problem encountered by managers is likely to involve a number of these disciplines. Whilst specialism by managers in any one of these disciplines is not unusual – e.g. finance, marketing, human resources – any manager should have a strong awareness of the other disciplines.

Chapter 13 is concerned with human resource management. Leisure is often termed a 'people business' not only because of the importance of customers but also because the main purpose of staff is to satisfy customers' demands. Managing staff, or human resources, involves key issues, including leadership and appropriate organisational structures to empower staff to perform to their potential.

The marketing of sport and leisure is covered in Chapter 14. It explains the marketing approach, the concept of social marketing, and the influence that marketing has on potential customer behaviour. Core concepts of marketing are explained, including mission and vision, market research, marketing strategies, market positioning, segmentation, and the use of the marketing mix to meet the objectives of marketing plans.

Chapter 15 examines one of the most important leisure management skills, that of programming for leisure services and facilities. Managers must have sufficient knowledge of programming because it is the principal means by which sport and leisure are delivered to customers and through which organisational objectives can be met. The chapter explains what programming consists of, different programming strategies, and programming methods for general and target markets.

Chapter 16 looks at vital aspects of contemporary management – quality management and performance management. Total quality management systems are commonplace in the sport and leisure industry, particularly Quest, a system devised specifically for sport and leisure organisations in the UK. There are numerous quality awards available, and the chapter reviews these and their relationship with organisational performance. Performance management is closely related to quality management and relies not only on accurate measurement of organisational performance, e.g. by benchmarking, but also on appropriate management processes to act on this information.

Chapter 17 examines core principles of financial management. On the one hand, an understanding of financial accounting is important as an essential context within which all managers operate. On the other hand, management accounting principles enable managers to act appropriately to improve financial performance.

Chapter 18 examines entrepreneurship and enterprise in sport and leisure. It explores the characteristics of entrepreneurs – are they born, or are they the products of their environments? Examining enterprise involves a set of principles and techniques, including feasibility assessment, business start-up financing, business planning, investment appraisal, and managing risk. It has a close relationship with many other management disciplines, particularly finance, marketing, and human resource management. Enterprise establishes best practice principles, not just for new ventures but also for innovation and change in businesses generally.

Chapter 19 is an introduction to the role of law in managing sport and leisure. Whereas managers are rarely legal experts, the law is an essential context for their decision-making. Basic principles of legal liability and negligence, working with children, employment law, and risk management will help managers to be aware of their legal responsibilities and how their decision-making is constrained by the law.

Chapter 20 deals with the planning and management of special events. Events are an important part of any comprehensive sport and leisure programme. Well organised, they can be a boon; badly organised, they can spell disaster and deter people from coming to such events in future. Leisure managers must be capable of controlling the planning and staging of events. This chapter demonstrates the importance of events at local, regional, and international levels. It covers the event planning process and demonstrates how events can be managed from beginning to end.

Last, but by no means least, Chapter 21 provides an opportunity to analyse the rapidly growing management consultancy sector that supports the sport and leisure industry. Management consulting is a fast-moving and constantly changing industry, reflecting the wider business environments within which the clients operate and the many commercial, market, competitor, operational, financial, and other challenges and opportunities they face. It is a sector that will continue to grow as sport organisations seek outside expertise to capitalise on opportunity.

1.4 Key Definitions

Before discussing the meanings of sport and leisure in depth, it is instructive to outline these and other definitions of key concepts involved in leisure. These concepts are not all mutually exclusive, and arguably the most all-embracing concept is leisure. Individual chapters, particularly in Part II of this book, provide further discussion of these and other concepts in leisure.

- **Leisure** is perceived in a variety of ways – as a type of time, as a set of activities, or as a state of being. At its most ideal, leisure can be perceived as experiencing activities, unpaid and chosen in relative freedom, that are personally satisfying and have the potential to lead towards self-actualisation, i.e. personal growth and fulfilment.

- **Recreation** is usually thought of as leisure-time activities which are more organised and institutional, and sometimes it is used as another term for leisure. In its purest sense, recreation is re-creation – an inner-consuming experience that leads to revival of the senses and the spirit. In this sense, recreation renews, restores, and 'recharges the batteries'. *Physical recreation* refers to physical activities which have this restorative value.
- **Sport** is an informal or formally organised physical activity, typically but not always competitive and typically governed by a set of rules and officials. However, as elaborated in the following text, there are many activities which are commonly labelled sports but which do not have one or more of the basic characteristics which typically define sport.
- **Creative industries** is a term that has come to be used in the UK to mean a set of creative and commercial activities, which include some leisure industries such as music, radio, television and film production, and performing arts; some industries that are partly leisure such as publishing and crafts; and some industries that lie outside leisure, such as advertising and architecture.

The two concepts at the core of this book are sport and leisure, and we explore their definitions further in the next two sections. Sport is a major interest of many further education (16 plus) and higher education (18 plus) courses in leisure and is therefore a specific focus throughout most of this book. Leisure covers a wide range of activities and organisations, the management of which is the main subject of this book.

1.5 Defining Sport

Identifying sports is relatively easy from a common-sense point of view, e.g. by listing activities that are considered to be sports. Core sports activities such as football, baseball, and athletics are clearly sports, but what about darts and snooker? The latter are reported in the media as sports, but many would dispute their identification as sports because they involve little physical effort. What about climbing and long-distance walking? They both require physical effort but typically are not competitive. It is in defining the characteristics of sport that difficulties arise, because characteristics such as physical effort and competition are not shared by all the activities that we label 'sport.'

For an activity to be identified as a sport typically requires one or more of several characteristics including physical activity, skill, competition and also regulations with officials to enforce them (e.g. referees, umpires). The European Sports Charter offers perhaps the simplest definition of sport:

> 'Sport' means all forms of physical activity which, through casual or organised participation, aim at expressing or improving physical fitness and mental well-being, forming social relationships or obtaining results in competition at all levels.

Gratton and Taylor (2000) add a more pragmatic criterion – that there is general acceptance that an activity is a sport, e.g. by the media and government sports agencies. They suggest three categories of sport:

1   A core of sports which have all the required attributes, such as football and athletics;
2   Physical, recreational, but mainly non-competitive activities, which include fitness activities, most swimming, and possibly long-distance walking;
3   Non-physical but competitive activities which have institutional organisation and are generally accepted as sports, such as darts and snooker.

However, both the media and government are biased and selective in their coverage of sports. The media is full of popular sports, but even world champions in minority sports hardly get a mention. Government recognition of sports, e.g. for funding purposes, is often conditioned by major events such as the Olympic Games, but these Games are very selective in what sports they include – a major debate in sport is always around what sports should be included in the Olympics, for example. At Tokyo 2020, we saw the inclusion of skateboarding for the first time, which many would still believe to be a recreation type of activity.

However, there is little doubt that the definition provided by the European Sports Charter is a very inclusive definition, embracing physical activities as well as competitive sports. It implicitly acknowledges a spectrum of sport and physical activity, with formal, competitive sports at one end and informal physical activities at the other. These activities share basic attributes, including health and wellbeing and social relationships.

However, no matter what definition we use there will always be conjecture with certain activities disputed as 'proper sport' or not. For example, sport typically includes some activities that involve aesthetic movement, such as gymnastics and ice skating. Dance is consistent with the Council of Europe definition – it is physically active, skilful, and at the elite end it is competitive – yet many would deny it is a sport. Another source of debate concerns competitive activities where the winner is decided by subjective judgement, e.g. gymnastics, ice skating, equestrian dressage, freestyle skiing, and even boxing (in cases where a knockout is not achieved).

How important are these definitional considerations to the sport and leisure manager? On the one hand, many such managers are involved at the community level. They recognise the competitive structure of sport and the desire of many sports participants to improve. They also must acknowledge and cater for the array of other reasons for sports provision, from the demand by individuals for relaxing, invigorating, and social sport, to broader objectives such as improving community health. Management to these non-competitive objectives will necessarily emphasise attributes such as enjoyment, health benefits, and social relationships. It will not make a distinction between sport and physical activity. On the other hand, fewer sport and leisure managers will be more narrowly focused on performance sport. Their efforts will be engaged in managing participants to improve their skills and competitive positions. Definitions of sport do matter, then, because they bring precision to the objectives of the manager.

1.6 Defining Leisure

What is leisure? This question has been discussed for a long time by philosophers, researchers, lecturers, sociologists, and leisure directors, managers, and students. The United Nations Universal Declaration of Human Rights states, 'Everyone has the right to rest and leisure time. There should be limits on working hours, and people should be able to take holidays with pay' (Article 24). 'Everyone has the right freely to participate in the cultural life of the community, to enjoy the arts and to share in scientific advancement and its benefits' (Article 27).

The word *leisure* appears to be a self-explanatory concept, and most people will have little difficulty, on a 'common sense' basis, describing what it means to them. Yet scholars have been unable to agree with clarity on descriptions of leisure, let alone define what the word means. Indeed, leisure has been debated for well over 2,000 years. For example, Edginton *et al.* (2003) provided over 200 definitions of leisure and recreation. If we were to review this list in 2021, then we might even add more to it, given how quickly the world has shifted in the last twenty years!

A starting point for understanding is the derivation of key words. The Greek word *schole* was synonymous with *leisure*, the implication being that leisure was non-work but also was associated with learning and culture. The English word *leisure* is derived from the Latin *licere*, 'to be permitted' or 'to be free'. So here, at least, there are common denominators conveying that for us to be 'at leisure' there must be an essential freedom to choose what we want to do and what we want to be.

The concept of leisure permits widely varying responses. Leisure is commonly thought of as the opposite of work, but one person's work can be another person's leisure, e.g. art and crafts. Freedom from obligation is often regarded as a key attraction of leisure, but many non-work activities involve considerable obligation, e.g. volunteering. Some regard leisure as being an opportunity for relaxation and pleasure, but often people spend their leisure time in dedicated service, study, personal development, or hard training. Whatever leisure is, it is important to people's quality of life. And it is important for leisure professionals to understand what leisure is and what it does for people – in a customer-focused industry, this is essential.

1.6.1 Leisure as Time

This approach treats leisure as a residual of time, after taking out of total time everything that is not regarded as leisure, i.e. paid work and 'obligated' time such as sleeping and personal hygiene. However, some uses of time are difficult to categorise in this way. Eating, for example, could be seen as obligated time but is definitely a leisure activity when it is a social occasion with family or friends. Do-it-yourself and gardening might be obligated chores to some but pleasurable choices for others.

In leisure time one has a choice over how to spend it – the terms *discretionary time* and *free time* have been used to describe such choice. However, such time is not always seen as leisure. Those people who are made to retire early or are made to feel redundant can find themselves feeling alienated, isolated, and robbed of a purpose in life. Such situations make it a mistake to consider 'leisure' as simply time free from work or obligations. Again, whatever the definition of leisure we employ, managers in sport and leisure organisations must be aware of the nuance of the term and that it means different things to different people. Understanding people's leisure needs and demands is key here as well as effective planning and programming so that there is always a range of activities to suit as many people as possible. You can never please everyone, but you must certainly try and include everyone in your approach to providing sport and leisure.

> ### Discussion Question
>
> What is the difference between leisure and free time? Give examples of people with one but not the other.

1.6.2 Leisure as Activity

Another classical understanding of leisure is that it is made up of an activity or a 'cluster of activities'. Dumazedier (1967), for example, suggests:

> Leisure is activity – apart from the obligations of work, family and society – to which the individual turns at will, for relaxation, diversion, or broadening his individual and his spontaneous social participation, the free exercise of his creative capacity.

Many look at leisure as activities freely chosen. However, in reality, some leisure activities are not freely chosen. Dumazedier (1967) coined the term *semi-leisure* to describe those activities which one was obliged to do but which brought about satisfactions in the doing, e.g. do-it-yourself, family obligations.

1.6.3 Leisure as a State of Being

In the society of ancient Greece – at least at the educated, privileged strata – the 'treasures of the mind' were the fruits of leisure which contained the joy and delight of life. Hence, Aristotle thought of leisure as a state of being, free from the necessity of work and characterised by activity for its own sake or as its own end. The 'ideal man' would strive for perfection in arts, music, sport, school, and in military service. This ideal leisure made for an advanced society and for good governance. Neulinger (1974), in similar vein, suggests:

> Leisure is a state of mind; it is a way of being, of being at peace with oneself and what one is doing. . . . Leisure has one and only one essential criterion, and that is the condition of perceived freedom. Any activity carried out freely without constraint or compulsion, may be considered to be leisure. To leisure implies being engaged in an activity as a free agent, and of one's own choice.

Pieper (1952) went further and stressed the idea from a spiritual perspective:

> Leisure it must be understood, is a mental and spiritual attitude – it is not simply the result of external factors, it is not the inevitable result of spare time, a holiday, a weekend or a vacation. It is, in the first place, an attitude of the mind, a condition of the soul.

Leisure, to Pieper, was not a means to an end, but rather an end in itself. Leisure, for Pieper, is a mental or spiritual attitude, a 'condition of the soul'. It produces an inward calm; it means not being busy, but letting things happen. Kraus (2001) also identifies a 'spiritual' dimension:

> Leisure implies freedom and choice and is customarily used in a variety of ways, but chiefly to meet one's personal needs for reflection, self-enrichment, relaxation, or pleasure. While it usually involves some form of participation in a voluntary chosen activity, it may be regarded as a holistic state of being or even a spiritual experience.

Discussion Question

Is it possible to have leisure as a way of life? Discuss what types of people might be able to do this.

1.7 The 'Pleisure' Principle

This term was devised by George Torkildsen in an attempt to get to the heart of the leisure experience. It is reproduced in his words as a testimony to his endeavour to go beyond the immediate concerns of leisure managers and to explore the fundamental meaning of the products they manage. The term *pleisure* was introduced by Torkildsen in 1992, and this section explains it and the implications for leisure managers.

Three concepts are the foundation stones for leisure management: play, recreation, and leisure. In debating and dissecting each concept, a case can be made for treating each as a distinct concept, and in common language we can all distinguish children at play, young people, and adults taking part in organised recreation, and being at leisure. However, the feelings we might experience could be the same whatever words we care to use. Why, then, the concern, one might well ask? It is tempting to dismiss this line of enquiry as mere semantics which simply add to the jargon. However, there is more to it than just words because we often provide for these three aspects of life in different ways. We provide play space, community recreation facilities, or multi-use and family leisure centres.

At the core of play, recreation, and leisure, there exist several similarities and overlaps, so much so that we can use each word at times to mean much the same thing. Indeed, several words, ideas, or themes are used frequently in describing something of their collective essence: freedom, absence of necessity, choice, self-initiation, self-expression, satisfaction in the doing, playfulness. There are, of course, differences. Playfulness and spontaneity are found more in children's play. Recreation carries a badge of respectability – doing things that are good for you. *Leisure* is a looser, more casual, less constrained term than *recreation*, and it encompasses a vast range of active and passive, casual and serious pursuits. Despite the differences and nuances, there are times, whether at play, recreation, or leisure, that people experience a feeling of immense satisfaction in the doing or of wellbeing or a quality of experience that can lead to revitalisation or an uplifting of the spirit. This can, of course, occur in many different life situations, including work, but it is when we are 'at leisure,' free to make choices and be ourselves, that we are more likely to achieve a quality we might describe as 'wholeness' or an inner-consuming experience. The experience goes beyond the description afforded by words – but it needs to be called something!

As there is no word to describe this experience in the English language, Torkildsen invented the word *pleisure*. Figure 1.1 illustrates better than words the concept of the pleisure experience at the heart of play, recreation, and leisure.

What implications does this 'discovery' have for leisure professionals and managers? The 'pleisure principle' implies that in meeting the needs of individual people, clients, and customers of leisure and recreation services, facilities, and programmes, it is the quality of the

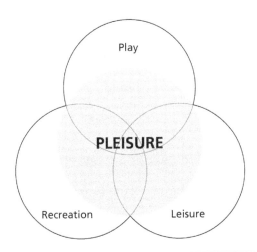

Figure 1.1 'Pleisure' at the heart of play, recreation, and leisure experience.

experience that is more important for them than the activities, programmes, numbers attend-ing, or the income generated. The activity itself may be quite secondary to what it does for a person, or what it means to him or her. Moreover, appreciating that leisure managers have business goals to fulfil, people are more likely to be attracted to and 'buy' activities that they perceive to be worthwhile or that bring satisfying experiences – pleasure.

1.7.1 From 'Pleisure' Principles to Leisure Management Actions

Putting principles into practice is not easy. Expediency is often the option we take and, understandably, management practices tend toward efficiency. If, as leisure professionals, we want to provide a choice of activities and the opportunity for people to experience and develop their leisure participation, then we must provide favourable environments: the right conditions, satisfactions, and positive outcomes.

- **The right conditions** – leisure programmes need to be designed with sufficient options for different people. There needs to be freedom of choice and the opportunity for some self-initiation and spontaneity.
- **Satisfactions** – for leisure to be satisfying, some of the following experiences need to be present: self-expression, challenge, novelty, stimulation, joy, playfulness, 'pleasure' experi-ences, re-creative moments.
- **Positive outcomes** – for leisure to be effective, there should be some positive outcomes; for example: accomplishment; physical, emotional, social, and psychological wellbeing; heightening of self-esteem.

Favourable experiences give satisfactions. Satisfactions lead to consuming interests. Consum-ing interests can lead to life-enhancing experiences, a goal of leisure. Providing for client and customer satisfactions can also lead to successful business outcomes.

Regrettably, it is not so simple. There are several individual and institutional barriers to providing services and programmes based on maximising the 'pleasure' experiences of people. The reasons are complex. People, generally, are not agents free to do as they please and are limited in their response to leisure services and programmes; some people have physical, mental, and social limitations or their environments limit choice (e.g. family, peer group, culture, resources). Leisure for others is eroded through obligations, lack of time, or through enforced free time without the means or motivation to use it. Activities one might consider as leisure, such as sport, can be practised in such a manner that the spirit of play and fair play are submerged and dominated by the desire to win at all costs. And there are inequalities of opportunity – physical, social, and economic.

Successful private sector organisations, although concerned with financial profits, realise that maximising 'pleasure' experiences can lead to greater profits. However, if as a society we want to provide 'pleasure,' then government, in particular, must have appropriate aims and objectives:

- Services should be open to all and meet individual needs, so that a person can choose activities in relative freedom;
- Priorities should be balanced to serve the greatest number and those in greatest need, recognising that those in greatest need may well be in the minority.

The question is: With the emphasis on freedom, can 'pleasure' actually be organised, planned, and managed? The activity can be organised but the experience cannot. What is the manager's role? Normally considered as managing resources, services, facilities, and programmes, sport and leisure managers have a wider remit. Their role is to:

- Consult and involve people and then create environments and services to match the market profiles and their expectations;
- Extend the range of activities to offer wide and varied choices;
- Help groups through supportive services – some can be enabled to create their own opportunities and manage themselves;
- Assist employers in giving their employees recreation activities at workplaces and outside work;
- Help provide leisure education for schools, colleges, and organisations to develop leisure skills (physical, social, cultural, and intellectual) which can help people, particularly young people, to make choices to realise their potential.

In these and other ways, leisure managers and other professionals can help to extend opportunities. These actions amount to an enhanced 'people approach' in public leisure services. This stems from the belief that everyone has worth, has a need to express himself or herself, and that society will benefit from citizens who have the ability and resourcefulness to be creative and find fulfilment in their lives through leisure.

1.8 Conclusions

Leisure is a complex concept and certainly not as simple as 'free time'. It involves fundamental principles of free and informed choice and appropriate opportunities. It requires a relationship with paid work which is not in conflict but is again a choice for the individual. It has the potential to become central to both a way of life and a sense of identity. And given the considerable constraints that exist, which often prevent the realisation of leisure's potential, there is a clear role for managers. Leisure managers need to know what leisure is in order to hope to satisfy the aspirations of their customers and to realise the potential benefits that leisure can provide for individuals and society.

Many of the earlier definitions feature freedom of choice, to which some add intrinsic motivations. What, then, is the role of management? If leisure is so self-determined, is management a contrived and redundant skill in leisure? The ethos of this book and of the leisure management profession is that management has key roles to play in facilitating leisure, however defined. Management of facilities and services provides opportunities for people to express their leisure demands. Even natural resources are typically the outcomes of man's management of the land, e.g. in the provision of footpaths and canals, and in access to coastal and inland amenities. Policy also has an important role – in Japan, for example, legislation was passed to limit the number of working hours; and in Europe the European Working Time Directive has a similar objective.

Customers are the starting point for sport and leisure management and are at the heart of many management decisions. Quality management begins with consideration of what the customer wants. Marketing may be seen by some as a manipulation of people's free expressions of choice, but for marketers themselves the mission is to develop the offer of products to consumers, i.e. to extend the choice of activities. Even human resource management, with an explicit concern for staff, is designed to enable staff to satisfy customer preferences.

> **Practical Tasks**
>
> Complete a diary recording your use of time and identify what percentage of it is leisure. Compare this with diaries recorded by other people in different situations, e.g. relatives, friends. Consider how important leisure is to each person.

Structured Guide to Further Reading

For numerous definitions of concepts related to leisure and recreation:
Edginton, C., Coles, R., & McClelland, M. (2003). *Leisure Basic Concepts*. AALR, Reston, VA.

For a consideration of the way in which definitions of leisure have developed to create a more complex and fundamental concept:
Goodale, T., & Godbey, G. (1988). *The Evolution of Leisure*. Venture Publishing, State College, PA.

For practical lists of leisure activities for a variety of countries:
Cushman, G., Veal, A. J., & Zuzanek, J. (Eds.). (2005). *Free Time and Leisure Participation: International Perspectives*. CABI Publishing, Wallingford.

References

Auger, D. (2020). Leisure in everyday life. *Society and Leisure*, 43(2), 127–128. doi:10.108 0/07053436.2020.1788780

Deloitte. (2021). The leisure consumer 2021. Retrieved from https://www2.deloitte.com/uk/ en/pages/consumer-business/articles/the-leisure-consumer.html

Dumazedier, J. (1967). *Toward a Society of Leisure*. W.W. Norton, New York.

Gratton, C., & Taylor, P. (2000). *Economics of Sport and Recreation*. E & FN Spon, London.

Kraus, R. (2001). *Recreation and Leisure in Modern Society*, 6th edition. Jones & Bartlett, Sudbury, MA.

Neulinger, J. (1974). *The Psychology of Leisure*. Charles C. Thomas, Springfield, IL.

Pieper, J. (1952). *Leisure: The Basis of Culture*. New American Library, New York.

Russell, B. (1935). *In Praise of Idleness*. Allen & Unwin, London.

Chapter 2

Sport and Leisure
A Historical Perspective

In This Chapter

- Why do sport and leisure managers need a historical perspective on sport and leisure?
- Where and how did leisure emerge in the UK?
- How can we explain the development of leisure as we know it today?
- To what extent do earlier forms of sport and leisure impact on how we experience sport and leisure today?
- What lessons can leisure managers take from history?

DOI: 10.4324/9780367823610-2

Summary

This chapter aims to show how understanding the historical development of leisure can be useful for a leisure manager today. In that regard, the approach taken here is different from the more conventional methods seen in historical accounts of leisure. Rather than outlining a set of dates and events that, added together and shown chronologically, make the history of leisure, this chapter examines some of the most important processes that have 'fostered a set of circumstances' within which leisure has developed. Processes, for example, of boredom, work and employment, industrialisation, and commercialisation are all key, it is argued, to understanding how and why leisure has emerged. Medieval times may appear to have been a long time ago, but the roots of leisure as we know it can be traced back to that period, and there are some similarities to why people engage in leisure today. Examining leisure through time, and comparing it to society today, shows how valuable lessons from history can be.

2.1 Introduction

Faced with a busy schedule of work, a leisure manager would be forgiven for considering the historical development of leisure as something rather insignificant to pressures faced in the 'here and now'. However, there are benefits to taking a longer-term view of the sector, and this chapter aims to demonstrate this. It is argued that the roots of many of the topics that dominate current debate in sport and leisure can be traced a long way back through time, and understanding this developmental nature of issues helps to shed light on, among other things, the complexity of the issues, how deeply rooted in culture they have become and, consequently, how difficult they can be to change and manage. Take health as an example. Scanning various media outlets from around the world, one would be forgiven for thinking that issues such as obesity, non-communicable diseases, or sedentary lifestyles are contemporary issues, and employment, lifestyles, diets, and habits have changed so much that as a society we face something of a health crisis. However, many of the developments relating to leisure and certainly those supported by government throughout history have been linked to a moral panic over health. The same could be said for social disorder and crime. In this regard, while acknowledging that management and leadership are often about change, it is also about understanding and appreciating what is *within the realm of possibility*. An understanding of history and the processes that have developed over time are crucial to a more realistic appreciation of what can be achieved in the present. Indeed, by taking a longer-term view of the sector, it sensitises us to the ways in which issues facing leisure managers are not actually new and, in that regard, lessons can be learned from history. Indicators on how to manage issues and not repeat mistakes are all skills that any leisure manager should value. This chapter, therefore, is a slightly different approach to a conventional historical perspective. It does not talk through events as they happen, rather the processes that have, over time, emerged and given rise to circumstances within which leisure can take place. The first step in doing that is to understand that history is socially constructed rather than a set of established facts.

2.1.1 History as a Social Construct?

In their book on the basics of sport management, Wilson and Piekarz (2016) note that history is fluid. By their own acknowledgement, this is an odd concept to grasp, as a general consensus would be that history is fact. It is what *happened*, and members of society have dedicated time to studying history. Any error in our understanding of history is, therefore, simply our failure to grasp those facts in their fullest sense. However, over the course of studying history, things can be challenged, which means history can change. Wilson and Piekarz (2016, p. 26) conclude that:

> The reality is that people write history, which can be influenced by what facts and events they select as evidence, which can be distorted and shaped by their own biases, be challenged by new evidence, or simply be examined and written in different ways as new questions are asked. For the sport manager, this acts as a reminder that what may initially be accepted as certainties and truth, can often have the potential to change.

If truth and certainty have the potential to change, then it seems futile and practically ineffective to provide a chapter for leisure managers that assumes they will not. For that reason, the underpinning assumption over the remainder of this chapter is that absolutes like truth do not exist. Accepting that history can be something constructed by those who were in it or study it is, one might argue, a starting point for a more reflective manager. Put another way, understanding that certain information, which has been accepted uncritically, might be a constraining force and exposing these 'taken for granted' views to investigation can only be helpful for progressing knowledge. Indeed, even if, in the process of an investigation, a leisure manager confirms their views, then something has been accomplished. But there is a second point. That leisure is often about perception. A perception of how much time one has, a perception of how busy you feel, a perception of how much you enjoyed an activity, or a perception of whether something was 'worth it'. So, notwithstanding that those studying leisure can point to events and changes in legislation or to new policies and changes in government, those actions and intended and unintended consequences that flow from them, are not based on fact; rather they are based on a perception with 'real' consequences.

2.2 Quest for Excitement

A very good illustration of these points is the work of Norbet Elias and Eric Dunning in *Quest for Excitement* (1986), and it is here where we will start our examination of the history of leisure. One of Elias' seminal pieces of work was *The Civilising Process*, in which he examined how, over time, as societies became more developed, people who made up those societies became more civil, more domesticated, more polite, and more obedient to perceived social rules. It is against the backdrop of this work that Elias and Dunning wrote *Quest for Excitement: Sport and Leisure in the Civilising Process*. In that work they show how, as societies become more civilised, there is a suppression of excitement, and, for Elias and Dunning, this is key to the way in which leisure has developed.

One of the more common debates regarding the emergence of leisure, which Elias and Dunning's work helps to explain, is the extent to which leisure is used as an escape from the mundane nature of 'real life' or whether leisure is an opportunity to rest, relax, and 'chill out' because of the stress and strain placed on the body and the fast pace of modern living. And this can be seen in other periods of time too. For example, a growing number of people entered paid employment through the period of industrialisation, and that work was heavily routinised. Were leisure time and the activities associated with it during the Industrial Revolution about escaping from such a routine? Or, on the contrary, at a time when manual jobs were common, did leisure act as a time to relax? So, rather than finding activities that provide escapism, leisure is often seen as 'down time', a chance to unwind from the pressure or tension created by things like employment, childcare, or education for example. Elias and Dunning argue that, over time, societies have become more civilised, one consequence of which is that 'situations which generate a tendency among people to act in a highly excited manner have become, as far as one can see, less frequent in the most developed societies' (Elias & Dunning, 1986, p. 44). In highlighting this point, Elias and Dunning suggest that in pre-industrial times, things like famine, flooding, a strong harvest, or drought would elicit spontaneous excitement among societies through despair or joy. However, in more developed societies, not only have the circumstances changed – these scenarios are more likely to be high levels of employment or a financial crash like the one seen in 2008 in the developed world – but also these situations are less likely to elicit spontaneous excitement. Over time, as societies have become more civilised, social and self-control have increased. As Elias and Dunning (1986, p. 44) put it:

> Uncontrolled and uncontrollable outbreaks of strong communal excitement have become less frequent. Individual people who openly act in a highly excited manner are liable to be taken to hospital or to prison.

This transfers to other areas of life as well. We may understand a young child crying uncontrollably, dancing with joy, or screaming with excitement. But these acts are, according to Elias and Dunning (1986), less acceptable forms of behaviour for adults and certainly when an adult is in public. These have become increasingly controlled, confined to our homes, supressed or, at best, a source of embarrassment if displayed in public. It is within this context then that Elias and Dunning link the use of leisure to a 'quest for excitement'. Their argument is that 'in advanced industrial societies, leisure activities form an enclave for the socially approved arousal of moderate excitement behaviour in public' (Elias & Dunning, 1986, p. 46). What the development of leisure has allowed, therefore, is a relaxation of restraints that people value in their everyday lives. Through music, dancing, sport, alcohol, recreational drug use, crafts, or films, among many other things, people can seek the excitement that they have been socialised into supressing in other areas of their life. Let us take the example of sport. The sight of an adult crying in public seems rather unusual (perhaps even more peculiar if the adult is male given the social constraints of gender) and would normally only be seen in circumstances of death or extreme crisis. However, while watching or participating in sport, it is seen as quite acceptable. Indeed, showing such emotion is often celebrated because it shows the passion that adult has for their sport. There are other areas in which this is the case, for example, gambling, going to the theatre, dancing, going to a concert, attending a comedy festival, watching television, climbing a mountain, or going to a party – areas of leisure where excitement and outbursts of extreme emotions are socially acceptable. These, Elias and Dunning argue, are part of a 'mimetic' class of leisure. They are the activities that people pursue in their leisure time because they may lead to forms of arousal not felt in other parts of life and, more importantly, these activities take place in arenas that allow occupational and social restraints to be disregarded for a period of time. This is not to say, however, that Elias and Dunning, among others, have not advocated that leisure also includes things like rest and relaxation. Indeed, they develop a typology of leisure in which they refer to things like sociability, private work, family management, rest, and catering for biological needs – which all have elements of leisure in them. For example, while sleep is a biological need, people also choose in their spare time to go for a short sleep or stay in bed longer in the morning because it is the weekend. Likewise, eating is a biological need, however, one might make time to eat out as a leisure activity. For Elias and Dunning, these activities are more likely to be used to fill spare time and are separate from the 'mimetic class' of activities that are used in that quest for excitement. So what does this mean for leisure managers now?

The conceptualisation of the growing need, in developing societies, for an area of life that allows a pursuit of arousal that is socially acceptable helps leisure managers to understand some of the reasons for engagement in leisure. It may seem obvious that leisure time is about enjoyment; however, the wider point here is that throughout history, it appears that people are seeking less suppression and environments where excitement can be normalised and encouraged. Of course, what is excitement to one person may not be the same as another person and understanding that among service users is also key. A term often related to leisure is *freedom*, and in many ways, this is closely related to freedom of expression. It is not necessarily that people have increasingly sought freedom in activities per se; things like sport, the cinema, and the theatre are well regulated with specific places for people to sit, stewards on hand to control behaviour, and so on. Rather, it is seeking an environment where freedom to be excited is allowed. The balance between regulations and freedom is a tension that often surfaces in leisure. Football hooliganism is an example of this and well documented in other work (see, for example, Dunning *et al.*, 1986). Having established something of a conceptual framework for why leisure has developed over time, let us now turn to how it has developed. For this part, there are three phases to consider. Importantly, the phases of the development of leisure are only split up for convenience and, as the following sections show, there is a lot of overlap between the phases. For people living in those times, the change from one phase to another will not have been sudden. Nevertheless, first is what is regarded as the pre-industrial phase of leisure, and it is there where we can start to understand how leisure emerged in the UK towards what we see today.

2.2.1 The Emergence of Leisure

Leisure as we regard it today, like any social process, did not start; it emerged. It emerged from a set of enabling and constraining factors in society, one consequence of which was time for people to spend doing what they want to do. Given this, it is very difficult, indeed impossible and unnecessary, to pinpoint a time in history we might call the beginning of leisure. Making this more complicated, leisure as we would describe it today is not necessarily what someone would describe as leisure one, two, or three hundred years ago. That is to say, the words or concepts we use to examine this topic are not constant – and some might suggest inadequate. An argument commonly debated in articles surrounding the history of leisure, for example, is the role played by industrialisation in the formation of leisure (see, for example, Burke, 1995). In short, pre-industrial 'leisure' in the period before the 1750s was nothing like the mimetic leisure activities we regard as leisure today. Indeed, it was more akin to festivals, gatherings, carnivals, religious communities, or rituals, and while there were some activities that *now* we regard as leisure like gambling, hunting, tennis, and cards (Burke, 1995), this was not seen as leisure as we now know it. The process of industrialisation was tied closely to the development of weekends, holiday periods and, consequently, leisure time as we now conceptualise it. So, there are two approaches here. Looking at leisure as a process that emerged in medieval Europe and over time has evolved through modernization into what we see today, or to understand it as something of a two-part process splintered by industrialisation – that is to say a pre- and a post-industrial phase of leisure. In the pre-industrial phase, because there was no regulated work, no weekends, no official time off, there was nothing to define where leisure was. Unfortunately, as Burke (1995, pp. 138–139) argues, 'the binary opposition between what one might call a "festival culture" and a "leisure culture", like many dichotomies and polarities, is as misleading as it is convenient' (Burke, 1995, p. 139). There is ample evidence from medieval Europe of words and language that suggested a withdrawal from obligatory activities. Again, here it is important not to use the word *work*, because in these times work, as we conceptualise it now, did not exist. Nevertheless, Romans, Church Fathers, and Monks all had terminology that suggested an act of withdrawing from obligatory activity was common at that time. The work of Burke (1995) is excellent for outlining the development of the process that must emerge correlatively with the development of leisure, that of the notional withdrawal from work or obligatory activity. In a similar vein, Burke notes that:

> the term *vacatio*, originally used to describe a state of mind, by the fifteenth century was applied to institutions in the case of the suspended activity or 'vacations' of the court of Rome, the lawcourts, the Inns of Court, and of course the universities. In Oxford and Cambridge, the term 'long vacation' was in use by the seventeenth century.

In the UK, before the Industrial Revolution, there were other words that had appeared, which give an indication that the process of withdrawing from obligatory activity (whatever that looked like) was part of society. Among other words, Burke notes that *play, pastime, recreation,* and *retirement* that were part of vocabulary in and around the seventeenth century. It is the word *pastime* that Burke makes the most prominent point for leisure managers of today. First recorded in the 1400s, *pastime* relates to the history of boredom and how people in medieval Europe became concerned with how to 'pass time'. Again, note the perceptual nature of this and how, even long before the idea of mundane jobs was part of society, people had some form of quest for excitement, something that made use of time that was perceived as spare.

Discussion Question

What are the parallels between perceived boredom in the 1400s and perceived boredom in modern society?

2.2.2 Industrialisation

Keeping in mind that this distinction is only being made to make the process of understanding the development of leisure more manageable, the increased pace of industrialisation that occurred in the middle of the 1700s in the UK and in other areas of the world like Europe and North America had a profound impact on the leisure lives of the people in those societies. The first one hundred years of this period saw growing urbanisation, more factory workers, and developments in technology. The second hundred years saw, among other advancements, the introduction of electricity into factories and the construction of electric power lines, railways, and canals. All these were central to the developments in employment and, consequently, pay that went alongside this work.

2.2.3 Work

A vital pre-requisite for being a successful leisure manager is to understand the role that work has, and continues to play, in the leisure lives of people. Generally, paid employment sits in opposition to leisure in that most people regard employment as an obligatory activity with little choice or freedom. In the social construction of neo-liberalist and capitalist ideologies, working is necessary to survive by buying food, land, shelter, and fuel for example. But work also has a relationship with leisure, which is illustrated well through industrialisation. The money we earn, the time we spend in work, and how physically fatigued we are from work are all factors that impact on where, when, and how we engage with leisure. Commenting on the process of industrialisation, Russell (2013, p. 16) claims that 'in 1850, the "normal" working week for the labouring classes in regular employment saw attendance from 6am to 6pm . . . from Monday to Saturday'. Notwithstanding the fact, as Russell argues, this 60-hour week generally included two hours for lunch each day, this was perceived as too high and, therefore, the time spent in employment each week would decrease over the proceeding one hundred years or so. Indeed, including the addition of 'weekends', where fewer hours were worked on Saturday and Sunday, Russell (2013, p. 16) concludes that 'by 1920, an employee might expect to work, effectively, one full day a week less than his or her 1850 counterpart, and two by the early 1960s'. In the first half of the twentieth century, there was also increasing pressure on employers to offer paid holidays. Holidays and vacations, again, as we think of them today, had their roots in the high levels of employment across society, affording families the opportunity to save money and take time away from paid employment. However, by the 1950s paid holiday had become 'effectively a universal entitlement' (Russell, 2013, p. 17). The offer of paid holidays spread exponentially through the employment sector from a point in the 1920s where Russell (2013) claims around one million labourers had paid holiday to 1940 when roughly four million people were entitled and, finally, to 1945 when an estimated 10 million people had paid holidays.

These may seem mute points when placed in the context of more contemporary society. However, the relationship between employment and leisure will be forever entwined. In Chapter 3, working patterns are explored in more detail, and understanding existing patterns of employment requires consideration from leisure managers. For example, brought sharply into focus by the COVID-19 pandemic and the technological advancement over the past 30 years or so, working from home is now considered a routine part of an increasing number of employment sectors in developed societies. Or, at the very least, more organisations are offering a 'hybrid' approach to working, where some time can be spent working remotely, usually at home, and some on site. Data gathered by the Office for National Statistics highlights this trend and can be seen in Figure 2.1. Notwithstanding that the context is different, the interdependence between employment, work, and leisure remains important. Working from home opens a more fluid approach to the way people approach tasks. Doing the washing, preparing dinner, doing exercise, and tending to pets can be fitted in during work when, ordinarily, they had to fit outside of the working day early in the morning or later at night. In a similar way, more flexibility is offered around when people can work. Working earlier in the morning or later in the evenings are seen as more acceptable even if they are not desirable. A similar change in employment conditions is being seen in the rise of 'zero-hour contracts', which is more of an informal agreement between employer and employee. A zero-hour contract means employees are not guaranteed any hours but, rather, they pick and choose when they work.

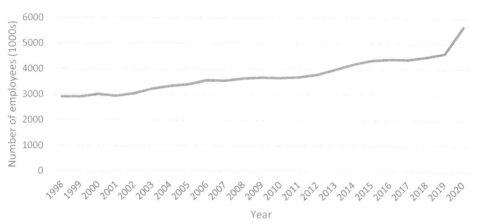

Figure 2.1 **Number of those in employment who work mainly from home in the United Kingdom from 1998 to 2020 (in thousands).**

Discussion Question

What do changes do you think will happen in leisure due to more people working from home and more 'zero-hour contracts'?

2.3 Pay

If the developments around industrialisation helped to free up time for people to spend on leisure, as Elias and Dunning (1986) and Russell (2013) have alluded to, this is only really useful if it is accompanied by resources to fulfil that time. In Russell's (2013, p. 17) account of the development of leisure, reference is made to the growth of wages in the second half of the nineteenth century, suggesting that 'falling basic commodity prices cause real wages for workers to rise by about 80% between 1850 and 1900'. The 'real' wage increase is worth reflecting on briefly. It is a process that continued in the main through the first half of the 1900s and beyond, however, not at such a rate. Nevertheless, it has not been seen in the first part of the twenty-first century. Indeed, in Figure 2.2, the average annual income is shown for the UK between 1999 and 2021. On the face of it, this is a positive picture; however, at the same time as the increase in income has been occurring, the price of basic commodities has also been increasing. In the report by the Office for National Statistics, which is the source of the data, it is argued that employees in the UK are economically poorer now when compared to the period prior to the 2008 financial crisis. And these consequences have not been distributed evenly across society either. For example the report goes on to suggest that in 2017, UK workers in their thirties earned 7.2% less than people of that age nine years earlier. This compared with a decline of just 0.7% for people in their sixties.

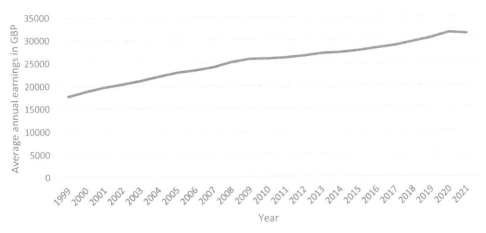

Average annual earnings for full-time employees in the UK
1999–2021

Figure 2.2 **Median annual earnings for full-time employees in the United Kingdom from 1999 to 2021 (in GBP).**

The complex interplay between pay and leisure is clear throughout history. As leisure has developed, even in times of declining 'real terms' wages, people have gravitated towards cheaper forms of leisure, such as alcohol consumption or watching television. For leisure managers, then, not only is it imperative to stay abreast of social trends like inflation, wage rates, and employment levels, but also to understand that changes in these areas are likely to have an impact on how people engage with their leisure time.

2.3.1 New Leisure?

One consequence of industrialisation is that an increasing number of people within more developed countries have additional time and disposable income to spend on their quest for excitement. One very clear example of that was the development of football clubs and, more specifically, the number of people who attended as spectators. Football clubs had started to emerge around the 1860s in the UK and, as more time was awarded for leisure, the use of a Saturday afternoon to go and watch football became increasingly popular. Before the turn of the twentieth century, attendances were averaging below 10,000 spectators. Between 1900 and 1920, there was an exponential growth in the number of people going to spectate, and by the middle of the 1920s, the top divisions comfortably averaged over 20,000 spectators for games, with some larger clubs like Chelsea, Liverpool, Everton, and Newcastle recording attendances in the high 30,000s. Around the same time, the development of technology was having an impact on cinema, and attendances were increasing in that genre too. By the 1930s, around 900 million admissions were recorded at cinemas. Incidentally, attendance at cinemas would increase throughout the following decade and became very popular during the years of the Second World War. These are just two examples of how changes in employment structure, brought about through various means like strike action and government legislation, impacted on the leisure lives of the population. One of the final points Russell makes on this relates to how, over the course of industrialisation, leisure moved from 'class' to 'mass'; association football and the cinema are good examples of this, as are theatres and vacations.

As we move away from the period of industrialisation, and towards the establishment of the welfare state, it is worth picking up on one important aspect that is explicit in the development of leisure over time. Russell (2013) notes that it is impossible to talk of the emergence of leisure, and here the focus is on modern forms of leisure, as the same process for everyone. Even if, as is largely the case in this book, focus is on one area of the world like the UK, within that specific region leisure has developed differentially for diverse groups of people. Gender, ethnicity, age, and social class, for example, are all ways in which experiences of the development of leisure can be stratified. It is noted at this point because the same can be said for industrialisation. This was not a uniform process for all; it was heavily gendered, for example. The consequences of, among other things, working conditions, pay, living conditions, state support for leisure, and commercialisation are not, and never have been, experienced the same by everyone in society, yet they are closely linked to the experiences people have of leisure. This is another good example of how the development of leisure can hold key indicators for current leisure managers. As other chapters in this book show (see for example, Chapter 3), over time, leisure participation has been different for different groups of society, and that continues today. As this section highlights, conceptualising leisure as one uniform process dismisses the nuances that have long been a part of this process and that impact on different people and their leisure lives.

2.3.2 The Welfare State

The process of industrialisation continued into the twentieth century, but it was another process that, by the early 1900s had started to impact leisure. Like all processes, the welfare state did not just start; the roots are embedded in the early nineteenth century. However, it had gathered pace, and the First World War and the Second World War only served to accelerate the process. *The welfare state* refers to the role that government has in people's lives, particularly in relation to education, employment, health, and security. During the World Wars government had to play a greater role in supporting people, and that provided the platform for what Coalter calls the 'post-war' welfare state. Coalter (1998, p. 27) continues by claiming that 'within this climate of opinion, a broad notion of "social service", combined with a local government commitment to "service development" to include increased investment in public leisure provision, was established'. Hence, as the range of goods and services that were funded and organised by the State grew in post-war Britain, leisure was swept up in that expansion. While Coalter (1998, p. 27) suggests there was little debate around it, he argues that 'a vague consensus emerged that access to various recreational opportunities was part of the rights of social citizenship', and a number of developments over this period show this (see Chapter 5). However, it is not until the 1960s that more coherent policies were developed for the provision of sport and leisure, when there was recognition of the importance of sport to individuals, society, and the economy and the determination that governments should support this. Provision and support for sport came through the establishment of the Sport Council in 1965. Again, it is worth turning to what this means for the current leisure manager. The state still plays a pivotal role in the services afforded to leisure, and, as can be seen throughout this book, the role it plays in leisure of those in disadvantaged areas of society are crucial. The final aspect to examine, however, is a move away from state involvement. As the 1980s emerged, a new political approach in many parts of the developed world shaped the relationships that people had with leisure.

2.3.3 Consumer Society and Leisure

Although the 1980s do not seem that long ago, certainly when compared with the years covered at the beginning of this chapter, there is one final process that needs to be covered, that of commercialisation. To reiterate, like all processes discussed before this one, commercialisation of leisure did not start in the 1980s; it emerged long before that. However, it rose to prominence as the political agenda of the time sought to expose services and goods previously held by the state to market forces. What occurred was a transfer of goods and services to the private sector, where financial profit is the aim rather than social good. Of course, this change in political ideology also had an impact on work and, through the 1980s and 1990s the balance between leisure and work shifted towards work. At the very least it seems for those working in full-time employment, there was a requirement to work extra hours. It is the beginnings of the resurgence of neo-liberalism in the UK, which the Prime Minister of the time, Margaret Thatcher employed. So, leisure, like other sectors of society were exposed to deregulation, market competition, withdrawal of funding from the state, and privatization. Neo-liberalism and the associated capitalist models continued through the next Prime Minister John Major and then taken on by New Labour following their landslide victory in 1997. The remains of this are still in evidence today. Together, the post-war welfare state and the neo-liberalist ideologies of free-market capitalism through the 1980s, 1990s, and into the early 2000s in particular show how the political ideologies of different periods can play into the leisure lives of people in society.

2.3.4 Conclusion

It is worth starting this conclusion with a brief reminder of why this chapter is in this book. It is about understanding how the history of leisure can help sport and leisure managers today. For that reason, let us recap on the main 'take-home' points of this chapter. First, there is, and always has, been a relationship between leisure and boredom. All aspects of leisure possess an element that is about passing the time. So for leisure managers, although it sounds simple, enjoyment and targeting times when people are likely to be looking to pass time is key. Second, as society has developed, so has a social requirement to supress public displays of extreme excitement. This is summarised in the work of Elias and Dunning, who show that, over time, an increasingly important aspect of leisure has been to provide environments where extreme excitement is accepted. Mimetic forms of leisure allow for things like dancing, singing, shouting, crying, and jumping about to take place without fear of judgement. Sport is a very good example of that. So how do leisure managers capitalise on this? Providing environments where people can escape the suppression of society and 'let themselves go' is essential; remembering that this might look different for different groups, is however, also vital. Third, of course there are aspects of leisure where people want to be on their own; however, throughout history, constant reminders exist of the social aspects of leisure. Spending time with people is a key component, which, ironically, is not the way that participation in sport and physical activity has gone over the past 30 years or so. But it is a point that leisure managers need to appreciate. Fourth, the relationship between employment and leisure is symbiotic, and leisure managers would be wise to maintain their understanding of trends and patterns in employment, including pay and working hours. This is something that is covered in this book. Finally, the role of the state is key to leisure provision and is something that can give an indication of the way leisure is moving.

> ### Practical Tasks
>
> **1** How do you think leisure policy and sport provision will change over the next decade?
> **2** What will new employment opportunities look like for sport and leisure managers, and what trends and patterns will they have to address?
> **3** How would you define 'new leisure'?

Structured Guide to Further Reading

Burke, P. (1995). The invention of leisure in early modern Europe. *Past & Present*, 146, 136–150.

Cunningham, H. (2016). *Leisure in the Industrial Revolution: C. 1780-c. 1880*. Routledge, Oxon.

Coalter, F. (1998). Leisure studies, leisure policy and social citizenship: The failure of welfare or the limits of welfare? *Leisure Studies*, 17(1), 21–36.

Reid, D. A. (1976). The decline of Saint Monday 1766–1876. *Past & Present*, 71, 76–101.

Reid, D. A. (1996). Weddings, weekdays, work and leisure in Urban England 1791–1911: The decline of Saint Monday revisited. *Past & Present*, 153, 135–163.

References

Burke, P. (1995). The invention of leisure in early modern Europe. *Past & Present*, 146, 136–150.

Coalter, F. (1998). Leisure studies, leisure policy and social citizenship: The failure of welfare or the limits of welfare? *Leisure Studies*, 17(1), 21–36.

Dunning, E., Murphy, P., & Williams, J. (1986). Spectator violence at football matches: Towards a sociological explanation. *British Journal of Sociology*, 221–244.

Elias, N., & Dunning, E. (1986). *Quest for excitement. Sport and leisure in the civilizing process*. Basil Blackwell

Russell, D. (2013). *The Making of Modern Leisure: The British Experience c.1850 to c.1960*. Routledge, Oxon.

Wilson, R., & Piekarz, M. (2015). *Sport Management: The Basics*. Routledge, Oxon.

Wilson, R., & Piekarz, M. (2016). *Sport Management; The Basics*. Routledge, Oxon.

Chapter 3

Trends in the Sport and Leisure Industry

In This Chapter

- How have the trends in leisure participation and spending changed over time?
- How much time do we spend participating in leisure activities, and has that changed?
- Has leisure inside and outside of the home changed?
- What are the wider societal trends we need to be aware of?

DOI: 10.4324/9780367823610-3

Summary

This chapter identifies trends in leisure at home and away from home. The former has increased in the face of technological innovation and other social factors. For example, the recession of 2008 and the COVID-19 pandemic that started in 2019 saw people spend more leisure time within the home. An examination of this change highlights important growth areas and changes within leisure, such as the use of the internet for streaming music, television programmes, and movies and the growth of social media. Despite this, leisure away from home is the focus for most leisure expenditure in the UK, with eating and drinking out and leisure travel being the largest sub-sectors. Although leisure is a growth industry, it contains some sectors which show strong growth compared to others, such as use of the internet, holidays, visiting coffee shops, and gambling. Similarly, it is important to note that the growth in certain leisure expenditure is not consistent across populations; it varies by age, for example. Other sectors seem to be reducing or remaining stable. It seems we might spend more on alcohol, but that does not necessarily suggest we are drinking more, and the same can be said for smoking. Likewise, between 2002 and 2018, spending on restaurants has remained relatively stagnant. The same note of caution needs to be added here with regard to different sections of society. Take, as an example, visiting restaurants and hotels. In 2018, the poorest 10% of UK households spent, on average, 7% of their total weekly expenditure on visits to restaurants and hotels (£18.20 a week) compared to those with the highest income, who spent 10% of weekly expenditure (£110.60 a week) on the same visits. This highlights that, in addition to leisure trends, it is also wise for leisure managers to be aware of more general demographic, social, and economic trends. These more general trends include changes in population levels and structures, changes in incomes and inequality, and changes in health.

3.1 Introduction

It can appear that humans are now enjoying higher standards of living with goods, services, activities, and opportunities that in past years seemed unimaginable. This has been fed by, among other things, rising incomes, technological advances, and greater mobility of people. However, many of the more developed economies have, simultaneously, increasing inequality between the 'haves' and the 'have nots'. And there are worrying trends in the proportions of populations who are overweight and obese – particularly in the USA and UK but also in other more developed countries. This chapter explores major trends relevant to sport and leisure and, although the core evidence used relates to the UK because of the availability of consistent data, there are places where data from other countries is included, and it is certainly the case that many of the issues covered relate to other countries, particularly those considered more developed or developing.

Commentators, forecasters, social scientists, and researchers provide information on trends in areas such as time, participation, expenditure, travel, and economic, social, and demographic changes, which all impinge on leisure in some way. Exploring the past and trying to predict the future in terms of leisure provision and participation are essential planning and management tools. They are used in numerous ways, including:

- to draw attention to specific areas of growth and decline;
- to predict the most likely future leisure activities of consumers;
- to plan leisure services and facilities strategically;
- to reduce the element of risk in decision-making on future provision and policy; and
- to provide information for use in marketing of future facilities, services, and programmes.

Trends are normally indications of national movements and, therefore, it is important for leisure planners and managers to remember that what is happening nationally may not be occurring locally. Moreover, some trends are short-lived, emphasising the volatility of the leisure industry. Also, forecasting future trends is fraught with uncertainty because the future does not always follow past trends – imagine predicting leisure activities beyond 2020 prior to the COVID-19 pandemic! It was predicted in the 1960s that in the UK, for example, employment would have moved to the 'three 30s' – i.e. 30 years of working life, 30 working weeks per year, and a 30-hour working week. This has only been partly achieved in the western world and for very few. Indeed, many people in full-time employment, particularly those who are highly educated, in higher-status jobs, and in dual-career households, are coping with higher workloads than 50 years ago (Gershuny & Sullivan, 2019).

3.2 General Leisure Trends

3.2.1 Leisure Participation

Let us start with a common trend between many countries. Men have spent and continue to spend more time on leisure activities compared to females – although this could be changing. Dahlberg *et al.* (2020), for example, used data collected in 1992, 2002, and 2011 on leisure participation in Sweden and found that, at each of these points in time, women were less active in leisure. Moving to the UK, in 2000, women spent just under 38.5 hours on leisure each week, while men spent, on average, just under 43 hours per week. By 2015, the gap had narrowed but not by much, with women spending, on average, just over 39 hours per week on leisure compared to 43 hours by males, according to the Office for National Statistics. Self-reported data collected by the Institute of National Statistics in Spain in 2003 and 2010 showed the same. In 2003, on average, males spent 320 minutes every 24 hours on 'social life and entertainment', 'sports and outdoor activities', 'hobbies', and 'the media', while females spent 266 minutes. Seven years later, the same patterns were found. Males spent, on average, 319 minutes on those activities and females 266 minutes. The trend in gender inequality is largely maintained for physical activity. For example, data gathered in 2014 from 26 European countries showed only six countries (Austria, Denmark, Finland, Germany, Iceland, and Sweden) where more females participated in sport, fitness, or physical activity as part of their leisure time than males. However, there is some data that seems to suggest the gap could be narrowing in some countries. In Flanders, over a 40-year period between 1969 and 2009, the gap in physical activity levels between males and females diminished. There are similarly some nuances in the type of activity (males are more likely to undertake their physical activity at clubs, for example) (Scheerder & Vos, 2011). Table 3.1 shows changes in leisure activities in different countries around the world.

Table 3.1 Changes in Leisure Activities in Selected Countries

County	Time period	Overall leisure time	Increasing		Decreasing		Source
USA	2009–2019	Unchanged	Computing and computer games	Thinking/relaxing	Socialising	Reading	American Time Use Survey
Germany	2000–2010	Increased	Watching TV and video	Computing and computer games	Reading		German Time Use Survey
Spain	2000–2010	Increased	Watching TV and Vvdeo	Computing and computer games	Thinking/relaxing		Spanish Time Use Survey
Belgium	2000–2010	Increased	Computing and computer games	Hobbies (not computer and computer games)	Reading	Thinking/relaxing	Belgium Time Use Survey
Finland	2000–2010	Increased	Computing and computer games	Hobbies (not computer and computer games)	Thinking/relaxing		Finnish Time Use Survey
Estonia	2000–2010	Increased	Eating out	Computing and computer games	Reading		Estonian Time Use Survey
Poland	2000–2010	Increased	Computing and computer games	Thinking/relaxing	Watching TV and video	Reading	Polish Time Use Survey
Norway	2000–2010	Unchanged	Watching TV and video	Computing and computer games	Reading		Norwegian Time Use Survey
Italy	2000–2010	Increased	Thinking/relaxing	Watching TV and video			Italian Time Use Survey
France	2000–2010	Increased	Thinking/relaxing	Computing and computer games	Reading		French Time Use Survey
South Korea	2014–2019	Unchanged	Computing and computer games	Reading	Socialising		Korea Time Use Survey
Japan	2016–2019	Increased	Physical activity participation	Media use (smartphone, television, and internet)	Volunteering		Japanese Time Use Survey

The most reliable long-term evidence of leisure participation rates in Great Britain was from the General Lifestyle Survey (previously the General Household Survey). This survey, however, was last conducted in 2011 and seems to have unearthed less about leisure than in previous iterations. Figure 3.1 shows how stable the participation rates of the main domestic leisure pursuits were in the last quarter of the twentieth century. Most of the activities in the figure were stable or rising in this period. Only dressmaking/needlework/knitting declined.

Discussion Question

What do you think happened to these activities after 1996?

Of the activities that were outlined in the General Household Survey data up to 1996, most have seen a decline in popularity. With regard to in-home leisure time, watching the television remains the top activity, although the data show this has dropped over the past 20 years or so. Data vary, but it seems to be between 65% to 80% of adults who watch TV weekly for leisure. There are other trends that show something similar. For example, children are spending fewer hours watching TV in 2019 than they were in 2014. The number of households with a TV is not increasing, a number that has been stable for the past ten years, and there is evidence that we are spending less time watching TV (although consuming TV programmes through phones, tablets, and laptops may be replacing this). Similarly, listening to music or the radio remains popular, but not to the same extent as in 2002. In the UK, just under 60% of people claim to listen to music or the radio in their leisure time in 2019. The way we listen to music has, perhaps unsurprisingly, changed. The percentage of people who listen to music via compact disc (CD) has fallen, while digital platforms have increased in popularity. Between 2011 and 2018, the percentage of people using free legal streaming services in the UK jumped from 7% to 25%. In that time, the use of any digital

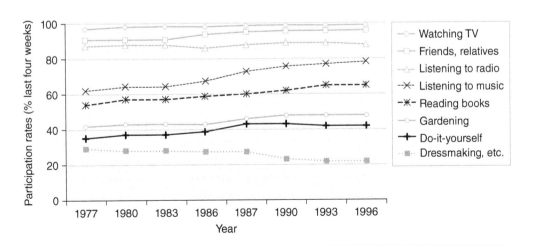

Figure 3.1 **Leisure trends in Great Britain, 1977–1996.**
Source: General Household Survey (ONS, 1996)

platform by music listeners rose from 25% to nearly 40%. Another notable difference seems to be the diminishing status of entertaining and visiting friends as a leisure activity. Up to the late 1990s, 'visiting or entertaining friends or relations' was undertaken by over 90% of the population in the UK; however, data from the ONS suggest that 'entertaining others at home' is now only done by 21% of the UK population. We can account for some of the difference from a change in the survey being used to gather the data, however, it remains an important trend to highlight. In the final 20 years of the twentieth century, the number of people within the UK who read books increased to around 65%. This growth has, however, reversed somewhat over the first 20 years of the twenty-first century. Notwithstanding that it remains a popular activity, the number of people reading books in their spare time had returned to around 50% of the UK population. DIY has also seen a slight decrease in popularity with around 30% of the population in the UK claiming to use their leisure time for DIY in the home. Finally, dressmaking/needlework/knitting saw a decline in participation between 1977 and 1996, which has stabilised at around 20% for the past 20 years or so.

One key development over the past 30 years or so has been the increase in internet use within the home. For example, in 2006 in the UK, 35% of the population used the internet daily. By 2020, that figure was 89%. Put another way, in 2020 only 5% of those asked had not used the internet in the past three months. In 2006 that figure was estimated to be 40%. The impact of this process seems to have been mirrored in our leisure activities with, for example, 34% of people in the UK currently surfing the internet in their spare time. Similarly, in 1996, 16% of people in the UK owned a mobile phone, but by 2020 that figure was 95%. The ownership of a mobile phone – and the advancement in its capabilities – has emerged correlatively with the growth of social media. Today, this forms a large part of our leisure time. In the UK, 38 million people use Facebook, which only came into existence in 2004. Indeed, across the world there are over 2.5 billion active Facebook users. Add in other social media platforms, such as Twitter, which has over 16 million users in the UK, and Instagram, with 28 million active users, and what has become apparent is there is a new virtual arena in which many people spend their leisure time.

Of the activities we undertake away from home, going out to restaurants, cafés, and bars remains a popular activity, and that is the case for all ages. In 2015, 33.7 million people used a coffee shop or café. By 2019, that had risen to 35.9 million. With respect to alcohol, there is a mixed picture. For example, there is some evidence that alcohol consumption is declining or stable. In Scotland, for example, the mean number of units consumed by males has dropped between 2003 and 2019 from 21.8 units per week to 15. However, across the whole of Great Britain, spending on alcohol to consume in the home has increased year on year between 2005 and 2019. As part of the same process, the number of pubs has declined over the past 20 years. There were just under 61,000 pubs in 2000 and just over 47,000 by the year 2019. Another activity outside of the home that remains popular for all age groups is travel and sightseeing. Although it is slightly more prevalent among older groups, it is comfortably in the top five activities people in the UK do. Indeed, between 2010 and 2019, the average number of holidays taken by people in the UK sat between three and four trips per year. The number of admissions to the cinema has grown from 156 million in 2001 to 176 million in 2019. This has also included more alternative venue screenings. Attending a music concert remains popular for all but is more likely to be done by younger groups, as is visiting a theme park. Finally, the desire to visit an art gallery does not seem to be impacted on by age, with around 25–30% of people in the UK using their spare time to make a visit, which has remained relatively stable since 2000.

Sport and Physical Activity

Sports and physical activities participation evidence for England is presented in Figure 3.2 and 3.3. This has been divided into two graphs, principally because the original data were collected using the *Active People* survey, while data from 2015 onwards has used the *Active Lives* survey. The data are, therefore, not comparable. However, taken in isolation, the two figures do show some trends in participation. For example, swimming seems to have shown a decline across the past 15 years, whether measured in once-a-week participation (Figure 3.2) or once in the past 28 days (Figure 3.3). Walking remains a popular activity, and there has been an increase in participation in 'fitness' activities in gyms.

Discussion Question

Why do you think participation rates in swimming have fallen in the 15 years prior to 2018?

When you move around the world, you find different trends in leisure and sport. Indeed, the work of Fadaaka and Roberts (2018) illuminates the way leisure in Saudi Arabia has developed.

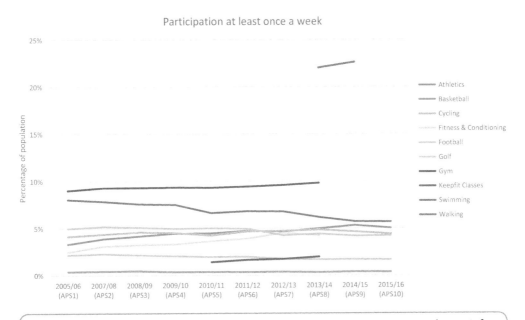

Figure 3.2 **Participation in selected activities between 2005 and 2016 for adults in England.**
Source: Sport England

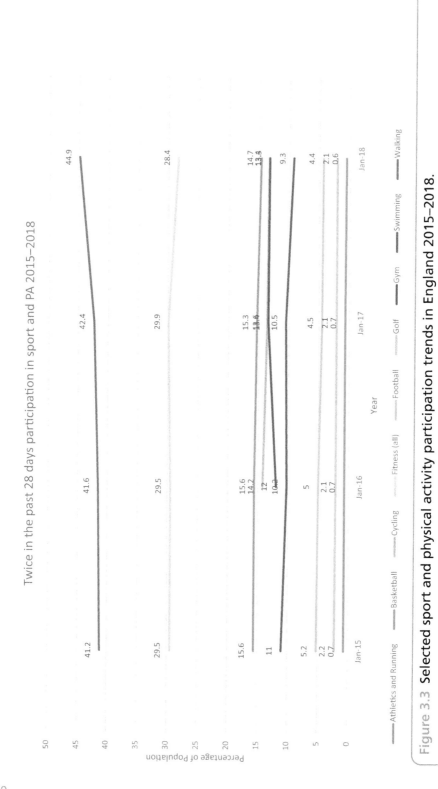

Figure 3.3 Selected sport and physical activity participation trends in England 2015–2018.
Source: Sport England

Leisure and Change in Saudi Arabia

Saudi Arabia is, by Fadaaka and Roberts' own admission, an extreme case to examine when it comes to leisure. The Islamic roots (specifically the Wahhabi version of Islam) and an absolute monarchy have combined to create a scenario where the types of leisure activities written about in previous sections are not available in Saudi Arabia. For example, religion 'prohibits most forms of out-of-home leisure that people throughout the rest of the world enjoy – consuming alcohol, cinemas, theatres, theme parks, concerts, galleries and exhibitions, for example' (Fadaak & Roberts, 2018, p. 128). In-home leisure, by contrast, has changed. From the 1990s onwards, Fadaak and Roberts (2018) note that Saudi households were able to watch satellite television. News channels from other gulf states were now available to watch, and this was followed by Al-Jazeera, CNN, and the BBC. 'News was followed quickly by entertainment channels with comedies, game shows, quizzes, dramas, music, films and shopping channels' (Fadaak & Roberts, 2018, p. 130). In addition to this, they found that from 1998, a mobile telephone service became available and in 2003, an internet service. What Fadaaka and Roberts uncover, therefore, is the way 'new media' has shaped leisure and, in many ways, wider society in Saudi Arabia, specifically for younger people. Table 3.2 and Table 3.3 are taken from their work and highlight the trend of media consumption over time.

What did they find? While there had been some initial resistance, the participants had all embraced the new forms of media as part of their leisure. The same can be said of mobile phones and the engagement with social media such as Twitter and WhatsApp. Together these make participants' 'private time and family time more varied and interesting' (Fadaak & Roberts, 2018, p. 134). Moreover, this shift in leisure has had ramifications for the wider political structures of the region. No longer constrained to state television channels, Saudi households can now watch debates, and royals have had to follow – by taking part in such television. The internet has helped to spread political debate through blogs and tweets. And the younger royals are responding. Public concerts have been held, and there are museums and discussions about the possibility for theme parks. It is a fascinating case study of the way leisure and society entwine.

Table 3.2 **Trends in Internet Activity in Saudi Arabia**

	2005	2006	2007	2008	2009	2010	2011	2012	2013	2014
Internet users (in millions)	3	4.8	7.6	9.3	10.3	11.4	13.6	15.8	16.5	19.6
Internet penetration as a percentage of the total population		13.0%	20.0%	30.0%	36.0%	38.0%	41.0%	47.5%	54.1%	55.1%	63.7%

Table 3.3 Mobile Phone Activity in Saudi Arabia

	2007	2008	2009	2010	2011	2012	2013	2014
Mobile service subscriptions (in millions)	28	36	44.8	51.6	53.7	53	51	53
Mobile phone penetration as a percentage of the total population	113.0%	138.0%	167.0%	186.0%	188.0%	181.5%	169.7%	171.4%

Source: Fadaak and Roberts (2018).

3.2.2 Leisure Spending

Figure 3.4 identifies the scale of spending on culture and recreation services since 2005 and, as you can see, shows that this part of the leisure sector is worth over £54 billion per year.

But there is more. Once tourism, eating out, and the growing spend on home entertainment are accounted for, the scale of spending on leisure becomes clear. Leisure away from home dominates leisure spending both in terms of market value and share of spending, and there have been significant increases in spending over the past ten years in areas such as holidays overseas, domestic holidays, and eating out. In-home leisure spending in terms of online gambling, home entertainment, and reading (with an increase in e-books) has also seen increases, while there seems to have been a reduction in spending on alcohol (note this is on alcohol alone, not with a meal, which has increased), home and garden, and active sports. Table 3.4 offers some comparison between the figures in 2008 and 2018. Likewise, Figure 3.5 shows the share of consumers spending on leisure in the United Kingdom (UK) in 2016 and 2019, and you can see the graph is dominated by out-of-home leisure.

Over the past ten years spending on leisure goods and services in the UK has risen by over 25% and this has occurred in some sectors more than others. This may be related to the increased availability of credit, which has recovered since the recession of 2008. However, it is leisure services that are the most dynamic element of leisure expenditure. A very good example of this is how, over the course of the COVID-19 pandemic, leisure services have been hit hard by a lack of consumer spending. There tend to be four categories of consumer spending in terms of trends over time: high-growth services, which include leisure services; high-growth goods, which include leisure goods; low-growth sectors, such as non-alcoholic drinks; and declining sectors, such as alcoholic drinks.

Discussion Questions

What are the main factors which determine how much you spend on leisure in a typical month? To what extent do you think the same factors are important in determining leisure spending at a national level?

Expenditure on recreational and cultural services in the UK 2005–2019

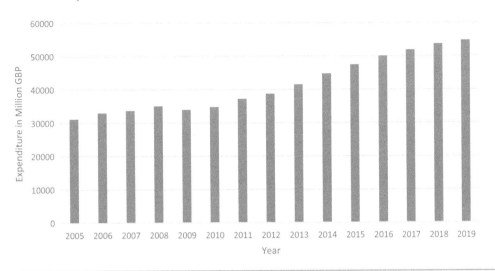

Figure 3.4 **UK leisure and recreation spending.**
Source: Office for National Statistics

Table 3.4 **Market Value in the UK**

Consumer spending on leisure	Market value in billion GBP	
	2008	*2018*
Reading	7.58	12.21
Home entertainment	22.06	68.11
House and garden	16.16	13.21
Hobbies and pastimes	9.72	*
Eating out	43.42	89.50
Alcoholic drink	43.26	21.27
Eating and drinking	86.68	110.77
Local entertainment	6.37	*
Gambling	9.94	14.30
Active sport	11.81	10.62
UK holiday accommodation	10.52	27.50
Holidays overseas	36.76	58.13

Share of consumers spending on leisure in the UK in 2016 and 2019, by category

■ Q1 2019 ■ Q1 2016

Figure 3.5 **Consumer spending on leisure in the UK.**
Source: Deloitte

Just like types of activities, patterns and trends in leisure spending are different in different areas of the world. Take for example Poland (Jung, 2005). Before the fall of communism in 1989, leisure spending in Poland was 10.5% of total household expenditure. By 1993 it had fallen to about 5% of household expenditure, and it stayed at 5 or 6% for the rest of the 1990s – the result of a greater concentration of expenditure on more basic goods and services at a time of national uncertainty and fundamental economic change (Jung, 2005). The objects of leisure spending changed too – in the late 1980s, spending was dominated by electronic equipment (colour televisions, video recorders), but by the late 1990s higher proportions were directed to tourism and reading materials.

3.2.3 Leisure Time

Over the past 40 years or so, there has been considerable discussion about whether people in more economically developed countries have increasing or decreasing amounts of leisure time. There was a trend towards the end of the twentieth century for increasing numbers of people to report feeling 'time poor' or that life had 'speeded up'. However, data seemed to show that we had more leisure time than ever. Robinson and Godbey (2010) suggested that the 'time squeeze' people reported was perceptual, created not by longer paid work time but by a growth in opportunities to spend time on different leisure activities and having to choose between them. Similarly, Gershuny and Sullivan (2019) note that this reporting coincided with the assumed emergence of a 24/7 society, the belief that people were increasingly multi-tasking to keep up, a tendency towards rushing quickly from one task to another, and growing pressures brought on by advances in technology. The latest data presented by Gurshuny and Sullivan, in fact, seem to show that fewer people in 2015 reported feeling 'always rushed' than they did in 2000. So, has this trend reversed? And how much time do we spend on leisure compared to the past? This is a very important consideration in designing sport and leisure services – to what extent do they need to be time flexible?

Overall, in the UK, the proportion of the day devoted to work, sleep, and leisure has remained stable over the past 50 years or so, however there are some subtle changes that could also account for some people feeling life has been 'speeding up'. For example, Gratton and

Taylor (2005) showed that for the last 25 years of the twentieth century, the actual working hours of manual and non-manual workers, male and female, had increased slightly. This is backed up by Gershuny and Sullivan (2019), who found that between the mid-1980s and 2015 there had been a small increase in time undertaking paid work. In 2015, 'full-time employed men and women worked on average 40.2 and 37.3 hours per week respectively, as against 26.1 and 23.8 for part-timers' (Gershuny & Sullivan, 2019, p. 86). Perhaps two points to note here are, first, while males have increased their paid work very slightly, there has been a higher increase in time females accumulate in paid employment over time. And second, in the period preceding this (1961–1985), time spent in paid work dropped for males and females.

Time in paid work for males on weekends (particularly a Saturday) has reduced over time; however, this seems to have resulted in males taking on more unpaid work relating to their home life. Gurshuny and Sullivan found that males now undertake more unpaid work, such as cleaning, looking after children, and shopping for food, when compared to the 1980s and the 1960s. Conversely, females do less unpaid work in the home than they did in the past but do more paid work than they did in 1961 (Gershuny & Sullivan, 2019). Adding together time spent in paid and unpaid work shows 'total time working' has reduced for both men and women. On average, females spend 494 minutes a day working compared to 483 minutes for males.

3.2.4 Changes in Leisure

What are the net effects on UK leisure time of leisure's increasing opportunities and of changes in paid and unpaid work time? Again, there has been no seismic shift. Despite how differently you may think UK society is now compared to the 1960s, leisure time has remained steady. According to Gershuny and Fisher (2000) leisure time increased from an average of 285 minutes a day per person in 1961 to an average of 305 minutes a day in 1995. And according to Lader et al. (2006) leisure time reached an average of 326 minutes per person per day by 2005. However, just like changes in employment patterns, changes in leisure time have not been felt equally. Gurshuny and Sullivan compared data collected in 1961, 1975, 1985, 2000, and 2015 and concluded that over that period 'leisure time increased by three-quarters of an hour for men, but by only five minutes for women, so that, while in 1961 men's and women's leisure time was somewhat equal, by 2015 men enjoyed over half an hour's more leisure on average per day than women' (Gershuny & Sullivan, 2019, p. 36). In 1961, weekend leisure time for females was almost exclusively in the home, while males' leisure time was largely away from the home. By 2015, Gurshuny and Sullivan had found this difference to have almost disappeared. This is hardly a dawning of a 'leisure age', as was once predicted.

There are examples of similar trends from around the world. In the Netherlands, for example, that stability in leisure time seems to have occurred over the past ten years or so. In 2006, on average, 42.9 hours per week were spent on leisure. By 2011 that had dropped to 42.7 hours per week, however it recovered to 43.8 hours in 2016. Moving to the USA we see that leisure time for males is higher than for females and has been all the way back to 2009. Figure 3.6 shows the hours per day spent on leisure and sports by US population between 2009 and 2019. While overall time has remained static, so has the difference between males and females.

> **Discussion Question**
>
> If leisure time is increasing over time in many countries, or at least staying the same, why do people feel under pressure for time?

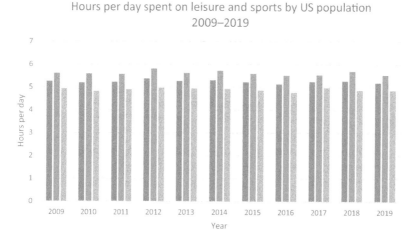

3.3 Leisure at Home

Although leisure at home appears out of reach of leisure managers, in fact it is heavily conditioned by leisure industries, which provide the choices for leisure at home, and by governments, which regulate many of the at-home activities. Furthermore, at-home leisure provides some important leads for away-from-home leisure managers – particularly in the use of technology and innovation to feed market growth. Leisure at home is a major competitor for leisure away from home, in the use of leisure time and in leisure expenditure, so it is important for managers of leisure services away from home to take note of the strategies and decisions of industries servicing leisure at home.

Leisure in the home can be divided into four categories, so let us examine the trends in each category. The first is home entertainment, which encompasses listening to music, watching films, and playing video games. Entertainment retail sales revenue in the UK rose from £5.5 billion in 2005 to £7.8 billion in 2019. However, the more significant change has been a shift from physical purchases to online purchases of home entertainment. In 2011 26.2% of purchases were digital, but by 2019 that was 81.7%. This has been mirrored in the number of retail shops for film, music, and video games, which have dropped from 2015 onwards. This trend has also been seen in television viewing. Over the past ten years or so, 'on-demand' services have been developed whereby viewers can watch 'catch-up' or classic programmes at times of their choosing. This is a good example of producing a time-flexible product to fit a perceived time-pressured market.

Second is the category of 'house and garden', and this has equally benefitted from moves to online retail. The amount spent per year on DIY tools and equipment increased by £2 billion between 2008 and 2018. The sector is now worth around £5.1 billion per year. There is, of course, a debate to be had over whether DIY is leisure or work. While some enjoy DIY, for others it remains a necessity. With respect to gardening, sales of plants have remained somewhat constant over this period. In the UK, the total revenue from the sale of plants was around £4.1 billion in 2008, and despite some slight fluctuations, by 2018 that figure was £4.2 billion.

The third category to consider is reading in the home. Reading, like other categories, has changed in the face of a technological revolution, and the process of downloading 'e-books' is something considered relatively mainstream within leisure. However, it appears that downloading has not taken over the reading sector to the extent it has with music and video. Between 2008 and 2020, revenue from digital book sales increased from around £100 million to just over £700 million, and this did replace some sales of physical books. However, there still appears to be something about the physical copy of a book that attracts us. Attitudes to reading have stayed largely the same over time, and that is supported by the amount of money we spend on books. Revenue from book sales rose from £3.1 billion in 2008 to £3.75 billion in 2019. However, there are several slight changes in behaviour to note. Over the past ten years or so, the number of people who have 'never visited a public library' has increased. Children's engagement with reading is dropping, and the number of this group who visit a library each year has dropped from 75.3% in 2008 to 61.2% in 2020. This could be replaced by buying books of course (for example, the online retail outlet Amazon is now the top location for purchasing books); however, a report from the Department for Digital, Culture, Media, and Sport in the UK seems to show participation dropping. They reported that between 2008 and 2020 participation among those aged 5–10 dropped from 87.7% to 81.1%, and for children aged 11–15 it fell even more sharply from 93.6% to 82.6%. The final category relates to 'hobbies and pastimes'. Essentially, this encompasses things that do not fall into the other categories, and while it can be hard to trace, there are some key trends to highlight. First, it seems that around the world people are spending more of their time and money on hobbies. In the USA, when considering hobbies, books, musical instruments, and sporting goods, the amount spent rose steadily from the early 1990s to 2007. And although things have stabilised since then, the sector is worth over $80 billion annually.

Technological advances have left a mark on other aspects of the leisure industry. Indeed, arguably the most significant growth trend over the past 40 years or so has been in the purchase of home computers and use of the internet. By 2018, 85% of adults aged between 16 and 74 within the European Union had used the internet during the previous three months, and in some countries, this was over 90%. Consequently, new leisure activities within the home have emerged. A good example of this is the streaming of movies, 'boxsets', and TV series via online platforms, such as Netflix, Amazon Prime, Rakuten, and NowTV. Watching movies has long been a part of people's leisure time, however, it has never been so accessible from the home. The same might be said of shopping for clothes, which can be done from the home via the internet. Similar patterns have occurred in other leisure areas. People can have friendship networks that are based solely online, they can read newspapers and books via the internet and, most obviously, the playing of computer games themselves can take place with people situated anywhere in the world via an internet connection. The implications for leisure managers are clear – a combination of technological innovation and affordability is a powerful attraction to leisure consumers.

Listening to music is another popular leisure activity heavily influenced by changing technology – from records to cassettes, to compact discs, to minidiscs, to DVDs that play music, videos, and games. However, further technological advances mean the biggest growth area relating to listening music is now online streaming via the internet. Furthermore, traditional home music systems are increasingly being replaced by tablets, mobile phones, and smart speakers. Through an internet connection, consumers can access a seemingly never-ending catalogue of music from companies such as Spotify, Deezer, Tidal, Amazon Prime Music, Apple Music, YouTube Music, and SoundCloud. Rather than buying the album or song, consumers can purchase subscriptions to these platforms and listen 'on demand'. In 2019, around 45% of internet users between the ages of 16 and 64 used streaming services to access licensed music during the day (Park *et al.*, 2019).

What are the advantages and disadvantages of technological change for the leisure consumer?

3.4 Leisure Away from Home

Leisure away from the home can also be sub-divided to help us understand some of the trends. These areas are eating and drinking, neighbourhood leisure (the entertainment element of which includes cinema, live arts, and other entertainments), and holidays and tourism. Figure 3.5 shows the share of consumer spending in these areas; however, let us explore the trends that are occurring.

The most common leisure activity outside of the home among adults in the UK is eating out. Depending on age, around 60% of people go out to eat in their spare time, which seems to have dropped over the past 20 years or so. Perhaps this is accounted for by an increase in takeaway food, which is something of a hybrid model – the food is bought out of the home but usually consumed in the home. In the UK, 95% of people eat out and/or order takeaway food. This has coincided with the emergence of companies specialising in the delivery of food, such as Deliveroo, UBER Eats, and Just Eat. This market has grown significantly over the past few years and is now worth $35.7 billion globally. Another sector that has grown in out-of-home leisure is coffee shops. In the UK, there were just over 17,000 in 2000, and that number had risen to around 29,000 by 2021. It was predicted to carry on increasing, however, we will have to wait and observe the consequences of the COVID-19 pandemic. This seems to have been in opposition to pubs, which have been declining.

Is the decline of the British pub inevitable? Should politicians be concerned because of the significance of pubs to local communities?

Holidays are a major form of leisure, and that is especially the case in the more developed countries around the world. Data from the Eurostat website help illustrate how tourism has developed, and some of the data are summarised in Figure 3.7. Over the past 20 years or so, there has been a clear trend within certain countries for more time to be spent on holiday (measured by night spent in accommodation). However, the story is slightly more complex, and there are some nuances in the data. As an example, data from the World Bank (see Figure 3.8) show that the amount spent on international tourism, as a percentage of money spent on all imports, has decreased in the UK, Germany, Italy, and the United States – interestingly, countries where the number of nights spent away from home has increased. Does this point to more 'staycations' in these countries? This is not to say international travel is not on the increase worldwide. In 2018, total expenditure on international tourism across the globe was around US$1.5 trillion and in 1996 was just under US$500 billion. Figure 3.9 shows that expenditure in some selected countries.

The gambling sector, despite being relatively small when compared to, for example, tourism, plays a significant role in many people's leisure. In the UK between 40% and 50% of people gamble at least once a month and collectively spend around £15 billion each year. Just like other industries, this sector has benefitted (or not, depending on your view of gambling) from the technological revolution, so much so that gambling can also be classed as

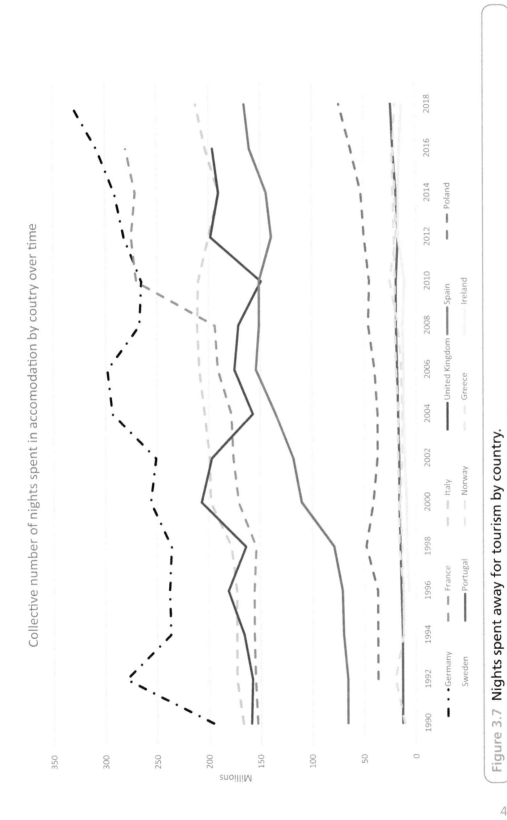

Figure 3.7 Nights spent away for tourism by country.

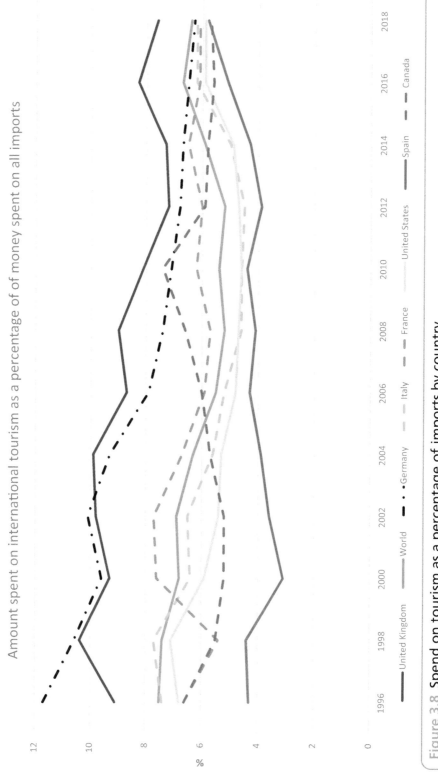

Amount spent on international tourism as a percentage of of money spent on all imports

Figure 3.8 Spend on tourism as a percentage of imports by country.

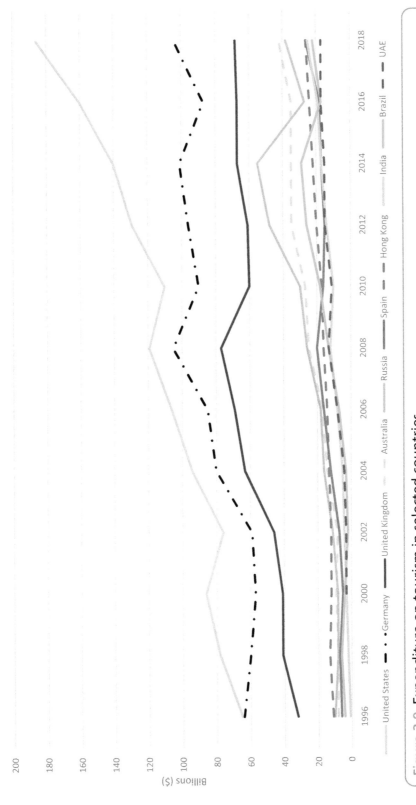

Figure 3.9 Expenditure on tourism in selected countries.

an in-home leisure activity. Between 2008 and 2019 the number of active online betting accounts in the UK rose from 16.1 million to 30.1 million, accounts that can be accessed from the comfort of our homes. Coincidentally, the number of people employed in the gambling sector dropped from roughly 130,000 in 2008 to just under 90,000 in 2018. Similarly, betting at the venues for horse and dog racing had been reducing for the past ten years. What is worth noting with regard to this sector is the significant role government regulation plays. A few examples of this are the introduction of the state franchised National Lottery in 1994, the 2005 Gambling Act (which included the formation of the gambling commission to oversee the sector), and the 2014 Gambling Act, which sought to regulate gambling for companies based overseas but wanting to deliver their service in the UK. The live arts sector (typically seen as comprising music, performance, and visual arts) has grown steadily in the UK for over a decade and before the COVD-19 pandemic had employed roughly 315,000 people. That figure had increased by around 100,000 on the previous decade. This progress is reinforced by attendances at both music concerts and festivals, which also saw increases. In 2012, for example, 2.79 million people attended a festival and 13.11 million a music concert. In 2019 those figures had increased to 5.2 million and 28.5 million respectively. Theatre attendance had remained constant over the same time. There is, of course, a note of caution here. This sector has been impacted significantly by the constraints of COVID-19, and the data over the next few years are likely to be less positive. Cinema remains a popular out-of-home leisure activity in the UK and has remained constant in terms of attendances since the turn of the century. This is not the case everywhere around the world. China, for example, has seen a dramatic growth in cinema attendance, while in the USA there has been a steady decline.

The final aspect to explore is sport and physical activity (PA) participation. Around 35% of adults in the UK participate in some form of sport at least once a week. Add in PA (walking for leisure, for example), and around 60% of people in the UK partake in 150 minutes a week. What is important to note is there has been very little change in either figure over the past decade. This overarching picture, however, does hide some subtle changes in participation worthy of note. One of the more interesting trends is that traditional sports such as Association Football, Rugby Union, and Netball have seen a reduction in participation levels. The traditional approach to being a member of a club, training and playing at set times, does not seem to marry with the way we can (or want to) spend our leisure time. Rather, people in the UK have moved towards sports and PA that they can do when they want, with whom they want, and for as long as they want. Indeed, these traditional sports have had to make changes to the organisation of their sports to appeal to this trend. 'Back to Netball', 'Walking Football', and 'Into Hockey' are all examples of more convenient offers for participants of traditional team sports. Walking for leisure is, by far, the most popular activity and, as can be seen from Figure 3.2 and Figure 3.3, many other sports and physical activities have mirrored the wider stability within sports participation.

CASE STUDY 3.2

Sport Physical Activity and Inequality

David Barrett and Professor Simon Shibli

In the UK, municipal investment in sports facilities was one of the consequences of the Wolfenden report, supported by the Sports Council during the 1970s. Gratton and Taylor (1991) detail how local authorities built some 137 sports centres and 190 swimming pools between 1974 and 1975, in order to spend surplus cash prior to amalgamation into new larger entities. Moreover, the 1975 Sport and Recreation White Paper enabled local authorities to provide sport and recreation as a discretionary service, and investment in facilities flourished towards the end of that decade. More recently, however, local authorities have withdrawn support for public facilities in response to reductions in funding from central government. As a discretionary service, sport and recreation has suffered disproportionately in the austerity era, resulting in closures and disposals. King (2012) found that there was some evidence of regional disparities in the scale and pace of budget cuts to leisure services, which were more easily defended by authorities in more affluent areas of the UK (King, 2012). Analysis of Sport England's Active Places database shows net change over time, which in turn highlights how deprived neighbourhoods compare unfavourably in terms of the provision of facilities, relative to the more affluent areas of the country (Table 3.5).

When mapped against the Indices of Multiple Deprivation, the net change in facility provision between 2000 and 2020 exhibits a distinct pattern which indicates that the supply of space in which to participate in sport has increased faster in more affluent neighbourhoods. Moreover, the increase in provision has been driven by growth among private and commercial operators such as David Lloyd and Virgin Active. In contrast, deprived areas have seen much lower growth, especially with regard to swimming pool space, while the number of grass pitches has fallen over the same period. The supply of new artificial grass pitches was more evenly distributed, but crucially, access to these spaces tends to be controlled by fencing, and participants are charged for their use. The loss of grass pitches in deprived areas is all the more significant since this implies a loss of lower cost (or in many cases free) pitch provision and a reduction in green space, which a number of authors have demonstrated to have significant amenity value for people living in deprived neighbourhoods (Mytton et al., 2012; Marmot, 2010).

More generally, the data demonstrate that while investment in new facilities has continued, even through a period of apparent austerity, the source, scope, and extent of that investment has varied significantly between deprived neighbourhoods and more affluent areas. The effect of this apparent inequality of resources is to pull the rug from under the various projects and programs aimed at increasing participation by people in areas of economic disadvantage.

Further evidence is provided by the users of public sports facilities. Data from Sport England's National Facility Benchmarking Service show that over time, it is users on lower incomes (in routine and casual occupations) who are increasingly under-represented in public sports halls and swimming pools, even in the best performing facilities (Figure 3.10). The graph shows representation scores for NS-SEC 6–7, where a score of 1 represents the expected number of users based on a facility catchment population profile. Based on facility catchment populations, the proportion of people from NS-SEC 6–7 using the best performing centres was 95% of the 'expected' level in 2014, but only 60% in 2019.

Widdop et al. (2018) use an analysis of participation data from the Active People Survey to contextualise reductions in local authority budgets for sport and recreation because of central government cuts to funding. Despite some evidence of service innovation, and an increase in funding from the health sector, the effects of ' "austerity measures" have disproportionately affected the working class'.

Table 3.5 Net Change in Sport Facility Provision 2000-2020

Facilities	IMD 2019 Deciles										
	More Deprived							Less Deprived			Total
	1	2	3	4	5	6	7	8	9	10	
Sports Hall n	109	42	124	100	131	159	176	179	237	274	1,531
%	7%	3%	8%	7%	9%	10%	11%	12%	15%	18%	100%
Swimming Pool n	10	18	32	47	44	44	78	85	95	94	547
%	2%	3%	6%	9%	8%	8%	14%	16%	17%	17%	100%
Grass Pitches n	-21	-118	-72	-104	4	61	113	91	239	217	410
%	0%	-3%	-2%	-2%	0%	1%	3%	2%	5%	5%	9%
Artificial Grass Pitch n	405	369	412	345	360	391	446	447	432	463	4,070
%	10%	9%	10%	8%	9%	10%	11%	11%	11%	11%	100%
Total n	503	311	496	388	539	655	813	802	1,003	1,048	6,558
%	8%	5%	8%	6%	8%	10%	12%	12%	15%	16%	100%

Source: Active Places Database, Sport England 2020

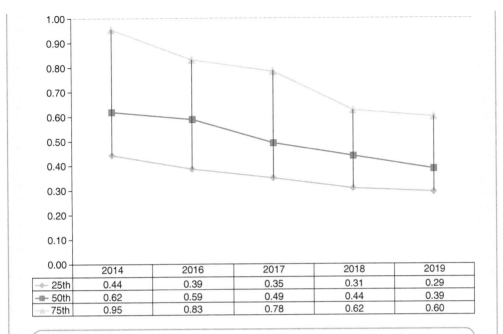

	2014	2016	2017	2018	2019
25th	0.44	0.39	0.35	0.31	0.29
50th	0.62	0.59	0.49	0.44	0.39
75th	0.95	0.83	0.78	0.62	0.60

Figure 3.10 Representation scores for NS-SEC 6–7 at public sports facilities in England.

Source: Sport England, National Benchmarking Service

3.5 General Demographic and Socio-Economic Trends

As has been demonstrated on several occasions throughout this chapter, we cannot compartmentalise leisure from wider social and economic trends. For example, note the impact that technological advancement has left in our leisure lives. To conclude this chapter, some of the more important general trends in society are explored from a leisure perspective.

3.5.1 Growing and Ageing Populations

According to the United Nations, the global population stands at around 7.8 billion people. But it is the growth in that population that merits consideration. In most regions of the world the population is growing. Of that, the highest rate of growth is in the Middle East and North Africa (MENA) region, where the annual increase can be over 3%. On the opposite end of the scale, Japan and a handful of Eastern European countries show a slight decrease in their population year on year. However, taken as a whole, the global population is increasing by roughly 1.1% each year. One further characteristic of the global population is that it is ageing. That is to say, the percentage of the population over 60 is increasing and has been doing so exponentially for the past 50 years. This trend is predicted to continue for the first half of this century at least. To give some context, in 1950 there were around 250 million people worldwide who were 60 or over; by 2020 that figure had reached 1000 million (1 billion), and it is forecasted that by 2050 that number will be just over 2000 million (2 billion). Over the same period, the number of people in the global population aged below 14 has started to plateau. Despite this age group growing from around 850 million people in 1950 to 1.9 billion people by 2020, there is likely to be very little growth in this age group over the next 30 years. This will have implications for leisure managers when put alongside the growth in older adults. If the participation rate for an activity – the percentage of the population who participates in it – stays constant but population size increases, the market expands. If both the population and participation rates in sport and leisure increase, then the growth in sport and leisure markets will be that much greater. Alternatively, if participation rates fall, as we have noted that some have in the UK recently, this may be 'compensated' by population increases such that the market for sport stays the same size or even increases. It is important for a leisure manager to anticipate such considerations, alongside demographic changes such as those reviewed in the following text, to forecast their future market size and plan provision accordingly.

Discussion Question

What are the threats and opportunities for leisure providers when considering the ageing population?

3.5.3 Social Structures

Inequality

In numerous areas around the world, wealth and income inequality is increasing. The UK is one such area. In 2020 the London School of Economics' International Inequalities Institute released a report (www.lse.ac.uk/International-Inequalities) into inequality and the impact it has on social mobility (Friedman *et al.*, 2019). In the foreword to that report (p. 3) it was noted:

> In 2005, the Sutton Trust published research on the decline of social mobility in Britain. It put social mobility on the map. It starkly demonstrated that opportunities to get on in life were unequal and many of the ladders to success for previous generations had gone. 15 years later it is clear that the gap in opportunity between those at the top of society and everyone else has still not been bridged. Today's report provides powerful new evidence of persistent inequality of opportunity.

Another useful resource for this issue is the World Inequality Database. Their 2018 report noted that in Europe, North America, China, India, and Russia, the percentage of a nation's total income that is accounted for by the top 10% of earners has been increasing since the 1980s. One of the sharpest increases has emerged in India, there was a very sharp increase in Russia during the 1990s, and in Europe there has been a steady increase over a similar period. In terms of the world regions, the Middle East is the most unequal part of the world, with an average of 61% of a nations' income resting in the hands of the top 10% of the population; however, it must be noted that this has been reducing slightly for the past 15 years or so. Income inequality in Brazil and Sub-Saharan Africa are high but, equally, are reducing steadily. What has accompanied this trend is the so-called stagnation of the 50%. Globally, and this can be mapped on to more local levels in Western Europe and the USA for example, growth in income has not been consistent across sections of the population. According to the World Inequality Database, the income share of the global bottom 50% has lingered close to 9% since 1980. Over the same 36-year period, the top 1% of the global population saw a growth in their share of income from 16% in 1980 to 22% in 2000 and then down slightly to 20% by 2016. The final point to make is that wealth and income inequality are linked to other forms of inequality, such as health inequalities, housing inequality, and inequality in education. As shown in Case Study 3.2, it is also linked to sport, PA, and leisure inequalities.

The second topic to address is that of the changing characteristics of 'the family'. In the UK specifically, between 1996 and 2019, there has been an increase in the number of families. However, the number of families that are made up of one mother and one father who are married is not growing. In fact, it is stable and the growth in families is occurring elsewhere. The most significant growth has occurred in two areas specifically – first, opposite sex partners who are cohabiting but are not married. In 1996 this accounted for 1.45 million families. By 2019, the number had increased to 3.4 million, just under 2 million of whom had no children. The second significant increase has been in the number of same-sex couple families. This sat at 16,000 families in 1996 but over the past 23 years has risen to just over 100,000 families. A large proportion of these families do not have children, although an ever-increasing number do. One other category of family worth noting are lone parent families. From 1996 there has been a slight growth in the number of such families from 2.4 million to 2.8 million. In 2019 these were made up of around 400,000 lone father families and 2.4 million lone mother families, both of which have slightly increased in number since 1996.

> ### Discussion Question
>
> Which leisure activities will benefit from (1) inequality? and (2) changes in the ways families are constructed?

3.5.4 Ethnic Diversity

At a very basic level, those who manage sport and leisure provision need to be aware of the shifts in the ethnic make-up of their markets, not least because those from different ethnic backgrounds have different leisure needs and demands. This becomes increasingly important when set against the context of growing global migration and, as a result, an increase in multi-cultural or multi-ethnic societies. In England and Wales the last data point we have as a reference is 2011. Indeed, at the time of writing this book, there is another census being taken across England and Wales. Not unexpectedly, those identifying as 'White British' make up much of the population, at 80.5%. This percentage is reducing; in 2001 that figure was 87.4%. So where have the changes occurred? Well, a major trend in Europe since 2004 is immigration from the eight former Eastern Bloc countries which joined the European Union, facilitated by regulations on the freedom of movement of labour within the EU. Out of 1.42 million people who arrived in the UK from May 2004 to November 2006, for example, 427,000 were people registering to work from these countries, with the vast majority coming from Poland. This is reinforced by data from the Office for National Statistics. Between 2001 and 2011 the percentage of the population who identified as 'Other White', which includes the groups from the former Eastern Bloc countries, saw the largest increase in their share of the population, increasing from 2.5% to 4.4%. Indeed, by 2011, there were 579,000 people residing in England and Wales who were born in Poland. Only those born in India (694,000) made up a larger proportion of the population. Over the same period there were slight declines in those identifying as 'White Irish', which dropped from 1.2% of the population to 0.9% of the population. Similarly, dropping from 0.4% to 0.3% of the population were those identifying as 'Mixed White and Black African'. However, the percentage of the population from a 'Black African' background doubled from 0.9% in 2001 to 1.8% in 2011.

3.6 Conclusions

This chapter has sought to highlight the complex link between trends in wider society and those within leisure. Indeed, while these have been separated out for the purposes of analysis, they are, of course, all part of the same process. Maintaining a handle on and, more importantly, understanding the consequences of changes over time is a key skill for any leisure manager. Over time there have been some areas where progress has been rapid, and it has impacted almost all our leisure, for example, technological advancements. But it is also worthy of note that there are some enduring activities that have stayed. Indeed, although the perception is often that current society is very different from the past, as this chapter shows, there are plenty of aspects within leisure that have not changed that much at all.

Practical Task

1 For a particular country, use the internet or other appropriate sources to find the changes over the last 20 years in participation rates for two sport or leisure activities of your choice, as well as changes in population over the same period. Calculate for these two activities what has happened to the number of people participating, i.e. to the size of the market. What are the implications of your results for planning the two sport or leisure activities?

Structured Guide to Further Reading

Active Lives Reports. Retrieved from https://activelives.sportengland.org/
Gershuny, J., & Sullivan, O. (2018). *What We Really Do All Day: Insights from the Centre for Time Use Research*. Penguin, Grantham.
International Inequalities Institute Annual Report. (2020) Retrieved from www.lse.ac.uk/International-Inequalities/Assets/Documents/W920-0124-III-REPORT-V20-2.pdf
Lyn Craig, B. C., & van Tienoven, T. P. (2019) Young people's daily activity in a globalized world: A cross-national comparison using time use data. *Journal of Youth Studies*. doi:10.1080/13676261.2019.1659941

Useful Websites

https://inequality.org/
www.lse.ac.uk/International-Inequalities
www.ons.gov.uk/
https://wid.world/

References

Dahlberg, L., McKee, K. J., Fritzell, J., Heap, J., & Lennartsson, C. (2020). Trends and gender associations in social exclusion in older adults in Sweden over two decades. *Archives of Gerontology and Geriatrics*, 89, 104032.

Fadaak, T. H., & Roberts, K. (2018). Young adults, new media, leisure and change in Saudi Arabia. *World Leisure Journal*, 60(2), 127–139.

Friedman, S., Savage, M., McArthur, D., & Hecht, K. (2019). *Elites in the UK: Pulling Away? Social Mobility, Geographic Mobility and Elite Occupations*. LSE, London.

Gershuny, J. I., & Fisher, K. (2000). *Leisure in the UK across the 20th Century*. In Halsey, A. Webb, J. (Ed.). (2000). *Twentieth-century British social trends*. Macmillan Press.

Gershuny, J. I., & Sullivan, O. (2019). *What We Really Do All Day: Insights from the Centre for Time Use Research*. Penguin, Grantham.

Gratton, C., & Taylor, P. (1991). *Government and the Economics of Sport and Recreation*. Harlow, Longman.

Gratton, C., & Taylor, P. (2005). The economics of work and leisure. In A. Veal & J. Howarth (Eds.), *The Future of Work and Leisure*. Routledge, London.

Jung, B. (2005). Poland. In G. Cushman, A. J. Veal, & J. Zuzanek (Eds.), *Free Time and Leisure Participation: International Perspectives*. CABI Publishing, Wallingford.

King, N. (2012). *Local Authority Sport and Recreation Services in England: Where Next?* APSE, Edge Hill.

Lader, D., Short, S., & Gershuny, J. (2006). *The Time Use Survey, 2005*. Office for National Statistics, London.

Marmot, M. (2010). *Fair Society Healthy Lives* (Full Report). The Marmot Review, London.

Mytton, O. T., Townsend, N., Rutter, H., & Foster, C. (2012). Green space and physical activity: An observational study using health survey for England data. *Health Place*, 18(5), 1034–1041.

Office for National Statistics (ONS). (1996). *General Household Survey, 1996*. ONS, London.

Park, M., Thom, J., Mennicken, S., Cramer, H., & Macy, M. (2019). Global music streaming data reveal diurnal and seasonal patterns of affective preference. *Nature Human Behaviour*, 3(3), 230–236.

Robinson, J., & Godbey, G. (2010). *Time for Life: The Surprising Ways Americans Use Their Time*. Penn State Press.

Scheerder, J., & Vos, S. (2011). Social stratification in adults' sports participation from a time-trend perspective Results from a 40-year household study. *European Journal for Sport and Society*, 8(1–2), 31–44.

Widdop, P., King, N., Parnell, D., Cutts, D., & Millward, P. (2018). Austerity, policy and sport participation in England. *International Journal of Sport Policy and Politics*, 10(1), 7–24.

Chapter 4

People's Needs and Leisure Demand

In This Chapter

- Do leisure needs exist?
- What is the difference between leisure needs, wants, and demands?
- What factors influence leisure participation?
- What are the planning and management implications of leisure demands?

DOI: 10.4324/9780367823610-4

Summary

All humans have the same basic needs that must be satisfied. In theories of motivation, need is seen as a force within the individual to gain satisfaction, enjoyment, and completeness as well as survival and safety. There are many levels and types of need, including important needs of self-actualisation and personal development that sport and leisure help to achieve. 'Leisure needs' as such may not exist; rather there are human needs which can find satisfaction through leisure. Need is not just an individual concept but should also be considered in the form of social need, which embraces several different types, including normative, felt, expressed, comparative, created, false, and changing needs.

Many discrete and interrelated factors condition people's choices and participation in leisure activities, which is the most obvious expression of their demand. These include personal factors, social and circumstantial factors, and opportunities presented by leisure providers. People's use of facilities and services is affected, to a considerable degree, by management policy and management actions, which should be designed to both fulfil customers' expectations and counter barriers to participation. Facilities must both be accessible and provide attractive leisure opportunities.

4.1 Introduction

The understanding of leisure helps us to meet some of the needs of individuals and groups of people and is therefore of value to the wider community. Leisure services are claimed by their providers to be based on the needs of the people they are intended to serve. However, is this always the case in practice? Do policy makers, planners, providers, and managers of leisure services have sufficient insights into people's needs? Should they be concerned with needs, wants, or demands, and what is the difference? Policy makers, facility managers, and club officers all seek to identify what their citizens, customers, and members need and how their demands can be satisfied.

This chapter first discusses the concept of need. It addresses such questions as: What are human needs? Can leisure meet some of these needs? and Do leisure needs exist? More pragmatically, leisure providers are faced with evidence of demand in the form of participation in sport and leisure activities. Therefore, after clarifying the distinction between needs, wants, and demand, we review evidence on demand. We attempt to clarify the major demographic and socio-economic influences on participation in sport and leisure, using evidence from the UK and beyond. Such evidence is important in informing policy makers and service managers who are interested in designing and managing appropriate opportunities for their citizens and customers. Participation evidence drives the market segmentation which managers, and particularly marketing managers, employ when planning, providing, and promoting services for specific groups of people (see Chapter 14).

4.2 Needs, Wants, and Demand

Leisure policy makers, researchers, planners, and managers often equate 'needs' with wants or demands. However, there are differences between the three:

- **Needs** are deficiencies which relate to fundamental human requirements. Arguably, sport and leisure are most relevant to health and self-development needs.
- Leisure **wants** are many and various, and they exist as responses to the desire to satisfy needs and preferences. They include the desire for new leisure experiences such as gym membership, holidays, online gaming, theatre shows, and football matches.
- Leisure **demands** are similar to wants but are often interpreted as actual, revealed demands, i.e. leisure activities and expenditures that have been realised. Many wants may not be so realised, e.g. simply because of the lack of sufficient money.

Policy makers and leisure planners have generally been concerned with identifying sport and leisure demands rather than understanding people's needs. Large-scale government and commercial surveys, for example, have identified certain demands but have not elaborated what motivates people to leisure and why people participate. Whereas a 'need' appears to be conceptually 'woolly' and operationally elusive, a 'demand' appears tangible, measurable, even predictable (Kew & Rapoport, 1975). However, Torkildsen, among others, believed that if researchers are to provide information of real value to policy makers and planners, they must explore people's needs and values, not just their demands. To reach a full understanding of demand, it is necessary to know not only what people do, as provided by social surveys, but also reasons for participation and non-participation and the needs that underpin demand, which are better explored by qualitative research.

4.3 Needs, Drives, and Motivation

One simple view is that human need is caused by something that is missing, a deficit. Of relevance to sport and leisure, for example, are the need for physical health when overweight, the need for relaxation when stressed, and the need for excitement when bored. Needs here are the causes of motivation, rather than the motivation itself. Drives are goal directed; they release energy. They are generally considered to be the motivating factors within human personality.

Many psychologists who see the motivational aspects of human needs as drives do so in conjunction with the concept of 'homeostasis', which is a fundamental need to maintain a state of relative internal stability. Homeostasis is easiest to understand in terms of physiological needs, for example the relief of cold or hunger. Needs which are more social in nature, such as the needs for achievement, self-fulfilment, and acceptance, are less easily accounted for in terms of homeostasis. However, the principle of 'psychological homeostasis' is used by Shivers (1967) as the basis of 're-creation', i.e. purposeful leisure.

Need is often used to denote some inner state that initiates a drive; for example, 'Humans need to sleep'. This is the approach taken by Maslow, whose analysis of the 'hierarchy of needs' is the most well-known theory of needs. Maslow (1954, 1968) discerned five levels of need. If humans are chronically hungry or thirsty, the biological and physiological need to secure food and water will be most powerful. After hunger and thirst needs have been met, other higher needs emerge. Next will be the needs for safety, orderliness, and a predictable world. When these have been met, the need for belonging and love (family, personal, and work relationships) is followed by the need for esteem (achievement, status, responsibility, reputation) and then finally the need for self-actualisation, i.e. for personal growth and intel-lectual fulfilment. It is at the highest levels of need – belonging, esteem, and self-actualisation – that sport and leisure have a role to play.

Doyal and Gough (1991), however, do not accept Maslow's 'Needs Hierarchy': 'Its strict temporal sequencing of motivations in question is simply false. Some people seem far more concerned with their self-actualisation than their safety – mountain climbers, for example'. Maslow's categories seem either to be combined or at times to conflict. Thompson (1987) takes a similar stance: 'One can have a drive to consume something, like lots of alcohol, which one does not need and at the same time have a need for something, like exercise or diet, which one is in no way driven to seek'.

Perceived need, therefore, may be a matter of individual preference. Subjective feeling, however, is not a reliable indicator of human need; it is more an expression of wants. We can strongly want things which are seriously harmful, such as recreational drugs or excess alcohol, and, in our ignorance, not desire things which we require to avoid harm, such as exercise. The message should not go unheeded by leisure managers. We can provide excellent, accessible ser-vices and programmes which are good for our health and charge nothing for them, yet people will buy alternatives which they desire but which are not good for their health, such as sweets and snacks. In practice, this is why management decisions on what to supply are typically based on revealed demand, rather than more fundamental concepts of need.

Discussion Question

Should a sport or leisure manager be more interested in what leisure activities people undertake or what leisure means to people?

Doyal and Gough (1991) reason that there are two main types of need: one concerned with survival, security, and health; and the second concerned with what they term 'auton-omy' and learning. By *autonomy*, Doyal and Gough mean they believe that a basic personal need is to recognise ourselves as distinct and separate individual people and that through learning and education we grow and develop. Human beings are not capable of growing up and developing alone; therefore, basic needs are provided for in a social context. Society has created 'institutions' to provide for the realisation of individual needs; among them, leisure facilities and organisations.

It appears to be a reasonable conclusion that there is a relationship between need and motivation. Significant contributions to the understanding of motivations in leisure are pro-vided by Csikszentmihalyi (1975) and Scitovsky (1976). Scitovsky analysed how people's preferences are formed and suggested, in contrast to the state of homeostasis, that optimum arousal was a key criterion for success in consumption. Csikszentmihalyi uses the term *flow* to describe a similar state of optimum consumption experience – 'a holistic sensation that people feel when they act with total involvement'. To take the example of playing a game of football, if the level of competition and standard of playing is too low, arousal is too low, and it will be a boring experience. If, however, the standard of play is too high, arousal is too high, and it will cause anxiety and dissatisfaction. When arousal is optimum, the game will be a pleasure to play.

According to Scitovsky, the key factors in determining optimum arousal are the degree of novelty of the consumption experience and the skill of the individual in coping with this nov-elty. For example, an experienced mountain climber has the skill to cope with very difficult and risky climbs and to optimise arousal. A beginner, however, may get just as much of a 'buzz' from a relatively easy climb. Many sports organisations organise activities, and particularly the learning of appropriate skills, in a way that implicitly acknowledges these principles of motivation by 'optimum arousal', and many aspire to a condition from playing sport that is equivalent to Csikszentmihalyi's 'flow'.

> ## Discussion Questions
>
> What needs and motivations does television viewing service? Do they justify television's importance in leisure participation?

4.4 Do Leisure Needs Exist?

Both 'leisure' and 'needs' have been shown to be complex concepts. Linking leisure to needs and asking the question, 'Do leisure needs exist?' is even more complex.

Despite the limitations of Maslow's theory, one benefit is that it emphasises the developmental needs of the individual. Need is not just seen as the reduction of a state of tension or the return to homeostatic equilibrium. In addition, people are striving towards self-actualisation and growth. If leisure has a place in this process, self-actualisation could be perceived as one of the goals of leisure or, indeed, the ultimate goal.

Tillman (1974) is one of many authors who have examined needs and identified those which are important to leisure. He listed needs for:

- New experiences like adventure;
- Relaxation, escape, and fantasy;
- Recognition and identity;
- Security – being free from thirst, hunger, or pain;
- Dominance – to direct others or control one's environment;
- Response and social interaction – to relate and react to others;
- Mental activity – to perceive and understand;
- Creativity;
- Service to others – the need to be needed;
- Physical activity and fitness.

> ## Discussion Questions
>
> What needs does sport and leisure fulfil for you? Are any of these needs not capable of being met by non-leisure activities such as paid work, household work, or community work?

However, the concept of 'leisure needs' is misleading. People have needs which can be satisfied in a variety of ways, including not just leisure but also other means such as housing, work, and family. One way of meeting needs may be through taking up leisure opportunities; but it is only one way. Leisure needs as such may not exist. The case study of empirical investigations of leisure consumers' benefits (Case study 4.1) relates three different leisure experiences to concepts very similar to some of the needs identified here.

Exploring Benefits for Leisure Consumers: Three Examples

How are leisure needs analysed in practice? This case study summarises three studies in *Managing Leisure: An International Journal* which attempt to empirically identify the benefits for customers of different services and which give important indications of the needs these services are satisfying. These examples are cricket spectators in the UK, visitors to a zoo in the USA, and children at a summer camp in Greece.

All three studies used quantitative techniques to identify benefits to, motivators for, and preferences of consumers. This involved questionnaire surveys, the responses for which were grouped, through factor analysis, to identify the main types of benefit. Whereas the questions did not use the term *need*, the results relate closely to some of the concepts of needs reviewed in this chapter.

In the cricket study (Kuenzel & Yassim, 2007) the purpose is to identify the relationship between the emotion of joy, customer satisfaction, the informal promotion by them of the experience by 'word of mouth', and the revisit intentions of customers. Sport spectating is described as hedonic consumption, in the pursuit of personal pleasure, and one of the principal drivers of customer satisfaction in such an activity is the feeling of joy it generates. Three variables are explored relating to joy:

1 **The quality of the game** – represented by the performance of the two teams, but particularly the team that the individual supports;
2 **Social facilitation** – represented by the spectator's interaction with friends, family, and other spectators, as well as sharing the experience of the game with others;
3 **Auditory elements** – represented by the atmosphere created by the different noises of the crowd.

The results of the study show a significant relationship between the three variables and joy, which influences customer satisfaction positively, which in turn influences word-of-mouth and revisit intentions favourably. Social facilitation was found to be the most important dimension of joy.

In the study of Fort Worth Zoo customers in the USA (Tomas *et al.*, 2002), four major benefits emerged as important for visitors:

1 **Family togetherness** – bringing the family together in an enjoyable experience;
2 **Companionship** – being with and doing things with friends;
3 **Wildlife enjoyment** – enjoying rare sights and discovering new elements;
4 **Wildlife appreciation and learning** – including learning more about wildlife, appreciating it more, and thinking what to do to help wildlife.

In the study of children at a Greek summer camp (Alexandris & Kouthouris, 2005), six factors emerged as the main motivations for respondents to attend the camp:

1 **Camp experience** – including memorable experiences, community life, and fun;
2 **Socialisation among old friends**;
3 **Socialisation with new friends**;
4 **Independence** – including feeling free and getting away from parents;

5   **Participation in activities** – i.e. the experience of sporting, outdoor, and water activities;
6   **Parents' decisions** – not really a benefit, just reflecting the fact that some children are sent to camp against their preferences.

Socialisation with new friends was identified as the most important motivation, with camp experience the second most important.

In all three of these investigations the socialisation element emerges strongly, and this relates closely to Maslow's 'belonging' need and to Tillman's 'response and social interaction' need. Other consumer benefits to emerge as important relate more to the specific experiences offered by the different services, i.e. the quality of the cricket match, wildlife attributes at the zoo, and camp experience at the children's camp.

These relate most closely to Tillman's need for 'new experiences' and possibly also to Maslow's 'self-actualisation' need.

Another aspect of these studies needs emphasising. All were undertaken to inform providers of what their customers valued most, in order for them to improve their services. These studies are very much in the spirit of finding out not just what your customers do, but what they need from and value about the service provided.

4.5 Social Needs

Needs, then, have important social dimensions. Bradshaw (1972) classified social needs into four categories: normative, felt, expressed, and comparative. Godbey (1976) and others expanded the number of classifications by adding additional categories: created needs, false needs, and changing needs. These seven needs are described here within the context of providing leisure services.

4.5.1 Normative Needs and Leisure

These represent value judgements made by professionals in the sport and leisure field, for example the standards that are set by policy makers for the amount of open space needed in local communities. They are usually expressed in quantitative terms and have been commonly used in sport and leisure planning. However, the use of such normative needs as the major determinant of leisure provision can be challenged on several points – a full discussion of the problems and benefits of standards is presented in Chapter 11.

4.5.2 Felt Needs and Leisure

These can be defined as the desires that an individual has but has not yet actively expressed; they are the determinants of what a person thinks he or she wants to do. Felt needs are largely learned patterns, from personal experience and the experiences of others. They are limited by an individual's knowledge and perception of available leisure opportunities. However, mass communication has expanded individuals' knowledge beyond the realm of their experience. Clearly sport and leisure managers have an opportunity to influence individuals' felt needs, by promotion.

4.5.3 Expressed Needs and Leisure

These are felt needs that have been able to be realised, i.e. activities in which individuals actually participate. They provide the leisure manager with knowledge about current leisure preferences, tastes, and interests and are typically the most common frame of reference for sport and leisure planning, if only because they are relatively easy to identify. However, if leisure resources, programmes, and services are based solely on expressed needs, there is less incentive to initiate new services and programmes. Expressed need itself does not give a total picture of felt need, or of why people do or do not participate.

4.5.4 Comparative Needs and Leisure

Often an individual or organisation will compare itself with another individual or organisation. This may be done purely out of interest, or it may provoke feelings of deficiency. Care must be exercised when utilising the comparative method in assessing needs – one cannot assume that what works well in one situation will automatically be effective in another.

4.5.5 Created Needs and Leisure

Godbey (1976) suggests that policy makers and professionals can create leisure interests. Created needs refer to those activities which organisations have 'introduced to individuals and in which they will subsequently participate at the expense of some activity in which they previously participated'. In other words, created needs refer to those programmes, services, and activities solely determined by the organisation and accepted by the participant without prior felt need or knowledge. Some analysts are critical of created needs, seeing them as stimulating demand simply to feed growth in commercial business. However, according to Edginton *et al.* (1980) the created needs approach can be useful to the participant and to the organisation:

> Many individuals are grateful to organizations for helping them identify an area of interest that previously they had not considered. In a sense, the approach is a form of leisure education that is an important component of the philosophy of recreation and leisure service organizations. The organization also benefits by serving as an agency that creates opportunities for stimulation and enrichment. As a result, individuals may look to the organization as a vehicle for providing innovative experience.

There are many examples within leisure of what might be seen as created needs which demonstrate innovation and enterprise, such as theme parks, 4D cinema, budget airlines, and even restaurant delivery services (e.g. Deliveroo, Just Eat). The ultimate judges of the value of such products are consumers, who vote with their feet and their money. It is probably more appropriate to term such products *created demands*, rather than *created needs*.

4.5.6 False Needs and Leisure

Needs may be created which are inessential, which are in fact false needs, i.e. there is a distinction between what an individual is aware of needing (felt needs), what are usefully 'created needs', and what is created but not needed. Marcuse (1964) suggested that society encourages the individual to develop certain sorts of 'need' which serve the interests of society as a whole but may be false needs for the individual. Thus, people acquire the 'need' for cars, laptops, smart phones, etc., which it is in the general interests of the economy to promote. However, they are false needs to the extent that they are not strictly essential. However, it is hard to prove the existence of false needs, and it is ethically dubious to challenge the expressed demands of customers who react positively to innovative products and services by labelling them 'false needs'.

4.5.7 Changing Needs in Leisure

Rhona and Robert Rapoport (1975) claim that although every person has needs, these needs change as one progresses from one phase of life to another. The Rapoports' thesis is that all people have a quest for personal identity. Each person is seen as having a 'career' consisting of separate but interrelated strands. Three major strands relate to family, work, and leisure. Each life strand produces changes in needs, interests, and activities at critical points in life such as marriage and the birth of children. It is important for sport and leisure providers to consider the needs attributed to each stage in the life cycle if they are to make the most appropriate provision for different age segments of the population.

Another dimension to social needs is social control. One of the assumptions made in this book is that what is fulfilling, meaningful, and worthwhile for the individual is in the main likely to be worthwhile for the community also. Leisure needs, therefore, should be considered in a social and community context. Stokowski (1994) suggested that leisure is a consistent feature of life in 'human gatherings', but often for social control purposes:

> leisure is something that human beings need just as they need food, shelter, warmth, security and protection. At the same time . . . leisure is seen as quite low down on the scale of essential social values. . . . Leisure is regarded as something to be given as a reward to the individual and society or withheld as a punishment or as a way of controlling social behaviour.

This view of leisure sees it as part of a social system, including family, employment, education, and government, which determines what an individual does, even to a large extent what he or she chooses to do. Leisure in this system is designed to provide opportunities for people which are controlled and conform to social norms. This is perhaps best demonstrated by an example of deviation from such social norms. UK government policy in response to riots in Brixton and Liverpool in 1981 included efforts to improve leisure opportunities, and one way of looking at this policy response is to see leisure as a tool to bring dissatisfied young people back within social control. Another more subtle example of social control is the way that unemployed people often reduce their formal leisure participation, not just because they have less income, but also because they feel unworthy of such leisure – they have not earned it.

Discussion Question

Discuss the key differences between wanting to know how sport and leisure can satisfy people's needs and being able to research more easily what people choose to do in sport and leisure activities.

4.6 Sport and Leisure Participation

Revealed demand is documented in many countries by data on participation. The most common indicator used is participation rates, i.e. the percentage of a population or sub-group that participates in an activity over a given time. Table 4.1 gives English participation rates for 2018–2019 in a variety of sport and leisure activities. This evidence is produced by an annual *Taking Part* survey of adults (16 years and older) conducted in England since 2005 (DCMS, 2019a). Another large national survey in England, *Active People*, concentrates on sports participation, so results from this survey are reviewed in Chapter 9.

The *Taking Part* survey illustrates some of the problems when moving from conceptual discussions about needs and demand to more practical expressions of demand through evidence. *Taking Part* is comprehensive, but it does not ask questions about needs, and it does not cover all leisure activities – it is confined to the five categories in Table 4.1. And within each category it is selective about which activities are included – in arts events, for example, it does not ask about cinema visiting. Nevertheless, it is a relatively comprehensive overview of national participation in leisure.

Table 4.2 provides some evidence of the leisure pursuits of young people aged 5–15 years in England (DCMS, 2019a). It demonstrates the differences between total participation and participation outside school, the latter being more voluntary. The data pertain to activities done outside of school and relate to more leisure-focused activities as opposed to sport participation. It is also split into two age brackets (5–10-year-olds and 11–15-year-olds) to provide some broader comparisons.

The *Taking Part* evidence in Tables 4.1 and 4.2 typically records what percentages of adults and children in England undertook each type of leisure activity at least once in the year. *Taking Part* asks other relevant questions about participation, including frequency of participation, which varies considerably.

The evidence on what people demand in leisure is vital as a set of signals to sport and leisure managers, expressing people's revealed preferences. Despite the huge variety of leisure activities engaged in, there are a few activities that are very popular, and in that sense leisure

Table 4.1 Annual Participation Rates for Adults in Various Leisure Activities in England, 2018–2019

Leisure activity	Percentage of adults participating in the year
Engaged with the arts	77
Visited a heritage site	72
Visited a museum or gallery	50
Visited a library	33
Used a social networking website or app	84

Source: DCMS (2019b). https://assets.publishing.service.gov.uk/government/uploads/system/uploads/attachment_data/file/879725/Taking_Part_Survey_Adult_Report_2018_19.pdf

Table 4.2 Annual Participation Rates in Leisure for Young People in England, 2018–2019

Leisure activity	Percentage of 5–10-year-olds participating	Percentage of 11–15-year-olds participating
Engaged with the arts	96	97
Visited a heritage site	71	67
Visited a museum or gallery	63	60
Visited a public library	64	70

Source: DCMS (2019c). https://assets.publishing.service.gov.uk/government/uploads/system/uploads/attachment_data/file/832510/Taking_Part_Survey_Child_Report_2018_19.pdf

demand is largely predictable. Participation evidence identifies which are the mainstream markets and which are minority markets, at least in terms of revealed demand.

4.7 What Factors Influence Leisure Participation?

Many factors influence people's leisure choices. The first group of factors relates to the individual: his or her stage in life, interests, attitudes, abilities, upbringing, and personality. The second group relates to the circumstances and situations in which individuals find themselves, the social setting of which they are a part, the time at their disposal, their job, and their income. The third group relates to the opportunities and support services available to the individual: resources, the quality of activities, facilities and programmes, and the management of them.

Table 4.3 summarises many of these different factors – it is an illustration of the complexity and variety of influences on an individual's leisure participation and expenditure decisions. In addition, even if people have identical circumstances and opportunities, one person may choose one activity and another something entirely different – personal preferences are important too.

In England, the *Taking Part* survey provided direct evidence of what individuals think prevents them from participating in various leisure activities. Table 4.4 summarises the top responses for 2018–2019. For arts and heritage activities, personal preferences are at the root of the most common constraint – a lack of interest. This is difficult for leisure managers to overcome because it indicates that these people may not even be potential attenders, although new interest might be generated by effective education and promotion. For sport the main constraint is perceived health status, which is more capable of being modified by managers. Physical activities can be designed to take into consideration all kinds of health problems, and indeed physical activity is typically promoted as a means of improving health status. For libraries the main reason for non-attendance is that there is no need to go – presumably because alternative sources of reading and reference materials are readily available, i.e. purchases and the internet.

By understanding the major relationships between leisure participation and the influences and constraints in Tables 4.3 and 4.4, leisure managers can foresee some of the difficulties

Table 4.3 Influences on Leisure Participation

Personal	Social and circumstantial	Opportunity factors
Age	Occupation	Resources available
Stage in life cycle	Education and attainment	Facilities – type and quality
Gender	Disposable income	Awareness
Ethnicity	Material wealth and goods	Perception of opportunities
Marital status	Car ownership and mobility	Recreation services
Dependants and ages	Time available	Distribution of facilities
Will and purpose of life	Duties and obligations	Access and location
Personal obligations	Home and social environment	Activities provided
Resourcefulness	Friends and peer groups	Transport
Leisure perception	Social roles and contacts	Costs: before, during, after
Attitudes and motivation	Environment factors	Management: policy and support
Interests and preoccupation	Mass leisure factors	Marketing
Skills and ability – physical, social, and intellectual	Population factors Cultural factors	Programming Organisation and leadership
Personality and confidence	Upbringing and background	Social accessibility
Health	Culture born into	Political policies

Table 4.4 Major Reasons for Adults Not Participating in Leisure Activities

	Percentages of non-participants citing:			
	Not really interested	Difficult to find the time	Health not good enough	No need to go
Arts event	43	33	20	
Heritage events	36	40	16	
Museums and galleries	36	39	12	
Libraries		19	5	58

Source: DCMS (2019b).

encountered by potential participants, and management approaches can be modified accordingly. Care is needed in examining the evidence, however, because the influences often interact in their relationship with leisure participation. For example, education, household income, and local area deprivation are all independently associated with inactivity. These differences are already evident in young adults and increase steadily with age. What is appropriate policy intervention? Reduce entrance charges to sports facilities for the poor? A targeted sports education programme in deprived areas? Would either of these have much of an impact when the culture people are born into and their upbringing might also be correlated with income and education? It is because of such problems that more 'joined up' policies are seen as the way to tackle social exclusion, which is itself the result of several interrelated factors.

4.7.1 Personal and Family Influences

The personality of an individual, his or her interests, physical and social ability, a person's will and purpose in life, and a whole range of other personal factors will influence choice and participation in sport and leisure. Some important personal factors are now reviewed.

4.7.1.1 Age and Stage in the Family Life Cycle

Age has an important influence on sport and leisure participation, but its effect will vary depending on the person, the opportunities, and the type of activity. For children, there is a rapid change in the space of a few years. For adults, participation profiles by age groups are different for different leisure pursuits, as shown in Table 4.5 for the six types of leisure activities covered by the *Taking Part* evidence for England.

In most of these categories participation rates increase until middle age then fall with older age. However, the opposite is the case for social media usage, which drops significantly in the older age groups. Such profiles are important in order for sport and leisure managers to understand who their main markets are and where the main problems of dropout occur. In leisure for example, given current understanding of the beneficial effects of physical activity

Table 4.5 **Age and Leisure Participation in England, 2018–2019**

	Age				
Activity	16–24	25–44	45–64	65–74	75+
Arts	77	79	80	79	64
Heritage	67	74	76	76	58
Museums and galleries	51	54	52	51	32
Libraries	26	39	31	34	30
Social networking apps	99	98	88	64	30
Volunteering	35	26	29	35	29

Source: DCMS (2019b).

for the physical and mental health of older people, the declining participation rates by age disclose a major challenge to policy makers and sports managers alike.

Discussion Question

Given the evidence of declining leisure participation by age, should leisure managers spend a lot of effort trying to get older people to attend their facilities or simply concentrate on the ages where they know demand is strong?

Age should not be considered in isolation, however. Age may be less restrictive for certain leisure activities than life cycle changes, such as getting married and having children. For some, participation may increase with age because of children leaving home or a person retiring from work. Although age may influence the level of fitness and energy, a reduction in family and work responsibilities may more than compensate for this.

4.7.1.2 Gender

The leisure patterns of males and females are typically different. Evidence for England is given in Figure 4.1 It demonstrates that for two of the leisure sectors covered, male participation rates are higher than female, but for four others female participation rates exceed those of men.

Men and women face different constraints on their leisure participation. A higher proportion of men work full time in the paid labour force in most countries, including the UK. However, women typically have higher time commitments to home and family obligations,

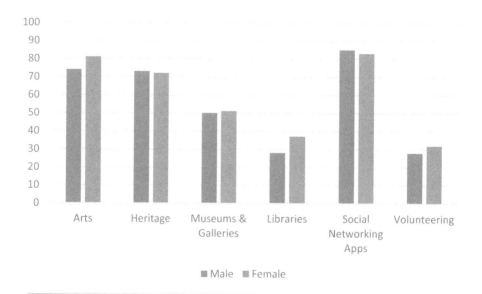

Figure 4.1 **Gender and leisure participation by adults in England, 2018–2019.**

particularly looking after children; and in England a high proportion have part-time paid work (Harmonised European Time Use Survey, 2015). The net effect of these different constraints, however, is that typically women have less leisure time than men.

Women have had, and continue to have, greater constraints placed upon them than men, which shows unambiguously in leisure time evidence. However, one of the misleading factors in looking for similarities and differences stems from the fact that most surveys have studied traditional leisure activities. Once a wider view of leisure is taken, encompassing the range of activities in and around the home, holidays, socialising, entertainment, etc., a more complex picture starts to emerge.

4.7.1.3 Ethnicity

As the flow of peoples between countries increases, whether for economic, political, or other reasons, so an increasingly important personal dimension to leisure participation is ethnic origin. Figure 4.2 shows some evidence of differences in leisure participation by different ethnic groups in England.

The highest participation rates are typically for white and mixed people. However, for libraries white people have the lowest participation rates, possibly reflecting a relationship between ethnicity and income. It is important to emphasise that within these broad ethnic groups there are considerable variations in participation rates, e.g. between different Asian groups.

In many other countries, evidence of leisure participation by ethnicity is not available. In the USA, however, evidence for outdoor recreation pursuits in Cushman *et al.* (2005) shows that people of Caucasian origin had higher participation rates than those of African American or Hispanic origins for all but 2 of 31 activities listed. This finding may be as much a reflection of cultural traditions and preferences as inequality of opportunity, although it is

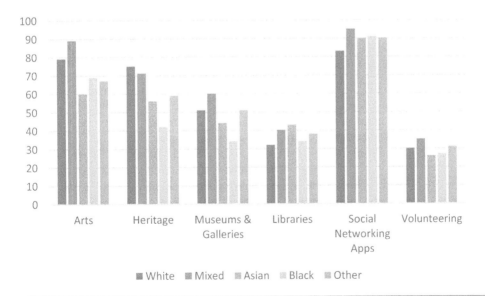

Figure 4.2 **Ethnicity and leisure participation by adults in England, 2018–2019.**

likely to be influenced by inequalities of income too. But it draws attention to the need for sport and leisure planners and managers, particularly in the public sector, to cater for diverse cultural needs and demands in contemporary communities.

Discussion Question

Are the lower participation rates in many leisure activities by ethnic minorities a sign of discrimination, or differences in culture, or are they due to other reasons?

4.7.1.4 Education

The type of education, the length of education and the educational attainment of people are closely related to upbringing, class, occupation, income, and other factors. In general, the higher the qualification, the greater the degree of participation in leisure activities. This is evidenced in many surveys over the past 20 years. A challenge for policy makers, however, is that female educational performance is increasingly stronger than male, yet the gender differences in activities such as sport persist.

4.7.2 Social and Circumstantial Factors

The range of social and situational circumstances that affect leisure participation include the home, school, work environment, income, mobility, time, social class, and social roles. Evidence for some of these in relation to leisure is reviewed here.

4.7.2.1 Time Availability

The most recent breakdown of leisure time in the UK is provided by the Office for National Statistics (ONS) in 2017 (data up to 2015). There are some key differences relating to leisure time noted in the report that link to some of the demographic factors already mentioned in this chapter. The main findings from the report are summarised as follows:

- Across all parts of the UK, men spent more time on leisure activities than women (an average of 6 hours and 9 minutes compared with 5 hours and 29 minutes per day respectively).
- The gender gap was greatest in Northwest England (men spent 7 hours per week more than women on leisure time) and smallest in Northern Ireland (identical for both men women).
- People in Southeast England spent the most time on leisure activities (5 hours and 2 minutes per day), compared with Northern Ireland, where they spent the least (4 hours and 22 minutes per day).
- The majority of leisure time for both men and women was spent consuming mass media, for example, watching TV, reading, or listening to music (16 hours and 24 minutes per week for men and 14 hours and 23 minutes for women).
- On average, men spent more time per week on sports, hobbies, and computer games than women (4 hours and 29 minutes and two hours and 29 minutes per week respectively), while women spent more time doing social activities (4 hours and 19 minutes compared with three hours and two minutes per week for men).

- The age group spending the most time on leisure activities was those aged 65 and over (7 hours and 10 minutes per day), at 50% more time in leisure than the 25- to 34-year-olds, who took the least leisure time (4 hours and 46 minutes per day).
- People who work in skilled trade professions spent the least amount of time on leisure (4 hours and 34 minutes per day), compared with people in sales and customer services professions who spent the most (5 hours and 21 minutes per day).
- Those from high-income households were more likely to be engaged in leisure activities on the weekends than those from low-income households, who were more likely to be working.
- Of the individuals who were working, on average, those employed full-time spent the least amount of time performing leisure activities (4 hours and 48 minutes per day), compared with those who were employed part-time (5 hours and 7 minutes per day); enjoyment of leisure was similar across all working groups.
- Of the individuals who were not working, those who were long-term sick spent the most time in leisure activities (7 hours and 57 minutes per day) and were least likely to enjoy their leisure time; retired people took slightly less leisure time (7 hours and 19 minutes) and enjoyed their leisure time more.

Source: ONS (2017)

It is clear from this report that there are still some barriers to overcome for certain groups in respect to access and availability to more leisure time. The amount of leisure time a person has continues to be dictated by demographic and social factors such as gender, education, income, and employment status.

4.7.2.3 Socio-Economic Class and Leisure Participation

The nature and meaning of social class are generally regarded as being problematic, because class relates not simply to income or occupation but also to upbringing and parental background. Social class is often regarded as grouping based on occupation, which is 'socio-economic class' rather than social class. Socio-economic class is more easily identified for most people because it is related to occupations. However, classification of those not in paid work is obviously more difficult – and is normally done by reference to the partner's occupation for those full time in the home, or previous occupation in the case of the unemployed or the retired.

Evidence of the effect of socio-economic class on leisure participation in England is shown in Figure 4.3. For most of the types of leisure covered, the relationship echoes that of income and participation – not surprisingly, because occupation and income are closely related. Upper socio-economic groups participate in the following activities more often than lower socio-economic groups, with the gap being a substantial one aside from use of social media apps, which is closer together (87% and 78% respectively). In respect to the other activities, the trend gap between groups has been consistent since the beginning of the *Taking Part* survey in 2005.

These findings in relation to socio-economic groups are not a new phenomenon. This pattern can be traced back throughout history also. As far back as 1976, the IFER/DART explored the issue of socio-economic class and referred to the importance of 'social climate', a complex of factors in addition to those which relate to age, gender, income, occupation, and education. The attitudes and values of people in their social setting are seen as enabling or inhibiting factors concerned with leisure choices. Their review of evidence relating to personal and social circumstances and leisure shows a powerful interrelationship between

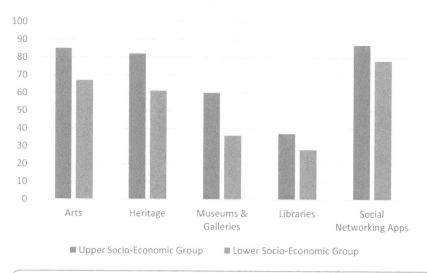

Figure 4.3 Socio-economic class and leisure participation by adults in England, 2018–2019.

factors such as income, education, and occupation, which leads to clear differences in leisure participation between those at one end of the scale and those at the other. People towards the top end of the income, education, and occupation scales have much higher participation rates in most leisure activities, i.e. sport, the arts, heritage. This conclusion extends to other leisure activities not covered in the evidence reviewed, e.g. tourism.

At the other end of the spectrum, the evidence points unambiguously to what are termed 'the socially excluded' – i.e. people with lower education attainment, lower income, lower skill jobs, etc. – with a much lower probability of engaging in many leisure activities. It is to this sector of society that public leisure policy has been directed in an attempt to improve opportunities. The very term *socially excluded* suggests that the low participation rates are because of constraints, but the extent to which they result from constraints rather than preferences is not well researched. This situation still appears to be present in the data for 2018–2019 and the trend in data since 2005 for the UK. One of the most common reasons given for lack of participation is 'not really interested'. However, the lack of interest may itself be partly determined by the socio-economic class a person belongs to.

4.7.3 Opportunity and Leisure Participation

The opportunities that sport and leisure managers provide through the facilities and programmes they offer are a form of social filter. For example, some swimming pools in England have adapted their facilities and staffing to programme Asian women's swimming sessions, with great success. There are both formal and informal social filters – programming is an example of formal, whilst the appearance and culture of a facility are informal, an example being the way many old people are deterred from using sports facilities because they have the image of only being for young, fit people.

The way people perceive their neighbourhood can have as significant an effect on leisure participation as the way they perceive local leisure provision. For example, if residents perceive their neighbourhood as being violent, the elderly in particular will be fearful of venturing out of the house at night. Sport and leisure management should include or interact with actions which might change people's perceptions for the better, not only of leisure facilities and their local neighbourhood but also of themselves.

4.7.3.1 Access and Leisure Participation

Leisure participation undertaken outside the home involves some travel. The method of travel can affect the level of satisfaction – it can determine time, distance, and destination. Apart from walking, all other means of travel incur a financial cost. The mobility conferred by the ownership of a car has revolutionised people's use of leisure time. For almost every activity the chances of participating in leisure activities in Britain are increased for car users by between 50% and 100%, according to General Household Survey evidence. Accessibility is also influenced by other important factors, particularly the location of a sport or leisure facility.

4.7.3.2 Awareness and Leisure Participation

If people do not know that something exists, then obviously they will not go to visit it, unless they stumble upon it. One of the key functions of leisure marketing is to inform potential users of the leisure opportunities provided for them (see Chapter 14). Leisure facilities are not sought in the same way as a shopping centre or place of work. Therefore, knowledge about them derives from seeing them, hearing about them, or reading about them. The influence of the media is critical in informing many leisure choices, as is the internet and social media channels.

4.8 The Influence of Planning and Management on Leisure Participation

People's take-up of leisure opportunities and use of leisure facilities are determined, as we have seen, by some discrete factors and several interrelated factors. Effective planning and management are no less important as an influence on demand. The way services and facilities are managed can have a profound effect on the extent to which they are used and who uses them.

Obviously the most direct way in which planning and management can affect leisure participation is through the quality of decisions by leisure providers. Planning the location and design of a facility, management policy, marketing, the attitudes of staff, sensitive customer service, skilled programming reflecting the 'needs' of the community – all such decisions go towards creating an accessible service, a welcoming atmosphere, an attractive image, and a set of leisure opportunities that is known and valued by potential customers. Even the administrative and booking systems at a leisure facility can consciously or unconsciously act as a type of social filter, encouraging some people from attending but possibly deterring others.

Although many of the constraints on leisure demand are seemingly beyond the reach of leisure managers – e.g. they can't alter a person's income or education – there are actions they can take to target and attract specific groups. In the public sector particularly, explicit management decisions are often taken to attract hard-to-reach groups such as the socially excluded. Even people who think they are not interested in an activity may be targeted by management efforts to persuade them that they should be interested! This is not unusual, for example, in management of sports facilities and outreach services (i.e. mobile services taken into specific communities).

People use leisure facilities for a variety of reasons. Sport centres, for example, can be places to go and socialise. The activity itself may be of quite secondary importance compared with getting out of the house, having 'quality time' with the children, and meeting and talking with friends. Management needs to be aware of such motivating factors in deciding on management policy and delivery.

Leisure planning and management exist, in large measure, to provide opportunities for individuals to participate actively or passively, seriously or casually in their time for leisure. People's preferences can be met, in part, by effective leisure planning and management, but only if the needs and demands of different people are identified. Therefore, a broad base of research, consultation, and (for the public sector) community involvement will help to plan appropriate provision. It is suggested that such an approach will provide:

- An increase in individual and community stakeholders' inputs and involvement in planning and decision-making;
- A better understanding of the community's needs;
- Accurate and up-to-date information on the activities in which people are involved, the activities in which they would like to be involved, and how these can be provided.

Chapter 11 includes an examination of demand forecasting techniques and public consultation alternatives.

4.9 Conclusions

There are many constraints on sport and leisure choices. This means that there are clear differences between leisure needs (what we must have), wants (what we desire), and what we actually demand and consume (what we commit time and money resources to doing). Leisure can offer significant options for individual actions and for personal decisions, should opportunities permit these decisions to be realised. As choice concerns the individual, two factors must be stressed. First, there is a strong link between leisure and other elements of life; and second, because it matters to the individual, the quality of the experience is of paramount importance.

People can still enjoy leisure, even though they might face severe difficulties and constraints in accessing leisure activities. Many people overcome the limitations of a poor education, family obligations, and personal handicaps and even overcome the obstacles of low income, insufficient facilities, and resources to find themselves satisfying interests, fulfilling experiences, and 'mountains to climb'. Sport and leisure management, therefore, has much to offer in the way of enabling people to discover themselves and achieve fulfilment in their leisure choices.

Practical Tasks

1   Interview two people of very different ages. Identify what they need from their leisure activities and assess the similarities and differences between them.
2   Visit a sport or leisure facility and assess the extent to which its offer is limited in the types of people it attracts (by age, gender, ethnicity, etc.), both by formal filters such as its programme and by informal filters such as its image and dominant user types.

Structured Guide to Further Reading

For a review of leisure and needs:
IFER/DART (Institute of Family and Environmental Research and Dartington Amenity Research Trust). (1976). *Leisure Provision and Human Need: Stage 1 Report (for DoE)*. IFER/DART, London.

For a review of sports participation concepts and economic influences on demand decisions:
Gratton, C., & Taylor, P. (2000). *Economics of Sport and Recreation*. E & FN Spon, London.

Search appropriate leisure and sport journals for case studies of specific target groups, analysing their needs and drawing implications for policy and management.

Useful Websites

For *Taking Part* survey reports and data:
https://assets.publishing.service.gov.uk/government/uploads/system/uploads/attachment_ data/file/879725/Taking_Part_Survey_Adult_Report_2018_19.pdf

For more information on leisure time in the UK:
www.ons.gov.uk/economy/nationalaccounts/satelliteaccounts/articles/leisuretimeintheuk/ 2015

References

Alexandris, K., & Kouthouris, C. (2005). Personal incentives for participation in summer children's camps: Investigating their relationships with satisfaction and loyalty. Managing Leisure, *10*(1), 39–53.
Bradshaw, J. (1972). The concept of social need. New Society, *30*(3), 640–643.
Csikszentmihalyi, M. (1975). *Beyond Boredom and Anxiety*. Jossey Bass, San Francisco, CA.
Cushman, G., Veal, A. J., & Zuzanek, J. (Eds.). (2005). *Free Time and Leisure Participation: International Perspectives*. CABI Publishing, Wallingford.
DCMS. (2019a). *Active People Survey*. DCMS Publishing, London.
DCMS. (2019b). *Taking Part Survey*. DCMS Publishing, London.
DCMS. (2019c). *Taking Part Survey, Child Report*. DCMS Publishing. London.
Doyal, L., & Gough, I. (1991). *A Theory of Human Needs*. Macmillan, London.
Edginton, C. R., Crompton, D. M., & Hanson, C. J. (1980). *Recreation and Leisure Programming*. Saunders College, Philadelphia, PA.
Eurostat. (2015). *Harmonised European Time Use Survey*. Eurostat, Luxembourg.
Godbey, G. (1976). *Recreation and Park Planning: The Exercise of Values*. University of Waterloo, ON.
Kew, S., & Rapoport, R. (1975). Beyond palpable mass demand, leisure provision and human needs – The life cycle approach. Paper presented to Planning and Transport Research and Computation (International) Company Ltd, summer annual meeting.
Kuenzel, S., & Yassim, M. (2007). The effect of joy on the behaviour of cricket spectators: The mediating role of satisfaction. Managing Leisure, *12*(1), 43–57.
Marcuse, H. (1964). *One Dimensional Man*. Sphere Books, London.
Maslow, A. (1954). *Motivation and Personality*. Harper, New York.

Maslow, A. (1968). *Towards a Psychology of Being*. Van Nostrand, New York.

Rapoport, R. and Rapoport, R.N. (1975) *Leisure and the Family Life Cycle*. Routledge & Kegan Paul, London.

Scitovsky, T. (1976). *The Joyless Economy*. Oxford University Press, New York.

Shivers, J. A. (1967). *Principles and Practices of Recreational Services*. Macmillan, New York.

Stokowski, P. A. (1994). *Leisure in Society: A Network Structural Perspective*. Mansell, London.

Thompson, G. (1987). *Needs*. Routledge, London.

Tillman, A. (1974). *The Program Book for Recreation Professionals*. National Press Books, Palo Alto, CA.

Tomas, S. R., Scott, D., & Crompton, J. L. (2002). An investigation of the relationships between quality of service performance, benefits sought, satisfaction and future intention to visit among visitors to a zoo. Managing Leisure, 7(4), 239–250.

Part II

Sport and Leisure Provision

Contents

Chapter 5

Government, Sport, and Leisure (Public)

In This Chapter

- How do governments get involved in sport and leisure?
- What is the rationale for government involvement?
- What are the roles of central and local government and non-department public bodies (NDPBs) in sport, physical activity, and leisure in the United Kingdom?
- What are the key elements of legislation affecting sport and leisure?
- How does the exchequer funding affect sport and leisure in the UK?

DOI: 10.4324/9780367823610-5

Summary

Governments influence leisure through direct provision, financial support, and both enabling and controlling legislation, all of which are delivered via different levels of government. Organisations like the European Union or the Organisation of American States exist at the international level, central governments at the national level, and in many cases regional governments and local authorities work with smaller communities. Within the UK, central government typically has the most pervasive influence, but most of this is indirect – it is Non-Departmental Public Bodies (NDPBs) and local authorities that tend to have the most direct effects on leisure markets. The rationale for government intervention in leisure is something of a balance. On the one side, governments want to allow people free choice of what they do in their leisure time. However, at the same time, governments are compelled to support leisure activities to increase access for disadvantaged groups and regulate aspects of leisure that maybe damaging to society and the population.

5.1 Introduction

Looking specifically at the UK, since Torkildsen's *Leisure and Recreation Management* was first published in 1983, there have been significant changes in central government and local government. For example, there has been devolution of many central powers to the Scottish Parliament and the Welsh and Northern Ireland Assemblies. Legislation over much of the last 40 years has had the effect, on the one hand, of tightening councils' budgets and, on the other hand, bringing flexibility and accountability into the ways in which services could be delivered.

There is one issue of terminology that it is important to get straight. Throughout this book the term *leisure* is used to encompass a wide range of activities such as sports, physical activity (PA), recreation, arts, play, heritage sites, etc. In government circles, and particularly in countries other than the UK, a more common term is *culture*. Ironically, however, *culture* is the term used in the title of the main UK government department responsible for leisure – the Department for Digital, Culture, Media, and Sport (DCMS) – although it is slightly confusing to identify sport separately because sport is part of culture. Another confusing matter is that culture in the UK is often seen more narrowly as a term covering the arts. In the USA, a more commonly used term for leisure in policy is *recreation*. In the UK (as in many other countries, including France and Japan), central government has a powerful role with regard to leisure; however, local authorities provide more leisure opportunities. The USA, Germany, and Australia are examples of a different model – a federal system – in which regional or state governments play a significant role. The regional role in the UK is at its most significant in the responsibilities devolved to the Scottish Parliament and the Welsh and Northern Ireland Assemblies.

5.1.1 Central Government

Central government does not typically provide leisure services directly but has a coordinating policy function. A good example of this was in response to the COVID-19 pandemic, where the UK central government allocated around £100 million to 266 local authorities across England to support the recovery of publicly owned leisure centres and gyms. In more federated systems, central government is largely concerned with matters of national interest, such as national sports teams, national parks, and world heritage sites. In the UK, the DCMS is responsible for government policy on the arts, sport, the National Lottery, tourism, libraries, museums and galleries, broadcasting, creative industries, press freedom and regulation, licensing, gambling, and the historic environment. The UK has a unitary system of government, and that has and continues to exist alongside a process of devolution. This process of devolution is in evidence through the provision of leisure, with leisure responsibilities existing in departments of the Scottish Parliament and Welsh and Northern Ireland Assemblies. It is also important to note that other central UK government departments have links and influence in respect of leisure policy. They include departments responsible for schools, higher education, local government, health, and the environment.

Central government makes decisions on national policy and sets out the legal framework for its regional and local networks, its agencies, and its institutions. It regulates the way local government can act and deliver services at the local level. The legal framework laid down by central government controls how the country is run; its laws apply to most aspects of life, including social lives and leisure, whether inside or outside the home. For example, the law sets down the rules governing radio, television, and press coverage; what age you must reach before watching certain films at the cinema or drinking alcohol in a public house; what standards of hygiene are enforced in restaurants; and a whole range of safety standards for funfairs, rides and slides, sporting events, concerts, and festivals.

Central government has a direct funding influence on national excellence in several types of leisure provision, for example in the UK:

- **Sport** – financing grassroots sport through Sport England and funding elite sport through UK Sport. In that regard, for the four years up to 2016, UK Sport invested just over £274 million supporting athletes preparing for the Rio de Janeiro Olympics and just under £73 million for athletes competing at the Paralympics;
- **Arts** – financing internationally famous venues such as the Royal Opera House and the Royal Shakespeare Company at Stratford;
- **Heritage** – financing major national heritage sites such as Stonehenge and Hadrian's Wall;
- **Museums and art galleries** – financing national museums such as the National Gallery and the Natural History Museum.

Discussion Question

Consider possible arguments for and against government funding of (1) a national sports stadium, such as Stade de France or Wembley Stadium; and (2) a national performing arts centre, such as the Royal Opera House or Sydney Opera House.

5.1.2 Non-Departmental Public Bodies

For actual delivery of leisure policies and services, many national governments rely on NDPBs to steer policy. NDPBs are separately constituted and typically run by an independent board of directors. However, they receive funding mainly from central government, so they are often heavily influenced by central government policy. There is a lot of political debate over the use of NDPBs. For example, from 2010 onwards the government of the time made no secret of its desire to reduce the number of NDPBs, and in 2017 the number of NDPBs the DCMS was responsible for dropped from over 50 to 34. Indeed, since the last edition of this book, the Museums, Libraries, and Archives Council has been one such NDPB to be dissolved. NDPBs can be susceptible when cuts in public spending are needed; however, in leisure they provide vital coordinating and focusing functions for government policy in their sectors. In the UK they include five sports councils (Sport England, SportScotland, Sport Wales, Sport Northern Ireland, and UK Sport); four arts councils (Arts Council England, Arts Council of Wales, Creative Scotland, and Arts Council of Northern Ireland); English Heritage (caring for over 400 historic monuments); as of 2017, 15 national museums directly funded by DCMS; and VisitBritain, which is the national tourism agency responsible for marketing Britain worldwide.

There are a lot of NDPBs in the UK because leisure is a very diffuse area of responsibility, and because policy responsibility in the UK is typically devolved to the four countries. In Australia, Lynch and Veal (2006) report over 30 NDPBs at the national level:

- Five responsible to the Department of Environment and Heritage, including the Commonwealth National Parks, Reserves, and Botanic Gardens and the Natural Heritage Trust;
- Over 25 responsible to the Department of Communications, Information Technology, and the Arts, including the National Library/Gallery/Portrait Gallery and National Museum, the Australian Broadcasting Corporation, the Australian Film Commission, the Australian Film Finance Corporation, Music Australia, Australian Sports Commission, and the Australian Institute for Sport; and
- One responsible to the Department of Tourism – Tourism Australia.

There are also NDPBs at the state level of government in a federal system such as Australia. Case Study 5.1 demonstrates how a health NDPB in the state of Victoria, Australia, has influenced sport organisations to take on more of a health remit. It also demonstrates an important government policy link between sport and health.

CASE STUDY 5.1

VicHealth: Building Health Promotion into Sport and Recreation Organisations

One of the key rationales for government intervention in sport and physical activity centres on health improvement. VicHealth is a health promotion foundation funded by the Victoria state government in Australia. Over the past 20 years or so, VicHealth has developed several strategies and programmes aimed at getting more Australians physically active. Indeed, one which started in 2000 set out to change Regional Sports Assemblies in Victoria from being narrowly focused on sports competitions to being concerned with facilitating community sport and recreation programmes as part of the state-wide health promotion strategy. Casey et al. (2009) examined this work and highlighted a four-stage approach to the programme. The first stage consisted of raising awareness by engaging in direct discussions with executive officers of the sports assemblies, funding community consultations to plan the implementation of health promotion, and finally, conducting a health promotion education programme with the assemblies' staff and board members. The second stage involved formal adoption by the Regional Sports Assemblies of a programme to promote participation in community sport and recreation. This process was facilitated by further funding from VicHealth to implement the programme. Third, the implementation of the programme involved an initial three years of VicHealth funding and workforce development, which helped to reorient the assemblies to health promotion activity. Finally, the fourth stage was to transform the Regional Sports Assemblies into health promotion agencies using sport and recreation. This was arguably the biggest test – could the transformation continue without continued VicHealth funding? The work of VicHealth in this area continues with, among other things, a new Physical Activity Strategy 2019–2023. This strategy, like programmes and strategies that have gone before, focuses on the groups who face the most barriers to participation and, like the work of 2000, engages in programmes away from traditional sport. In 2013, VicHealth set a ten-year goal that 300,000 more Victorians would be physically active by 2023. In the latest strategy, which reaffirms this target, the organisation has three 'focus areas': fear of judgement experienced by women; social sport, active recreation, and play; and walking and active travel. It remains funded by the Department of Health.

Source: Derived from Casey *et al.* (2009)

Discussion Question

What are the advantages and disadvantages to organising public policy for leisure through a group of NDPBs, rather than organising policy and strategy in a government department and providing funding to organisations directly?

5.1.3 Local Authorities

Arguably it is local authorities that have the largest scope of leisure services in many countries. They have several identifiable elements and spheres of influence, which are summarised in Figure 5.1. Different local authorities will have some or all of these elements, depending on the location and the size of the authority, its policies, and its responsibilities.

Most obvious is how local authorities in the UK provide facilities. The public has access to many facilities, such as urban and country parks, playgrounds, libraries, museums, nature trails, and beaches, and these are paid for indirectly by the public through taxes. Local authorities also provide facilities where there is a direct payment by the user, albeit often at highly subsidised charges, such as swimming pools, playing fields, golf courses, marinas, arts centres, theatres, and sports centres. Local authorities, however, are not simply providers of facilities. They support organisations of all kinds – private institutions, voluntary organisations, and even commercial companies – when it is believed to be advantageous to the public. For example, local authorities can make their own resources (buildings, labour, and skills) available for use, with or without charge. They can also provide financial grants. Another, less apparent role of local authorities in leisure is their function as planning and housing authorities. Indirectly, they enable leisure provision through planning decisions and assisting with the availability of land and resources. They can simultaneously assist with leisure

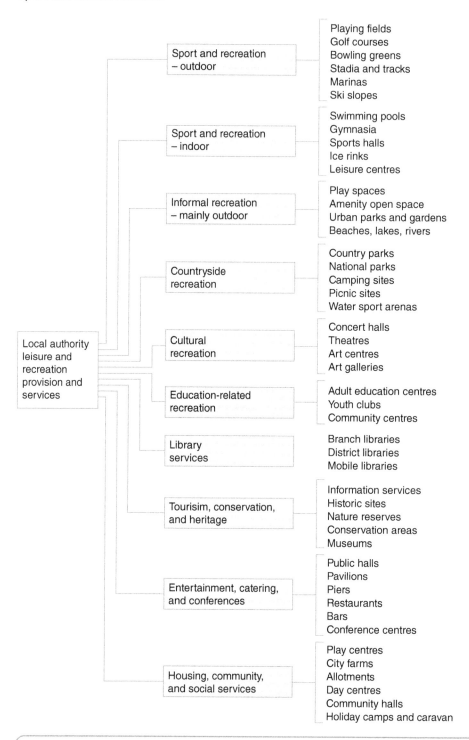

Figure 5.1 Examples of local authority leisure facilities and services.

around the home, in streets and walkways, in neighbourhood play areas and open spaces. All of this is, however, done with guidance from central government.

A political curiosity underlies local authority provision of leisure in the UK. Local authorities have a legal duty to provide leisure opportunities through education, museums, and libraries. However, they only have discretionary powers in England and Wales to assist the arts, sports, informal recreation, countryside recreation, entertainment, tourism, and youth and community services. This matters when cuts in public expenditure are sought, because it is discretionary services which are likely to bear a heavier share of the cuts.

Discussion Question

Why do you think local authorities in England and Wales finance the provision of sport and recreation when they are not obliged to do so?

5.2 The Development of and Rationale for Public Sector Leisure Services

In this section, we will use the UK as the example; however, the wider point the section makes is how government interest in sport and leisure has developed over a long period of time. This is the case in most countries as is shown in Case Study 5.2. Here we explore more recent developments around leisure policy in a relatively new country, Israel.

CASE STUDY 5.2

Leisure Policy in Israel

The first major study of leisure and culture in Israel, in 1970, was sponsored by the Ministry of Education. It led to two government committees considering the results and developing policies for a shorter working week and culture and the arts. Ruskin and Sivan (2005) identify a remarkably logical and fundamental set of issues driving the policy makers at this time:

- Whether there is need for an explicit cultural policy in a democratic society;
- How Israel can blend disparate ethnic cultures into a national culture;
- How to blend religious tradition with secular modernisation;
- Whether the mass media can avoid the international free flow of information, which is dominated by politically and culturally strong nations;
- Whether Israel should take on European culture, arts, and values or a blend of this and other cultures;
- What the population should do with more leisure time;
- What cultural opportunities are created by more leisure time and the role of leisure education;
- How cultural policy makers might help the less well-educated generation to overcome the constraints of age;
- How equal opportunities might be guaranteed in the provision and consumption of leisure.

Consideration of these and other issues led to the formation of leisure policies in a series of workshops with government practitioners. Two significant developments in the 1990s helped to consolidate the leisure policies. First, a national curriculum was developed for leisure education – 'intended to develop in pupils the skills, knowledge, attitudes and values to be wise consumers of leisure time, and have carry-over value for their future as adults' (Ruskin & Sivan, 2005, p. 148). Second, a leisure management administration was established in the key government-backed organisation, the Israel Association of Community Centres, which coordinates these key local providers of community services, including leisure.

It is the first of these initiatives that is ground-breaking for government policy. According to Sellick (2002), Israel is the first and only country to place leisure education directly into the education curriculum. To do so required the appointment of a National Commissioner of Leisure Education, the training of over 200 teachers in specific leisure education details, and the recruitment and training of a variety of health professionals to develop leisure education courses suited to their areas of expertise.

Source: Derived from Ruskin and Sivan (2005)

5.2.1 The First 100 Years: Mid-Nineteenth Century to Mid-Twentieth Century

The origins of public sector leisure in the UK go back to the nineteenth century, where government became increasingly concerned for the moral and physical welfare of the urban working classes and social control. So, government sought to modify freely chosen activities of the populace into acceptable forms necessary for political and social progress. A good example here is the Baths and Wash-Houses Act of 1846 from which swimming pools were built. Despite a focus on personal cleansing and hygiene, this also enabled leisure bathing. Similarly, the Town Improvements Act 1847 allowed local authorities to provide places for leisure and the Museums Act 1845 and the Libraries Act 1850 fostered more public buildings and amenities for recreational purposes. They are examples of what has been termed the 'rational recreation movement' (Coalter *et al.*, 1986). The beginnings of public sector leisure, however, were permissive, i.e. allowing local authorities to make provision if they wanted. The Public Health Act 1875 was the first major statutory provision enabling urban authorities to purchase and maintain land for use as public walks or pleasure grounds. From here we see the roots of local authority involvement in the parks movement. Parks departments expanded their sphere of authority and took over areas for organised outdoor sports, entertainment, and festivals.

According to Coalter *et al.* (1986), by the end of the nineteenth century the principles of public leisure policy were clear, i.e.:

- Improvement of the quality of life of the urban working classes;
- Improvement of physical health, productivity, and fitness for war reasons;
- Improvement in moral welfare, by providing 'better' alternatives to those available in private markets;
- Social integration and control;
- Promotion of self-improvement; and
- Government facilitating rather than directly providing leisure opportunities.

> **Discussion Question**
>
> How relevant do you think the nineteenth-century reasons for government intervention in leisure are today?

The beginning of the twentieth century saw a continuation of government concern for these principles. Interestingly, the Physical Training and Recreation Act 1937 was the first major Act to use the word *recreation*. Notably, however, it was introduced because of unrest in Europe and there was an urgent need for a strong, fit nation.

5.2.2 Post-Second World War Initiatives

Following the Second World War, the rationale for government involvement in recreation included 'national excellence' and, during this period, government established several NDPBs to help implement its policies. For example, the Central Council for Physical Recreation and the Arts Council. Through such agencies, government invested in national assets in leisure, particularly in sport, the arts, heritage, museums, and galleries. Other provision followed. The Town and Country Planning Act in 1947 allowed authorities to define the sites of proposed public buildings, parks, pleasure grounds, nature reserves, and other open spaces. The National Parks and Access to the Countryside Act of 1949 gave local planning authorities the opportunity to provide accommodation and camping sites and to provide for leisure. An Education Act in 1944 gave education authorities permissive powers to make it mandatory on all education authorities to provide adequate facilities for 'recreation and social and physical training' for primary, secondary, and further education. This resulted in the growth of the Youth Service, adult education, and physical education (and hence sport), and facilities such as sports grounds, swimming pools, larger gymnasia, and halls.

5.2.3 The 1960s: An Age of Leisure Enlightenment

Up to the 1950s, governments consistently viewed recreation as a 'means to an end'. However, the report of the Wolfenden Committee in 1960 was something of a watershed moment and led to the recognition by Parliament of recreation's intrinsic merits. The Committee (Lord Wolfenden, 1960) examined the factors affecting the development of games, sports, and outdoor activities in the UK and, alongside the Albermarle Report on the Youth and Community Service (Ministry of Education, 1960), stressed the need for more and better facilities for indoor sport and recreation. There followed one of the most significant developments in the history of leisure provision – the growth of multi-use, indoor leisure centres.

Around this time, youth and community services were developed by education authorities; country parks were promoted by the newly formed Countryside Commission; and library services and the arts were also part of this leisure renaissance. For example, the Public Libraries and Museums Act 1964 placed a duty on every library authority to provide a comprehensive and efficient library service. There was a growing realisation that thousands of schools and education facilities were potential community leisure and recreation centres. The Department of Education and Science and the Ministry of Housing and Local Government advanced a new policy guideline which encouraged use of such facilities by schools and the public.

Were the 1960s an age of enlightenment in leisure policy or the signal of a 'nanny state' developing?

5.2.4 The 1970s and Local Government Reorganisation

The Maud Commission into the structure of local government in England (Lord Redcliffe-Maud, 1969) led to a reduction in the number of local authorities. Local government reorganisation also coincided with an important government document. The 1975 White Paper *Sport and Recreation* (Department of the Environment, 1975) stated that provision of recreational facilities is 'part of the general fabric of the social services'. Some analysts feel that this period was one of restructuring of government-funded social infrastructure for a new post-industrial age. However, another significant change in the late 1970s was that it marked the start of a long-term squeeze on local government spending.

5.2.5 The 1980s and Compulsory Competitive Tendering

From the 1980s the rationale for public sector involvement in leisure in the UK changed. In the Conservative administrations that remained in charge up to 1997, economic justifications were important. It was a period of 'marketisation' of public leisure services (Henry, 2001), not only because of the emphasis on an economic rationale but also because of the main legislation to affect local government leisure provision – Compulsory Competitive Tendering (CCT). From 1997, various administrations have had a more even-handed rationale, continuing to promote the economic benefits arising from public investments in leisure but also promoting wider social benefits. What has been consistent over this period, however, has been the emergence of what is termed 'new managerialism' (Robinson, 2004). This concerns the adoption of commercial business practices resembling strategic planning, customer orientation, and performance measurement. The public sector leisure manager is now managing a facility to improve effectiveness and increase efficiency.

Central government has the most powerful effect on public leisure services, even though most provision is by local authorities. CCT is a good example of this. Although CCT was general legislation, it is a good demonstration of the top-down influence of government legislation on leisure provision. Two acts in 1988 and 1989 introduced CCT and extended it to the management of local authority sports and leisure facilities. CCT required that contracts to run leisure provision be open to competition should organisations other than the local authorities choose to bid for them. Local authorities still owned the facilities and had control over some aspects through the contract specifications. However, CCT opened the door to management of some of these public assets by commercial companies, charitable leisure trusts, management buyouts, and other management hybrids (Chapter 7 examines non-profit organisations). At its heart, CCT was about improving financial performance, and early evaluations of CCT emphasised this. A survey of local authorities in 1996 by the Centre for Leisure and Tourism Studies identified the main effect of CCT in leisure management as being cost reductions brought about by several measures, including reduced services, staff cuts, facility closures, and maintenance cuts. The cost reductions were accompanied by price increases above inflation and increased income generation. This is consistent with many observers' fears of CCT – that it would lead to over-concentration on 'the bottom line' at the expense of, for example, satisfying the needs of disadvantaged customers. Although CCT is no longer in operation, many of the procedures that had their roots in CCT are still evident nationally and internationally, for example, the European Transfer of Undertakings Directive 2001 and the Transfer of Undertakings (Protection of Employment) Regulations 2006 (TUPE).

> ### Discussion Question
>
> What are the respective advantages and disadvantages of a local leisure centre being managed by a local authority team or by a commercial company?

5.2.5.1 The 1990s and Best Value

Seeking a compromise between right-wing and left-wing political concerns, 'Best Value' was introduced as part of a 'Third Way' in 1999. Best Value championed a new culture in public service administration, which sought to retain the benefits of the previous government's emphasis on efficiency and improve service effectiveness. Best Value was structured around six key components:

1 **Performance indicators** – national indicators were developed, and each authority was expected to set targets, publishing its performance in annual local performance plans;
2 **Performance standards** – government identified benchmarks for minimum acceptable standards of performance;
3 **Performance targets** – set locally for strategic objectives, including efficiency, cost, effectiveness, quality, and fair access;
4 **Performance reviews** – to ensure that continuous improvements to all services are made. Quality schemes such as Investors in People, Quest, and Customer Service Excellence also have important roles in achieving Best Value (see Chapter 16);
5 **Competition** – as an essential management tool. Ways to test competitiveness included benchmarking against a range of alternative providers, contracting out services after competition between external bidders, partnership or joint ventures, asset disposal or sell-off. CCT is replaced under Best Value by Voluntary Competitive Tendering and a more flexible choice of management options;
6 **Audit and inspection** – new arrangements with rigorous external checks on the information provided in local performance plans.

The Local Government Act of 1999 identified four key aspects of the Best Value process. The first was to *challenge* what the local authority was doing. Was it the right function, the right time, the right level, and delivered in the right way? Second, it was important to *compare* the authority's performance to the performance of other organisations using a range of relevant indicators. Third, to *consult* with stakeholders such as providers, users, non-users, and employees at all stages of a review. And finally, to *compete* to determine the ideal way of delivering services. The duty of Best Value required local authorities to deliver services by the most economic, efficient, and effective means available to meet the requirements of local communities and to secure continuous improvements. But did it work? Case Study 5.3 looks at performance evidence for public sports and leisure centres during the period of Best Value, comparing 2001 with 2006.

The Performance of English Sport and Leisure Centres under Best Value

The National Benchmarking Service (NBS) has been collecting performance data for sports and leisure centres since 2001 and provides evidence to demonstrate whether these public leisure facilities have achieved improvements in both efficiency and effectiveness. The 2019 report, carried out by the Sport Industry Research Centre at Sheffield Hallam employed 51 performance indicators across five areas:

- 14 access (use by target groups, visit frequency, number of unique visitors);
- 20 efficiency (subsidy, income, expenditure, throughput);
- 2 utilisation (usage, market penetration);
- 14 attributes scored by customers for satisfaction and importance (accessibility, quality, cleanliness, staff, value for money); and
- The Net Promoter Score (assessing loyalty).

Based on the 2019 report, let us look at some key efficiency indicators over time. First is the usage, measured by 'visits per square metre'. On the following graph, the twenty-fifth, fiftieth, and seventy-fifth quartile are shown between 2014 and 2019. Albeit at different rates, there has been an increase in visits per square metre.

Two other indicators of efficiency are cost recovery as a percentage and operating costs per visit. Cost recovery for the top 50% of centres has been on or above 100% since 2016 (see Figure 5.3), meaning centres recover all (and then some) of their costs for running the facility. The other good news story appears to be the staff costs as a percentage of total income. This is shown in Figure 5.4. This shows, along with cost recovery, a more efficient use of staff, and it is also worthy of note that the bottom 25% quartile has closed the gap to the other two reference points between 2014 and 2019.

Visits per square metre (usable space)

	2014	2016	2017	2018	2019
25th	68	70	79	67	77
50th	95	95	105	108	114
75th	129	136	144	158	165

Figure 5.2 Visits per square metre shown over time and by quartile.

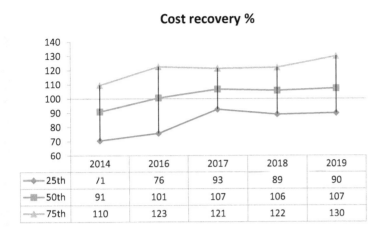

Cost recovery %

	2014	2016	2017	2018	2019
25th	71	76	93	89	90
50th	91	101	107	106	107
75th	110	123	121	122	130

Figure 5.3 **Cost recovery as a percentage over time.**
Source: Sport Industry Research Centre

Staff costs as % of total income

	2014	2016	2017	2018	2019
25th	88	66	68	65	61
50th	67	55	53	53	51
75th	51	45	45	44	43

Figure 5.4 **Staff costs as a % of total income.**
Source: Sport Industry Research Centre

It is important to point out that Best Value is not the only change to have occurred in the provision of public services since 2001. Whilst it has an important influence, so do other factors such as the changing levels of financing of local government services, the changing priorities of local authorities, the obligations imposed by other legislation, competition from other facilities, and the changing demands of customers. Therefore, the data presented here are not just the results of Best Value policy, but of a complex array of influencing factors.

5.2.5.2 *2000 Onwards and a Focus on Elite*

A feature of the last 30 years or so has been a strengthening commitment from government, through policy statements and funding support, to the national excellence rationale for financing in leisure. It is nowhere more evident than in sport, where considerable funding of elite sportspeople and facilities led to significant improvements in Great British performance at the Olympic Games of Beijing in 2008, London in 2012, and Rio in 2016 and, following this, £342 million was allocated to sports for the Tokyo Olympic cycle. There has been substantial UK government investment in new facilities, most notably perhaps for the hosting of the Olympic Games of 2012. However, subsequently, Wembley Stadium; the National Velodrome in Manchester; and English Institute of Sport facilities in Bath, Birmingham, Loughborough, Manchester, Sheffield, and elsewhere were all examples of such investment. The same is happening for the 2022 Commonwealth Games in Birmingham. Indeed, following 2012, successive governments have sought to attract large scale events such as the Commonwealth Games, the Rugby Union World Cup, Hockey World Cup, the Rugby League World Cup, the Netball World Cup, and the Cycling Road World Championships to name a few.

5.2.5.3 Children, Education, and Disability

As far back as the 1980s, major Education Acts have had substantial effects on leisure. The Education Acts of 1986 and 1988 aimed to make the education service 'more responsive to consumer needs', devolve responsibility to local levels, and reduce bureaucracy. The 1986 Act encouraged greater community use of premises. The 1988 Act included the National Curriculum and local management and devolved budgets of schools. It makes sound educational, social, and economic sense to provide for the community within existing community structures such as schools. There can be benefits for all parties, but only given appropriate policies, facilities, and management. One of the basic issues with these school-community collaborations is the extent to which the facilities are 'school' facilities or 'community' facilities. Three types of ownership and management arrangements have been common:

1 **Dual use** – where leisure facilities have been provided solely under local education authority powers and are managed entirely by the school, but they are open to community use at certain times. The educational budget can only be used for school purposes and curricular activities, so the community use must not be subsidised;
2 **Joint provision** – a facility, whilst forming part of (or being adjacent to) the school and used by the students, financed at least partly by other agencies, such as the local authority. These other agencies are typically involved in the day-to-day running of the facilities;
3 **The Community School** – a school which engages in non-school activities and in which the governing body has control over as well as the responsibility for those members of staff who are wholly or partly engaged in non-school activities.

Leisure services departments and leisure managers can play an important role in achieving the best from community use arrangements with schools. For example, they can:

- Advise school governing bodies and informally provide help and advice on community sport and leisure, sharing with schools ideas relating to marketing, programming, pricing, and operational management;
- Achieve levels of parity, for example, in pricing, between different agencies;
- Facilitate collaborative programming;
- Offer to manage the non-educational use on a contract basis;
- Organise courses for leaders, coaches, and teachers;
- In collaboration with the local education authority, Sports Council, Arts Council, and the local authority, appoint Development Officers to work with schools;
- Promote links between schools and local clubs;

- Provide collaborative promotion, awareness, and publicity of the facilities and activities offered at the school; and
- Advise on applications to the National Lottery, grant-making bodies, and sponsors.

Discussion Questions

Should schools be obliged to open their sports facilities to public use, rather than leave the decision to the head teacher and the school governors?

The Children Act 1989 was a significant legislative change on behalf of children in the UK. This Act affected the management of leisure, play, and sport by providers of services for children, providers of facilities, employers of paid staff and volunteers, and providers of information. The 1989 Act contains regulations, duties, and powers that affect everyone who is responsible for planning, managing, and delivering services to children, particularly those to children under the age of eight. The clear direction and commitment behind the legislation is to put children at the heart of, and give priority to their needs in, all those processes which affect their lives.

For the first time in the sphere of play and recreation, the local authority had a statutory duty to provide services. One of the practical outcomes of the Act is the requirement for registration – any person or organisation providing services for children under eight years old, whether in public, voluntary, or commercial sectors, must be registered. The facilities affected by the Children Act included:

- Crèches, play groups, child minding services;
- Before- and after-school clubs;
- Playschemes, outdoors and indoors;
- Activities in leisure centres, e.g. mini-gymnastics, ballet, trampolining, football, and swimming classes;
- Activities in museums and art galleries;
- Adventure playgrounds;
- Commercial play centres;
- City farms;
- Theme parks;
- Play spaces in shopping centres and supermarkets;
- Holiday schemes in libraries, theatres, and sport centres.

Another Children Act in 2004 gave legislative backing to a government programme to improve the welfare of children and young people from birth to the age of 19. This programme was called Every Child Matters and aimed to support every child in the UK, whatever their background or circumstances, to:

- Be healthy;
- Stay safe;
- Enjoy and achieve;
- Make a positive contribution;
- Achieve economic wellbeing.

The Children Act 2004 created Children's Trusts in each area, through which the legal 'duty to cooperate' is enforced. The Act also requires each area to have a Children and Young People's Plan to cover all relevant government services, including relevant leisure services.

One major concern of recent times in the wake of the Children Acts is that of child protection. This has implications for all leisure and recreation services, whether in the public, private, or voluntary sectors. Whilst there is almost universal acknowledgement of the need for child protection, there is also concern about the level of bureaucracy that all voluntary leaders and helpers are having to be put through, particularly being checked for a relevant criminal record. Getting the balance right, between child protection and burdening willing volunteers with requirements, is difficult.

Discussion Question

Should parents who regularly take their and other children to a voluntary club's events have to undertake a formal check of their criminal record in the interests of child protection?

5.2.5.4 Disability Discrimination Acts

Acts in 1995, 2005, and 2010 in the UK sought to protect disabled people from discrimination by giving them rights enforceable by law. These rights include rights of access to facilities and services, rights against discrimination in the workplace and wider society, and rights regarding the functions of public bodies. Service providers, including leisure managers, are now obliged to make 'reasonable adjustments' to premises or to the way they provide their services. The government advice specifically identifies everyday services, including hotels, pubs, theatres, and voluntary groups such as play groups.

Under this legislation, it is now against the law for service providers to treat disabled people less favourably than other people for a reason related to their disability. The 'reasonable adjustments' which leisure managers are expected to make include:

- Installing an induction loop for people with a hearing impairment;
- Providing an option to book tickets by email as well as by phone;
- Providing disability awareness training for staff who have contact with the public;
- Providing larger, well-defined signage for people with impaired vision; and
- Putting a ramp at the entrance to a building as well as steps.

Clearly, these measures have resource implications for services that have not previously undertaken them. Beyond this, in 2021, the UK government released a new National Disability Strategy. Within it, the Strategy made explicit reference to leisure and promised to:

- Widen participation in arts, culture, and sport;
- Make the UK the most accessible tourism destination in Europe;
- Improve access to paths; and
- Make playgrounds more inclusive.

5.3 The Links between Central Government and Local Government

As well as legislation, such as the ones listed earlier, UK central government also partly funds local authorities. For example, in 2002 the DCMS estimated that nearly 90% of central government spending on sport and recreation goes to local government, and this accounts for over half the spending by local authorities on sport and recreation. In return for their major contribution to the funding of local authority services, it is not surprising that central government requires local authorities to conform to national policies and to be accountable for the efficiency and effectiveness of their services. However, there has been something of a change over the past decade or so. Indeed, successive governments have cut the money they give to local authorities by 38% in real terms between 2009–2010 and 2018–2019, from £34.6 billion to £24.8 billion per year. This has meant local councils have had to increase council taxes – although they have not been able to increase them enough to offset the reduction completely. Several approaches to managing the performance of local authorities have been used. First was the Comprehensive Performance Assessment (CPA), which was a system of performance indicators that local authorities were obliged to report. Then there were Comprehensive Area Agreements, with a slimmed down set of national performance indicators. And finally, Public Service Agreements (PSA), which specify objectives and targets for NDPBs and local authorities. However, the coalition government removed these in 2010, coincidentally as the money they afforded local authorities started to reduce. The coalition government introduced Structural Reform Plans, which were designed 'to replace the old, top-down systems of targets and central micromanagement' and put more power 'into the hands of people and communities'. One of the major underpinning forces here was the Big Society concept. The first Structural Reform Plan for the DCMS focused on the 2012 Olympics and Paralympics, boosting the Big Society, media reform, universal broadband, and encouraging competitive sport in schools, all of which had implications for local leisure.

The coalition government also signalled its intention to reduce the 'top-down' approach to monitoring by removing any local area agreements. In theory, it would be up to local authorities to decide how they would monitor themselves. So, for local authorities, the past decade has seen less accountability but also less spending power.

Discussion Question

What are the implications for local authorities of less accountability but less spending power?

5.4 The National Lottery

The National Lottery was launched on 14 November 1994 to raise money for a variety of good causes which are beneficial to the public and enhance the quality of life of people living in the UK. The National Lottery Act 1993 established five areas to benefit from the Lottery: sport, the arts, heritage, charities, and to promote the year 2000 (this is now closed). In addition, the National Lottery Act 1998 created a sixth good cause, NESTA (National Endowment for Science, Technology and the Arts), a national trust endowed from the Lottery but operating independently of government. NESTA's aim is to help talented individuals (or groups of such individuals) to achieve their potential, to help people turn inventions or ideas into products and services, and to contribute to public appreciation of science, technology, and the arts.

The Lottery is included in this chapter on government because it is essentially a government-controlled operation. The Lottery is regulated by the National Lottery Commission, which is an NDPB funded by the DCMS. DCMS has responsibility for the policy framework for the

National Lottery but remains at arm's length from the regulation and operation of the Lottery. The responsibility for distributing proceeds from the Lottery at the time of writing rests with 16 distributing bodies, many of them NDPBs:

- Four national Arts Councils:
  - Arts Council England
  - Scottish Arts
  - Arts Council of Wales
  - Arts Council of Northern Ireland

- Four national Sports Councils:
  - Sport England
  - SportScotland
  - Sports Council for Wales
  - Sports Council for Northern Ireland

- UK Sport;
- Olympic Lottery Distributor;
- Heritage Lottery Fund;
- The Big Lottery Fund – for improving communities and the lives of people most in need;
- Awards for All – for local communities;
- UK Film Council;
- Scottish Screen;
- NESTA.

The early years of the Lottery resulted in substantial sums being raised, exceeding expectations. Then there was a substantial drop in ticket sales, followed by a stabilisation of revenues in recent years. At least three clear messages for change have been identified. First, too many grants were being awarded to large prestigious projects. Second, certain geographical areas in the UK were benefiting more than others. Third, certain types of activities and organisations, particularly those that were well organised in terms of being able to handle the whole application process, were being successful and other well-deserving causes were not coming forward or were not getting through the process. To ensure a greater spread of awards, the Lottery distributors have recently been committed to focusing funding into areas not previously funded. Small projects, for example, have benefited from the introduction of Awards for All.

The criticism of awards for large national projects being made at the expense of many smaller awards for community projects is one that endures, particularly because of the 2012 London Olympics. In total the National Lottery raised £750 million towards the Games, with many leading figures in other good causes claiming that meant less money for their areas. The Olympic Games Lottery funding also reopens another criticism which was made at the start of the National Lottery – that Lottery funding substitutes for government funding and therefore does not represent a net addition to total funding. However, this is difficult to verify because it raises the impossible question of what would have happened if the National Lottery had not happened. In respect of the 2012 Olympic Games, the UK government funded considerably more than the National Lottery funds, but without the latter it would have had to pay more. The funding of elite sport has continued to gather pace. Table 5.1 highlights the latest round of funding that Olympic and Paralympic sports will receive in the run up to the 2024 Games in Paris.

Table 5.1 UK Sport Investment for Paris Cycle, 2021–2025

	Tokyo Award	Paris Award (as at Dec. 2020)	Paris Award (as at Dec. 2021)
Olympic Sport	**(2017–2021)**	**(2021–2025)**	**(2021–2025)**
Archery	£930,379	£2,134,257	£2,612,674
Athletics	£23,007,531	£22,175,520	£22,175,520
Badminton	£665,100	£3,154,358	£3,154,358
Boxing	£12,084,436	£11,395,507	£11,557,507
Canoeing	£16,344,693	£12,108,836	£12,292,241
Cycling	£24,559,306	£27,601,684	£28,713,669
Diving	£7,223,280	£8,463,542	£8,680,542
Equestrian	£12,541,195	£11,085,964	£11,746,626
Gymnastics	£13,408,688	£12,510,990	£13,075,314
Hockey	£12,905,612	£12,376,622	£12,669,845
Judo	£6,564,334	£5,446,804	£6,106,538
Modern Pentathlon	£5,498,321	£4,391,183	£5,093,383
Rowing	£24,655,408	£22,212,008	£22,452,008
Sailing	£22,249,000	£21,338,088	£22,208,411
Shooting	£6,008,790	£5,802,749	£6,130,091
Swimming	£18,731,645	£16,590,017	£18,084,340
Taekwondo	£8,223,805	£7,776,898	£7,963,598
Triathlon	£7,049,372	£6,806,550	£6,935,550
TOTAL	£222,650,895	£213,371,575	£221,652,213
Paralympic Sport	**(2017–2021)**	**(2021–2025)**	**(2021–2025)**
Boccia	£3,094,483	£3,473,835	£3,539,835
Para-Archery	£2,669,092	£2,633,644	£2,668,644
Para-Athletics	£8,937,070	£9,065,401	£9,065,401
Para-Badminton	£949,595	£1,106,833	£1,106,833
Para-Canoe	£3,017,671	£3,032,881	£3,471,115

(Continued)

Table 5.1 (Continued)

	Tokyo Award	Paris Award (as at Dec. 2020)	Paris Award (as at Dec. 2021)
Para-Cycling	£5,661,328	£7,829,158	£8,043,492
Para-Equestrian	£3,294,056	£3,011,243	£3,052,243
Para-Shooting	£2,076,000	£1,692,915	£1,941,168
Para-Rowing	£2,614,482	£3,139,577	£3,238,577
Para-Swimming	£8,805,943	£7,829,247	£8,291,915
Para-Table Tennis	£2,726,060	£3,717,787	£3,750,787
Para-Taekwondo	£523,470	£563,162	£660,662
Para-Triathlon	£2,852,775	£3,814,618	£3,988,618
Powerlifting	£1,097,075	£1,612,722	£1,734,722
VI Judo	£1,968,986	£847,617	£955,776
Wheelchair Basketball	£4,603,219	£4,197,157	£4,399,572
Wheelchair Fencing	£650,044	£1,599,819	£1,695,819
Wheelchair Rugby*		£2,650,289	£2,950,289
TOTAL	£55,541,349	£61,817,905	£64,555,468

Discussion Question

Is it fair that £750 million of National Lottery funds were designated for the 2012 London Olympics?

Lottery funding to local authorities can be significant, though it is increasingly very difficult to obtain, as competition for funding mounts and available funds have decreased. Local authorities can apply for direct financial assistance for projects at council-owned facilities and enable organisations within the district to obtain funding for projects that complement existing provision and fit into local strategies. To harness these opportunities effectively requires a coordinated and focused approach by local authorities and leisure managers. The creation of a leisure strategy (or wider cultural strategy) is an important step towards effective use of total resources, and bids for lottery funding would be expected to fit in with such strategies.

5.5 Conclusions

Government has a very strong influence on sport and leisure provision, at both the local and national levels. Its main agents for influence at the national level are a range of NDPBs and other partners. It influences sport and leisure not only by direct provision but also by laws and regulations, funding support, and policies which are implemented through NDPBs and local authorities. Leisure managers cannot escape responsibilities and constraints imposed by government. And, of course, many leisure managers are working directly for government. The rationale for government intervention in leisure began by concentrating on the beneficial individual and social effects of leisure, including health, moral behaviour, and social control. It then developed into a recognition that leisure in its own right was good for society – one UK government paper suggested that it was part of social services. More recently the rationale has been more focused on the social benefits (and costs) of leisure, including health, economic importance, excellence, social inclusion, and social control. However, the power of this rationale is arguably about to face its sternest test. As more developed economies emerge from the recent recession, one of the inevitable consequences of the fiscal stimulation employed by many governments to help recovery is that in the next decade or so there will have to be severe cuts in government spending to reduce levels of public sector borrowing. A key question for the medium term, therefore, is how much will government support for leisure be reduced? This is particularly pertinent in the UK when one of the main agents of government support, local authorities, have few mandatory obligations to provide for leisure – most of their support is discretionary. Some sectors of leisure might be more sheltered from the government expenditure cuts to come. For example, excellence in sport has received substantial government funding in the UK the 2012 London Olympics being a significant example. One of the ways in which government spending on, and support for, sport and leisure can be defended is by evidence that it produces a social return. In the past, public sector leisure has been criticised for not providing sufficient evidence of what is gained by government support. It will be increasingly important that in the coming years such evidence is collected and used effectively to defend the rationale for a hands-on government role in leisure.

Practical Tasks

Find and read some of the media coverage of the 2012 London Olympics and Paralympics (e.g. use libraries and the internet). Did the media show any recognition of the rationale for public funding of these Games?

Structured Guide to Further Reading

Houlihan, B., & Lindsey, I. (2013). *Sport Policy in Britain*. Routledge, Oxon.
Hoye, R., Nicholson, M., & Houlihan, B. (2010). *Sport and Policy: Issues and Analysis*. Routledge, Oxon.
Vic Health Strategy. (2019–2023). Retrieved from www.vichealth.vic.gov.au/media-and-resources/publications/physical-activity-strategy
Wilson, R., & Platts, C. (Eds.). (2018). *Managing and Developing Community Sport*. Routledge, Oxon.

Useful Websites

For information on DCMS policy:
http://europa.eu/pol/cult/index_en.htm
www.gov.uk/government/organisations/department-for-digital-culture-media-sport

For information on National Lottery distribution bodies:
National Lottery Distribution Fund Account 2020-2021 - GOV.UK (www.gov.uk)

For information on the EU and culture:
www.oas.org/en/
www.tnlcommunityfund.org.uk/
www.vichealth.vic.gov.au/about

References

Casey, M. M., Payne, W. R., & Eime, R. M. (2009). Partnership and capacity-building strategies in community sports and recreation programs. *Managing Leisure*, 14(3), 167–176.

Coalter, F., Long, J., & Duffield, B. (1986). *Rationale for Public Sector Investment in Leisure*. Sports Council and Economic and Social Research Council, London.

Department of the Environment. (1975). *Sports and Recreation*, Cmnd 6200. HMSO, London.

Henry, I. (2001). *The Politics of Leisure Policy*, 2nd edition. Palgrave Macmillan, Basingstoke.

Lord Redcliffe-Maud. (1969). *Report of the Royal Commission on Local Government in England 1966–1969*. HMSO, London.

Lord Wolfenden. (1960). *Report of the Wolfenden Committee on Sport, Sport and the Community*. Central Council for Physical Recreation, London.

Lynch, R., & Veal, A. J. (2006). *Australian Leisure*, 3rd edition. Pearson Education, Sydney.

Ministry of Education. (1960). *The Youth Service in England and Wales: Report of the Committee November 1958* (Albermarle Report), Cmnd 929. HMSO, London.

Robinson, L. (2004). *Managing Public Sport and Leisure Services*. Routledge, London.

Ruskin, H., & Sivan, A. (2005). Israel. In G. Cushman, A. J. Veal, & J. Zuzanek (Eds.), *Free Time and Leisure Participation: International Perspectives*. CABI Publishing, Wallingford.

Sellick, J. (2002). *Leisure Education: Models and Curriculum Development*, RLS 209. California State University, California.

Chapter 6

Sport and Leisure Provision in the Commercial Sector (Private)

In This Chapter

- What does commercial sport and leisure consist of?
- What are the objectives of commercial sport and leisure providers?
- What is the typical structure of commercial sport and leisure industries?
- How does globalisation affect commercial leisure?
- What are the key drivers of commercial leisure?
- What are the major commercial leisure industries, and how have they evolved?

DOI: 10.4324/9780367823610-6

Summary

The commercial leisure sector is typically the largest, at least in terms of monetary dimensions. It involves more expenditure than either the public or the voluntary sector.

The structure of the commercial leisure sector can be identified in two main ways: first, by the activities supplied and second, by the size structure of companies in each industry, i.e. the proportion of market sales from the largest firms. The major commercial leisure industries by financial size typically include alcohol production and distribution, eating out, home entertainment (TV, games, music, etc.), and holidays. A typical size structure of commercial leisure in more developed countries is oligopoly, with a few firms dominating market supply.

Commercial leisure firms, like commercial firms generally, are motivated by profit. It is profit that enables them to satisfy shareholders, increase their value on stock markets, reinvest, grow, diversify, and merge with or take over other firms – so profits are linked to many other objectives.

Key drivers for commercial leisure companies have historically included society-wide factors which influence all sectors, such as the amount of leisure time available, and to whom it is available; the income people have to spend; laws laid down by government; and technological changes.

Several important commercial leisure industries are reviewed, i.e. eating and drinking out, betting and gambling, commercial sport, cinemas, leisure parks, theatres, nightclubs, and theme parks.

6.1 Introduction

In 2016, the leisure sector in the UK was worth £117 billion (Deloitte, 2016). At the time, this accounted for 7.4% of GDP and had seen a 5% annual growth rate since 2010. More recent estimates from the London Stock Exchange Group suggest that this figure fell slightly in 2019 to £111 billion, but there is still little to doubt in terms of the size and scope of the sector. A large proportion of this spending is in the commercial sector, as is the case in other developed economies. Millions of people buy domestic and overseas leisure tourist trips, sports equipment, and cinema tickets, eat out socially, drink alcohol, gamble, watch television, and are entertained in their leisure time through services and products provided commercially.

Commercial leisure providers are often defined as those which make profit, but that simplification ignores some important complications. Many other types of providers often use 'commercial practices' to achieve their objectives, such as efficiency savings (i.e. cost cutting, for example in the public sector), target marketing (all sectors), and quality management (important in the public as well as the commercial sector).

6.2 The Commercial Leisure Sector: An Overview

There are two main kinds of commercial leisure business:

1 Commercial operators managing commercial activities for profit, e.g. public houses, ski holiday companies;
2 Commercial operators managing not-for-profit or public sector facilities/activities, such as UK contract companies Leisure Connection, DC Leisure Management.

In addition, there are two other forms of business that have commercial characteristics:

1 Not-for-profit operators managing some activities commercially to improve financial performance, for example to help repay capital costs, pay for minor investments or cross-subsidise non-profitable community activities, e.g. health suites and cafés in public sector leisure centres;
2 Commercial companies providing resources for not-for-profit organisations in return for publicity, brand awareness, beneficial image, and possible increases in sales; this, of course, is commercial sponsorship, and it is discussed in Chapter 14 as an important marketing tool.

The London Stock Exchange Group provide some estimates as to what the average family spends (in the UK) on some activities linked to these types of providers. For example, in 2019, they estimated that each year the average family spends approximately £190 on trips to theme parks; £180 on activities such as bowling, mini golf, and visiting arcades; £170 on trips to the zoo; and £170 on trips to the cinema. On a weekly basis, the average household spends more than £79 on recreation and culture, the largest proportion of which contributes towards package holidays.

The types of exercise and holiday travel the UK is spending money on is also changing. An increase in boutique exercise classes has seen a rise in fitness spending, reaching over £22 billion (compared with £17 billion in 2010), while individuals are spending more on holidays that specifically include some sort of class or workshop. Of course, these figures will undoubtedly change again in a post-COVID world, but it will take a few years yet for us to see real trends in the data linked to this.

6.3 Commercial Sector Objectives

The major difference between a commercial organisation and a public or voluntary organisation is that a primary objective of the commercial operator is to achieve financial profit or an adequate return on investment. The other sectors may also make financial surpluses on occasion, but they are established primarily for other reasons. Yet, profit-making and not-for-profit organisations in leisure have similarities – they must both attract sufficient clients, customers, or members, or they will fail. Public and not-for-profit managers increasingly use some of the skills and techniques of commercial operators, such as market research, targeted promotion, and product innovation, and development.

Despite the fundamental objective of making profit to both survive and prosper, many private businesses do not make profits. In such a climate, many commercial leisure organisations find it hard to stay in business and, compared to public sector services, competition is fierce, and many companies may fail. Leisure is a volatile market, and changes in leisure spending add to this uncertainty.

Making profit is a simplification of the objectives of the commercial provider. There are many other short-term and medium-term commercial sector objectives which either need profit to accomplish them or are designed to increase profit. These include:

- Increasing stock market value, which is often but not always related to short-term profitability;
- Growing, through organic, endogenous means of product and market developments, or through merger and acquisition;
- Maximising sales, which can sometimes be risky in terms of profitability and is closely related to the growth objective;
- Increasing market share, which is a means of gaining power in the market;
- Controlling risk, e.g. through diversification – moving into other markets to develop a portfolio of activities is a strategy which can reduce the risks of confining supply to one market in a sector which can have quite volatile movements in demand.

6.4 The Size Structure of Commercial Leisure Companies

The commercial leisure industry is made up of many thousands of businesses, from independent gyms and craft shops to giant multinationals producing sports clothing and footwear or alcoholic drinks. It is the large companies that tend to dominate in several commercial leisure industries. Examples of large companies operating in this sector include British Airways, Centre Parcs, David Lloyd Leisure, Expedia, InterContinental Hotels Group, Odeon Cinemas, and P&O Cruises.

This concentration of market power in a few large companies is termed an 'oligopoly', and it is characterised by both interdependence and uncertainty. The companies are interdependent because one large company's actions in supply influence the other large companies, e.g. a price decrease by one company can cause a reduction in demand and sales for another company. This can cause stability, in that no one company wants to 'rock the boat'. Sometimes oligopolistic companies collude illegally in cartels, for example to fix prices and prevent price competition. There are national and international laws (e.g. for the European Union) against such behaviour, and large penalties are imposed if companies are proven guilty.

Other oligopolistic markets are characterised by extreme competition, which is the source of considerable uncertainty and instability, and which can threaten the financial viability of even large companies. This has happened, for example, in the package holiday market in the UK, where even the market leaders have gone out of business. The most recent example here is the collapse of Thomas Cook in 2019. It is also increasingly the case with airlines, with budget airlines competing fiercely on price and some large conventional airlines suffering consequently. This situation has been further exacerbated in light of COVID-19 and restrictions on international travel.

Discussion Question

What are the main advantages and disadvantages of an oligopoly market structure in the production of beer?

6.5 Globalisation

Many commercial markets have in recent decades become more global, with multinational companies serving customers on a global basis. Leisure provides many of the most quoted examples, i.e.:

- McDonalds and KFC, which are globally recognised fast food restaurants, reaching as far as Russia and China;
- Disney, with not only theme parks in the USA, Paris, Tokyo, and Hong Kong, but also films and merchandise which are universally recognised;
- Large international hotel chains, such as Hilton and Best Western, which aim to ensure the same standard of facilities and service wherever they are in the world;
- Sports clothing and footwear producers such as Adidas and Nike.

These brands are classic examples of what has been called *globalisation*, a term which is used in a variety of disciplines to mean different things. In economics it signifies expanding international trade, international supply chains, and particularly the economic significance of large multinational companies producing and trading in a global market. In politics and international relations, it refers to the increasing importance of global relations and the diminishing importance of nation-states. In sociology and cultural studies, the term has been used to signify the emergence of a global society, with common values driven by international media, and standardisation of culture internationally, often denigrated with terms such as 'Cocacolanisation', 'McDonaldisation', or 'Disneyfication'. Clearly it is an interdisciplinary concept, but one thing is at the heart of it – commercial activity. From these examples, it is obvious that commercial leisure provides some of the most conspicuous examples.

Many simplified claims have been made under the banner of globalisation, and such is the international recognition of leading multinational brands that it is easy to use them to portray a global normality in terms of product and service offerings, and customer needs and values. This is reinforced by the market concentration referred to earlier, with many large multinational companies having significant proportions of market sales, not just nationally but also internationally. It is also reinforced by the exponential increases in communications, driven by technology – particularly through the media, the internet, and mobile phones – which free many people from restricted national communications.

Nevertheless, it is easy to overstate the significance of globalisation. For example, the international presence of McDonald's may be significant, but a large majority of the eating out business is conducted in independent restaurants and food outlets with distinctive characteristics that attract customers. Factors such as strong national (and local) cultures, language, religion, and politics remain as important defining characteristics of nation-states, which are the main reference points for developing international business. Technology has facilitated international communications but has also enabled increased sensitivity to the needs of local markets. Brands often cross international boundaries, but there are examples where they are hidden behind local brands which have more credibility in a particular country.

There is no disputing the rise in international business activity, the presence and power of some international brands, and the mobility of international capital to find the most cost-effective production locations. However, to assume that this is where most commercial leisure business is positioned would be an overstatement. For the commercial production and distribution of leisure goods, globalisation is an economic reality. However, in leisure services much commercial activity is rooted in local communities, particularly those elements that rely on direct personal service. In such circumstances the scope for globalisation is limited.

> **Discussion Question**
>
> Discuss the advantages and disadvantages of globalisation to the production
> and distribution of a sports shoe compared with a fitness centre.

6.6 Key Drivers for the Commercial Leisure Business

This section reviews four key drivers for commercial leisure – time, money, government, and technology. These factors determine the scale and nature of commercial leisure business and constrain, liberate, or actively facilitate commercial leisure development. They are derived from common considerations in the relevant literature.

6.6.1 Time

Chapter 3 identifies time as a key determinant and constraint of leisure demands with free time in the UK comprises on average 23% of the 24 hours a day available. Even though this has not changed a great deal (Gratton & Taylor, 2000; Gershuny, 2000), there is clear evidence that people feel more time pressured, i.e. they perceive that they have less time for the things they want to do, including work and leisure (Robinson & Godbey, 1999). Time availability is a key determinant of people's demand for leisure, whatever sector is supplying it. It is also the most cited constraint on leisure demand. The implications for leisure managers are clear – time convenience is an important attribute for leisure services.

Another crucial feature of time availability is its variation across different types of people, particularly by age and working status. For example, older people have the longest amount of leisure time per day out of the categories compared (see Chapter 3 for further information). Combined with the ageing population, which is common across many more-developed economies, this results in an important, growing market for commercial leisure. Many holiday companies, for example, have identified the growing importance of older people, with specifically targeted promotions at off-peak times of the year.

Time constraints can be lessened by appropriate design of services and appropriate use of technology. Some commercial leisure businesses have been very astute at doing this – none more so than broadcasting, with on-demand streaming services such as Netflix, Amazon Prime, and Disney + enabling viewers to watch programmes when they want, rather than when they are scheduled.

6.6.2 Money

For demand to be realised in the commercial sector, it is necessary to have not only the time but also money. A rising trend in leisure expenditure, whether in the home or away from it, is disposable income, especially across more-developed economies. OECD statistics disclose a common feature over the last 20 years or more: rising disposable income for most of the period, even after allowing for inflation. In real terms, gross national disposable income increased between 1988 and 2008 by 68% in the UK, 73% in the US, 90% in Japan, and 98% in Australia. Some of this increase will be accounted for by population growth and inflation, but generally inflation rates were fairly low during this period, and much of the increase signifies real increases in spending power.

Discussion Question

What is the most important constraint on buying more leisure goods and services, time or money? Consider this question for yourself and others in different employment circumstances to you.

6.6.3 Government Regulation

Government both facilitates and constrains commercial leisure markets. There is no better example of this than the sale of alcoholic drinks in licensed establishments in the UK. In recent years there has been a general deregulation of licensing such that there are more opportunities to drink alcohol now, and these opportunities last longer in the average day. However, as Case Study 6.1 shows, government regulation has also had a significant effect on the ownership of public houses, breaking up an oligopoly by the large brewing companies in the supply of beer to consumers.

CASE STUDY 6.1

Government Regulation of Public Houses in the UK

By the end of the 1980s, the market for beer production was dominated by six national brewers – an oligopoly typical of many commercial industries. They accounted for three-quarters of UK beer production and controlled over half of all public houses (pubs) – 32,000 pubs out of a total of 60,000 – and a substantial proportion of off-licence sales. The brewery-owned pubs were 'tied' to selling the brewer's beers only, and many other independent pubs (not owned by a big brewery) also entered into agreements with the big brewers to supply their beers in return for loans at favourable interest rates.

In 1986 the UK government's Director General of Fair Trading asked the Monopolies and Mergers Commission to investigate the beer market. The Commission reported in 1989 that the beer market was controlled by a 'complex monopoly' which favoured the brewers, who controlled not only the production but also the distribution of beer. This prevented competition and restricted choice for consumers. The report recommended that the number of pubs which brewers were allowed to own should be capped.

The government then legislated in 1989 with 'Beer Orders'. These required brewers with more than 2,000 pubs either to dispose of their breweries or release from their 'ties' half of the pubs above the designated threshold by November 1992, i.e. they had to pull out of production or radically cut their control over distribution. The Beer Orders also legislated that the remaining 'tied' pubs must sell one brand of cask beer and one brand of bottled beer from any supplier – so-called guest beers – to give consumers more choice. Furthermore, the Orders forbade any ties concerning non-alcoholic beers, low alcohol beers, and non-beer drinks, many of which had higher profit margins and were also controlled by the major breweries.

The reaction to the legislation by the major brewers was to sell their pubs. From owning 32,000 pubs in 1989, by 2004 they owned none. Instead, through acquisition and merger activity, there emerged a new oligopoly of what are termed *pubcos*, i.e. pub-owning companies whose main business is running pubs. The House of Commons

Select Committee report (House of Commons, 2004) identified seven pubcos with more than 1,000 pubs each, the largest two owning over 8,000 pubs each. The top six pubcos own about 40% of all pubs. However, all the pubco pubs are leased to tenants, who run the pubs independently.

Therefore, the government regulation of the beer market has led to a radical restructuring of the industry, splitting what was previously a vertically integrated set of companies which controlled production and distribution into two separate industries – one for production, the other for distribution. Ironically, the market concentration of beer producers is as high as ever – the top six brewers supplied 84% of sales in 2003. And a new oligopoly has emerged for distribution, the pubcos. But breaking the ownership link between the two has led to what the government has described as 'a reasonable amount of competition'. Furthermore, as the ties between production and distribution have been broken, the Beer Orders became irrelevant, and they were revoked in 2003. Job done!

Source: Adapted from House of Commons, 2004

Government also has significant effects in several other major commercial leisure industries, such as broadcasting and gambling (see Chapter 5). In broadcasting, governments not only allow public funding of public service broadcasters, such as the BBC in the UK, but also regulate the structure of broadcasting. In gambling, national and sometimes regional governments dictate through both law and planning regulations exactly what gambling is allowed in what premises. This leads, for example, to very different gambling regulations in different states in the USA.

6.6.4 Technology

Technology has had a longstanding historical effect on commercial leisure. Think of the impact of the railways on domestic holiday-taking and the development of traditional seaside resorts in the UK. Think also of various developments in air transport and the effects on leisure trips – the most recent being budget airlines.

The internet has arguably had the most dramatic technological impact on commercial leisure today. E-commerce has grown rapidly (and continues to do so), and all commercial sectors are actively examining the opportunities and threats it brings. The internet has changed the structure and delivery of leisure products and services. This is particularly the case with holidays and leisure trips, where increasing numbers of customers are planning and booking their own travel and accommodation online. It is also the case with home entertainment, with online games and downloading or streaming of music, films, and television programmes (see Chapter 10). The home fitness market has also grown substantially in recent years with products such as DIY home workouts linked to fitness and nutrition providers and products such as Peloton, which allow people to exercise from their own home whilst simultaneously connecting with friends around the globe.

Discussion Question

Besides time, money, government, and technology, what other key drivers of commercial leisure can you identify, and why are they important? Take one of the key drivers and discuss the main implications of recent changes for managers in a sport or leisure industry of your choice.

6.7 Commercial Leisure Industries: A Review

This section reviews some major commercial leisure industries to illustrate contemporary developments. It concentrates on commercial leisure away from the home: Chapter 10 reviews the major at-home commercial leisure industries – reading, home entertainment, DIY, gardening, photography, toys and games, and pets. It also excludes consideration of major tourism-related industries – accommodation and transport.

6.7.1 Eating and Drinking Out

The alcohol production industry is dominated by the few major breweries, as indicated in Case Study 6.1. However, as is typical of oligopolistic industries, consumer demand also sustains many small, independent breweries. One institution which performs a unique and distinctive function in the UK is the public house and, as the case study also shows, the ownership of pubs has changed dramatically in the last 20 years. As a focal point for social activity, the selling of alcohol and food, and often the staging of live music events, the pub caters for a variety of demands. It remains one of the most popular free-time activities outside the home among adults, although, as noted in Chapter 4, it is in sharp decline.

In the long term, the decline in pubs is because of changing preferences, e.g. 40% of all alcohol sold in the UK is now for home drinking, before the Coronavirus pandemic saw that rise, and there is fierce competition on alcohol prices from supermarkets particularly. Other negative influences on pubs include drink-driving laws; health-conscious eating and drinking; and, for pubs in the south of England particularly, cheap purchases from France and Belgium. In the shorter term, many commentators have pointed to the ban on smoking in enclosed public spaces as the main reason for the decline in pubs in the UK. The ban was introduced in Scotland in 2006 and the rest of the UK in 2007.

Another major influence on the industry is taxation – a favourite target of governments being alcohol. In 2008, for example, the UK government introduced higher-than-average tax increases for alcohol, which one study estimated would lead to a loss of 75,000 jobs in the industry in the following four years. However, times have changed in this regard more recently, primarily due to the COVID-19 crisis, and more recently in March 2021 the *Financial Times* reported that the tax on alcoholic drinks in the UK was to be frozen for only the third time in 20 years as part of a series of measures announced in the budget to support the hospitality industry after months of enforced closures due to the pandemic.

> **Discussion Question**
>
> Has the pub had its day? Think of a successful pub you have visited, and consider the reasons for its success.

Nevertheless, the public house market has shown that it can adapt to the changing nature of demand and to its changing circumstances. A growing diversification of products and segmentation of the market have been brought about by the growth in sales of pub food. Food expands the market to a wider public, and profit margins on food are greater than on drinks. Family pubs are increasingly characterised by the provision of indoor and outdoor play areas and children's soft play facilities so that families can enjoy meals out. Although sales of beer are in long-term decline in pubs, the sales of food are increasing, and 'gastro pubs' are expanding in number. According to Mintel (2019) the value of the eating-out market was expected to hit £76.8 billion with over 89% of people surveyed stating they had eaten out or had a takeaway in some format during the last year.

In the UK, there are over 50,000 enterprises in the licensed restaurant industry, including fast food and takeaway outlets. The market structure of the eating out industry varies according to the type of venue. The eating out sector is very competitive, particularly with many small independent restaurants in a very price-competitive market. However, coffee bars and fast-food chains have a different structure.

Coffee bars are in an oligopolistic market in many of the more developed economies. In the UK, three companies dominate the market, and between them Starbucks and Costa have over half the market share. Branded fast-food restaurants are also dominated by a few large companies. Demand for fast-food outlets is strong, but they have been criticised for selling unhealthy foods and have been the subject of protesters' actions as symbols of globalisation and capitalism. Nonetheless, the McDonald's logo is said to be the most recognised worldwide.

Although a varied and dynamic industry with plenty of new entrants, eating out is also a risky business. Hospitality businesses such as restaurants, hotels, pubs, and bars are much more likely to fail than other businesses. The reasons for this include the time it takes to establish a customer base and the difficulty of raising working capital against the typically small assets of independent restaurant owners.

6.7.2 Betting and Gambling

The gambling industry is growing in the United Kingdom (UK). The gross gambling yield (GGY) in Great Britain increased from roughly £8.4 billion in 2011 to approximately £14.4 billion in 2018 (Statista, 2020). The GGY refers to the amount retained by gambling operators after the payment of winnings prior to operating cost deductions. Since legislation for remote gambling changed in 2014, the considered GGY for remote gambling accounts for the largest share of the market. The gambling industry provided jobs for some 100,000 employees in the UK in 2018, of which the majority works in the betting sector, followed by casino and bingo (Statista, 2020). It is a service industry and therefore shares many of the service management requirements of the rest of the leisure industry. It has particular ethical and legal issues, however, of which managers have to be aware.

In 2020, a report found that 32.2% of adults gamble once a week, and other figures suggest that around 47% of people in the UK have gambled in some way in the last 4 weeks. In this regard, gambling is clearly a mass participation leisure activity. In the UK gambling is dominated by sports betting, scratch cards, gaming machines, and the National Lottery, which together account for about 57% of the market. Other forms of gambling are relatively small scale, including bingo and the football pools, which were traditionally very popular during the 1980s and 1990s but have been replaced as gambling trends have shifted towards online and virtual participation. Indeed, over 460 high street betting shops were closed in 2020 owing to a surge in online gambling, lockdowns due to the COVID-19 pandemic, and a government crackdown on fixed-odds betting terminals which were at the heart of the issue for a number of problem gamblers.

The government has a strong influence on the gambling industry, through several means. UK examples include introducing the National Lottery in 1994 and significant deregulation of gambling in the early 2000s. More recently, the UK Government have also cut the maximum bets allowed on fixed-odds betting terminals in 2018. Additionally, in the UK, there is a non-departmental public body which was set up by the 2005 Gambling Act to regulate commercial gambling – the Gambling Commission. Its regulatory objectives are to keep gambling crime free, to ensure players are not exploited, and to protect children and vulnerable people from the dangers of gambling – these are the ethical considerations which good managers in the gambling industry will be watchful for.

The UK gambling industry contains some elements which are in decline, e.g. bingo, and others which are growing, such as online betting. For example, there are currently believed to be over 80 different online bookmakers licensed to operate in the UK. It remains big business, not only in its own right but also in relationship with other leisure sectors, particularly sport. The review that follows does not include lotteries, because the National Lottery is really a government initiative and is reviewed in Chapter 5, whilst other lotteries are typically run by charities, sporting clubs, and cultural bodies, so they are not commercial operations.

6.7.2.1 Betting and Racing

The horseracing industry is another significant part of the commercial gambling sector. The most recent overview of this industry was provided by Deloitte in 2013. They summarised that the total direct and indirect expenditure of British racing was £3.45 billion and that British racing provided a tax contribution of over £275 million (Deloitte, 2013). There are 60 racecourses in Britain, with a combined total attendance of over 5.6 million in 2013. The horse racing industry generates direct expenditure of over £1 billion a year and employs 17,400 people (Deloitte, 2013). It remains one of the most popular sport spectator events in the UK, and flagship races such as the Grand National, Cheltenham Gold Cup, and Epsom Derby generate significant attendance and broadcast income from around the globe.

6.7.2.2 Casinos

There were 156 casinos in the UK in 2020, which was a slight increase from 153 in the previous year. There are three companies that own the majority of casinos in the UK – Gala Coral Group, Grosvenor, and Genting Casinos – another oligopoly. The location of casinos is strictly regulated in the UK.

Changes in the law have benefited casinos through, for example, longer licensed drinking times; the abolition of the 'cooling-off' period, i.e. the time between joining a club and being allowed to gamble; and payment for chips with debit cards. The main growth in competition recently is from online casinos and the shift to more online participation in gambling outlined earlier in this chapter.

6.7.2.3 Bingo

Bingo was first developed in the sixteenth century in Italy as a game for the *intelligentsia*, but then it came to be regarded as an undemanding 'working class' pursuit. However, bingo does have surprising social benefits. It is one of the few leisure activities which has good participation by lower socio-economic groups, lower income groups, divorced/separated people, the long-term unemployed, older people, and women (Wardle *et al.*, 2007). There are lots of subsidised public sector leisure providers that would like that profile of users! However, bingo revenues have declined in the past decade owing to the shift in online gambling. Many online betting providers now offer virtual bingo, so there is no need for people to physically leave the house to participate.

The Gambling Commission (2019) reports that Great Britain had 650 licensed bingo clubs operating as of September 2018, a small decrease of 1.1% from March 2018. This shows some resistance to the online trend that has threatened to wipe out the physical nature of how people gamble, but the number of bingo clubs still in operation retains some hope for this part of the sector for now. It will be interesting to see how bingo fares in a post-COVID environment given the age demographics of people who play largely falling into the 'vulnerable' category.

6.7.2.4 Gaming Machines

Amusement machines are a major source of income for many leisure providers. During the period April 2019 to March 2020, it is estimated that the average number of gaming machines across all sectors in Great Britain amounted to 191,286 (Statista, 2020). This represents a 6% increase on the previous year's total. The number of gaming machines in Great Britain has gradually increased in the past decade, although the government decision to limit the maximum stake on fixed-odds betting terminals from April 2019 might have an impact on this area of gambling in the future. The decision means that the maximum bet on these terminals was reduced from £100 to £2. It was done to discourage high stakes gambling and to expose people to the risk of gambling harm. The machines have been called the 'crack cocaine' of gambling by campaigners who say they let players lose money too quickly, leading to addiction and social problems. However, this decision will also have a knock-on effect for the industry, as fixed-odds betting terminals made up 57% of betting shops profit in 2017. That suggests that bookmakers are becoming increasingly reliant on them as a source of profit and outlines one of the ethical and moral problems with this industry with corporations potentially putting company profit before the health and safety of their customers.

> ### Discussion Questions
>
> Should the maximum bet on fixed-odds betting terminals have been lowered? What implications might it have moving forward for all parties concerned?

6.7.3 Sport

The global sport market is currently worth an estimated $471 billion dollars, and the commercial sector accounts for a large proportion of this market (Statista, 2021). The market is not only growing (showing year-on-year growth since 2011), but it is also a very diverse and complex sector. It includes things such as manufacturing, retail (including sports goods), events and venues, leagues and teams, commercial leisure, business services, media, sponsorship, and gaming/esports. The following sections provide a brief overview of some of these areas.

6.7.3.1 Spectator Sport

Commercial spectator sports are dominated worldwide by football, motor sports, and horse racing, whilst different countries have their own favourites, e.g. American football, ice hockey, baseball, and basketball in the USA. The most popular sports attract large numbers of spectators and huge television audiences. In the UK, consumer expenditure on spectator sports was valued at £1.468 billion in 2019 and had shown year-on-year growth every year since 2015 (Mintel, 2020). Of course, the COVID-19 pandemic has had a huge impact on live spectators given that most sports around the world had to play behind closed doors for over a year between March 2020 and May 2021. Indeed, Mintel predicted that the sector should have achieved another year of growth in 2020 had it not been for the pandemic. However, this also puts the market in a strong place to bounce back quickly, just as it did after the last recession between 2007 and 2012. The appeal of sport, and the demand for live spectator sport, makes it a sector that is often resilient against crisis, at least on a general level. Moreover, major sporting events can also be an important contributor to economic growth. This is evidenced in the UK by the hosting of the Rugby Union World Cup in 2015 and the Cricket World Cup in 2019, which both added value to the market (Mintel, 2020).

The highest attended sporting events will always be the more infrequent mega events such as the World Cup in football or the Olympic Games, but the majority of spectator spending occurs in the most dominant national sports in respective countries. In the UK, this is football. Consumer expenditure on spectator sports in the UK is dominated by football, which typically accounts for around 60% of all spending (Mintel, 2020). In the English Premier League (the top tier of English football) the capacity utilisation rate has remained above 95% for the last decade or so, and some professional teams in England can boast waiting lists for season tickets with demand far outstripping supply.

This has not always been the case, however, and the sporting product of the English Premier League remains one of the greatest sporting success stories (from a commercial perspective) in recent times. Live spectator numbers for football fell in the UK from the late 1940s to the mid-1980s. Several factors then contributed to a strong recovery in attendances (although not to the levels of the 1940s). These included stadia improvements following the Bradford and Hillsborough disasters, the formation of the English Premier League in 1992, the flotation of some clubs on the Stock Market, the increasing revenue from and coverage on television, and more international stars attracted to the Premier League.

As businesses, professional sports often live up to the cliché 'it's a funny old game', and they provide the most tangible evidence that so-called commercial businesses are often not just in it for profit. Year after year the professional football industry in the UK, for example, demonstrates that, apart from a few notable exceptions, many clubs operate with financial losses, and many are technically insolvent and only sustained by rescheduled debts. For example, in the English Football Championship (tier 2 of English football) the clubs made a combined loss of £309 million in 2018–2019. These clubs were spending 107% of their revenue on player wages which contributes to the huge losses we see in the English game. Despite its dominance as a global league and the ability to command huge broadcasting revenues, it is not the clubs that get rich from this but rather the players. Nice work if you can get it!

Nevertheless, there are outstanding examples of business success in professional sport. In football the most conspicuous example is Manchester United, a club which, despite its large debts at the time of writing, generates significant profits and enormous revenues from merchandise and media rights as well as from live spectators attending matches at Old Trafford. Furthermore, there are other examples of football clubs at every level of the professional game that are successful businesses in the conventional manner of making profits. The trouble with professional sport is that commercial success is never enough – sporting success is equally and often more important. One of the most conspicuous examples of the business 'knife edge' walked by some professional football clubs is Leeds United, which went from being one of the top Premier League sides in England to a League 1 side in a few seasons – principally because of financial problems, in particular escalating debts.

6.7.3.2 Sport Media

Whereas professional football often presents a poor image of commercial business, sport media provide some of the most successful examples of commercial success. An example featured in Case Study 10.2 is football and television, in particular the success of Sky television. There is a powerful, symbiotic relationship between the commercial sport and television industries, which the case study illustrates.

The relationship between professional sport and the media is a very important business alliance. Professional sport gets valuable revenue for media coverage, which helps to overcome the gap between costs and the revenue from finite live spectator numbers. The media can reach many more people interested in professional sport and make successful businesses out of this communication. Gratton and Solberg suggest:

> The most significant change in the sports industry over the last 20 years has been the increasing importance of broadcast demand for sport which has led to massive escalation in the prices of broadcasting rights for professional team sports and major sports events.

> (Gratton & Solberg, 2007, p. 1)

The escalation in the prices of broadcasting rights, however, has shown the risks involved in sport media. Setanta, having paid part of a record fee for Premier League football broadcasting rights in England and Scotland, then did not realise sufficient subscription income, and their business folded in 2009. This left more than a few football clubs in financial trouble, such has been their increasing dependency on television revenues. The Setanta failure demonstrates the difficulties of breaking into a sport broadcasting market which is dominated by a few large companies. At present, it is Sky Sports and BT Sport hold this privileged position in English football (with Sky Sports being the clear number one in terms of market position). However, new players are beginning to enter the market such as Amazon Prime, and we may see further movement in this space from some of the other over-the-top (OTT) streaming style providers in the future such as Netflix, Google, and Facebook. The rise in the 'on-demand' culture of consuming media is driving market change, but the problem with live sport is it can never be 'on-demand' by definition. That said, the big tech companies are fully aware of the insatiable consumer demand for sport, and it will come as no surprise to many if these providers look to purchase more content rights in the coming years.

6.7.3.3 Sports Clothing, Footwear, and Equipment

Although the sports industry is dominated by expenditure on sports services, there is also a significant amount of consumer spending on sports goods, most notably in fitness equipment and sports goods. This involves the manufacture, distribution, and retailing of a vast range of goods, from yachts, canoes, tents, bicycles, and hang-gliders, to tracksuits, specialist footwear for a variety of different activities, rackets, balls, snooker tables, dartboards, trampolines, and goalposts. In the UK in 2019, sales from the manufacture of sports goods totalled £414 million, and the annual turnover of sports goods manufacturers totalled £828 million (Statista, 2020). Over 1 million people in the UK spent under £100 on purchasing fitness equipment in 2019, with around 45,000 people spending £500 or more. This trend has been rising in recent years with a shift to more 'home fitness' style routines and companies such as Peloton now selling static bikes for home exercise that can also connect people with friends and colleagues around the world in the form of virtual exercise classes.

In relation to the retail sportswear market, the sales of outdoor apparel in the UK totalled £838 million in 2017 with Adidas being the clear market leader. These big brands have had to align their apparel business to changing fashion trends over the last decade or so, but they have continued to show significant growth and commercial profits which have always been boosted significantly by the footwear market.

Manufacture of sports clothing and footwear is very often 'outsourced' to countries with low labour costs, such as Taiwan, China, and the Philippines. This raises ethical issues about 'exploitation' in less developed countries, but the commercial logic is that it keeps production costs low and allows high wholesale and retail margins in more developed countries.

> ### Discussion Question
>
> Is it 'exploitation' when a multinational sports goods company organises production in a less developed country?

6.7.3.4 Health and Fitness Clubs

The fitness sector is comprised mainly of commercial providers, although fitness facilities are common in public sector leisure centres too. It is a sector that has seen substantial growth in the past two decades. In the UK, the number of members of clubs stands at around 10.4 million in 2019. In Europe, only Germany has more with 11.7 million. The next highest is France (6.2 million), Italy (5.5 million), and Spain (5.5 million). Together, these five countries account for 65% of the total market in Europe (Statista, 2020). In the UK alone, the market size of the gym, health, and fitness club industry was worth £2.12 billion in 2020, and that figure had risen from £1.1 billion in 2011 (Statista, 2020).

Commercial sector growth has been driven by a significant increase in the number of commercial fitness clubs, with development by several chains, including Bannatyne's, Cannons, David Lloyd, Esporta, Fitness First, LA Fitness, and Virgin. Most of the clubs are standalone, but some are in hotels and run by the hotel or by outside contractors. On a less expensive scale, there has also been considerable growth in the budget gym industry, with organisations such as Pure Gym making significant market gains. The appeal of these types of gyms is low cost, no contract, and 24-hour opening times. The clubs are minimalistic in terms of equipment and staffing (which keeps costs low) but can offer flexibility to their members as their doors are (literally!) always open.

Health and fitness clubs have evolved over the past 40 years into a widespread, sophisticated market leader. With a move towards individual health and fitness, supported by government policy, a burgeoning market has grown in the private sector with new kinds of equipment – resistance, cardio-vascular, treadmills – and these have led to highly sophisticated, computerised machinery that incorporates club members' personal workout information. Personal trainers are an important development from this industry. Indeed, the number of personal trainers in the UK has increased 34% in the last decade from 15,197 in 2011 to 23,143 in 2020.

The nature of some clubs has been moving from physical fitness to health and wellbeing, a shift which forward-thinking leisure managers should take seriously. This trend will no doubt continue in the future as physical and mental health become an increasing public health agenda. Commercial fitness firms will have a role to play in this as the market expands, and we have already seen private health care companies acquire health and fitness clubs in the past (e.g. Nuffield Health, who acquired Cannons Health and Fitness Clubs in 2007).

It is not uncommon today to find private health companies with a range of services which have a synergy with health and fitness clubs, i.e. treatments and therapies including acupuncture, the Alexander technique, aromatherapy, chiropractic therapy, homeopathy, hypnotherapy, massage, meditation, osteopathy, reiki, reflexology, relaxation training, sports injury clinics, t'ai chi, and yoga. While it provides a few of such services, the trend in the private fitness sector is more towards the concept of 'wellness' and health spas, which have been extremely popular in parts of Europe for the last hundred years. The American wellness market sector has also moved towards provision of health spas and holistic approaches.

6.7.4 Cinema and Theatre

Cinema and theatre are arguably two of the leisure pursuits that are most at risk (in a physical sense) as we enter the post-COVID-19 world and beyond. Even before the pandemic, there were suggestions that the number of cinema and theatre admissions were falling, although the UK Cinema Association reported cinema admissions in the UK of 176.1m in 2019. However, in 2020 this figure fell to just 44m, a damning inditement of the impact that COVID-19 has had on the industry, with cinemas and theatres suffering complete closures for over a year in 2020.

With reference to theatre, in the UK, commercial theatres are largely centred on London. There are estimated to be around 1,1000 active theatres in the UK, but only a very small proportion of these will have access to substantial government subsidies (e.g. Royal Opera House, London Coliseum, National Theatre, Sadler's Wells). The London commercial theatres are another oligopoly, with 5 companies owning 29 London theatres between them: Ambassadors, Delfont Mackintosh, Live Nation, Nimax, and Really Useful Group.

There are still positives for the theatre industry in relation to pre-pandemic figures. There were 44,135 theatre performances in the UK in 2018, and 18.8m tickets were sold. The average price of a ticket was £27.10, which is relatively affordable in comparison to other leisure pursuits. However, both the cinema and the theatre face challenges moving forward.

Indeed, the cinema industry is also under another threat from streaming platforms such as Disney + who have started to sell 'Premier Access' to their newest releases that allows people to consume them on the same day that they air in cinemas. This price is currently a one-off few of £20 in the UK, which is also around the average cost of one cinema trip itself. Again, the shift to a more online and on-demand culture will prove to be a big challenge for sectors such as this where the 'liveness' of the event is not as unique as the world of spectator sports.

6.7.5 Leisure Parks

Leisure parks are clusters of leisure and other developments in one location, such as cinema, tenpin bowling, restaurants, and clubs. Leisure experiences in attractive, safe environments attract families and the older age groups and provide an alternative to home entertainment. However, different groups in the community have different demands; these are largely age related and lead to a fragmented market. To cater for each separate market would be costly and less attractive to the family market. Multi-facility leisure schemes are increasingly being developed to attract a wide range of users within one complex.

In the 1990s interest from developers in the leisure park market was stimulated by evidence of increasing numbers of cinema-goers, greater interest in tenpin bowling and bingo, and the popularity of nightclubs. As a result, nearly all leisure parks designed during this time are anchored by multiplex cinemas and restaurants, which then become a catalyst for other elements, particularly tenpin bowling and health and fitness clubs, but also bars/pubs, bingo, and nightclubs. In retail parks with leisure, cinemas and restaurants are also the main anchors, with tenpin bowling the next most common leisure element.

6.7.6 Nightclubs

Despite the nightclub scene going through a sustained period of growth in the early 2000s, the overall market currently appears to be in decline. The market size, as measured by revenue, of the nightclubs industry is £171.6 million in 2021, but this shows a decline of 87.7% when measured against the previous year. Of course, the closure of nightclubs from the COVID-19 pandemic will have played a part here, but the sector itself has shown decline in the last five years with an average decline of 38.3% per year since 2016. There will be some growth back into the industry following the reopening of nightclubs in July 2021, but forecasters from Ibis World do not offer long-term growth prospects for the industry, predicting that revenue is not expected to recover to pre-COVID-19 (Coronavirus) pandemic levels over the period due to the expected permanent closure of many nightclubs in the current year. Moreover, competition from alternative late-night venues and regulations designed to curb binge-drinking and lower levels of violent crime are anticipated to weigh on industry performance.

One of the issues for this sector has always been (and will continue to be) a clash of cultures. On the one hand there is the promotion of sales of alcohol and exciting entertainment, as these make for profitable business for the industry (and through taxes, also for the government) as well as satisfying the demands of consumers. Yet on the other hand there is public and policy concern about health, anti-social behaviour, and crime, which gives rise to calls for further regulation. Leisure managers and other professionals need to identify ways in which appropriate compromises are reached, ensuring customers' demands are still satisfied, whilst protecting them and others from the excesses that can arise. Leisure education, in its widest sense, is one of the means of helping young people to make their own choices to meet their needs for excitement and fun without causing social concern.

6.7.7 Theme Parks

Theme parks have become popular since the creation of Disneyland, which resurrected the amusement park industry in 1955 in the United States. Disney's philosophy has been one of providing excellence, cleanliness, courtesy, and safety. They create an atmosphere of fantasy, glamour, escapism, prestige, and excitement. Disney theme parks are successful in Tokyo, Hong Kong, and Paris, as well as Florida and California, and they are world leaders. In the US version of Disneyland, for example, the park attracted global visitors of 155.99 million in 2019.

Britain's first theme park was Thorpe Water Park at Chertsey, with a theme of maritime history. Its development encouraged the provision of other 'theme' facilities elsewhere in the UK. Britain's largest, Alton Towers in Staffordshire, is the tenth largest theme park in Europe, with over 2 million visits in 2019. Apart from Disney, four other companies dominate the operation of theme parks in Europe: Merlin Entertainments, Parques Reunidos, Grevin et Cie, and Aspro Ocio. Merlin Entertainments operates some of the largest UK theme parks

– Alton Towers, Thorpe Park, Legoland, Madame Tussauds, Sea Life centres, and Chessington World of Adventures – as well as the London Eye and theme parks in Italy and Germany.

Theme parks are a magnet for children and young people and are therefore attractive for day trips and family outings. They take up large amounts of land, so they need to be located at distances from urban settings, requiring longer travel times than to local facilities. They are marketed as a 'day out' and have benefited during times of recession from the trend towards 'staycations' – holidays at home.

The biggest commercial challenge is to generate sufficient visitors and revenue to cover not only the high running costs but the high capital costs of new, eye-catching major rides, which have become a necessity to encourage repeat visits. Generating visits is only partly controlled by management actions – particularly investment, advertising, and pricing. Other major influences are the state of the general economy and, of course, the weather.

There are positive trends for theme parks in the future, as they will remain a sought-after leisure pursuit. However, recent research by Mintel (2020) stated that they will also have to find new ways to win over families by continuing to capture kids' attention while some of the most desired attractions will be paused (because of COVID-19) and to meet the desires of the entire family in new and safe ways. For example, 56% of families in the US who have children under the age of 18 in the household say their child has input in where their family goes on vacation.

6.8 Conclusions

Commercial providers of facilities, services, and products for leisure consumption have by far the greatest influence on people's use of leisure time, compared to other providers. This chapter has reviewed some general considerations and some of the commercial markets for leisure away from home. However, there are other major commercial leisure interests covered in other chapters, particularly leisure in the home (Chapter 10) and sponsorship (Chapter 14).

Commercial businesses must make profits, or in the end they go out of business. To reap the best profits and returns on investment, management policies, approaches, and techniques are important. Several factors determine commercial leisure success, including:

- Accessibility and location, either in town centres or in out-of-town sites;
- The range of facilities and activities;
- The catchment area and the market competition (not just from similar facilities but also other opportunities for children and families);
- The quality of products and services;
- Investment in new products;
- Pricing;
- Promotion;
- Catering and social opportunities;
- Facilities and services for different market segments;
- Car parking.

The commercial sector, whilst having to maintain profitability, does not operate in isolation from other sectors. Government is a key influence on commercial business, both facilitating and constraining. The commercial sector does generate important positive and negative social outcomes, which it is showing increasing regard for – it must, otherwise it loses the support of communities and ultimately consumers.

Practical Tasks

1 Visit a commercial leisure organisation. Identify how many ways it tries to get you to spend money. Identify other possible ways in which it could tempt you to spend money.
2 Visit the venues of two major operators in any *one* of the following industries: cinema, bingo, fast food, coffee bars. Consider the similarities and differences between the sites and decide whether oligopoly is good or bad for customer choice and quality of service.

Structured Guide to Further Reading

For market reviews of different commercial leisure markets, international and UK:
Mintel report and Statista

For an overview of gambling in the UK:
www.gamblingcommission.gov.uk/

For sports broadcasting:
Gratton, C., & Solberg, H. A. (2007). *The Economics of Sports Broadcasting*. Routledge, London.

Useful Websites

For international disposable income statistics, from the OECD:
www.oecd.org/LongAbstract/0,3425,en_2649_33715_36864949_1_1_1_1,00.html

For household expenditure statistics in the UK, from the Office for National Statistics:
www.ons.gov.uk/peoplepopulationandcommunity/personalandhouseholdfinances/expenditure

For information on horse racing in Great Britain:
www.britishhorseracing.com/

For information on the 2005 Gambling Act:
www.culture.gov.uk/what_we_do/gambling_and_racing/3305.aspx

For information on cinema in the UK:
UK Cinema Association, www.cinemauk.org.uk/

References

Deloitte. (2013). *The Economic Impact of British Racing, 2013*. Deloitte Publishing, London.
Deloitte. (2016). *Passion for Leisure A View of the UK Leisure Consumer*. Deloitte Publishing, London.

Gambling Commission. (2019). *Licencing Authority Bulletin, Bongo*. Gambling Commission Publishing, London.

Gershuny, J. I. (2000). *Changing Times: Work and Leisure in Postindustrial Society*. Oxford University Press, Oxford.

Gratton, C., & Taylor, P. (2000). *Economics of Sport and Recreation*. E & FN Spon, London.

House of Commons. (2004). Trade and industry second report. Retrieved from www.publications.parliament.uk/pa/cm200405/cmselect/cmtrdind/128/12802.htm

Mintel. (2019). *Eating Out Review - UK*. Mintel Publishing, London.

Mintel. (2020). *UK Sports and Outdoor Fashion Market Report*. Mintel Publishing, London.

Robinson, J., & Godbey, G. (1999). *Time for Life: The Surprising Ways Americans Use Their Time*. Pennsylvania State University Press, Pennsylvania, PA.

Statista. (2020). *Gambling Industry in the United Kingdom (UK) – Statistics and Facts*. Statista Publishing, London.

Statista. (2021). *Global Sport Market – Statistics and Facts*. Statista Publishing, London.

Wardle, H., Sproston, K., Orford, J., Erens, B., Griffiths, M., Constantine, R., & Pigott, S. (2007). *British Gambling Prevalence Survey 2007*. National Centre for Social Research, London.

Chapter 7

Sport and Leisure Provision in the Third Sector (Voluntary)

In This Chapter

- What is the scale and scope of volunteering in sport and leisure, and what motivates volunteers?
- What benefits and problems are there for volunteers in sport and leisure?
- What are the major barriers and incentives for volunteering in sport and leisure?
- How does government interact with the third sector in sport and leisure?

DOI: 10.4324/9780367823610-7

Summary

The 'third sector' contains a diverse set of sport and leisure providers, including voluntary and charitable organisations and provision for staff in commercial companies. Many providers employ paid managers, although voluntary organisations are typically managed by volunteers. Voluntary organisations are important for sport and leisure provision, with hundreds of thousands across a range of leisure interests. They range from small local clubs with a handful of members to large national organisations with millions of members. They bring benefits to members, but they also have problems, the most important of which appears to be a shortage of volunteers. At the local level in the UK an increasing number of public sector leisure assets, such as museums and sports centres, are managed by charitable trusts, which do not utilise many volunteers. Charitable status brings both advantages and disadvantages.

The relationship between the third sector and the public sector needs careful management at national and local levels. At the national level, the government promotes the social outcomes of the third sector because they align to government objectives. The government is also interested in promoting what is termed 'capacity building' in the third sector, i.e. making it more effective. However, there is a sensitive balance to be achieved between supporting the third sector with public funding and attempting to steer it towards a greater conformance with government policies.

7.1 Introduction

The 'third sector' referred to in this chapter has traditionally been labelled the 'voluntary sector'. However, increasingly, it is called the 'third sector' because it contains various organisations run by paid staff, not volunteers. Similarly, private non-profit organisations such as non-government organisations (NGOs) – one of the best-known examples in sport being the International Olympic Committee (IOC) – also sit in this sector. So, this chapter considers the management of volunteers, but volunteers are not the only concern of this chapter. The third sector embraces any organisation that is not profit-making but also not a government organisation. These can include:

- **Voluntary organisations** – primarily run by volunteers, although quite a few have paid employees for key functions – for example, managers of larger clubs and governing bodies, some bar staff at clubs, increasing numbers of coaches in sports clubs;
- **Charitable trusts** – often run by paid employees. Many trusts have been set up to operate public sector leisure assets (e.g. leisure centres, parks) at the local level in the UK;
- **Social enterprises** – businesses operating for a social purpose, often with charitable status;

- Commercial companies that provide non-profit sport and leisure opportunities for their employees – financed by profit-making organisations but run for the welfare of employees and often organised by paid employees.

This chapter starts with an exploration of volunteers and voluntary organisations in sport, leisure, and PA – the largest part of the third sector. Ironically, volunteers do unpaid work in their own leisure time, using their energy, skills, and often their own money, because they want to do it. In this sense, volunteering – giving service to others – is a leisure activity, and the concept of *volunteerism* embraces this. Volunteering is often categorised as either *formal*, volunteering for clubs or organisations, or *informal*, volunteering on a more ad hoc basis. One global example of volunteering (both formal and informal) within PA is Parkrun. Parkrun utilises volunteers each week to deliver a 5 kilometre 'fun run' at various parks around the world. Some volunteers are formal, for example the 'Event Director', however, each individual Parkrun has less formal volunteering roles, and those running Parkrun are encouraged to volunteer when they can. It is a good example of a blend of formal and informal volunteering.

7.2 The Scale and Scope of Volunteering

In the UK volunteering has been reducing slightly over the past decade. In 2013 for example, according to Sport England data, around 70% of adults volunteered at least once a year and 44% at least once a month. By 2020 that had dropped to 64% and 39% respectively. The sport sector is the most popular environment for volunteering in the UK, followed by the arts, heritage, and then museums and galleries. Indeed, while volunteering generally has gone down, the share of those who do volunteer has increased in sport. Potentially, Parkrun has been the defining factor in that trend. Looking at Europe, there is evidence to suggest this trend in decreasing volunteering is mirrored across the continent. Table 7.1 shows the percentage of the population who volunteer in sport, comparing 2013 to 2017. Looking at 2017, the Netherlands, Sweden, and Denmark had just under 20% of the population volunteering in sport, while Romania, Italy, and Portugal have the lowest percentage. However, the table is ordered in change in percentage.

Table 7.1 **Percentage of Population Who Volunteer in Sport in Selected Countries**

Country	2013	2017	Change
Sweden	25	19	−6
Austria	12	6	−6
Ireland	15	10	−5
Croatia	8	3	−5
Estonia	12	8	−4
Germany	10	7	−3

(Continued)

Table 7.1 (Continued)

Country	2013	2017	Change
United Kingdom	10	7	−3
Slovakia	6	3	−3
Finland	13	11	−2
Slovenia	12	10	−2
Czech Republic	10	8	−2
France	7	5	−2
Hungary	6	4	−2
Lithuania	5	3	−2
Luxembourg	13	12	−1
Romania	3	2	−1
Italy	3	2	−1
Portugal	2	1	−1
Denmark	18	18	0
Belgium	9	9	0
Cyprus	5	5	0
Spain	4	4	0
Greece	3	3	0
Poland	3	3	0
Bulgaria	3	3	0
Netherlands	18	19	1
Latvia	8	9	1
Malta	4	6	2

Source: European Commission

Table 7.2 Distribution of Volunteers in 2018, by Type of Organization in Scotland

Distribution of adults who had provided help in the last 12 months in Scotland in 2018, by type of organization or group	
Youth/children activities outside schools	24
Local community or neighbourhood groups	21
Children's activities associated with schools	20
Health, disability, and social welfare	17
Hobbies/recreation/arts/social clubs	16
Sport/exercise (coaching or organising)	15
Religious groups	15
The elderly	7
Environmental protection	6
Domestic animal welfare	6
Education for adults	5
Culture and heritage	5
Justice and human rights	4
Safety, first aid	3
Political groups	3

Source: Scottish Government

Table 7.3 Volunteering Activities Undertaken over the Past 12 Months in the UK

Activity	Percentage
Organising or helping to run an activity or event	35.3
Other practical help	29.1
Member of a committee	21.7
Raising or handling money/taking part in sponsored events	19.8
Visiting people	17.5

(Continued)

Table 7.3 (Continued)

Activity	Percentage
Giving advice/information/counselling	16.6
Coaching or tuition	16.4
Befriending or mentoring people	13.9
Leading the group	13.2
Providing transport or driving	11.8
Secretarial, administrative, or clerical work	10.2
Representing	6.9
Officiating – e.g. judging, umpiring, or refereeing	6.3
Trustee	6.2
Campaigning	5.8
Conservation/restoration	5.3
Other answers	2.8
Steward	1.5
Work in a charity shop [Coded data only]	1.1

Source: Department for Digital, Culture, Media, and Sport (UK)

Overall, the data show more countries with a decrease in the number of volunteers in sport and only three countries – the Netherlands, Latvia, and Malta – where an increase has occurred.

WHERE DO PEOPLE VOLUNTEER, AND WHAT DO THEY DO?

To give an idea of where people volunteer, we can break down volunteering by sector. In England, for example, of those who volunteer, in 2020, 20.1% do so in sport, 7.7% volunteer in the arts, 5.2% in heritage, 2.6% at museums and galleries, 1.9% in libraries, and 0.6% in archives. More specifically, data from another country, Scotland, shown in Table 7.2 gives a more detailed analysis of the types of organisations people volunteer in, the most popular being youth or children activities outside schools and local community or neighbourhood groups. The other useful data that help us understand volunteering in England is displayed in Table 7.3. This is a detailed look at what activities those volunteers have undertaken over a 12-month period, which ranges from being a member of a committee, befriending or mentoring people, to undertaking secretarial, administrative, or clerical work.

7.3 Who Are the Volunteers?

Leisure management interest in volunteers is largely confined to management of volunteers in organisations which produce leisure outputs, so reference is made here to specific characteristics of volunteers in sport and leisure.

7.3.1 Gender

In a 2001 a Citizenship Survey (Home Office, 2003) found a difference between volunteering activities of males and females. Men were more likely to be engaged than women in sports and exercise and hobbies/recreation/arts/social clubs. Indeed, the male bias in sports volunteering was common across all EU countries (GHK, 2010) and also in Australia and Canada (Cuskelly *et al.*, 2006). Low *et al.* (2007) also found that women were more likely to volunteer than men overall, across all fields of interest. And in youth/children's activities (outside school) and environment/animals, women are more likely to volunteer than men. Data in 2020 from Sport England show that a difference remains in England. More females (34.6%) volunteer than males (30.1%), but when it comes to sport and leisure in England more males (3.56 million) volunteer compared to females (2.54 million). The top three activities for females are 'Provided any other help', 'Provided transport', and 'Admin or committee role', while males are most likely to have 'Coached or instructed' and then 'Provided transport' or undertaken an 'Admin or committee role'. This reflects the gender division in sport coaching more broadly.

7.3.2 Age

Age also seems to have a relationship with volunteering. In 2010, a GHK survey suggested that for most EU countries volunteering was mainly undertaken by people aged between 30 and 50; but in a minority of countries, including the UK, it was the age group older than that according to data from a Community Life Survey. As can be seen in Figure 7.1, those aged 65 to 74 have, since 2013, provided the most volunteer support. This is not the same when we look at sport as an aspect of leisure. In England, approximately 6 million people volunteered in sport in 2020. Of these, the highest number came from those aged 45 to 54, where 1.24 million people volunteered. Next, 1.08 million people volunteered who were aged between 16 and 24, and 1.03 million aged between 35 to 44. Those aged 65 to 74 were only the sixth largest group. Data from Sport England in Figure 7.2 show that the role people undertake is also impacted by age.

7.3.3 Ethnicity

Perhaps the starkest example of how volunteering is stratified in sport comes when we look at the groups who are socially excluded. When we look at volunteering in general, there is a relatively equal distribution across different ethnicities, 33% for those who identify as White, 32.3% as Black, 27.8% as Asian, and 31.6% as Mixed. This is very different in sport and physical activity. Table 7.4 shows the ethnic breakdown of those who volunteer in sport and reflects wider issues in sport and physical activity.

7.3.4 Education and Income

The 2001 Home Office Citizenship Survey (Home Office, 2003) showed that people at the highest end of the social spectrum, i.e. with the highest levels of education, from the higher socio-economic groups, or with the highest levels of household incomes, were most likely to be involved in formal or informal voluntary activity. Ten years later, GHK (2010) reported

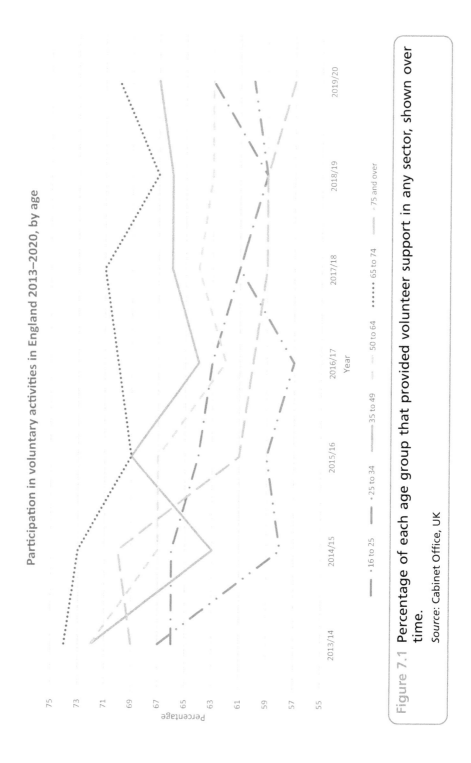

Participation in voluntary activities in England 2013–2020, by age

Figure 7.1 Percentage of each age group that provided volunteer support in any sector, shown over time.

Source: Cabinet Office, UK

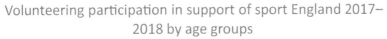

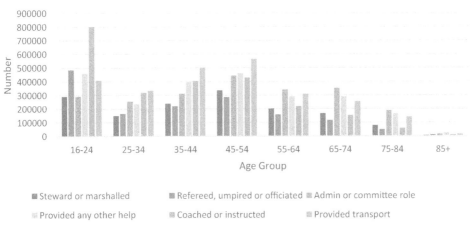

Volunteering participation in support of sport England 2017–2018 by age groups

- Steward or marshalled
- Refereed, umpired or officiated
- Admin or committee role
- Provided any other help
- Coached or instructed
- Provided transport

Figure 7.2 **Sport volunteering by age and activity.**
Source: Sport England

Table 7.4 **Volunteering Participation in Support of Sport in 2019, by Ethnicity Group in England**

Number of people who volunteered to support sport and physical activity in England in 2019, by ethnicity group

White British	5,321,300
White Other	203,700
South Asian	331,200
Black	198,000
Mixed	99,300
Other ethnic group	32,000

that, in EU countries generally, people with higher education degrees or vocational training are more likely to volunteer in sport. And not much has changed in England when we look at more recent data. There remains the bias in volunteering towards those from higher socio-economic groups. In 2019, for example, 35.5% of those from upper socio-economic groups volunteered, while 19.7% of those from lower socio-economic groups volunteered. And work status does not determine this. In 2020, 32% of those who were employed volunteered in some form, and 32% of those who were not working volunteered. However, the type of work, or indeed, education matters. See, for example, Figure 7.3, which shows that full-time or part-time students are most likely to volunteer in sport and physical activity, followed by those working full-time or part-time and those who have retired. Interestingly,

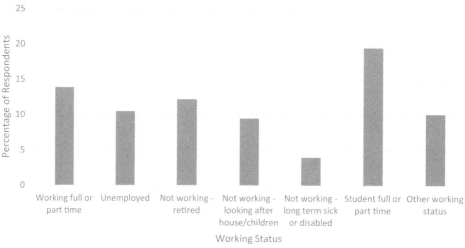

Figure 7.3 **Volunteering participation by working status.**
Source: Sport England

the lowest group are those who are long-term sick or disabled and, like other sectors of the sport and physical activity sector, those who have mental or physical impairments are often marginalised in volunteering. These issues are all very relevant to managers in voluntary organisations: When seeking new volunteers, should managers select the easiest option, the more affluent base from which existing volunteers come? Or should they make the extra effort required to recruit from the lower volunteering sections in the community?

7.4 The Nature of Volunteering

People exhibit wide variations of behaviour in expressing their individual and collective needs in leisure. There are religious, community, and welfare groups; groups for men, women, old people, and young people; advisory and counselling groups; paramedical and military groups. Some people join clubs and associations that are culturally 'uplifting' or educational. Some join acting, ballroom, jazz, line dancing, slimming, singing, operatic, or pop groups; large numbers play sport in groups, sail the seas with yachting clubs, and climb with mountaineering groups. Many leisure groups identify themselves by wearing badges or special clothing such as uniforms to create an alternative identity – a leisure identity. Some uniforms identify a way of living, for example members of the Salvation Army, who in their own leisure time give help to the needy. Some groups meet virtually; the development of the internet, social media platforms, and video capabilities allows groups to meet in virtual spaces and increase their global networks. This became increasingly important during the COVID-19 pandemic, of course. Although the work was done a few years ago, the work of Cnaan *et al.* (1996) help us identify the key dimensions of 'the volunteer' (see Table 7.5). The alternatives within these four dimensions illustrate the variability of volunteering, with one or two of them challenging the very concept of volunteering, i.e. having an obligation to volunteer, which can occur, for

Table 7.5 **Key Dimensions and Categories in Definitions of the Volunteer**

Dimensions	Categories
Free choice	1 free will (to choose voluntarily)
	2 relatively uncoerced
	3 obligation to volunteer
Remuneration	1 none at all
	2 none expected
	3 expenses reimbursed
	4 stipend/low pay
Structure	1 formal
	2 informal
Intended beneficiaries	1 benefit/help others/strangers
	2 benefit/help friends or relatives
	3 benefit oneself (as well)

Source: Cnaan *et al.* (1996)

example, on becoming a member of some clubs, and receiving a stipend (a fixed or regular payment, although typically a low figure).

This table demonstrates that volunteers often gain something for themselves through volunteering. Consider volunteer coaches (particularly parents), for example, looking for glory from the achievement of their children in a team, and think of the status conferred upon presidents and chairpersons in clubs and societies. Volunteering is undertaken with different motives and in pursuit of different purposes. Parker (1997) identifies four types of volunteering, each sharing certain elements with one or more of the others:

1   Altruistic volunteering as giving of time and effort unselfishly to help others;
2   Market volunteering as giving something 'freely', but expecting (later) something in return;
3   Cause-serving volunteering as promoting a cause in which one believes;
4   Leisure volunteering as 'primarily' seeking a leisure experience.

Motivations to volunteer in sport were reported on an EU-wide basis by GHK in 2010. They identify the following important motivators, which they suggest are different from other fields of interest due to the leisurely and relaxing context that the sports sector provides for its volunteers:

- Personal interest in a particular club, e.g. parents volunteering in a club where their children play and ex-participants giving something back to their club;
- Personal interest in the sport, such that volunteers can enjoy themselves and interact with people sharing the same interests;
- Social benefits, including building new relationships;
- Social responsibility, e.g. helping to keep a club going and strengthening the community's social fabric;
- Acquisition of new skills and experiences, which can be useful in looking for paid work;
- Opportunities to participate in big sports events and possibly meet famous sportspeople.

Table 7.6 **Reasons for Formal Volunteering in the England in 2020**

Reasons for formal volunteering in England in 2020	Percentage
I wanted to improve things/help people.	65.4
The cause was really important to me.	40.1
I felt there was a need in my community.	34
I had spare time to do it.	33.8
I thought it would give me a chance to use my existing skills.	23.6
It's part of my philosophy of life to help people.	21.6
It was connected to the needs of my family/friends.	21.1
I wanted to meet people/make friends.	19.2
I thought it would give me a chance to learn new skills.	16.2
My friends/family did it.	12.9
It's part of my religious belief to help people.	11.9
I felt there was no one else to do it.	9.2
It helps me get on in my career.	7.4
It gave me a chance to get a recognised qualification.	2.2
I felt I needed to do it to get into a paid position.	1.9
None of these	1.9

Source: Sport England

To quantify this, in more recent times, Sport England collected data on why people undertake formal volunteering roles within sport, and the findings can be seen in Table 7.6. By far the most popular reason for volunteering is the more altruistic aspects of wanting to improve things or help people, but other popular reasons include 'the cause was really important', 'there was a need in the community', or simply that people 'had spare time'. Interestingly, the least popular answers all related to using volunteering to further a career.

Having started volunteering, many people continue for a considerable time, particularly in formal volunteering. Stebbins (2004) identifies ongoing involvement with a voluntary organisation as one of three principal types of 'serious leisure' (the other two being amateurs and hobbyists). Others label it as 'formal volunteering' and 'constructive leisure'. Stebbins' term *serious leisure* acknowledges the presence of a serious orientation to leisure. He uses the following definition:

> the systematic pursuit of an amateur, hobbyist, or volunteer activity that participants find so substantial and interesting that, in the typical case, they launch themselves

on a career centred on acquiring and expressing its special skills, knowledge and experience.

(Stebbins, 2004, p. 49)

The use of the term *career* in this respect signifies that many volunteers commit to a continuous engagement with their roles, which distinguishes them from the episodic, occasional, volunteering contributions of other more casual volunteers. Many sports and leisure clubs depend on core volunteers of this type to fulfil key management positions. The committed, career volunteers in sport have been labelled 'stalwarts' (Cuskelly, 2004; Nichols, 2005).

Discussion Question

What does the nature of volunteering tell us about the distinctions between work and leisure?

Whilst stalwarts are essential for club sport, they also bring management problems, especially when they want to, or have to, stop volunteering. It becomes even more important than normal to plan for succession in such positions, and job splitting is almost certainly likely to be necessary.

7.5 Benefits of Volunteering and Problems for Volunteers

Volunteering in sport and leisure brings about benefits for both society in general and for individual volunteers. One of the main social benefits is the way it contributes to social capital. The term *social capital* refers to:

> social networks based on social and group norms which enable people to trust and cooperate with each other and via which individuals or groups can obtain certain types of advantage.

(Coalter, 2007, p. 1380)

Using Putnam's (2000) view of social capital, it is clear there are two main types of social capital:

1   **Bonding capital,** among homogeneous types of people who are highly likely to associate with each other;
2   **Bridging capital,** between more heterogeneous types of people who are less likely to associate with each other.

It is thought that social capital can help with community spirit and cohesion, citizenship, neighbourliness, trust, and shared values. Indeed, when asked about benefits of sports volunteering to wider society 71% of respondents identified 'increased social cohesion and inclusion' and 61% acknowledged 'benefits to the local community' (GHK, 2010). However, social capital generated through volunteering is most likely to be of the bonding type, rather than bridging, because many clubs are exclusive in nature, bringing 'like people' together through common interests. Over 20 years ago, Arai (1997) used empowerment theory to help understand changes in volunteering and concluded that it can have both desirable benefits and undesirable elements, such as tensions in power relationships at a personal and community level. Among the benefits community volunteers described were:

- Opportunities for shared learning;
- Opportunities to contribute to community;
- Development of camaraderie, feeling connected to community.

Thus volunteering is connected not only to psychological empowerment (self-conception, self-efficacy, locus of control) but also to social empowerment (increased access to information, knowledge, skills, and resources; increased social connections) and political empowerment (access to decision-making processes, power of voice, and collective action).

Specifically in relation to sport, Sport England (2018) found volunteering linked to people being able to meet the goals they set themselves, continuing to try when they find things difficult and, finally, feeling that people in their local area can be trusted. However, as well as a general level of satisfaction, there are specific issues which significant minorities of volunteers are concerned about. According to Low *et al.* (2007), 31% of regular, formal volunteers agreed that 'things could be better organised', and 28% felt there was 'too much bureaucracy'. In 2003, Sport England reported problems for volunteers within sport. Nearly three-quarters of core volunteers surveyed in sports clubs agreed that 'there are not enough other people willing to volunteer in the club', and 65% of the same sample agreed that 'increasingly the work is left to fewer people'. Sport England (2018) have also noted that volunteers within sport are not reflective of wider society when it comes to gender, ethnicity, and social class. This means that those groups are missing out on the potential benefits of volunteering and, perhaps more interestingly, reinforces that the social capital gained from volunteering is more bonding than the presumed bridging.

Discussion Question

If volunteering has benefits for the individual, why is there often a shortage of volunteers in sport in more developed countries?

Coalter (2007) cites Putnam (2000) in pointing to society-wide changes that have impacted negatively on volunteering, including suburban sprawl, increasing time pressures, greater use of television, and other home entertainment and the privatisation of public services. In sport, such factors impact not only directly on volunteering but also indirectly through changes in sports participation. A decline in traditional team sports and an increase in individualised sports activities such as fitness are apparent in several countries (Coalter, 2007), and the latter requires far less volunteering than the former. Data gathered by the Sport Industry Research Centre (SIRC) for Sport England (2018) suggested that there was little evidence to suggest an imminent decline in the number of sports club volunteers, with only 12% expected to withdraw their services in the next 12 months. However, reasons for considering withdrawing time were a lack of time (44% of respondents), work commitments (38% of respondents), and family commitments (34% of respondents). Indeed, for a while, there has been a consensus that 'not enough time' is by far the most common reason for withdrawing volunteer services. This was given as a reason by 41% of ex-volunteers in Low *et al.* (2007), and 23% of ex-volunteers in sport blamed the lack of spare time in 2003 (Sport England,

2003a). Clearly, if there is a shortage of volunteers, there is a major recruitment challenge in at least some parts of the voluntary sector. And the signs are that this is the case. In the SIRC research, 75% of clubs felt they did not have enough volunteers. So that are the barriers to recruitment?

7.6 Barriers to and Incentives for Volunteering

In 2007, the work of Low *et al.* identified the principal barriers to formal volunteering for those who do not volunteer at all. Time, again, was by far the most common response, and this seems to have remained. In 2019, a report from France titled 'The Evolution of Voluntary Associations in France' found that 'lack of time' (46%) was the most cited reason for not commencing volunteering. As was discussed in Chapter 3, this may be a *perceived* lack of time, however, the consequences are just as damaging for clubs and organisations. Following this, people cited lack of opportunity (29%) and to devote oneself to one's own work (23%) as further barriers.

A potential barrier to volunteering in the UK which has received a lot of media attention is child protection legislation, particularly the requirement for volunteers working with children and vulnerable groups to undertake criminal records checks. However, research undertaken with Scottish sports club volunteers (SportScotland, 2008) suggested that a large majority see the need for such legislation and checks, and only a relatively small minority of volunteers are sufficiently put off by these procedures that they might stop volunteering. The Scottish research suggested few potential volunteers are deterred by criminal records checks; they are much more likely to be deterred by a general lack of time or the demands of their paid work.

So, how do clubs and organisations get people involved? Apart from attacking the barriers to their involvement, what can managers do by way of incentives to attract more volunteers? The work of Nichols *et al.* (2019) is outstanding in this respect. They synthesise several

Table 7.7 **Barriers Preventing People in France from Doing Voluntary Work, 2019**

Reasons preventing people in France from becoming volunteers in a charity organization in 2019	
Lack of time	46%
Lack of opportunity	29%
To devote oneself to one's own work	23%
Considers that he or she lacks the required abilities/qualities	12%
Other reasons	12%
Association organization is not suitable	9%
Not concerned with volunteering	7%

Source: France Volunteering

studies from around the world and from a variety of time periods. In their work, Nichols *et al.* (2019) argue that 'promoting volunteering through appealing to self-interest' should be avoided, as it promotes 'values that may undermine it [volunteering] in the long run'. Policies within the UK have shifted in recent years to emphasise that volunteering is good for the volunteer as, among other things, it can supposedly improve wellbeing, help develop skills, and create contacts. However, as Nichols *et al.* (2019) highlight in their work, this presumes the public are only interested in personal gain from volunteering rather than altruistic reasons. There are three principal issues with this. Frist, if personal gain is promised to recruit volunteers rather than altruism, then there is a risk that personal gain becomes a prerequisite for future involvement. Second, this ignores that at different stages of a person's life, their involvement in volunteering opportunities is underpinned by different reasons. For example, young people are likely to be following their parents' example, and those who are retired are likely to be 'giving back' to clubs or organisations they care about. Finally, there is scant evidence to show that these personal gains are certain. In their research paper, Nicholls et al. suggest, for example, there are questions about whether volunteering causes better wellbeing or those who have a higher level of wellbeing are more likely to volunteer?

In conclusion, Nichols *et al.* (2019) offer some policy recommendations, which can be useful for leisure managers and, as such, are worth reflecting on here. First, it is important to see volunteering within an organisation as a 'growing natural resource'. Emphasising that the organisation requires volunteers to exist and tapping into the moral obligation of society are more likely to foster committed volunteers over a longer period. That being said, given the deep-rooted tendency of some people *not* to volunteer, an approach that also emphasises the personal benefits might be needed – especially to recruit completely new volunteers. Speaking of new volunteers, it is important to present new volunteers with simple tasks and support to help the volunteers. It cannot be assumed that volunteers know what to do or will automatically bring benefits to the organisation. Finally, it is important to note that a more equal society would likely bring about more volunteering. It is, of course, outside the control of leisure management; nevertheless, it is an important point when considering how we encourage volume.

7.7 Third Sector Organisations

The number of volunteer-involving organisations is subject to considerable estimation. However, according to the National Council for Voluntary Organisations (NCVO) more than 166,000 voluntary organisations contributed around £18.2 billion to the UK economy in 2017–2018. The NCVO is the largest umbrella body for voluntary organisations in the UK, and their website has a lot of useful resources to explore. Third sector bodies vary greatly in size and type, and these are listed in Table 7.8.

The third sector has national bodies representing almost every main field of social organisation. Leisure has a wide range of national organisations, including those for children's play, sports, arts, heritage, tourism, and the environment. Some types of organisations, such as environmental organisations, have experienced very high levels of growth in membership. The National Trust, for example, had a membership of over 5.6 million in 2021, more than 20 times the 1971 figure of 278,000. Some more traditional third sector movements, for example young people's church groups, have witnessed a decline in numbers. Scouting and Guiding have been struggling with declining numbers of members in recent years, but they are still major young persons' organisations. There are 400,000 members of the Scouts in the UK, with 100,000 adult volunteers according to their latest annual reports, and the numbers

Table 7.8 **Range of Third-Sector Organisations**

Community organisations	National Council for Voluntary Organisations, community associations, community councils
Children's groups	Pre-School Playgroups Association, Toy Library Association
Youth organisations	Scout Association, Girlguiding UK, National Council for YMCAs, National Association of Youth Clubs, DJ clubs
Women's organisations	National Federation of Women's Institutes, National Union of Townswomen's Guilds, Mother's Union, Women's Voluntary Service
Men's groups	Working men's clubs, servicemen's clubs
Old people's groups	Darby and Joan Clubs, Age Concern
Disabled groups	Gardens for the Disabled, Disabled Drivers' Motor Club, Gateway clubs
Adventure organisations	Outward Bound Trust, Duke of Edinburgh's Award, National Caving Association
Outdoor activity organisations and touring groups	Camping Club of Great Britain and Ireland, Youth Hostels Association, Central Council of British Naturism, Ramblers' Association, British Caravanners' Club
Sport and physical recreation organisations	Football Association, National Skating Association of Great Britain, Cycle Speedway Council, GB Wheelchair Basketball Association
'Cultural' and entertainment organisations	British Theatre Association, Museums Association, English Folk Dance and Song Society, British Federation of Music Festivals
Educational organisations	National Institute of Adult Education, Workers Educational Association, National Listening Library
Hobbies and interest groups	National Association of Flower Arranging Societies, Citizens Band Association, Antique Collectors Club, Handicrafts Advisory Association for the Disabled, British Beer Mat Collectors' Society
Animals and pet groups	Pony Club, Cats Protection League
Environmental, conservation, and heritage groups	National Trust, Friends of the Earth, Royal Society for the Protection of Birds, Keep Britain Tidy Group, Save the Village Pond Campaign, Rare Breeds Survival Trust, Greenpeace groups
Consumer groups	Consumers' Association, Campaign for Real Ale

for Girlguiding are similar. In 2018, there were around 400,000 Girl Guides in the UK and just over 100,000 volunteers.

According to the Active People Survey, around 9.8 million people are members of sport and physical activity clubs in 2016, and in 2019 Sport England claimed that figure had risen to 11.1 million. Within this, 75% of the volunteering that takes place in sport and physical activity is done within a club environment. That is not an unsubstantial number of people. As a result, in England, it remains one of the largest areas of interest for volunteers. But these clubs face challenges. In 2019, Sport England developed a 'clubs plan', which highlighted some of the issues facing clubs. They were:

- Attracting and retaining new members or participants;
- Recruiting and retaining leaders, organisers, and coaches;
- Increased costs, reduced income, and the need to generate new income streams;
- Over-reliance on a single source of funding;
- The need to improve or extend facilities;
- A high level of dependence on local authority and school facilities at a time of falling budgets;
- A heavy reliance on volunteers;
- High levels of volunteer turnover, making it difficult to develop and retain knowledge.

For comparison with the UK position, Case Study 7.2 provides details for sports clubs in Germany. It demonstrates that the importance of sports clubs and sports volunteers in Germany mirrors their importance in the UK. It also shows that different countries share similar problems, particularly in acquiring sufficient sports volunteers in clubs.

CASE STUDY 7.2

Sports Clubs in Germany

In 2007 a national survey of over 13,000 sports clubs was conducted which led to estimates that Germany has over two million volunteers in sports clubs, giving a total of 36.6 million hours. This volunteering, as in the UK, is 'the most important part of civic involvement' (Breuer & Wicker, 2008, p. 1).

Sports clubs provide a substantial part of the sport infrastructure in Germany – 42% of clubs own their own sports facilities. These include many gyms/fitness centres, sports halls, sports fields, swimming pools, shooting ranges, and horse-riding facilities. In addition they provide important social amenities, with over 30,000 club houses and over 11,000 youth centres. Thirty percent of clubs have programmes with explicit health promotion/rehabilitation objectives, in addition to the obvious health benefits from their normal sports activities. Nearly 70% of clubs cooperate with schools in some way.

Sports clubs in Germany are seen to provide an important function for specific age groups: 63% of clubs have opportunities for children under six years, and 93% have opportunities for people over 60 years old. Participation in voluntary sports clubs in Germany is typically not expensive. Membership fees are very reasonable – with medians of €3.50 a month for children, €7.50 a month for adults, and €14 for family memberships. And over half of the clubs do not charge admission fees (rising to 64% of clubs in the case of children).

As well as volunteers, one-third of German sports clubs employ paid staff, largely in the functions of coaching/supervision, technology/maintenance, and management/administration. Not surprisingly, the largest cost item for sports clubs was for coaches/

trainers. Other large cost items included the maintenance of the clubs' facilities and the costs of sports equipment and clothing. In revenue terms, the largest contribution by far was membership fees, followed by donations.

When asked about problems at their clubs, the one with the highest score was 'adherence/acquisition of voluntary workers', echoing the problems in UK sports clubs discussed earlier in this chapter. For over 4% of German sports clubs it is a problem which they suggest threatens their existence. Second and third most important problems in German sports clubs were 'adherence/acquisition of adolescent competitive athletes' and 'adherence/acquisition of trainers'. So human resources in various guises are the main focuses of managerial concern.

The German study is a good example of how evidence helps to show the importance of the voluntary sector, in this case to German sport. It led Breuer and Wicker to state: 'The contribution of sports clubs to the sports supply of the population is irreplaceable in Germany' (2008, p. 3).

Source: Distilled from Breuer and Wicker (2008)

The previous edition of this book gave a brief outline of clubs and their future. Given the time of the release, it would be remiss not to mention the impact of COVID-19. This is particularly the case because in that previous edition, it was noted that third sector clubs were rather precariously placed. Together with the Sport and Recreation Alliance, the Sport Industry Research Centre at Sheffield Hallam released a report on the impact of the COVID-19 pandemic. It is a useful resource, not least because 1,400 community sport providers involved in the delivery of more than 75 sports and activities took part in the survey. Some of the headline findings were as follows. Voluntary organisations lost on average 60% of their members during the pandemic, and those providers with cash reserves saw them decline by 18%, while liabilities increased by an average of 20%. Further, one in three providers operate without any financial cushion. The report also found that organisations with more ethnically diverse communities will be under additional stress as they restart. They were already operating with low reserves – around 17% of their annual income – and this has dropped to just 10%. It is not all bad news. Volunteers in administrative and facility maintenance roles seem to have 'stayed at the wheel' during lockdown, and 98% are predicted to return. Overall, voluntary clubs expect to lose only 4% of their overall volunteer workforce. For paid roles the picture is not as good. Paid coaches were the individuals within the sport and physical activity workforce who suffered the most significant fall in numbers, dropping by 63% during the pandemic.

7.7.1 Implications for Managers

The nature of voluntary clubs and associations means there is a lot for the leisure manager to consider. These considerations are also important for managers in third sector organisations to acknowledge.

- All the clubs tend to be, at least partially, exclusive. Open to all in principle, clubs 'guarantee' their exclusiveness with enrolment fees or memberships. If a voluntary organisation seeks funding from or partnership with the public sector, a more inclusive outlook is necessary.
- Clubs are not static. The leisure manager hoping to work with or in the third sector should bear in mind, therefore, that new clubs are likely to change in membership structure, and leadership priorities and styles, in the first few years.

- Clubs are social groupings. It is important for leisure managers working with voluntary organisations to accommodate the imperative within clubs to keep members happy.
- Clubs are often dependent on support services like hired premises, and local authorities can help by providing support services. The local authority's enabling role plays an important part.

7.8 Charitable Status

Within the third sector there are organisations of different legal status, and a common type is a charity. Many but not all sport and leisure organisations in the UK are charities. The Charities Act 2006 provides a clear description of 'charitable purposes', which mainly concern public benefit. The activities that are listed as providing public benefit include some relevant to leisure:

- The advancement of citizenship or community development (including the promotion of volunteering and the voluntary sector);
- The advancement of the arts, culture, heritage, or science;
- The advancement of amateur sport – identified as sports or games which promote health by involving physical or mental skill or exertion;
- The advancement of environmental protection or improvement.

Of the leisure related charities, the Arts Council of England and the National Trust are the largest, with annual income of £743.3 million and £680.9 million respectively.

7.8.1 Advantages and Disadvantages of Charitable Status

There is continuing change in the management of public leisure assets in the UK, particularly an increase in the number being managed by charities. Examples include organisations such as Greenwich Leisure Limited, which is a non-profit charitable Social Enterprise, or Sheffield City Trust, which is a charitable trust. It is, therefore, relevant to explore the advantages and disadvantages of being a charitable trust.

Advantages include the following:

- Management autonomy and control are increased rather than having decisions imposed by key stakeholders. This compares favourably with the influence of politicians in the public sector and shareholders in the commercial sector.
- The opportunities for partnership are easier to establish.
- Fiscal benefits: Charities can take advantage of financial benefits such as tax relief.
- Financial and forward planning: Monies can be borrowed and invested with greater flexibility, provided the governing instrument permits it.
- Charities can fundraise to support both capital and operational budgets. With further tax relief on charitable donations, they are better able to attract grants and sponsorship.
- As a voluntary enterprise, a charity can encourage a strong spirit of belonging and community endeavour. Even paid staff can feel a greater sense of personal commitment.
- Compared with the public sector, management has executive control, streamlining decision-making.

The **disadvantages** of charitable status include:

- Charities cannot undertake certain political, campaigning, and pressure group activities. They cannot trade 'permanently', although charities often need to trade in order to provide the funds for the charity to do its work. Some charities set up separate trading companies, which covenant their profits to the charities.

- Often, there is a need to raise substantial sums of money, particularly in starting up a charity.
- A charitable body, whether run by paid staff or volunteers, can be at the mercy of local councils, needing to approach them for assistance. A charity can charge reasonable prices, but they should not be so high that the charity endangers its charitable status by ceasing to benefit a sufficient cross-section of the public.
- Charities constantly need to raise money, and some are having to sell/lease land to help fund projects.
- Some charities make surpluses, but care must be taken in case doubt is cast upon the 'public benefit' of what the charity is doing.
- There can either be too few staff or low paid staff, many giving service beyond the 'call of duty'.
- The key people on the management committees carry a heavy burden of responsibility and are usually busy people, often in paid employment elsewhere and sometimes engaged in many causes in the community.
- People may not know, or even care, that a theatre or sports centre is being run by a charitable trust. To the public, it is a 'public' facility.

> ## Discussion Question
>
> **Is the growth of local leisure charitable trusts mainly because they are a way of saving public expenditure?**

7.9 Government and the Third Sector

The relationship between government and voluntary sport differs in different countries. For example, in Germany and the Netherlands the government is responsible for the provision of infrastructure and facilities, which voluntary sports clubs then use. In the UK, more clubs own their own facility and others hire facilities from local authorities or education establishments for example. Indeed, in many cases, third sector organisations are inextricably linked to public providers and public money. Charities can be partly sponsored by local authorities or largely subsidised, and local councils support many voluntary groups and projects. The interdependence between many third sector organisations and public authorities is part and parcel of the wide framework of public community services, including sport and leisure.

An example in UK sport is that Sport England, a government agency, promoted 'Clubmark' from 2002. Clubmark was an accreditation system awarded to sports clubs which met minimum operating standards in four areas: playing programme, duty of care and safeguarding and protecting children and young people, sport equity and ethics, and club management. By 2015, around 12,000 clubs had the Clubmark accreditation. Sport England also promotes Club Matters, which provides free resources, support, guidance, and workshops to grassroots sports clubs, groups, and community organisations. It also aims to improve the professional workforce that supports grassroots sports clubs, groups, and community organisations.

The national government in the UK is keen to encourage links between the public sector and the third sector. Government, increasingly, recognises the role played by the third sector, particularly in community and 'caring' organisations. Also, an increasing number of public and community services are delivered by third sector organisations on behalf of the government at national level and on behalf of local authorities at local levels – an example being trust management of sport and leisure centres in the UK. Indeed, formal volunteering, encouraged by government, has both economic and social benefits – because of the volunteering alone, it provides cost-effective services, and it is a key factor in active citizenship.

A twin track approach to the relationship between government and the third sector is evident in the UK:

1 Relying on the third sector to be an 'agent' of government policy in service delivery (and using government funding to 'leverage' the sector's compliance in this respect);
2 Seeking to improve the effectiveness of the sector.

However, there is balance to be struck between supporting volunteering and seeking to control it. Blackmore (2004) identified a danger of 'mission drift', with resources in voluntary organisations diverted to delivering funders' priorities. She also warned against the growing audit and performance measurement culture in government, which may spill over into its expectations of the voluntary sector and undermine its distinctive character. Finally, Collins and Kay (2003), for example, expressed reservations about the capabilities of the voluntary sport sector in delivering the government's social inclusion objective. The ISLP review suggests:

> While there may be a temptation to see voluntary sports clubs as a policy tool for delivering participation and performance goals, to treat them as such may lead to a lack of volunteer commitment and problems in recruiting and retaining volunteers. . . . That is not to say that voluntary sports clubs may not be able to contribute to these policy aims, just that considerable care needs to be taken when developing policy that encourages them to do so.
>
> (ISLP, 2005, p. 40)

Discussion Question

Why would the involvement of government and its agencies in sports clubs undermine attempts to recruit and retain volunteers?

7.10 Conclusions

Third sector organisations give people the chance to participate and to become involved in all levels of organisation and management of sport and physical activity. In terms of community sport and leisure, managers must be aware that the third sector, more than other sectors, holds many of the keys to individual self-fulfilment, one of the main goals of effective leisure management. It is important, therefore, for leisure managers to understand what it means to be a volunteer. A problem in this sector is that organisations are often composed of unpaid volunteers, who in the main shun the concept of 'management'. Nevertheless, any organisation should be interested in providing its members with effective services and not wasting their membership income, so good management is still valid in this sector. And many third sector managers have some significant issues to contend with, particularly a shortage of volunteers in several areas of voluntary leisure provision, e.g. sport and young persons' organisations.

This is likely to be key to any 'recovery' after the COVID-19 pandemic. The relationship between the voluntary and public sectors is a very 'live' issue at national and local levels. At the national level, government is clearly interested in the role of voluntary organisations in promoting national policy objectives. At the local level, partnerships between local authorities and charitable trust organisations are growing in number. However, it is important at both national and local levels that the independence of the third sector is both recognised and valued – and not undermined by undue political pressure.

Practical Tasks

1 Volunteer for one day with a sport or leisure organisation of your choice. Write a diary of your experience, including the way you were treated as a new volunteer, the 'management' of volunteers, and the attitude of your fellow volunteers to their tasks.
2 Interview a couple of volunteers in a sport or leisure organisation of your choice. Find out why they volunteer, what benefits they get out of it, and how important it is for them. Are your findings consistent with the literature?

Structured Guide to Further Reading

Barrett, D., & Coleman, R. (2021). *Returning to Action: Evaluating Organisational Preparedness in the Wake of the Covid-19 Pandemic*. Project Report. The Sport and Recreation Alliance. Sheffield.

Barrett, D., & Coleman, R. (2021). *Returning to Action: Evaluating Organisational Preparedness in the Wake of the Covid-19 Pandemic*. Project Report. The Sport and Recreation Alliance, Sheffield.

Barrett, D., Edmondson, L., Millar, R., & Storey, R. (2018). *Sports Club Volunteering* (Unpublished report submitted to Sport England). Sport Industry Research Centre, Sheffield Hallam University, Sheffield.

Nichols, G., Hogg, E., Knight, C., & Storr, R. (2019). Selling volunteering or developing volunteers? Approaches to promoting sports volunteering. *Voluntary Sector Review*, 10(1), 3–18.

Useful Websites

www.ncvo.org.uk/about-us/
www.sportandrecreation.org.uk/policy/research-publications/research-archive
www.sportenglandclubmatters.com/

References

Arai, S. (1997). Volunteers within a changing society: The use of empowerment theory in understanding serious leisure. *World Leisure and Recreation*, 39(3), 19–22.

Blackmore, A. (2004). *Standing Apart, Working Together: A Study of the Myths and Realities of Voluntary and Community Sector Independence*. National Council for Voluntary Organisations, London.

Breuer, C., & Wicker, P. (2008). *Sports Clubs in Germany*. German Sports University, Cologne.

Cnaan, R., Handy, F., & Wadsworth, M. (1996). Defining who is a volunteer: Conceptual and empirical considerations. *Non-profit and Volunteer Sector Quarterly*, 25, 364–383.

Coalter, F. (2007). *A Wider Social Role for Sport: Who's Keeping the Score?* Routledge, London and New York.

Collins, M. F., & Kay, T. (2003). *Sport and Social Exclusion*. Routledge, London.

Cuskelly, G. (2004). Volunteer retention in community sport organisations. European Sport Management Quarterly, *4, 59–76*.

Cuskelly, G., Hoye, R., & Auld, C. (2006). *Working with Volunteers in Sport: Theory and Practice*. Routledge, London.

GHK. (2010). *Volunteering in the European Union, Educational, Audiovisual and Culture Executive Agency*. Directorate General Education and Culture, Brussels. Retrieved from http://ec.europa.eu/citizenship/news/news1015_en.htm.

Home Office. (2003). *2001 Home Office Citizenship Survey: People, Families and Communities*. Home Office, London. Retrieved from www.homeoffice.gov.uk/rds/pdfs2/hors270.pdf.

Institute of Sport and Leisure Policy (ISLP). (2005). *Academic Review of the Role of Voluntary Sports Clubs*. ISLP, Loughborough University, England.

Low, N., Butt, S., Ellis Paine, A., & Davis Smith, J. (2007). *Helping Out: A National Survey of Volunteering and Charitable Giving*. Office of the Third Sector/Cabinet Office, London. Retrieved from www.cabinetoffice.gov.uk/media/cabinetoffice/third_sector/assets/helping_out_national_survey_2007.pdf.

Nichols, G. (2005). Stalwarts in sport. *World Leisure*, 2, 31–37.

Nichols, G., Hogg, E., Knight, C., & Storr, R. (2019). Selling volunteering or developing volunteers? Approaches to promoting sports volunteering. *Voluntary Sector Review*, 10(1), 3–18.

Parker, S. (1997). Volunteering – Altruism, markets, causes and leisure. World Leisure and Recreation, *39*(3), 4–5.

Putnam, R. D. (2000). *Bowling Alone: The Collapse and Revival of American Community*. Simon & Schuster, New York.

Sport England. (2003a). *Sports Volunteering in England, 2002*. Sport England, London, Retrieved from www.sportengland.org/volunteering-in-england.pdf

Sport England. (2018). Fresh insight into volunteer habits. Retrieved from www.sportengland.org/news/fresh-insight-into-volunteer-habits

Sportscotland. (2008). *Child Protection Legislation and Volunteering in Scottish Sport: Summary Report*. Sportscotland, Edinburgh.

Stebbins, R. A. (2004). *Between Work and Leisure*. Transaction Publishers, New Brunswick, NJ.

Chapter 8

Cross-Sector Collaboration

By Mathieu Marlier

In This Chapter

- Why is cross-sector collaboration important to the future of sport management?
- How do the 'three sectors' need to come together?
- What roles can each sector play to improve participation in sport?
- How can we understand the 'need' of cross-sector collaborations?
- What frameworks make cross-sector collaborations work?
- What are the key success factors for successful cross-sector collaborations?

DOI: 10.4324/9780367823610-8

Summary

Cross-sector collaborations are regarded as one of the most promising and needed ways to solve interdisciplinary, complex, often multi-faceted problems. In sport and leisure, cross-sector collaborations show great potential to increase participation in sport and leisure. Using the knowledge, skills, and resources of the social, health, and private sectors is a sure way to reach more people who are not yet engaging in sport and leisure activities. However, in many cases, sport organisations still adopt an isolated approach and do not know how to engage in cross-sector collaborations. This chapter introduces the needs of cross-sector collaborations in sport and leisure, it provides insights in key success factor of cross-sector collaborations, and it offers a practical and easy adaptable framework that can guide sport and leisure organisations in starting the use of cross-sector collaborations to reach their objectives.

8.1 Introduction

The importance of collaborations has been apparent throughout our history. Julius Caesar's 'divide and conquer' policy provides a good example. He was all too aware of the power of a united enemy. Indeed, the only time the Gallic tribes stood a real chance of pushing away the foreign Roman invaders was when Vercingetorix was able to unite the different tribes through cross-tribal collaborations.

Today, due to an increasing complex environment and specialization, collaboration becomes an even greater necessity to deal with problems of society. Problems that are inter-related, complex, and multidimensional are called 'wicked' problems. Solving them is only possible through cross-sector collaborations.

Wicked problems are very much present in the sport realm as well. In the last decades the role of sport has changed from a means of leisure to a means of increasing physical activity, mental health, and social cohesion (Marlier *et al.*, 2015b). Many organisations in the sport sector (sport clubs, sport city services, sport federations) are struggling to cope with this new role in society. Many find themselves alienated from other sectors because of a legacy of operating within silos. Throughout this chapter, the case of increasing sport participation through cross-sector collaborations will be used to make the theory of cross-sector collaborations more tangible.

To better understand and integrate cross-sector collaborations, the following chapters will exist out of three parts. The first part focuses on *the why* of cross-sector collaborations, emphasising the need for cross-sector collaborations. The second part explores *the how* of cross-sector collaborations by explaining some of the most critical success factors of cross-sector collaborations. The third part elaborates on a practical tool that provides guidelines for sport and leisure organisations on *how to start* engaging in cross-sector collaborations. This practical tool will be applied to the case of creating vital cities to better understand how this practical tool can be used.

8.2 The Need for Cross-Sector Collaborations

To be able to explain the need for cross-sector collaborations it is first necessary to understand what is meant by collaborations. *Collaboration* can be defined as 'a dynamic relationship among diverse actors which actions concern sharing "goods" and "knowledge" between the partners' (adapted definition from [Brinkerhoff, 2002]). Similar concepts to collaborations are partnerships, coalitions, alliances, networks, and interorganisational relationships. Both in theory and practice, these concepts are used interchangeably. In this chapter we will stick with *collaborations*.

Cross-sector collaborations, in turn, can be defined as 'partnerships involving government, business, non-profits and philanthropies, communities, and/or the public as a whole' (Bryson *et al.*, 2006, p. 44). The basis of these concepts is that they constitute relations between two or more organisations in different sectors to perform a common task or to create a certain benefit.

There are three pertinent reasons why cross-sector collaborations are needed. First, because wicked problems cannot by managed by one organisation. Second, because it is the fastest way to get innovative results. Third because it creates better access to more resources and thus creates a competitive advantage. These reasons are further elaborated in the next paragraphs.

8.3 Wicked Problems Cannot Be Managed by One Organisation

Wicked problems are problems that address multidimensional challenges and cannot be managed by one organisation alone (Turrini *et al.*, 2010). These wicked issues present a special challenge to organisations, companies, and government because they defy precise definition, cut across departments and policy, and resist service solutions offered by a single agency. Traditional bureaucratic hierarchical arrangements such as departmental programs not only fail to overcome these issues, but they add to the problem by further fragmenting services and people. Solving these wicked problems requires a collaborative, cross-sector approach. The use of these cross-sector collaborations is intuitively appealing because they enable integrated and holistic responses to these wicked problems (Zakocs & Edwards, 2006). This is one of the reasons why companies, governments, and public agencies are engaging increasingly in intersectoral collaborations, networks, alliances, or partnerships with public, non-profit, and for-profit organisations.

> **CASE**
>
> # Increasing Sport Participation – Sports Delivery Paradox I
>
> *Societal changes in the twentieth and twenty-first centuries have led to a bigger gap between rich and poor, an increased social diversity, and a decrease in social cohesion and social capital in our Western civilization (Putnam, 2007). The sport sector aims to inspire every individual to participate in sport, and in recent decennia the sport sector has been appealed to put more effort in including ethnic minorities and people of lower social class. This is however where the sports delivery paradox comes in. On the one hand sport organisations struggle to reach disadvantaged target groups due to a lack of skills and knowledge to deal with these groups. On the other hand, health, social, youth, and cultural organisations use sport as a vehicle to capture the attention of these disadvantaged groups and to reach physical, social, and mental health gains, but they lack sport-specific skills and resources to reach their goals. To dissolve this paradox and to reach and strengthen each other's goals, the need to collaborate between sport, health, social, and other sectors is pertinent.*

8.4 Building Innovation

Humans have the tendency to solve problems with their current understanding of things. It is a natural and normal thing. Take the meatgrinders of the First World War as an example. For a couple of years, generals were unable to break the defences of their enemies at the trenches. Both forces of the Allies and the Central Powers lost millions of soldiers because of perceptions of old-fashioned strategies. Using old strategies in a new world caused them to send wave after wave of brave men just to be mowed down by artillery of the enemy. It was only after engineers were more involved in strategy to overcome the trenches that airplanes and tanks were able to cross no-man's land (the land between enemy lines) and create a breakthrough.

This is one of the crucial elements that shape the importance of cross-sector collaborations. If we are to find new solutions to problems that we are constantly confronted with, collaborations are one of the best ways to overcome tunnel vision and break out of our silos.

CASE

Increasing Sport Participation – Using Innovation

In sport we see the same stalemate position regarding sport participation. For the last 20 years in Europe, we have seen a stagnation of sport participation rates. About 40% of people are engaging in sport. The answer to increase sport participation is very simple: Find ways to engage the 60% of people who are not engaging in sport.

One answer lies in better adopting and integrating new innovations into sport through better collaborations with the tech-sector. One example is the recent innovations of exergaming and virtual reality. Preliminary research has been found effective to engage a broad population in an active lifestyle, also in people who are less motivated to engage in sport participation (Kari, 2014). The Wii, Kinect (Xbox), and Pokemon Go are the precursors of a new era of exergames that will allow to effectively use games to increase sport participation. Sport organisations of all kinds can make use of these new strategies to engage people who are not (yet) engaging in sport participation. To be successful in doing this, closer collaborations with technology, early adopters, and change agents will be needed.

8.5 Better Access to More Resources

The example of getting access to more resources is quite evident: When you share the knowledge, skills, infrastructure, and financial means of different people and organisations in different sectors, you expand your organisational capacity. You are more effective as an organisation because you can reach a broader target group with more means. This in turn influences the problem-solving strategy, the creativity, and the flexibility of your organisation: (a) A better problem-solving strategy is possible because you tap into the different problem-solving tactics of different people, organisations, and sectors. In problem solving theory one of the aspects to come to a better solution is the number of solutions that you can choose from; (b) More creativity is often the results of having a larger diversity of perspectives around one table. This is often what is needed to attract more people to events and activities; and (c) More flexibility and agility are a result of facing up to the challenges that to new creative problem-solving strategies bring forth. It makes an organisation more flexible and ready to react to environmental change (Cox & Blake, 1991).

The rationale behind this problem-solving strategy, creativity, and flexibility has to do with increasing the frame of references. Each person's frame of reference is because of upbringing, past experiences, social network, etc. Everything we read, hear, and experience goes through this filter. In general, we need this filter to process all impulses of our complex society, but consequently they limit our possibilities in finding various solutions to a problem. Often, in one specific sector, people have a similar mindset. This is where cross-sector collaborations step in and add value because they enable more potential solutions, creativity, and in time, more flexibility because of integrating different persons with a different frame of reference. Having a culturally diverse team can provide the same competitive advantage (Cox & Blake, 1991).

CASE

Increasing Sport Participation – Connecting Resources between the Sport, Social, and Health Sector

One specific study that focused on cross-sector collaborations in sport found a 20% higher sport participation rate in communities where the sport, social, health, and youth sector were connected, compared to similar communities without these connections (Marlier et al., 2014). The most important reason for this difference was related to creating better access to more resources. Sport organisations could better reach people in disadvantaged situations because they would get more referrals through the network of social, health, and youth organisations. Reciprocally, this connection enabled the social, health, and cultural organisations to improve access to sport-specific infrastructure, information, and skills. The connection between the different organisations lowered barriers for people in disadvantaged situations and increased overall sport participation in the communities (Marlier et al., 2020).

8.6 Success Factors of Cross-Sector Collaborations

By now the need for cross-sector collaborations should be evident. The question that remains is: Why don't all organisations engage in cross-sector collaborations, if these are so needed and effective? One quote by Huxham and Macdonald (1992, p. 50) illustrates this very well: 'There is a fine balance to be struck between gaining the benefits of collaborating and making the situation worse'. Several barriers that hinder organisations to engage in cross-sector collaborations are the fear to lose autonomy, distrust in partners, considering partnerships too complicated, and the belief that they are too time consuming (Williams, 2005).

To this end, it is crucial to understand how and under which circumstances collaborations can be effective. Cross-sector collaboration effectiveness can be defined as the 'effects, outcome, impact and benefits that are produced by the network as a whole and that can accrue to more than just the single member organisations and sector in terms of increasing efficiency, client satisfaction, increased legitimacy, resource acquisition, and reduced costs' (Turrini *et al.*, 2010, p. 529).

The question whether and under what specific circumstances partnerships are effective is one of crucial importance (Kenis & Provan, 2009). In this section we will discuss six of the most mentioned success factors in cross-sector collaborations: having a clear purpose, horizontal organisational structure and the right leadership to steer this structure, overcoming miscommunication, developing trust, dealing with conflicts, and evaluating the process and outcomes or the cross-sector collaborations. It is important to understand that these success factors are not independent from one another. They interact, strengthen, and are interdependent on each other.

For those wanting a broader overview of success factors, I refer to the works of Emerson *et al.* (2012), Turrini *et al.* (2010), Parent and Harvey (2009), and Ansell and Gash (2008). To make this part more relevant, it might be helpful to envision collaborations and relationships in your own life (for example current or past relationships, friend groups in your sport club, music band, youth organisation). After all, transferring your own knowledge with the theoretical success factors found here might make you more successful in future collaborative adventures.

8.7 Purpose

The purpose or the reason why several actors engage into a collaboration is critical. A clear purpose can be used to kindle a sense of unity in diversity that allows sufficient common ground to emerge, despite the variety of actors and their positions (Klitsie *et al.*, 2018). It is the inspiration and drive that keeps partners going in good times and the glue that keeps partners together at times when motivation is low, or when the cross-sector partnerships experience some difficulties.

Depending on whether the partnership can live up to its purpose and reach its goals will define in many cases the added value of the collaboration. Some partnerships have a clear purpose at the outset; for other partnerships a clear purpose develops over time (Waddock, 1988). The former is characterised as goal-directed networks, the latter as serendipitous networks. Whether this purpose is clear from the beginning or develops over time is not of crucial importance. What is important is whether there is an agreement on the partnership goals (Kenis & Provan, 2009). Conflicts between the individual organisational goals and the partnership goals impedes performance of the partnership (Mandell & Keast, 2008). In collaborations, to have a clear purpose that is aligned with the organisational goals is thus considered as one of the crucial determinants of collaboration effectiveness.

8.8 Organisational Structure and Leadership

The typical organisational structure of an organisation is top-down and hierarchical. It is an illusion, however, that this always needs to be the case. When looking at nature, ants are a great inspiration. Ants function without a leader or central coordination and adopt themselves through self-organising mechanisms. They are excellent adopters to environmental conditions e.g. creating bridges when there are gaps in the roads or creating self-made rafts when flooded. Much like ants, currently an interesting phase in organisational structure is developing with experiments of more agile and flatter structures as project designs and self-managed work teams (Gibbons, 2015). These new structures make it easier to create alliances with different organisations and sectors as every person is freer to look for opportunities outside the normal fixed structures. Instead of using the imagination and problem solving of one person, you can now tap into the 5 billion neurons of a multitude of persons all aiming to get to the same results, but who use their own imagination to get there.

This of course implies that different leadership styles are needed. There are no 'followers' in collaborations; instead there are equal, horizontal relationships (Mandell & Keast, 2009). Leaders need to shift from a controlling to a coaching position, where trust is key and process evaluation support the evaluation of the results. Adopting a collaborative leadership style has been advocated as one of the identifying characteristics of leaders of the future.

8.9 Overcoming Miscommunication

It is safe to say that without communication there is no collaboration. One reason why cross-sector collaborations are difficult is because you have more levels to consider: In 'normal' collaborations, you can have problems of communication between different persons and different organisations. In cross-sector collaborations, you can have communication problems between different sectors as well, because they use a different terminology and have a different cultural identity.

Terminology and use-specific language exist in all different sectors. It is difficult for people in that sector, who use this terminology each day, to grasp that other people do not understand what they are saying. If they do realise this is a problem, it is still difficult to explain in layman's words what is meant. Take the following case for example.

CASE

Miscommunication between a Sport Entrepreneur and an App-Developer

A sport manager has this great idea to develop an application that connects people who want to play football, basketball, or frisbee at any time. When he talks to an application developer she talks about creating a mock-up and vertical slice of the application in Java rather than Python, integrating a 3D technical artist, and subcontracting another company to polish the game. The entrepreneur nodded the whole time, but the app was never developed.

Cultural identity also plays a great deal in miscommunication. Each sector has a different set of values and a different cultural identity. Being able to relate to the culture of the other partners is of crucial importance to avoid miscommunication in collaborations (Stegeman et al., 2012). One example:

Increasing Sport Participation – Cultural Identity

In our cross-sector case of collaborating with sport, health, and social organisations, sport organisations tended to be more action-oriented, whereas social organisations invested more time in creating a shared vision before taking action. Health organisations tended to rely more on evidenced-based programs as a basis for their actions. Understanding these cultural differences gave way for overcoming language barriers.

It is thus crucial to understand the language, culture, and priorities of other sectors' organisations (Stegeman et al., 2012). One item that might facilitate this communication and avoid misunderstandings is having staff in your own organisation who come from the different sectors that you want to collaborate with (Marlier et al., 2015a).

8.10 Trust

Trust is quintessential to every human relationship. It relates to the mutual confidence in the abilities and intentions of the actors in the partnership. It is important to know that trust is something that takes time to develop, and its development should not be rushed; it needs to grow through a process of mutual learning or through shared accomplishments (Parent & Harvey, 2009). The popular author and speaker Simon Sinek eloquently describes trust as giving someone the power to destroy you and trusting that they will not use it.

Personal contact and external focus are crucial aspects to foster trust (Marlier et al., 2015a). *Personal contact* refers to the match between the individuals who will collaborate. Selecting the most qualified members in your team to cross bridges is thus very important to increase trust. Several aspects are important to consider when talking about creating trusting relationships. For instance, people who are open, extraverted, and likeable are in most cases best suited to foster trust among different organisations ((Stegeman et al., 2012). External focus relates to the extent a person looks to reach own organisational benefits by creating organisational benefits for other organisations. One study concerning crossing bridges in Europe found that the fastest way to reach own organisational goals is through the perspective of 'what is in it for them' (Stegeman et al., 2012).

8.11 Dealing with Conflicts

Conflicts are evident and intrinsic to the structure of collaborations. Some say in order to evolve as a collaboration conflicts are positive and sometimes needed (Kenis & Provan,

2009). However, even more important are clear agreements on how to deal with these conflicts (Lucidarme *et al.*, 2013).

Five different methods are identified by Mohr and Spekman (1994): joint problem solving, persuasion, leadership skills (sometimes referred to as 'smoothing' in this context), domination, harsh words, and arbitration. Joint problem solving is in most cases the best option because it has the best chance of reaching a mutually satisfactory solution. In many cases, however, persuasion is used by a partner with more power to adopt particular solutions (Mohr & Spekman, 1994). Leadership skills will have a great effect on the outcome of this persuasion and influence (Mandell & Steelman, 2003). Domination, harsh words, and arbitration, but also ignoring the problem, affect the trust between the different partners which has a negative influence on partnership outcomes (Robins *et al.*, 2011).

To elaborate on the most successful of the five methods – joint problem solving – a couple of experts have initiated the Harvard Negotiation template, which has proven a useful instrument in conflict resolution (Fisher *et al.*, 2011). It is a five-step template that covers the following aspects: (a) Don't bargain over positions; (b) Separate the people from the problem; (c) Focus on interests, not positions; (d) Invent options for mutual gain; and (e) Insist on using objective criteria. These steps are best explained with an example.

CASE

Increase Sport Participation – Joint Problem Solving Using the Harvard Negotiation Template

Imagine the responsible of sport and the social sector in city x who want to improve integration through sport. The goal for the sport responsible is to increase sport participation; the goal for the socially responsible is to give more opportunities to people in disadvantaged situations. There is a conflict regarding who should pay what part to whom. The sport responsible says the socially responsible needs to pay more; obviously the socially responsible says the opposite. In previous partnerships over the last three years, there have always been difficulties and problems, so over the years some sort of dislike between the two has grown.

To try to overcome their differences, they are willing to use the Harvard negotiation principle. (a) To stop bargaining over positions, they stop to discuss who needs to contribute what to whom. (b) They try to separate the people from the problem by setting aside their feelings of previous experiences and focus on the issue at hand. (c) They question each other about the interest behind their position. The sport responsible asks the socially responsible in a sincere way to try to explain to him what makes it difficult for her and her team to engage into the project. The social partner says that in the last five years they have seen their workforce reduced to half the amount of the people, due to cuts in the social budget of the city. She explains that this was also the reason why the previous projects did not run as smoothly as desired. The socially responsible asks the same question to the sport responsible. He answers that a lot of people in his team feel unable to contribute to the project because they do not have affinity with people in disadvantaged situations; it makes them feel uncomfortable. (d) They think about mutual gains, and the socially responsible says that two persons of her workforce can guide his team to understand how to best deal with people in disadvantaged situations from an empowerment perspective. In return, the sport responsible answers that his sport team can take the lead in the project to increase the experience of the sport team and reduce the input of the social team. (e) They decide on objective criteria to evaluate the project. They will check whether the sport team feels more comfortable to deal with people in disadvantaged situations and to what extent the guidance of the social team helped them. They will also check with the social team as to what extent this project put extra strain on them and whether they considered the project as valuable for them as well.

I welcome everyone to apply this template to resolve current conflicts; maybe it can offer novel insights to bury some slumbering frustrations.

8.12 (Process) Evaluation

As in all projects, having clear criteria to evaluate the outcomes is of crucial importance, as they help in creating clarity in communication. Participation in goal setting and planning of cross-sector collaborations is essential in order to come to a valuable (process) evaluation (Mohr & Spekman, 1994). Evaluating the process is important because it can nip potential conflicts in the bud, and it makes you flexible to adapt to the context and steer the cross-sector collaboration in the right direction if it is heading off course.

In cross-sector collaborations, evaluating the outcomes can be complex because you need to consider views of a variety of stakeholders and outcomes at different levels. As mentioned in the first success factor (Purpose), the goals for one partner to enter in the collaboration can be interrelated, competing, or shared (Babiak, 2009). This means you can evaluate the outcomes for each organisation but also on the network level (i.e. Did the collaboration result in dealing with the wicked problem?). It is useful to understand that cross-sector partnerships take time to produce tangible outcomes on a network level (Sydow, 2004). In general, three to five years are needed to produce these outcomes.

8.13 The Five-Step Model of Cross-Sector Collaborations

But exactly how do you start to collaborate with other sectors? The next section is devoted to providing a guideline for people and organisations that want to engage in cross-sector collaborations in the setting of promoting sport or leisure. Figure 8.1 depicts a five-step model to start cross-sector collaborations.

A **first step** is defining the organisational goals that you want to reach with the cross-sector collaborations. As mentioned before, having a clear purpose for engaging in cross-sector collaborations is a key success factor.

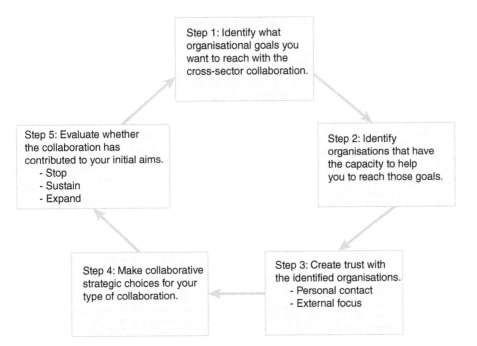

Step 1: Identify what organisational goals you want to reach with the cross-sector collaboration.

Step 5: Evaluate whether the collaboration has contributed to your initial aims.
- Stop
- Sustain
- Expand

Step 2: Identify organisations that have the capacity to help you to reach those goals.

Step 4: Make collaborative strategic choices for your type of collaboration.

Step 3: Create trust with the identified organisations.
- Personal contact
- External focus

Figure 8.1 The five-step model to guide the start of cross-sector collaborations.

CASE

Increase Sport Participation – Different Goals of Different Organisations in Different Sectors

Different goals were noted in the cross-sector collaborations between sport, health, and social organisations to reach ethnic cultural minorities and people of lower social class: (a) For sport organisations and sport clubs the goal was to increase the number of people participating in sport, increase the number of club members and volunteers, and take up their social role in the community; (b) for social organisations the goal was to empower this target group by means of sport and to create places where they could meet, interact, and focus on their talents instead of their problems; (c) for health organisations the goal was to increase opportunities for this target group to be more physically active; and (d) for cultural and youth organisations the goal was to reach more participants to their activities and create a more efficient and effective leisure offer (Marlier et al., 2020).

A **second step** consists of identifying the partners in your surroundings who have the capacity to help to accomplish the organisational goals you want to achieve with the collaboration. Starting and leveraging available capacities in your context is one of the core principles of capacity building (NSW Health Department, 2001). Ideally, capacities of all organisations in the field are known, and rational decisions can be made to which organisations would be best suited. However, in most cases this knowledge is absent, and this second step in the model presents itself as probably one of the hardest ones to take. This is especially true for the sport sector, as in many cases these sport organisations work in silos and consequently are not aware of the capacities of other organisations that could help the sport organisations in attaining their goals (Barnes et al., 2007). Some people and organisations specialize in connecting information, skills, and resources and can help to identify the right organisations to team up with. Of course, other possibilities can help to overcome this step. A broad personal network of the organisation's leader is generally important in identifying the right partners.

A **third step** is contacting the organisations and developing trust at an early stage. Much is dependent on the person who is engaged in the collaboration. It should be someone with an open and extraverted personality who can enthuse other partners with the aspirations of the collaboration and who can relate to the cultural identity of the other partners. Engaging in a collaboration should always start from an external focus and the question: How can I strengthen my partner's goals with my own goals? Arguably, developing trust is the single most important feature of collaborations because it has the power to overcome miscommunication and potential conflicts. To use a metaphor: If cross-sector collaborations were a flock of birds, trust would be the wind that carries their wings.

A **fourth step** concerns making the collaboration concrete and involves making strategic decisions in close participation with the involved partners. This implies that the organisations in the collaboration must decide on the purpose of the collaboration, divide the tasks, delineate roles, make the desired objectives SMART (specific, measurable, achievable, relevant, time-bound), and address how they will be in contact with each other and how they will evaluate both process and outcome. This step is, however, not so straightforward as it assumes to be. Translating mutual goals in actions is often a difficult process (Kaats & Opheij, 2012). Often the only practical way forward is to get started on some action without fully agreeing to the aims. A clear role and task delineation results in higher trust to reach the mutual objectives of the partnership. Process evaluation enables partners to share more skills and knowledge with others in the CSDP. Of course, much relies on what you want to achieve. This can range from promoting the partners' activities in your facilities, organizing a mutual activity involving sport or physical activity, building mutual infrastructure, and sharing staff members. Deciding on the best type of governance will largely be influenced by the type of collaboration you engage in. For example, a collaboration concerning building a new type of sport infrastructure will need to be more formalized than a collaboration concerning a mutual sport camp.

A **fifth and final step** consists of the evaluation of Step 1: Did the cross-sector collaboration add value to obtain one of the organisational goals that you wanted to accomplish through this collaboration? If not, you can choose to stop the collaboration; if it did, you can continue and even expand your collaboration. One crucial aspect to consider in this phase, however, is time. In most to all cases it takes time to get results from the collaboration. Results of collaborations can be like pouring ketchup: It clogs in the beginning, but once the first results roll in, everything follows smoothly. Therefore, it is crucial that you have established clear ways to evaluate the partnership. Positive results will create legitimacy of the partnership; bad results will make it easier to dissolve the partnership. These assessments are not possible if your results cannot be measured. Positive collaborations create legitimacy and stimulate the strategy to engage in other collaborations (Marlier et al., 2015a). This notion is closely linked to the phenomenon of the 'Matthew effect', which indicates that advantage breeds more advantage. This has much to do with Step 3, where trust needs to be created. It takes time for each partner to understand the language and culture of the partners of the other sectors (M. B. Edwards, 2015). Therefore, it is advised for organisations new to collaborating to start with smaller projects and to gradually build the needed capacity to collaborate. Of course, if you notice that the potential is missing in the specific collaboration, it is better to focus time and energy on other partners. If you find the collaboration valuable to reach your own organisational goals, you want to make them sustainable and maybe engage in other and more mutual activities to reach different organisational goals. To increase sustainability, you need to make sure the needed resources are available (Babiak & Thibault, 2009). The reputation of being a reliable and good partner will encourage other partners to start collaborating with you.

8.14 Case: Vital Cities – Application of the Five-Step Model of Cross-Sector Collaborations

This section provides an applied case of designing a vital city with the aid of the five-step model of cross-sector collaborations.

Making cities more active and vital is one of the most pressing needs for modern societies. Two main reasons underpin the necessity for vital cities. First, about 55% of the world's population lives in cities (United Nations, 2018). In 2050 this number will amount to 68% (United Nations, 2018). If we want acceptable levels of air pollution and traffic congestion, more people will need to make use of active transport e.g. walking, biking. Second, physical inactivity and sedentary behaviour are one of the leading factors for death worldwide (WHO, 2018). Humans are designed to move, and integrating a healthy amount of physical activity at school, at work, and at home is no less than a necessity for living a healthy life.

Just by describing these needs it becomes evident that creating vital cities integrates a whole variety of departments and stakeholders at various levels. It touches upon aspects such as what bike lane is most urgent to fix, in what area would a new playground have most effect, in which park would seniors need more benches to be able to rest during their walk, in what area could additional city lights help so adults would feel safe to run in the evening/at night, how cars can be avoided from the city centre, etc. A multitude of different departments are thus intertwined to enable the design of a vital city – the department of urban planning, mobility, economy, sport, statistics, youth, education, social integration – all have valuable input to make. For example, the department of urban planning designs what the city should look like in the future, making sections car-free, integrating parks, and creating bike and walk-friendly routes to create the needed conditions for people to transport in an active way. But mutually the mobility department will decide on what sections can be car-free and when and how safer bike lanes can be integrated in the current situation. The sport department will need to advise where new sport infrastructure for what target group needs to be installed to have the most effect. Furthermore, the statistics department will need to provide data so policy makers can make decisions based on evidence related to the pollution levels, safety levels of pedestrians and cyclists, and accessibility levels to recreation and sport infrastructure. Smart detecting systems and sensors are built nowadays throughout the entire city to provide big data on these aspects.

It is thus not possible to have a departmental approach to solve the wicked problem of developing a vital city. To resolve this multidimensional challenge, many cross-sector collaboration initiatives have been developed, e.g. Active Design (Sport England, 2015), Vital Cities (2018), and Active City (P. Edwards & Tsouros, 2008). The aim is basically to have a horizontal (different departments) and vertical integration (citizens, local organisations, practitioners, policy makers) to come to a strategic roadmap of becoming a vital city.

To make this more tangible, here is a specific example of how Bruges, a city in Belgium, is tackling its vital city strategy with the five-step model of cross-sector collaborations.

1. Step 1: Identify organisational goals you want to reach with the cross-sector collaborations.

   a. The network goal: Make Bruges a vital city where active transport is encouraged, air pollution is reduced, and people are given as many opportunities as possible to be active, come together, and feel good.
   b. Organisational goals of different sectors in the vital city project:

      i. Urban planning department: Design a city which is liveable and ready for the future for its inhabitants;
      ii. Mobility sector: Create a safe and accessible city for citizens and local businesses;
      iii. Sport sector: Increase the number of people participating in sport and being active in Bruges;
      iv. Social sector: Create more places where citizens can meet to combat loneliness, and improve integration of different groups in Bruges;
      v. Health sector: Increase physical activity and mental health of the citizens in Bruges;
      vi. Youth sector: Create more play and recreation opportunities for youth in Bruges;
      vii. Statistics department: Use big data to provide added value for the city of Bruges.

2. Step 2: Identify organisations that have the capacity to help you to reach those goals.

   a. The task force in Bruges exists of seven members who represent the organisations of each of the sectors/departments mentioned earlier. Each member is responsible to identify and involve the different organisations in their sector that have the capacity to add value to create a vital city. The aim is to collect data on how the citizens of Bruges want to shape their city into a more vital one through co-creation sessions.

3. Step 3: Create trust with the identified organisations.

   a. To value this step, in the different work groups, several teamwork games and challenges are given to get to know each other better and to create trust in a stimulating context.

4. Step 4: Make collaborative strategic choices for your type of collaboration.

   a. Vital city roadmap:

      i. Data-informed decision making

         1. The most crucial vital city priorities are based on objective data of the statistics department and the co-creation sessions with different citizens and organisations.
         2. A meeting between policy makers and the vital city task force is set up. Based on the data, policy makers in Bruges decide to focus their main efforts to increase active transport. Specifically, they aim to increase active transport in Bruges from 5% to 10% over the next four years.

      ii. Selecting priorities per community

1. Together with field organisations, practitioners, and inhabitants the task force sets up a plan to increase safety and active transport in the different communities.

ii. Develop well planned and integrated strategies: Together with field organisations and practitioners of the different sectors and the inhabitants of the community, the task force sets up a plan to increase safety and active transport per community with SMART objectives. (See the following text for an example of one intervention.)

1. Intervention 1: For children from 6 to 12 years old, they set up a 'get safely to school' project together with one school of the community and an innovative company. Four pillars are built at four locations, 800 metres from the entrance gate of the school. With an interactive bracelet, the children are rewarded with move coins every time they touch the pillar with their bracelet.
2. Intervention 2: For adults, they set up together with a couple of companies in the community a challenge for the most 'bike-friendly' company. An app tracks the active transport of the employers during a couple of months. After a few months, the participants are celebrated, and the winners get an award that values them for their efforts.

5. Step 5: Evaluate whether the collaboration has contributed to your initial aims.

   a. Stop, sustain, expand:

   i. Intervention 1 – Sustain: Although quite successful to raise active transport to the school, the technological part sometimes failed. The different members of the project sat together to wrinkle out these technological bugs to improve the program.
   ii. Intervention 2 – Expand: The app-tracker inspired 280 individuals to participate in the program. Next year, more companies will participate to become the most bike-friendly company, and the program will be expanded to other communities. In these new communities, it is imperative that the program will be adapted to the context in order to make it successful.

8.15 What Comes Next?

In this chapter we discussed the necessity and the practicalities of cross-sector collaborations. Cross-sector collaborations are what will drive the future forward by providing innovative solutions to wicked problems. However, they are not easy, as cross-sector collaboration increase complexity, take time to work, and implicate the loss of some autonomy for an organisation. Although not easy, being able to collaborate between teams, organisations, and sectors is an indispensable competence that managers will need to comprehend and apply if they want to be ready for the future. In sport and leisure, cross-sector collaborations are in many cases still in their infancy. To this end, this chapter described some important success factors and presented the five-step collaboration model that shows how collaborations could be initiated, developed, and evaluated by building trust through a participative approach.

Discussion Questions

Need for Cross-Sector Collaborations

1. Think about a problem you would like to resolve related to sport or leisure, or an issue that you would want to improve in the sports industry. How could cross-sector collaborations help you in solving this problem?

Success Factors

1. Write down one specific situation in which you experienced the positive sides of collaborating.
2. Explain what made this collaboration stand out; why did it work out the way it did?
3. Are your answers related to the success factors described in this chapter? Or are they independent of them?
4. Write down one specific situation in which you experienced the negative sides of collaborating.
5. Explain what made this collaboration a bad experience; why did it not work out the way you wanted it to?
6. What success factors described in this chapter were lacking in this collaboration?

Five-Step Cross-Sector Collaboration Model

1. Think about a goal that you want to achieve in one of the organisations that you are in. Apply the five-step model to help you to set out your strategy.

References

Ansell, C., & Gash, A. (2008). Collaborative governance in theory and practice. *Journal of Public Administration Research and Theory*, 18(4), 543–571.

Babiak, K. (2009). Criteria of effectiveness in multiple cross-sectoral interorganizational relationships. *Evaluation and Program Planning*, 32(1), 1–12.

Babiak, K., & Thibault, L. (2009). Challenges in multiple cross-sector partnerships. *Nonprofit and Voluntary Sector Quarterly*, 38(1), 117–143.

Barnes, M., Cousens, L., & MacLean, J. (2007). From silos to synergies: A network perspective of the Canadian sport system. *International Journal of Sport Management and Marketing*, 2(5), 555–571.

Brinkerhoff, J. M. (2002). Government-nonprofit partnership: A defining framework. *Public Administration and Development*, 22(1), 19–30. https://doi.org/Doi 10.1002/Pad.203

Bryson, J. M., Crosby, B. C., & Stone, M. M. (2006). The design and implementation of Cross-Sector collaborations: Propositions from the literature. *Public Administration Review*, 66, 44–55.

Cox, T. H., & Blake, S. (1991). Managing cultural diversity: Implications for organizational competitiveness. *Academy of Management Perspectives*, 5(3), 45–56.

Edwards, M. B. (2015). The role of sport in community capacity building: An examination of sport for development research and practice. *Sport Management Review*, 18(1), 6–19.

Edwards, P., & Tsouros, A. (2008). This planning guide provides a range of ideas, information and tools for developing a comprehensive. In *World Health Organization*. Retrieved from WHO Europe website www.euro.who.int/__data/assets/pdf_file/0012/99975/E91883.pdf

Emerson, K., Nabatchi, T., & Balogh, S. (2012). An integrative framework for collaborative governance. *Journal of Public Administration Research and Theory*, 22(1), 1–29.

Fisher, R., Ury, W. L., & Patton, B. (2011). *Getting to Yes: Negotiating Agreement without Giving in*. Penguin, Grantham.

Gibbons, P. (2015). *The Science of Successful Organizational Change: How Leaders Set Strategy, Change Behavior, and Create an Agile Culture*. FT Press, London.

Huxham, C., & Macdonald, D. (1992). Introducing collaborative advantage: Achieving inter-organizational effectiveness through meta-strategy. *Management Decision*, 30(3).

Kaats, E. A. P., & Opheij, W. (2012). *Leren samenwerken tussen organisaties: Samen bouwen aan allianties, netwerken, ketens en partnerships*. Kluwer, Norwell, MA.

Kari, T. (2014). Can exergaming promote physical fitness and physical activity?: A systematic review of systematic reviews. *International Journal of Gaming and Computer-Mediated Simulations (IJGCMS)*, 6(4), 59–77.

Kenis, P., & Provan, K. G. (2009). Towards an exogenous theory of public network performance. *Public Administration*, 87(3), 440–456. https://doi.org/DOI 10.1111/j.1467-9299.2009.01775.x

Klitsie, E. J., Ansari, S., & Volberda, H. W. (2018). Maintenance of cross-sector partnerships: The role of frames in sustained collaboration. *Journal of Business Ethics*, 150(2), 401–423.

Lucidarme, S., Marlier, M., Cardon, G., De Bourdeaudhuij, I., & Willem, A. (2013). Critical success factors for physical activity promotion through community partnerships. *International Journal of Public Health*, 1–10.

Mandell, M. P., & Keast, R. (2008). Evaluating the effectiveness of interorganizational relations through networks. *Public Management Review*, 10(6), 715–731. https://doi.org/Doi 10.1080/14719030802423079

Mandell, M. P., & Keast, R. (2009). A new look at leadership in collaborative networks: Process catalysts. *Public Sector Leadership: International Challenges and Perspectives*, 163–178. Retrieved from https://books.google.be/books?hl=nl&lr=&id=yYljZSpL68gC&oi=fnd&pg=PA163&dq=Keast+personal+network&ots=I3jjA9qzSc&sig=JIq3NEkpsLcBN6Pz6LkmFV29E3U#v=onepage&q=Keast personal network&f=false

Mandell, M. P., & Steelman, T. (2003). Understanding what can be accomplished through interorganizational innovations The importance of typologies, context and management strategies. *Public Management Review*, 5(2), 197–224.

Marlier, M., Cardon, G., De Bourdeaudhuij, I., & Willem, A. (2014). A capacity building approach to increase sports participation in disadvantaged urban communities: A multi-level analysis. *Journal of Urban Health*, 91(6). https://doi.org/10.1007/s11524-014-9879-2

Marlier, M., Constandt, B., Schyvinck, C., De Bock, T., Winand, M., & Willem, A. (2020). Bridge over troubled water: Linking capacities of sport and non-sport organizations. *Social Inclusion*, 8(3). https://doi.org/DOI: 10.17645/si.v8i3.2465

Marlier, M., Lucidarme, S., Cardon, G., De Bourdeaudhuij, I., Babiak, K., & Willem, A. (2015a). Capacity building through cross-sector partnerships: A multiple case study of a sport program in disadvantaged communities in Belgium. *Bmc Public Health*, 15(1), 1. Retrieved from http://bmcpublichealth.biomedcentral.com/articles/10.1186/s12889-015-2605-5

Marlier, M., Lucidarme, S., Cardon, G., De Bourdeaudhuij, I., Babiak, K., & Willem, A. (2015b). Capacity building through cross-sector partnerships: A multiple case study of a sport program in disadvantaged communities in Belgium health policies, systems and management in high-income countries. *BMC Public Health*, 15(1). https://doi.org/10.1186/s12889-015-2605-5

Mohr, J., & Spekman, R. (1994). Characteristics of partnership success: Partnership attributes, communication behavior, and conflict resolution techniques. *Strategic Management Journal*, 15(2), 135–152.

NSW Health Department. (2001). A framework for building capacity to improve health. In *NSW Health*. Better Health Care Centre, Gladesville.

Parent, M., & Harvey, J. (2009). Towards a management model for sport and physical activity community-based partnerships. *European Sport Management Quarterly*, 9(1), 23–45. https://doi.org/Doi 10.1080/16184740802461694

Putnam, R. D. (2007). E pluribus unum: Diversity and community in the twenty-first century the 2006 Johan Skytte Prize Lecture. *Scandinavian Political Studies*, 30(2), 137–174.

Robins, G., Bates, L., & Pattison, P. (2011). Network governance and environmental management: Conflict and cooperation. *Public Administration*, 89(4), 1293–1313.

Sport England. (2015). Active design: Planning for health and wellbeing through sport and physical activity. Retrieved from www.sportengland.org/media/3426/spe003-active-design-published-october-2015-email-2.pdf

Stegeman, I., Kuipers, Y., & Costongs, C. (2012). Crossing bridges: Working together for health and well-being. Retrieved from www.health-inequalities.eu/HEALTHEQUITY/_images/annex_14_final_crossing_bridges_publication_eng_low_res.pdf

Sydow, J. (2004). Network development by means of network evaluation? Explorative insights from a case in the financial services industry. *Human Relations*, 57(2), 201–220.

Turrini, A., Cristofoli, D., Frosini, F., & Nasi, G. (2010). Networking literature about determinants of network effectiveness. *Public Administration*, 88(2), 528–550.

United Nations. (2018). World urbanization prospects. Retrieved from https://population.un.org/wup/Publications/Files/WUP2018-KeyFacts.pdf

Vital Cities. (2018). VITAL CITIES: Urban sports promotion for social inclusion, healthy and active living. Retrieved from https://urbact.eu/sites/default/files/vital_cities_final_synthesis_report.pdf

Waddock, S. A. (1988). Building successful social partnerships. *MIT Sloan Management Review*, 29(4), 17.

WHO. (2018). Key facts physical activity. Retrieved from www.who.int/news-room/fact-sheets/detail/physical-activity

Williams, T. (2005). Cooperation by design: Structure and cooperation in interorganizational networks. *Journal of Business Research*, 58(2), 223–231.

Zakocs, R. C., & Edwards, E. M. (2006). What explains community coalition effectiveness? A review of the literature. *American Journal of Preventive Medicine*, 30(4), 351–361.

Chapter 9

Sport, Physical Recreation, and Physical Activity

In This Chapter

- What are the differences between sport, physical recreation, and physical activity?
- Who provides these?
- Who participates in them, and why are they important?
- How are sport, physical recreation, and PA organised and funded in the UK?

DOI: 10.4324/9780367823610-9

Summary

Sport is ever present in news in the media, and sport at the top level gives us some of the most enduring cultural images. However, this is only really the 'tip of the iceberg' when it comes to understanding our relationship with sport and, specifically, sport participation. In fact, many would argue that sport is not the thing most of us participate in; it is, in fact, physical recreation or physical activity. Sport is usually defined as having definitive rules, being competitive, and usually time bound. Activities like walking, running, swimming, or cycling, which are all popular activities, are not sport at all. And this is where the bulk of activity takes place. In this chapter we will try and unpack how these three areas interact and what that means for leisure managers. Indeed, the 'participation challenge'– how do we get people into sport, physical activity, or physical recreation and then keep them there – is one of, if not the, most important challenge facing leisure managers and others within the leisure industry.

9.1 Introduction

The place to start here is with the definitions of each of the aspects of this chapter. The Council of Europe's definition of *sport* is:

> all forms of physical activity which, through casual or organised participation, aim at expressing or improving physical fitness and well-being, forming social relationships, or obtaining results in competition at all levels.

Using this definition, it appears sport extends well beyond a narrow concept of elite, competitive, organised activity we so often read about in the media. Given this, it is argued in this chapter that a more nuanced set of definitions is required to appreciate the various components the Council of Europe is referring to. Indeed, this chapter will talk separately about sport, physical recreation, and physical activity. This is not to say that these three sectors do not, in places, overlap. Debates exist among academics and practitioners concerning this; for example, where does play fit in?

Nevertheless, for leisure managers, being clear on what activity is being used and, importantly, *why* it is being used matters. So, when referring to sport, what is being discussed in this chapter is a competitive, goal-directed activity that includes physical skill or prowess. Sport has a set of rules which participants agree to, and these rules are designed to limit the most efficient way of achieving the goal. Then this chapter refers to physical recreation. Writing in 1994, Henderson and Bialeschki (p. 1) claimed that 'physical recreation is freely chosen, enjoyable activity which involves movement of the body and may be described as sport, exercise, fitness, dance, or outdoor activities'. In that regard, some sport may be physical recreation, and some physical recreation may be sport; however, clear differences exist. Specifically, there is a greater element of free choice in physical recreation, and there are less rules around time, space, and place, which is not usually the case with sport – particularly traditional ones. Second, the goal of physical recreation is enjoyment, which is often not the goal of sport. Perhaps one way to conceptualise this is that sport is more about enjoying the outcome (winning or succeeding), where physical recreation places more emphasis on enjoying the process. Finally, this chapter includes physical activity. As Piggin (2020) notes, perhaps because of a growing concern for health, there has been a tendency for physical activity to be defined physiologically, epidemiologically, or biomechanically. For example, the World Health Organisation advocates, as a definition, 'bodily movement that requires energy expenditure' (WHO, 2018, cited in Piggin, 2020). However, Piggin argues this is a rather narrow definition and ignores the social, political, and cognitive dimensions of physical activity. For that reason, Piggin (2020, p. 5) offers an alternative definition, claiming that 'physical activity involves people moving, acting and performing within culturally specific spaces and contexts, and influenced by a unique array of interests, emotions, ideas, instructions and relationships'. This can, therefore, include a wider array of activities that have been discussed in other parts of this book. Gardening and DIY, for example, fall under this definition. Understanding the areas of sport, physical recreation, and physical activity – the differences and the areas they overlap –sensitises leisure managers to the complexity surrounding activities people undertake in their leisure time and guards against confusing or conflicting aims or objectives. To illustrate this, let us start with sport and how, particularly via political use, it has emerged as a tool for solving social problems.

9.2 The Importance of Sport

9.2.1 Politics and Globalisation

Nelson Mandela, at the Rugby Union World Cup in South Africa in 1995, announced, 'Sport has the power to change the world'. What transpired in the following 31 days and the impact on South African national identity gave further credence to the role sport can play in wider social objectives. Indeed, other politicians in other countries did the same. John Major introduced *Sport: Raising the Game* in 1995, which had a focus on using traditional sport in schools to foster lifelong participation and teach children about societal values in the UK. Tony Blair, despite strategically rejecting the idea of using mega events for wider social good, backed the successful 2012 London Olympic bid to 'inspire a generation'. Finally, in the USA, Presidents George H. W. Bush and Bill Clinton both advocated the Midnight Basketball programmes that aimed to reduce inner-city crime. Sports became 'patriot games' in the late nineteenth century, and their significance has grown ever since, often involving governments at the highest levels. For example, several governments boycotted the 1980 Olympic Games in Moscow and then others the 1984 Los Angeles Games. And sport is also drawn into the 'theatre' of war, the most serious example being a World Cup qualifying match between El Salvador and Honduras in 1969, which sparked riots leading to a war – the so-called Football War.

Sport today is beamed across the globe, engaging the interest of billions of people worldwide. The mass media and professional sport are now inextricably merged and economically dependent. The introduction of cable and satellite delivery systems gives 24-hour access to sports channels and pay-per-view audiences. The media has accelerated the globalisation of sport. A conspicuous example of this is the Olympic Games. Gratton and Solberg (2007) report that in 1956 just one nation broadcast the Summer Olympics in Melbourne. By 1976, 124 nations broadcast the Montreal Summer Olympics, and by 2004 the number had risen to 220 nations for the Athens Games. In parallel, the revenue from broadcasting rose exponentially, as Table 9.1 shows.

Table 9.1 Summer Olympic Games Broadcast Revenue, 1960–2016

Broadcast revenue from the Summer Olympic Games from 1960 to 2016 (in million US dollars)

1960	Rome	1.2
1964	Tokyo	1.6
1968	Mexico City	9.8
1972	Munich	18
1976	Montreal	35
1980	Moscow	88
1984	Los Angeles	287
1988	Seoul	403
1992	Barcelona	636
1996	Atlanta	898
2000	Sydney	1332
2004	Athens	1494
2008	Beijing	1739
2012	London	2569
2016	Rio	2868

Source: International Olympic Committee

The relationship between the media and sports stars is also worthy of note. Those at the top of elite sport (specific ones in particular) earn a lot of money, and they are also a marketing manager's dream as an attractor for sport. Whenever a major sports programme is launched, it is likely to be fronted by a major sports star – this is the simple 'hook' that, it is suggested, gets a lot of potential participants interested.

9.2.1 Economic and Social Importance

Arguably the clearest evidence of the national benefits of sport relate to economic benefits. In the UK, for example, according to the Office for National Statistics the total value of consumer spending on recreational and sporting services in 2017 was £11.6 billion. Clearly this was impacted by the COVID-19 pandemic, however, it remained above £10 billion in 2018 and 2019. Sporting goods also make up part of this. Sales within the UK and then exported around the world add around £1 billion to this figure. And then there is gambling, which is not included. Growth (at least pre-pandemic) in consumer sport spending demonstrates not only the increasing relative economic importance of sport but also the need for competent managers to help sustain this growth.

The growing significance of sport in the lives of people and the economy is often the catalyst for an unwavering belief in the 'power of sport' for helping treat society's problems. Two main aspects are used in the drawing of this conclusion. First, because people are interested in sport, this can be a medium through which to engage them. Second, because sport is inherently good, it can teach values such as abiding by rules, understanding how to win and how to lose, teamwork, and how to overcome adversity. And what is more, there are a plethora of sporting stars who can display such behaviours. However, this is an oversimplification of the argument. First, let us take participation. According to Sport England data, 25% of the population do less than 30 minutes of sport and physical activity a week. Indeed, while around 60% of the population claim to undertake 150 minutes of physical activity per week, that leaves 40% of the population who do not engage at recommended levels. Participation in traditional sport like football, golf, or netball is declining or static, and while 25% attend live sports events, this leaves 75% who do not. This is not to say participation levels in the UK are bad. In fact, they are good, but it does start to undermine the pervasive view that sport is for everyone and that everyone enjoys it. Second, sport is not always a good thing that brings out the best in people, and we cannot ignore the dark side of sport. Cheating; gamesmanship; performance enhancing drug use; sexual, physical, and emotional abuse; corruption; and pain and injury are all part of competitive sport. This, it seems, has started to be reflected in the strategies of those who provide sport, physical activity, and physical recreation in the UK. It is to those organisations we now turn.

9.3 Provision for Sport, Physical Activity, and Physical Recreation

Provision for sport, physical activity (PA), and physical recreation (PR) is shared by all three of the major supply sectors – commercial, third sector, and government – but not in equal measure. Sport-related employment (including PA and PR) in England was estimated to be around 445,000 in 2018. That may seem a lot, but when you compare that to the volunteers in the third sector, it is not. In 2019, 2.3 million people coached or instructed in a voluntary capacity, while 94,000 coaches or instructors were in paid employment. Likewise, 1.3 million people voluntarily refereed or officiated, 2.1 million voluntarily took up an administration or committee role, and 1.4 million volunteered as a steward or marshal. Although the commercial sector makes up the largest section of paid employees, without third sector organisations and the volunteers that help run them, sport, PA, and PR would look very different in the UK.

9.3.1 Facilities

Perhaps because of the more organised nature of sport, participation depends to a large extent on sports facilities, whereas physical activity and recreation not so much. Using data from the Sport England Active Places Power website, Table 9.3 shows the count of different types of facilities in England from all sectors. For some, we can show how that number has changed over the past ten years, highlighting a marked increase in synthetic turf pitches, grass pitches, health and fitness suites, and sports halls.

This contrasts with the latter part of the twentieth century, when owners of many playing fields, often local authorities or schools, sold the land for development in order to relieve

Table 9.2 Count of Facilities in England, 2009 and 2018

Facility type	2009	2018	Change
Athletics track	379	759	380
Golf	3,019	2,826	-193
Grass pitch	56,097	68,548	12,451
Health and fitness suite	6,737	7,521	784
Ice rink	44		
Indoor bowl	366		
Indoor tennis centre	325		
Ski slope	159		
Sports hall	9,311	11,418	2,107
Swimming pool	5,005	5,041	36
Outdoor tennis court		20,391	
Studio		7,462	
Squash court		3,858	
Synthetic turf pitch	1,651	6,992	5,341

their budgets. Another problem is ageing facilities, particularly the indoor facilities such as sports centres and swimming pools, where considerable sums are needed to bring them up to modern standards (Carter, 2005). For physical activity and physical recreation, the picture is a little more complicated. Here the facilities being used are more likely to be parks, paths, pavements, roads, or open spaces; indeed, one might argue some of these are not facilities at all. However, some are; but it just needs a different way of thinking about facilities. Over 100 million people visit the UK's 15 national parks each year, and they need maintaining and managing.

CASE STUDY 9.1

National Parks

There are 15 national parks across the UK, vast areas of countryside that are free for people to visit, and a wide range of activities take place there including walking, cycling, swimming, climbing, running, orienteering, canoeing, sailing, and paragliding. These areas also have residents (just under 500,000 people), so the areas need careful management. Each one of the 15 national parks is managed by a National Park Authority, and each Authority has a set of board members (not full-time employees) who seek advice about how the national park should be run. According to their website, each of the 15 National Park Authorities employs between 50 and 200 people undertaking various roles from office work to guides and rangers who work outside on the land. Notwithstanding the paid employees, like other parts of sport, physical activity, and physical recreation, volunteers are the 'lifeblood' of the national parks. The volunteers help by 'leading guided walks, fixing fences, dry stone walling, planting trees, checking historic sites and surveying wildlife', which are all vital roles in the management and maintenance of these landscapes. We may not think of national parks as facilities, however, they are places where many people spend their leisure time and, in that respect, they need to be managed. They are the site of a lot of physical activity and recreation. These areas do face problems, however; despite being free, they do not attract a diverse range of the population. Participation data show a low proportion of minoritised ethnic groups accessing the parks and low numbers from low socio-economic groups. Why do you think that is? The social, mental, and physical benefits of spending time outdoors in places like national parks are well documented. So encouraging more people to visit the sites is good for society; however, this means a more complex set of circumstances within which these 'facilities' need managing.

9.3.2 Voluntary Clubs

In 2013, it was estimated by the Sport and Recreation Alliance (SRA) that around 151,000 voluntary clubs organise sport for roughly 8 million people in the UK. Most of these clubs are affiliated with national governing bodies of sport, but they do fall under the definition of physical activity and recreation too. For example, in this data, cycling, swimming, sailing, snow sports, canoeing, and angling are included, but that is not to say all participants are involved in the competitive aspects of these pursuits. The 151,000 clubs are predominantly run by administrators, coaches, and helpers who freely give of their time. Whilst this is big business, the management of voluntary organisations and volunteers is a very delicate balancing act between serving members' interests and balancing budgets, and between welcoming and nurturing volunteers and producing good quality sport at reasonable cost. One thing to note here is that, during the various 'lockdowns' experienced by the UK during 2020 and 2021, clubs were able to 'demonstrate an incredible resilience in the sector, with volunteers continuing to support their clubs across the lockdown period' (SRA, 2021). This is one advantage of the sector being built on the willingness and generosity of volunteers who are largely undertaking their role because of their love for the club. Where paid employees may seek alternative employment in a 'safer' sector, volunteers are bonded to their clubs in ways paid employees are not.

Discussion Question

Voluntary clubs are very important providers of sport, PA, and PR, but they often struggle with insufficient numbers of volunteers. Does this mean that such clubs are not the future for this type of provision?

9.4 Participation in Sport and Physical Activities

The 'throughput' of people in sports facilities is large scale. Over 11 million people attend live sports events each year and, in the UK, the largest sector is professional football. There were just over 14.5 million visits to Premier League grounds in the 2018–2019 season, for example. Aside from this, over 1 billion visits are made to UK public parks each year, many for formal or informal sport, PA, and PR. Over 4.5 million people swim indoors regularly, meaning an estimated 80 million visits are made to UK local authority swimming pools each year. Participation in sport, PA, and PR has a clear impact on management, be that management of facilities, management of events, or management of workforce. It is, therefore, briefly considering participation.

A major source of data on adults' sports participation in England has been the *Active Lives* survey (previously called *Active People*). When it was *Active People*, the survey sought data from those over the age of 16, however, a re-brand to *Active Lives* also included a change in sample frame to include those over the age of 5, which gave more insight. This is a national survey with a sample size of around 190,000, although it has been nearly double that at times. Either way, it is one of the largest surveys of sport, PA, and PR participation in Europe. Some of the headline results for 2019–2020 are shown in Table 9.3, indicating the percentage of people who participated in sport, PA, or PR at least twice in the last 28 days based on a range of societal stratifications.

Overall participation has not moved too much over the past 30 years or so, however, there are some patterns within the latest data that are vital for any leisure managers to grasp. For example, it remains the case that those from higher social classes (measured by the National Statistics Socio-Economic Classification, known as NS SEC) participate more than those from lower classes. Of those who fall into NS SEC 1–2, 83.8% participated twice in sport, PA, and PR within the previous 28 days, whereas, for those from NS SEC 3–5 and NS SEC 6–8, the figures were 75.2% and 64.2% respectively. Similarly, sport, PA, and PR remain more inaccessible for those who have mental or physical impairments, compared to those viewed as 'able-bodied' (79.4%). For those who had one impairment, participation fell to 70.2%, falling further to 64.1% for those who had two impairments, and to 52.6% for those with three impairments. Finally, participation remains segregated based on ethnicity. Those who classify themselves as 'Mixed' (78.1%), 'White British' (77.4%), and 'White other' (75.5%) are most likely to have participated in sport, PA, and PR twice in the last 28 days, while those identifying as 'Black' (67.8%), 'Asian (excluding Chinese)' (63.5%), or 'Other (56.7%)' ethnicities were the lowest in terms of participation. These figures point to long-standing issues around participation, however, at the same time, they are contemporary. They clearly relate to wider structural issues within society, such as inequality, however, leisure managers must contemplate their role in encouraging participation from disadvantaged groups.

The data from Sport England also show some more encouraging signs in that participation between genders seems to have equalled out. This is, in some way, down to the inclusion of more recreation activities and physical activity in the data; however, there is some evidence that more females are participating. The use of more questions around PA and PR in *Active Lives* also seem to show that activity levels do not perhaps drop off over the life course as we previously thought. There is a drop after the age of 16, however, activity seems steady between the groups 16–34 (77.8%), 35–54 (76.4%), and 55–74 (76.4%). This appears to contradict the commonly held belief that the older we get the less active we are. There are, however, two primary points to be made here. This is activity measured as twice in the past 28 days, not by the amount recommended by the scientific community for health

Table 9.3 **Participation in the Last 28 Days: At Least Twice in the Last 28 Days**

	Nov. 2019–2020
NS SEC 1–2 (higher)	83.8%
NS SEC 3–5 (middle)	75.2%
NS SEC 6–8 (lower)	64.2%
NS SEC 9 (students and other)	75.5%
Male	75.8%
Female	75.2%
In another way	58.6%
Heterosexual or straight	75.6%
Gay or lesbian	79.2%
Bisexual	76.2%
Other sexual orientation	57.3%
Aged 16–34	77.8%
Aged 35–54	76.4%
Aged 55–74	76.4%
Aged 75+	63.9%
No disability or long-term health condition	79.4%
One impairment	70.2%
Two impairments	64.1%
Three or more impairments	52.6%
Mixed	78.1%
White British	77.4%
White other	75.5%
Chinese	70.9%
Black	67.8%
Asian (excluding Chinese)	63.5%
Other ethnic origin	56.7%

Source: Sport England

improvement (5 bouts of 30 minutes per week). This approach, therefore, will 'catch' more people in the data. Indeed, when looking at those who are considered 'active' (they participate in at least 150 minutes of activity a week), despite a levelling through the mid-life period, there is a drop across the life course between ages 16–24 (70.1%), 25–34 (65.7%), 35–44 (64.3%), 45–54 (65.5%), 55–64 (61.8%), and 65–74 (57.3%). Again, if the aim for leisure managers is to facilitate participation, then reviewing the barriers faced by the different age groups is important. Managers of all types of providers should be interested in participation statistics such as those in Table 10.3. For commercial managers, the statistics identify those

Table 9.4 **Participation in the Last 28 Days by Activity, 2020**

	At least twice in the last 28 days
Walking for leisure	47.6%
All cycling	18.2%
Running or track and field athletics	15.6%
Fitness class	14.0%
Running or jogging for leisure	12.9%
Dance of all types	9.6%
Gym session	9.0%
Weights session	5.3%
Swimming	5.2%
Body weight exercises	4.6%
Yoga	4.2%
High intensity	3.6%
Football	3.0%
Circuit training	2.9%
Pilates	2.6%
Dance-based class	2.2%
Creative or artistic dance	2.0%
Golf	1.8%
Free weights	1.7%
Tennis	1.5%
Weights-based class	1.5%
Badminton	1.2%
Cross training	1.1%
Gymnastics, trampolining, or cheerleading	1.1%
Fell running	0.8%

Source: Sport England

with more potential to participate, which is important for marketing purposes. For public sector managers, the statistics identify those who are most deserving of special attention – e.g. through specific programmes, targeted promotion, price discounts – because they have relatively low participation rates.

Table 9.4 identifies the most popular activities in England by the same measure of participation at least twice in the last 28 days. It demonstrates clearly how important non-competitive activities are. They comprise at least some, if not all, of the top ten places. Even when athletics are considered alongside running, the track and field part comprises less than 1% of the population, which suggests around 13% take part in running in a semi-serious way, for example, at a Parkrun event. Even then, this is only a competitive environment if you want it to be, and there are few external pressures to turn up every week. Furthermore, many of these non-competitive activities are characterised by individual participation, rather than in teams or with playing partners and are also time flexible – with the participant being able to participate whenever he or she chooses. These non-competitive, individual, time-flexible activities are the ones to have shown most growth in the last three decades, and many of them are available in gyms – it is not difficult to see what has fuelled the development of so many commercial fitness centres. Walking has always been the most popular of activities in Britain since the first national surveys were conducted in the 1970s. Improvements in rights of access will only have increased the incentive to walk in the countryside. Furthermore, the ageing population that is emerging in England will lead to a growth in recreational walking activity because walking does not suffer as much as other activities do from the decline in physical mobility with age. However, there is a note of caution. Curiously for something that is free to access, participation in 'walking for leisure' and 'hill walking' is split along ethnic and social class lines, again highlighting the wider social processes that are at work.

Discussion Questions

What do the top five activities in England (walking, cycling, running, fitness, and dancing) say about the different motivations of people who participate?

This move to more individual, less time restricted, and less competitive forms of activity is why this chapter sought, at the very start, to differentiate between sport, PA, and PR. If they are merged, leisure managers run the risk of missing important information about participation. So what has the impact been on team sports? Let us take football as an example. Over the past five or six years, football has seen a decline in participation from around 5.2% of the population to 3% of the population. This decline has occurred in 11-a-side football and small-sided football. The only area that has remained stable is walking football, a version of football introduced for those with lower levels of mobility. It remains the case that national interest in football is more from spectating and media interest than from participation, and this validates the view that watching sport, PA, or PR does not necessarily translate into participation. Notwithstanding a largely successful 'Back to Netball' campaign, netball participation has not really grown, only stayed where it was. This suggests any recruitment into the sport is being offset by those leaving. Field hockey participation has nearly halved over a 5-year period, and there has also been a decline in Rugby Union, Rugby League, and Cricket. There is no doubt that it is an awkward picture for those in charge. Managing how to make these traditional sports fit into the lives of people who want to participate when they want, with whom they want, and for how long they want may be the key. Interestingly, the data collected by Sport England in *Active Lives* also sought to understand the motivations people had for taking part in any sport, PA, or PR. Most participants strongly agreed or agreed that motivations for taking part were enjoyment, the opportunity to be physically active, feeling they had the ability, feeling guilty when they do not take part, and because it is important to participate regularly. Most disagreed or strongly disagreed that a motivation for taking part was to not let someone else down. It is a further indication that being part of a team is becoming less of a reason for why people participate.

As noted in Chapter 7, volunteering remains a necessity for the provision of sport, PA, and PR. Indeed, 21.3% of the population volunteered in some capacity within the past 12 months, with 33.9% of those having volunteered for over five years, 28.7% volunteering for between two and five years, and 37.4% volunteering for under two years. Volunteering plays such a vital role that managing volunteers is a job in itself. Volunteers underpin most sport, PA, and PR clubs, which are still popular. Just over 40% of the population participate in sport, PA, or PR through a club (when measured as at least twice in the past 28 days). These clubs would not exist without the dedication of volunteers. But, at the same time, there is some evidence in the latest data that volunteering can help reduce things like loneliness and help with overall wellbeing.

Most of the evidence available on sports participation in England is for adults; however, the data from *Active Lives* now also include some questions for those aged 5–16, which gives a wider insight into sport, PA, and PR over the life course. In Table 9.5, the top 20 activities (undertaken at least once a week) are shown for three age groups. First are children at infant school age (ages 5–7), then junior school age (ages 7–11) and, finally, those who are secondary school age (ages 11–16).

So what can we glean from this data? Taking one theme from this chapter, the role of team and organised sports appears to be different at different stages of the school cycle. In the early years of school (infant school) there are ten activities that can be considered organised

Table 9.5 **Top 21 Activities Undertaken in Leisure Time by Children and Young People by School Age**

Infant school	Junior school	Secondary school
Walking to get to school or other places	Playing it, tag, chase, sardines, or other running games	Walking to get to school or other places
Playing it, tag, chase, sardines, or other running games	Walking to get to school or other places	Going on a walk
Going on a walk	Running, jogging, cross-country, the Daily Mile	Football
Climbing or swinging in the playground, garden, or park	Football	Kicking a ball about

Infant school	Junior school	Secondary school
Dance	Kicking a ball about	Running, jogging, cross-country, the Daily Mile
Swimming (and diving)	Dance	Dance
Kicking a ball about	Going on a walk	Cycling for fun or fitness
Riding a scooter	Swimming (and diving)	Playing it, tag, chase, sardines, or other running games
Cycling for fun or fitness	Cycling for fun or fitness	Trampolining (including in a garden, at a trampoline centre, or as part of a club)
Football	Trampolining (including in a garden, at a trampoline centre, or as part of a club)	Basketball
Trampolining (including in a garden, at a trampoline centre, or as part of a club)	Basketball	Swimming (and diving)
Running, jogging, cross-country, the Daily Mile	Gymnastics	Cycling to get to school or other places
Gymnastics	Climbing or swinging in the playground, garden, or park	Rugby
Frisbee, throwing and catching, or skipping	Riding a scooter	Netball
Judo, karate, taekwondo, and other martial arts	Frisbee, throwing and catching, or skipping	Badminton
Cycling to get to school or other places	Dodgeball and benchball	Boxing
Tennis	Cycling to get to school or other places	Dodgeball and benchball
Climbing (including indoors)	Rugby	Climbing or swinging in the playground, garden, or park
Skateboarding, roller skating, blading	Netball	Hockey
Dodgeball and benchball	Tennis	Gymnastics

Source: Sport England

on some level (dance, swimming and diving, football, trampolining, running, gymnastics, various martial arts, tennis, climbing, and dodgeball or benchball), with only football being a competitive team sport. By the next stage (junior school) rugby, basketball, and netball appear as the impact of the school curriculum is seen with climbing and the martial arts dropping out. By secondary school, 13 of the activities are organised activities and, by this point, field hockey and badminton have been added to rugby, basketball, football, and netball in the competitive team sport genre. It shows that over the course of time in schools, students are moved to more traditional forms of physical activity and sports. Of course, the glaring questions is, how reflective is this of the pupils' wider lives and the activities they *want* to do in their leisure time? There seems a disconnect between activities undertaken at school age and activities we choose to undertake when we leave school and head into later life.

Discussion Question

What are the consequences for leisure if school-based sport and physical activity curriculum does not match the sport, physical activity, and recreation that people choose to undertake later in their life?

It has long been argued that the fall in participation rates among young people when they leave education represents significant lost potential for leisure in the UK, and government has spent considerable policy effort and funding trying to reduce the post-school drop-out. For the first time, however, *Active Lives* data show the activities that young people do inside and outside of school. A summary of this is provided in Table 9.6.

Table 9.6 During School Hours or Outside of School Hours Participation by Activity (Years 7–11)

In school		Out of school	
Walking to get to school or other places	35.80%	Walking to get to school or other places	44.10%
Football	27.60%	Going on a walk	30.20%
Kicking a ball about	25.90%	Kicking a ball about	28.30%
Going on a walk	23.40%	Football	28.30%
Running, jogging, cross-country, the Daily Mile	21.40%	Running, jogging, cross-country, the Daily Mile	23.70%
Dance	16.10%	Dance	19.10%
Playing it, tag, chase, sardines, or other running games	16.10%	Cycling for fun or fitness	18.90%
Cycling for fun or fitness	14.90%	Playing it, tag, chase, sardines, or other running games	16.90%

In school		Out of school	
Basketball	12.50%	Trampolining (including in a garden, at a trampoline centre, or as part of a club)	13.10%
Trampolining (including in a garden, at a trampoline centre, or as part of a club)	11.00%	Basketball	11.10%
Netball	8.60%	Swimming (and diving)	10.30%
Cycling to get to school or other places	8.40%	Cycling to get to school or other places	10.00%
Rugby	8.30%	Rugby	7.80%
Swimming (and diving)	7.40%	Netball	7.10%
Badminton	7.10%	Boxing	7.10%
Dodgeball and benchball	6.60%	Climbing or swinging in the playground, garden, or park	6.20%
Boxing	5.70%	Badminton	6.10%
Hockey	5.60%	Gymnastics	5.40%
Climbing or swinging in the playground, garden, or park	4.70%	Dodgeball and benchball	4.90%
Gymnastics	4.60%	Frisbee, throwing and catching, or skipping	4.50%

Source: Sport England

The policy has centred on achieving a consistent 'five-hour offer' nationally, i.e. two hours a week of high-quality physical education plus three hours a week of high-quality extra-curricular opportunities. In recent years, in the UK, this policy effort has extended to include primary schools through the establishment of the PE and sport premium. According to the government at the time, in 2019, primary schools were given around £320 million in government funding 'to make additional and sustainable improvements to the quality of the PE, physical activity and sport offered through their core budgets'.

9.5 The Administration of Sport in the UK

The structures for administering and delivering sport in the UK are complex, but it is important for sports managers to know what organisational networks can help them with information or funding. They can be structured according to four levels:

1   National (government);
2   National (non-government);

3 Regional;
4 Local.

Even at the national level there are a multitude of relevant organisations, both government and non-government, as shown in Table 9.7.

9.5.1 National Organisations

Although the principal UK government department responsible for sport is the Department of Digital, Culture, Media, and Sport (DCMS), several other central government departments are relevant to sport, PA, and PR. These include those responsible for health, children, schools, further education, higher education, local government, criminal justice, and

Table 9.7 **Examples of National Sports Organisations in the UK**

UK government department	Department for Digital, Culture, Media, and Sport
Non-departmental public bodies	UK Sports Council
	Sport England
	SportScotland
	Sport Wales
	Sports Northern Ireland
	English Institute for Sport
	SportScotland Institute of Sport
	Welsh Institute of Sport
	Sports Institute Northern Ireland
	UK Anti Doping
Independent non-government organisations	British Olympic Association
	British Paralympic Association
	Football Foundation
	UK Coaching
	Women's Sports Foundation
	Youth Sport Trust
	National Governing Bodies of Sport
'Umbrella' organisations	Sport and Recreation Alliance
	Scottish Sports Association
	Welsh Sports Association
	Northern Ireland Sports Forum
Professional associations	Chartered Institute for the Management of Sport and Physical Activity
	Chief Cultural and Leisure Officers Association
	UK Active

transport. This reflects the fact that sport, PA, and PR contribute to a number of cross-cutting agendas within government.

There are also several non-departmental public bodies (NDPBs), funded by government and with sport in their remit. Sports councils, as an example, are considerable sources of funding for leisure managers for specific programmes. A good example is the £160,000 of funding Sport England has given to International Mixed Ability Sport since 2016. Away from participation, national sports institutes help the country's top sportsmen and women to win medals in major tournaments like the Olympics, the Commonwealth Games, and world championships in different sports. Aiding the development of national facilities, for example, helps athletes in their pursuit of success. The National Cycling Centre, Manchester; the eight English Institute of Sport sites across England; and a network of facilities under the banner of 'St Georges Park' provide high-quality opportunities for elite and improving sportspeople, but many also have access for community groups, so they represent high-profile opportunities for leisure managers in nearby locations. National sports organisations are constitutionally independent of government. They are not-for-profit organisations; most are charitable and rely on funding from member clubs. However, some national sports organisations like UK Coaching receive a substantial proportion of their funds from government. Next, individual sports are run by independent governing bodies, the majority of which are 'recognised' national governing bodies (NGBs). Some NGBs have a UK structure, some a GB structure, and most are constituted separately in England, Wales, Scotland, and Northern Ireland. Many of the major NGBs receive substantial funds from the government via the national sports councils. Any leisure manager organising development in specific sports should develop a close relationship with the appropriate NGBs.

9.5.2 Regional Organisations

In England there were nine Regional Sports Boards (RSBs), grant-aided by Sport England; however, these were disbanded in 2009. This means that Active Partnerships (previously known as County Sport Partnerships) are probably the most prevalent regional organisations in sport, PA, and PR. There are currently 42 Active Partnerships in England, and they work with national and local organisations to 'join up' the approach to increasing activity levels. Their position regionally means they provide an in-depth understanding of the needs of the local communities and focus on the groups in communities who are not active.

9.5.3 Local Organisations

Local organisations are at the heart of sport, PA, and PR provision in the UK, and probably sports clubs and local authorities are the most significant. For example, around three-quarters of sport facilities in the UK are local authority owned. That being said, there is an increasing trend for facilities to be owned by sport and leisure trusts. These organisations are not-for-profit but allow local authorities to outsource the running of facilities. The trusts aim to make some profit; however, these profits are reinvested back into the facilities.

9.6 Why Are Sport, Physical Activity, and Physical Recreation Important?

Today, governments play a crucial role in terms of policy, sponsored agencies, and funding of sport, PA, and PR. In the main, this is because of the supposed associated benefits that participation accrues for individuals and society. For governments around the world it is seen as a 'win-win' situation. Sport, PA, and PR can help address wider social issues and, at the same time, government ministers appear in touch and current because of their interest in sport. Let us turn to the following case study of the European Union to help illustrate this.

CASE STUDY 9.2

The European Union and Sport

By their own admission, the European Union (EU) are in favour of using sport for wider social goals. They claim that 'sport represents an integral part of the lives of millions of Europeans'. For this reason, it is seen as a tool that can be used for 'social good'. The EU also claim that 'sport builds community cohesion, grows social inclusion and leads to an enhanced sense of European identity. Sport is also a key facet of . . . European economies; the sector employs millions of European citizens and adds billions in revenue'. For this reason, the EU have developed and maintains several initiatives including:

   BeActive Awards: These were created to support projects and individuals dedicated
      to promoting sport and physical activity across Europe.
   BeInclusive EU Sport Awards: Every year, the European Commission awards
      organisations whose work recognises the power of sport to improve social
      inclusion for disadvantaged groups.
   European Week of Sport: Levels of physical activity are currently stagnating, and
      even declining, in some member states. The European Week of Sport aims to
      respond to this challenge.
   EU Sport Forum: This is a European Commission-led initiative and supports a
      yearly event – it brings together policy makers, private enterprise, educational
      and other experts to discuss challenges, opportunities, and the future of sport
      in the EU.
   Erasmus+ Sport Info Day: A conference, the aim of Erasmus+ Sport Info Day is to
      allow important policies in this field to be translated into concrete actions on the
      ground. It is a day for disseminating information on procedures, best practice,
      common mistakes, and engaging in debate around sport.
   SHARE initiative: The SHARE initiative is designed to increase knowledge
      surrounding the role of sport and physical activity, specifically in relation to
      regional and local development. In doing this, the initiative aims to ensure that
      sport and PA is part of policy and investment decision-making at European,
      national, and regional levels.
   HealthyLifestyle4All initiative: This is a campaign run over two years to link sport
      and active lifestyles with health, food, and other policies. It sheds light on the
      European Commission's commitment to promoting healthy lifestyles for all.

As well as these initiatives, the EU also provides a role in governance of sport, physical activity, and physical recreation. There is an understanding that sport organisations are autonomous, however, the EU promotes compliance among member states and the organisations that underpin sport, physical activity, and physical recreation. In particular, the EU promote democracy, transparency, accountability in decision-making, and inclusiveness in the representation of interested parties.

Like the EU, the UK has a long history of using participation in sport, PA, and PR for wider social goals. Indeed, 60 years ago, the Wolfenden Report (Lord Wolfenden, 1960) identified the need for a Sports Council, which was established 1965. Three other national councils followed, for Scotland, Wales, and Northern Ireland. Similarly, in 1973, the Select Committee of the House of Lords on Sport and Leisure (House of Lords, 1973) called for action to remedy deficiencies in sporting opportunities, claiming:

> The state should not opt out of caring for people's leisure when it accepts the responsibility of caring for most of their other needs. The provision of opportunities for the enjoyment of leisure is part of the general fabric of the social services.
>
> (House of Lords, 1973)

At a similar time, central government pushed the notion that sport and leisure opportunities could help to alleviate anti-social behaviour and many ills of the world. This belief was documented in *Policy for the Inner Cities* (Department of the Environment, 1977) and the report of the Scarman Inquiry into riots in Brixton, London (Scarman, 1981). Perhaps the next notable development came some 15 years later when, in November 1994, the National Lottery was launched, which turned out to be one of the most influential decisions ever made for the sustained development of sport and physical recreation in the UK. A year later, *Sport: Raising the Game* (Department of National Heritage, 1995) was published by the conservative government of the time, placing emphasis on using traditional sport, in particular in schools, to help build character and teach the values needed for society to work. Following a landslide election win, New Labour sought an opportunity to build on the work of John Major and his government when they released *A Sporting Future for All* in 2000. Despite paying some attention to elite sport, this document had more of a focus on 'sport for all' ideals and how participation could assist in communities, teach morals, and improve health. Not two years later, another national sport policy was delivered, and *Game Plan*, published by New Labour in 2002, paid no less attention to the wider role of sport. In fact, it placed more emphasis on it. *Game Plan* included aspects of physical activity and not just sport, stressing the role that participation can play in improving health, reducing crime, increasing social inclusion, raising employment, and helping with attainment at school. *Game Plan* echoed the wider 'joined up government' approach taken by New Labour and encouraged the use of sport, PA, and PR to help address wider government agendas. Importantly, seeking funding from other departments such as health, justice, and communities was seen as reasonable for those involved in sport, PA, and PR. These moves by successive governments heightened the importance of sport, PA, and PR in government. While in and of itself participation in any of these three areas was seen as important, it was the increasing emphasis on tackling wider social problems through sport, PA, and PR that moved it up government agendas. However, this is only part of the story.

The evidence that sport, PA, and PR can tackle wider social issues such as crime, health, social exclusion, inequality, education, and employment is weak, or mixed at best. The work of Geoff Nichols on crime, Mike Week on health, and Fred Coalter on all aspects of society are given as further reading from this chapter and are well worth your time. In short, it is far too simplistic to link leisure participation in sport, PA, and PR to improvements in wider societal issues. Take sport (as defined at the start of this chapter) as an example, which, as data presented in this chapter highlight, can be both inclusionary and exclusionary. Access to sport for those who are from minority ethnic backgrounds, those with an impairment, and those from lower social classes is difficult. So how can we use sport to 'bridge' between communities, classes, and ethnicities? Sport can be good for health, but it also has negative impacts on health through injury. This more balanced view creates something of a problem for leisure managers and those working in sectors that use sport, PA, and PR. It does, however, give an opportunity for those in the sector to think differently about how sport, PA, and PR are delivered. What works for who? When does it work? Why does it work? What is clear is that re-branding sport, PA, and PR but delivering the same product will simply maintain the status quo.

> ### Discussion Question
>
> Taking the three definitions from the start of this chapter, in what ways will sport, physical activity, and physical recreation fit in with the lives of the different groups discussed in this chapter and why?

9.7 Conclusions

The 'power of sport' has long been used as a justification for government involvement in sport. However, studies into the claims made on behalf of sport show a much more complex picture, and claims that increasing sport participation will improve society are far too simplistic. It is for this reason that those involved in leisure are better off conceptualising sport, physical activity, and physical recreation as different things. They are, by their very nature, different activities and as such will suit different people and have different consequences. Taken in their entirety, participation rates have stayed stable, however, this hides some more nuanced trends. A move to more informal, less time bound, and less serious physical activities and recreation are replacing more traditional forms of sport. Sport, physical activity, and physical recreation are delivered by a complicated network of organisations, but responding to the changing appetite for sport, physical activity, and leisure is key for these organisations if the sector is to remain relevant in the eyes of government, policy makers, and, of course, funders.

> ### Practical Tasks
>
> 1 Find five people you know. Ask them about the activities they do in their spare time. How does this compare with the activities they did when they were young? What are some of the reasons they have changed activities?

Structured Guide to Further Reading

Coalter, F. (2007). *A Wider Social Role for Sport: Who's Keeping the Score?* Routledge, Oxon.

Nichols, G. (2007). *Sport and Crime Reduction: The Role of Sports in Tackling Youth Crime*, 1st edition. Routledge. https://doi.org/10.4324/9780203089156

Weed, M. (2016). Should we privilege sport for health? The comparative effectiveness of UK Government investment in sport as a public health intervention. *International Journal of Sport Policy and Politics*, 8(4), 559–576. doi:10.1080/19406940.2016.1235600

Useful Websites

https://activelives.sportengland.org/
www.eis2win.co.uk/
www.mixedabilitysports.org/
www.sport.wales/
www.sportengland.org/
www.sportireland.ie/
https://sportscotland.org.uk/
www.ukcoaching.org/
www.uksport.gov.uk/

References

Carter, P. (2005). *Review of National Sport Effort and Resources.* DCMS, London. Retrieved from www.culture.gov.uk/images/publications/Carter_report.pdf.
Department of National Heritage. (1995). *Sport: Raising the Game.* Department of National Heritage, London.
Department of the Environment. (1977). *Policy for the Inner Cities,* Cmnd 6845. HMSO, London.
Gratton, C., & Solberg, H. A. (2007). *The Economics of Sports Broadcasting.* Routledge, London and New York.
Henderson, K. A., & Bialeschki, M. D. (1994). Women and the meanings of physical recreation. *Women in Sport & Physical Activity Journal,* 3(2), 21
House of Lords. (1973). *Second Report from the Select Committee of the House of Lords on Sport and Leisure.* HMSO, London.
Lord Wolfenden. (1960). *Report of the Wolfenden Committee on Sport, Sport and the Community.* Central Council for Physical Recreation, London.
Piggin, J. (2020). What is physical activity? A holistic definition for teachers, researchers and policy makers. *Frontiers in Sports and Active Living,* 2(72). doi:10.3389/fspor.2020.00072
Scarman, L. (1981). *For the Home Office, the Brixton Disorders: First Report of An Inquiry,* Cmnd 8427. HMSO, London, 25 November.
Sport and Recreation Alliance. (2021). *Our Strategy 2021–25.* SRA Publishing, London.

Chapter 10

Leisure in the Home

In This Chapter

- How is leisure in the home relevant to leisure management?
- How significant is spending on leisure in the home?
- What drives the growth and change in home entertainment?
- How important are DIY and gardening?
- How are hobbies and pastimes changing?
- Is gambling at home a problem or an opportunity?

DOI: 10.4324/9780367823610-10

Summary

Leisure in the home includes some of the most vibrant parts of the leisure market, none more so than home entertainment. It is often simplified as 'watching television' because of the amount of time we spend doing this; however, there is a lot more to it than that, and the developments it contains offer important lessons to the whole of the leisure industry – including the speed of adoption of technological change, the use of contemporary media, the importance of the pricing decision, the transformation of consumers' spending behaviour, and the simplification of consumer choices. Moreover, leisure in the home is not now confined to the home – technology allows us to take television viewing, listening to music, gambling, and playing computer games on our travels. Governments have a potentially important regulatory role in leisure in the home, particularly in organising broadcasting and media infrastructures. In recent years increasing pressure for regulation of social media has emerged, which is a way in which we meet our friends virtually – something that was almost unheard of 20 years ago.

10.1 Introduction

What is leisure in the home doing in a book about leisure management? Well, leisure in the home may not be managed directly, but indirectly it is supported by, and the target of, considerable business interests. Table 10.1 shows the leisure activities people did in their homes in the UK between 2019 and 2020, and many of these activities are fed by large industries that make them possible. Although leisure in the home might appear at first sight to be beyond the remit of management, in fact very similar management principles apply to the industries that service leisure in the home as to industries providing leisure out of the home. The only major difference is that the customer is remote from the industry, so direct personal service is less of a feature (but it is still often an element, e.g. home deliveries or virtual contact).

Table 10.1 Activities People Do in Their Spare Time at Home in the UK 2019–2020, by Age

	18–24	25–34	35–44	45–54	55–64	65 or older
Listening to music/radio	64%	63%	59%	60%	55%	46%
Watching television	56%	65%	65%	69%	68%	69%
Cooking and baking	47%	55%	54%	52%	49%	43%
Playing video games	43%	34%	27%	20%	16%	17%
Surfing websites	33%	39%	37%	34%	31%	31%

	18–24	25–34	35–44	45–54	55–64	65 or older
Reading books	32%	47%	51%	51%	53%	54%
Arts and crafts	31%	30%	30%	26%	27%	23%
Photography	30%	23%	19%	16%	16%	18%
Home DIY	25%	32%	30%	31%	29%	28%
Solving puzzles, e.g. crosswords, Sudoku, jigsaws	24%	32%	34%	33%	38%	47%
Entertaining others at home	23%	28%	23%	22%	18%	12%
Playing a musical instrument	15%	9%	7%	6%	6%	4%
Sewing, knitting, dress making	12%	16%	17%	19%	28%	26%
Gardening	11%	22%	26%	34%	42%	47%
Computer programming	10%	9%	8%	6%	5%	7%
Car/motorbike mechanics and maintenance	9%	8%	8%	6%	6%	7%
Reading newspapers	7%	12%	14%	16%	19%	34%
Collecting (e.g. stamps, magazines)	6%	6%	5%	5%	5%	6%
Model building (e.g. train, airplanes, etc.)	6%	6%	5%	3%	3%	5%
Astronomy	6%	6%	6%	5%	5%	4%
None of the above	3%	3%	3%	2%	2%	3%

Source: Dunnhumby Beyond

Discussion Question

Does leisure in the home need 'managing'?

10.2 Spending on Leisure in the Home

Leisure in the home is worth a lot to the economy. For example, in the UK in 2019, £4.7 billion was spent on various TV subscriptions, licences, and watching films at home, and the industry surrounding 'takeaway' food reached £5.6 billion. Table 10.2 documents data from the Office for National Statistics from 2019 on the amount each household spends, on average, per week on a range of leisure activities in the home. Spending on food dominates, and the rise of delivery services, such as Deliveroo, UBER Eats, and Just Eat have contributed to this – it has never been easier to get food delivered. After this comes home entertainment in

Table 10.2 **Spending on Leisure at Home in the UK, 2019**

Pets and pet food	£5.80
Other takeaway and snacks	£5.60
Takeaway meals eaten at home	£5.40
TV, satellite subscription, TV licenses	£4.50
TV, video, and computers	£3.50
Gardening equipment and plants	£3.20
Games, toys, and hobbies	£2.90
All gambling (in and out of home)	£2.60
Newspapers	£1.40
Books	£1.20
Computer software and games	£1.00
Audio equipment and accessories	£1.00
Magazines and periodicals	£0.60

Source: Office for National Statistics

the form of TV, film, and computers. Finally, there is, towards the bottom, a group that can come under the heading of 'reading' which includes newspapers, magazines, and books.

10.3 Changes in the Home Leisure Market

As was noted in Chapter 3, there have been changes in consumer spending in leisure in the home markets over time. For example, in the UK, revenue from entertainment retail increased from £5.5 billion in 2005 to 7.8 billion in 2019. The amount people were spending per year on DIY increased by £2 billion between 2008 and 2018, and there was a sharp increase in the revenue from digital book sales to just over £700 million by 2018. Indeed, revenue from book sales climbed from £3.1 billion in 2008 to £3.75 billion in 2019. But there are some other trends to examine when we look at in-home leisure spending. By 2021, for example, the takeaway food market was predicted to be worth over £11 billion. However, interestingly, the proportion of the population who claim to have eaten a takeaway in the past week in the UK has remained relatively stable at circa 30% to 35%, suggesting those who do eat takeaways are spending more. Listening to music remains popular, but the trend is towards spending less on physical copies of CDs and records and more on digital subscriptions. In 2005, the UK spent around £38 million on digital forms of music; this was £280 million in 2020, according to the Entertainment Retailers Association. Since the last edition of this book, technological advances mean we no longer need to purchase videos or DVDs; we can watch video 'on demand' (VOD). Spending on VOD increased between 2007 and 2014 to a peak of around £150 million per year. In each subsequent year, the spending on VOD has dropped and, in 2019, it was below 2007 levels at £85 million (offset by subscriptions to film viewing platforms like Netflix). We can also access video games in the same way. Consumer spending on digital consoles and online games in the UK has increased from £890 million in 2013 to just under £2.4 billion in 2020. Another popular pastime is reading, and consumer spending has increased here too – again with more digital downloading available. For DIY, it has been a mixed picture over the past ten years or so. Revenue of DIY stores rose between 2008 and 2011 to a turnover of £7.5 billion, but it then fell sharply in 2012. Since then revenue has been recovering slowly and in 2018 was £7.1 billion, with more purchases online. Indeed, the past ten years or so have seen an increase in the number of shops relating to clothes, food, music, reading, and other leisure activities that are *only* online. Capgemini reports that in 2011, in the UK, spending in retail online was £68 billion; by 2019 that figure was £178 billion. Of course, not all this increase has come from leisure; for example, buying essential groceries online has increased, as has buying cleaning products or personal hygiene products. However, data from the ONS presented in Table 10.3 show that, not only is 'retail therapy' from the home now considered a leisure activity, but much of that spending goes towards other aspects of leisure in the home.

Table 10.3 **Most Popular Goods Purchased Online in Great Britain, 2020**

Clothes (including sports clothing), shoes, and accessories	55%
Deliveries from restaurants, fast-food chains, or catering services	32%
Printed books, magazines, or newspapers	29%
Furniture, home accessories, or gardening products	28%
Computers, tablets, mobile phones, or accessories	24%
Children's toys or childcare items	22%
Cosmetics, beauty, or wellness products	22%
Cleaning products or personal hygiene products	18%
Consumer electronics; for example TVs, stereos, cameras, or household appliances	18%
Sports goods (excluding sports clothing)	17%
Food or beverages from stores or from meal-kit providers	13%
Medicine or dietary supplements such as vitamins	13%
Physical copies of films or series	13%
Physical copies of music	12%
Bicycles, mopeds, cars, or other vehicles or their spare parts	8%

Source: Office for National Statistics

> **Discussion Question**
>
> What are the implications for leisure managers of an increasing amount of leisure being available online and, as a result, in the home?

10.4 Reading

Newspapers and magazines are in general decline in the UK, although there is a mixed picture in other countries. The reasons for such a decline are probably a mixture of, first, increasing competition from television (e.g. 24-hour news channels), radio, and particularly the internet and second, rising prices of newspapers and magazines (largely because of the costs of raw materials). Data from Ofcom show that, in 2005, people in the UK reported they spend on average 9.9 hours a week on the internet. Over the following 15 years, that increased year on year up to 2020, when people reported an average of 24.9 hours a week on the internet. The teenage magazine market has suffered particularly, because this is the age group most likely to use the internet for a range of reasons but especially for social networking.

The market for books, like other markets, has become a sales battleground between the traditional retail outlets, supermarkets, and the internet, once again illustrating the importance of the pricing decision. Supermarkets can discount bestselling books to a greater extent than traditional bookshops can afford, sometimes as 'loss leaders' to attract customers, whilst the internet offers the convenience of shopping from home.

CASE STUDY 10.1

Harry Potter Books

The *Harry Potter* series of books was a publishing phenomenon. Each issue in the series coincided with growth in overall book sales in the UK, and the economic cycle in books there became dependent on the *Harry Potter* publication dates. The final book of the series surpassed all previous book launches, with simultaneous releases in 90 countries in July 2007, and joint UK and US sales topped 11 million in the first 24 hours. This exceeded the achievements of the sixth book in the series, which sold 9 million copies in the first 24 hours in the UK and USA. Prior to the final book, cumulative sales worldwide exceeded 325 million, in 63 different languages.

The *Harry Potter* books have transformed their publisher, Bloomsbury, from a small company to a significant player in the industry, demonstrating the power of a successful product. The books also illustrate the struggle taking place in book retailing internationally between traditional booksellers, supermarkets, and the internet. Asda heavily discounted the final *Harry Potter* book (£5 each) in the UK, selling nearly all its 500,000 copies in the first 24 hours. Amazon, meanwhile, had 2.2 million orders worldwide. Traditional bookshops became resigned to losing the bulk of sales to their competitive rivals, hoping instead to benefit from a general increase in reading by children.

It is claimed that the *Harry Potter* books not only were a reason for the success of the book industry in the last decade, but they also introduced a whole generation of new children to reading books for pleasure, particularly boys, who are characterised more by their IT literacy than reading. A survey in Australia found a significant proportion of children were more interested in reading after reading the *Harry Potter* books and had since read several other titles. The books they read after *Harry Potter* encompassed a wide range of genres and titles and included fantasy, fairy tales, science fiction, historical fiction, realistic fiction, and reference books.

In the UK, a survey by the book retailer Waterstones suggested that children and teachers alike believe that *Harry Potter* has had a significant impact on children's literacy levels. Almost six out of ten children surveyed said that *Harry Potter* books had helped them improve their reading skills, and nearly half said that *Harry Potter* books made them want to read more books. Over eight out of ten teachers said that *Harry Potter* had a positive impact on children's reading abilities, and nearly seven out of ten teachers said that *Harry Potter* had helped turn non-readers into readers.

An interesting development in the reading market is electronic reading, which allows for e-books to be consumed on tablet devices, mobile phones, or specific e-book devices. Table 10.4 shows consumer book sales revenue in selected countries worldwide in 2018. In the UK and the USA, more revenue was generated from e-books.

This has had profound implications on where consumers purchase their books, if not on how much we read. In 2018, in a survey of people who regularly use e-books, Ofcom found that 69% of respondents had used Amazon in the past three months to stream/access or share e-books through the internet. Notwithstanding the next site was Waterstones, which is recognised for selling books, only 13% had used the site, and the next most popular service was Apple's iTunes/iBookstore/AppStore. The pace of change in this area is such that, while in the last edition of this book, e-readers were something of a new phenomenon, by 2020, they had become considerably cheaper and, most notably, Sony had decided not to make any new versions of their e-reader. So, what is the current picture? In the UK the number of the population who own an e-reader sits at around 30%, and in the USA, it was at around 20% in 2016 but with signs of a big increase over the next four years. Between 2011 and 2019 the number of adults in the USA who had read a book on an e-reader or tablet rose slightly from 17% to 25% and, importantly, this was in a context where the percentage of the population who said they had read a book in any format dropped slightly. The percentage of the population who

Table 10.4 **Revenue in Billion US Dollars**

	Printed and audio books	*E-Books*
United States	7.94	8.69
Japan	6.18	1.93
Germany	6.05	0.78
China	4.01	0.38
Italy	2.35	0.39
Great Britain	1.41	1.45

Source: Office for National Statistics

listened to audio books also increased over this period from 11% to 20%. But there is some evidence to the contrary too. The average annual expenditure on digital book readers in the USA is declining. It peaked at just over $30 in 2013 and has been declining year on year. In 2019 the figure sat at $19. So, while more people seem to be using e-reader devices, we do not spend as much on books to read on them. In the USA, this has resulted in e-book sales revenue remaining relatively stable. As a side note, with respect to Case Study 10.1, in 2019 the third most popular book for download in the USA was *Harry Potter and the Sorcerer's Stone*.

Discussion Question

Have you bought or would you buy an electronic reader? Discuss the reasons why or why not.

10.5 Home Entertainment

Home entertainment is the electronic hardware which is increasingly prevalent in leisure in the home, i.e. watching television, streaming music, and the use of tablets and phones for leisure purposes. It is the largest sub-sector of leisure in the home but also has seen significant changes over time, largely because of changes in technology.

10.5.1 Television

The television market has been significantly influenced by technological changes throughout its history, and the past ten years have been no different. Indeed, in the UK, Netflix is now the most popular watched 'channel' (if channels exist anymore), which is an online platform that did not appear until 1997. The competition between terrestrial, satellite, cable TV, and online platforms like Netflix has resulted in an upsurge in choice for the consumer. To add some context, in 2006, revenue from online TV viewing was around £11 million in the UK, and by 2020 it was over £3.8 billion. In that time, there has also been an expansion of the channels that are free to watch via digital.

There is an argument that one consequence of greater competition is on the quality of TV productions, i.e. the effects of limited budgets outweighing any high-quality programme aspirations. On the other hand there is an argument that greater competition among TV channels and production companies should drive standards higher, not lower. This 'cost versus quality' dilemma, i.e. seeking high quality and lower cost at the same time, or attempting an appropriate compromise between the two, is quite common in leisure markets (e.g. hotels, holidays) and is an important consideration for leisure managers.

Discussion Question

Does increased competition and choice in television supply mean that quality of programmes is falling?

In a trend that echoes other sectors of leisure (for example, physical activity), the way we consume TV has shifted. This is encapsulated in the latest Ofcom report into viewing, which suggests, on average, people in the UK 'watch' TV for 5 hours and 40 minutes per day. However, less than half (47%) of that viewing is live TV, and that is reducing. Subscription video on demand (for example, Netflix and Amazon Prime), broadcaster video on demand (for example, BBC iPlayer, ITV Hub, and 4OD), YouTube, playback of recorded shows, and watching via games consoles are now more popular than ever and show that there has been a diversification in how we access TV. So, not only have the choices increased, but consumers are able to access what they want when they want via a device that suits them. It is a further example of leisure adapting to fit into the lives of those who consume it. This shift has also changed the way commercial TV broadcasters generate funding. Between 2016 and 2020, for example, revenue from online video advertising rose from £0.5 billion to £1.3 billion, and revenue from subscriptions increased from £0.9 billion to £2.1 billion. This offset a reduction in revenue from more traditional streams like commercial public service broadcasters. This is a further indication that consumers will spend on leisure if it offers the product they want and if that product requires flexibility and choice.

CASE STUDY 10.2

Football and Television

Broadcasting and sport have had a close relationship for a long time. As ownership of first radios and then televisions became universal in more developed countries, so sport became an important feature of broadcasting. In the UK, the BBC dominated sports broadcasting for a long time, and consequently sport received little financial reward for being broadcast. The arrival of ITV in 1955 ended the BBC's monopoly in the purchasing of broadcasting rights, and competition and fees increased gradually until the 1990s.

In 1992, BSkyB entered the competition for the broadcasting rights for Premier League football in England and brought a much more competitive ethos. Whilst ITV, a free to air terrestrial channel, had paid £44 million in rights fees in 1988 for four years of live first-division football coverage, BSkyB paid £191.5 million in rights fees in 1992 for five years of live Premier League football coverage. Fifteen years later, BSkyB and Setanta together paid £1,700 million for three years' rights (Gratton & Solberg, 2007). They paid such historically high sums because they calculated there would be sufficient increases in subscriptions and therefore subsequent advertising revenues. However, this was not the case for Setanta, which later went out of business.

Football is a key driver for television subscriptions. BSkyB's total subscriber numbers in the UK and Ireland rose from 3.9 million in 1994 to 6.9 million in 1998. Out of the latter, 2.7 million (nearly 40%) were subscribers to one of more of Sky Sports channels. Of these, 82% regularly watched football, and for 47% football was their favourite sport to watch (Gratton & Taylor, 2000). When asked in research what the main reason was for subscribing to Sky Sports channels, 40% answered sport, 10% answered football, whilst 5% identified live Premier League football. Other sports were each identified by less than 1% of subscribers (Monopolies and Mergers Commission, 1999). It is now more difficult to isolate the subscriptions to Sky by sport, as they have changed the way they package their channels, but in the second quarter of 2021, Sky had 23.2 million subscribers in total. Sport, and in particular football, remains high value to Sky in driving that subscription number.

It is not only BSkyB that has benefited from broadcasting live Premier League football. The distribution of the higher television revenues to Premier League clubs meant that it became a very significant proportion of most clubs' income. In 1996–1997, for example, income from BSkyB's television coverage represented 20% or more of total revenue for 11 out of the 20 Premier League clubs (Gratton & Taylor, 2000). By 2021, some Premier League clubs' television revenue accounts for 60–70% of revenue, and the value of that revenue to the clubs is worth roughly £100 million per year. Growth in the overseas broadcasting market and the future potential of streaming services at club level may change the landscape (and revenue position) of football and broadcasting in the future.

The move to more subscription-based TV is something that has occurred in other countries around the world, although at different rates. Data collected in 2020 for example showed that, on average, in the USA for every 100 households there were 104 TV subscriptions – that is more than one per house, of course. In China the number was 94 TV subscriptions for every 100 houses; in Canada, 82; in Turkey, 71; in Argentina, 69; and in Chile, 59.

10.5.2 Radio and Podcasts

Listening to the radio is a very popular form of home entertainment in many countries including the UK. For those who do listen to the radio, the amount of time spent listening has remained steady over the past ten years or so – it is around 20 hours a week. It also seems that roughly the same amount of people area is 'reached' by radio in 2021 as in 2010, just under 50 million people. By far the most popular place to listen to the radio is at home, and the national broadcaster, the BBC, is, by some distance, the most listened to. This stability does mask some more complex changes in the sector. For example, listening on demand, just like watching on demand, is on the rise. However, radio has held more live listeners than TV has held live viewers. Around 70% of radio listening is to live broadcasts in the UK. Although listening on demand has increased in radio, this has only been marginal, rather the expansion has come from the increasing popularity of podcasts, which were only really developed at the turn of the century. Podcasts, which are audio files that can be downloaded and opened whenever the listener wants, are listened to by around a quarter of the population in the UK and are most popular when people are commuting, doing housework, or driving. In that regard, they could have been included for leisure inside or outside the home. Perhaps the most noteworthy aspect of podcasts are the devices used for listening. Mobile phones, smart speakers, and laptops are the most popular medium through which podcasts are consumed, and this further emphasises a point made earlier. Several leisure activities have morphed in a way that allows the consumer to access them when they want, how they want, and for as long as they want.

10.5.3 Format Wars

The trends being seen in home leisure are nothing new. Home entertainment is a commercial battleground between different formats – again showing the power of technological change. In recorded and recordable media these battles have included Betamax and VHS in video tapes in the 1980s (won by VHS) records, tapes, and CDs in the 1980s and 1990s (won by CDs); videos and DVDs in the late 1990s (won by DVDs); and Blu-ray and high definition (HD) in the first decade of the twenty-first century (won by Blu-ray), although it could be argued HD had the last laugh given its growth in TV reception. This has continued since 2010 in a battle between more conventional approaches to home entertainment and the advancement of streaming, with streaming platforms currently having the advantage. Some companies, such as Love Film, attempted a hybrid model, but none have been able to match the convenience of streaming services it seems. As before, the lessons are clear for anyone involved in the home entertainment businesses – always look for the next format, and retain competitiveness in technology. Are these lessons also applicable to other areas of leisure?

Discussion Question

Is there such a thing as too much choice for consumers? Discuss in relation to electronic devices for leisure in the home.

10.5.4 Listening to Music

Listening to music had already become a portable leisure activity through the 1980s and 1990s with portable cassette and CD players; however, streaming of music via the internet has now become the most popular way of accessing music. Data from 2020, for example, showed that of all 'listening time' undertaken in the UK, 3% was done using CDs, while 14% was done via online streaming services. To add some context here, 72% of listening was done via the radio, showing that, unlike live TV, live radio has remained more resistant to other forms of music and audio entertainment. Where the change has happened is the reduction in purchases and consumption via CD. Another trend to note since the last iteration of this book is the decline in MP3 players. The clear market leader in the previous version of this book was Apple's iPod; however, following a peak in sales around 2008 and 2009 at roughly 55 million units, there has been a steady decline in sales year on year. In 2014, the latest data available, 14 million units were sold worldwide. However, this change is not a reflection on how much we listen to music, rather a change in how people access the music. The growth in streaming services (some of which require a payment and some that do not) such as Apple Music, Amazon Music, Google Play, SoundCloud, Spotify, and YouTube, coupled with technological developments in mobile phones, tablets, and speaker systems has made MP3 players like the iPod and traditional Hi-Fi systems less important for accessing music. Data gathered in Mexico found that 97% of respondents used smartphones for streaming music, 33% used a computer, 23% a tablet, and 25% a SmartTV. Only 6% used an iPod. This point is further reinforced by data on the number of people who subscribe to music streaming services around the world, which increased from 76.8 million in 2015 to over 400 million in 2020. This is now a significant revenue generator for the companies who stream the music. To give some examples, as of 2020, streaming music generated $3.7 billion in the USA, about ₹12 billion in India, $1.1 billion in Germany, $580 million in France, and $335 million in Italy. In the previous edition of this book, it was argued that, when it comes to playing music, 'consumers are faced with an almost confusing choice of devices to play music on and in such circumstances there is a tendency to support market leaders to reduce the uncertainty'. By the early 2020s, it seems clear that consumers have chosen streaming services as their preferred choice for now.

10.5.5 Computers and Electronic Games

Computers are very important for home entertainment and leisure more broadly. Not only are they a site of leisure in the home, they also now allow us to plan holidays, sign up and pay for experiences, or search for activities in areas we live. Importantly, the number of houses around the world with access to a computer (whether that be a tablet computer, a desktop, or a laptop) is increasing steadily. As an example, it is estimated that by 2025 around 330 million households in Europe will have a computer. In 2010 the figure was 206 million households, and in 2020 it was 294 million. There is a note of caution here, however. The picture on the use of computers and especially around games is difficult to unpack. There has been a 'blurring of the lines' between the functions of different devices. For example, a mobile phone can be used as a personal computer, a tablet computer can be used as a personal computer, and a personal computer can be used as a phone – and in some cases – also a tablet. So when it comes to the use of computers, the reality is consumers can use a phone, tablet, laptop, console, or desktop computer to play games, surf the internet, or enjoy social media. When looking at the UK specifically, around 24% of households have a desktop personal computer, 52% have a tablet computer, and 57% have a laptop. However, there are, of course houses that have a combination of these and, in some cases, all three: 5% have a desktop PC only, 15% have a tablet computer only, and 19% have a laptop computer only. This picture also highlights the context from which 'second-screen syndrome' has emerged – the act of using two devices at the same time for different tasks, such as, watching a film and being on social media.

With regard to gaming, this remains a popular activity for using computers, be it consoles, tablets, laptops, or desktop computers. In 2013 consumer spending on digital consoles and online games in the UK was just over £891 million, and by 2019 it was around £2 billion. This proved a popular activity during the COVID-19 pandemic 'lockdowns', and spending jumped to £2.39 billion in 2020. Given this is a chapter about 'in the home' leisure, it would be remiss not to note that 'mobile games' – games downloaded onto mobile devices like tablets and phones – is the largest sector of revenue generation. It generates more than double the revenue of downloads and online gaming.

Broadband connection is a major technological change which is vital for the high speed downloading important to so many of the internet services referred to earlier. It is an important government objective in many countries as connectivity is vital, not only for leisure but for other areas of business, commerce, education, health, and transport for example. Importantly, the fifth generation of cellular network (known as 5G) is being established around the world, which will have an impact on the speed and amount of, among other things, streaming and downloading people can undertake. It is, of course, unlikely that 5G will be realised in each country at the same time or at the same speed. Computers and video games are commonly blamed for the reduction in physical activity among 'Generation Y', particularly boys. However, it is too simplistic to blame one element of the competition for young people's time for any lack of physical activity. Television, parents, schools, eating behaviour, peer group pressures, and many other factors contribute to physical activity behaviour. One trend has been the use of technology in promoting physical activity in the home. It started with concepts like Nintendo Wii or DDR (Dance Dance Revolution), however, other companies like Peloton or Zwift have now joined in.

Discussion Question

What are some of the challenges and opportunities for leisure managers, given the advances in home entertainment technologies?

10.6 House and Garden

This sector consists of two main parts – DIY and gardening. In terms of consumer spending in the UK, DIY is about twice the scale of gardening, but both are among the largest expenditure elements of leisure in the home.

10.6.1 DIY and Gardening

Since much of DIY is maintenance of the home, cars, domestic equipment, etc. to either solve or prevent problems, there is an issue about whether such expenditure is truly leisure expenditure or more akin to housework. Nevertheless, it is usually included in categories of leisure in the home. In the long term, DIY benefits from home ownership, however, this has been reducing in the UK since 2007 and has stagnated at around 65% of UK households. In the shorter term, the DIY market tends to fluctuate in line with the housing market generally, such that the housing boom in the UK in 2001–2004 was accompanied by annual growth rates in DIY spending of between 7% and 11% in real terms. In contrast, a stalling house market in 2005 was accompanied by a decline in the value of the DIY market. In 2008, as the housing market and consumer confidence fell, together with bad summer weather, so DIY spending fell again. Clearly the COVID-19 pandemic impacted on the housing market around the world and on our activities. Without the ability to undertake other out-of-home leisure, decorating and gardening became an alternative focus for more people. Indeed, plants, seeds, and bulbs for the garden and paint for indoors were the most purchased products during the pandemic in the UK. There is some other evidence that the pandemic did not impact on DIY as much as other sectors. Table 10.5 shows the areas where people in the UK, Germany, and the USA spent less on during the pandemic. DIY was close to the bottom.

Table 10.5 **Products and Services People Spend Less on Due to the COVID-19 Pandemic, 2020 in %**

	Germany	United Kingdom	United States
Going out (e.g. restaurants, cinemas, pubs/bars)	74	83	77
Travel (e.g. public transport, vacations)	67	77	70
Services (e.g. hairdresser)	61	76	69
Clothing	41	60	49
Consumer electronics, household appliances, furniture	28	39	34
Hobbies	27	30	26
Investments	31	25	26
Food and drinks (e.g. shopping, takeaways, delivery)	16	23	23

(Continued)

Table 10.5 **(Continued)**

	Germany	United Kingdom	United States
Childcare	19	22	22
Home entertainment (e.g. video, games, books)	11	19	19
Insurance	13	17	19
Housing, energy, maintenance (e.g. electricity, waste disposal, DIY)	12	14	13
Health and hygiene (e.g. medicine, hand sanitizer)	7	6	8
Household cleaning products	8	8	8

Source: Statista

There is a paradox to the tendency for DIY spending to follow the housing market. If the housing market went into decline, it would be logical to expect DIY spending to increase, because this would protect the value of the house owner's major asset. However, this does not normally happen. The largest element of DIY consumer spending in the UK is household maintenance, i.e. fixing or preventing problems. Other significant elements of DIY spending are paint, wallpaper, timber, and equipment hire. Supply of DIY products is dominated by large retailers in the UK, including B&Q, Wickes, and Homebase, and Halfords for cars and bikes.

> **Discussion Question**
>
> Is time spent on DIY and gardening leisure or housework?

10.7 Hobbies and Pastimes

This is an incredibly difficult section to analyse, for the simple reason that hobbies and pastimes can be anything for anyone. However, to add some context, Figure 10.1 shows the top hobbies and interests in the UK. Of the activities that occur primarily in the home, owning pets, photography, and arts and crafts are the ones not really covered so far in this chapter. So, let us turn our attention to those for a moment.

10.7.1 Photography

Photography, like home entertainment, is an activity that is clearly not confined to the home, but it is conventionally treated as an in-the-home leisure activity. In the photography market, the biggest change in recent years has been stimulated by the change to digital technology.

In 2008 *Leisure Forecasts* (Leisure Industries Research Centre, 2008) estimated that ownership of digital cameras grew from 11% of UK households in 2002 to 59% of households in

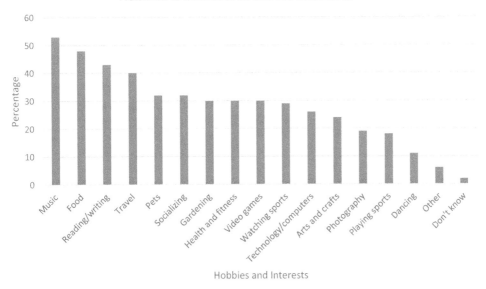

Figure 10.1 **Hobbies and interests of adults in the UK in 2021.**
Source: Statista Global Consumer Survey

2008. However, in 2021 that figure was suggested to be 47% by the Global Consumer Survey, and one of the reasons for this is the development in mobile phones (known as smart phones), which now act as a camera and video recorder. Perhaps more importantly, the quality of the pictures and films that smart phones can capture has also improved. The rise of digital cameras over the past 20 years or so has boosted the relative importance of photographic equipment sales for those with a keen interest in photography. Mobile phone cameras have also led to a steep decline in the demand for throwaway film cameras. Another important driver for the photography market is the rising popularity of social networking and photo editing sites on the internet. Such sites as Flickr and Snapfish have facilitated the sharing of digital photographs.

10.7.2 Owning Pets

In the UK, the expenditure on pets is increasing and has been doing so from 2005, when £2.9 billion was spent annually. This has increased significantly, and in 2020 the figure stood at £7.8 billion, nearly triple the figure from 15 years previous, and it is one of the most consistently expanding markets in the UK. Of the UK population, 59% own some form of pet with, perhaps unsurprisingly, dogs (33%) and cats (27%) being the most popular kind of pet. Indeed, in the UK, no other pet is owned by more than 2% of households. Pet ownership and expenditure is influenced by changes in demographics and the housing market, but sometimes these effects are uncertain. The greater number of single-person households caused by higher divorce and separation rates, for example, might be a positive influence on pet ownership because pets are good company for single people. Alternatively, it might be a negative influence because families are the traditional mainstay of pet ownership. The tendency for couples to have children later in their lives typically means lower numbers of children, which has a negative effect on pet ownership. However, many childless couples might see pets as almost surrogates for children, in which case the lack of children has less of a negative effect. Finally, increased life expectancy could have a positive influence on pet ownership because pets are good companions for older people, or a negative influence because of other expenditure priorities for older people and restrictions on their housing tenancy agreements. Perhaps the other point to note here is that this is a sector impacted by the COVID-19 pandemic. Both dog and cat ownership jumped in 2020–2021 as people spent more time in their homes. In 2016 the People's Dispensary for Sick Animals (PDSA) undertook research into why people had pets. Of respondents, 93% claimed owning a pet 'makes me happy', 88% suggested it 'improves my life', 80% said it 'makes me mentally healthier', and 61% said it 'makes me physically healthier'.

10.7.3 Arts and Crafts

There are a lot of different parts to the 'arts and crafts' sector. Some examples include floral crafting, edible arts, paper crafts, needle work, wood crafts, home décor, beads and jewellery, sewing and fabric, kids' crafts, knitting, or painting and drawing. Despite this being seemingly distant to the 'technological revolution' talked about elsewhere in this chapter, there are a few ways in which this sector has embraced technology. The use of YouTube for tutorials, for example, means that (often for free) people can stay in their homes and follow experts from the field and develop their skills. The same could be said of musical instruments, for example. There are also several ways in which materials for various arts and crafts can be purchased via the internet and, conveniently, delivered to the consumer's house. A good example of this is the online retailer Etsy. Founded in 2005 in the USA, Etsy focuses on vintage or handmade items and also sells craft supplies. It is a success story. In 2012, Etsy had revenues of $74.6 million, however, by 2019 revenues had jumped to $818 million. A further example of how the COVID-19 pandemic helped some sectors, Etsy saw revenue in 2020 more than double to $1.7 billion! Staying with the USA, participation in this form of hobby seems to have increased slightly. In 2010, 56% of households had participated in a craft, a number which rose to 63% by 2016. The spending on this area is slightly more for younger groups (18–24) than it is for older groups (over 55).

10.8 Gambling

Gambling is a leisure activity that is switching location from out of the home to in the home in the UK and around the world, largely because of the internet and particularly the spread of broadband and 4th Generation (4G) mobile network. However, several countries have acted to either outlaw or severely restrict online gambling, including the USA, Japan, China. Pakistan, Hong Kong, and the Netherlands. Internationally, therefore, the greatest uncertainty for online gambling lies in legislative and taxation action – either continued restriction or possibly liberalisation.

   The reasons for some countries being more restrictive in allowing online gambling are partly fiscal, to protect tax revenues from land-based gambling enterprises, and partly moral, in fear of an explosion of uncontrollable gambling through people's homes. For example, in 2006 the USA brought in regulations which outlawed the processing of bets taken online by banks and credit card companies, which came into law in early 2009 and effectively blocked internet gambling. There are, however, some states where this is now legal, although different forms of online gambling (casino, poker, or sports for example) are accepted and prohibited in various states. In the UK a more pragmatic and liberal line was taken, and in 2007 a 15% remote gaming tax was introduced. This was clearly designed to protect tax revenues whilst not hitting the gambling industry too hard – many major gambling companies have diversified into online gambling. As a result, online gambling was the fastest growing element of the UK gambling market, growing 650% in the period 2002–2007. In the past edition of this book, it was noted that this growth came from a very small base, and in 2008 online gambling was still only 7% of the total gambling market (Leisure Industries Research Centre, 2008). However, online active accounts have doubled between 2008 and 2020 while betting shops have been reducing, suggesting a further shift. Likewise, between 2008 and 2013, on average about 4 million new accounts were set up with online bookmakers. Between 2016 and 2019, this number was around 30 million a year. Of course, this could be the same people holding multiple betting accounts. Live sports attract the most bets, followed by casino games, and this has been the case for quite a while.

Discussion Questions

How much regulation should there be for online gambling? And for what reasons?

10.9 Conclusions

Leisure at home has been impacted significantly by the technological advances within our society. However, a note of caution needs to be taken. This is not a revolution in the activities we undertake in the home, rather a change in the ways we access and consume them. Perhaps the only real outlier in this is the growth of social media over the past 20 years or so, which has added a rather substantial leisure activity to our lives. Notwithstanding this, traditional activities like watching TV, reading, hobbies, listening to the radio, and keeping pets all remain a staple of in-home leisure. But there are some aspects that are worthy of note. These activities are increasingly done at irregular times, and the way they have been adapted to fit around other activities is interesting. Increasingly, it seems people want leisure activities to be there when they want them rather than people being there when leisure activities are offered. TV, music, and other gaming activities are examples of this. Is this more adaptable approach to leisure something leisure managers can learn from? Are there ways that leisure that was once accessed outside of the home can be gradually offered inside the home? Leisure pursuits are activities we access after the completion of other obligatory activities; it seems some activities have been able to flex around those obligatory activities better than others.

Practical Tasks

1   Conduct an audit in one house or flat of:

   (a) The percentage of space in the home that is used for leisure;
   (b) The percentage of each member of the household's time spent on leisure at home;
   (c) The value of the leisure equipment in the home (you will need to estimate this).

   What conclusions do you reach about the importance of leisure to this household?

2   Design and conduct a pilot survey of young people (16–24 years) and older people (50+ years) who you know to find out:
    (a) How dependent they are on technology for consuming leisure in the home (i.e. television, computer, audio equipment, etc.);
    (b) How competent they feel in using such leisure technology. What are the implications of your results for the prospective marketing of a new piece of leisure technology?

Structured Guide to Further Reading

Blackshaw, T. (Ed.). (2013). *Routledge Handbook of Leisure Studies*. Routledge, Oxon.
López-Sintas, J., Rojas de Francisco, L., & García-Álvarez, E. (2017). Home-based digital leisure. *World Leisure Journal*, 59(Sup1), 86–92.
Ofcom. (2021). Media nations UK 202021, 5 August. Retrieved from www.ofcom.org.uk (accessed 19 October 2021)

Useful Websites

https://ec.europa.eu/eurostat
www.ons.gov.uk/
www.statista.com/

References

Gratton, C., & Solberg, H. A. (2007). *The Economics of Sports Broadcasting*. Routledge, London and New York.
Gratton, C., & Taylor, P. (2000). *Economics of Sport and Recreation*. E & FN Spon, London.
Leisure Industries Research Centre. (2008). *Leisure Forecasts 2008–2012*. Leisure Industries Research Centre, Sheffield.
Monopolies and Mergers Commission. (1999). *British Sky Broadcasting PLC and Manchester United PLC: A Report on the Proposed Merger*. The Stationery Office, London.

Chapter 11

Planning for Sport and Leisure

DOI: 10.4324/9780367823610-11

Summary

In this chapter, leisure managers are encouraged to understand key elements of the planning process and their potential involvement in it. The role of the government, the tiers in the planning system, and planning processes are considered, with a focus on the UK to give the review of processes coherence. Practical techniques for sport and leisure planning are also examined, with a focus on understanding leisure demands.

The accurate assessment of leisure demand is at the heart of good leisure planning. This mirrors the importance of knowledge of the market in marketing (Chapter 14) and the importance of customers to quality management (Chapter 16). Several methods of assessing and forecasting demand are reviewed, with strengths and weaknesses identified. Many of these are quantitative estimation techniques, although an understanding of why people demand leisure is also important.

This chapter finishes with a suggested ten-point planning process for leisure managers to consider. Thereby, leisure managers can identify what roles they might play in this process. It is important for leisure managers to get involved in leisure planning at all levels of provision: local, regional, and national. Their specialist knowledge of the nature of leisure demands is a vital ingredient in ensuring that supply matches demand.

11.1 Introduction

This chapter deals with local planning for sport and leisure, i.e. the considerations that government in particular lays down for the effective and appropriate planning of sport and leisure provision and development. Business planning, by individual organisations for a new sport or leisure development, is included in Chapter 18. Local planning is not irrelevant to commercial and third sector businesses, however, because any commercial sport and leisure development will be influenced by local plans. Local plans will also affect local communities more generally because a key element in their construction is how accessible sport and leisure facilities and amenities are, and whether they fit local needs.

Government planning has always been concerned, albeit often peripherally, with the provision of facilities for leisure. The evolution of the planning movement was closely associated with the nineteenth-century fight for the retention of open spaces and commons, which were threatened by unplanned urban development. The movement has evolved from a concern for public health, education, and moral standards to problems of inner cities and countryside recreation and conservation. Leisure planning as a discipline is not a new phenomenon. Indeed, leisure planning was at the forefront of the planning of the Garden Cities in the UK by Ebenezer Howard in the early twentieth century.

This chapter is not a text for planners, but instead it provides information about planning processes and systems. It also reviews practical techniques for sport and leisure planning. The context for planning involves legislation, government regulation, direction and guidance, public debate and consultation, the geography of an area, land use, and the need for sport and leisure facilities and amenities to fit within community plans and cultural strategies.

The planner's objective is to provide the right facilities, in the best location, at the right time, and at an acceptable cost for the people who need them. Planning is not a static process but a dynamic and changing one. Planners themselves are only part of the planning process. They do not directly acquire and manage land and amenities. They identify locations for facilities according to acceptable planning principles. They seek to minimise conflicts of interest, traffic, noise, pollution, and congestion. Planners help to make towns functional, attractive, and healthy places; they also safeguard the public interest and help to conserve (and foster good use of) the environment.

One of the fundamental drivers of leisure planning is equitable distribution of opportunities. This is open to a variety of interpretations of the concept of 'equity', and equity is not necessarily synonymous with equality. Equal distribution of leisure facilities does not necessarily provide either equal opportunity or equal participation. Often, the more affluent people are the predominant users of public sector facilities, despite attempts to provide amenities in disadvantaged areas.

The leisure manager should be involved in the planning process at the earliest stage to assist in assessing need and demand, identifying gaps in provision, and proposing appropriate services and facilities. Unfortunately, however, there are too many examples of poor planning. The most common failure is that leisure facilities are often placed on land which is available because it is owned by the local authority, but which is not in an appropriate location for their market. In such circumstances, they are unlikely to achieve optimum levels of usage, and hence they require increased levels of subsidy. Community-built facilities located on the periphery of centres of population or away from main transportation routes, or alongside physical barriers such as rivers or difficult road systems, suffer from poor access and inevitably result in a restricted catchment.

11.2 The Role of Government in Planning

Planning systems regulate development and land use and contribute to government strategy for sustainable development in towns, cities, and the countryside. The systems help to plan for homes, schools, factories, transport, etc. and in doing so protect the natural and manmade environments. They differ in different countries, so the UK is used as an example. In England there are 365 planning authorities, including regional planning bodies, district councils, unitary authorities, and national park authorities. At a national level, policy is set out in a series of Planning Policy Statements. At a local level, planning decisions are set out by county councils, district, borough, or city councils and parish or town councils.

Planning issues in Wales are implemented by 24 local planning authorities. In Scotland there is a National Planning Framework, with 34 planning authorities to help implement it. The most recent, National Planning Framework 4, sets out the development plans for Scotland in 2050. In Northern Ireland, a Regional Development Strategy has been written for the period up to the year 2035.

The planning system aims to ensure that development occurs in the right place and that inappropriate development is prevented. However, no matter what planning systems are in place, planning and development decisions are taken by politicians, and therefore the political influence is important. For example, at the local level in the past it was not unusual for sport and leisure developments to favour the constituencies of specific politicians in power at the time.

The case of playing fields in the UK demonstrates how the government has felt the need to act on a national concern – the development of playing fields for other purposes, e.g. housing, retail, and the consequent loss of sport and recreational opportunity. Legislation brought in the late 1990s requires any proposed development plans involving playing fields to be referred to the national sport agency, Sport England. This demonstrates how specific, reactive legislation is sometimes needed to support sport and leisure planning, in this case responding to a perceived threat to sport and leisure provision. Enforcement of the legislation is not through the courts but rather through a sport agency.

11.3 Key Planning Processes

This section reviews a selection of planning processes in England, to illustrate the complexity of planning but also to show how planning procedures are constructed. The processes are different in different countries – they are even slightly different in the four countries that make up the UK. It is therefore not possible to review the processes in detail for different countries.

11.3.1 Planning Policy Statements/Guidance

In England, there has been a National Planning Policy Framework in place since March 2012, which was been updated and revised in February 2019. It provides a framework within which locally prepared plans for housing and other development can be produced. Within this framework is guidance on planning relating to leisure facilities (both indoor and outdoor) and the use of open space. This is managed in parallel with Sport England. The following sections focus on the guidance provided by Sport England on their website in relation to the planning system for sport and physical activity that links to the National Planning Policy Framework. Sport England break their guidance down into four specific sections: planning for sport guidance, playing fields policy, planning applications, and assessing needs and playing pitch strategy guidance. We begin with the assessing needs section as this is vitally important in the planning process. If you cannot clearly articulate the need and the opportunity, then it is unlikely that the planning will be accepted.

11.3.2 Assessment of Needs and Opportunities

Sport England provide guidance specifically on how to undertake and apply needs assessments for sports facilities. They provide a handy checklist document that covers the three-stages approach to undertaking a needs assessment for sport facilities. There is also a link to a full guidance document on their website that provides detailed advice on how to undertake each stage and individual step. The stages and procedure are listed here and are explained in more detail on the Sport England website under the section 'Planning for Sport'.

Stage A: Prepare and tailor the approach.
Stage B: Gather information on supply and demand.
Stage C: Assessment – bring the information together.

11.3.3 Planning for Sport Guidance

Sport England provide a downloadable Planning for Sport guidance document that is ideal for anyone involved in, or looking to engage with, the planning system in England. This includes local authority officers and councillors, planning inspectors, developers, and consultants through to parish/town councils, neighbourhood forums, public health leads, sports clubs/organisations, community groups, and individuals. The guidance includes 12 planning for sport principles which are split into four categories: overarching, protect, enhance, and provide (further detail provided on the Sport England website under the section 'Planning for Sport').

11.3.4 Playing Fields Policy

Playing fields are one of the most important resources for sport in England. They provide the space for team sports on outdoor pitches and form part of a network of open spaces and wider green infrastructure in an area. To help protect the spaces where people get active, local planning authorities are required by law to consult with Sport England on planning applications they receive that affect playing fields. Consequently, Sport England have developed a Playing Fields Policy to help them assess and respond to such applications. They also provide publicly available guidance alongside the Playing Fields Policy to give clarity and advice to external parties on how individual assessments are made. These include details on the definition of key terms and how Sport England interpret them, how the policy relates to government policy, how Sport England apply the policy, and how to consult with Sport England regarding any applications. The guidance document on Playing Fields Policy is constantly being updated to link to the broader guidance provided by the government to link to the National Planning Policy Framework and the Playing Fields Policy guidance that was last updated in August 2018.

11.3.5 Planning Applications

Any planning application is also assessed and linked to wider government legislation such as the Statutory Instrument 2015/595. This sets out how local planning authorities are required to consult with Sport England on planning applications for development affecting playing field land. The government, within its Planning Practice Guidance, also advises local planning authorities to consult in cases where development might lead to:

- Loss of, or loss of use for sport, of any major sports facility;
- Proposals which lead to the loss of use for sport of a major body of water;
- Creation of a major sports facility;
- Creation of a site for one or more playing pitches;
- Development which creates opportunities for sport (such as the creation of a body of water bigger than two hectares following sand and gravel extraction);
- Artificial lighting of a major outdoor sports facility;
- A residential development of 300 dwellings or more.

Any applications are then assessed using the Playing Fields Policy and Guidance and must be in line with the 12 planning for sport principles highlighted here. Major new developments, such as residential, are also covered under this guidance, and any new major residential development should ensure that the needs it generates for sport and physical activity provision will be met and that the environments they create facilitate and enable people to lead active lifestyles.

11.3.6 Planning Techniques

The most authoritative source of information on planning techniques for sport, leisure, and tourism is Veal (2017). Much of the review that follows is informed by Veal's work.

Underpinning many of these techniques is both an understanding of demand for different sport and leisure activities and knowledge of the quantity and quality of existing sport and leisure opportunities. The fundamentals of sport and leisure planning are to compare demand with supply and then plan to remedy any likely unmet demand with changes in supply. In reviewing the planning techniques, it is important to identify how both supply and demand can be measured. In the case of demand, this is more difficult because for planning purposes it is not just present demand that needs to be measured but also future demand. This needs to be forecasted for the period ahead appropriate to the plan – the 'planning horizon'.

The techniques examined are:

- Those focused more on supply:

  - standards of provision;
  - hierarchy of provision;
  - spatial analysis;

- Those focused more on demand:

  - expressed demand and demand forecasting;
  - public consultation;

- Those focused on both supply and demand:

  - matrix analysis;
  - social area/need index;
  - facilities planning model;
  - U-Plan system.

11.3.7 Standards of Provision

One of the most developed and widely used approaches to the 'equitable' distribution of recreational services is the use of standards of provision, whereby the standards identify what type of provision should be made, typically for a specific size of population. There are many examples cited in Veal (2017) including provision for local sport centres and open space planning standards including playing fields and informal space.

Many standards are not based on empirical research but on long-accepted assumptions of what is 'needed'. Standards appeal to politicians and planners. Someone 'in authority' has done the thinking for you. Standards are simple and efficient; they invite the same level of provision area to area; they act as an external authoritative source; and they can be measured, monitored, and assessed. Standards are important and useful when they have been based on sound methodology and are used with flexibility and local knowledge. They give yardsticks against which to measure existing provision, they are easy to understand and communicate, and they cover many of the facilities provided by local authorities.

However, while standards have advantages, they also have disadvantages:

- Standards can become institutionalised, unmovable, and given greater strength and importance than they merit.
- Standards vary. Most major pursuits have standards – pitches, pools, indoor sports centres, libraries, and so on, but sometimes the same activity has different standards, which prompts the question: Which one to choose?
- The validity of some standards is open to question. Playing space standards, for example, are based on participation rates, but participation is largely dependent on the level of

supply. Changes in provision will lead to changes in participation, but the implications for possible changes in standards are unclear. As both supply and demand change over time, so standards can become out of date. The growth of fitness centres, driven by increased demand, may mean that the standards for provision for these facilities are too weak; whilst the decline in squash may make standards of provision too generous. Hence, some standards of just a decade ago are no longer valid or appropriate.

- Standards should always be tempered by local knowledge and circumstances. If they are unrealistic, they will be ignored. For example, national open space standards cannot be achieved in inner-city areas.
- While standards are easy to understand, they can be misinterpreted and used as a justification for taking no further action. Some authorities have been known to interpret standards to suit their own purposes. For example, they may say that they have more than adequate indoor playing space, but analysis might reveal that most of the total space is made up of small units unsuitable for activities in demand or that access by the general public is restricted.
- Standards are inanimate, inhuman. They are concerned with quantitative and not qualitative aspects of provision. They take no account of the leisure potential of the specific areas, i.e. local needs, local priorities, local differences, and local environments.
- Many leisure pursuits are amenable to standards of provision, but many are not. Water recreation, tourism, heritage, entertainment, and arts have no comprehensive basis for evaluation.

In summary, standards of provision can involve a crude assessment of demand. As they are based on national information, they can often bear little relationship to local circumstances; they deal in quantities, thereby ignoring the quality of provision as well as key aspects of distribution, use, and management. At best, standards of provision can be used as a starting point by providing a benchmark for measuring the adequacy of facilities and for identifying under- or over-provision, while recognising that most standards indicate minimum levels of provision. However, more recently, standards have been replaced by more sophisticated techniques which attempt to measure supply and demand.

11.3.8 Hierarchy of Provision

A modified version of the standards approach is the hierarchy of provision approach, normally applied to a range of facilities for a given population size. It has been used in the development of new towns, where the planning of leisure facilities and services is seen as a prerequisite for attracting people to the towns. For example, a town might have a three-tier hierarchy for sport:

- A school level using facilities and services for school and community – a grassroots tier;
- Specific club facilities and services, e.g. hockey or tennis at a second tier;
- Flagship central facilities and services at the third tier.

A hierarchical approach helps to settle the debate over whether to provide a large centrally located facility or numerous smaller facilities strategically placed throughout the district. With scarce resources, often a choice must be made. There will probably be savings in the capital costs if only one large centre is provided, as economies of scale would apply in both the construction and operation of the facility, e.g. the construction costs per cubic metre of internal space are lower for large buildings than for smaller buildings. However, the closer a person resides to a leisure facility, the more likely they are to use the facility, and the more

Table 11.1 Suggested Hierarchy of Leisure Provision and Estimates for Leisure Facilities in the UK

Community size	Recommended facilities	Activities offered
1 Hamlet/small village, 500–1500 population	Community hall, community open space, mobile library	Badminton, Keep Fit, yoga, football, cricket
2 Small country town, 2500–6000 population	See previous plus tennis courts, sports hall, swimming pool	See previous plus tennis, netball, gym, hockey
3 Town	See previous plus specialist sports venues, golf courses, skateboard parks, bowling green	See previous plus bowling, golf, skateboarding, judo, karate
4 City	See previous plus sports stadia, athletics grounds	See previous plus home grounds of sports clubs (football, rugby, hockey, athletics grounds)
5 Capital city	See previous plus national sports centre for selected sports	See previous but for national teams

Source: Adapted from Nagle, G. and Cooke, B., (2017). Geography: Course Companion. Oxford University Press

frequently, compared with a person who resides some distance away. This is the principle of 'distance decay'.

Within this, there is also the issue of a threshold population, which is the minimum number of people required for that facility to be viable. The smaller the threshold population, the smaller the sphere of influence. However, it is very hard to find accurate and reliable figures for threshold populations in relation to leisure facilities. Some estimates for leisure facilities linked to the hierarchy of provision argument are provided in Table 11.1 by Nagle and Cooke (2017).

Of course, this list is subjective in many ways, as it is not always a perfect fit, and there are many facilities/sports that are missing. National centres are not always located in capital cities either. In the UK, for example, the English Institute of Sport (home to many NGBs) resides in Sheffield not London. Additionally, many towns have professional sport teams in the UK, and these are not just confined to big cities. Nonetheless, it does serve as a usual tool to gain a sense of scale in the planning of leisure activities and facilities and the importance of space and location.

Discussion Question

When they are accused of being a nuisance on the streets, it is often claimed by young teenagers that there is 'nothing to do' and 'nowhere to go'. How would you construct a hierarchy of sport and leisure facilities and services for young teenagers in your area?

11.3.9 Spatial Analysis

When asked to list the three most important factors in the development of hotels, Conrad Hilton cited 'location, location, location'. This equally applies to most leisure facilities. Ideally, a public leisure facility should be located near a main road that is well served by a public transport system, near other facilities. In recent years in the UK, extensive user surveys have been taken of many leisure facilities, and from these an indication of the size of a leisure facility's catchment area can be made. Using this approach, the geographical area covered by the facility's perceived catchment area can be identified, with areas beyond that, theoretically, not being served.

This is a useful planning tool, because by putting together the calculated catchment areas of all the facilities in an area for a specific purpose, e.g. multi-use leisure centres, it is possible to identify geographical gaps in provision. It also enables identification of the degree of overlap of catchment areas, which may have implications for the programming of 'competing' facilities.

However, there are several important issues which need to be considered when conducting such a spatial analysis, including:

- The quality of existing facilities, whether they have spare capacity or whether their demand exceeds supply;
- The density of population in the relevant areas;
- The shape of the catchment areas of leisure facilities, which are not circular but are distorted due to many factors, e.g. physical barriers such as rivers, railway lines, and busy roads can restrict a catchment area, while access to a facility along a major road can extend the catchment area along its route;
- The respective catchment populations of different leisure facilities, which may differ in size, affluence, mobility, and social composition.

11.4 Expressed Demand and Demand Forecasting

Information on expressed demand is often provided by large scale, national participation surveys – such as the *Active People* surveys for sports participation in England and the *Taking Part* surveys for leisure participation in the UK. National surveys identify the way in which participation in a variety of leisure activities varies by gender, age, socio-economic group, ethnicity, etc. National surveys are often conducted by public agencies, and the results are in the public domain.

A problem with most large-scale national surveys, however, is that the samples for local areas are insufficient for detailed analysis. This leads to national demand evidence being assumed to be relevant to a local area, which is not necessarily the case. However, the *Active People* survey of sports participation in England was designed to produce 1,000 respondents in every local authority, which enables detailed analysis and is therefore useful for planning purposes at the local level.

As well as national surveys, it is often the case that information on expressed demand is collected locally. The analysis of sports facilities' booking sheets, for example, can reveal the amount of spare capacity available and may indicate whether the demand for specific facilities at certain times exceeds the supply available – this would depend on records being kept of failed attempts to book because capacity was full. The level of demand for existing facilities can therefore provide a useful guide to whether additional facilities are required in an area.

How would you measure excess demand for a particular activity in your area? Could this be done on a continuous basis, rather than by occasional measurement?

It is not just knowledge of current or recent demand that is important to planning. Through the use of survey information, it is possible to forecast what will happen to participation if population levels or structures change – for instance a growing population, an ageing population, or a population with higher numbers of immigrants from certain countries. Such forecasts can be achieved by quantitative techniques such as time series, regression analysis, or the simpler cohort analysis.

11.4.1 Time Series

If there is sufficient data over time on demand, from repeated surveys which are consistent, time series is a statistical method by which trend data over time can be extrapolated into the future to provide a forecast of demand. This is done by calculating a 'moving average' which exposes the underlying trend in the data over time as well as identifying normal seasonal fluctuations in demand (here is not the place for a detailed statistical explanation – you need to refer to a statistics textbook). The technique can be used for particular leisure activities and for specific population sub-groups, if there is sufficient reliable data for these. There are two main problems with this technique, however. First, it assumes that the future will exactly replicate demand patterns from the past, which often isn't the case. Second, the technique offers no explanation for changes over time – a problem which regression and cohort analyses attempt to remedy.

11.4.2 Regression Analysis

In this technique, it is necessary to have data for whatever is being explained, called the 'dependent variable' – in this case a measure of sport or leisure demand – and data for the 'independent variables' which have an influence on demand, such as age, gender, ethnicity, education, socio-economic group, income, car ownership, etc. All these data are inputted into multiple regression software, which then estimates the separate effects of each of the independent variables on the dependent variable. This regression analysis will also disclose the statistical significance of each effect and the explanatory power of the whole model.

With such a model calculated using recent data, it is then possible to input forecasted values for important independent variables in the future, e.g. an older population, to estimate the effect this has on demand. However, such analyses are rarely conducted by local authorities or even regional authorities because of either the lack of sufficient data or the lack of expertise to run regressions. They are mostly conducted by academic analysts and national agencies. As such, regression analysis is not really feasible for local leisure plans.

11.4.3 Cohort Analysis

This is a simpler technique than regression analysis. A cohort is simply a sub-group of the population, e.g. by age, gender, income, etc. Two pieces of information are needed to forecast demand for any cohort in the population: first, a forecast of the population changes for the planning area over the planning period; and, second, an estimate of the participation rate of that cohort in the leisure activity being planned – usually drawn from survey data. Multiplying the forecasted population by the estimated participation rate will provide the number of people it is anticipated will be interested in an activity.

With survey data also providing likely frequencies of participation, this technique will help to identify likely demand in the future for any specific cohorts, if specific and reliable data exist on population forecasts and expected participation rates. The 'explanation' for these forecasts lies in the different cohorts selected for analysis – acknowledging the major structural variables which affect likely participation, such as age, gender, etc.

11.4.4 Latent Demand

The level of expressed demand identified by surveys and used in techniques to forecast demand is to an extent dependent upon the level of provision. It does not take into consideration latent demand. This is demand that is real but is not yet realised because of major constraints, such as lack of supply. Occasionally, however, surveys include questions on latent demand. With the help of survey evidence, forecasts of demand can integrate not just expressed demand but also estimates of latent demand. In the case of swimming in England, for example, if latent demand were converted into actual swimmers, another 4.3 million swimmers would be added to the 5.55 million swimmers already active (Bullough et al., 2010).

11.4.5 Public Consultation

Public consultation, along with intelligence on expressed demand, is an important indicator of public demand. The weakness is that people may demand facilities but never use them. In addition, the more articulate and organised leisure groups are often the most vocal. Nevertheless, public consultation remains invaluable in gauging local feeling and opinion. Not only is it politically desirable to consult with people, but the planning process itself is incomplete unless people are consulted about their leisure needs and demands, their perception of existing facilities and services, and their expectations of future provision. Without such consultation, the planning process is paternalistic – dictating provision for people as opposed to planning with the people.

As with other methods, public consultations are not without their shortcomings. These are normally associated with the expressions of demand not being representative of the community, and with the subjective nature of many of the responses.

The major methods of consulting with the public include:

- Community surveys;
- Leisure facility user surveys;
- Surveys of clubs, societies, and organisations;
- Public meetings;
- Working parties;
- Stakeholder interviews;
- Focus groups.

11.4.6 Community Surveys

Four surveys which have been used regularly are household interviews, street surveys, postal surveys, and telephone surveys. More recently online surveys are becoming popular, as much for their economy in implementation as their effectiveness in generating results. The face-to-face household interview is a sound approach but can be both time-consuming and expensive to administer. To avoid unnecessarily alarming residents, particularly the elderly, household interviews are best undertaken following an introduction, e.g. by telephone or post, which requires even more time. A face-to-face alternative is the street survey. This requires achieving randomised quota sampling, e.g. a reasonable cross-section of males and females, different age groups, etc. It also calls for trained, sensitive interviewers. The postal survey is much easier and cheaper to administer, although it has limitations. The response rate can be very low unless some interest has been created in the local media or an incentive is associated with the return of the questionnaire. A low response rate then raises the issue of sample bias – were the people who responded of a particular type? A telephone survey using skilful, sensitive researchers is comparatively easy to undertake, provided the questionnaire is short and simple. The problems are those of contacting the selected people and getting accepted. Many sales personnel use the telephone to sell products such as financial products and double glazing. Hence, there is resentment towards this form of consultation.

11.4.7 Leisure Facility User Surveys

User surveys conducted in a face-to-face approach or by self-completion questionnaires can be informative, providing information on the user profile, the facility's catchment area (and the areas not being served), participation data (e.g. activities, frequency), perceptions of provision, how it is managed, and expectations for the future. When the questionnaires are self-administered, user surveys tend to be less representative and the response rate is reduced, although this method is easier and cheaper. Identifying users also provides a broad picture of the non-users when comparisons are made with local population characteristics.

11.4.8 Surveys of Clubs, Societies, and Organisations

The voluntary organisations for sports and arts are often the backbone of leisure groupings. Hence, in any leisure planning process their contribution is essential. A survey of local clubs and societies can provide valuable information regarding membership levels, resources, and current and future requirements. The drawbacks are that often databases of key contacts are out of date because of changes in club officials, and there is often a delay in the responses because of the seasonal nature of some clubs. Furthermore, many clubs are independent in outlook and are not prepared to look at aspects beyond those that directly affect their members. Levels of response from such organisations are often low.

11.4.9 Public Meetings

Although opinions given at public meetings are not necessarily those representing the entire community, they do give an indication of the strength of the support or opposition to particular proposals. Good promotion is necessary to ensure that reasonable and hopefully representative attendances are achieved at the meetings and that those who 'shout loudest' or have vested interests do not hold sway. Working with the press to give balanced reports of such meetings is also important, and it requires good public relations.

11.4.10 Working Parties

A much under-used approach is that of a working party, whereby relevant stakeholders get together with officers and members from the local council in a working party that has delegated authority to propose recommendations. A formal example of this approach in planning for sport in England is Community Sport Networks, which are working parties of local leaders in sport, set up to help plan the development of sport in their communities. It is important that such working parties have the authority to influence decisions, or they simply become talking shops and soon lose enthusiasm.

The advantages associated with this approach are considerable. It is democracy at work and, hopefully, the realistic expectations of the local community can be fulfilled. Unfortunately, in such a situation decision-making can be slow, and the commitment of members will wane if progress is not seen to be made. But the greatest problem may be associated with working party members making unrealistic demands that require excessive amounts of space and finance to fulfil.

11.4.11 Stakeholder Interviews

Interviews with community leaders, including politicians, teachers, leisure leaders, play-workers, youth leaders, social workers, police, ethnic minority representatives, disadvantaged and disabled groups, and the business community can be an invaluable source of information. Likewise, informal interviews with shopkeepers, publicans, postal workers – all those who encounter a wide range of residents – help to build a picture of how different people perceive the current provision, how it is managed, and what deficiencies they think exist.

The main advantages of interviews – either semi-structured, with the main issues for discussion identified, or unstructured, with only the main topic identified – are that the interviewee drives the decision about which issues are covered and the responses. This contrasts with structured questionnaires, where the respondent is only required to address the specific questions asked, and these may not consider other issues important to the respondent.

11.4.12 Focus Groups

The focus group differs from other methods of consultation in three ways:

1   All those interviewed have been involved in a real situation relevant to the subject.
2   The 'content' for the discussion has been previously identified, so participants have had time to think about it.
3   The discussion facilitates conflict and consensus between interested parties – it is not just a matter of adding up different responses, but also a matter of the strength of opinion and the judgement reached by the discussion.

The focus group interview generally involves 8 to 12 individuals who discuss a particular topic under the direction of a moderator. The moderator promotes interaction, makes sure that everyone has a say, and ensures that the discussion remains on the topic of interest. Smaller groups may be dominated by one or two members, while larger groups are difficult to manage. A typical focus group session will last for up to two hours. Depending on the intention of the research, the moderator may be more or less directive with respect to the discussion but is more often non-directive. The moderator might begin with a series of general questions but then directs the discussion to more specific issues as the group proceeds.

11.4.13 Other Consultations

There is a range of other methods, including consultation clinics for individuals or small groups, stakeholder panels, local press and media, and website interactions.

At present, there is no one way of determining the level of potential leisure demand for a particular activity. All the approaches reviewed have different advantages and limitations, and to be able to make a fairly accurate projection of the likely demand for a facility or service, it is desirable to use a range of different methods. Planning for people means putting people into the planning process. To make future leisure provision appropriate and meaningful, a greater understanding is required of people's needs and demands, what leisure means to people, and the role it plays in their lives.

11.4.14 Matrix Analysis

This approach is more of a management technique than a planning approach, but it has an important function in specific situations, for example where planning criteria have been established for a range of possible developments on a particular site, or where the facilities within a park or geographical zone must meet the demands of all sections of the community. If the community is divided into different cohorts, e.g. pre-school, young children, teenagers, adults, etc., listing their needs and matching these against the facilities available, each cell in the matrix will identify the degree of match between a particular population cohort and a particular type of provision. This will lead to the identification of deficiencies. Further applications can be used to place a list of facility/service deficiencies into a priority ranking order, or to select the most appropriate site from a range of possibilities.

11.4.15 Social Area/Need Index

The Social Area or Need Index approach determines whether a deficiency in provision exists in relation to need and places different local areas into a priority ranking. At present, most of the methods of assessing demand concentrate upon the relationship between the resources available and potential users, but little emphasis is attached to the concept of need. It is logical to assume that those areas with a low resource level as well as a high level of need should have a higher priority than areas with a high level of resources and a low level of need.

More recently, needs are often represented by a government-produced Indices of Deprivation. This provides statistics on relative deprivation in small areas in England.

11.5 Facilities Planning Model

The Facilities Planning Model is used by SportScotland and Sport England as a method of assessing the demand for sports facilities (sports halls, swimming pools, synthetic turf pitches, and indoor bowls centres) at the community level of provision. The basic structure of the model is to compare demand for facilities with supply, considering how far people are willing to travel to a facility. The model has been developed to help users:

- Assess the requirements for different types of community sports facilities on a local, regional, or national scale;
- Help local authorities determine an adequate level of sports facility provision to meet their local needs;

- Test 'what if' scenarios in provision and changes in demand, including testing the impact of opening, relocating, and closing facilities and the impact major population changes would have on the needs of the sports facilities.

The Facilities Planning Model can be used in urban and rural settings. It is a substantial improvement on a standard approach to planning facilities. However, it deals only with known demand and not with latent demand, or demand generated by new marketing efforts or innovative management. It calculates likely demand for facilities based on an appropriate level of provision, but this is driven by a national model – it is not driven by local data on demand. The model relies on consistent information about existing facilities. It is also important to realise that it is only a planning tool which helps providers make decisions – it is not a policy-making instrument which makes the decisions for them.

11.6 U-Plan System

Veal (2017) has devised a system for leisure planning which is called U-Plan. Although it is a participation-based approach, it entails three core components:

1 **Objectives and outcomes** – establishing broad targets for the planning exercise, related to the organisation's mission and the key criterion of participation;
2 **Participation** – measuring existing participation and evaluating likely future patterns;
3 **Supply** – identifying the facility/service implications of the targets and projections from the participation analysis.

These components are broken down into 18 planning tasks, including several tasks reviewed earlier, i.e. surveying residents' leisure participation, surveying users of facilities/services, forecasting participation changes, and auditing the existing supply of facilities/services. However, these tasks are prefaced by the refinement of organisation objectives, the clarification of decision-making responsibilities, and the setting of budget constraints, which echo important features of other chapters in this book (see Chapters 17, 18, and 21). Veal's U-Plan system is therefore more than a planning technique – it is a coherent and holistic approach to planning for leisure provision. And it is driven by participation, which echoes the importance of customers to both marketing (Chapter 14) and service quality (Chapter 16).

11.7 A Ten-Stage Leisure Planning Process

The leisure planning process, in conceptual terms, is a simple model based on identifying leisure needs and demands and providing services and facilities to meet those demands. However, the process is far more complex. Figure 11.1 identifies a ten-stage leisure planning approach, representing best practice based on leisure theory and current practical application from a leisure management perspective, which summarises much of what has been reviewed in this chapter. This planning process runs parallel to, and in collaboration with, the formal planning process and local plans.

To explain this process a little more:

- **Stage 1: Review policies, goals, and objectives.** This concerns the philosophical basis of providing for the community and the roles of the key stakeholders (e.g. as providers, enablers, partners, etc.).
- **Stage 2: Evaluate provision.** This stage identifies the type, range, and ownership of facilities, whether public, voluntary, or commercial. It also evaluates effectiveness and

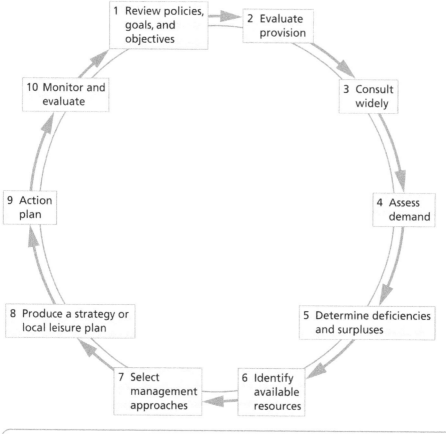

Figure 11.1 **A leisure planning process.**

efficiency, usage, and management. It determines levels of demand and spare capacity. A population study will identify resident concentrations and specific sections of the community that require special consideration, while a transport analysis will highlight the accessibility of existing and potential leisure sites.

- **Stage 3: Consult widely.** This creates the opportunity to find out what needs to be provided for those the plan is intended to serve. Consultation is needed with residents, workers, and organisations. A range of techniques should be used. Consultation is also needed with agencies such as arts and sports governing bodies, with education authorities and schools, and with neighbouring authorities to avoid overlap and duplication.
- **Stage 4: Assess demand.** Although there is no single leisure planning technique that can accurately indicate what the potential demand may be for a particular activity or facility, a good indication can be obtained by using different leisure planning techniques, including demand modelling. These include national and, more specifically, local data; population profiling; the results of consultation; and identifying known and latent demands.
- **Stage 5: Determine deficiencies and surpluses.** This stage analyses the supply-demand relationship. Comparing the level of potential demand with the actual provision should, theoretically, produce a list of deficiencies. It would be unrealistic for any authority to

contemplate redressing all the perceived deficiencies; rather, the deficiencies should be ranked in order of priority.

- **Stage 6: Identify available resources.** It will be necessary to examine all potential sites for leisure development, and these should be assessed in terms of their suitability (e.g. size, terrain, accessibility, environmental considerations). A feasibility study should be undertaken, which should lead to a business plan encompassing capital and revenue costs, management, and use. Grants and planning obligation opportunities will need to be considered.
- **Stage 7: Select management approaches.** There now exists a range of management options, and it is incumbent on local authorities to provide value for money. Options include commercial contractors, trust management, buy-outs by existing managers, business concessions, partnerships, or a mix of these for different operations. Different facilities and services may well require different management approaches.
- **Stage 8: Produce a strategy or local leisure plan.** Leisure managers will also need to prepare a local leisure plan or series of specific plans (e.g. Arts; Sport and Recreation), incorporating short- and medium-term development plans for the area, with the council's role in these developments being clearly defined. A local leisure strategy will set out the roles of the council, the policies, the development and management objectives, and a plan of action.
- **Stage 9: Create an action plan.** To implement the strategies, it will be necessary to produce an action plan with clear objectives, targets, and methods of measurement. Areas of responsibility will need to be assigned to key committees and officers with delegated areas of responsibility. To ensure that the tasks are completed on time, it is advisable that a detailed critical path analysis network be drawn up.
- **Stage 10: Monitor and evaluate.** The progress made will need to be monitored and results measured. This should include the effect of the actions upon the community. The strategies will need periodic review in the light of economic, social, and environmental changes.

11.8 Conclusions

The nature and scale of leisure provision are often the result of inheritance, and possibly this may be the reason why local authorities often had no philosophy for the allocation of leisure resources – no stated purpose for their expenditure on leisure services or their planning for other providers. With greater recognition of leisure as a meaningful part of local, regional, and national infrastructure, this ad hoc approach to leisure planning has changed, in the UK and in other countries.

As with marketing, a knowledge of customers is important to sport and leisure planning. However, there is no one method of accurately determining the demand for leisure activities or amenities. Each of the methods of assessing demand reviewed in this chapter has its strengths and its limitations; and used appropriately they can provide a good indication of the extent to which demand is unsatisfied. It would be wise, if resources allow, to use more than one method, as a form of triangulation – examining the same problem with different methods is a test of the validity of the results.

Leisure planning is an important discipline. Approached logically, it should result in eliminating previous examples of poor leisure planning, where provision is inappropriate to the market it is meant to serve. Leisure planning differs from general planning, as leisure outside the home is made up of an extremely wide variety of activities and choices; and leisure behaviour is not always predictable. Nevertheless it is important for the leisure manager to understand and participate in appropriate planning processes. This will ensure an appropriate fit between supply and demand, moderated by the resources available.

Resources are also important to the scope and scale of leisure planning undertaken at the local level. It requires a lot of time and expertise to use the techniques reviewed in this chapter and, whilst external consultants can help, all such planning efforts will be constrained by the local authority's resources.

Practical Tasks

1   Local plans:

   (a) Select an area. Find a local development plan/framework (usually publicly available through the local authority's website) and identify what elements of leisure are acknowledged in this plan.

   (b) For the same area, find a local leisure/cultural plan and identify what processes of consultation were undertaken to inform this plan.

   Is it possible to identify from these plans the importance of leisure to policies and people in the local area investigated?

2   Cohort analysis:

   (a) Find current population figures and population forecasts for a specific area. Identify specific population cohorts and their likely populations now and in ten years' time.

   (b) Identify participation rates for a specific activity for the cohorts, using appropriate survey data. Assuming likely scenarios (e.g. policy initiatives, industry changes), estimate how these participation rates are likely to change in the next ten years.

   (c) Multiply the current populations for the cohorts by their current participation rates to identify the number of people participating. Multiply by average frequency of participation to calculate average number of visits in a given period. Repeat the process to calculate the number of people and visits in ten years' time.

   (d) What are the implications of your results for planning provision?

Structured Guide to Further Reading

For guidance on planning principles:

National Planning Policy Framework. Retrieved from www.gov.uk/government/publications/national-planning-policy-framework – 2

Sport England Planning for Sport. Retrieved from www.sportengland.org/how-we-can-help/facilities-and-planning/planning-for-sport?section=planning_for_sport_guidance

For a review and discussion of planning techniques:

Veal, A. J. (2017). *Leisure and Tourism Policy and Planning*, 4th edition. CABI Publishing, Wallingford.

Useful Websites

For planning policy in England and Wales and a guide to Local Development Frameworks: www.planningportal.gov.uk/

For planning policy in Northern Ireland:
www.infrastructure-ni.gov.uk/articles/planning-policy

For planning policy in Scotland:
www.gov.scot/publications/scottish-planning-policy/

Reference

Bullough, S., Moriarty, C., Wilson, J., & Panagouleas, T. (2010). *The Nature of Latent Demand Compared to Expressed Demand, Using Active People 2, A Strategic Insights Paper*. Sport England, London.

Chapter 12

Global Economics of Sport and Leisure

*By Girish Ramchandani
and Darryl Wilson*

In This Chapter

- Understand the size and shape of the sport market;
- Identify the key sectors of the sport market and their influence on GDP;
- See the relationship between the supply of sport and the demand for sport;
- Appreciate the impact of global trends on the international sport market;
- Understand the importance of broadcasting and sponsorship;
- See the impact of government involvement in sport.

DOI: 10.4324/9780367823610-12

Summary

Sport has massively increased its profile as an area of economic, social, and cultural activity. It is now a major global industry. In most developed economies it accounts for around 2% of GDP, in some a lot more. The economics of sport used to treat the sport market as a national market, looking at the demand side and the supply side of the market and analysing the main factors affecting each. An increasing and hugely important part of every country's sport market is international or global. A lot of the rise in the economic importance of sport in recent years is due to the developments in broadcasting and sponsorship, which is covered in this chapter. This chapter also considers the role of government in the global sport market.

12.1 Introduction

Prior to the 1960s sport was predominantly a local activity, and the sport market was dominated by mass participation sport. Elite sport was mainly amateur except for some professional team sports where rewards were modest. Broadcasting rights income, government funding of elite sport, and sponsorship income were negligible. In the 1960s and 1970s, international sporting competitions became increasingly important, creating the need for national policies and strategies for elite sport. National agencies for sport were set up in many countries, signalling the increasing importance of government in sport. Since the early 1980s, the sport market has become increasingly global, driven by increasing commercial sector interest in sport, and this globalisation of the sport market is the focus of this chapter. Gratton *et al.*'s (2012) *Global Economics of Sport* provided a detailed analysis of how this global market for sport has emerged, and this chapter synthesises the contents of that book with some new content and updated examples.

12.2 The Economics of Sport

Figure 12.1 shows the hierarchical nature of the sport market as first conceived by Gratton and Taylor (2000), with a relatively small group of elite athletes at the top of the pyramid competing in national and international competitions. At this top level of sport, money flows into sport from sponsorship, from paying spectators, and from television companies eager to broadcast this high standard of competition. Although this elite end of the sport market appears to be essentially commercial, it is also subsidised by governments. There is a national demand in every country for international sporting success. Governments fund the top end of the sport market to 'produce' sporting excellence and international sporting success. At the bottom of the pyramid is recreational sport – people taking part in sport for fun, for enjoyment, or maybe in order to get fitter and healthier. Government subsidies at this level are much higher than those directed at the elite end of the sport market.

The supply side of the sport market is a mixture of three types of provider: the public sector, the voluntary sector, and the commercial sector. Government supports sport both to promote mass participation and to generate excellence, but government also imposes taxation on sport. The commercial sector sponsors sport both at the elite level and at the

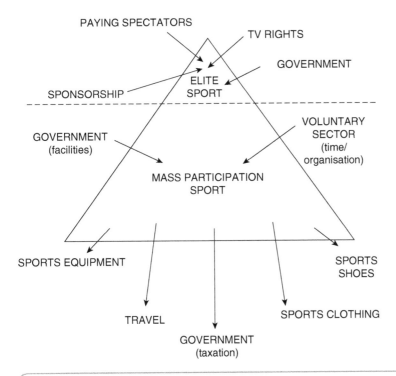

PAYING SPECTATORS

TV RIGHTS

GOVERNMENT

SPONSORSHIP

ELITE
SPORT

GOVERNMENT
(facilities)

VOLUNTARY
SECTOR
(time/
organisation)

MASS PARTICIPATION
SPORT

SPORTS EQUIPMENT

SPORTS
SHOES

TRAVEL

SPORTS CLOTHING

GOVERNMENT
(taxation)

Figure 12.1 **The sport market pyramid.**
Source: Gratton and Taylor (2000)

grass roots. Some of these sponsors (e.g. Nike, Adidas, and Reebok) do so to promote their sports products and receive a return on this sponsorship through expenditure by sports participants on their products. Most of sports sponsorship is, however, from the non-sports commercial sector (e.g. Coca-Cola, McDonalds, etc.), where the motives for the sponsorship are less directly involved with selling a product to sports participants. Squeezed in between government and the commercial sector is the voluntary sector, putting resources into sport mainly through the contribution of free labour time, but needing also to raise enough revenue to cover costs since the voluntary sector cannot raise revenue through taxation as government can.

If the supply side of the sport market is complicated, then so is the demand side. The demand for sport is a composite demand involving the demand for free time; the demand to take part in sport; the demand for equipment, shoes, and clothing; the demand for facilities; and the demand for travel. Taking part in sport involves, therefore, the generation of demand for a range of goods and services which themselves will be provided by the mixture of public, commercial, and voluntary organisations discussed earlier. To this complexity of the demand to take part in sport can be added the complication that the sport market is a mixture of both participant demands and spectator demands of different types. As we move up the hierarchy towards elite sport, there is an increasing demand to watch sporting competitions. Some of these spectators may also take part, but many do not. The spectators may go to a specific sports event or watch at a distance on television. Alternatively, they may not 'watch' at all, preferring to listen on the radio or read about it online or via social media. All these activities are part of the demand side of the sport market.

In fact, market demand is even more complicated than this rather complex picture since Figure 12.1 only represents the flows into and out of a national sport market. A small, but increasing, part of every country's sport market is international or global.

12.3 The Development of the Global Sport Market

Even before the First World War some of the basic ingredients of the global sport market were already in place. Three elements, however, were missing: sports broadcasting, sponsorship, and transnational corporations in sport. The whole of the period from 1914 to the present saw the increasing commercialisation of sport and the rise in economic significance of the sport market both nationally for developed countries and internationally. Broadcasting was developed relatively early in this period, but the significance of global sports corporations and sponsorship are much more recent developments.

Commercialisation and globalisation, prompted by global television media and multinational corporations, have radically transformed the nature of modern sport, turning it from an amateur-based pastime into a serious multi-billion-dollar global business and established industry, which has grown astronomically over the last 50 years (Gratton *et al.*, 2012). The global sports market in 2019 was valued at US$ 458.9 billion by The Business Research Company (2020). The same source also estimated the global sports market to shrink in 2020 to US$ 446.5 billion mainly due to economic slowdown across countries owing to the COVID-19 outbreak and the measures to contain it, but then recover and grow from 2021 onwards to reach US$ 556.1 billion in 2023. North America is the largest region in the global sports market, accounting for 35% of the market in 2019, followed by the Asia Pacific region at 30% (The Business Research Company (2020).

The globalisation of the sport market has taken place over a relatively short time period since the early 1980s and is the culmination of a series of trends as identified by Westerbeek and Smith (2003):

- Huge expansion in the number of broadcast hours devoted to sport on television and other media;
- Increasing international standardisation of sports media output so the same sports pictures are broadcast across the world;
- Increasing value of 'global sport properties', most notably athletes and major sports events;
- Increasing market power of top global sports corporations, including sport-centred media companies;
- Growth in the economic importance of sport both within national economies and globally;
- Increase in number of top global corporations, mainly from the non-sport sector, using sport as their major global sponsorship vehicle.

Although the main process of globalisation takes place at the elite end of the sport market, the bottom end of the market is provided for by global sports corporations such as Nike and Adidas, who supply the shoes, clothing, and equipment that make up the largest share of the sport market. There are commercial companies that produce, distribute, and market their product on a global basis. Gratton *et al.* (2012) describe how Nike designs its sports shoes in Oregon, USA; contracts out the production of these shoes to factories in Thailand, Indonesia, China, and Korea; and markets the shoes on a global basis using a symbol (the swoosh) and, in the past, three words that were understood throughout the world ('Just Do It').

Despite recent focus on the amount of money involved in sport at the elite level in terms of sponsorship, payments of broadcasting rights, transfer fees, and players' salaries, in fact consumer expenditure on sport is not dominated by payments related to major professional sports. Instead, consumer expenditure in the sport market consists in the main of expenditure related to the consumer's own participation in sport rather than as a spectator. By far the largest sector of the sport market consists of all the products which are bought for use in sport, such as sports clothing and footwear, equipment, and services such as subscription fees to sports clubs and entry charges to sports facilities. Analysis by the Business Research Company (2020) indicates that of the estimated US$ 458.9 billion global sport market in 2019, the 'participatory' sector accounted for US$ 314.7 billion, whereas the 'spectator' sector accounted for US$ 144.2 billion.

We now examine some of the key drivers that have contributed to the development of the global sports market.

12.4 Broadcasting

It is the development of global sports broadcasting and the formation of the sport/media/business nexus that has had a decisive impact on the nature of sport, changing its purpose, way of production, organisation, and consumption (Gratton *et al.*, 2012). A feature of the global market for sports broadcasting is that it operates under imperfect competition. It all depends on whether the market is in short supply (excess demand) or short demand (excess supply). The short side of the market usually imposes its transaction conditions on those competing together on the long side of the market. Andreff (2008) identifies four different forms of the sports broadcasting market, as described here:

a) A monopoly, when only one organiser supplies his/her exclusive sports event to competing TV channels (consider the IOC offering the Olympic Games, FIFA with the football World Cup). In a monopoly market, price is relatively high, broadcasting rights expensive, and revenues accruing to the organiser big.
b) An oligopolistic monopoly, when only one event organiser is facing very few potential buyers – TV channels (e.g. the UEFA Champions League). Broadcasting rights are still high, though lower than in the monopoly case due to fewer competitors on the demand side.
c) A bilateral monopoly, when a single public TV channel monopolises the demand side of a domestic market or when a European cartel of public channels (ERU) merged all demands for a sports event to be broadcast on a European scale. In the case of bilateral monopoly, economic theory teaches that the transaction price is determined by the relative bargaining power (not necessarily economic or financial) of the monopoly and the monopsony. Usually the price is lower than the price emerging in the presence of a pure or oligopolistic monopoly.
d) A monopsony, when professional clubs are competing for the sale of their individual broadcasting rights to a single TV channel (the French football championship in the 1970s) instead of the league pooling the rights for all clubs. Then, in such a case, the lowest price is reached, as well as the lowest revenues for sports organisers since they are competing on the long side of the market in the face of a single buyer.

The development of television technology and its spread across the globe changed the nature of sports production and consumption and hence the economics of sport. The FIFA World Cup was televised for the first time in 1954, and the Rome Olympics in 1960 were the first to take advantage of the 'Eurovision link' to broadcast live around Europe (Whannel, 2005). Television broadcasting has significantly increased the global popularity of both events and contributed significantly to globalisation of sport in general.

In the case of the Olympic Games, broadcast programming is generated by Olympic Broadcasting Services (OBS), which captures the broadcast signal from each Olympic venue and delivers the signal to the Olympic broadcast partners to air over various media platforms throughout the world. From the full range of available material, each Olympic broadcast partner can deliver those events and images that it determines to be of greatest interest to the target audience in its home country or territory. Increased host broadcast coverage has afforded the Olympic broadcast partners greater programming opportunities in more sports and enabled the broadcast partners to deliver more complete Olympic coverage to their audiences around the world. The IOC works in partnership with its broadcasters to ensure that an increasing amount of live coverage is available and that the latest technologies, including HDTV, live coverage on the internet, and coverage on mobile phones are available in as many territories as possible. The global audience reach (i.e. the number of people who saw at least one minute of the Olympic Games coverage on television) and the hours of content provided to the rights-holding broadcasters for recent Summer and Winter Games are presented in Table 12.1.

According to global broadcast figures published by the IOC (2020, pg. 30):

● Half the world's population watched the Olympic Games Rio 2016, with viewers having access to more Olympic content than ever before. The average TV viewer watched over 20% more coverage of Rio 2016 than London 2012, with 584 TV channels, more than 270 dedicated digital platforms, and hundreds of official broadcaster pages on social media.

● More than a quarter of the world's population followed the Olympic Winter Games PyeongChang 2018 across various media platforms. In total, the IOC's global broadcast partners made more coverage available from PyeongChang than any previous Olympic Winter Games, offering a combined 157,812 hours – an increase of 38% from Sochi 2014. The increased digital coverage helped make PyeongChang 2018 the most digitally

Table 12.1 **Olympic Games TV Global Audience Reach and Host Broadcast Feed Hours**

Edition	Games	Global television audience reach (billion)	Host broadcast feed hours
Summer	Beijing 2008	3.5	5,000
Winter	Vancouver 2010	1.8	2,700
Summer	London 2012	3.6	5,600
Winter	Sochi 2014	2.1	3,100
Summer	Rio 2016	3.2	7,100
Winter	PyeongChang 2018	1.9	5,600

viewed Olympic Winter Games ever, with 670 million global online users viewing digital broadcast coverage – 120% more than watched Sochi 2014.

Similarly, it has been estimated that 3.6 billion people watched some official broadcast coverage of the 2018 FIFA World Cup in Russia (equivalent to 51% of the global population), including 3.3 billion in-home TV viewers plus 0.3 billion people who did not watch coverage in home but did see coverage on digital platforms, in public viewing areas or in bars and restaurants (FIFA, 2018a). The final between France and Croatia was seen live by 1.12 billion people. There was an unprecedented level of viewing on digital platforms, as highlighted by the following data presented from different countries (FIFA, 2018a, pg. 7).

- In Russia, 4 million unique users accessed Channel One's digital coverage of the Russia v. Croatia quarter final, almost four times the total of the top match in 2014 (1.3 million for Brazil v. Germany). Across all three broadcasters in Russia there were 171 million video views of 2018 FIFA World Cup content.
- In China CCTV's digital platform CNTV received 6.5 billion views for simulcast and VOD coverage, seven times the figure achieved in 2014. Digital sub licensees Migu and Youku received a further 4.4 billion and 2.5 billion views respectively.
- Around 38 million unique users accessed digital content on the owned and operated digital platforms of FOX in the USA, generating 60 million hours of viewing. NBC Telemundo (Spanish) apps and websites generated a further 30 million hours of viewing.
- In the UK over 2 million unique users saw coverage of Sweden v. England on the BBC's digital platforms, almost double the peak from 2014 (1.1 million for Brazil v. Germany). In total the BBC and ITV generated 255 million video views and over 52 million hours of viewing.
- Despite not being involved in the tournament, 0.43 million unique users in Italy watched live coverage of the final on Mediaset's website. Italy v. Uruguay, the top performing match for broadcaster RAI in 2014, had only 0.28 million unique users.

The potential for huge audiences, even during the day and late at night, and usually during the slack summer season as is the case of the summer Olympic Games, has led to growing competition between television networks for exclusive broadcasting rights for major sports events (Whannel, 2005). This competition brings significant sums of money into sports and helps to transform the economics of global sports and sports events. The combined global value of all sports media rights was nearly US$ 50 billion in 2018 (SportBusiness Media Consulting, 2018) and is projected to reach around US$ 56 billion in 2022 (SportBusiness Media Consulting, 2019). A significant driver of growth is expected to be the deeper penetration of new 'non-traditional', i.e. non-pay TV players such as technology platforms and social media companies (Delta, 2019).

According to SportBusiness Media Consulting (2018), the sports with the highest share of global media rights value in 2018 were football (40.6%), American football (15.6%), basketball (8.6%), and baseball (7.4%). European football and the North American major leagues accounted for all top ten most valuable sports media rights properties in that year. Huge domestic deals for the National Football League (NFL), National Basketball Association (NBA), and Major League Baseball (MLB) make the USA the most valuable market, accounting for 44.2% of global sports media rights value. This percentage however represents a continued trend downward over recent years, with USA's market share now 2.4% lower than in 2016. The NFL is by far sport's most valuable media rights property, earning nearly US$ 7.8 billion annually from its media rights agreements. Table 12.2 shows the value of broadcasts rights fees paid for past summer and winter Olympic Games. Olympic broadcast

Table 12.2 IOC Broadcast Revenue Generation, 1993–2016

Olympiad	Summer Games (US$ millions)	Winter Games (US$ millions)	Overall (US$ millions)
1993–1996	898	353	1251
1997–2000	1,332	514	1845
2001–2004	1,494	738	2232
2005–2008	1,739	831	2570
2009–2012	2,569	1,280	3850
2013–2016	2,868	1,289	4157

partnerships have provided the Olympic Movement with a secure financial base and helped to ensure the future viability of the Olympic Games.

For some properties, where there has historically been consistent and rapid growth, most recent auctions have plateaued in rights value, which signifies a potential market correction or a point of reflection (Delta, 2019). In contrast to the North American major leagues, which earn most of their media rights revenue domestically, European football properties benefit from broad-based international fan interest and are earning an increasing percentage of their rights revenues offshore. This point can be appreciated by considering the case of the English Premier League (EPL). The EPL is the most-watched sports league in the world, followed in 188 countries by a cumulative global TV audience of 3.2 billion during the 2018–2019 season. Global audience figures have become of increasing importance for the EPL after a dip in the value of its domestic television rights from GBP 5.4 billion (for the 2016–2019 cycle) to 5 billion (for the 2019–2022 cycle). Despite this decline, the EPL's total income from domestic and international TV rights will increase from GBP 8.5 billion during the previous three-year cycle to GBP 9.2 billion for the 2019 to 2022 term, as a consequence of substantial growth in league's international rights (KPMG, 2019). In 2018 the EPL earned some 38% of its revenue from international rights (SportBusiness Media Consulting, 2018). The GBP 4.2 billion overseas broadcast rights revenue for the 2019–2022 cycle is 46% of the league's total broadcasting revenue. As international revenues are set to grow, in the next distribution cycle (2022–2025) the EPL is likely to see its overseas broadcasting income surpass its domestic rights for the first time (KPMG, 2019).

Broadcasting rights fees have become a major, sometimes predominant, source of revenue for many sports properties. The EPL's financial supremacy is largely due to its success in securing lucrative broadcasting deals since its formation. The EPL has always sold its media rights collectively, enjoying stronger bargaining power, and also on a 'no single buyer' basis, creating a competitive environment (KPMG, 2019). Olympic broadcast partnerships have been the single greatest source of revenue for the Olympic Movement for more than three decades. In the case of the Olympic Games, broadcast rights accounted for 73% (US$ 4.157 billion) of total revenue for the period 2013–2016 (IOC, 2020). In the 2018 financial year, the lion's share of FIFA's total revenue (55%) was attributable to the sale of television broadcasting rights for the 2018 FIFA World Cup in Russia (FIFA, 2018b). The explosive growth of television sport and the huge sums of money generated by broadcasting rights fees has changed the economics of sport, turning it into a highly commercialised commodity.

12.5 Sponsorship

Popular sporting events that can attract a global audience via broadcasting become ideal vehicles for corporate sponsors seeking to raise the global profile of their brands. Such events 'transcend cultural differences and, being universal in appeal, open up access to consumer markets around the world in a way that few other social and cultural practices can equal' (Smart, 2007). As such, they offer multinational corporations a unique platform for brand building and global marketing. Gratton *et al.* (2012) note that it has only been in the last quarter of the twentieth century, in association with developments in sports television broad-casting, that corporate sponsorship began to have a marked impact on sports. From the late 1970s and early 1980s, corporate sponsorship of global sports events began to grow dramatically.

FIFA was the first global sports organisation for which corporate sponsorship became a major source of revenue generation, with the World Cup becoming the main tournament for securing lucrative global commercial sponsorship agreements and for auctioning the sale of global television broadcasting rights (Smart, 2007). FIFA currently operates a three-tier sponsorship structure. FIFA partners have the highest level of association with FIFA and all FIFA events as well as playing a wider role in supporting the development of football all around the world. FIFA World Cup sponsors have rights to the FIFA Confederations Cup and the FIFA World Cup on a global basis. The main rights for a sponsor in this tier are brand association, the use of selected marketing assets and media exposure, as well as ticketing and hospitality offers for the events. The Regional Supporter level is the third level of FIFA's sponsorship structure, allowing companies within five pre-defined global regions to promote an association with the FIFA World Cup in the domestic market. This tier provides regional sponsorship rights to up to 20 brands from North and Central America, South America, Europe, the Middle East and Africa, and Asia (FIFA, 2018c). FIFA signed up 14 new sponsors in the 2015–2018 cycle, resulting in seven FIFA partners (Adidas, Coca-Cola, The Wanda Group, Gazprom, Hyundai-Kia, Visa, and Qatar Airways), five FIFA World Cup sponsors (Budweiser, McDonalds, The Mengniu Group, Vivo, and Hisense), and eight Regional Sup-porters. Seven of these companies were from China, and as such Chinese businesses had an unprecedented presence at the 2018 FIFA World Cup. Marketing rights afforded to sponsors were the second most important source of revenue for FIFA in the 2018 financial year (after the sale of television broadcasting rights), accounting for US$ 1,143 million or nearly 25% of FIFA's total revenue (FIFA, 2018b).

Olympic sponsorship programmes have contributed significantly to the growth of the Olympic Movement, the Olympic Games, and sport worldwide. It is generally recognised that the 1984 Los Angeles Olympics was a watershed in the commercialisation of the Olympic Games and providing a model in financing major events in general. Until that point, global sporting events such as the Olympics were increasingly regarded as a financial burden to organisers. The 1984 Games is described as inaugurating the most successful era of cor-porate sponsorship in Olympic history (Gratton *et al.*, 2012). The Olympic Partners (TOP) Programme is the worldwide sponsorship programme created by the IOC in 1985 to develop a diversified revenue base for the Olympic Games and to establish long-term corporate part-nerships that would benefit the Olympic Movement as a whole. To control sponsorship pro-grammes and the number of major corporate sponsorships, the IOC constructs and manages

Table 12.3 TOP Programme Partners and Revenue by Olympiad

Olympiad	Games	Number of TOP Partners	Revenue (in US$ millions)
1985–1988	Calgary/Seoul	9	96
1989–1992	Albertville/Barcelona	12	172
1993–1996	Lillehammer/Atlanta	10	197
1997–2000	Nagano/Sydney	11	579
2001–2004	Salt Lake City/Athens	11	663
2005–2008	Turin/Beijing	12	866
2009–2012	Vancouver/London	11	950
2013–2016	Sochi/Rio	12	1,003

programmes in which only a small number of corporations participate. The TOP Programme provides each Worldwide Olympic Partner with exclusive global marketing rights and opportunities within a designated product or service category. The TOP Partners may exercise these rights worldwide and may activate marketing initiatives with all the members of the Olympic Movement that participate in the TOP Programme. Table 12.3 shows how the TOP Programme has evolved since its creation in 1985. Over the last eight Olympiads, TOP Programme marketing rights has grown from US$ 96 million (1985–1988) to US$ 1,003 million (2013–2016), and the revenue generated from the TOP programme now accounts for 18% of the IOC's revenue during the 2013–2016 Olympiad (IOC, 2020).

In addition to the revenue that the TOP Programme generates for the IOC, the Olympic Games domestic sponsorship programme is managed by the local organising committee within the host country under the direction of the IOC. The domestic sponsorship programme grants marketing rights within the host country or territory only. For the 1993–1996 Olympiad, covering the 1992 Lillehammer Winter Games and the 1996 Atlanta Summer Games, the total revenue generated from the domestic sponsorship programme was US$ 534 million. For the 2013–2016 Olympiad, this figure had increased to US$ 2,037 million. The amount of revenue that is generated by the Olympic Games domestic sponsorship programmes is considerably greater than the amount generated through the TOP programme, but not as much as that generated by broadcast partnerships.

Though less in total than the amount raised through the sale of broadcasting rights, the rate of growth in sponsorship income has mirrored that of broadcasting. That is no coincidence. Sponsors are attracted to events that attract large television audiences. The summer Olympic Games and the Football World Cup attract the largest cumulative television audiences on the planet. As a result, these events are sponsored by global corporations aiming to enhance their global market position. Most of these sponsors are non-sports corporations simply because most major global corporations are in the non-sports sector. According to international sports marketing agency Two Circles (Nicholson, 2020), the top five sectors in terms of global sports sponsorship spending in 2019 were financial services (US$ 12.58 billion), automotive

(US$ 5.93 billion), technology (US$ 5.58 billion), telecoms (US$ 3.14 billion), and retail (US$ 2.87 billion). Companies in these five sectors collectively accounted for around 65% of the total global sponsorship spend in that year. The widespread prevalence of non-sport corporations forming associations with the global sport market can be appreciated further by looking at the identities of the 14 corporations that currently participate in the ninth generation of the IOC's TOP Programme, known as TOP IX, each with global product-category exclusivity. These include (IOC, 2020):

- Airbnb (unique accommodation products and unique experiences services);
- Alibaba Group (Cloud infrastructure, Cloud services, and e-commerce platform services);
- Atos (information technology products, services, and solutions);
- Bridgestone (tyres, restrictive automotive vehicle services, non-motorised bicycles, and diversified [rubber] products);
- Coca-Cola (non-alcoholic beverages);
- Dow (chemicals, raw materials, and compounds used across selected industries);
- GE (selected industrial equipment for systems used in energy, healthcare, transportation, and infrastructure industries);
- Intel (processors, chips, and similar silicon platforms and drones);
- Omega (time pieces; timing, scoring, and venue results systems and services);
- Panasonic (audio/TV/video equipment);
- Procter & Gamble (personal care, healthcare, and household care products);
- Samsung (wireless communications and computing equipment);
- Toyota (vehicles, mobility support robots, and mobility services);
- Visa (payment services, transaction security, pre-paid cards).

These sponsors are not promoting sport. They are promoting their products that are marketed on a global basis with the events that have the largest global reach. There will continue to be a healthy market for sponsors at this top end of the events hierarchy. However, not all sports have events that achieve this level of global television coverage. For many sports, achieving major sponsorship deals can prove very difficult. Lower down the events hierarchy, sports are often faced with sponsors ending their sponsorship when faced with difficult economic conditions in their industrial environment. For these, sports sponsorship can be a highly risky form of funding because of the volatility of sponsorship demand when sponsors are faced with the difficult trading conditions seen around the world since the global economic crisis of 2008–2009. Indeed, the global sports sponsorship spend fell by 37%, from US$ 46.1 billion in 2019 to US$ 28.9 billion in 2020 as the result of the COVID-19 pandemic.

It is not only events though that attract sponsorship. Teams, kit, stadia, and the athletes themselves are all targets of sponsors. There are six broad categories of sports sponsorship mainly in the context of the sports sponsorship industry in the United States. The six categories include sports governing body sponsorship, sports team sponsorship, athlete sponsorship, broadcast and media sponsorship, sports facility sponsorship, and sports event sponsorship. The corporations that tend to enter sponsorship with governing bodies like FIFA and IOC tend to be larger, national, or multinational companies, mainly due to the large financial investment required with these sponsorships. Again though, the motivation of the sponsor is that all of these will be showcased in the broadcast at major events.

In addition to considering how broadcasting and sponsorship have contributed to the globalisation of sport and sporting events, it is also worth looking at the role of government in an increasingly global sport market.

12.6 Government Intervention in the Sport Market

The importance of sports has risen steadily in emerging economies, resulting in the increase in government spending on the development of the sports industry, specifically into setting up sports infrastructure, building teams in sports, and attracting large investments. For example, the plan of the Chinese government to increase the value of the sports industry in the country to US$ 813 million by 2025 is resulting in the flow of large investments into sports activities that include events, facilities, teams, leagues, and other programs. Similarly, for 2018–2020, the federal government of India has set aside a US$ 262 million budget for the 'Khelo Program' to promote the sports industry in the country (The Business Research Company, 2019).

Economic welfare principles provide us with reasons for government intervention in the sport market. When a private market operates successfully, but still it fails to cater adequately for the full effects of the market on the welfare of society, economists call this a 'market failure' situation. There are several causes of market failure which are relevant to the market for sport. In each case the existence of market failure is in principle a reason for government intervention, since intervention has the potential to prevent or compensate for the market failure (Gratton & Taylor, 2000). As examples, here we use the relationship between sport and health and the public good nature of international sporting success.

As Gratton *et al.* (2012) argued, it is now generally accepted that sport and physical activity can have an important positive impact on health. In particular:

- Regular physical activity decreases the risk of cardiovascular mortality in general and of coronary heart disease mortality in particular.
- Regular physical activity prevents or delays the development of high blood pressure and reduces blood pressure in people with hypertension.
- Physical activity is also important in helping people to control their body weight and in controlling diabetes.
- Specific forms of physical activity can help to reduce the risk of falls and accidents.
- Physical activity improves bone health and helps to maintain strength, coordination, cognitive functioning, and balance.
- Physical activity reduces the risk of colon cancer, and evidence is growing to support links with other forms of cancer.
- Moderately intense physical activity enhances the immune system.
- Physical activity reduces the risk of depression and has positive benefits for mental health including reducing anxiety and enhancing mood and self-esteem.
- Physical activity can play a valuable role in the prevention and treatment of non-specific chronic low back pain.

There is evidence to suggest that a more efficient means of achieving health policy objectives may be to redistribute resources from health services to direct expenditure on the provision or subsidisation of active recreation services in order to improve the health of the population (Gratton *et al.*, 2012). The relationship between sport and health is not the only market failure to support the argument for government intervention in the sport market, but it is one of its strongest arguments.

The most recent strategy for sport in the UK – *Sporting Future: A New Strategy for an Active Nation* – sets out five outcome areas that define why the government invests in sport. These include physical wellbeing, mental wellbeing, individual development, social and community development, and economic development. Studies have shown that sport is an important sector of economic activity in terms of both Gross Domestic Product (GDP) and employment. Research funded by the European Commission (2018) found that sport-related GDP was 279.7 billion Euro or 2.12% of total GDP within the European Union (EU). In addition, 5.67 million EU employees could be attributed to sport, a share of 2.72%. However, these economic indicators do not capture the full extent of the externalities of sport. According to a review of international literature on the social impact of sport (DCMS, 2015):

- Sport and exercise prevent or reduce physical and mental health problems and save on health care costs.
- Sports participation improves pro-social behaviour and reduces crime and anti-social behaviour, particularly for young men; promotes bonding social capital and collective action, particularly volunteering; and has a positive effect on educational outcomes, including psychological and cognitive benefits and educational attainment.
- There is a positive relationship between sport participation and subjective wellbeing, i.e. life satisfaction or happiness for individuals.

Recently, Davies *et al.* (2019) valued several outcomes linked to health, education, crime, subjective wellbeing, and social capital that they identified from the literature as having a strong relationship with sports participation. Using a Social Return on Investment (SROI) framework, they quantified that these outcomes were collectively worth £44.75 billion in England in 2013–2014 and that for every £1 invested in sport, £1.91 worth of overall social impact was generated. Subjective wellbeing was the largest component of social impact, generating £30.43 billion, or 68% of overall social impact from sport.

A rather different argument relates to government intervention in elite sport to generate international sporting success. Gratton and Taylor (2000) argue that international sporting success is a public good (also referred to as 'collective goods'). The principal characteristics attached to such goods are that they are non-rival and non-excludable in consumption. *Non-rival* means that one person's consumption does not prevent another person from enjoying the same product at the same time. *Non-excludable* means that no consumer can be prevented from enjoying the product. Under these two conditions, private market provision is not worthwhile, so public goods will be underprovided by the private market. Because many of the benefits of international sporting success (e.g. improved national morale, increased interest in sport) are such that nobody can be prevented from feeling them, they are non-excludable. Because everyone can enjoy these benefits together with no congestion in consumption, they are non-rival. A free market would underprovide such public goods because there is always the temptation for consumers to become 'free riders', benefiting from the products without paying for them. Governments can ensure that adequate provision is made for excellence in sport to be produced and that those who benefit from this public good pay, through taxes.

These are only two examples of market failure in the sport market, and we do see government intervention in the sport market in many countries both to encourage more sports participation for health reasons and to support elite sport, in particular Olympic sports since many countries now have elite sports strategies aiming to maximise success at the Olympics.

In recent years the competition between nations for success in elite sport has intensified, as is evidenced by the increasing sums of money being invested by some nations into elite sport development programmes. This development has been referred to as a 'global sporting arms race' (De Bosscher *et al.*, 2006). To illustrate this point, Table 12.3 shows the amount of money invested by UK Sport (the nation's high-performance sports agency investing in Olympic and Paralympic sport) through its World Class Performance Programme in recent years.

The combined amount of elite sport funding for Summer Olympic and Paralympic sports increased from around £264 million in the four years leading up to the Beijing 2008 Games

Table 12.4 Elite Sport Funding in the UK

Years	Summer Olympic Sports	Summer Paralympic Sports	Winter Olympic Sports	Winter Paralympic Sports
2005–2008	£235,103,000	£29,545,872		
2007–2010			£5,776,000	£650,000
2009–2012	£264,143,753	£49,254,386		
2011–2014			£13,444,638	£755,600
2013–2016	£274,465,541	£72,786,652		
2015–2018			£28,353,135	£3,909,223

to more than £347 million in the four years leading up to the Rio 2016 Games. The data in Table 12.3 also illustrates that there has been considerable growth in the funding allocated to Winter Olympic and Paralympic sports in the UK. Because of public investment in elite sport, there is increased scrutiny and accountability as to the efficiency and effectiveness of how those public funds are used.

Several researchers have sought to investigate the determinants of success in elite sport based on macro-level factors such as population size, economic welfare, climate, geographical circumstances, and political systems (e.g. Bernard & Busse, 2004). Research has shown that over 50% of international success by countries can be expressed by three variables, namely population, wealth, and communism (De Bosscher, 2006). However, as nations have become strategic in their approach to elite sport development, they rely less on these passive macroeconomic variables and more on critical success factors that can be influenced by well-considered polices. De Bosscher *et al.'s* (2015) SPLISS framework identifies nine pillars of policy components that can contribute to increased success in elite sport, namely: (1) financial support; (2) elite sport structures and policies; (3) sport participation; (4) talent identification and development systems; (5) athletic and post-career support; (6) training facilities; (7) coaching and coach development; (8) national and international competition; and, (9) scientific research.

Thibault (2009) identified three major negative consequences from the globalisation of sport: the international division of labour with global sports corporations using labour from developing countries to manufacture sports clothing, shoes, and equipment; the migration of top athletes from their country of origin to countries willing to pay the highest salaries; and the increasing involvement of global media conglomerates in sport. The negative economic consequences of sports globalisation identified by Thibault (2009) are effectively market failures in the global sport market. Economics tells us that governments should intervene to correct such market failures. But there is no world government to carry out such interventions.

12.7 Conclusion

The economics of sport used to treat the sport market as a national market, looking at the demand side and the supply side of the market and analysing the main factors affecting each. Although this approach is still relevant to some extent, increasingly it is more appropriate to talk about the global sport market. As Maguire *et al.* (2002) point out: 'dominant, emergent, and residual patterns of sport and leisure practices are closely intertwined with the globalisation process'.

An increasing and hugely important part of every country's sport market is international or global. The major globalising forces are: the increasing globalisation of media coverage of major sports events (e.g. the Olympics and the FIFA World Cup); the creation of new global sports events (e.g. the Cricket World Cup, the Rugby World Cup) driven by the eagerness of global sports organisations to promote their sport; global television coverage of what were formerly domestic events (e.g. the English Premier League); global recognition of the top athletes competing in these events; and association of these athletes with global sports brands (e.g. Nike, Adidas). The characteristics of the global sport market that emerged were: escalation in the price of broadcasting rights to the top sports events; global marketing of major sports products by using images (not words) recognisable worldwide; sports celebrities becoming the most important part of these images; and escalation in the price of sponsorship deals for events and athletes by both sport (e.g. Nike, Adidas) and non-sport (e.g. Coca-Cola, McDonalds) sponsors.

The globalisation of the sport market has created mutual dependencies between sport, broadcasters, and sponsors, and the relationships between them have driven the globalisation process. The whole point about the globalisation of sport is that it is supranational. Global sports organisations, broadcasting companies, and sponsors are operating in the world market for sport. It is certainly the case that new developments in technology and in sport will provide greater opportunities for further globalisation.

Discussion questions

1. What are the key factors that have contributed to the globalisation of the sport market?
2. Why has sport seen such an escalation in the price of broadcasting rights, and is this escalation restricted to mega-events like the Olympic Games and FIFA World Cup?
3. Why do non-sport corporations sponsor sport?
4. What outcomes are government investment in sport expected to achieve at elite and grassroots levels? To what extent do these outcomes actually occur?

References

Andreff, W. (2008). Globalisation of the sports economy. *Rivista di Diritto ed Economia Dello Sport*, 4(3), 13–32.

Bernard, A., & Busse, M. (2004). Who wins the Olympic Games? Economic resources and medal totals. *Review of Economics and Statistics*, 86, 413–417.

The Business Research Company. (2019). Sports market by type (participatory sports, spectator sports, sports team & clubs, racing & individual sports and spectator sports), by competitive landscape and by geography – global forecast to 2022. Retrieved from www.thebusinessresearchcompany.com/report/sports-market (accessed 2 June 2020)

The Business Research Company. (2020). Sports global market report 2020–30: Covid 19 impact and recovery. Retrieved from www.thebusinessresearchcompany.com/report/sports-global-market-report-2020-30-covid-19-impact-and-recovery (accessed 8 June 2020).

Davies, L., Taylor, P., Ramchandani, G., & Christy, E. (2019). Social return on investment (SROI) in sport: A model for measuring the value of participation in England. *International Journal of Sport Policy and Politics*, 11(4). www.tandfonline.com/doi/full/10.1080/19406940.2019.1596967

DCMS. (2015). A review of the social impacts of culture and sport. Retrieved from https://assets.publishing.service.gov.uk/government/uploads/system/uploads/attachment_data/file/416279/A_review_of_the_Social_Impacts_of_Culture_and_Sport.pdf (accessed 10 June 2020).

De Bosscher, V., De Knop, P., Van Bottenburg, M., & Shibli, S. (2006). A conceptual framework for analysing sports policy factors leading to international sporting success. *European Sport Management Quarterly*, 6(2), 185–215.

De Bosscher, V. Shibli, S., Westerbeek, H., & van Bottenburg, M. (2015). *Successful Elite Sport Policies: An International Comparison of Sport Policy factors Leading to International Sporting Success (SPLISS 2.0.) in 15 Nations*. Meyer & Meyer Sport, Maidenhead.

Delta. (2019). Sports rights: Not yet the 'slam dunk' for OTTs. Retrieved from www.deltapartnersgroup.com/sites/default/files/The%20Delta%20Perspective%20-%20Sports%20rights%20-%20Feb2019.pdf (accessed 8 June 2020)

European Commission. (2018). Study on the economic impact of sport through sport satellite accounts. Retrieved from https://op.europa.eu/en/publication-detail/-/publication/865ef44c-5ca1-11e8-ab41-01aa75ed71a1 (accessed 20 June 2020)

FIFA. (2018a). 2018 FIFA world cup Russia global broadcast and audience summary. Retrieved from https://resources.fifa.com/image/upload/2018-fifa-world-cup-russia-global-broadcast-and-audience-executive summary.pdf?cloudid=njqsntrvdvqv8ho1dag5 (accessed 22 June 2020)

FIFA. (2018b). FIFA financial report 2018. Retrieved from https://resources.fifa.com/image/upload/xzshsoe2ayttyquuxhq0.pdf (accessed 22 June 2020)

FIFA. (2018c). FIFA world cup sponsorship strategy. Retrieved from http://fifa.pressfire.net/media/newsletter/FWC-Sponsors-Background-Paper-English-version.pdf (accessed 22 June 2020)

Gratton, C., Liu, D., Ramchandani, G., & Wilson, D. (2012). *The Global Economics of Sport*. Routledge, Abingdon.

Gratton, C., & Taylor, P. (2000). *Sport and Recreation: An Economic Analysis*. Routledge, Abingdon.

IOC. (2020). Olympic marketing fact file 2020 edition. Retrieved from https://stillmed.olympic.org/media/Document%20Library/OlympicOrg/Documents/IOC-Marketing-and-Broadcasting-General-Files/Olympic-Marketing-Fact-File.pdf (accessed 12 June 2020)

KPMG. (2019). Broadcasting revenue landscape – big money in the "big five" leagues. Retrieved from www.footballbenchmark.com/library/broadcasting_revenue_landscape_big_money_in_the_big_five_leagues (accessed 18 June 2020)

Maguire, J., Jarvie, G., Mansfield, L., & Bradley, J. (2002). *Sport Worlds: A Sociological Perspective*. Human Kinetics, Leeds.

Nicholson, P. (2020). Global sports sponsorship spend to drop by 37% to $28.9bn. Retrieved from www.insideworldfootball.com/2020/05/18/global-sports-sponsorship-spend-drop-37-28-9bn-says-report/ (accessed 20 June 2020)

Schwartz, E., & Hunter, J. (2008). *Advanced Theory and Practice in Sport Marketing*. Elsevier and Butterworth-Heinemann, Oxford.

Smart, B. (2007). Not playing around: Global capitalism, modern sport and consumer culture. *Global Networks*, 7(2), 113–134.

SportBusiness Media Consulting. (2018). Global media report 2018. Retrieved from https://media.sportbusiness.com/2018/11/sportbusiness-consulting-global-media-report-2018/ (accessed 20 June 2020)

SportBusiness Media Consulting. (2019). Global media report 2019. Retrieved from www.sportbusiness.com/consulting/sportbusiness-consulting-global-media-report-

2019/#:~:text=Global%20sports%20media%20rights%20hit,rights%20accounting%20
for%20%2420.8bn (accessed 20 June 2020)

Thibault, L. (2009). Gobalization of sport: An inconvenient truth. *Journal of Sport Management*, 23, 1–20.

Westerbeek, H., & Smith, A. (2003). *Sport Business in the Global Marketplace*. Palgrave Macmillan, Basingstoke.

Whannel, G. (2005). The five rings and the small screen: Television, sponsorship, and new media in the Olympic movement. In K. Young & K. B. Wamsley (Eds.), *Global Olympics: Historical and Sociological Studies of the Modern Games*. Elsevier, London.

Part III

Functions of Sport and Leisure Management

Contents

Chapter 13

Managing People in Sport and Leisure

By Chris Wolsey

In This Chapter

- What are the relationships between changing customer needs, organisational behaviour, human resource processes, people management, and business objectives?
- Why is it important to develop an empowered, skilled, and motivated workforce?
- How important are effective leadership, management, and communication?
- How are formal and informal organisational structures linked to organisational context and strategies?
- How can an understanding of organisational behaviour and human resource strategy be developed and implemented?

DOI: 10.4324/9780367823610-13

Summary

It is often said that people form a critical component of virtually all organisations worldwide. This truism is particularly appropriate to the sport and leisure sector of the economy. This sector often relies upon the lowest paid staff to provide the 'front of house' customer service that is pivotal to successful customer interactions and retention. This is essential in an increasingly complex business environment.

There can be no 'one size fits all' prescription relating to how this is achieved in practice. What does exist, however, are several principles, often represented by conceptual models that seek to frame some of the key considerations, questions, and possible solutions. Broadly, these can be better understood and developed within the theoretical frameworks provided by the organisational behaviour literature. It is the dynamic interplay between a range of competing and complex business and human factors that organisations must seek to rationalise. Ideally, this should be accomplished in a way that balances the needs of the business with the demands of the external environment and the complementary range of managerial decisions designed to navigate appropriate pathways forward.

Given the ongoing issues associated with the COVID-19 pandemic, it is more critical than ever that such decisions are cognisant of local considerations, with a clear sensitivity to the evolving needs and wants of both staff and customers. This chapter looks at these issues by identifying appropriate structural and leadership models, based upon an understanding of changing customer and staff needs. Increasingly, this is seen to require staff engagement in order to elicit a better understanding of the local context, in all its various guises. The extra and essential ingredient is to frame such decisions in the context of organisational resources, priorities, objectives, strategies, and related actions. In this way, the people management role fulfilled by 'personnel' departments becomes a more fundamental managerial function, designed to extract maximum value from its 'human resources' on behalf of a variety of related stakeholders However, this often leads to several tensions that have to be recognised and managed in a process of continual review and improvement. Such dynamic processes are complex and by no means mutually exclusive, constantly evolving at individual, group, and organisational levels.

This chapter interrogates such issues and concludes that there is a need to push beyond more traditional models of management based on 'command and control' in favour of a more flexible and creative approach, designed to deliver an evolving customer and staff experience that promotes innovation and stakeholder engagement.

13.1 Introduction

Leading and managing people is fundamental to the successful operation of virtually all organisations and businesses. This is particularly true of sport and leisure organisations, whose market 'product' often contains a substantial service element. This relies heavily on the real-time interplay of customers, employees, and other related stakeholders. Often, it is such relationships that deliver ongoing competitive advantage and that are pivotal to customer perceptions of both value and quality. An understanding of organisational behaviour seeks to provide a conceptual framework in which the interactions and motivations of individuals and groups can be better understood and subsequently managed. This is not a simple linear process but represents a dynamic set of behaviours and actions that are very likely to generate both positive and negative performance consequences at the level of the individual, team, and organisation. The trick is to understand these better, to maximise the positive(s) whilst minimising the negative impact(s) for a variety of interrelated stakeholder outcomes.

Human resource management (HRM) should seek to provide a more functional and sensitive 'human' representation of business management decisions. Unfortunately, this is often translated into a corporate desire to squeeze as much value as possible from an organisation's employees. However, organisational and individual performance is often difficult to measure accurately (see Chapter 16). It should be considered relative to customer requirements, an understanding of staff members, the goals of the organisation, the available resources, the actions of competitors, and the ever-changing external environment. In this context, the COVID-19 pandemic is likely to prompt a need for a fundamental rethink of both customer and staff requirements within an ever-changing resource envelope. Simply being challenged to do more with less is unhelpful, unless complemented by a sometimes required and radical rethink of strategic and related operational imperatives.

In an ideal world, once there is sufficient clarity around such issues, decisions can then be made about how employees at all levels can make a significant contribution to a competitive and profitable customer experience. Assuming one has a clear understanding of current and developing customer requirements, it is then important to design organisational structures that facilitate a flexible and appropriate fit between customer requirements, organisational constraints, individual/group needs, and future business opportunities.

Human resource structures, systems, and processes should be designed to both deliver and develop all levels of staff in relation to organisational objectives and customer value. An understanding of organisational behaviour helps consider the potential consequences of management decisions in this regard. Consequently, this chapter seeks to provide a better understanding of the strategic fit between the deployment of staff and the needs of customers, organisations, markets, and industries within the sport and leisure environment.

Excellent staff are as important as excellent facilities in meeting customer requirements. Therefore, senior professionals and managers must have knowledge, experience, and understanding of human resource issues: motivation, organisational structures, and the impact of these important areas on both organisation and staff performance.

Staff – full-time, part-time, casual, or voluntary – are the most important resource in any sport/leisure organisation, and their cost should be regarded as a highly valued investment rather than an expensive and superfluous item of expenditure. The right staff need to be employed, trained, nurtured, and enabled to perform well for their organisations and for themselves. As customer habits are impacted by the COVID-19 pandemic, organisations must quickly adapt to such changes by adopting ever more refined business models, including the fundamental requirement to recruit, retain, and invest in high quality staff, capable of skilfully driving the business forward.

13.1.1 Sport and Leisure Employment

It is difficult to estimate the precise numbers of people employed in sport/leisure-related jobs, not least because of the definitional difficulties of this very broad industrial sector. Eurostat (2021) report a steady increase in the pre-pandemic numbers employed by the sport sector, continuing a well-established trend of attracting a comparatively younger workforce who, in the main, appear to be increasingly better qualified. However, as many customer-facing staff are forced to revaluate their employment decisions, both during and after the COVID-19 pandemic, organisations must recognise this in the evolution of related HR policies and strategic practices. In a global survey of approximately 1,000 sport leaders and workers, the pandemic resulted in considerable uncertainty and unemployment within the sector. This is particularly acute for the many forward-facing staff, such as those employed within the events industry. As the UK's Office for National Statistics (ONS) reveals, a gradual improvement in employment levels, following the efficacious uptake of COVID-19 vaccines and the opening of the UK economy, there is a clear message that

> Events of 2020 have been instrumental in increasing the speed of change. Our work lives have been redefined and in doing so has impacted people's career motivations and the values in the employers and the opportunities they choose. Today's employees, fuelled also by a new generation of job seekers, have a new set of requirements for their employers. Job seekers are looking for employers that are focused on supporting their work life balance and professional development with 69% of employees wanting more flexible working structures. No longer are the more traditional incentives of salary, travel and security high priorities that professionals seek.
>
> (GlobalSportsJobs, 2020)

Unsurprisingly, the newly inaugurated survey of UK Wellbeing, by the ONS, reveals that it is the low paid (to May 2021) who reported being negatively affected by COVID-19, whilst the higher paid reported the negative implications of sustained home-working in terms of cultivating working relationships and the blurring of boundaries between work and home. Similarly, five out of six distance learning resources offered by Skills Active (the Sector Skills Council for Sport & Recreation in the UK) in 2021, allude to related wellbeing issues, such as:

- Mental Health: Body & Mind
- Becoming a Wellbeing Champion
- Work-Life Balance
- COVID-19 Infection Control
- Wellbeing for Teachers

Sport and leisure organisations must be cognisant of such issues in their ongoing HR policies and actions. Nike, for example, has given staff employed in its corporate headquarters a week of paid leave to be taken just before they are required to return to work following the vaccine roll-out. This is against a backdrop of other large employers continuing to support home working. It is also worthy of note that this benefit is not available to all Nike employees, just those employed at head office. Clearly, as sport/leisure organisations adapt to the different business conditions post-pandemic, they must give equal and sustained consideration to the efficacy of their HR policies in relation to all staff and the subsequent positive and negative impact(s) that such policies/decisions may generate. Continuing to view this relationship in purely transactional terms and failing to appropriately differentiate between the changing needs and motivations of important stakeholders, particularly full-time, part-time, and casual staff, would be a mistake.

13.2 The Importance of Staff Training and Development

Education and training are of vital importance at all levels of sport and leisure management. Without men and women of vision and standing, and without qualified and trained staff, no sport/leisure organisation can hope to be efficient, let alone effective in meeting the needs and aspirations of its various stakeholders, most notably its staff and customers. Staff are an investment; training helps to get the best out of them, for their own job satisfaction and for the organisations of which they are an integral part. However, there exists some confusion over the use of the two terms *training* and *development*. At times these terms appear to be interchangeable, and sometimes one term may be all-embracing, encompassing both meanings at once.

Overall, training is about learning specific, often vocationally oriented skills and knowledge that can be applied directly to work-based practice, typically in the short term. Broadly, it deals with relatively narrow questions with respect to 'what' and 'which' things should be done. In other words, it perpetuates current practice. Development, however, is a wider educational concept that promotes personal growth. This encourages an approach to learning which is much broader and deeper, allowing a greater understanding of related issues and opportunities for the transfer of knowledge into a variety of problem-solving situations. This promotes questions such as 'Why are things done in this way?' and gives the necessary insight and confidence to challenge prevailing orthodoxies by suggesting improvements and innovations to current practice. This, in turn, allows more flexible and progressive approaches to daily performance-related issues that affect customer value. There can be no question that both are needed in the contemporary context of sport and leisure organisations and their evolving markets.

13.2.1 The Need for a Coherent Training Structure

Unlike many professions, leisure does not have obvious educational or professional pathways, with clear entry qualifications leading onward to training and advancement. The profession covers a wide variety of specialisms including sport, the arts, tourism, heritage and countryside management. It is closely related to many other careers, such as planning, business management, marketing and teaching. Skills from these professions are often relevant and create opportunities to cross over into the leisure profession.

(Griffiths & Randall, 2004)

Any coherent system of training and development must be structured around the management and staffing needs of sport and leisure organisations, combined with related resource considerations. If training, in its widest sense, is to be effective, we need to ask, 'Why is it needed?' and 'Who is it for?' before we ask, 'What should it be?' Organisations should make training judgements based upon evidence-based systems that deliver proven and increasingly prioritised performance outcomes. This provides a rational justification for the allocation of resources to support the required investment in this important area of both HRM and business practice. As the UK Commission for Employment and Skills (2009) argues, this means 'creating a modular and flexible qualification system in which only employer recognised and accredited learning and qualifications that meet industry requirements are eligible to receive significant public funding'. However, despite this sentiment, the sport and leisure industry has, until more recently, failed to fully embrace the need for a coherent plan in this regard.

In the UK, the Chartered Institute for Physical and Active Recreation (CIMSPA) was inaugurated in 2011, after many years in the making. This now represents the professional body for this sector and is gradually getting to grips with the need for a more coordinated and coherent management/leadership/training and professional development structure. CIMSPA looks to define, and quality assure, professional standards through partnerships with professional training and educational associations and an individual route to membership that is broadly defined by continual professional development (CPD). CIMSPA 'Member' status looks to provide an assurance that current competence is maintained through related training, whilst the Chartered 'Fellow' status implies a higher level of development/education aligned to excellence and 'significant impact over time'. However, this relies heavily on the quality assurance of third-party training providers. Whilst vocational training provider accreditation has seen significant and positive movement, the area of management and leadership development in the sector has been slower to develop.

13.3 Leadership and Decision-Making

A successful manager must have both the management skills to ensure that customer needs are catered for and the people skills to inspire and lead a group of staff. Effective leadership requires an understanding of the goals of the organisation, the services, facilities, programmes, resources, and the people involved. Leadership is an important aspect of management – the ability to lead effectively is one of the factors that produces an effective manager. Leadership has been described as a mixture of art, craft, and humanity. It is an essential part of a manager's job.

Adair and Reed point to the need for leadership:

> Management has the overtone of carrying out objectives laid down by someone else. Moreover, there is nothing in the concept of management which implies inspiration, creating teamwork when it isn't there, or setting an example. When it is the case that inspiration and teamwork exist, you may well have managers who are in effect leaders, especially if they are the source of the inspiration. But it is, I believe, unfortunately more often the case that management does not ring bells when it comes to people.
>
> (Adair & Reed, 2003)

Discussion Questions

Is it possible to be a good manager without being a good leader? Conversely, is it possible to be a good leader without being a good manager?

What is also critically important is a firm understanding of the political and power context in which the organisation is operating. This has consequences for leadership and management. Often sport and leisure organisations are dependent on other stakeholders such as central government for funding and, sometimes, for survival! This context will influence the leadership and managerial behaviours. Therefore, leadership and management cannot be fully understood unless there is a clear appreciation of the context faced by the organisation.

A good leader is concerned both with people and results. *Leadership* is a word with positive connotations. We look to leaders to inspire, direct, and pave the way. In sport and leisure management, there is a need for excellent leaders at all levels – policy makers, executives, middle managers, and operational personnel. Sometimes, managerial leadership skills come from within the team or are exercised so subtly that they are not always evident. We can see evidence of this with some conductors of an orchestra, directors of a theatre production, or with some coaches and captains in sport who quietly get the best out of their players without shouting from the rooftops. This requires more than a dose of humility and the self-confidence to support colleagues in the co-production of improved performance – allowing staff, not management, to take centre stage!

Much of the literature on leadership includes a range of interrelated concepts, variables, and theories. These include concepts and theories of leadership attributes such as personal qualities, trait theories, power theories, behavioural theories and, more recently, situational theories. There can also be an element of teaching and coaching within the leadership model, as well as the need to understand the increasingly dynamic role of those who 'follow'. Far from simply being subordinates who carry out the instructions of managers/leaders, today's 'followers' should be encouraged and supported to make a clear and positive contribution to organisational development decisions. Co-workers, not subordinates, should be actively encouraged to work with managers/leaders to mould an appropriate way forward. This, in turn, is likely to have positive benefits in terms of employee engagement, recruitment, and retention in a post-COVID era that places increased importance on such issues. Clearly there is much to consider, learn, and apply in the complex world of the leader. It is useful, therefore, to reflect on the leadership styles of those sport and leisure practitioners who have been considered successful in their leadership roles. One such person is John Wooden (see Case Study 13.1).

CASE STUDY 13.1

John Wooden

John Wooden is one of the most successful basketball coaches in American NCAA basketball history, with his team, UCLA, winning 10 national basketball titles in 12 years. What is unique about John Wooden is the quiet and professional approach that he adopted on the sideline during games. Occasionally, he would become animated, but for the most part, he was reserved and in control, with his team often coming out on top. This was very much in contrast to his contemporaries, who would often be seen shouting instructions to players throughout the matches. It would appear, to the uninitiated observer, that Wooden was somehow different in his approach. His players, without doubt, had great respect for him, and it seems clear that he had equally great respect for them. There is certainly something about John Wooden that all sport and leisure managers can learn from.

What was it about his leadership, coaching, teaching, and management style that led to his success? John Wooden developed what he called the 'pyramid of success'. This was based on years paying great attention to detail. Wooden would keep meticulous records

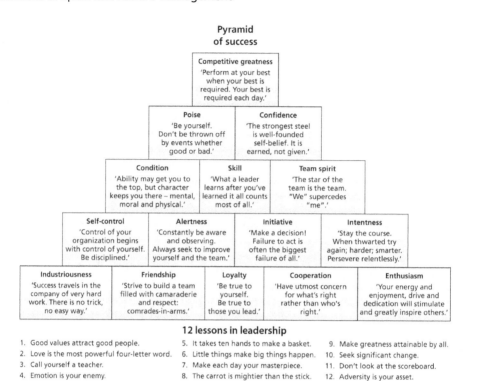

Pyramid of success

Competitive greatness
'Perform at your best when your best is required. Your best is required each day.'

Poise	Confidence
'Be yourself. Don't be thrown off by events whether good or bad.'	'The strongest steel is well-founded self-belief. It is earned, not given.'

Condition	Skill	Team spirit
'Ability may get you to the top, but character keeps you there – mental, moral and physical.'	'What a leader learns after you've learned it all counts most of all.'	'The star of the team is the team. "We" supercedes "me".'

Self-control	Alertness	Initiative	Intentness
'Control of your organization begins with control of yourself. Be disciplined.'	'Constantly be aware and observing. Always seek to improve yourself and the team.'	'Make a decision! Failure to act is often the biggest failure of all.'	'Stay the course. When thwarted try again; harder; smarter. Persevere relentlessly.'

Industriousness	Friendship	Loyalty	Cooperation	Enthusiasm
'Success travels in the company of very hard work. There is no trick, no easy way.'	'Strive to build a team filled with camaraderie and respect: comrades-in-arms.'	'Be true to yourself. Be true to those you lead.'	'Have utmost concern for what's right rather than who's right.'	'Your energy and enjoyment, drive and dedication will stimulate and greatly inspire others.'

12 lessons in leadership

1. Good values attract good people.
2. Love is the most powerful four-letter word.
3. Call yourself a teacher.
4. Emotion is your enemy.
5. It takes ten hands to make a basket.
6. Little things make big things happen.
7. Make each day your masterpiece.
8. The carrot is mightier than the stick.
9. Make greatness attainable by all.
10. Seek significant change.
11. Don't look at the scoreboard.
12. Adversity is your asset.

Figure 13.1 John Wooden's pyramid of success.
Source: Taken from Wooden (2005). For further information, visit Wooden's website: www.coachwooden.com

of every training session. He would have detailed notes on every player and would regularly discuss each player's performance with them, with suggestions for adjustment and improvement. This not only included player performance but genuinely caring for the player as an important member of the team. Successful leadership, according to Wooden, included such attributes as industriousness, friendship, loyalty, cooperation, enthusiasm, self-control, alertness, initiative, intentness, condition, skill, team spirit, poise, confidence, patience, and faith – all working together to create the structure for successful leadership and competitive greatness (Wooden, 2005). These attributes are combined to create Wooden's pyramid of success (see Figure 13.1).

In distinguishing leadership from other management functions, it has been suggested that most management functions can be taught, whereas leadership skills must be learned through doing. Leadership stems largely from a manager's personal dealings and personal influence over others. Leaders need to inspire, communicate, support, and direct. However, it is important to recognise that 'virtually every employee in the 21st century will be called upon to display leadership behaviours at some point in time' (Landy & Conte, 2009). Consequently, leadership is as much about the need to address the changing perceptions of 'followship' as it is about leadership per se. Leadership will need to become an important enabling behaviour rather than what has been traditionally accepted as a controlling function. (Co)workers should not merely be viewed as subordinates, but as active participants in producing better quality outcomes. Sport provides an excellent exemplar of this concept, where professional athletes are trusted to make important decisions during pivotal and pressured times of sporting preparation and performance. In 2008 Paul Azinger successfully introduced the 'pod' system, utilised by US Navy Seals, to provide a way to instil teamwork in a US golf team of very successful, but very individual players. Each of the 12 individuals played within a four-person self-managing pod, which cultivated communication, respect, teamwork and, ultimately, an appropriate performance response for the Ryder Cup-winning team. Leaders, such as Azinger and John Wooden, prepare both individuals and teams of individuals who are invested in the process and in an overarching unifying goal/desire to succeed. In this context, the rollout of HR initiatives such as 360-degree feedback and upward appraisal, where subordinates give feedback to superiors on their managerial behaviours and performance, is to be encouraged. These help to redefine antiquated notions of the dynamic and symbiotic interplay between the ever-evolving notions of leadership and followship.

13.3.1 Leadership Styles

There are several appropriate leadership styles (see Figure 13.2). It is not always possible to define precisely what good leadership is but, unlike good leadership, a person with poor leadership exhibits a wide range of easily recognisable traits: aloofness, insensitivity to others, intimidating manner, abrasiveness, overbearing, over-supervising, failing to delegate, seeking praise first instead of giving praise to colleagues, blaming, finding scapegoats, indecision, and so on.

A leader's style should be flexible enough to change to suit the situation. Leaders must balance the big picture – the vision – with the details. Little things matter – sensitivity, care, attention to detail. A false assumption is often made that a leader is one of autocratic,

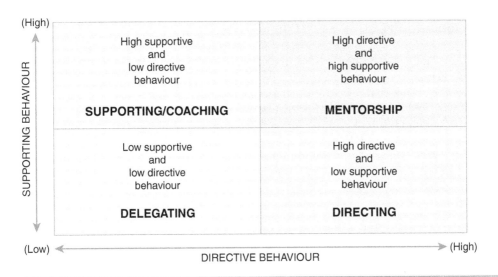

Figure 13.2 **Leadership styles.**

democratic or 'laissez faire'. However, most leaders tend to use a combination of styles but with a leaning towards one, depending on their prevailing personality, experience, and the current internal and external business environment. In emergencies and critical situations – e.g. swimming pool safety or problems in opening a major event on time – autocratic and directive leadership is eminently suitable. The authoritarian/directive style can also be very effective when toughness is needed under certain conditions, even at some personal emotional cost to the leader. Leadership is not an easy option. It requires commitment, resilience, sensitivity, nuance, and skill.

The 'art' of leadership involves the juxtaposition of both hearts and minds, where a blended balance is needed between the characteristics of the manager, the characteristics of the team, the type of organisation, the nature of the problem, and the pragmatics of resource allocation. It is in the strategy and the tactics of handling the problem that the manager's leadership skills are put to the test. Can they raise the level of employee motivation? Can staff and key user groups be persuaded to accept or even embrace change? Can the quality and effectiveness of managerial decisions be improved? Can teamwork, morale, and staff development be enhanced along with increased levels of satisfaction for the clients and customers?

Discussion Questions

For a named sport of your choice, what tensions exist between the needs of the individual, the group, and the organisation? For example, in professional sport there always seem to be perpetual battles between club and country. Who is best placed to resolve such issues and how?

13.3.2 Team Building

A distinction needs to be made between the manager as the leader and leaders of discrete teams within the organisation, e.g. specific 'offensive' and 'defensive' teams within many sports, particularly in North America. Heller offers the advice:

> A leader must always be aware of the ultimate goals of the organisation, and know how their own objectives fit in with them. Once these goals have been established, you must ensure that your team understands the direction in which they are heading and why, and the purpose of their own activities within the overall plan. The ultimate objective should be broken down into attainable, yet challenging goals that ideally will be inspiring and motivating for the whole team. Aims should also relate directly to the specific skills of each individual within the team. Working together towards a shared goal gives people a sense of ownership and responsibility, and builds an atmosphere of team spirit.

> (Heller, 1998)

Heller (1998) suggests that for a team to function most effectively, there are key roles that should be filled, including coordinator, ideas person, critic, external contact, implementer, team leader, and inspector. It is vital that all members of a team work together to maximise team performance. Each member should be able to cover the role of at least one other member; members should be given responsibility to act on their own initiative within a team, but

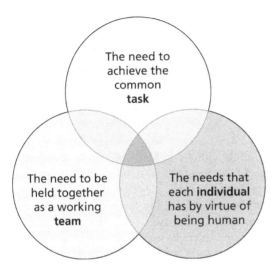

The need to
achieve the
common
task

The need to be
held together
as a working
team

The needs that
each **individual**
has by virtue of
being human

Figure 13.3 **Unifying a team.**
Source: Heller (1998)

a large task will be better handled by the whole team being responsible for the entire project. Heller suggests that most teams place too much focus on the task and not enough on the individual. His model, shown in Figure 13.3, illustrates an 'ideal situation in which the needs of the individual, the dynamics of the group, and the requirements of the task coincide . . . to produce a unified, effective working team' (Heller, 1998).

The modes of behaviour within groups have been termed *task-oriented, maintenance-oriented*, and *self-oriented*. Both 'task' and 'maintenance of the team' are important in varying situations, depending on the objectives of management, whereas the behaviour within self-interested groups hinders the achievement of common goals. This behaviour can arise, for example, because individual goals/behaviours subvert those of the group/team. For example, many health clubs operate a sales system based on individual numbers and associated commissions. This can create competitive tensions and conflict within the group of sales staff, which could, in part, be resolved by introducing a commission system based more upon team vs. individual targets. Of course, this can also create tensions; particularly if you were to consider yourself a top performer within such a team!

Argyris (1966, 1976) suggested ten criteria, based on empirical research, that are necessary for group competence and effectiveness:

1 Contributions made within the group are additive.
2 The group moves forwards as a unit, is team spirited, and there is high involvement.
3 Decisions are mainly made by consensus.
4 Commitment to a decision is strong.
5 The group continually evaluates itself.
6 The group is clear about goals.
7 It generates alternative ways of thinking about things.
8 It brings conflict into the open and deals with it.
9 It deals openly with feelings.
10 Leadership tends to go (or move) to the person most qualified.

Think of a successful team environment that you have experienced. Did a leader exist? What were the characteristics of the team that contributed to the overall success? How was success defined?

Leaders must deal with conflict and cooperation within and between groups. Conflict is not, in itself, undesirable. It is only through the candid and skilful expression of differences that good problem-solving is promoted. For everyone to agree is as unrealistic as expecting that no agreement is possible. But conflict so severe as to disable the participants and prevent the continuation of problem solving is unacceptable. One answer is to find an overriding 'superordinate' goal – one which both (or all) groups accept as essential to reach and which all can reach. For example, the success of professional team sports is predicated upon maintaining a competitive balance between the teams and ensuring the uncertainty of outcome and thus excitement for the customers or fans. Even though competition between teams is intense, there is a collective recognition that equalising the power of teams is in the best interests of all major stakeholders. This applies to a range of different contexts, from Formula One motor racing to the draft pick system in American sports, where the weakest teams can recruit the best college players with the most potential. Of course, even here there are possible tensions, for example, where player recruitment in US sports, appears to be influenced by a variety of factors, including COVID-19 vaccination status!

Bennis (1989) suggests that ingredients for good leadership include a guiding vision, passion, integrity, trust, curiosity, and daring. A great deal depends on what we want to accomplish. As Covey (1992) says, 'Begin with the end in mind'. Adair and Reed (2003) have a chapter entitled 'Humility' – leadership as a form of service. Adair and Reed use the strapline: 'The task of leadership is not to put greatness into humanity, but to elicit it, for the greatness is already there'.

In summary, the manager must be a successful leader in order to be effective. The manager must seek to better understand themselves, their staff, and their customers. The manager recognises that a high degree of staff-centred behaviour, in helping to run an organisation, raises employee teamwork and morale. But this does not mean that a manager leaves all decisions to the staff. Situations vary and staff vary. Staff readiness and ability are important. The successful leader will behave appropriately in the light of their perceptions of the people and the situations. In addition to leading personally, the manager must recognise that many subordinates fulfil important leadership roles themselves. They too need training in the 'art' of effective leadership. Leadership may result in the successful completion of a task, but effective leadership occurs when the team of staff not only completes the task, but does so willingly and, typically, is involved in the decision-making process that produces positive results.

13.3.3 Management Communication

Rather than persuading, communication should ideally be two-way. The argument for two-way communication is not only a moral one; it is also a practical one because the manager will become more effective by encouraging the group members to make full use of their abilities. Drucker put the argument against the purely persuasive approach to communication in the following way:

In many cases human relations has been used to manipulate, to adjust people to what the boss thinks is reality; to make them conform to a pattern that seems logical from the top down, to make them accept unquestioningly what we tell them. Frankly, sometimes, I think it is better not to tell employees anything rather than to say, 'We tell them everything, but they must accept it, and it is our job to make them accept it'.

(Drucker, 1955)

Forcing one-way communication on people without their understanding and without understanding them makes for poor management. Such decisions could be classed as misjudgements, particularly where 'the boss' may not have the legitimate authority to make such decisions.

13.3.4 Coaching, Mentoring, and Motivational Leadership

Like sports players and teams, sport and leisure management staff and teams can benefit from coaching and mentoring. Coaching and mentoring can inspire learning through practical experience and help promote real personal performance gains. Moreover, they may both facilitate and enhance personal learning by an associated development in self-awareness. Through both approaches staff can be encouraged to undertake new tasks, improve performance, develop new skills, learn how to solve problems, and become even more valuable members of the team.

Good business coaching will work with staff to help release their latent potential, by encouraging them to become more aware of their individual motivations and decision-making processes. Good business coaches need to be very good listeners and work closely with staff, usually over the relatively short term, to help them solve their own business or sometimes personal challenges. They will encourage and facilitate self-reflection through asking open questions such as: 'What would you say is the real issue here?', 'What's the most important priority?', 'What barriers exist?', 'What options do you have?', 'What are the first steps in moving this forward?', and 'How will you know when you have achieved this?' As such, business coaches do not offer specific advice, but they skilfully encourage learners to solve their own problems.

A mentor, on the other hand, is an experienced guide – a believer, an understander, promoting the cause and showing the way – who can make a lasting impression on an individual's life, over the longer term, by offering advice and guidance based upon direct personal experience. An effective mentor-mentee relationship provides a helping hand, inspires mutual trust, loyalty, and friendship and, unlike businesses coaching, can be directive in nature by offering advice such as, 'I don't think that's the best way forward' and 'I think, based on my experience and knowledge, what you need to do is this'.

The bond between mentor and mentee is an emotional one, based upon mutual respect, and requires time to mature. In this process, the mentee absorbs an approach, a style, a life-view which can shape their future. The mentor can open doors for their mentee for which, without them, it's unlikely there would be a key. In contrast, business coaching works with employees, when required, and offers no direct advice, instead helping the participants to develop their own, bespoke, problem-solving skills in response to specific performance-related objectives.

We have considered the different interpretations of management versus leadership and shown how important the human side can be to the effective management of sport and leisure. Leadership, decision-making, communications, and an understanding of group behaviour are key components. Management must be appropriate to different situations, and the manager must adapt his or her style of management to changing situations. A manager armed with only one style of management may be ill equipped for the variety of different tasks and people to be handled – just like a golfer with only one club!

The business of sport and leisure requires staff to be flexible and work unsocial hours, and it calls for styles of leadership in keeping with providing good customer service and care of staff. In these circumstances, the 'democratic' manager with a professional 'executive style' is more likely to succeed. Such a manager will see the job as effectively maximising the efforts of others. The manager's commitment to both tasks and relationships will be evident to all. These managers often work with a team; ideas can come from any quarter; and the greater number of possibilities explored, the better the understanding of the problem. As Hammer (1996) argues, 'Managers will coach and design rather than supervise and control'. However, they still must lead – they cannot hide behind the team – and they still must make the ultimate decision; but both manager and staff feel involved in the successes and failures. Setanta, the sports broadcasting media organisation, provides a good example of this. After the collapse of its funding in the UK, caused by the worldwide financial crisis of the time, employees stood up and applauded when the owners told them that the company was to go into administration (Robinson, 2009). Staff appeared genuinely appreciative of the hard work and openness with which they had all attempted to push through the crisis and were aware that the factors contributing to the business failure of Setanta Sports, in the UK, were largely outside the business' control.

Of course, whilst issues of leadership are critical to the involvement, motivation, and development of staff, they will always exist within the structural context of the organisation.

13.4 The Impact and Importance of Organisational Structure

An organisation's structure represents the way in which the work is organised and shared out and the way an enterprise is managed. Every sport or leisure organisation, from the smallest to the largest, has an organisation and staffing structure of some kind. Used effectively, the structure provides the framework through which the work processes are operationalised to achieve organisational objectives.

Of course, whilst there are many 'structural' models that help us to understand such fundamental organisational building blocks, their 'effective' operation is always subject to a range of tensions. These include the developing needs of the customer in relation to constantly changing levels of competition. Such issues act collectively and cumulatively to create either a positive organisational culture or one that subverts the original intention of the initial structural arrangements. In other words, it is rarely as simple as merely delegating the roles and responsibilities needed for the organisation to fulfil its overall mission and underlying business objectives. In the real world, the ability to understand and respond positively to such challenges is critical to the role of the manager.

13.4.1 The Need for Appropriate Structures

There is a considerable variance in the staffing structures, the types of staff, and the levels of staffing needed within sport and leisure organisations. For example, in public leisure, subsidised by the public purse and subject to local government administrative systems and standardised procedures, one might expect to find a considerable level of uniformity. However, different localities have different facilities and different circumstances, and wide variations can and do exist in the structures employed by local authorities. Moreover, there are also likely to be differences in the backgrounds, interests, and aspirations of staff at all levels of the organisational hierarchy, as well as differences in their employment status, e.g. full-time, part-time, temporary, casual, and voluntary.

Discussion Question

Identify the likely similarities and differences between full-time, part-time, casual, temporary, and voluntary workers in terms of knowledge, experience, commitment, and motivation. For a major sporting event such as the New York Marathon, what possible differences will the employment status of workers make to customer experiences?

Many sport and leisure facilities, particularly in the voluntary sector, are managed by a leader and volunteers. They take responsibility for facilities, machinery, programmes, and personnel. However, as is often the case with voluntary sport organisations, there is a lack of formal human resource systems and processes. Reporting on non-profit organisations in New South Wales, Australia, Taylor and McGraw (2006) found that 'despite pressures to become more strategic in their people management, only a minority of these sport organisations have formal HRM systems'.

This is also often the case in professional sports organisations, which typically have a relatively small number of employees and struggle to justify the expense of a functional human resources department or even human resources specialists. This leads to a particular culture within an organisation which can be difficult to change, as Case Study 13.2 demonstrates.

CASE STUDY 13.2

Manchester City FC

Manchester City Football Club has seen huge changes during the period 2005–2010, particularly during the latter part of the decade, with £200 million worth of new football talent brought into the club during 2009. This followed the takeover of the club, in September 2008, by the Abu Dhabi United group and a newly appointed club chairman, Khaldoon al-Mubarak, making it one of the richest football clubs in the world.

On-the-pitch changes had also been matched by off-field changes in the long-term strategic management and organisation of the club, including the decision by Garry Cook, the club's Chief Executive at the time, to initiate quarterly staff meetings at the new Eastlands Stadium. However, whilst this may seem great news for the club, it is not without its problems. The Guardian journalist, David Conn, commenting on his observation of the meetings, reveals:

His shtick is not, it has to be said, going down noticeably well with the people who receive it mostly in silence, arms folded. Cook introduces Mark Allen, head of the newly established human resources department and part of an executive team recruited after Khaldoon expressed his shock at the 'amateurish' structure of the club on his arrival. Allen unveils an impending culture of appraisals, formal feedback and pay reviews, sweetened by a significant new benefit.

> 'We will be announcing,' he says proudly, 'private medical cover for all staff'. Even this is not greeted with quite the whooping and hollering that Cook might have expected in his previous job, at Nike's US headquarters. Manchester City have always been more of a National Health Service, not private medical cover, kind of a football club.
>
> (Conn, 2009a)

It, clearly, takes many staff time to adjust to newly instigated human resources processes, focused around the needs of the key stakeholders (customers, players, etc.). Such organisational change processes need to be handled sensitively, particularly if they involve a fundamental change to the prevailing organisational culture. As such it is likely that there will be tensions between the old working practices and the new professional approach, in this case, adopted by the new owners. Clearly, Cook appears to be adopting a 'carrot and stick' approach that identifies and rewards appropriate behaviours as a prelude to a more substantive shift in organisational values and performance. As Khaldoon explains, 'We like to take a long-term view. . . . As long as the foundations are there, you have to allow the business to run. It is no different in football' (quoted in Conn, 2009a).

Cook's professional, business-oriented, and customer-focused approach is, according to Conn (2009a), reported to have gone down well with another key set of the club's stakeholders, i.e. the Manchester City fans. These are reported to be eager to embrace the new era for the club and the newfound sensitivity to their needs. This is nothing overtly radical in management terms, but it merely represents a willingness to listen to the needs of consumers in the new, professional culture of service provision and management. It is inevitable, therefore, that this will be reflected in the way that staff are organised and managed.

The way in which such organisational change is implemented will be key to ongoing performance enhancements. Conversely, at least over the short term, this may result in negative consequences as individuals struggle to adapt. This is equally applicable to the players. As Johnson *et al.* (2008) suggest, 'Poor performance might be the result of an inappropriate configuration for the situation or inconsistency between structure, process and relationships'. In other words, the structure of Manchester City might seem right in managerial terms, but this may not reflect the uniqueness of the football club culture, established over may years prior to the Abu Dhabi takeover. In real terms, this is likely to take some time to become embedded in the foundations and habitual practices of existing employees.

For most sport and leisure organisations, staffing takes the largest share of operating costs. This is particularly the case in professional sports, where player wages and transfer fees can have a significant effect upon the operational bottom line of the organisation. After 21 years playing for Barcelona Football Club, the multi-award winner, Lionel Messi, completed a move to the French side Paris Saint-Germaine (PSG). Messi, regarded by many as the best footballer in the world, was all set to sign a new five-year contract with Barcelona and had accepted a 50% pay cut, in order to keep within the Spanish La Liga restrictions and the European Football Governing Body UEFA's Financial Fair Play guidelines. However, despite accepting the maximum pay reduction allowed under Spanish law, Barcelona cited 'financial and structural obstacles' as the reason that the deal still couldn't be secured to keep Messi, and his family, at Barcelona – something that all sides appeared to want. This leaves PSG to navigate similar financial tensions in their quest for European Champions League glory. However, for the owners of PSG, Qatar Sports Investments, this is part of a much wider strategy, including the 2022 Qatar Football World Cup, to strategically reduce Qatar's historical reliance on gas and oil revenues and to diversify into other sustainable areas, such as tourism. Like the English Football side, Manchester City, ostensibly owned by another oil-rich Gulf state, the United Arab Emirate (UAE), the financial resources available to such sports teams gives them a clear competitive advantage that operates outside the more normal business models found within professional sports.

If the business model is not set up to deal with market variations, then companies can find themselves in financial difficulty. In times of external environmental shocks, such as COVID-19, economic stringency prevails and furlough schemes lead to a fundamental rethink, from both staff and organisations, about their future working relationships. Reductions are a common method of reducing deficits and/or increasing net returns. It is therefore important to provide a clear justification for the most appropriate levels and methods of organising staff for the prevailing organisational objectives and market environment. Otherwise, there is a risk of indiscriminate staff cuts, which may harm organisational performance.

Portsmouth Football Club became the first Premier League club in England to go into administration during March 2010. According to Kelso (2010), 'Drastic cuts saw 20 full-time and 65 part-time staff made redundant across all departments of the club, reducing the staff from 320 to 235 with the possibility of more redundancies to come'. Paradoxically the most expensive staff, the players, are not for sale, as the administrator's objective was to sell on the club as a going concern. To accomplish this goal, it was deemed necessary to retain the club's prize assets in order to attract potential buyers. However, such short-term decisions may lead to longer-term negative revenue consequences, as both the staff and the customer experience are likely to be diminished. Paradoxically, the opposite appears true for Michael Jordan's Chicago Bulls and his multi-NBA winning championship side in the 1990s. An ESPN documentary details the 'The Last Dance' of the highly decorated side during their final 1997–1998 championship winning season, where the owners had already decided to dismantle the side and its coaching staff. The documentary suggests that this may have been, at least partially, due to their own success and the negative commercial consequences of paying the contracts and bonus payments of their expensive superstars. Clearly, any business model must exist within a sustainable financial/resource envelope. This makes the innovative utilisation of talented and productive employees even more critical to ongoing business success.

Staff flexibility is required in sport and leisure because of the multiplicity of tasks and the typically long opening hours. This should be mirrored by organisation and employer flexibility. It needs mutual dependency and interest to work together in the spirit of teamwork. This is difficult to achieve, but when it is achieved the impact can be dramatic. Arguably, one of the greatest team sporting achievements of recent times is by the Great Britain track cycling team, which won 9 out of a possible 18 gold medals at the 2008 Beijing Olympics. Although the performance director, Dave Brailsford, is formally the leader, in reality:

> For a sports team at the highest level, it is a highly unusual structure. This is no one-man operation headed by a forceful individual; while Brailsford is where the buck stops, the four senior managers seem to enjoy an equal say in decision-making at a strategic level.
>
> (Fotheringham, 2008)

One of GB track cycling's senior managers is the ex-Olympic gold medallist Chris Boardman, who is responsible for equipment and coach development. For Boardman, the critical ingredient is that they all had the same strategic goal of being the best in the world. This overrides any other personal agendas and produces a true team performance, designed to produce the very best track performances by blending management, coaches, athletes, and equipment in perfect harmony. This approach progressed to deliver transferrable success for the Road Racing 'Team Sky', with multiple Blue Ribboned event wins, such as the Tour de France, during the ensuing years. If only such ingredients could be easily replicated across all sport and leisure organisations!

13.4.2 The Principles of Management that Affect Staffing

Some top-level managers and senior personnel are called upon to formulate policies and organisational structures. Most managers, however, are appointed to positions in existing organisations, to which they must adapt. It is important that managers at all levels understand the organisational structure, the principles on which it is based, and the components which go to make it up.

According to the International City Management Association (1965), three basic principles of management must be considered in establishing an organisational structure, namely unity of command, logical assignment, and span of control. In this context, it is also important to consider two further variables, namely employee engagement, and authority and power.

13.4.2.1 Unity of Command

This principle states that everyone in an organisation should be responsible to only one superior. Adherence to this principle establishes a precise chain of command within the organisation. However, situations exist in sport and leisure organisations which do not follow such a principle. For example, the head groundsman can play a pivotal role in the outcome of any number of sporting encounters. However, always assuming the availability of appropriate staff at critical moments, does the groundsman answer to the chief executive, the stadium operations manager, the coaches, the sporting captain, the 'star' players, or the referee/umpire? All represent important stakeholders in the process. Just with this relatively simple example, one can easily detect the potential for miscommunication, misunderstandings, and structural problems to emerge.

Consequently, sport and leisure managers need to be careful when considering unity of command, as it is grounded in very traditional approaches to structure and management, based on the principle of command and control. This has benefits in terms of clarity of role and lines of responsibility and may function better in organisations where there are many habitual and non-contestable tasks to perform. However, in an increasingly dynamic and competitive environment, requiring more, not less, flexibility, sport and leisure organisations need staff who can take the initiative and welcome autonomy.

> ## Discussion Questions
>
> Traditionally, it would be the decision-makers, towards the top of the organisational hierarchy, who would dictate structural arrangements within sport and/or leisure organisations, e.g. in a sports centre or a theatre. To what extent do you think staff would be comfortable engaging in the process of deciding organisational structures? What would be the advantages and disadvantages of involving staff in this process?

13.4.2.2 Employee Engagement

MacLeod and Clarke (2009) wrote a seminal UK government report looking at the issue of employee engagement. This has many different facets, but central to it is the following supposition:

> If employee engagement and the principles that lie behind it were more widely understood, if good practice was more widely shared, if the potential that resides in the country's workforce was more fully unleashed, we could see a step change in workplace performance and in employee well-being, for the considerable benefit of the UK.
>
> (MacLeod & Clarke, 2009)

Despite this, there is recognition that there are a significant number of employees who do not feel engaged in their working life. This has much in common with the central concept of 'empowerment' developed throughout this chapter. MacLeod and Clarke (2009) identify several barriers to this within the workplace in both public and private sector organisations. There are many managers who cannot see the potential use of the idea and/or do not understand the concept or how to introduce it. Those managers who do recognise the potential relevance of employee engagement may not be well supported by others. Unsurprisingly, the report identified that leadership and management were seen to be pivotal to employee engagement. Leadership is fundamental to offer an appropriate organisational culture based on mutual trust and integrity. Management should then enable a greater staff voice by supporting and encouraging staff participation, requiring regular feedback and appropriate coaching for staff, working towards common operational and strategic goals.

13.4.2.3 Logical Assignment

This principle states that staff doing the same work should be grouped together and that work is planned and scheduled in a logical order. Without logical assignment, there can be duplication or overlap, confusion, and power struggles. Effective structural arrangements can help to reduce the negative consequences of such micro-politics. Managers need to give much more consideration to wider issues of organisational health through actively promoting behaviours designed to deliver openness and trust within the organisation. This has as much to do with a consistent leadership style and organisational culture as it has to do with structural arrangements.

In September 2008, Kevin Keegan walked away from his job as manager of Newcastle United Football Club over a dispute with the owner concerning player recruitment. Keegan alleges that he was assured he would have the final word over player recruitment, while the club's owner at the time, Mike Ashley, had recruited several 'inexperienced people to key positions because, it is said, they were his friends and he trusted them' (Conn, 2009b). These included an executive director of football, a vice president in charge of player recruitment, and a technical coordinator. When it became clear to Keegan that his authority had been usurped by these structural arrangements, he decided that his position was untenable. Keegan's position was vindicated by the Premier League's arbitration panel when, in October 2009, he received £2 million in compensation for 'constructive dismissal'.

This was arguably the most high-profile case of its kind at the time, but it was also reflective of a trend amongst Premier League clubs to move to a more 'continental system' of structuring football clubs. Under this system, managers are appointed to run the non-playing side of the game, with various titles such as 'Director of Football', whilst 'Head Coaches' are appointed to take care of first-team football. This represents standard operating practice for several successful European clubs such as Bayern Munich, AC Milan, Barcelona, and Real Madrid.

Professional sport often represents a multi-million-pound business, and so it is logical to argue that one person should not be responsible for all aspects of the organisation, particularly when their only qualifications might be sports coaching related. Historically, football managers in the UK are appointed because of their football knowledge, not because of their business qualifications and experience. The lesson here is that what might appear logical on paper may prove unworkable in practice, as local context and sensitivities also need to be understood and accounted for.

13.4.2.4 Span of Control

Span of control is a rather limited concept, as the need to 'control' staff must be balanced with the need to both empower and engage them. A better term might be *span of engagement*. It is not possible to state the exact number of people a manager should 'control'. Much depends upon the organisational context, i.e. customer requirements, organisational culture, organisational systems, organisational resources, competence of subordinates, and the manager's own knowledge, ability, time, energy, personality, and leadership.

Organisations with narrow spans of control, i.e. a relatively small number of employees to supervise (see Figure 13.4), enhance the manager's ability to balance the need to both control and engage staff. This can improve horizontal communication within levels, but it is likely to work against vertical communication up and down an increased number of hierarchical levels. Hence, narrow spans of control tend to require more tiers of management, more managers, and more expense, as in the previous example from Newcastle United. Alternatively, wider spans of control may result in more limited direct control but should give managers greater 'reach' across the organisation's functions (see Figure 13.5).

As a rule of thumb, organisations should only have as much structure as is needed. Structural layers can always be added later, but they are notoriously difficult to remove once they

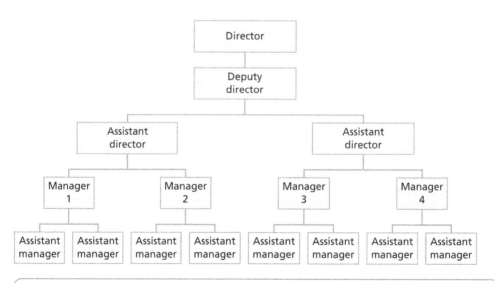

Figure 13.4 An organisation with a narrow span of control.

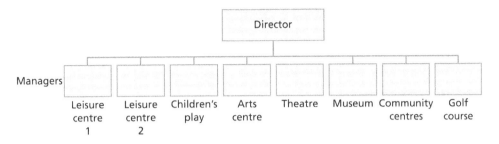

Figure 13.5 **An organisation with a wide span of control.**

are in place. There is a correlation between the number of managerial layers and the degree of managerial control. The more layers, the more control. The more control, the less potential there is for autonomy and therefore innovation. This is a tricky balancing act to achieve because where the span of control is too wide, both managers and their staff can become overloaded and performance can dip. Conversely, a narrow span of 'control' makes it possible to supervise work tightly but may not give staff the opportunity to make decisions or feel a sense of ownership, engagement, commitment, and achievement.

Discussion Questions

What are the main differences between span of control and span of management? How do these differences affect your view on whether a manager working closely with a small number of staff (i.e. a narrow span of control) is a good idea?

13.4.2.5 Authority and Power

Too often these words are mistakenly treated as being synonymous with each other. Authority is based upon a person's position within the organisational structure, incorporates the person's responsibilities, tasks, etc. and is, in theory, accepted by his/her subordinates as 'legitimate'. Power on the other hand is a much broader concept and relates to the person's ability to influence or persuade others to take a particular course of action. Power can come from being a leader, even without positional authority, and power can also come from being an expert – the power of knowledge. It can also come from being the most dominant but not, necessarily, the most knowledgeable person in the room!

Ideally, power will be exercised both explicitly (through direct decisions) and implicitly (through the prevailing organisational culture) for the common good of all stakeholders. Therefore, employees will be both extrinsically and intrinsically motivated to perform well against their given role. However, what may be claimed to be good for wider organisational objectives may be to the detriment of staff, who are repeatably asked to do more with less, without requisite levels of resources and support.

Increasingly the role of a manager should be more about enabling and empowerment than it is about the use of managerial power as a form of command and control. Empowerment, in a human resource context, implies a genuine caring for colleagues and their development, in line with the prevailing organisational objectives, resources, and customer requirements. This is seen as a more effective way of achieving objectives than a model that is based on subordination and control. Unfortunately, many sport and leisure organisations are still dominated by more traditional roles, based on hierarchy, power, and subordination of the many to the position and power of the few. This problem is illustrated by Case Study 13.3.

CASE STUDY 13.3

Formula One Motor Racing

Max Mosley was the president of the Fédération Internationale de l'Automobile (FIA) from 1993 until he agreed to relinquish the reins in October 2009, following a power struggle with key stakeholders in Formula One. The FIA is a non-profit organisation that controls worldwide motor sport. However, despite overseeing many positive developments, Mosley's reign was controversial during his final years and nearly led to the demise of Formula One motor racing, with many of the major teams threatening to start their own race series, complaining of the autocratic style of Mosley and his unwillingness to listen to their views. This demonstrates that sports governing bodies must seek to tread a fine line between exercising appropriate levels of control and balancing this with a willingness to listen to the views of stakeholders to develop the sport.

Importantly, it also demonstrates the key role that personalities and leadership style can play in fashioning the future of sport. Jean Todt, Mosley's successor, was elected FIA President on the promise of more collaboration, not conflict, and the prospect of a new commissioner for all FIA world championships. This represents another tier in the structure but does not provide a means by which one person can work with the differing stakeholders involved in each of the FIA's worldwide race portfolios. Arguably, this provides a more appropriate span of management by providing a better unity of command and logical assignment of roles. The new structure provides the opportunity for much more constructive dialogue to develop between all the stakeholders who are fundamental to the future development of the sport.

What this example shows is that sport and leisure organisations do not exist in a vacuum and must look at both external and internal factors when considering changes to the way in which staff are managed. This, in turn, is influenced by the way that both formal and informal communications are cultivated between key stakeholders and the prevailing structural arrangements that are designed to facilitate positive and productive working relationships. Much easier said than done!

The traditional approach does have short-term benefits, as it is often perceived to be both quicker and easier for managers to communicate 'one-way' instructions than it is for them to engage in the trickier and more time-consuming process of 'two-way' dialogue and decision-making. In the longer term however, there is greater potential for commitment, motivation, and innovation in an organisational culture based on empowerment and mutual development. This is particularly important for sports organisations, many of which are reliant upon governing bodies to both control and develop their sport.

Clearly, the environment (internal and external) is rarely fixed but instead is in a state of flux around changing perceptions of who holds the most power. For example, in October 2009 Jack Warner, a highly influential member of FIFA's Executive Committee, commenting on England's bid for the 2018 football World Cup warned, 'My [FIFA] colleagues are saying very quietly that the guys who are coming to them are lightweight. This is the type of thing that loses you a bid' (quoted in Watt, 2009). Arguably, such comments precipitated difficulties within the England bid team, leading to resignations, recriminations, and a restructuring of the team. It also led to a more high-profile involvement from world sports stars such as David Beckham and to a subsequent meeting between Jack Warner and the UK's Prime Minister at the time.

Discussion Questions

To what extent are authority and power barriers to effective employee engagement? Are there any circumstances when it is not sensible to engage/empower staff?

13.5 Formal and Informal Organisations

There is a need to distinguish between informal and formal organisations. A formal organisation has a clearly defined structure that establishes relationships and differences in status, role, rank, and levels of authority. There will be both written and unwritten rules with respect to channels of communication, accepted forms of behaviour, and the manner in which key tasks have to be undertaken. Additionally, such organisations have defined outcomes and, to achieve these, the overall work is divided amongst the workforce in a coordinated way so that they function as a unit or a department. In contrast, an informal organisation has a much less defined structure. It is also likely to be much smaller in size and more likely to have a shorter lifespan. In certain circumstances an informal organisation will be converted into a formal one, e.g. an interest group forming a club or society with rules and a constitution.

Handy's work on organisational culture is worth considering in relation to formal and informal organisational types. Handy (1985) usefully categorises organisations into four cultural types:

- **Role culture** – based on rules and procedures;
- **People culture** – based on the needs of individuals;
- **Power culture** – based on the dominance of powerful individuals and groups over others;
- **Task culture** – based on the need to carry out and achieve tasks.

This last cultural type is the most effective, as it focuses on activities and jobs of work. In practice each of the cultural types exists side by side in most organisations, often with one dominant culture being evident.

Informal relationships facilitate lateral communication, rather than 'going through the channels', even in formal organisations. Informal, two-way communication can lead to improved understanding with both internal and external stakeholders. Much of the important 'human' work which makes an organisation 'tick' is undertaken through informal communication. While formal structures are required, managers should also encourage effective informal structures to enable the essential human dimension and improve decision-making. For example, at Disney, the park designers regularly consult cleaning supervisors, as they are best placed to receive market intelligence from around the parks concerning what works and what doesn't for customers. This process, which is both formal and informal in nature, cuts across organisational boundaries and space and time allocations for staff.

Discussion Question

Do you think the balance of formal and informal processes differs between the three main sectors of provision: commercial, public, and third sector? Think of sport or leisure examples to illustrate your discussion.

13.5.1 Designing Formal Structures

Forming an organisational structure is like creating a structure from building blocks – the work unit or the job of an individual worker is the smallest building block in the structure as a whole. Organising is the process of dividing up the work in a structured framework. Managers have distinct tasks in setting up the staffing structure:

- Dividing the work tasks into jobs that are considered important to the customer experience;
- Grouping similar tasks, usually by forming sections, units, or departments;
- Specifying and controlling the relationships between the groups;
- Delegating authority for carrying out the jobs or group of jobs – this is normally done via 'chains of command';
- Specifying the authority or control over the groups, which can be centralised or decentralised to varying levels.

In designing these structural arrangements, managers need to be aware of the extent to which employees have control of the nature, flow, and type of work that is allocated to them through the formal structural arrangements. Butler (1991) defines structure 'as providing a relatively enduring set of rules for decision making'. This is important, as the nature of decision-making will have an impact on employee engagement and the crucial relationship between managers and staff. Professional sport provides a good illustration of this. Sports coaches and managers are heavily involved in the preparation and training stages before matches. However, once the contest begins, there is only limited support that can be given. Ultimately, it is the responsibility of the sportsmen and women to make the correct choices during the sporting contest. It is incumbent upon the support staff to prepare front-of-house staff to produce the results demanded by the customers.

CASE STUDY 13.4

The Ryder Cup, Whistling Straights, Wisconsin, USA, Sept. 2021

The Ryder Cup is one of golf's premier events and represents a biannual, three-day competitive match between Team USA and Team Europe. It is quite unique in that it represents a team competition in an otherwise very individualised sport. Typically, golfers must be very self-centred in their pursuit of sporting glory, and they very rarely have anything more than a small support team travelling with them. Team events such as this involve a much more collective approach that is not typical of the rest of the golfing calendar year.

The United States had a very young team, with six first-time 'rookies' and an average age of 29. Team Europe had an older and more experienced team, many of whom had tasted victory before.

The Americans, on paper, clearly had the best team. However, this was also the case at previous competitions, and Europe had still emerged victorious in 9 of the last 11 outings. However, in a highly competitive game of very small margins, it appeared to be all to play for.

In the event, the result went resoundingly with the form book, and the US successfully completed a record-breaking win over Europe. This provides an insight into several issues related to the management of people and subsequent performance. As Graeme McDowell, one of the European vice-captains commenting on the preparations observed,

'Padraig's a very cerebral captain. He's a very process-orientated person. . . . It's really a study of the people'.

The two Ryder Cup captains both felt that they had prepared their respective teams well. For Team Europe, the emphasis appeared to be on cultivating the team cohesion that had proved pivotal in the historic success of similar European teams. There can be little doubt that the European Captain, Padraig Harrington, would have been very happy with this objective before the start of the first day of competition and, despite trailing the US team after the first four morning matches, he decided to stick to his original plan of using every European player during the afternoon play. It later emerged that Harrington's original plans changed at the eleventh hour. Reports allege that the European team had failed to consider that some of their player pairings used different golf balls, something that is significant in a 'foursomes' match where one golf ball is shared by both players. This alleged oversight may have had an important contribution to Harrington's best-laid plans and the subsequent ability of the American team to start well and then maintain such momentum throughout the 'home' match!

The US captain, Steve Stricker, was looking to build upon the lessons from previous Ryder Cups, where the American teams often found it difficult to replicate the team ethos of their competitors. Unlike Team Europe, the American team was rarely stronger than the sum of its parts and had repeatedly punched well below its combined weight of talented players during recent competitions. Steve Stricker counteracted this by instigating a variation on the previously successful 'pod' system utilised by the former Ryder Cup Captain, Paul Azinger in 2008, where players were grouped into smaller teams or 'pods' to better cultivate team cohesion and tactics.

In some ways Stricker used his preparation time to exercise all possible advantages. In 2017 he also captained 'The President's Cup', where Team USA played against the 'Rest of the World' and was able to try out and refine such an approach. Throughout the Ryder Cup, Stricker looked to exercise some flexibility with his player pairings, something which was built into the refined pod system. He exercised home-team advantage by bringing the whole team together at Whistling Straights two weeks before the tournament started to help with planning and preparation. This was not really possible for the European Team, who had to contend with COVID travelling restrictions. In addition, Stricker exercised the discretion afforded to him, due to the COVID-19 pandemic, by opting for six 'Captain's Picks' when recruiting his team of golfers. This allowed him more flexibility than the original and more rigid qualification system. Harrington, already constrained by a more complicated qualification system, opted to keep things as they already were.

Due to the Coronavirus, there was a very one-sided crowd at Whistling Straights. Team Europe had spent some time attempting to placate and nullify the impact of an extremely partisan crowd during the practice rounds, prior to the start of the competition. For example, they had emerged on the first tee wearing Cheesehead hats to signify the local NFL team, the Green Bay Packers, in a charm offensive designed to help mitigate to obvious home-team advantage.

However, in the event, the home advantage was overwhelming. The quality of the American Team, combined with its considered leadership proved impossible for the Europeans to match. Stricker's ability to control the controllables, whilst using flexibility when needed, proved an irresistible force for the very talented and on-form American team. As Stricker commented on his preparations, leadership style, and the trust he had in his team,

'They're just so talented. . . . So it was really just getting out of their way'.

Chandler (2005) suggests that structure should follow strategy. However, the creation of strategy is, in itself, a challenging task and does not always account for the political realities that managers face in their daily work situations. Sport and leisure managers often have to react to changes in the external environment that dictate the flow, pattern, and types of decisions that are eventually taken. Structures need to be suited to strategy but also flexible enough to service change and innovation.

13.5.2 Departmental Structures

To be effective, managers must divide the workload into manageable parts. The main purpose of dividing the work is to establish methods of determining section responsibilities, the distribution of authority to individuals, and the processes of delegation. The most widely used method of dividing work is departmentalisation – dividing the workforce into units and departments. In constructing work patterns it is important, as far as possible, to match the needs of individuals to the needs of the work to be done, building in the essential requirement for innovation and staff engagement.

Sport and leisure managers need to be careful when dividing workloads up so that the process does not become overly mechanistic. This may stifle innovation and restrict the possibilities created by dynamic change and staff empowerment. Clearly a balance is needed between dividing work up and creating enough space for innovation, creativity, and the ability to respond to dynamic change.

13.5.3 Different Organisation Structures

The various organisational structures used by sport and leisure organisations fall on a continuum between a mechanistic model which is rigidly structured, at one extreme, and an organic model which is flexibly structured, at the other (see Figure 13.6). The different models are outlined here, together with their characteristics: either more 'vertical' or more 'horizontal', and more or less 'bureaucratic'. Within the compass of these various parameters are some specific 'models', and four are considered briefly: bureaucracy; the 'pyramid'; the matrix structure; and hybrid structures.

The mechanistic extreme is comprised of formal structures, hierarchical communications, and standardised tasks, and power resides at the highest level. The organic extreme is more likely to have informal structures, with more lateral communication and shared ownership of tasks for those with the appropriate knowledge and experience. Control, authority, and communications at the organic extreme move through a wide horizontal network.

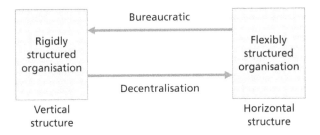

Vertical
structure

Horizontal
structure

Figure 13.6 **The mechanistic-organic continuum.**

13.5.3.1 Bureaucracy

The bureaucratic model is the most widely implemented form of organisational structure. It is a vertical structure. Authority is located at the top of the hierarchy and flows downwards through the organisation. The division of labour emphasises the hierarchical structure and establishes a superior/subordinate relationship. This allows the various activities to be sub-divided into a specific set of tasks, with the roles of individuals clearly defined. There is great benefit in such an approach in terms of clarity of role and lines of communication and authority.

However, in Handy's terms the role of cultures in this model is based on rules and proce-dures. In such organisational cultures there is the potential for what has been termed 'goal displacement'. This is where the means and ends get confused. In other words, the rules become more important than the outcomes. So, for example, it would be more important to follow rules and procedures even if objectives, customer needs, and performance were nega-tively affected by this type of behaviour and action.

13.5.3.2 The Pyramid

Peter (1986) demonstrates the ways in which proliferating bureaucracies sap human resources. He perceives that the problem with major organisations is that they are constructed upside down, with the point of the operation almost invisible underneath the baggage of top-heavy administration. Instead, the pyramid should be turned upside down so that all senior staff are supporting more junior staff at the point of customer delivery – the primary purpose of most organisations in this area. Paradoxically, a sport/leisure organisation, looking to prune expenditure, often cuts jobs at the lower, delivery levels. The customer service elements, such as receptionists, grounds staff, coaching staff, cleaners, and attendants often provide a mis-placed solution that is least likely to affect a positive change. Indeed, it may in fact be more likely to impact negatively on customer satisfaction, retention, and longer-term profitability.

13.5.3.3 The Matrix Structure

The matrix structure (Figure 13.7) is normally a combination of a functional, departmental structure with an overlay of project managers who are responsible for completing specific topics, e.g. a feasibility study for a new sport/leisure facility. In this example the project manager can call upon the expertise in the different departments to assist in the production of the feasibility study: personnel services on staffing aspects, technical services on produc-ing the designs, and projections of capital costs, etc. The advantage of this structure is that it concentrates on the task in hand; technical experts are used as and when required.

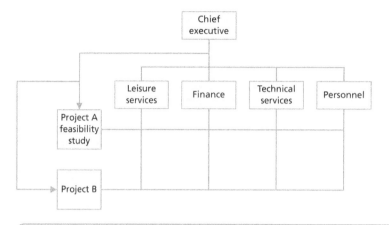

Figure 13.7 **Matrix organisation.**

For example, part of the project brief for many new sports stadia involves a consideration of environmental impact and sustainability. Examples include the Olympic stadium for the London 2012 Olympics and the new stadium and training ground for Tottenham Hotspur Football Club. This requires specialist expertise to be integrated into an eco-friendly design brief, both for altruistic reasons and to promote a more acceptable image to future stake-holders, particularly sponsors, whilst increasing the flexibility of use afforded to such large revenue generating facilities.

Unfortunately, problems can also be encountered when using this form of organisation such as role conflict and role ambiguity – is he or she working for the department or for the project? This situation can produce tensions, work overload, or provide inadequate or too much authority to the project manager. Inadequate resources and authority can delay the proj-ect and result in time-consuming negotiation and meetings. To make a matrix organisation effective, there is a need for a multi-disciplinary team and effective teamwork. Objectives need to be clearly defined and accepted, whilst related resources need to be appropriately deployed.

13.5.3.4 Hybrid Structures

The delivery of sport/leisure products and services calls for flexibility and adaptability – different forms of organisational structure will suit different situations. Commercial sports management, charitable trust management, partnership management, and volunteer manage-ment have different psychological, structural, and resource needs. As such, they may require a variety of 'hybrid' structural arrangements. Sports, arts, and outdoor leisure often call for specially created forms of 'looser' organisational structures. In such leisure environments, with outreach workers, wardens, coaches, teachers, and voluntary support groups, there will be a need to cultivate a flexible management regime. The roles and responsibilities may be fluid and subject to an iterative process of negotiation. As Wolsey and Whitrod-Brown argue:

> The management of people, in sport, represents a number of unique challenges for the industry. Whilst traditional industrial relationships are governed by employment contracts and the exchange of personal time and effort for monetary gain, this does not apply to many volunteers working across the industry. As a consequence, it is the

psychological contract that is fundamental to understanding the perceptions, behaviours and success of many volunteers in this area.

(Wolsey & Whitrod-Brown, 2018, pg. 244)

Therefore, the motivations of a variety of full-time, part-time, casual, and volunteer workers must be taken into account when considering the correct combination of organisational structures. For example, the ongoing training and development needs of an Olympic athlete are very different from those of a short-term volunteer at a one-off sporting event. Both need guidance and inspiration to give their best performance. However, whilst athletes may be willing to run through brick walls in the pursuit of personal excellence, this is not the primary goal for most sports volunteers. The organisational structure must reflect such differences and must serve to enhance personal motivations, not stifle them.

If used wisely, organisational structures provide a framework in which individual and group ambitions can flourish. For most volunteers, for example, the requirement to adopt a more professional approach is often viewed as a bureaucratic imposition from full-time governing body staff. Because most structures emphasise hierarchies, they confer status and 'pecking orders'. Some managers therefore become over-concerned with preserving and enhancing the organisational structure itself and their own position within it, rather than using it to serve the aims and objectives of the organisation.

All organisations, particularly those involved in sport and leisure, represent a social network of relationships and ongoing transactions, leading to the fulfilment, or otherwise, of customer requirements, individual needs, and organisational objectives. The trick is to ensure that all these factors are catered for simultaneously and in a way that offers something valuable and unique to the market, particularly with reference to the people who work hard to deliver such products and services within sport and leisure organisations.

13.6 Conclusions

This chapter has demonstrated that sport and leisure management requires high-quality leaders, managers, and staff. Managers in the industry will need continuing professional development to respond positively to the dynamics of the external government and business environments. Managers need to be aware of more flexible ways of working to deliver a committed, dynamic, and highly motivated workforce. This workforce needs to be well placed to respond to both current and future competitive challenges in this important and expanding area of the economy. To accomplish this, there is an increased need to consider more progressive models of management, which are more about employee empowerment and development than about the traditional prescriptions based only upon 'command and control'. This requires sensitivity, skill, and, above all, effective leadership.

Practical Tasks

1   Consider the structural arrangements of the sport/leisure organisation that you work(ed) for or that you are familiar with. Describe them in relation to the structural types outlined in this chapter (i.e. bureaucratic, pyramid, matrix, and hybrid). Is this structure fit for purpose – does it service the organisation's objectives? What are its advantages and disadvantages for individual, group, and organisational performance? How could it be improved?

2   Using generic and leisure-specific literature, identify the characteristics that are considered to differentiate sport and/or leisure provision from other areas of the economy. For example, what are the differences between providing products and services? Are there differences between sport and other parts of the leisure industry? What implications exist for people management and human resource practices in such areas?

3   Consider a sport governing body that you are aware of. Identify how it is structured by using its website or other documents. Who are the key stakeholders? Who are the key power brokers (individuals and organisations), and why? How does this relate to Handy's typology of organisational culture? What evidence can you find regarding how effectively the various stakeholders work together?

References

Adair, J., & Reed, P. (2003). *Not Bosses but Leaders*, 3rd edition. Kogan Page, London.

Argyris, C. (1966). Interpersonal barriers to decision making. *Harvard Business Review*, 44(2), 84–97.

Argyris, C. (1976). *Increasing Leadership Effectiveness*. Wiley, New York.

Bennis, W. (1989). *On Becoming a Leader*. Business Books, London.

Butler, R. (1991). *Designing Organisations: A Decision Making Perspective*. Routledge, London and New York.

Chandler, A. D., Jr (2005). *Shaping the Industrial Century*. Harvard University Press, Cambridge, MA.

Conn, D. (2009a). *How the Takeover of Manchester City Came Just in Time to Rescue a Club in Disarray*. The Guardian, London.

Conn, D. (2009b). Kevin Keegan's case at Newcastle sheds light on the grubby deals we seldom see. Retrieved from www.guardian.co.uk/football/blog/2009/oct/02/kevin-keegan-newcastle-united-arbitration-panel (accessed 12 March 2010).

Covey, S. (1992). *The Seven Habits of Highly Effective People*. Simon and Shuster, London.

Drucker, P. F. (1955). *The Practice of Management*. Pan Books, London.

Eurostat. (2021). Employment in sport. Retrieved from https://ec.europa.eu/eurostat/statistics-explained/index.php?title=Employment_in_sport (accessed 27 August 2021).

Fotheringham, W. (2008). Revolutionaries. Observer, Sport Supplement, 23 November, 53.

GlobalSportsJobs. (2020). The impact of 2020 on the people of the sports industry. Retrieved from https://intelligence.globalsportsjobs.com/the-impact-of-2020-on-the-people-of-the-sports-industry (accessed 3 June 2021).

Griffiths, H., & Randall, M. (2004). *Careers in Leisure, Institute of Leisure and Amenity Management*. ILAM House, Lower Basildon, Reading.

Hammer, M. (1996). *Beyond Reengineering*. HarperCollins Business, London.

Handy, C. B. (1985). *Understanding Organisations*, 3rd edition. Penguin Books, Harmondsworth.

Heller, R. (1998). *Managing Teams*. Dorling Kindersley, London.

International City Management Association. (1965). *Basic Concepts of Organisation*. Bulletin 3, Effective Supervisory Practices. ICMA, Washington, DC.

Johnson, G., Scholes, K. and Whittington, M. (2008) Exploring Corporate Strategy, 8th edition, Pearson Education, Harlow

Kelso, P. (2010). Portsmouth dismiss 85 staff as Peter Storrie takes 40 per cent pay cut. *Telegraph*, 10 March 2010. Retrieved from www.telegraph.co.uk/sport/football/leagues/

premierleague/portsmouth/7415616/Portsmouth-dismiss-85-staff-as-Peter-Storrie-takes-40-per-cent-pay-cut.html (accessed 12 March 2010).

Landy, F. J., & Conte, J. M. (2009). *Work in the 21st Century: An Introduction to Industrial and Organisational Psychology*, 3rd edition. Wiley-Blackwell, Malden, MA.

MacLeod, D., & Clarke, N. (2009). *Engaging for Success: Enhancing Performance through Employee Engagement*. Department for Business, Innovation and Skills, London. Retrieved from www.berr.gov.uk/files/file52215.pdf

Peter, L. (1986). *The Peter Pyramid*, Allen & Unwin, London.

Robinson, J. (2009). Setanta thought it had a sporting chance. *It lost*, Observer, *Business and Media Section*, 28 June, p. 4.

Taylor, T., & McGraw, P. (2006). Exploring human resource management practices in non-profit sport organisations. *Sport Management Review*, 9, 229–251.

UK Commission for Employment and Skills. (2009). *Towards Ambition 2020: Skills, Jobs, Growth*. UK Commission for Employment and Skills, London, October.

Watt, N. (2009). World Cup 2018: Gordon Brown meets FIFA's Jack Warner to back England's bid. *Guardian*, 27 November. Retrieved from www.guardian.co.uk/football/2009/nov/27/gordon-brown-jack-warner-meeting (accessed 15 January 2010).

Wolsey, C., & Whitrod Brown, H. (2018). Human resource management and the business of sport. In D. Hassan (Ed.), *Managing Sport Business: An Introduction*, 2nd edition. Routledge, London.

Wooden, J. (2005). *Wooden on Leadership*. McGraw Hill, New York.

Chapter 14

Marketing of Sport and Leisure

In This Chapter

- What is marketing, and who are the customers it is aimed at?
- How can information on customers be organised to help marketing?
- What is relationship marketing?
- How does assessing the internal and external environments contribute to marketing?
- What is the 'marketing mix'?
- How important is sponsorship to marketing in sport and leisure?

DOI: 10.4324/9780367823610-14

Summary

Much of the modern emphasis in sport and leisure businesses is on the customer. Satisfying customers is at the centre of notions of service quality. This chapter follows a marketing planning process which begins with identifying the organisation's objectives and understanding customers, particularly the market segments of interest to the organisation; proceeds through analysis of the organisation's internal and external environments and its market positioning; then involves a range of decisions about the 'marketing mix' before implementing an action plan and monitoring whether or not marketing objectives have been achieved.

Eight marketing mix decisions are considered in this chapter, because sport and leisure are largely service industries. This marketing mix consists of product, price, place, promotion, people, physical evidence, process, and sponsorship. These are not separate considerations, however, but interrelated and interdependent parts of an integrated plan. The one element of this mix which is different from many other industries is sponsorship, which is particularly important to some parts of the sport and leisure industry.

14.1 Introduction

Marketing is an essential part of good management practice. It is a process of identifying customer needs, wants, and wishes, and satisfying them. Sport and leisure services and facilities depend on satisfied customers, or they go out of business. Marketing involves creating appropriate goods and services and matching them to market requirements. Therefore, far from being just about selling, marketing is from the beginning an integral part of the business process. Marketing does the following:

- Assesses the needs and wants of potential customers;
- Analyses the internal organisational and external market environments;
- Segments the market appropriately;
- Positions the product in the market;
- Implements a number of decisions, termed the 'marketing mix';
- Secures appropriate relationships with customers;
- Analyses, evaluates, and adjusts.

However, marketing is as relevant to not-for-profit organisations, in the private and public sectors, as it is to the commercial profit-making sector. Any providers should be motivated to supply their customers with what these customers want. In the commercial world, marketing has proved to be an effective means of staying in business and making greater profits. For leisure services in the public and voluntary sectors, it can help to achieve a more complex set of objectives. The common link is the customer, because it is through satisfying customers that any organisational objectives are achieved. As Chapter 16 makes clear, the essence of quality management is satisfying customers.

Marketing is not a single function in a business or service organisation. It is a business philosophy, a business way of life. Traditionally, many companies used to be process led and product oriented; having a predetermined product or service, they found customers and convinced them to want their product. The approach is 'This is what we've got – now sell it'. Local government services have often worked in this way. For example, facilities are built, equipment is installed, markings are put on to the floors, programmes are devised, times are decided, charges are determined, systems are established, and the council will proudly announce that the facility is open. Councillors might then say of the facility, 'It is there for them to use; if they don't use it that is their lookout. We provide plenty of opportunity in our town'. This approach is concerned with providing predetermined products.

The marketing approach reverses the process and starts with the customer. It is market led. It requires the manager to find out what the customer wants and then design, produce, and deliver what is required to satisfy customers and achieve the organisation's objectives. Blake (1985) said: 'Sports centres, pools, theatres, art galleries, libraries, museums, gymnasia, are merely warehouses holding tangible and intangible products that have no value except that brought to them by customers'.

14.1.1 The Concept of Social Marketing

Marketing can be interpreted as much broader than just economic exchange and can also include exchanges dealing with social issues. Kotler and Zaltman (1971) define social marketing as '[t]he design, implementation and control of programmes calculated to influence the acceptability of social ideas and involving consideration of product planning, pricing, communication, distribution and market research'. Marketing can encompass political campaigns, community programmes, and social causes such as environmental issues, healthy living, child protection, disability issues, anti-smoking campaigns, and equal opportunities. Social marketing, however, is less concerned with finding out what consumers want, and more concerned with convincing consumers that certain decisions are in their own interests and worth acting on for social reasons.

14.2 The Marketing Planning Process

To market successfully, there needs to be a marketing plan. Sometimes this is used to mean the selection of the marketing mix, but it is a more holistic process than this. Figure 14.1 illustrates a ten-stage marketing planning process. This process establishes the structure for the rest of this chapter. Whilst each element is reviewed separately, it is important to remember that this is an integrated set of issues and decisions which are dependent on each other.

14.3 Organisational Vision, Mission, and Objectives

Concise organisational statements of vision and mission are very important, not only to steer marketing planning but also for all stakeholders in an organisation, whether they are customers, staff, shareholders, or partner organisations. An organisation's vision statement is a clear statement of where it wants to go. Its mission statement identifies the organisation's main reason for existing and indicates the values guiding its policies and strategies. The vision and mission statement are equivalent to aims, but they do not contain sufficient detail to enable them to be confidently translated into operational details and targets. For this, objectives are necessary.

1 Identify the organisation's mission, vision, and objectives

2 Research and understand customers

3 Analyse internal and external market environments

4 Set marketing objectives

5 Devise marketing strategies

6 Decide the specific market mix

7 Set budgets

8 Write the marketing action plan and communicate

9 Implement the plan and control

10 Monitor, review, and update

Figure 14.1 **The process of marketing planning.**

To be operationally useful, objectives need to have certain attributes – often summarised in the term 'SMART', but this is modified and has an extra letter added to form the term MASTER (Measurable, Achievable, Specific, Time-specified, Ends not means, Ranked) (see Chapter 17). The essential point is that it must be possible to identify if and when objectives have been achieved.

> ### Discussion Question
>
> Arts Council England's vision statement reads: 'By 2030, we want England to be a country in which the creativity of each of us is valued and given the chance to flourish, and where every one of us has access to a remarkable range of high-quality cultural experiences' (www.artscouncil.org.uk/our-vision). How useful is this as a steer for marketing the arts?

14.4 Understanding Customers

An essential part of analysing external and internal environments for an organisation is understanding customers. Customers include:

- Individuals;
- Organisations (who buy for others);

- Supporters;
- Spectators;
- Schools;
- Clubs;
- Parents of young users;
- The community.

Even non-users might be seen as potential customers and are therefore worthy of consideration from a marketing perspective. Different customers have different needs, a principle which is at the heart of market segmentation (see Chapter 14).

Chapter 4 identifies some dimensions to the concepts of customer need and market demand. Understanding customer needs and demands is a foundation stone for marketing. Market research and demand forecasting are tools to help with this (see Chapter 14). There are several other techniques to help, including customer profiling, market segmentation, and analysis of customer relationships. Before reviewing these techniques, it is important to understand consumer behaviour.

14.4.1 Consumer Behaviour

This is a branch of marketing analysis which examines the reasons for customer purchases. It centres on needs and motivations, which have already been reviewed in Chapter 4. Many theories of consumer behaviour are based on logical processes. For example, the theory of reasoned action suggests that consumer behaviour is driven by intentions, which are themselves driven by a variety of internal and external factors. Consumers have attitudes towards prospective purchases which will be driven partly by their perceptions of value, partly by their personal circumstances, and partly by the social environment they live and work in (Pope & Turco, 2001).

Mullin et al. (2007) identify a range of environmental and individual factors which influence consumer behaviour, either positively or negatively. Such factors include:

- Environmental:
  - significant others, such as parents, teachers, and peer group leaders;
  - cultural norms and values, which may be inherited but may also be influenced by the media;
  - class, race, and gender relations;
  - climatic and geographic conditions;
  - market behaviour of sport organisations.

- Individual:
  - self-concept, including self-image and self-confidence;
  - life-cycle stage;
  - physical characteristics;
  - income and employment;
  - education and learned skills;
  - perceptions;
  - motivations, including physiological, psychological, and social;
  - attitudes.

In short, sport and leisure marketers have a significant task in understanding why consumers behave the way they do.

14.4.2 Market Segmentation

Knowledge of consumer behaviour leads to the conclusion that customers are not one set of people with the same characteristics and preferences. Instead, customers comprise numerous groups of individuals within each of which there are similarities in needs, characteristics, motivations, etc. It is no longer appropriate to believe that an organisation is providing a service for all people. Even local authorities, with arguably the broadest remit in terms of a potential customer base, now recognise that if they indiscriminately market their services to all, it will probably result in particular types of people being over-represented among their customers and some groups, particularly the disadvantaged, being under-represented. Remedying this requires market segmentation and target marketing.

A market segment, then, is any relatively homogeneous subdivision of a market that is likely to be attracted to particular products or services. Several forms of market segmentation are available:

- **By demographics** – e.g. age groups, gender groups, ethnic groups, tourists;
- **By socio-economics** – e.g. by income, occupation, housing type, car ownership;
- **By geography** – i.e. different areas, from countries to communities, the latter often coinciding with socio-economic variables in formal classification systems;
- **By behaviour and benefits** – i.e. how customers respond to and what they get from the service, e.g. off-peak visitors, fitness motivated customers, visitors motivated by education/skill improvement;
- **By psychographics** – typically different attitudes, lifestyles, and values.

Many practical segmentation exercises involve a mix of these different methods. It is possible to conduct clear and simple segmentation by using descriptive statistics such as age, gender, and socio-economic profiles of populations to identify major market segments suitable for marketing actions. It is unlikely that many sport and leisure organisations will have the resources to undertake a complex statistical analysis, such as that illustrated in Case Study 15.2 – particularly small and medium-sized enterprises and organisations in the voluntary sector. Sport England's segmentation analysis enables relevant organisations to utilise a ready-made system for identifying market segments and what motivates them, allowing organisations to design appropriate marketing communications.

CASE STUDY 14.2

Sport Consumers Segmentation in England

Consultants Experian have produced for Sport England a 19-segment classification of people in respect of sport – using national survey data to identify their activity levels, their socio-demographic characteristics, their motivations, and their attitudes. This segmentation was conducted to provide those working in community sport with both an insight into the sporting behaviour, barriers, and motivations of existing participants and a practical marketing tool. The 19 market segments are summarised in the following link: https://segments.sportengland.org/pdf/summarySheet.pdf

They comprise:

1 Competitive male urbanites;
2 Sports team drinkers;

  3 Fitness class friends;
  4 Supportive singles;
  5 Career-focused females;
  6 Settling down males;
  7 Stay at home mums;
  8 Middle England mums;
  9 Pub league team mates;
 10 Stretched single mums;
 11 Comfortable mid-life males;
 12 Empty nest career ladies;
 13 Early retirement couples;
 14 Older working women;
 15 Local old boys;
 16 Later life ladies;
 17 Comfortable retired couples;
 18 Twilight year gents;
 19 Retirement home singles.

Detailed information on the size and composition of these segments has been produced at different geographical levels – street, community, local authority, and region.

It is also available for individual sports and broader sport groups (e.g. by type, such as racquet sports or martial arts, by facilities used, by individual/team). The information extends to how sport and active recreation fit into each segment's lives, the type of marketing communications messages they respond to, the communications media they respond to, the brands they identify and associate with, and how they make decisions. This is all very important for the detailed marketing planning for each segment.

Sport England also provides advice on how its market segmentation can be used for a variety of purposes, including catchment area analysis, funding decisions, planning new facilities, project evaluation, attracting new members, and identifying appropriate partner organisations. In addition there are case studies demonstrating how County Sports Partnerships (sub-regional organisational networks) have used the segments for a variety of purposes. Humber County Sports Partnership in the northeast of the country, for example, has used it to develop new marketing strategies for its constituent local authorities, matching programmes to motivations for key segments and modifying marketing communications, taking into account the decision-making processes of these market segments.

The process of segmentation needs good market research to identify the different segments. It requires strategies and matching of segments to products within the overall service – using tools such as the Sport England segmentation analysis. In practical terms, market segmentation requires that the selected segments are measurable, substantial (of sufficient size to be worth separate marketing planning and implementation), and easily identified and accessible, so that marketing communications can be directed at them effectively and efficiently.

14.4.3 Customer Relationships

Relationship marketing is an approach to marketing which is designed to improve the relationship between the customer and the service provider. Being led by considerations of what matters for customers, it contrasts with product-led and process-led marketing. Relationship marketing is increasingly important in sport and leisure marketing, as the many examples in Ferrand and McCarthy (2009) demonstrate. Through this approach, the understanding of customers is structured by their relationship with the product, the brand, and the organisation. Sport is an excellent example of this. At one extreme are fans of sports teams – the most loyal of customers who turn out to support their teams no matter what, often home and away, who purchase associated merchandise in larger quantities than other supporters, and who provide the most vocal sounding board for any matters the organisation wants to test, e.g. through fanzines. At the other extreme are commercial fitness clubs, whose greatest problem is often poor retention of members because their customers tend to shop around to find the service most appropriate to their needs and at the best price.

The rationale for relationship marketing is undeniable, especially in sport and leisure. More loyal customers spend more and cost less than new or less loyal customers. Customers with a good relationship with the product, brand, and organisation will act as ambassadors or agents for attracting further customers – their word of mouth is a powerful medium. Relationship marketing translates market segments into individuals because a key objective is to establish a relationship with each individual customer.

The main marketing implications of relationship marketing are that it is important to:

- **Build new and stronger relationships** – e.g. through personalised marketing communications to selected market segments;
- **Retain and develop existing relationships** – e.g. through loyalty offers and rewards and added value services;
- **Recover from problems with existing relationships** – e.g. through fast identification of problems and effective action to resolve them.

These are principles which any marketing strategy should adopt. However, Ferrand and McCarthy (2009) promote relationship marketing as an alternative strategic approach to more traditional marketing approaches such as that identified in Figure 14.1. Their model consists of three key stages:

1 Change the internal marketing structure of the organisation to focus on developing relationships.
2 Create and develop relationships with targeted customers, i.e. with the market.
3 Create and develop relationships with key stakeholders, i.e. with the network or organisations relevant to supply.

Discussion Question

Discuss the difficulties of professional sports clubs simultaneously developing good relationships with corporate clients, 'fair weather supporters', and relatively low-income, long-term fans.

14.5 Analysing Internal and External Environments

Understanding customers is really part of a first stage of marketing planning, which involves auditing and analysing the internal (organisational) and external (market) environments of the organisation. This involves assembling appropriate data and then analysing it. The types of data which are relevant include:

- Internal:
  - mission, vision, and objectives;
  - customers, e.g. satisfactions, dissatisfactions, expectations, relationships;
  - resources, e.g. management structure, staff, finance, technology;
  - stakeholders, e.g. staff, partners, funders, relationships.

- External:
  - PEST – Political, Economic, Social, and Technological considerations which impact on the organisation's activities (also called STEP);
  - potential customers – needs, motivations, profiles, behaviour, and locations;
  - competitors, both direct (same products) and indirect (appealing to similar customer needs) – profiles, market shares, critical – success factors, limitations, strategies, trajectories over time;
  - markets – size, growth, product developments, prices, distribution characteristics, promotion norms, and development.

14.5.1 SWOT

A traditional means of summarising the internal and external environmental analysis which is still in common use is SWOT: Strengths and Weaknesses summarise the internal analysis of the organisation; Opportunities and Threats summarise the external environment for the organisation. SWOT analysis is typically concise, attempting to select the key issues important to marketing decisions. It is also often descriptive, but the word *analysis* is important – it needs to both justify the importance of the selected SWOT features and make clear the marketing implications for the organisation.

Discussion Question

Consider the main strengths, weaknesses, opportunities, and threats of a sport or leisure organisation in your locality. What are the marketing implications of your conclusions?

14.5.2 Marketing Objectives and Strategies

Marketing objectives should aspire to the same attributes as organisational objectives, and they should be shared by the whole organisation, not just the marketing manager/department. They should specify marketing targets in relation to appropriate performance indicators. Marketing objectives are also likely to be specific to selected market segments. Examples include reaching a certain number of members from a particular demographic section of the catchment area, such as older people, and reaching a target for secondary income per attendance, from merchandise and catering.

Discussion Question

For a sport or leisure organisation of your choice, discuss possible organisational objectives and marketing objectives to illustrate the differences between them.

A marketing strategy is a calculated approach to achieving objectives and targets. The strategy sets a direction for the specific marketing instruments – the marketing mix. One important element of the strategy is market segmentation. Another is market positioning.

14.5.3 Strategic Positioning

'Positions' are people's perception of where products fit in the market. A product's position can be easily recognised, and favourable positions encourage continued sales. Products and services have long-term 'personalities', just like people. For example, the Bank of England – normally safe and dependable; Wimbledon – the pinnacle of tennis and its traditional values; Apple products – innovative and creative. Disney, McDonald's, Nike, and hundreds of other brands have a position in our minds and in the marketplace. Positions, however, can be favourable or unfavourable. Local authority leisure services for years have had to battle with the public perception of their facilities as basic and cheap, in comparison with higher-quality commercial sector facilities.

Positions are established through well-targeted marketing communications. Many modern-day marketing communications, especially brands aimed at young people, are being driven through social media, for example, as people on average spent just under two hours a day on social media in 2019. Other companies look to leverage market position and market share through commercial deals linked to sport teams, products, and athletes.

Repositioning is possible. The drink Lucozade used to be sold in chemist's shops for people who were ill. However, TV promotions using Olympic gold medal winners, like Daley Thompson, repositioned Lucozade as a refreshing energy drink for athletes – from a position of a drink for the sick to a drink for the fit. Crompton (2009) views repositioning as vitally important for the future of public leisure services. It is his claim that leisure services are still not central to public service provision, because they are not sufficiently positioned alongside major social concerns. Their future, therefore, depends on repositioning public sport and leisure so that the public and politicians associate them with solutions to such concerns, e.g. poor health, obesity, crime and vandalism, children's safety, etc.

Two other commonly cited tools can help in positioning products within the marketplace and within the organisation's portfolio of products. These are the Boston Matrix and the Ansoff Matrix.

14.5.4 The Boston Matrix

This matrix, shown in Figure 14.2, was designed for the Boston Consulting Group as a device to help analyse sources of cash flow within an organisation. Its two axes, market share and market growth rate, are associated respectively with cash generation and cash usage. The organisation's business units, or alternatively brands or products, can be positioned in this matrix using data and judgement. The matrix helps to identify the balance of the portfolio of business units, brands, or products, although not all the quadrants of the matrix are of equal merit with respect to cash flow:

- **Cash cows** – with high market share but low market growth, these are often described derogatively as mature and boring, but in fact because they are highly likely to be net cash generators, they are very valuable assets, with a market position which should be defended by rejuvenation tactics. In the UK, at indoor sports centres, five-a-side football leagues might be seen as cash cows.

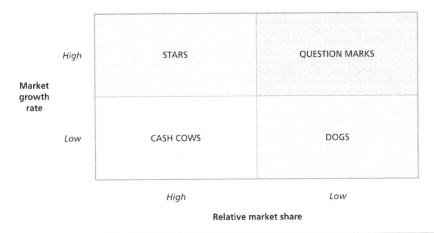

Figure 14.2 **The Boston Matrix.**

- **Stars** – with high market share and high market growth, these typically attract all the at-tention as the best performers, although the high growth rate requires high cash usage. Personal trainers and sport nutritionists in indoor sport and leisure centres in the UK are a current example of 'stars'.
- **Question marks** – with low market share and high market growth, these are net cash users, and although they may increase market share as a result of high market growth, there is a risk that their growth rate falls and they become 'dogs'. Specific forms of exer-cise class are possible 'question marks' because there is always uncertainty about whether they will become established or be replaced by a new form of exercise.
- **Dogs** – with low market share and low market growth, these are not worth continuing. In recent years in the UK, squash has been of this nature and has been disposed of by several indoor sports centres.

The Boston Matrix gives a clear positioning of an organisation's products, but it requires a detailed knowledge of the market to be accurate. It does not reveal the profitability or social impact of the organisation's products. It is therefore useful for analysis of cash flow and its potential, but it should not be interpreted as more than this. Nevertheless, cash flow is impor-tant to organisations in all three sectors, not just commercial companies. And it is from this perspective that the Boston Matrix gives implications for marketing priorities and activities, e.g. defensive marketing for cash cows against threats to market share and demarketing or disposing of 'dogs'.

14.5.5 The Ansoff Matrix

This matrix, shown in Figure 14.3, was devised to help organisations and their marketers identify the strategic choices for growth in their business. Each quadrant represents different potential for growth and risk:

- **Market penetration** offers probably the lowest growth potential but also the lowest risk, i.e. more of the same product to the same market. Growth can be achieved by capturing customers from other suppliers, attracting non-users, or encouraging existing users to buy/visit more frequently.

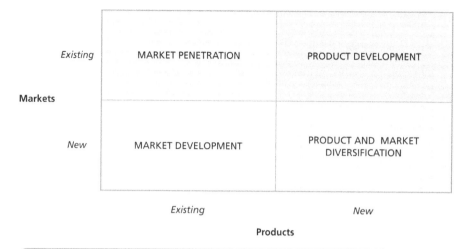

Figure 14.3 **The Ansoff Matrix.**

- **Market development** requires marketing activity in new markets. These may be new geographical areas or new market segments that were previously not targeted. Outreach services are a typical form of market development in sport and leisure, i.e. taking the services into geographical areas where usage is low. The growth prospects are higher than market penetration, but so are the risks – the new market may not be as suitable as the existing market.
- **Product development** requires identification, supply, and promotion of new products to existing customers. The growth prospects and risk depend critically on designing the right new product for the market – customer research is essential to reduce the risk. Commercial fitness centres are very good at developing new fitness products for their existing customers.
- **Diversification** is the riskiest strategy and the one requiring most research because both the products and markets are new. Several sports, for example, have developed new variants of their activities for very young participants.

The Ansoff Matrix, like the Boston Matrix, is a descriptive device to categorise products. These devices are not prescriptive and need careful interpretation with respect to marketing strategies for brands, products, and markets.

14.6 The Marketing Mix

Marketing is concerned with providing the right products and services, and then forging the best relationships between customers and those products and services. The 'marketing mix' is how that relationship is developed. It has several ingredients, each of which will have a greater or lesser influence in different settings. The first four are commonly referred to as 'the four Ps', while the last three are usually added in consideration of services marketing to make 'the seven Ps':

1 Product (including service);
2 Pricing;
3 Place;

4   Promotion;
5   People;
6   Physical evidence;
7   Process.

An eighth element of the marketing mix which is particularly relevant to sport and leisure is sponsorship. The sections which follow review these components.

14.6.1 The Sport and Leisure Product

The product (including the service) is the basis of all marketing. It is the unit of exchange with the client or customer. If it offers customers satisfaction, they may continue to buy it. Sport and leisure products are opportunities for customers, and they can be of different types, including tangible and intangible elements. They include one or more of the following:

- Goods, e.g. sports clothing and footwear;
- Facilities, e.g. tennis courts, museums;
- Services, e.g. a lesson, a guided walk, outreach opportunities;
- Events, e.g. a sports competition, a music festival;
- Programmes (see Chapter 15), e.g. a Shakespeare production, a mother and child swimming session, an aerobics class.

These are the vehicles for realising demands. When these products successfully match customer demands, it leads to the realisation of service outcomes, the benefits sought by customers. People want to enjoy, to be with friends, to learn, to look better, to feel better, to be skilful, to win. If customers do experience such benefits, they will want to 'buy' them again. Customers help to create the final product, which is the participation experience – this is the inseparability of leisure service products and consumption. Another key characteristic of many sport and leisure experiences is that they differ on each occasion. Every sports game is different, every drama production is different, every concert is different, even when there are some standard infrastructure elements supporting the delivery of the final product. It is this difference, or novelty, that is said to be a key driver of leisure demands (see Chapter 4).

The provision of services, facilities, and programmes is important in providing opportunities, but the purpose of the product is not realised until it is utilised. In this sense the sport and leisure product is highly perishable; for example, an unsold seat at a theatre production represents the permanent loss of an experience. Matching products to likely demand is a very difficult task, not just in terms of the timing of opportunities (around peak and off-peak fluctuations in demand, seasonal changes) but also in terms of the quantity and quality of the product offer. A sports centre which is too big for its catchment area, for example, will give rise to continual capacity utilisation problems, which represent a waste of product. Products exhibit life cycles. With most commercial products, that life cycle consists of:

- Product start;
- Growth;
- Development;
- Decline and replacement by better products.

In sport and leisure services, many products have been with us for a long time, but a number are relatively new (e.g. various forms of aerobic exercise classes), and some have declined (e.g. squash). Product development provides a continuous stream of new or changing products which fit customers' needs. Cinemas have changed from single to multi-screen. Tenpin bowling and bingo have changed to social venues with a wider range of products. In public sector sport, it is apparent that needs and motivations have changed over the years, with less demand for competitive team sports and growing demand for non-competitive, individual, fitness activities (see Chapter 9). This is not supply led, but rather is determined by changing motivations towards health- and fitness-related outcomes, such as losing weight for health reasons or looking good for social reasons.

Leisure products, like any other products, need testing and changing to suit customer needs. Hence market research and product testing need to be undertaken to have the best chance of matching products with markets. Capturing interest with the product is essential, and novelty is a desirable attribute. Good marketers should encourage levels of originality and be prepared to take risks. This is particularly the case in the arts, where new products are an important element of attracting repeat business. Originals and 'firsts' capture interest and can also create a lasting impression.

Packaging different products can generate customer benefits at all levels of participation, e.g. a daytime public leisure centre package might include sports activity, dietary clinic, sauna, and a crèche for the children. Marketers have identified three levels of product, and the packaging of products is clearly aimed at embracing all three:

1   The **core** product is the main motivation for the customer, e.g. a visit to an exhibition or a fitness class.
2   The **actual** product wraps certain elements around the core product, such as changing facilities in the case of sport.
3   The **augmented** product includes a variety of optional extras, such as merchandising, drinks, food, or transport arrangements.

Most sport and leisure programmes, even those designed with a specific activity in mind, tend to market more than one product. A combination of facilities can attract greater use, be more economical, and provide the spin-off to other activities, expanding the market.

Discussion Question

Think of a core product, e.g. enjoying a theatre production, a game of sport, an art exhibition. Now think of additional product items that can be offered to create added value for the customer. Are all these typically on offer, and if not why?

14.6.2 Brands

Another form of product augmentation which has become important is brands. A product is the basic functional item for sale, whether it is a physical good or an intangible service. Often it can be easily copied. However, a brand is fundamentally an identifier, such as a logo, which helps to distinguish one seller from its competitors – it cannot be copied. Aaker (2002) suggests that brands add several intangible associations which augment the product, such as customer relationships, emotional benefits, and user imagery.

The brand helps position the product in the market. A product takes on added value from a brand, because of the intangible associations and benefits which consumers relate to the brand. This added value is termed 'brand equity', which can be financial (such as increased sales and profits) and consumer based (such as perceived higher quality, brand associations, and brand loyalty). The marketer uses brands because they help to enhance the relationship with the customer, generating greater customer loyalty and more repeat purchasing of the product.

> ### Discussion Question
>
> Many customers buy only branded sports clothing and footwear, typically at considerably higher cost than unbranded equivalents. What are the main 'added value' reasons for this behaviour?

14.6.3 Pricing

It is important not only to match people's needs with appropriate products but also to do so at prices they are willing to pay. Otherwise demand remains latent, not revealed. Price is an important signal to both consumers and producers in the market system. Economists begin an explanation of the market system with a demand and supply diagram, with price as the controlling variable for both. Often the importance of price is overstated. In some art forms, where demand is dominated by customers without socio-economic disadvantage, evidence suggests that price is not very important compared with the product – the performance, e.g. theatre and music concerts. Nevertheless, for many products, demand is more price sensitive, particularly in markets where there is strong competition between alternative providers or for market segments which suffer from socio-economic disadvantage, such as older people without private pensions, the disabled, and the unemployed.

Prices perform valuable functions for providers – they raise revenue, they ration demand, and they can help discriminate in favour of certain types of customers. They are also important signals for customers, who may perceive prices as indicators of quality, e.g. low pricing may suggest low product quality, whilst high prices reinforce perceptions of high quality and exclusivity, e.g. exclusive holidays and yachts.

Pricing policy is an important factor in financial planning and a vital part of marketing. Important pricing decisions for any product include:

- **The level of price which is appropriate to the organisation's objectives and its market demand** – too low and there could be considerable excess demand, with queues for services and waiting time for goods; too high and there will be underutilised capacity in services and unsold stocks of goods. Even a free product should involve an explicit decision by the provider because it should match the organisation's objectives and a way needs to be found to recoup the costs of provision.
- **The structure of prices,** including whether to have different prices for different customers – in arts or sports events this is normal, with higher prices for better audience positions. In tourism, higher prices are charged in peak seasons. Many other leisure organisations charge discounts for various reasons such as socio-economic disadvantage, promotion at slack times of the day or week, to attract new customers, to build relationships, or to reward loyalty and repeat purchasing.

In principle, pricing decisions should be made with respect to a number of criteria:

- **The financial and marketing objectives of the organisation,** which can vary from maximising profits, through maximising utilisation, to maximising social benefits such as health improvement and reduction in crime and vandalism.

- **The costs of provision to the organisation** – not just the operating costs but also capital costs.
- **Strength of demand**, particularly in response to changes in prices. In economics this is termed 'price elasticity of demand', i.e. the relative strength of response of demand to a change in price. For many sport and leisure services, demand is typically price inelastic – examples include attendances at professional team sports events, sport and leisure centres, and arts venues such as theatres and concerts – meaning that the percentage change in demand is less than the percentage change in price.
- **Strength of competition**, not only from within the sector, e.g. between commercial firms, but also across sectors, e.g. between commercial firms and local authority providers. The greater the competition, the more responsive or 'elastic' demand is to changes in price, because it is easier for customers to find substitutes.

In practice, evidence suggests that not all these criteria are typically employed when pricing decisions are made. In the commercial sector the most common pricing determinant is costs, e.g. cost-plus pricing, where prices are decided by calculating average cost per unit of supply and adding a profit margin. There is sometimes fierce competition in the commercial sector which must be considered (see Chapter 6), and which in an oligopoly situation (a few major competitors) sometimes leads to stable prices, for fear of a price war between competitors.

In the voluntary sector, the most likely pricing level is one which will result in a break-even on operational costs for the organisation, so again costs are the major criterion for setting membership fees. This is because most clubs in the voluntary sector are non-profit; e.g. Chapter 7 shows that the average financial surplus in UK sports clubs is very small. Aiming to break even, however, requires an appreciation of both the costs of supplying opportunities for members and how sensitive members are to different prices. One way of linking prices to costs more directly is to charge prices for different elements of costs, e.g. membership fees (for club overheads), NGB affiliation fees, and match fees (for match-day costs).

In the public sector, pricing has largely been based on tradition, e.g. previous prices plus an increment, with some consideration of what is an 'acceptable' level in other authorities ('copycat pricing'). Subsidies are common in the public sector, so the pricing decision needs to consider what subsidies are reasonable and can be afforded from the public purse and how big the subsidies should be. Figure 14.4 illustrates a common charging continuum for public sector leisure services. The bulk of public sector leisure activities are priced at a subsidised level, with the primary objective of making activities accessible to disadvantaged segments of the community.

> **Discussion Question**
>
> In attempting to attract a wide cross-section of the community to a public leisure attraction, what are the relative merits of (1) generally low prices for all customers, and (2) specifically targeted price discounts for disadvantaged people?

14.6.4 Place

Products – facilities, programmes, activities – need to be accessible to the people they have been developed for. Place, or distribution, is the final contact with the customer, after other marketing decisions such as product, price, and promotion have been taken. Once customers

	SUBSIDY		PROFIT	
Type of charge	No charge	Some charge	Economic charge	Commercial charge
Basis of policy	Social service – all residents have a recreational need – facilities available to all	Many people and groups have needs for specialist activities for health and recreation	Participants are main benefactors – hence have to pay full costs	Benefits participants exclusively. Charges include full costs and profit charges based on what market can bear. Profit used to subsidise other facilities
Types of facilities	Parks Libraries	Swimming pools Public tennis courts Arts centres Community centres	Entertainments Golf courses	Indoor tennis Health and fitness Squash Sauna Sunbeds
Profile of users	Representative of neighbourhood	High proportion of local people Youths/young people	Middle income groups Young adults	Middle to high income groups

Figure 14.4 The pricing policy continuum for public sector sport and leisure.

attend a facility or a service opportunity, or purchase a sport or leisure product, it is a sign of effectiveness in distribution. In sport and leisure services the product is often centred on a particular type of facility, which means that instead of the distribution of goods to customers, as in manufactured goods, the customer very often has to attend a facility, e.g. a sports centre, a theatre, a country park. In these circumstances, one key product decision, facility location, is simultaneously a place decision.

Distribution decisions should be based on the market research about customers, their home and work locations, transportation, and other accessibility factors. A critically important decision for facilities is where to locate them in relation to their anticipated markets. This is arguably the most important marketing decision (see Chapter 14), because whilst programmes, activities, prices, and promotion can all be changed in the short run, within weeks if necessary, facility location is typically only changed in the long run, every 30 years or more.

It is therefore very important for services and facilities to be placed in locations that customers can get to easily. Accessibility can also be influenced with directional signs, maps, an attractive welcoming entrance, and by lighting the parking areas and walkways. The general awareness of the leisure facility can be reinforced by attractive displays and exhibitions in public places and by leaflet distribution. Place is also important within facilities, i.e. locating key elements within facilities with customer convenience in mind, e.g. changing rooms near playing areas, crèche adjacent to outdoor play space, good viewing for spectators.

Time and information are also key aspects of accessibility. Activities need to be in the right place at the right time, so programming is essential to distribution. Different market segments have potential for visiting at different times, so conventional programming – such as evenings for the theatre and concerts, weekday evenings and weekends for sport and physical activity – may be restricting accessibility unnecessarily. Less conventional programming times can work, with the right products and promotion, such as theatre matinees on weekday afternoons (attracting older customers) and early morning fitness opportunities (attracting people in 9-to-5 jobs). Similarly, information centres for sport and leisure opportunities often close in the evenings and weekends, when they may be most needed, although the internet has facilitated round-the-clock information.

Distribution of sport and leisure is often direct, from producer to consumer, e.g. participating in local public sports facilities, visiting a local library, museum, or art gallery. Other forms of sport and leisure are increasingly distributed indirectly, i.e. by agents or intermediaries. A major example is music and sport events, with internet agencies such as Ticketmaster in the UK taking increasing shares of ticket purchasing rather than the venues themselves. Other examples such as books, recorded music, and sports equipment and clothing are increasingly showing a switch of agents, from normal retail outlets to online purchasing. Whether distribution is direct or indirect has an effect on accessibility and price – typically indirect distribution increases both accessibility (by promotion to a wider set of potential customers) and price – either to the customer through a booking fee or to the supplier through a commission on sales.

Many leisure facilities will be inaccessible to segments of the population, for example people living in rural areas. In these cases, needs can be met by organising mobile services, e.g. mobile library, play bus, travelling theatre, and by appointing artists in residence, 'animateurs', and sports development officers. Community facilities such as village halls can be utilised to widen the distribution of sport and leisure services. In the arts, many drama and music companies have devised innovative alternative locations to traditional indoor venues for summer productions, using parks and the gardens of historic houses. Some of these are designed to be more attractive places for existing customers, rather than places which appeal to new market segments, but they demonstrate the effectiveness of imaginative place decisions.

14.6.5 Promotion

Many people mistakenly use the word *marketing* when they really mean *promotion*. Promotion's purpose is twofold: creating awareness of the opportunities provided by the supplier and seeking to attract and persuade customers to purchase the particular service or product. It is a process of familiarising and creating, and reinforcing favourable images, attitudes, and a willingness to buy. Through this process it is also a means by which customer relationships can be enhanced.

Promotional activity can be defined as an exercise in communications. There are many factors affecting demand, some of which consumers may not be conscious of. Restricted impressions or preconceptions, for example, can determine consumer responses, e.g. 'sports facilities are only for young, fit people', 'theatres are only for educated, well-off people', 'classical music is only for older people'. It is the job of promotion to correct such misimpressions and motivate anyone with a potential interest in an opportunity into moving towards the purchase stage.

Promotional communications can provide information about such things as the existence of the opportunity, opening times, etc., or they can simply create and reinforce a favourable image through symbolic association. The general functions of promotion are summarised by the acronym AIDA, i.e.:

- Attention – drawing the customer's attention to the product;
- Interest – creating interest in the product, through promotion of its benefits;
- Desire – stimulating a desire to purchase the product;
- Action – purchase and consumption of the product.

Promotion can set off an important additional round of communication about the product through word of mouth and recommendation – a large proportion of sport and leisure customers come with friends and like-minded groups of people. Masterman and Wood (2006) demonstrate the complexity of the communications process, which involves:

- The organisation encoding the messages it wants the market to notice with the required images and information;
- The potential customer decoding the message with the required interpretation;
- 'Noise' – external distractions in the communications process, which need to be minimised.

A promotional strategy should be built around a proper brief, taking account of:

- The benefits of the products to consumers;
- Target markets;
- The information and messages to be conveyed to potential customers;
- The media and promotional methods to be used;
- Offers and inducements.

Promotion consists of one or more of the following key components:

- **Personal selling** – a direct 'presentation' to one or more potential customers with the objective of selling a service or a product;
- **Advertising** – a paid form of non-personal presentation about the organisation and/or the opportunities it offers;
- **Incentives/promotions** – financial offers or 'gifts' that are made to potential customers with the objective of encouraging them to purchase a particular service or product;
- **Publicity/public relations** – favourable communication in the media (e.g. print or broadcast) which may be achieved at no direct cost to the organisation concerned.

These four methods are not necessarily independent of each other, and different methods can be used to enhance both the message and the customer relationship, e.g. an incentive to introduce a friend to an organisation, promoted by direct mail, will provide added value for existing customers. Sponsorship is sometimes identified as a fifth promotional vehicle, but in this chapter, it is covered later as another element of the marketing mix.

14.6.6 Personal Selling

Personal selling is important to sport and leisure and does not typically take place through such means as telesales, but rather through face-to-face contact with frontline staff, such as bookings or reception staff. To be effective in personal selling, it is necessary that the person concerned does it with enthusiasm, so that he or she is perceived as being able, efficient, and caring. The function of personal selling involves a two-way communication process and can provide valuable feedback about existing and potential programmes and activities.

14.6.7 Advertising

Advertising encompasses many forms of communication and includes:

- Posters – in prominent, eye-catching locations;
- Brochures and leaflets that describe the facilities, services, and programmes on offer;
- Advertisements placed in the local media, i.e. newspapers and radio;

- Newsletters and fully paid supplements in the local newspapers;
- Direct mailing enclosing new information, e.g. offers of new benefits in new programmes;
- Internet advertising, social network sites, texts.

Advertising is not just aimed at potential new customers but is also important for existing customers, i.e. to expand sales to people already buying the product, either by increased frequency of purchase or by purchase of different products from the same supplier. For example, a customer who has used a travel agent for a certain type of holiday may, through targeted advertising, be attracted to other types of holiday arranged by the same travel agent.

Advertising does not provide immediate feedback and can be an expensive form of promotion. Television advertisements are extremely expensive, as are paid advertisements in the press. In contrast, a 'mail shot' using an agency address list or compiling a database can be an effective (and cheaper) way of getting directly to a target audience.

The message to leisure managers appears to be to look at the whole variety of ways of communicating, to try out various forms and 'shop around' and then act positively, measure results, and make appropriate adjustments. Self-testing criteria for an advertising communication are that it should produce positive answers to the following questions:

- Is it eye-catching?
- Is the layout attractive?
- Do the headline and text stimulate the reader to proceed further?
- Does it provide adequate information?
- Is the message clear and simple?
- Is the text persuasive and credible?
- Does the advertisement create a favourable public image of the organisation?

However, no matter how well designed an advertising communication is, it needs to be effectively targeted at appropriate market segments to achieve success in promoting sales.

Discussion Questions

What advertising do you particularly remember and why? Did you purchase any of the associated products?

14.6.8 Incentives

Incentives in the form of an 'offer' have become a prime means of persuading people to buy. In contrast to the other forms of promotional activity, incentives should not be used on a regular basis but when offered should be restricted to a limited period of time. The main objective of using incentives is to stimulate participation from identified target markets, particularly from new customers. The incentives can take the form of an introductory offer, such as no joining fee at a fitness centre for a specified period, discounts, two-for-one purchases, and gifts.

Financial incentives can be persuasive. We all like to think we are getting something for nothing. The offer of discounts such as reduced off-peak pricing without adequate promotion and publicity, however, is unlikely to have a great impact. One of the cardinal principles of attracting a positive and warm response is to give freely and generously. Professional sports clubs, for example, knowing that the capacity of their home venue is unlikely to be sold out for certain matches, often give free tickets to local schools – this attracts new customers and creates a better atmosphere at the match.

14.6.9 Publicity

Publicity normally takes the form of press releases or feature articles, and in some instances a theatre or leisure centre may write its own weekly column in the local newspaper. Since most local authority leisure services departments have a minimal promotional budget, this has often resulted in many concentrating more on publicity than other forms of promotion. Local presses are often in need of appropriate features, and they are unlikely to be critical in editing these features. Publicity is a useful method of informing the community of the results of programmes, fixtures, and forthcoming events. To keep a facility continually in the public's mind, it is necessary periodically to have general interest stories relating to the facility in the local newspaper, since not all readers read the arts and sports pages.

Although publicity does not directly involve financial expenditure, the true cost of preparing the publicity material may be considerable, particularly if many senior personnel are involved. Publicity carries the risk that the press editorial staff may reject the 'press release' or prepared copy on the grounds that it is not adequately newsworthy. The press can sometimes give a negative image very forcefully, and they can be seen as challenging and questioning towards a local authority. Therefore, the only effective approach is to influence the press coverage by well-organised public relations. This includes informing and involving the press, keeping them up to date with news. Good press coverage will help the public to say that taxpayers' money spent on leisure services is well spent.

Rather than treat the four elements of promotion as separate decisions, Masterman and Wood (2006) promote an integrated marketing communications approach. This requires one integrated communications strategy embracing all relevant mechanisms, a focus on building relationships with customers, and specific targeting of customer groups.

14.6.10 People

Because sport and leisure are often services, people are an essential part of the marketing mix. One of the defining characteristics of services is the inseparability of production and consumption. Face-to-face interaction between the supplying organisation and the customer is inevitable, and the success of a service is very dependent on this people relationship. Avoiding this relationship is not a solution – a commercial fitness centre once tried to dispense with its line staff to reduce costs by making everything card-swipe controlled, including entry and use of all facilities. It failed as a business.

In Sport England's National Benchmarking Service for sport and leisure centres (see Chapter 16) staff attributes are typically ranked among the highest for customer satisfaction, particularly the helpfulness of staff and the standard of instruction. These 'people' attributes are also ranked by customers in the top half of the attributes for importance. Personal service, with genuine good intentions for the customer, is a core attribute for sport and leisure services. This needs careful recruitment of staff with appropriate interpersonal skills and training in customer care. It also needs a customer orientation for all staff, not just the line staff working at the 'customer face'.

Bad news travels fast. It is passed on more readily than good news. Sport and leisure marketers must therefore be concerned not only with what motivates people to take part in sport and leisure, but also what demotivates them. Nothing demotivates customers more than being poorly handled: rudeness; a 'take it or leave it' attitude; double bookings; ruined expectations; dissatisfactions; and broken promises. At the heart of these risks to service success is the quality of the people delivering the services.

When did you last encounter a 'bad' people experience in consuming a leisure service? What might the organisation have done to prevent this experience from happening?

14.6.11 Physical Evidence

Another defining characteristic of services is that they are intangible, yet ironically it is often the physical circumstances or 'tangibles' of a service that are most important to customers. In Sport England's National Benchmarking Service for sport and leisure centres, out of 20 service attributes certain tangibles are among the most important to customers, i.e. water quality for swimmers, cleanliness of changing areas and activity spaces. These tangibles relate to the core or actual product. Other tangibles which are part of the augmented product are less important to customers, e.g. quality of food and drink, quality of car parking.

The setting of a sport and leisure experience and the design of a facility are further important ingredients of the physical evidence. They can reinforce the image of a service when they excite, when they give a sense of occasion. Alternatively, there may be a danger of deterring the customer if these 'atmospherics' are missing and the setting/facility is dull and uninspiring.

14.6.12 Process

Because of the inseparability of consumption and production in services, the process of service delivery is under the spotlight throughout. This process runs from finding out about opportunities, through booking an activity, finding the facility, parking, entering the facility, finding the way round the facility, engaging in the activity, possibly buying food and drink, to leaving the facility. The whole process of service delivery determines the relationships between the organisation and its customers.

An obvious way to demonstrate an active and dynamic relationship with customers is through publicising customer suggestions and organisational responses to demonstrate and promote a process of continuous improvement. For example, many facilities have a section on their website titled 'You said, we did' in which there is a monthly update of customer suggestions and the centre's responses. Typically, these are about minor matters, such as the difficulty of opening doors, the range of food and drink, and the telephone response times for queries. But as the adage goes, it is the small things that matter.

14.7 Sponsorship

For sport and the arts, sponsorship is another significant element of the marketing mix. Sport and leisure organisations are attractive vehicles for sponsorship because their products, services, and events are associated with positive feelings, strong brand images, and clear target markets. Sponsorship is different from other elements of the marketing mix, however, because rather than the marketing *of* sport's products, it is the marketing of the sponsor's brand *through* sport (Hoye et al., 2009).

Meenaghan provides one of the clearest definitions of sponsorship:

> Commercial sponsorship is an investment, in cash or in kind, in an activity, in return for access to the exploitable, commercial potential associated with that activity.
>
> (Meenaghan, 1991, p. 36)

Sponsorship differs from patronage, where the finance or professional expertise is given by a commercial company for philanthropic reasons, without it looking for any material reward or benefit and often with it remaining anonymous. It differs from advertising in that the promotional messages are much less direct, and the sponsor has much less control over the marketing communications.

The exact amount of sports sponsorship expenditure is difficult to ascertain. Many companies are reluctant to reveal exact information; and in addition to the payment for sponsorship rights, sponsoring companies spend two or three times this amount on 'leverage expenditure', i.e. complementary marketing activities to fully exploit the commercial value of the sponsorship. The total spend on sport sponsorship worldwide was estimated to be worth $48.4 billion in 2020. Nevertheless, sponsorship expenditure is small compared with advertising – Masterman (2007) reports sponsorship as probably about 10% of sponsors' overall market and communications budgets, compared with about 35% spent on media advertising. However, sponsorship is rising partly because advertising is a very congested medium, and it is increasingly fragmented as the print, broadcast, and internet media multiply. Sponsorship of a major event ensures consistent exposure across different media.

The scale of sponsorship can vary enormously, from contributions of millions of pounds from a multinational company for national sports to the donation of a cup or prize by a small sports shop to a locally run competition. Indeed, most local teams in sport have a sponsor. It is the major companies investing heavily in sponsorship that dominate the market financially. Sponsorship growth, worldwide, can be attributed in large measure to increased television coverage of major events in both sport and the arts. Mega events are extremely costly to the sponsor and potentially extremely beneficial – the Olympics and the football World Cup reach audiences of billions. Technology advances such as cable and satellite television and internet coverage will increase sponsorship further still.

Sponsorship is conventionally seen as a transaction, an exchange. On the one side it benefits sport and leisure organisations. Most obviously it brings in revenue, services, or resources from the sponsor – without sponsorship, many events would be uneconomic even with large audiences and ticket sales. Sponsorship can also create interest, stimulate media coverage, and consequently increase attendance numbers. It can help to attract major 'players' in sport or the arts, and it can assist in bidding for events or other projects. Sponsorship can also support good causes, e.g. social and environmental.

On the other side of the exchange, sponsorship benefits the sponsoring company in several ways:

- By helping to reinforce or change its corporate image, by association with the sponsored organisation's product and brand;
- By increasing publicity and improving public relations;
- By improving trade and employee relations (e.g. through corporate hospitality);
- By increasing awareness of the sponsor's brands;
- By possibly increasing sales, market share, and gaining competitive advantage;
- By complementing other marketing activities.

There are also costs to both parties. In particular the sponsor pays 'leverage expenditure' to realise the full marketing value of the sponsorship, whilst the sponsored organisation can devote considerable resources to servicing sponsors' needs, e.g. ensuring that corporate hospitality arrangements are suitable, and that star players or performers are available for corporate occasions and publicity.

Sponsorship is of local as well as national significance, and sponsors can raise their 'respectability profile' with the public and with government when sponsoring good causes, particularly those advocated by the government. Governments can get actively involved in promoting sponsorship. For example, Sport England has several grassroots sports sponsorship incentive schemes which are funded by the Department for Culture, Media, and Sport.

14.8 Key Issues in Sponsorship Management

For sport and leisure managers, the key issues in sponsorship management depend on understanding the sponsor, just as the key issue in marketing management is understanding the customer. The key issues are as follows:

- **Objectives** – identifying not only what the sport or leisure organisation wants from sponsorship but what a potential sponsor is likely to want and how the sport can satisfy these business objectives. They may be similar to the benefits to sponsors listed earlier, but they are likely to be specific to the sponsorships being considered.
- **Sponsors' selection of organisations** – a key factor is synergy of target markets for the sponsor and the sport or leisure organisation. This synergy provides opportunities to realise benefits by both partners, but it enables the sponsor to benefit from increasing awareness of its brand by appropriate market segments that are attracted to the sport or leisure activity.
- **Costs and likely returns for both partners** – it is important for both partners to budget for the costs of servicing or leveraging the sponsorship and to have as clear an idea as possible of the evaluation criteria through which the returns can be assessed.
- **Implementation** – exclusivity is an important attribute of most sponsorship deals for the sponsor, and defences need to be made clear against 'ambush marketing', where a commercial company associates itself with the sport or leisure product without actually sponsoring it. Other operational requirements include the need for clear lines of communication and for the sport to help service the marketing objectives of the sponsor, e.g. awareness, media exposure, content of communications, corporate hospitality, merchandising.
- **Evaluation** – historically the weakest part of the package. It is likely to include awareness and attitude surveys, and sales of the sponsor's products before, during, and after the sponsorship deal. A commonly used measure is media coverage and equivalent cost, but this is problematic because the main purpose of the media coverage is to raise awareness of the activity, not the sponsor; therefore the quality of the marketing message for the sponsor is variable, and the effectiveness of the marketing message received by the audience is difficult to measure. Evaluation is not a task that should necessarily be left to the sponsor – the sponsored organisation can usefully help in the task as part of its support services for the sponsor.

Discussion Question

Select a sponsorship partnership in sport and leisure and discuss the synergies between the sponsor's products and brands and the customers of the sport or leisure organisation which is receiving the sponsorship.

14.9 Conclusions

This chapter has considered the marketing approach to sport and leisure services and facilities and the benefits that can accrue to organisations from systematised and detailed marketing planning. The marketing approach ensures that when a product or service is made available to the consumer, it has been planned, designed, packaged, priced, promoted, and delivered in such a manner that the customer is not only persuaded to buy but also to repeat the experience. While impulse buying, like attending an event or 'having a go', is important, repeat visits and repeat purchasing are even more so. Marketing affects people's awareness, attitudes, and behaviour. Managers of sport and leisure should encourage people to look more favourably on their organisations and their products, services, and brands.

Although this is not covered explicitly in this chapter, an appropriate and approved budget is needed for effective marketing. Very often, particularly in the public and private non-profit sectors, marketing budgets are inadequate for the task in hand. This is sometimes because marketing is seen as a cost, rather than as an investment. Yet the returns from investment in marketing are more interest in the products of the organisation, more purchases, and more customer satisfaction.

Practical Tasks

1 For a sport or leisure organisation that you are familiar with, use what data you can obtain on customers and/or members to suggest and justify a simple market segmentation appropriate to the organisation's objectives. Identify what other data would help with this task.

2 Visit a local leisure facility which you have not visited before, critically assess whether it is in a good location for its market, and decide whether accessibility is good both externally and internally. What place marketing recommendations can you make?

Structured Guide to Further Reading

For lots of examples of relationship marketing:
Ferrand, A., & McCarthy, S. (2009). *Marketing the Sports Organisation: Building Networks and Relationships*. Routledge, London.

For lots of examples of sports marketing:
Mullin, B. J., Hardy, S., & Sutton, W. A. (2007). *Sport Marketing*, 3rd edition. Human Kinetics, Champaign, IL.

Useful Websites

For participACTION:
www.participaction.com

For Change4Life:
www.change4life.co.uk

For Sport England's market segmentation:
www.sportengland.org/research/market_segmentation.aspx

For worldwide data on sponsorship expenditure:
http.//www.sponsorship.com/Resources/Sponsorship-Spending.aspx

References

Aaker, D. A. (2002). *Building Strong Brands, Simon and Schuster*. Free Press, New York.

Blake, T. (1985). Image. *Leisure Management*, 5(11), 14–15.

Crompton, J. (2009). Strategies for implementing repositioning of leisure services. *Managing Leisure: An International Journal*, 14(2), 87–111.

Hoye, R., Smith, A., Nicholson, M., Stewart, B., & Westerbeek, H. (2009). *Sport Management: Principles and Applications*, 2nd edition. Butterworth-Heinemann, Oxford.

Kotler, P., & Zaltman, G. (1971). Social marketing: An approach to planned social change. *Journal of Marketing*, 35(July), 3–12.

Masterman, G. (2007). *Sponsorship: For a Return on Investment*. Butterworth-Heinemann, Oxford.

Masterman, G., & Wood, E. (2006). *Innovative Marketing Communications: Strategies for the Events Industry*. Butterworth-Heinemann, Oxford.

Meenaghan, T. (1991). The role of sponsorship in the marketing communications mix. *International Journal of Advertising*, 10(1), 35–47.

Pope, N., & Turco, D. (2001). *Sport and Event Marketing*. Irwin/McGraw-Hill, Roseville, NSW.

Chapter 15

Programming Sport and Leisure Services and Facilities

DOI: 10.4324/9780367823610-15

Summary

Programming provides the services and products that sport and leisure managers are in business to deliver. It is the mechanism for meeting the needs of customers and organisational objectives. Programming is a continuous process characterised by repeated cycles of planning, implementation, evaluation, and review.

Programmes can be classified by function, by geographical areas and facilities, by types of customers, and by the expected outcomes. The classification into functional activities such as education, fitness, etc. is the most common in public sports facilities. There are different approaches to and methods of programming. Two major strategic directions are 'social planning', where the locus of control is with the authority and professionals, and 'community development', which is a more people-oriented direction. It is possible to combine the best of both approaches.

Within the broad strategic alternatives, there exist a variety of specific methods of delivery. Good programming requires strategy, structure, and coordination. This chapter finishes with a clear specification of programming stages, which clarifies the practical functions of the sport and leisure programmer. It consists of a logical sequence of actions through which leisure programmes may succeed.

15.1 Introduction

Programming is one of the most important functions of leisure managers. Everything that a service or department is concerned with – facilities, equipment, supplies, personnel, budgets, marketing, public relations, activities, timetabling, and administration – is solely to ensure that opportunities exist for people to enjoy or experience leisure in ways satisfying to them. Studies of various leisure activities have indicated that the most important element in people's decision on whether to visit is the programme. It is not the only means by which opportunities are provided for people to enjoy their leisure time – natural amenities, for example, are typically provided without a set programme to adhere to – but for many types of leisure provision, it is the mechanism by which the objectives of an organisation are realised.

Programming is equally important to sport and leisure managers in the public, commercial, and voluntary sectors – all have to attract the public or they fail. A commercial fitness club manager must programme the right activities at the right times to generate and retain a maximum number of members willing to pay the required fees. A voluntary sector club administrator must programme sufficient playing and social opportunities to keep members satisfied. A public sector manager must set a 'balanced' programme of opportunities to reflect an array of policy objectives, from the quasi-commercial to those explicitly for community benefits.

Balance is important to all providers, i.e. an appropriate balance between the competing demands for the opportunities which a supplier can provide. A balanced activity programme at a public sector leisure complex, for example, is likely to have some of the following features:

- Opportunities to participate in a range of leisure activities on a structured or an informal basis;
- Opportunities to take part actively (as a participant) or passively (as a spectator);
- Opportunities to be involved as an individual or with a club or group;
- Time set aside for a regular core programme of activities as well as time set aside for a variable programme of one-off opportunities, e.g. events.

Programming is equally important for a leisure facility with fixed spatial accommodation, such as a cinema or theatre with fixed seats, as it is in a more flexible space such as a sports hall which can be configured in a variety of ways. Major programming decisions in a theatre are about the appropriate artistic mix of performances and their timing and the duration of their run. In a relatively flexible space such as a sports hall, programming choices include choosing between many different activities that are possible, with some being continuous and others being one-offs. Programming decisions in the public sector extend to outreach services too, where delivery is taken to local communities, rather than expecting customers to always travel to purpose-built facilities.

An example of a programme for a leisure facility – in this case a swimming pool – is provided in Table 15.1. This programme demonstrates programming by types of user (e.g. schools, adults, club) and different purposes (e.g. Learn to Swim, Aqua Fit, Public Fun, birthday parties). It also shows how facilities can offer multiple sessions at once by dividing up the pool. In this case, the pool has six lanes which are divided up for different sessions. The number of lanes available for each session is denoted in brackets in Table 15.1.

A programme provides order and structure; people know where they stand – they know when to come, what they can expect. This chapter concentrates on the programming process and the manager's role in that process. The rationale for excellent programming is basically to make the best use of resources – time, space, staff, money. This has the following requirements:

- The need to resolve conflicting claims of time and space for available facilities and alternative use of resources to provide opportunities;
- The need to utilise capacity as much as is feasible – sport and leisure experiences are among the most 'perishable' of services in the sense that an unsold space at a particular time is a permanently lost revenue opportunity;
- The need for balance in the programme, to accommodate a wide range of clients and potential customers – particularly in the public sector, where social inclusion is an important objective.

Discussion Question

Consider what would be likely to happen if a community sports centre was opened without a programme being specified, i.e. activity on demand, meaning that people just turn up and play what they want, when they want, for as long as they want. What would be the implications for choice and variety of activities, for the setting up and breaking down of activities' equipment, and for customer satisfaction?

Table 15.1 An Example of a Swimming Pool Programme: Go! Active @ The Arc, Leisure Centre in Clowne, Chesterfield, England

---

Monday

06.00	09.00	Public Swim (3) & Lane Swim (3)
09.00	11.00	Staff Training (6)
11.00	12.00	Adult Lessons (3) & Fitness Swim (3)
12.00	13.30	Public Swim (3) & Lane Swim (3)
13.30	15.00	Schools (4) & Lane Swim (2)
15.00	17.30	Public Swim (3) & Learn to Swim (3)
17.30	19.00	Public Swim (2), Chesterfield Swim Club (1), & Learn to Swim (3)
19.00	21.00	Public Swim (3) & Lane Swim (3)

Tuesday

06.00	10.00	Public Swim (3) & Lane Swim (3)
10.00	11.00	Aqua Fit (6)
11.00	12.00	Public Swim (3) & Lane Swim (3)
12.00	13.00	Aqua Jog (6)
13.30	15.00	Schools (4) & Lane Swim (2)
15.00	18.00	Public Swim (3) & Learn to Swim (3)
18.00	19.00	Aqua Fun Flume Session (6)
19.00	20.00	Aqua Fit (6)
20.00	21.00	Public Swim (3) & Lane Swim (3)

Wednesday

06.00	13.30	Public Swim (3) & Lane Swim (3)
13.30	15.00	Schools (4) & Lane Swim (2)
15.00	19.00	Public Swim (3) & Learn to Swim (3)
19.00	20.00	Aqua Jog (6)
20.00	21.00	Public Swim (3) & Fitness Swim (3)

Thursday

06.00	09.00	Public Swim (3) & Lane Swim (3)
09.00	10.00	Aqua Fit
10.00	12.00	School Swim (4) & Lane Swim (2)
12.00	13.30	Public Swim (3) & Lane Swim (3)
13.30	15.00	School Swim (4) & Lane Swim (2)
15.00	16.00	Aqua Fit (6)
16.00	18.00	Learn to Swim (3) & Public Swim (3)
18.00	21.00	Learn to Swim (2), Public Swim (2), & Chesterfield Swimming Club (2)

Friday

06.00	09.00	Public Swim (3) & Lane Swim (3)
09.00	11.30	School Swim (4) & Lane Swim (2)
11.30	13.30	Public Swim (3) & Lane Swim (3)
13.30	16.00	School Swim (4) & Lane Swim (2)
16.00	18.00	Learn to Swim (3) & Public Swim (3)
18.00	19.00	Aqua Flume Fun Session
19.00	20.00	Aqua Jog (6)
20.00	21.00	Aqua Fit (6)

Saturday

08.00	12.00	Learn to Swim (3) & Public Swim (3)
12.30	15.00	Aqua Fun
15.00	18.00	Pool Party Hire

Sunday

08.00	09.00	Learn to Swim (3) & Public Swim (3)
09.00	15.00	Family Swim & Flume Session (6)
15.00	17.00	Public Swim (3) & Lane Swim (3)
17.00	18.00	Private Hire

Source: Go! Active @ The Arc, www.goactive.org.uk

15.2 What Constitutes a Programme?

What makes a programme? Does it have to be a schedule of activities, a timetable of bookings, or a list of events? Or can it be the planned availability of a supervised playground, mobile attractions, or a community event? Or can it exist through the organised distribution of services such as a sport and leisure information service which collates all that is going on? A programme is all these things and a good deal more. Rossman and Elwood Schlatter (2008) define a programme as 'a designed opportunity for leisure experience to occur', the critical word being *designed* – it is a management responsibility to ensure relevant and diverse opportunities, subject to the resources available. A practical interpretation is that programmes revolve around activities, amenities and facilities, services, staff, money, and time:

- **Activities** can range from the completely spontaneous to the highly structured and all stages in between. Informal activities can be anticipated within a community programme by creating opportunities, encouraging spontaneity, and having resources available such as space, time, and equipment, e.g. a ball to kick about, a wall to scribble on, or deckchairs to sunbathe on. Structured activities, for programming purposes, fall into several major categories, such as: arts, crafts, dance, drama, entertainment, games, sport, health and fitness, hobbies, music, nature, social recreation, travel, and tourism.
- **Amenities and facilities** cover open spaces, buildings, supplies, and equipment. These can be designed and constructed for special purposes, for example public arts centres or swimming pools. Alternatively, they can be designed for self-directed or spontaneous activity, for example an urban park, the natural resources available to the public such as riverside walks, forests, and beaches. Or they can be mobile resources to facilitate outreach services in local communities, such as a mobile library or a sports bus with sports development staff.
- **Services** cover all methods and means through which people are enabled to enjoy sport and leisure. Primary services include the leadership of or guidance for activities provided by key people such as coaches, tutors, and animateurs. Support services include information services, promotion and publicity, transport, discount card schemes in local authorities, member direct debit schemes in private clubs, and crèches.
- **Staff** are the enablers, connectors, and controllers, including: duty managers, supervisors, coaches, countryside rangers, teachers, technicians, cleaners, stage hands, librarians, museum curators, sports development officers, youth and community workers, and receptionists. They are all responsible for the programme provided for customers.
- **Money** is needed for the resources to set up and run services, facilities, and programmes. All programmes are subject to the reality check of what resources can deliver.
- **Time** is a key element in programmes, in respect of both the specific times that opportunities for customers are available and the duration of opportunities, both for a single visit and over the weeks, months, or seasons covered by the programme.

Discussion Questions

Just as 'not enough time' is the most cited constraint for leisure consumers, is time the most binding constraint to effective programming for leisure? And what scope does the leisure manager have to increase the time available for the programme? Consider the cinema as an example.

The sport and leisure manager/programmer must use the available resources efficiently to deliver programmes. The programme, however, is not a series of individual activities strung together. It is a carefully integrated and planned combination of many opportunities selected based on individual and group interests and motivations. These opportunities are organised to achieve the objectives of the organisation and simultaneously meet the needs and demands of individuals and groups.

15.3 Programme Classification

The type of programme needs to be known to communicate with the potential market. Programme classification should describe and communicate the different activities in the programme. It also helps in providing programme balance through analysis of each category. The commercial sector is particularly adept at 'segmenting' market sectors for profitable outcomes.

Simple classifications can aid communication and administration and make it easier for clients and customers to understand. 'Fun sessions' at a swimming pool will give a warning signal to adults that these sessions may best be avoided. Programmes can be classified in several ways, and four are commonly used:

1 **By function** – the most usual classification, normally by listing a number of activities or groups of activities, such as sports, arts, crafts, social; often the functional classification is linked to the motivations of the customers: casual, classes, fitness, education, club training, etc.;
2 **By facilities and areas** – e.g. pitches, swimming pools, rooms and halls to be let; and by local communities in the case of outreach programmes;
3 **By groups of people** – who the programme is intended for, such as casual users, members, family days, over 50s, parents and toddlers;
4 **By outcomes** – e.g. 'Learn to Swim' and other beginner sessions, skill development, keep fit, weight loss.

Discussion Question

Compare the most common classifications for programmes in a sports centre, an arts centre, a museum, and a country park.

Sociologists and psychologists tend to group people for classification into life-cycle stages, i.e. determined by such factors as age, dependency on others, marriage, having children, etc., which are relevant to customers' motivations, their appropriate market segments, and their desired outcomes. However, these can be merged for many programmes (e.g. youth, teenager, and young adults can be grouped together), or the groups can be further broken down (e.g. pre-school into toddlers, infants, and pre-school). Further classification can be made regarding the activities themselves: passive/active, structured/unstructured, planned/self-directed, high risk/low risk, etc. Marketers often identify market segments for the purposes of key decision-making, including programming. Market segmentation is covered in Chapter 14.

15.4 Planning Strategies for Sport and Leisure Programming

Two extremes of strategic directions for public-related sport and leisure programmes are:

1   **Social planning** (Edginton *et al.*, 2004), i.e. programmes planned by professionals such as local authority officers, sport and leisure managers, or club officials – often termed 'top down';
2   **Community development programmes,** i.e. which emanate from the community itself via community engagement in the decision-making processes – often termed 'bottom up'.

The social planning approach is the most common. The basic assumption underlying this process is that use of professional expertise and knowledge is the most effective way of meeting community needs and demands, balancing programmes, and meeting organisational objectives. In programmes for theatres or art exhibitions, for example, there are experts in the art forms on whom reliance is frequently placed for programming decisions. In practice many strategies for programmes are developed by professionals, often in consultation with key stakeholders and possibly with customers, but with little decision-making engagement by customers. This is increasingly seen as paternalistic, even when community consultation occurs.

Community development, on the other hand, is a programming strategy in which the role of the leisure manager is to enable individuals and organisations to get involved in the programming process (see Case Study 15.1 for a Canadian example led by ideas from the community). The locus of control is the important factor. The social planning strategy is professional and authority-controlled. Community development relinquishes at least some of the control of programme development to representatives of the community.

CASE STUDY 15.1

Kitchener's Festival of Neighbourhoods: An Example of the Community Development Strategy

The Festival of Neighbourhoods is an initiative of the City of Kitchener in Canada. Since 1994 the city authority held a draw for an annual $20,000 neighbourhood improvement grant, which local communities can apply for. It is designed to encourage individuals and families to build stronger relationships with their neighbours and celebrate their community. Applications for the draw need to be activities, projects, or events hosted in neighbourhoods and open to everyone, with the object of bringing people together.

The ideas suggested on the festival's website are largely leisure oriented and include evening walks, a music festival, a street party, a baseball game, a bike rodeo, a barbeque, and a funfair. The winners of the draw since its inception include six park improvement projects, half of which incorporated playground improvement, a nature trail improvement and extension, and a skateboard park. They might more accurately be called projects rather than programmes, but the essence of community development is at the heart of the Festival of Neighbourhoods, not just for the winners of the draw, but for all the community groups that complete applications.

Essentially, the programme for Festival of Neighbourhoods is planned by communities, although they get support in their applications and planning from city officers, and, of course, the winners get funding support from the draw. Research by Johnson *et al.* (2009) focused on the role of the community representatives who act as voluntary liaisons between public officials and neighbourhood residents. They identified very positive responses in the main from these community representatives regarding, first, their relationship with public officials and, second, their relationship with neighbourhood residents.

Key to these successful relationships were the flexible and trusting nature of the public officials, who were willing to let community groups lead in the planning of their projects, and the help the public officials gave the neighbourhood groups in seeking additional funding from alternative sources. Regarding the relationships between the community representatives and neighbourhood residents, the main issues that arose were the importance of the representatives soliciting views and support from their neighbourhoods on key issues regarding their proposals and resolving fears and conflicts regarding the nature and effects of the proposed developments.

It seems that community representatives rose to their responsibilities commendably, in having to cope with the two types of relationships important to their communities' development. A couple of the community representatives who were interviewed in the research lamented a disappointing number of 'new people' in their neighbourhoods willing to get involved in the collective action. But in the main their responses were very positive. The Festival of Neighbourhoods provides a successful example of publicly funded urban regeneration, using leisure, aimed at marginalised neighbourhoods, and led by the communities themselves.

Source: Derived from Johnson *et al.* (2009)

The community development strategy is ambitious. It typically needs capable, trained people 'out in the field'. Community developers have become known by many names: *encourager, enabler, catalyst, friend, adviser, activator,* and *animateur*. Animateurs are well-trained, capable, and sensitive professionals who work towards stimulating individuals to think about their own development and the development of other people in the community, through community programming. They work to develop the leadership capabilities of others – typically volunteers. They assist by supplying information about methods and procedures; they enable others to act for themselves.

Experience in the UK has shown that, on the whole, outreach programmes are only successful as long as the support is available over a sustained period of time. When the programmes cease, through lack of funding, for example, most of the newly formed groups flounder after a period of time, due partly to the lack of physical, psychological, or organisational support. Systems are needed which provide pathways and networks to maintain and sustain new programme developments. Or at the very least, exit routes should be clear and facilitated for people who want to continue participating in the activity elsewhere.

Traditionally, local authorities have often undertaken the social planning strategy, with much of the work being administered centrally, even remote from facilities. Such an approach, on its own, has the following disadvantages:

- The decision-makers are distant from the potential users of the facilities and even the immediate service providers.
- There is generally a lack of consultation and sensitivity concerning the needs and demands of the community.
- The facility staff are less likely to be involved in the decision-making process, and this can lead to a lack of accountability and commitment at facility level – this can manifest itself in poor staff motivation and low job satisfaction.

- Decision-making tends to involve committees, it may be slow, and it can result in repetitive and unimaginative programmes.

Looking across the broad spectrum of leisure programming, it seems clear that to adopt one direction – social planning or community development – to the exclusion of the other would be inappropriate. The community development approach fosters participant independence but can nevertheless lead to inefficiencies and to frustrations for the professionals. Both strategies have merit. A blend of the two is not only possible, but also desirable. Bolton *et al.* promote such a compromise: 'Rather than accepting the rather hackneyed and sterile debate of "bottom-up" or "top-down", we argue that there is a need for practitioners to develop a more central position in relation to community development' (2008, p. 100). They propose a partnership between community, citizens, and providers, each with clear roles in the development and delivery of programmes.

Discussion Question

As a member of a community, would you prefer to be helped to create leisure programmes for yourself, or would you rather a professional organised the programmes and gave you options to choose from?

15.5 Specific Approaches to Programming

Within the broad framework of the two main programming strategies lies a range of specific approaches to programming. Providing leisure opportunity is so diverse and complex a task that there is no one approach, system, or method which is suitable for all organisations, all situations, or all types of customers. The different approaches are known by a variety of names; most of them have no agreed formal titles in practice.

The programming methods employed depend on the organisation, the aims, the community to be served, the strategy, staff skills, money, facilities, and a wide variety of other factors. Most sport and leisure programmers do not use a single method. Most use a number of methods, but if they are poorly planned, they can be an untidy mix, lacking coordination. This section groups together around 30 approaches which have been identified, including those of Farrell and Lundegren (1991), Edginton *et al.* (2004), Kraus and Curtis (1977), and Rossman and Elwood Schlatter (2008), into 13 approaches or methods. They each have benefits if used along with other methods. They are:

1 **The lettings 'policy' or laissez-faire approach** – commonly found in the management of smaller community centres. The facility is provided and promoted to the local community; the programme is decided by bookings and usage, rather than a designed programme. Optimal usage and balance are seldom achieved because the programming is entirely reactive to demand.

2 **The traditional approach** – whereby what has gone on in the past and is generally successful is likely to be repeated. It relies on the same format as the past and therefore assumes that this is sufficient. It is not necessarily based on needs but on what has worked before. It does not consider new ideas and changes in demand. Its main merit is continuity and stability. As a single approach, however, it is ineffective. It can be far more useful as part of a process which learns from the past and makes modifications for the future.

3 **The current trends approach** – this relies on reacting to recent trends or activities in vogue. This has benefits in meeting some new demands. However, the approach is totally

experimental. It is likely to serve only a segment of the market, and what may work in one area may be a total failure in others. It is also likely to be unpopular with those seeking a continuous, predictable set of opportunities, e.g. many sports participants want to play their activities regularly. It is important to provide for fads, but they must be seen in context. It is a useful method to include in order to test the market.

4 **The expressed desires approach** – by asking people through surveys, focus groups, etc., and then programming for their wishes, the intention is to provide what they want. But will this result in actual participation? And which activities will meet which desires? Such an approach is difficult to administer, but it is a valuable tool for the programme planner; it gives information about people's desires. This approach has its limitations, however, as many respondents may not really know what they want until they try it; and they cannot predict with any degree of accuracy what their future leisure behaviour is likely to be.

5 **The authoritarian approach (also the 'prescriptive' approach)** – clearly a method derived from the social planning strategy. Reliance is placed on the judgement of the leisure manager. The assumption is that he or she understands what the needs are and what the community wants. This is a quick and tidy approach at its design and planning stage, but participants are denied any involvement in the programme process. Such an approach makes it difficult to adapt to more of a community development strategy. Programming by the manager's perception of what a community wants is a tempting approach to adopt because it appears to be based on needs, as interpreted by the professional. However, without community involvement there is a risk that the professional's diagnosis is not accurate for the population in the potential market.

6 **The socio-political approach** – where pressure from groups, often linked to social causes, is used as a basis for a community programme. Such causes often provide political advantage and carry local authority support. For example, crime, poverty, deprivation, discrimination, and social disorder may call for certain kinds of programming, concentrating on specific target groups and areas. Leisure managers in the public sector do not operate in a political vacuum but must respond to political and social pressure and to changing conditions. This approach, however, needs careful handling by an experienced leisure manager who can add practicality to the political ideal while programming for the overall goals of the organisation.

7 **The action-investigation-creation plan approach** – a three-phase plan to programming (Tillman, 1974). The *action* element is a reaction to demands generated by the community. The *investigation* element is concerned with fact-finding about the nature of demands and service requirements. The *creation* element is the interactive relationship between participants and professionals. The professionals use their own expertise and actively seek the views and involvement of participants. This approach is a compromise between the social planning and community development strategies.

8 **The external requirements approach** – means that the programme is basically dictated by a key stakeholder, e.g. the local authority, a school or college, or a governing body. It tends to have uniform standards, leadership, and resources across local organisations, and external assessment is conducted for the stakeholder's requirements. A Scout or Girl Guide troop, for example, will satisfy the association's requirements. Such organisations normally have vertical management structures, a hierarchical leadership pattern, similar resources, administration, and an external reward system. This approach may also be relevant for some commercial organisations, such as fitness centres, where a centralised approach is demanded of local clubs.

9 **A cafeteria-style approach** – with a variety of choices available for customers to sample. This is useful in that people may not know what they want and can try things out. Additionally,

such an approach can help to meet the diverse needs of clients, such as family groups where individuals can choose different activities. It is a safe approach but tends to be expensive. While it appears to be the answer to the leisure manager's dilemma, it is inefficient in the use of resources because it can plan and provide services which then go unused because they have not been chosen. In addition, it is very difficult to set objectives and measure success – some activities will be winners and others will be losers, but the reasons may not be known. For example, poor marketing rather than a lack of demand may be the cause of poor utilisation. Nevertheless, any comprehensive sport and leisure programme will need to indulge in a cafeteria approach for some of its programmes, if only as an initial tactic to establish demand patterns.

10 **The demand approach** – offers what people want. It is a common form of programming. Clubs, associations, and interest groups make known their demands, and managers devise a programme to match these. Managers are faced with scores of applications requesting specific facilities. However, the most vocal, the most aware, and the socially articulate will make their demands known most readily. The approach is not concerned with equitable distribution and may result in a narrowly focused programme. Many people and groups will not even be aware of the options and benefits. Because there is lack of understanding of the complexity and importance of programming, community leisure services and facility programmes are often a mix of the traditional and demand approaches. A broader mix of programming methods would be more suited to the task.

11 **The community orientation approach** – a process where individuals are involved in the planning process. This approach is clearly derived from the community development strategic direction. It is typically facilitated by using skilled professionals, or community volunteers, to meet people on their own patch, for example through outreach programmes, associations, and community counsellors. The discovery approach is an extension and continuation of community orientation. It assumes that people can work together without superior or subordinate relationships. One person's knowledge, skills, abilities, and interests are used to meet another's needs, without necessarily imposing value systems or external expectations. The approach is a people-to-people approach of interactive discovery, which probably requires skilled community leadership to make it effective.

12 **The community leadership approach** – consisting of community and consumer inputs channelled through advisory boards, user committees, tenants' groups, or other action groups. The concerns of the community are represented in a more structured way than in the previously described approach. Community leadership assumes that individual interests are represented by their group. This, of course, is not wholly possible, but it does indicate community interaction and a level of democracy. At least it opens channels of communication between providers and consumers, and as such it can be a valuable tool for the sport and leisure programmer. Few community leisure service programmes emanate from the community itself without an externally imposed structure and leadership. This kind of programming is difficult, time-consuming, and expensive in terms of paid personnel, usually requiring subsidy or management by volunteers.

13 **The outcomes approach (or benefits approach)** – designed to secure the outcomes, particularly for individual participants, that the objectives for the programme identify. This approach was originally devised for at-risk youth, with specific personal outcomes from the programme in which young people engage, such as self-confidence, self-efficacy, social skills, etc., being identified and the programme being designed to achieve them. A similar approach can be taken for a variety of specific target groups with different needs and motivations, e.g. ethnic minorities, older people, young mothers, overweight people. In fact every participant has needs and motivations, so in principle the outcomes approach can be taken for all programmes.

Is the cafeteria approach the most democratic of those reviewed because it relies on people 'voting with their feet' and because all votes are equal? Explain your reasoning.

15.6 Programme Planning

Whatever approach is taken to sport and leisure programming, it is vital, as in many other aspects of leisure management, to set out a programme plan before implementing it. A programme plan gives structure and logical process to programmes. It should minimise the 'nasty surprises' that require hasty decisions. And it is a clear specification of the reasons for the programming decisions and the detailed programming decisions themselves, which others can pick up and run with, or adapt for any new circumstances.

Table 15.2 identifies the key elements of a programme plan (adapted from Rossman & Elwood Schlatter, 2008). Many of these are either self-explanatory or covered elsewhere in this chapter or book (e.g. Chapter 13 for staffing, Chapter 15 for promotion, Chapter 18 for

Table 15.2 **Elements of a Programme Plan**

1 Programme name
2 Organisational mission and objectives = rationale for the programme
3 Objectives of the programme
4 Programme elements
   - activities
   - places and facilities
   - legal requirements
   - equipment and supplies
   - staffing and animation
   - flow chart and/or Gantt chart
   - promotion
   - pricing
   - budget
   - management/control/monitoring plan
   - cancellation contingency
   - set-up and breakdown
   - risk assessment and risk management
5 Evaluation of programme
6 Sustainability or exit routes for participants
7 Criteria for continuation and change

Source: Adapted from Rossman and Elwood Schlatter (2008)

budgets, Chapter 19 for risk assessment). Some of the elements need further explanation. A flowchart identifies the critical stages and responsibilities in a programme. A Gantt chart identifies specific timings and responsibilities for the stages; it provides a specific schedule for the preparation and implementation of the programme. The cancellation contingency defines the circumstances in which a programme would not be offered, or would be stopped – e.g. severe weather, a health scare – and plans for the procedure to implement cancellation. Risk assessment considers what in the programme might cause harm to people – either customers or staff – and the organisation, and how such risks can be minimised.

Sustainability in the context of a programme plan means whether the programme will be sustainable after the planned programme period. Sustainability is a particularly important element for community development programmes because it is likely that any public sector support, financial or from officers, will have a finite duration. Will the community be able to take over the management and operation of the programme? If a programme is likely to stop at the end of the planned duration, it is important to plan exit routes for participants, i.e. where can they continue to participate in such activities when the programme stops, and how can the transition to other opportunities be facilitated?

15.6.1 Co-Ordinating the Approaches to Programming

In terms of leisure programming, organisations are therefore faced with two levels of decision-making. First, which strategic programming direction should be taken? Second, which methods should be adopted to meet the strategic objectives? This is where leisure managers should come into their own, because of their contextual knowledge and their training and experience. One of the guiding principles will be that programming must be situationally and culturally specific. There are different communities, facilities, and areas providing different contexts, demands, and challenges. A good manager must be a realist and use whatever approaches and options are open to meet needs and demands effectively and to be resource-efficient in planning and operating the programme.

Needs assessment is complex (see Chapter 4). Part of the solution is gradually to make it possible for people to interpret and express their own needs and which types of programmes best suit them. Managers must, therefore, involve people in programme planning, if only in consultation. The leisure manager must:

- Understand the lessons to be learned from the various strategies and approaches;
- Understand the problems and opportunities within current leisure programming;
- Understand the requirements of customers, actual and potential;
- Devise a logical and objective approach to the situation, bearing in mind the goals of the organisation and the resources available.

15.6.2 Targeting Specific Groups

Leisure facilities in all sectors are used more by those who are more affluent and mobile than those who have social, economic, and other forms of disadvantage. In the commercial sector this is not an issue – attracting paying customers and making profits are important objectives. A commercial leisure service will target groups which will serve its objectives, and this means people with money and education – the latter being an important driver for demand in many forms of leisure, including the arts, heritage, countryside, and sport (see Chapter 4). There are national data which will help commercial organisations target particular geographical areas. National survey data also identify the activities and programmes most likely to attract paying customers from higher socio-economic areas, not only across different leisure forms, but also within specific leisure activities, such as sport. *Active People* surveys in England, for example, provide details for each sport and activity of how participation varies with income, employment status, socio-economic group, car ownership, house ownership, and other variables. Such information can help a commercial provider set programmes which are likely to attract paying customers.

Public sector organisations have a wider brief, however, and will be interested in providing opportunities for all, with a possible focus on people suffering disadvantages – the socially excluded. Socio-economic disadvantage in relation to leisure participation is well documented by the same data sources referred to earlier, particularly national survey data (see Chapter 4). Effective public sector leisure management can be measured in part by the degree to which a reasonable balance of the various population market segments within a community has been attracted across the range of services. However, evidence typically shows that those least likely to use leisure facilities are characterised by having low socio-economic status, low income, low educational achievement, and poor mobility. Out-of-home leisure in the form of sport, arts, and heritage does not appear to be of much relevance to many disadvantaged people, due to constraints such as the unrelenting pressure of parenthood, lack of money, no use of a car, etc. and due to preferences which lead many of them to other uses of their leisure time. This is a major challenge for public sector leisure programmers.

Yet the options for achieving greater representation in the use of public sector leisure opportunities are many and varied. Table 15.3 summarises some of them and demonstrates that the programming of existing facilities is not enough. It needs to be accompanied by

Table 15.3 Positive Programming to Encourage Wider Community Use

Financial
- Cost subsidies
- Reduced/free memberships
- Discount cards or free passes (not just for children)
- Avoidance of lump sum payments
- Bus passes

Programmes
- Play schemes and family holidays
- Young mothers' programmes
- Transport, e.g. minibus shuttle
- Crèches at minimal or no cost
- Leisure skill learning – arts, crafts, sports
- Taster courses
- Family events
- Open days
- Social and community programmes

Outreach
- Assistance to self-help groups
- Babysitting services
- Neighbourhood contacts
- Neighbourhood facilities
- Mobile facilities

Marketing
- Leisure counselling
- Advertising benefits
- Helpline services
- Leisure information service
- Links with other community services and voluntary groups

appropriate outreach programmes and by financial and marketing decisions to complement the programmes.

The single most limiting factor for many disadvantaged groups is often perceived to be the cost of taking part. Yet, even when providing facilities free of charge, the manager will still need to promote and provide support and backup services, such as more crèche facilities, taster sessions, and mother and child activities. Attracting people through promotion and incentives, however, is not enough. The style of management and operational services is also important. Those people lacking in confidence are the most vulnerable to 'take-it-or-leave-it' services and will be easily put off. First impressions count. The approach of sport and leisure staff to some users is easily interpreted as 'intimidating', particularly at receptions. Procedures, regulations, membership cards, and having to ask for information about concessions, for example, are off-putting for some potential customers. The benefits of leisure are most successfully promoted by face-to-face communication. Therefore, staff training in customer service is of vital importance.

15.7 Programming Leisure Centres

Multi-purpose leisure centres provide some of the greatest challenges for leisure programmers. These typically comprise of a sports hall, swimming pool, gym, activities rooms, and possibly outdoor pitches. Such leisure centres require programmes which use the same space in a variety of ways. Swimming pools, for example, can be programmed for lane swimming, water fun, water aerobics, water therapy, galas, and canoeing. Sports halls are used for concerts, antique fairs, dances, fashion shows, and Christmas parties, in addition to a large range of sports and other physical activities. Even gyms have flexible spaces for classes such as spinning, Pilates, circuit training, tai chi, and boxing-related exercise.

An example of programming for a large leisure centre is provided in Case Study 15.2. It demonstrates a mixture of programming approaches, as well as key issues relating to excess demand. However, it is not just the large centres that need good programming. Small centres with limited space and resources need even greater skill at times. For example, in a one-court sports hall (four badminton courts) programming may include a variety of sports (for schools, clubs, coaching, and casual use), concerts, dances, exhibitions, and antique fairs. The typical problem with such a multi-purpose space is a huge array of options for the programme but limited capacity to accommodate them, particularly at peak times of the day, week, and year. The programming decision is the designed solution to this problem.

CASE STUDY 15.2

Ponds Forge International Sports Centre

This centre in Sheffield, England, is one of the most technically advanced centres in Europe. Its facilities include three pools – an international competition pool, an international diving pool, and a leisure pool – as well as a sports hall large enough for ten badminton courts and international volleyball, which has seating for up to 1,000 when set for a sports event. This case study concentrates on the 50-metre competition pool, which can be configured as one large pool, or two or three smaller pools, for programming purposes – an important element of flexibility. A consideration of the programming for the range of water activities highlights the need to have firm general policies, which include a balance between local and international, community and club, casual and group, training and recreation. Programming problems for the management to overcome include competition demands versus participation, club squad and structured activity versus casual use, and income earning activities versus development of excellence and social needs criteria from the owner, Sheffield City Trust.

The problem of interrupted continuity is all too evident from the programme alterations signalled on the website for this facility. In a single month, for example, 32 hours of lane swimming were unavailable on two successive weekends because of national and local events; 15 hours of swimming or diving lessons were cancelled; and nine days of normal programmes were unavailable in the sports hall because of events. The dilemma is that Ponds Forge is a major events venue as well as one which has a regular sports activities programme for the usual array of customers, from casual participants to elite members of clubs. Events are held on all but four weekends in the year, and they raise a lot of income, so inevitably the regular participants have to establish routines which incorporate the centre's weekend events programme.

Ponds Forge was built as a nationally important events centre, and this is fully accepted by Sheffield City Trust. Events bring a lot of media attention and economic benefits to the city. There had been many complaints about the lack of public recreational swimming opportunities. Then a major review of the swimming programme resulted in more public swimming opportunities being available. Furthermore, Ponds Forge has been very proactive in keeping regular swimmers informed of cancelled times because of events – not only through the website but also through press releases, Facebook, and Twitter. The emphasis in these marketing communications is not just on informing customers about the cancellations due to events, but also on promoting revised and new opportunities for regular swimmers to maintain their swimming during events, e.g. by switching to evenings, when competition swimming is over, by using the leisure pool, or even by using other swimming pools in the city at weekends.

The programme must accommodate a variety of demands apart from events and casual recreational swimming, including elite and development squads, lane swimming for fitness, swimming lessons, and a variety of water-based activities such as water polo and canoeing. There is a general state of excess demand in a successful facility such as Ponds Forge – clubs would like more training time, the public would like more lane swimming, there are waiting lists for swimming lessons, and there are more events than can be accommodated. Therefore, compromise and balance in programming are important, as is creative thinking about making more space/time available. Since the review, there have been no major problems with the programme, so any changes have been minor, e.g. holding four swimming lessons at the same time in one-third of the main pool to free up space for other activities. Many of the changes and experiments with new elements in the programme are in reaction to customer feedback.

Discussion Question

What can Ponds Forge do to placate regular users who express dissatisfaction when their regular programmes are interrupted by events?

> **Discussion Questions**
>
> Faced with a number of competing demands (including various clubs, classes, casual users, and local firms) for a limited capacity sports hall on a Monday evening, which of the approaches reviewed earlier will cause the least trouble? Does that make it the best approach?

15.8 Programming Stages

The basic assumption was made at the start of this chapter that programming is a process. It is logical therefore to make programming a systematic process which takes a wide and open view of the variety of possibilities. First, the approach must be capable of incorporating either, or a mix, of the major strategies – social planning and community development. Second, the approach must be capable of handling any of the detailed options, from the authoritarian approach at one extreme to the community orientation approach at the other.

Different approaches will suit different situations at different times. But all programming is undertaken in stages, which are repeated to form cycles of preparation, delivery, and review. Torkildsen (2005) referred to his specification of programming stages as 'Programming by Objectives', but in practice any programming approach should be driven by clear and measurable objectives. And most programming involves similar functions of clarifying objectives, setting targets, planning, implementing, monitoring, evaluating, and reflecting. It is a practical approach which breaks the tasks down into sequential stages. It echoes similar processes in marketing (Chapter 14) and planning (Chapter 15).

Essentially, programming results in people taking part in leisure activities and benefiting from leisure experiences. One thing we know about leisure behaviour is that if the experience is satisfying it can become habitual. Programmes therefore need to offer levels of continuity. Once established, programmes are difficult to change in a hurry. Moreover, time is needed to set up programmes and resources, and finances are needed to promote and organise them. Hence, participation programmes need to run for at least a few months, unless, for example, they are short-term holiday or one-off weekend programmes, or tasters.

Leisure programming, therefore, in most cases is an ongoing cyclical process. Once a programme has been set in motion, it can go on in repeated cycles like a long-running saga. While it may be easier to just let matters take their cyclical course with the same content, good programmers will constantly review the programme, introduce new initiatives or refine them, re-plan, implement afresh, run the programme, evaluate, and then review again; and so the cycle goes on. Demands change, markets change, and leisure managers have to match their programmes to the market.

The process outlined in the next section is concerned largely with setting up the programme in the first place. But most programming is concerned with dealing with ongoing programmes with regular cycles of review, forward planning, implementation, and evaluation.

15.8.1 Interpret Policy, Establish Aims and Objectives

Understand the purpose of your organisation, its philosophy, and its fundamental beliefs. To do this you need to:

- Produce a 'mission statement' or 'statement of purpose', i.e. the aims and goals of the organisation;
- Produce programme policy guidelines and directional strategies.

Where no written philosophy/policy exists, top managers should interpret the organisation's purpose, communicate with others, produce a written policy statement, and obtain endorsement.

15.8.2 Assess Current and Potential Needs and Demands

Produce a profile of the current and prospective consumers and the type of services and activities required to meet their needs and demands. You should:

- Evaluate the current performance of facilities and services, and determine the level of spare capacity and excess demand;
- Collate all marketing information, including user surveys, complaints and suggestions, customer panels, resident surveys, and information from community councils and other relevant organisations;
- Establish a profile of relevant populations – i.e. the individuals and groups likely to participate – and their likely needs and motivations;
- Assess forthcoming opportunities, e.g. historic celebrations, national and international events;
- Identify market gaps and determine areas of deficiency in terms of services and programmes.

15.8.3 Assess Organisational Resources

Specify the existing and potential capacity of the organisation for delivering programmes. To do this:

- Identify current resources, facilities, organisations, services, programmes, and opportunities;
- Evaluate existing staff for delivering programmes, their skills, and potential development;
- Evaluate the actual contributions made by other agencies, e.g. voluntary sector, commercial enterprises, education and industrial clubs;
- Evaluate the potential for enhanced resources, e.g. partnerships, sponsorship;
- Evaluate potential community contributions to programme planning.

15.8.4 Set Objectives

Translate policies, market demands and available resources into practical objectives, prioritise and make each objective measurable and within a timespan (see Chapter 17). As part of this:

- Involve key stakeholders in the setting of objectives;
- Set short-range targets in each area of the facility, or each geographical area, within a precise time period: weeks (e.g. holiday programmes); months (e.g. beginner courses); and years (e.g. financial targets, social objectives, etc.);
- Set an appropriate balance between different programming approaches;

- Set an appropriate balance between passive and active leisure, between different activities for different purposes, e.g. self-improvement, fitness, social, entertainment, to meet objectives;
- Agree on performance indicators, including participation and financial ratios, and targets (see Chapter 17).

15.8.5 Plan the Programme

Adopt the programmer's motto: 'Proper prior planning prevents poor performance'. To plan:

- Consider how the programme fits into the marketing strategy, e.g. corporate approach to marketing, specific promotions;
- As time is the basis on which most programmes operate, identify hourly, daily, weekly, and seasonal patterns of use;
- Consider both fixed and flexible timetables;
- Determine programme areas, i.e. types of activities;
- Determine programme forms, i.e. casual, clubs, courses, events, etc.;
- Recognise the different needs of different people: relaxation, competition, beginners, high standard for different age groups, genders, ethnic groups, etc.;
- Choose and analyse activities which collectively are most likely, within resources, to meet objectives;
- Establish priorities between conflicting claims on the programme from different types of user and different activities;
- Consider not only the programme's implications for utilisation and revenue, but also its requirements for resources and costs;
- Plan for added value elements to the programme, e.g. in fitness clubs the development of new classes led by a skilled animateur;
- Build flexibility into the programme – it will lead to variety, wider use, and greater balance;
- Account fully for the resources and time necessary to set up and break down for programme changes, especially new events;
- Consider the staffing implications and management style, division of labour, responsibilities, training, etc.;
- Try to ensure that any community development programmes have fully considered sustainability, or exit routes to similar opportunities;
- Avoid administration problems by establishing easily handled and easily understood systems and methods which are easy for the user and easy for the organisation;
- Make full use of information technology and modern computerised systems.

15.8.6 Implement and Manage the Programme

The stages in this are as follows:

- Activate the agreed marketing strategy, using aspects of the marketing 'mix' to complement the programme, e.g. promotion, pricing, and place (see Chapter 14).
- Attend to staffing requirements – where community development is relevant, staff/helpers are needed to support newly formed groups until they become self-supporting; consider outreach skill development.
- Try new technologies for programming, e.g. video, computers, giant screen for information, visuals to show availability in spaces and programmes, self-service, do-it-yourself bookings, etc.; use information technology to your advantage.

- Ensure flexibility to meet changing situations – the flexible approach needs skilful management to enable individuals to participate in the way they want to.
- Control the programme through appropriate staffing and delegation of authority, financial and operational systems.
- Design monitoring systems to provide management with information relating to the current level of usage, the profile of users, changing trends.
- Anticipate the likely problems and be ready with alternatives.
- Avoid incompatible activities in terms of health and safety, noise, age, level of play, etc.
- Expand the programme with new activities, new methods, and new people.
- Programme 'packages', not just single items.
- Try some experiments; try out regionally or nationally fashionable activities; yet always enhance local success.
- Extend product life cycles through changes, variety, and new forms of delivery.
- Keep all stakeholders and particularly potential and actual users informed of what is going on – use a variety of communication systems.

Programme control is a management function; it helps if one manager has overall responsibility. It is important that the way the programme is delivered meets or exceeds customer expectations and that staff are fully committed to the success of the programme. Programming success is often hampered by seemingly small items, such as double bookings, which cause problems far beyond the relatively minor mistake.

15.8.7 Evaluate the Programme

How else will you know whether you are doing a good job? To what extent have the programme's objectives been met? You should:

- Evaluate inputs – what has gone into planning the programme: resources, staff, time, costs?
- Evaluate the process – what has occurred in carrying out the programme from start to finish?
- Evaluate the outcome, the results – how did they compare with objectives and targets? Were clients and customers generally satisfied with the opportunities provided by the programme?
- Measure the efficiency of the operation – how well has the job been carried out? How adequate has the staffing been? How well have staff performed?
- Use several criteria, not just financial, to measure the performance of each element of the programme.
- Use both quantitative and qualitative measures, i.e. not only throughput, socio-economic profile of users, income generation, cost-effectiveness, levels of sponsorship achieved, etc., but also attitudes by users to such attributes as ease of booking, helpfulness of staff, range of activity choices, the timing of activities, etc.
- Identify any changes in user profiles, catchment areas, etc. compared with previous programmes.
- Obtain feedback from users and possibly non-users, e.g. through community groups and representatives.
- Assess the effectiveness of the marketing strategy, e.g. awareness levels, attractiveness of opportunities, clarity of information, distribution of outreach services.
- Determine the effectiveness of the changes in the programme.

15.8.8 Modify the Programme Appropriately

- Reinforce and possibly expand the successful elements of the programme.
- If the programme or elements of it have been unsuccessful, first determine the reasons from the monitoring and evaluation; second, act to counteract the reasons, e.g. by changes to the components of the programme, staff training or retraining, staff areas of responsibility, or complementary elements of the marketing mix such as pricing or promotion.
- Modify targets according to levels of performance – targets should be challenging but realistic (see Chapter 17).

15.9 Monitoring and Evaluation

The vital function in ensuring that programming is a cyclical process is monitoring and evaluation. It is this which leads to comprehensive and systematic review, from which the programme stages start again, even possibly starting with reconsideration of the organisation's aims.

15.9.1 Monitoring

Monitoring involves continuous and regular collection of relevant information as part of the normal management information systems for the programme. Because this information is collected systematically, it can be checked regularly, and appropriate short run actions can be taken to remedy any emerging problems or to benefit from any unexpected opportunities. The information collected might include:

- The identities and registration details (if collected) of participants, their attendance records;
- The total number of visits to each session, compared with the plan;
- Total revenue collected, compared with the budget;
- The costs of operating each session, compared with the budget;
- Comments and suggestions from customers (and staff, if they are collected systematically).

15.9.2 Evaluation

Evaluation is more of a one-off, extra effort to collect information with which to judge a programme's successes and weaknesses. It may take place at selected points in time during the programme, but more typically it is conducted at an appropriate time towards the end of the programme's season. Evaluation will employ the monitoring information already collected, to which it will add information from any number of other methods, such as surveys, focus groups, and interviews with key individuals. Evaluation should seek the views of customers, key stakeholders, staff, and managers. It should produce an action document – i.e. what to do next – because it feeds into the re-planning of the programme.

Resources are typically constrained in operating a programme, no more so than in evaluation. Indeed, many programmes take place without any evaluation, which is a serious mistake. The key resource decision is who will do the evaluation. Evaluation can be undertaken by one or both of two main sets of people:

1 **Internal evaluation by staff** can be more sensitive to staff feelings, but it is more likely to be biased and less objective, and more likely to justify failures or to exonerate from blame. Furthermore, internal staff typically have enough to do running the programmes

and see evaluation as an unnecessary extra if they are not sufficiently briefed about its importance.

2 **External evaluation, e.g. by educational establishments or management consultants,** is likely to be more objective, but it can be hampered by staff suspicion or worry about the outcome and lack of detailed knowledge of programme implementation. And it is typically more expensive than utilising internal staff.

Whichever resource is utilised for evaluation, the important decision is to include an explicit component in the programme's budget for evaluation. Then it is more likely to be done.

15.10 Learning from Past Mistakes

One of the hallmarks of good programming, whatever the organisation, is the extent to which objectives have been met and client satisfaction has been paramount. Managers should learn from the successes and the problems of many of the programmes currently practised. Outlined here are a number of problem areas which have been found at community leisure centres. They are in no particular order of significance:

- Demands and needs are not being assessed (see Chapter 4).
- Objectives, so called, are not measurable (see Chapter 17).
- Programmes tend to be too traditional, static, and much 'the same old thing' – the same activities, the same delivery.
- Programmes lack variety and novelty.
- Often a 'take it or leave it' approach is adopted, regardless of whether the programme is appropriate to the target groups in the community.
- The advantages and disadvantages of different user systems (e.g. casual user, member, discount cards) are not evaluated fully.
- The balance of casual use with club use and events is not based on policy but expediency.
- The need to analyse the benefits of different activities is rarely considered.
- Regular, habit-forming activities (e.g. weekly sessions) are interrupted by insensitive one-off programming, which breaks into the pattern without consultation.
- Programme patterns, such as seasonality, are not given due consideration.
- Incompatible activities are sometimes programmed together.
- Insufficient flexibility is built into programming to adapt to new demands.
- Ways of expanding an already busy programme are insufficiently explored (e.g. early/late bookings).
- IT and computer systems are not being put to best advantage to aid efficiency (e.g. self-service); bureaucracy and cumbersome administration systems still abound.
- Programme worth is increasingly judged on numbers allied to financial viability; qualitative programming gives way under such strain.
- Risk avoidance leads to a lacklustre approach, with a lack of creativity, stifled programmes, lack of adventure, and non-appeal for young people.
- Some community facilities are used for few purposes, which occupy only a proportion of time and attract a narrow market segment.
- Programmes do not consider outreach possibilities; many potential satellite resources remain unused for the community: schools; church buildings; and clubs, business, and industrial sport and leisure facilities.
- Programme monitoring and systematic evaluation are not often carried out to change and improve programme content and presentation.

Not all poor programmes can be changed overnight. It may well take several cycles of the programme, for example, due to established patterns and 'sitting tenants'. However, most problems can be ironed out by making changes in easy stages.

Discussion Question

In a leisure facility or service that you are familiar with, do you recognise any of the failings listed here?

15.11 Conclusions

Good programming can offer choice, provide balance, attract the markets being aimed at, and be responsive to the needs and wants of stakeholders and customers. Conversely, poor programming results in the organisation's objectives not being met, limited choice, and too many dissatisfied customers. The centrality of the product in marketing, which in leisure services is the programme, is the rationale for this chapter. However, the programme needs support from other parts of the marketing mix, such as pricing and promotion (see Chapter 14), and from other aspects of management, including finance and human resources.

One of the key tensions in programming is between continuity and innovation. On the one hand, existing customers like stability and predictability, particularly in sports programmes. On the other hand, innovation and new opportunities attract existing and new customers alike, particularly in the arts. The virtues of continuity can lull a leisure manager into thinking conservatively about their programme – play safe, play the odds. However, creativity is an important attribute, and although it is accompanied by risks, particularly the risk of a weak response by customers, it is a gamble that must be taken.

Innovation and creativity in programming require boldness in forecasting future demands. Chapter 4 includes a review of demand forecasting techniques, but one of the main problems is that many forecasting techniques are based on previous patterns of demand – back to continuity again. Innovation in programming, particularly in the arts, means making bold decisions, taking risks, and accepting some programme failures. But if failures occur, it is important to learn from them through incisive evaluation. Even successful programmes need to be analysed to identify the key drivers of success within the programmes. Perceptive analysis of failures and successes can yield valuable lessons for future programming.

Practical Tasks

1 For the same leisure facility or space, have one person design a week's programme using the authoritarian approach and a second person design a week's programme using the cafeteria-style approach. Compare both the resulting programmes with the current programme and debate the merits of the different approaches.
2 For a leisure facility or service of your choice, obtain a typical week's programme and identify what the weakest elements of the programme are in terms of numbers of customers. Consider why such elements are on the programme and the costs of these elements.

Structured Guide to Further Reading

For an overview of programming issues and a summary of programming theories:
Edginton, C. R., Hudson, S., Dieser, R., & Edginton, S. (2004). *Leisure Programming: A Service-Centred and Benefits Approach*, 4th edition. McGraw Hill, New York.

For a workbook of how to undertake programming effectively and a review of key decisions relevant to programming:
Rossman, J. R., & Elwood Schlatter, B. (2008). *Recreation Programming: Designing Leisure Experiences*, 5th edition. Sagamore Publishing, Champaign, IL.

For evaluation of programmes:
Henderson, K. A. (2008). Evaluating and documenting programmes. In G. Carpenter & D. Blandy (Eds.), *Arts and Cultural Programming: A Leisure Perspective*. Human Kinetics, Champaign, IL.

Useful Websites

For Ponds Forge International Sports Centre:
www.ponds-forge.co.uk

For Clowne Leisure Centre:
www.goactive.org.uk

References

Bolton, N., Fleming, S., & Elias, B. (2008). The experience of community sport development: A case study of Blaenau Gwent. *Managing Leisure: An International Journal, 13*(2), 92–103.
Farrell, P., & Lundegren, H. M. (1991). *The Process of Recreation Programming*, 3rd edition. Venture Publishing, State College, PA.
Johnson, A. J., Glover, T. D., & Yuen, F. C. (2009). Supporting effective community representation: Lessons from the Festival of Neighbourhoods. *Managing Leisure: An International Journal, 14*(1), 1–16.
Kraus, R. G., & Curtis, J. E. (1977). *Creative Administration in Recreation and Parks*, C.V. Mosby, Saint Louis, MO.
Tillman, A. (1974). *The Program Book for Recreation Professionals*. National Press Books, Palo Alto, CA.
Torkildsen, G. (2005). *Leisure and Recreation Management*. Routledge, London and New York.

Chapter 16

Quality and Performance Management in Sport and Leisure

In This Chapter

- What are quality and performance management?
- What are the important elements of quality frameworks?
- What do different quality awards cover?
- How do quality awards improve organisational performance?
- What are good organisational objectives?
- How do you design a good performance indicator?
- What is benchmarking, and how does it help?

DOI: 10.4324/9780367823610-16

Summary

Quality management and performance management are important contemporary redefinitions of what good management of organisations is about. Their popularity has grown in recent years, and there are now several systems available with which to promote and recognise good management. Many systems are generic to all organisations or to public sector services. However, there are a few systems which are sport and leisure specific.

Quality management concerns processes which are designed to achieve continuous improvement in an organisation, and which are aimed at meeting and hopefully exceeding customers' expectations. Generic frameworks to promote self-assessment of quality management within organisations include the European Foundation for Quality Management, whilst the Culture and Sport Improvement Toolkit is an example of a framework specifically designed for sport and leisure services. Such frameworks translate the principles of quality management into practical evaluation criteria which organisations can use.

Performance management covers very similar principles to quality management, with more of a focus on specifying measurable objectives, selecting appropriate performance indicators, setting targets, measuring performance, and using the evidence to review objectives and actions. Performance management is facilitated by generic systems such as the Balanced Scorecard. There is also an array of performance measurement systems which promote performance management in sport and leisure organisations.

Finally, it is desirable to put an organisation's performance into perspective, and benchmarking is a technique which does this. The performance measurement systems include comparison of an organisation's performance with other similar organisations in the sport and leisure industry.

16.1 Introduction

Quality is a key determinant in satisfying customers in the sport and leisure industries, as in other industries. Whether managing in the commercial, public, or voluntary sectors, people have to be attracted to the services and facilities, and these should be managed with excellence – that is, with quality. However, quality does not just happen. It must be worked for. It must be managed.

Deming is renowned as the first guru of total quality management (TQM). TQM concerns a shared vision among all in an organisation and a continuing process of organisational improvement. Deming's quality improvement work revolutionised Japan's industrial productivity after the Second World War. He is noted for the Deming cycle, or PDSA cycle, a continuous quality improvement model consisting of a logical sequence of four repetitive steps – Plan, Do, Study, and Act – through which continuous improvement is achieved (Deming, 1986). Another important figure in the development of quality principles is Juran, who did much to consolidate a holistic, integrated concept of quality management (Juran, 1988), with an emphasis on communication and people management, and 'fitness for purpose' or 'quality' of a product or service defined by a focus on customers.

In the 1990s the popularity of quality programmes in the public sector in developed countries, including public leisure services, accelerated. This was stimulated by a number of considerations (Robinson, 2001; Williams & Buswell, 2003), including:

- An increasing strategic focus on customers;
- Promotion of quality management by key professional agencies;
- Rising customer expectations, driven by higher service standards in commercial services;
- Greater government pressure and legislation for accountability in public services.

The Chartered Quality Institute in the UK defines quality management as 'an organisation wide approach to understanding precisely what customers need and consistently delivering accurate solutions within budget, on time and with the minimum loss to society'. This institute describes quality in terms of innovation and care, as indicated in Figure 16.1, which demonstrates how all-embracing the concept of quality is.

Robinson (2004) reproduces definitions for several other terms important in quality management:

- **Quality** – how consistently the product or service delivered meets or exceeds the customer's expectations and needs (from Clarke, 1992);
- **Quality control** – the operational techniques and activities that are used to fulfil requirements for quality (from BSI, 1987);
- **Quality assurance** – all the planned and systematic actions necessary to provide confidence that a product or service will satisfy given requirements for quality (from BSI, 1987).

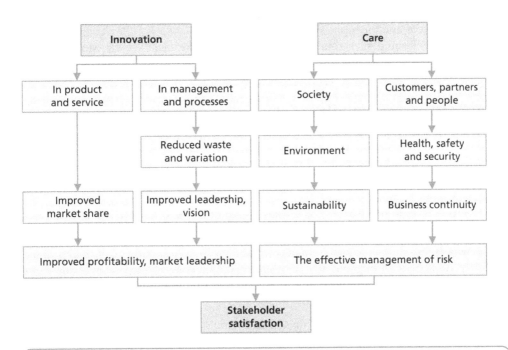

Figure 16.1 Chartered Institute of Quality principles of quality.

The term *performance management* covers very similar principles to *quality management*, with a focus on performance measurement and consequent actions. It informs management decisions with appropriate planning, objectives, targets, performance measurement, and review.

There is a wide range of quality management systems. Many require evidence of an organisation having gone through a formal process of applying quality management procedures and techniques, to then be awarded certification by an external body. These procedures are likely to involve consultation with customers, critical appraisal of the organisation, and continuous quality management improvement. Certification can also provide a competitive edge. However, quality management systems can be costly, particularly for small organisations and those in the voluntary sector. Quality management certification is particularly useful in local government; it can help in meeting government's standards designed to assess how well a council delivers its services.

> ### Discussion Question
>
> What is quality certification most useful for, improving management or reporting to stakeholders?

16.2 Total Quality Management

Total quality management (TQM) is an approach to improving the effectiveness of a business as a whole – i.e. a process which involves every person in an organisation – to ensure customer satisfaction. TQM thus focuses on customer needs and builds a logical linkage between these needs and the business objectives.

The principles behind such total quality management are identified by Mosscrop and Stores (1990):

- Excellence as the objective and getting it right first time;
- Everyone is a customer or a supplier in every transaction – every transaction in the business, every link in the chain, has a supplier and a customer;
- Absolute clarity about customers' needs; the perceptions of customers are paramount;
- Commitment from the top;
- Measurement of all key outputs;
- Prevention, not blame; sharing responsibility;
- Training and education;
- Integration of total quality into the business – a core business activity which permeates every aspect of leisure operations.

In other words, excellence is called for and is worked for by every person in all aspects of the operation. All activity throughout all operations is continuously directed at satisfying client and customer requirements. Clearly this is an ideal and will never be completely achieved. Challenges in achieving TQM include the following:

- Organisations do not often act in unison and harmony but are often characterised by separate departmental interests.
- Identifying all customers' changing needs is very difficult, and identifying customers' expectations is even more difficult.

- Organisational objectives are often not specified in a way that promotes TQM because they are too general and non-measurable.
- Measuring all outputs consistently is difficult and can be very resource intensive.

Some of these issues are explored in more detail in the following sections. Case Study 16.1, meanwhile, addresses an important consideration in quality management which is often overlooked in the quest for perfection – how to deal with mistakes. This is enhanced, as you will see in the case study, by the world of social media and the ease at which people can spread their word of dissatisfaction quickly to a global audience.

Discussion Question

In the light of its considerable requirements and challenges, is total quality management achievable?

CASE STUDY 16.1

Service Failures and Recovery in the Restaurant Industry: The Danger of Social Media

Much of the quality literature concentrates on positives – what to do right to improve quality – whilst principles such as 'right first time' suggest there is no room for mistakes. However, mistakes do occur, and in service industries the mistakes are all too quickly apparent. Furthermore, the received wisdom is that negative word of mouth resulting from dissatisfied customers is passed on to more people than positive word of mouth from satisfied customers.

A study by Israeli, Lee, and Karpinski in 2017 investigated this area by looking at how the dynamics of service failures in restaurants influence customers' attitudes and electronic Word-of-Mouth (eWOM) intentions on social media (SM). They focused on failure types, failure severity, and recovery efforts. One of their main findings suggests that customers' negative eWOM becomes more aggressive as the service failure escalates. Recovery efforts are also critical here, especially in the world of social media. It does not take long for bad news to spread on the internet. Indeed, in a time before social media, communications between managers and customers about customers' dissatisfying experiences were shared predominantly with staff, family, or friends. Nowadays, as Israeli, Lee, and Karpinski point out, such communications can be shared with the public through various social media platforms (e.g. Facebook, Twitter, Tripadvisor). Thus, it is important to understand customers' post-service failure incidents on social media platforms, since their postings may influence other prospective customers who review the contents.

Because customers who leave reviews on social media sites are not generally seeking commercial benefits from endorsing (or not!) a product or service, they are seen as credible and can have a huge bearing on future business. They have become one of the most important factors that influence the consumer decision-making process, such as purchase intentions.

Mistakes do happen, of course and nobody is perfect. In the restaurant trade in particular, service failures are common. However, perhaps more surprisingly, there is often little focus on service recovery training (Israeli *et al.*, 2017). This may seem strange given the growing popularity of social media and the increasing tendency of customers to communicate over social media platforms which enable customers to vent their frustration.

The implications in this study are clear, however. You must try to anticipate causes of service failure and prevent them. When mistakes are made, acknowledge them to the customer. You can also plan and implement effective recovery tactics to minimise negative word of mouth. There is evidence to suggest that most people can be forgiving. A study of service failures and recoveries in restaurants suggests that customers tend to forgive technical failures (e.g. burnt food) if recovery attempts are made. However, customers may not completely forgive service problems (e.g. long wait times, rude staff), even when there are subsequent recovery attempts (Silber *et al.*, 2009). Perhaps it is in this area where more service recovery training (or indeed staff training!) is needed.

Source: Derived from Israeli *et al.* (2017)

16.3 Quality Frameworks

Quality frameworks have been designed to help managers assess and promote total quality management in the workplace. They do not involve awards but rather establish a set of practical processes through which total quality management can be achieved. Two frameworks are summarised in the following sections: (1) one of the most commonly referred to generic models, the European Foundation for Quality Management's Excellence Model; and (2) a recent government initiative in the UK specifically for sport and cultural services, the Culture and Sport Improvement Toolkit.

16.3.1 The European Foundation for Quality Management Excellence Model

The European Foundation for Quality Management (EFQM) was founded in 1988 to enhance the competitive position of European organisations and their effectiveness and efficiency. The EFQM Excellence Model, also known as the Business Excellence Model, is a management framework that can be used to facilitate continuous improvement in an organisation. It is non-prescriptive and works based on self-assessment against relevant criteria which go to make up quality performance.

By comparing the organisation against the model's criteria, it is possible to identify strengths and weaknesses, providing a clear indication of those activities which distinguish the organisation from World-Class or Best-in-Class organisations.

The EFQM Excellence Model was updated in 2020 and is based on seven criteria. Two of these link to 'Direction' and include the purpose and strategy of the organisation. Three of the criteria link to 'Execution' and involve items such as engaging stakeholders and creating sustainable value. The final two link to 'Results' and include stakeholder perceptions and strategic and operational performance. The 2020 EFQM Excellence Model aims to give organisations the opportunity to take a holistic perspective and appreciate that each organisation is a complex but, at the same time, organised system. More information on this model can be found on the EFQM website.

The EFQM is the most widely used organisational framework in Europe and has become the basis for the majority of national and regional quality awards, for example the UK Business Excellence Award, Investors in Excellence, and Quest.

16.3.2 Culture and Sport Improvement Toolkit (CSIT)

CSIT is a national framework for performance management in cultural services in the UK. CSIT is a self-assessment toolkit for improvement planning, designed to complement other quality systems such as EFMQ, Quest, and Investors in People. It is described as an 'improvement journey' because it is a continuous process of improvement. Continuous improvement is necessary because of ongoing changes in both community needs and customer expectations. CSIT incorporates not only self-assessment but also '360 degree feedback', a process of engagement with internal staff and clients and external stakeholders, through which alternative views of the service are generated.

CSIT is designed for all organisations and partnerships with strategic and capacity-building responsibilities within the culture, sport, green space, and tourism services. It can be used by the following:

- Portfolios of local authority culture, sport, green space, and tourism functions (these might be in various departments) or single services (e.g. sports development, arts, museums, parks);
- Contracted delivery partnerships (e.g. between local authorities and commercial or not-for-profit organisations);
- Regional, sub-regional, or national strategic bodies (e.g. national cultural agencies, CSPs, NGBs of Sport);
- Wider partnerships (or consortia) comprising a range of different bodies in an area;
- Regional or sub-regional public sector collaborations (see the next section on peer-supported improvement).

Another important feature of CSIT is validation, accomplished largely by independent review and challenge, which includes interviews with staff and review of the documentary evidence used in the self-assessment. Peer review is another option. Once assessment and validation are completed, an improvement plan is written to convert the results into actions.

16.4 Quality Awards Schemes

Quality award schemes encourage and promote good practice in quality management. Awards, however, not only give recognition and status to an organisation; many come because of training, considerable collective effort, application of quality management systems, and improvement. As such, they are significantly more than certificates and trophies.

Quality awards are based on assessment of an applicant organisation against criteria specified by the awarding body. Some are competitive, recognising the best; but others have no limit on the 'winners' because they are simply judged against the award criteria. There are international, national, and regional awards, as well as industry-specific awards. Examples of international awards include:

- European Quality Award (now referred to as the EFQM Excellence Award), established in 1992 and offered by the European Foundation for Quality Management;
- Asia-Pacific Area Golden Quality Award;

- Deming Prize, established in 1951 (becoming international in 1984) and offered by the Japanese Union of Scientists and Engineers.

An example of a national award is the Malcolm Baldrige Award, established in 1987 by the US Congress and named after a former Secretary of Commerce. It aims to provide quality awareness and is based on a weighted score of seven categories of performance criteria: leadership; strategic planning; customer and market focus; measurement, analysis, and knowledge management; human resource focus; process management; and business results. Another national award is the UK Excellence Award, which is run by the British Quality Foundation, a National Partner Organisation of the European Foundation for Quality Management.

There are also industry-specific awards. The White Flag Award, in Ireland, is a quality award endorsed by Failte Ireland and the Irish Hotels Federation. It is aimed at swimming pools, sports halls, gymnasiums, and other indoor leisure facilities. The Green Flag Award, in England and Wales, is designed to recognise and encourage quality public parks. The Green Flag Award is managed by a consortium of Keep Britain Tidy, BTCV (the British Trust for Conservation Volunteers), and GreenSpace.

Many leisure, sport, and recreation institutions have award schemes. Examples in the UK include the Institute for Sport, Parks, and Leisure (ISPAL) Leadership Award; the Innovation Award; and the Health and Physical Activity Recognition Programme. In Australia, awards include the Parks and Leisure Australia Awards of Excellence. In the USA, the Gold Medal Awards from the National Parks and Recreation Association are given to communities which demonstrate excellence in long-range planning, resource management, and agency recognition.

16.4.1 British and International Standards

In the late 1970s, the British Standards Institute (BSI) developed the BS 5750 system to improve quality throughout the management process by using a structured system of standards and procedures. During the 1980s, the Department of Trade and Industry (DTI) encouraged British industry to compete internationally using quality initiatives. In 1994, three existing standards – British, European, and International – were merged and called ISO 9000 (Williams & Buswell, 2003). The relevant standard is now BN EN ISO 9001:2015.

This standard comprises a system which covers eight principles: customer focus, leadership, involvement of people, process approach, systems approach to management, continual improvement, factual approach to decision-making, and mutually beneficial supplier relationships. It is a system of quality assurance rather than total quality management, however, because it concentrates on identifying whether stated operational procedures are followed, rather than on ensuring that outcomes are achieved.

16.4.2 Customer Service Excellence

This is the UK government's standard for excellence in customer services in the public sector. It replaced another accredited standard, Charter Mark, in 2009. Customer Service Excellence is designed to act as a driver of continuous improvement, via an online self-assessment tool; it is a skills development tool, and it is an independently validated accreditation. It has five criteria for excellence:

1 **Customer insight** – i.e. an in-depth understanding of customers, through identification, engagement, and consultation, and through measurement of customer satisfaction;

2   **Organisation culture** – i.e. a customer-focused culture via appropriate leadership and policy, and the professionalism and attitude of staff;
3   **Information and access** – i.e. with an appropriate range and quality of information for customers, accessible services, and cooperative working with other providers;
4   **Delivery** – i.e. excellent standards of service delivery, meeting customer expectations, and dealing effectively with problems;
5   **Timeliness and quality of services** – i.e. via measurable standards, timely outcomes, and timely delivery.

Because the standard is designed for public services, three of these principal criteria are centred on the customer's experience, whilst the other two concern the extent to which the organisation is customer-facing and informed of customers' needs and satisfactions. This is a narrower focus than frameworks such as the Culture and Sport Improvement Toolkit, which includes more consideration of the service organisation itself (e.g. partnership, resource management, people management, performance, and learning).

16.4.3 Investors in People

Investors in People UK is a non-departmental public body, established in 1991 by the government as a business support and advice service. The Investors in People (IIP) Standard provides a framework for improving business performance and competitiveness through good practice in human resource development. They currently offer three different types of accreditations, including investment in people, wellbeing, and apprenticeships.

As leisure is often called a 'people industry', it is appropriate that IIP concentrates on performance in human resource management (HRM). A firm principle underlying IIP is that success in HRM will impact on wider organisational performance. Two studies in recent years have tested this relationship. Cowling (2008) investigated its effect on gross profit per employee, using a dataset of 2,500 UK private sector organisations. The results suggest that companies with IIP had gross profits per employee of £128.38, compared with a figure of £34.40 for companies without IIP. Furthermore, the research suggests that this higher performance is not just the result of better performing organisations choosing to undertake IIP.

Bourne et al. (2008) further endorsed the effectiveness of IIP. Their study used ten in-depth case studies of private commercial organisations, together with 196 responses to a survey from commercial organisations. The research concluded that IIP, through improvements in human resources policies, improved the organisations' social climates (trust, cooperation, and engagement) and improved their employees' flexibility. This led to improvements in non-financial performance (including quality of products and services, customer satisfaction, and attraction and retention of employees), which in turn led to improvements in financial performance. However, it should be emphasised that both the Bourne and Cowling studies used commercial company data and covered a wide range of industries – they were not leisure specific.

16.4.4 Investors in Excellence

Investors in Excellence (IiE) was developed in the UK by Midlands Excellence in 2003. It is a not-for-profit and non-membership body with a range of quality improvement activities. Its IiE Standard is described as a framework for coordinating improvement activity, increasing performance, and achieving recognition. The criteria against which achievement is assessed are those of the EFQM Excellence Model.

16.4.5 Quest

Quest is also based on the EFQM Excellence Model, but it is distinctive because it is the UK's quality award scheme for sport and leisure. It has been operating since 1996 and is managed by PMP, a sport and leisure consultancy. It has three awards:

1   **Quest Facility Management,** aimed at sport and leisure facilities in the commercial, voluntary, and public sectors;
2   **Quest Sports Development,** aimed at sports development units in local authorities, national governing bodies, and voluntary organisations;
3   **Quest Active Communities,** aimed at local communities and linked to the Facility Management Award.

Quest is recommended by the British Quality Foundation for UK sport and leisure operations and is endorsed and supported by the four Sports Councils in the UK, plus a range of industry-representative organisations which have played an important role in developing the scheme. There are three main stages to achieving Quest:

1   **Self-assessment,** in comparison to industry standards and best practice – this stimulates the right organisational culture for improvement, and it facilitates the identification of strengths and weaknesses and the development of action plans;
2   **External validation** – undertaken by independent assessors and, for facilities, including a mystery customer visit;
3   **Ongoing maintenance to retain registration for two years** – this involves an assessor visit and includes a further mystery customer visit in the case of facilities.

16.4.6 Quality Awards and the Performance of Leisure Facilities

An important 'bottom line' in most quality programmes is better performance by the organisation which succeeds in attaining the quality management award. Investors in People, for example, describes itself as 'a business improvement tool designed to advance an organisation's performance'. Robinson (2004) found that the two most cited reasons for using quality programmes given by leisure facility managers were to improve services and to improve efficiency. Is there any evidence, then, that quality awards lead to better performance?

Two studies of IIP have been noted earlier, but they were not leisure specific. Ramchandani and Taylor (2011) investigated the effect of four different quality awards on the performance of sport and leisure centres, using a sample of 98 centres which had been processed through Sport England's National Benchmarking Service. Between them these centres had several awards, including Quest, Charter Mark, Investors in People, and ISO 9002. Ramchandani and Taylor analysed 37 performance indicators, covering access to the centres by disadvantaged groups, finance, utilisation, satisfaction, and importance-satisfaction gaps. They concluded that there was a statistically significant difference between centres with and without any quality awards for only one indicator out of the 37 – the percentage of visits which were first visits at the centre – and for this indicator it was centres without any awards that had the higher performance. Ramchandani and Taylor also investigated the effects of individual awards and concluded that:

- Charter Mark was associated with higher access performance;
- Quest was associated with better finance, utilisation, and customer satisfaction performance;

- Investors in People was associated with better utilisation and customer satisfaction performance;
- For all awards, some dimensions of performance are stronger in centres without the awards than in those with the awards.

Ramchandani and Taylor concluded that choosing to achieve a quality award does not necessarily improve all aspects of performance, and the selection of which award to go for depends on what aspects of performance are priorities for an organisation.

Discussion Question

If you had to choose a quality management award for a leisure organisation to work towards achieving, which would you recommend, and why?

Another study which investigates the impact of a quality system on the operations of organisations in sport is featured in Case Study 16.2. It demonstrates the design and effectiveness of sport-specific quality systems.

CASE STUDY 16.2

Quality Management in Flemish Sports Organisations, Belgium

The Flemish government published a Strategic Plan for Sporting Flanders (the northern, Dutch-speaking part of Belgium) which emphasised a shift to quality and performance management in all sports systems and structures. This, it was intended, would lead to all providers of sporting services – including federations, clubs, and public services – monitoring the quality and effectiveness of their systems. It would also facilitate 'more professional quality and competence . . . in exchange for subsidies and other forms of support'. Federations and clubs are typically supported by government and local authorities.

The systematic promotion of total quality management in Flemish sport was related to other changes, particularly demands from some club members for a more contemporary approach to management, and a decrease in experienced volunteers. It was hoped that quality and performance management would help organisations to better deal with their internal and external challenges.

Van Hoecke *et al.* (2009) examine gymnastics clubs which have used IKGym, which began as an initiative to produce a guide to gymnastics clubs, including their service quality, but also set out to implement principles of quality and performance management, inform stakeholders about critical success factors, provide volunteer board members with professional advice and support, and improve the management of gymnastics clubs to enhance output and performance.

The IKGym system consists of an external audit to measure a club's performance over seven strategic dimensions (organisational management and strategic planning, internal communications procedures, external communication and image building, organisational culture, organisational structure, human resources management, and organisational effectiveness) and four operational dimensions (coaching; training group size, composition and intensity of training; quality of facilities and equipment; and performance and outcome). Each of these dimensions has an array of measures. A total score is calculated, and certification of performance is provided, which lasts for three years, along with quantitative and qualitative reports which identify strengths and weaknesses.

Seventy-two gymnastics clubs which had participated in IKGym agreed that it provided a very good picture of their organisational performance (Van Hoecke et al., 2009). In half of these clubs, the process of conducting the audit stimulated improvements in their organisation before the result was known. Nine out of ten clubs undertook targeted actions to correct weaknesses identified by the audit. IKGym was therefore an important influence on the change process in these organisations.

IKGym has been adapted in other more general quality systems for sports organisations in Belgium – including IKSport for sports clubs and PASS for youth academies in sports clubs. Research by Van Hoecke et al. (2009) suggests that these systems have been welcomed by their participating clubs for the accuracy of their audits and their usefulness in informing quality improvements.

Source: Derived from Van Hoecke *et al.* (2009)

16.5 Performance Management Principles

Performance management is a cyclical, continuous process which relies on:

- Specifying suitable objectives for the organisation;
- Employing appropriate performance indicators to represent these objectives;
- Setting challenging but realistic management targets for the performance of the organisation;
- Taking the required actions to realise these targets;
- Measuring performance;
- Reviewing achievements and reconsidering objectives, indicators, targets, and actions.

Discussion Question

Many sport and leisure organisations do not measure performance very well. Discuss the possible reasons for this. If possible, use examples of organisations you are familiar with.

16.5.1 Objectives

An essential first stage in performance management is setting specific organisational objectives. An objective is a desired future position. There are several desirable attributes for organisational objectives:

- Objectives should be specified so that, at the end of an appropriate period, it is clear whether they have been achieved. This means that objectives need to be measurable. Each objective requires appropriate performance indicators, by which measurement of performance is possible.
- Objectives are concerned with ends, not means. For example, it is not an objective to 'set low prices for disadvantaged groups in the community'. Rather, the objective here is 'to increase visits to the service by people from disadvantaged groups'.

- The prioritisation of objectives is important, because sometimes objectives may conflict with each other. For example, 'increase revenue' might conflict with 'increase usage of a sport facility by disadvantaged groups'. Where trade-offs between conflicting objectives are apparent, priorities need to be identified. Otherwise, managers are put in a situation where failure is inevitable.

Such attributes for objectives can be summarised with the acronym MASTER:

- Measurable;
- Achievable;
- Specific;
- Time-specified;
- Ends not means;
- Ranked.

Often, particularly in the public sector, organisational objectives are expressed vaguely or generally, so that it is difficult if not impossible to identify whether they have been achieved. Examples of such mis-specified objectives include 'achieving sport for all' and 'serving the community's needs'. These are 'aims' rather than objectives – they are broadly based and non-measurable. They require more specific, measurable objectives to be monitored through performance indicators and used for management decision-making.

Public sector sport organisations have a more complicated task in framing appropriate objectives than commercial organisations, because social objectives are important to public sector organisations, such as usage by disadvantaged groups, the satisfaction of local communities with services, and even impacts such as diversion of 'at-risk' youth from crime, as well as the more conventional financial and customer satisfaction objectives. Social impacts such as reduced crime and vandalism and improved health and citizenship are typically less easily expressed in a measurable form than more operational objectives such as usage and finance.

16.5.2 Performance

Performance for leisure organisations can mean any number of things, depending on what objectives are specified. This section identifies different aspects of performance that leisure managers will be most likely to be interested in:

- **Finance** – this is the most conventional dimension of performance found in the private sector. It is often specified simply as profits, but in fact financial performance covers much wider ground (see Chapter 17).
- **Economy** – this is concerned only with costs, i.e. inputs to the production process. Economy improves if inputs are acquired at lower cost. Overemphasis on economy, of course, carries some risk – for example if the inputs are of lower quality. For example, a major input in leisure services is typically labour, and to reduce the costs of labour risks a 'false economy', with such problems as higher labour turnover or lower skilled labour.
- **Effectiveness** – this is concerned with outputs and reaching targets. A basic measure of effectiveness is throughput, such as the number of visits in a week. However, this is a rather basic indicator because it contains no indication of the types of visitors that have been attracted, or the extent to which the service has met the needs of the visitors – both of which can easily be measured by market research of customers. Assessing the effectiveness

of such services may well extend to impacts in the local community, i.e. beyond the immediate use and satisfaction of customers.

- **Efficiency** – this is concerned with achieving objectives and targets at minimum cost, so it simultaneously takes into consideration both outputs and inputs. It is sometimes called *cost-effectiveness* or *cost efficiency* and is also what is meant by the terms *productivity* and *value for money*. A contemporary term in much use in recent years, particularly in public sector services, is *efficiency savings*; but this requires maintaining service outputs whilst cutting costs – a very difficult thing to achieve.
- **Equity** – this is particularly relevant to public sector services and means measuring fairness in the distribution of services to different types of customers, e.g. by age, gender, ethnicity, and ability. It can be interpreted in several ways, for example fairness in the accessibility of services for all local citizens (i.e. equal opportunity) or fairness in the service received by different types of customers.
- **Customer satisfaction** – this is at the heart of quality management. It can be measured directly by such methods as questionnaire surveys, comment slips, or complaints. Sometimes satisfaction with service attributes is compared with customer expectations of these attributes, and sometimes it is compared with the importance of the attributes to customers. In the public sector, it is also important to measure the satisfaction with services by local citizens, regardless of whether they have used the service. This may seem contradictory – if a person has not used a service, how can they possibly comment? However, it is often the case that the community has a collective interest in the performance of a service, not least because they have collectively paid for it. An example is sport and leisure services for 'at-risk' young people. A wide range of people in local communities will have a view on whether such services are satisfactory, from parents and neighbours to anyone with a fear of nuisance – or worse, from bored young people.

Discussion Question

Are social impacts too difficult to measure as performance dimensions for public sport and leisure facilities? Discuss in relation to such commonly cited impacts as improvements in health, reductions in crime and vandalism, and improvements in educational achievements.

16.5.3 Performance Indicators

A performance indicator is a piece of empirical data which can be used to measure the performance of an organisation, and which can be compared over time or between organisations. Table 16.1 outlines some criteria for what good performance indicators should look like.

Devising a set of performance indicators that fulfils all the criterion in this table is challenging. For national indicators, performance indicators should be clearly defined, comparable, verifiable, unambiguous, and statistically valid. Indicators that are published for the benefit of the local community should first and foremost be relevant and easy to understand. It is also important that performance indicators should be capable of being measured for separate parts of a leisure service, since it is likely that different objectives and different targets are applicable to different parts of the service, even within one facility.

Table 16.1 **Criteria for a Good Performance Indicator**

Criteria	Explanation
Relevant	An indicator should be relevant to the organisation's strategic goals and objectives and cover all relevant performance dimensions.
Clear definition	A performance indicator should have a clear and intelligible definition to ensure consistent collection and fair comparison.
Easy to understand and use	A performance indicator should be described in terms that the user of the information will understand.
Comparable	Indicators should be comparable on a consistent basis between organisations, and this relies on there being agreement about definitions. They should also be comparable on a consistent basis over time.
Verifiable	The indicator also needs to be collected and calculated in a way that enables the information and data to be verified. It should therefore be based on robust data collection systems, and it should be possible for managers to verify the accuracy of the information and the consistency of the methods used.
Cost effective	There is a need to balance the cost of collecting information with its usefulness. Where possible, an indicator should be based on information already available and linked to existing data collection activities.
Unambiguous	A change in an indicator should be capable of unambiguous interpretation so that it is clear whether an increase in an indicator value represents an improvement or deterioration in service.
Attributable	Service managers should be able to influence the performance measured by the indicator.
Responsive	A performance indicator should be responsive to change. An indicator where changes in performance are likely to be too small to register will be of limited use.
Avoids perverse incentives	A performance indicator should not be easily manipulated because this might encourage counterproductive activity.

(Continued)

Table 16.1 (Continued)

Criteria	Explanation
Allows innovation	An indicator that focuses on outcome and user satisfaction is more likely to encourage such innovation to take place than one that is tied into existing processes.
Statistically valid	Indicators should be statistically valid, and this will in large part depend on the sample size.
Timely	Data for the performance indicator should be available within a reasonable timescale.

Discussion Question

A very common performance indicator in use in sport and leisure facilities is annual visits per square metre of floor space. Discuss the extent to which this indicator fulfils the criteria in Table 16.1.

Good quality data is the essential ingredient for reliable performance information, so it is vital that the data used for the construction of performance indicators are up to the task. The additional consideration for performance data of completeness is an important reminder that validity and reliability are as much dependent on what is missing as on what is collected. However, it should be emphasised that in practice any set of indicators is unlikely to fulfil all these properties. These data qualities are difficult to achieve, and managers should, whilst striving to achieve them, accept and be open about the limitations of the data they use.

16.6 Private, Commercial Sector

For a private, commercial organisation, performance is largely specified in financial terms, although there are other important considerations. Financial ratios are designed principally for planning purposes (strategic appraisal) and control purposes (operational appraisal). Financial ratios are concerned not just with profit, but also with growth, liquidity, asset utilisation, defensive position, and investment performance. A sample of such ratios is given in Table 16.2.

Ratios must be interpreted very carefully. Many are more appropriate for comparing a single firm's performance over time than for comparing different firms, particularly if the firms are from different industries or sectors. Some ratios involve estimates which can be made in various ways, so comparing like with like can be problematic – for example valuing inventories and intangible assets. Some ratio values are annual averages, so getting the information from balance sheets is unreliable, merely averaging the beginning and end of the year situations, when more observations during the year are really required, e.g. liquidity ratios.

Table 16.2 **Performance Ratios for Commercial Organisations**

	Explanations
Growth	Year on year percentage changes in key variables, e.g. income, expenditure, profit, assets, liabilities.
Profitability	Gross profit ratio or net profit ratio. No rules of thumb. It varies widely between industries and firms.
	'Return on capital employed'. No standard definitions, so care is needed in making comparisons between firms and industries.
Liquidity	'Current ratio'. Rule of thumb = at least 1:1 and preferably higher.
	'Acid test', 'Quick' or 'Liquidity' ratio. A more discriminating test of ability to pay debts.
	'Cash ratio'. A more conservative measure which ignores less-liquid assets such as stock.
	Average collection period of trade debts, i.e. average number of days before accounts are paid.
Asset utilisation	Indicates the effectiveness in using fixed plant to generate sales.
	'Stock turnover'. Varies a lot between industries.
	Indicates revenue productivity of labour.
Defensive position	Indicates shareholders' interest in the business. (Net worth is ordinary shares + preference shares + reserves.)
	'Gearing ratio'. An indication of the riskiness of the capital structure.
	'Debt ratio'. An indication of the powers of creditors over an organisation.
Investment	'Dividend yield'. Indicates rate of return on investment in shares.
	Earnings per ordinary share.
	'Price/Earnings ratio'. Indicates the market's evaluation of a share.

Sources: Gratton and Taylor (1988); Wilson and Joyce (2010)
Note: Details of the use of these ratios can be found in any good accounting text.

Private firms are also interested in other aspects of performance apart from financial ratios. Market share is an important objective that is normally measurable, even at the local or regional level. Market share is one of several possible indicators for the demand for the product. It is vital for any organisation to be informed about the nature of, and changes in, demand for the service it is providing. Market research is a typical means of generating this evidence.

Most large private leisure organisations have marketing departments with market research functions. As well as continually monitoring demand for their goods and services by this means, they regularly employ outside market research agencies or consultancies to conduct specialist market research. In addition, some consultancies produce regular reports with market research information alongside financial data for different industries. One example of this is Mintel, a global and award-winning provider of market research. They produce business intelligence reports that deliver top-class data, market research, trends, and insights to impact businesses. Mintel provide reports across the sector of hospitality, sport, leisure, and tourism, including all sectors such as voluntary, public, and private.

16.7 Public Sector

Public sector services have been subject to increasing pressure for accountability in recent decades. Accountability does not just mean spending the money as they should; it also refers to achieving value for money from public spending. This requires appropriate performance indicators. In the UK the process of reporting to standard performance indicators has been driven in recent years by Best Value legislation, which has since been revised (in 2015) to Best Value Duty. This legislation sets out some reasonable expectations of the way authorities should work with voluntary and community groups and small businesses.

At the individual service level, much more comprehensive lists of performance indicators can be found. For example, Sport England's National Benchmarking Service for public sport and leisure centres (NBS) calculates 47 performance indicators across four dimensions of performance.

This NBS list is comprehensive, but even so it does not cover all the aspects of public facilities' performance that managers and politicians would like it to. The NBS does not measure most of the wider social impacts of such facilities, such as improvements in health, improved quality of life, reduced crime and vandalism, or education benefits – these are considered too difficult to measure regularly in the specific context of these facilities. The NBS does not measure non-users' attitudes and barriers – this would require research in local communities, which is expensive. The NBS also does not record the views, behaviour, etc. of young people under 14 years old, who are not considered suitable for the questionnaire survey employed. These exclusions demonstrate the compromise that is often necessary in practical performance measurement systems between what indicators are desirable and what indicators can be measured reliably and at reasonable cost.

It is the responsibility of each organisation to choose a manageable array of indicators to reflect its objectives. For a public sector provider, this may include throughput indicators for groups of clients, such as women, the elderly, lower socio-economic groups, and the disabled, since this would monitor the effectiveness of the organisation in dealing with such target groups. It may also include very conventional indicators of financial performance, particularly for parts of the service which have no particular 'social service' function, such as the bar, café, vending machines, and other merchandise sales.

How often should performance indicators evidence be produced? It is very common for performance indicators to be calculated on an annual average basis. However, there are good reasons for wanting operational performance indicators to be available on a far more regular basis. Decisions about promotion, programming, and staffing arrangements may be modified at any time, so a regular flow of up-to-date information assists such decisions. Such a consideration reminds us that the primary purpose of performance measurement is to help management decisions. A secondary purpose, albeit important, is to report performance to the organisation's stakeholders.

16.8 Targets

Targets are precise statements of what is to be achieved and by when. They support the process of performance management because they are tangible manifestations of the aim of continuous improvement, and they are important reference points against which improvement can be monitored. A target is typically quantitative, e.g. to increase the number of visits by ethnic minorities by 5%.

How is a target decided? The most appropriate basis is evidence of previous performance by the organisation and evidence of the performance of similar organisations elsewhere. Such evidence enables the target setter to reach the difficult but necessary balance between ambition and realism. Targets need to be challenging, but they also need to be achievable. If they are too easily reached, or if they are impossible to reach, they quickly fall into disrepute. Targets can and do change in the course of time. They need to remain under continuing scrutiny for their relevance to the operating circumstances of the organisation.

> **Discussion Question**
>
> How easy is it to set targets for the following objectives: (1) improve customer satisfaction; (2) increase the diversity of visitors; and (3) increase off-peak utilisation of a facility?

16.9 The Balanced Scorecard

The Balanced Scorecard was devised by Kaplan and Norton (1996). It is a system of performance measurement which is generic and used by a wide variety of organisations in all sectors and across the globe. A primary motivation for the Balanced Scorecard was to add strategic non-financial performance measures to the traditional financial measures to give a more 'balanced' view of organisational performance. The structure of the Balanced Scorecard is represented in Figure 16.2.

The figure demonstrates not just the development of performance measurement beyond the financial, but also a consistent process of specifying objectives, devising measures for these, setting targets, and devising initiatives to achieve the targets. It is the last of these processes that turns the Balanced Scorecard into a performance management system, not just a performance measurement tool.

16.10 Benchmarking

So far, we have been discussing the performance measurement that it is appropriate for an organisation to conduct, so that its managers can identify how the organisation is performing and whether changes are occurring as a result of their decisions. However, it is also likely that the organisation will want comparisons to be made with other similar organisations, to put their own performance into perspective. Benchmarking is a process which facilitates this, and there are two main types:

1 Data benchmarking involves comparison with numerical standards (e.g. averages) calculated for performance indicators in a particular service. The benchmarks are typically organised into relevant 'families' of similar organisations.

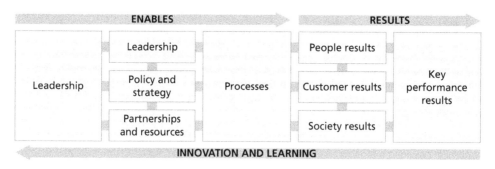

Figure 16.2 The Balanced Scorecard structure.
Source: Adapted from www.balancedscorecard.org/

2   Process benchmarking involves comparison of different procedures adopted in different organisations. Used in conjunction with performance data, process benchmarking helps a manager understand how to improve performance. It is often facilitated by 'benchmarking clubs' of similar organisations.

External benchmarks for performance are important because they identify the performance of an organisation relative to other similar organisations. They also enable other agencies to assess the relative performance of all organisations participating in the benchmarking exercise. This is particularly important in the public sector, where central government is typically interested in monitoring the relative performance of individual local government services. In many countries this job is done by independent auditors.

Comparative performance information is available in both the private sector and the public sector. In the private sector, for example, financial information for individual companies is available through the government via a website called Companies House. In the public sector in the UK, benchmarks are provided for sport and leisure by the Chartered Institute of Public Finance and Accountancy (CIPFA). Three other explicit benchmarking services can be identified for sport and leisure – one in Australia and New Zealand (CERM), the other two in the UK (APSE Performance Networks and NBS).

16.11 CERM Performance Indicators

Operating in Australia and New Zealand, the CERM PIs Project is run by the Centre for Environmental and Recreational Management at the University of South Australia. It has clients from the public sector and from voluntary and commercial facilities. Originally designed for public aquatic centres and leisure centres, it now extends to a range of sport and leisure services, including golf courses, caravan and tourist parks, campgrounds, skate parks, and outdoor centres.

CERM PIs provides benchmarks for 26 operational performance indicators, including services (e.g. programme opportunities per week), marketing (e.g. promotion cost as a proportion of total cost), organisation (e.g. cleaning and maintenance cost per visit), and finance (e.g. surplus/subsidy per visit). It also provides customer service quality benchmarks, covering gaps between customers' expectations and satisfaction in relation to several service attributes.

16.12 APSE Performance Networks

APSE Performance Networks covers over 200 UK local authority service areas, including civic, cultural, and community venues; culture, leisure, and sport; sports and leisure facility management; roads, highways, and transport; and trading standards, among others. APSE collects data across multiple dimensions and compares an individual local authority's performance with other local authorities of a similar type, determined by similar overall scores for a series of drivers, which comprise facility type and size, location characteristics, competition, transport, car parking, pricing policy, programming, and investment.

16.13 Sport England's National Benchmarking Service

The NBS measures performance standards for indoor sports and leisure centres. The NBS results for access, efficiency, and utilisation performance are compared with benchmarks for four families which have been empirically tested and proven to have structural effects on performance:

1 **Type of facility** – wet, dry (with/without outdoor facilities), and mixed (with/without outdoor facilities);
2 **The socioeconomics of a facility's location** – high deprivation, medium deprivation, low deprivation – measured by the percentage of the catchment population in the bottom two socio-economic classes;
3 **Size of the facility** – small, medium, large, and very large;
4 **Management type at the facility** – external partner, local authority, local trust.

Three benchmarks are employed. The 25%, 50%, and 75% benchmarks are the quarter, half, and three-quarters points in the distribution of scores for a performance indicator, if all the centres' scores were organised from the lowest score at the bottom end of the distribution to the highest score at the top end.

> **Discussion Question**
>
> If you managed a sport and leisure organisation which, according to benchmarking data, performed in the bottom quartile for an important performance indicator such as visits by young people, discuss the steps you would then take. (This should not include resigning!)

For the importance and satisfaction attributes, the NBS reports in three ways:

1 The satisfaction scores in comparison with industry averages for different facility types;
2 The gaps between importance and satisfaction mean scores from customers – the largest gaps being the strongest indication of problems;
3 The percentage of customers dissatisfied with each attribute.

16.14 Benefits of Benchmarking

Benchmarking in the sport and leisure public sector provides the ability to learn from those authorities that have performed particularly well in order to improve service delivery. This is what both the APSE and NBS are designed to do. APSE organises advisory groups, benchmarking meetings, and seminars to promote this shared learning, whilst NBS clients have demonstrated a number of general learning responses to the processes of performance management, such as:

- Generating the right information;
- Interpreting the results meaningfully;
- Utilising the results in performance planning, i.e. immediate action plans, and longer-term contract specification and strategy development.

Case Study 16.3 discusses the benefits to facility managers in one English local authority which has been utilising the NBS for several years.

CASE STUDY 16.3

The Benefits of NBS to Milton Keynes Leisure Centre Managers

Milton Keynes has put five of its centres through the National Benchmarking Service (NBS). For Milton Keynes Council, a key benefit of the NBS is that it enables them to monitor the performance of the different centres in a consistent and comparable manner and to compare them with national standards. It also provides performance data for inclusion in annual reports and cabinet/committee reports, and it helps to lever in funding for improvements and for further research.

Milton Keynes Council takes a collective approach to the discussion of performance, and the NBS facilitates this. When the reports are completed, the council convenes a workshop for all the centres' managers, plus the key officers from the council, led by the national lead for the NBS technical service. As a result of these workshop discussions, the following benefits from NBS participation have been discussed:

1. Awareness of performance – facility managers are provided by NBS with an objective, externally validated set of performance measures. Local managers can explain and discuss this information with their knowledge of local circumstances. As one pointed out, though, it is only a 'snapshot' of performance in respect of customers, because the user survey is only over nine days.

2. Education of stakeholders – the NBS data help to educate politicians about the realities of performance at the leisure centres. Indeed, one local politician has attended all the NBS workshops at Milton Keynes. Two of the centre managers feel that there are limits to the extent to which NBS information can be used for this purpose. They have not used it to inform customers, for example, because they feel the data need appropriate background knowledge for them to be properly understood.

3. Challenges to preconceived ideas held by managers and politicians – in fact, the NBS data often confirm preconceived ideas, but they occasionally throw up some unexpected surprises, both negative and positive, for managers. This has led to some detailed discussions at Milton Keynes, not just about revised expectations in

the light of the NBS evidence, but also about the accuracy of the NBS evidence. For example, local knowledge can challenge the catchment area for a facility, which the NBS derives from a national model.

4   Expectations and targets – NBS data help managers and other stakeholders to form realistic expectations about what performance is possible, given not only the performance of their own centres but also comparisons with national benchmarks. At Milton Keynes the NBS data inform a process of pragmatic discussion between officers from Milton Keynes Council and the centres' managers, from which there are shared expectations for the year to come. The council then 'incentivises' the centres' improvement plans by making 10% of their funding conditional on improvement in certain performance indicators' scores. One centre manager feels that the NBS data help Milton Keynes Council to identify different expectations for each centre, according to their strengths and their local circumstances.

5   Evidence-based management culture – experience of collecting data and receiving benchmarking reports helps to develop an awareness of further information needs. An example is qualitative research needed to identify exactly why customers have given a relatively weak satisfaction score to a particular service attribute. Although one centre manager feels that the current research is sufficient, others acknowledged that NBS performance data can lead to further research questions. However, there is then the matter of finding resources to address such questions.

6   Process benchmarking – benchmarking data facilitate the selection of partners with whom to discuss how to generate better performance for specific performance indicators. The Milton Keynes managers' NBS workshops are good examples of this process at a local level, with a refreshing openness to the discussions of both strengths and weaknesses in performance. One manager uses other NBS clients outside Milton Keynes to make comparisons and identify best practice.

7   Provide data for quality management systems – this benefit was endorsed strongly by most of the Milton Keynes managers. Their centres also participated in Quest, and they emphasised how complementary the two systems are: NBS providing data, particularly from customers, to inform key requirements of Quest.

In addition, one Milton Keynes manager suggested that the NBS data give Milton Keynes Council the opportunity to examine how authority-wide systems are working – for example their leisure (discount) card system.

16.15 Conclusions

Quality and performance management are in effect restatements of what good management is all about. Many of the principles in the examples reviewed in this chapter are similar, and they are all underpinned by the ethos expounded by Deming – Plan, Do, Study, Act. They service the aspiration for continuous improvement, and this improvement is designed to better meet the needs of customers. They promote good systems for the collection and use of appropriate evidence.

It is idealistic to think that the culture of total quality management can be achieved, i.e. that every single person in an organisation is united by an excellence culture. Rather, it is an aspiration, a culture to be aimed for, and part of continuous improvement is to take the organisation closer to the TQM ideal.

Good performance evidence enables weaknesses to be identified, plans to be made, actions to be taken, and outcomes to be improved – these are the essentials of performance management. However, acquiring appropriate evidence is not an easy matter. Some objectives, particularly in the public sector, are difficult to represent in performance indicators at reasonable cost. Generating accurate and consistent measurement data can also be a problem, e.g. financial data which can vary despite accounting regulations, and market research data which can all too easily fall prey to errors such as biased samples or misleading questions.

Another essential element of good performance management is to compare performance with other organisations. This is where benchmarking helps. However, rather than making comparisons within informal professional networks, a key advantage of the benchmarking systems reviewed in this chapter is that they offer objective, like-for-like comparisons. However, particularly for public leisure services, benchmarking systems do not cover everything – they do not cover very well the ever-important impacts of public services on their local communities. This weakness exposes a limit to performance management, which it is important to acknowledge – if measuring certain types of performance is too difficult, then managing them will be that much more difficult.

Practical Tasks

1 Begin the process of taking a sport or leisure organisation that you are familiar with through the CSIT system (Section 16.3.2). To what extent does it help you to identify the strengths and weaknesses of the organisation? What other advantages do you perceive in adopting this framework?

2 Specify three objectives for a sport or leisure organisation that you are familiar with, e.g. a local club or facility. Design a set of performance indicators by which performance of these objectives can be measured. Identify what data would be needed to measure performance for your selected indicators. Evaluate the major problems the organisation would have in collecting such data.

Structured Guide to Further Reading

For detailed discussion of quality issues:
Williams, C., & Buswell, J. (2003). *Service Quality in Leisure and Tourism*. CABI Publishing, Wallingford.

For rounded discussions of both quality and performance management in the public sector:
Robinson, L. (2004). *Managing Public Sport and Leisure Services*, Chapters 7 and 8. Routledge, London.

For the principles of performance measurement:
Audit Commission. (2000a). *Aiming to Improve: The Principles of Performance Measurement*. Audit Commission, London.

For details of performance management systems:
IDeA. (2010). *Culture and Sport Improvement Toolkit*. IDeA, London.
Kaplan, R. S., & Norton, D. P. (1996). *The Balanced Scorecard*. Harvard Business Press, Boston, MA.

Useful Websites

For quality frameworks:
Chartered Quality Institute, www.thecqi.org/
Culture and Sport Improvement Toolkit, www.idea.gov.uk/idk/core/page.do?pageId=8722761
EFQM, http://ww1.efqm.org/en/Home/tabid/36/Default.aspx

For IDeA, the UK agency for improvement and development of local government services (work on culture, tourism, and sport):
www.idea.gov.uk/idk/core/page.do?pageId=11216202

For quality awards:
British and International Standards, www.bsi-global.com
Customer Service Excellence, www.cse.cabinetoffice.gov.uk/homeCSE.do, and www.cse.cabinetoffice.gov.uk/UserFiles/Customer_Service_Excellence_standard.pdf
Green Flag Award, www.greenflagaward.org.uk/
Investors in People, www.investorsinpeople.co.uk
Quest, www.questnbs.info/
UK Excellence Award, www.bqf.org.uk
White Flag Award, http://81.17.252.145/~whiteflag/

For performance measurement systems:
APSE Performance Networks, www.apse.org.uk/performance-network.html
Balanced Scorecard, www.balancedscorecard.org/
CERM Performance Indicators, http://unisa.edu.au/cermpi/
National Benchmarking Service, www.questnbs.info/

For performance measures:
CIPFA statistics, www.cipfastats.net/
ICC British Company Financial Datasheets, http://library.dialog.com/bluesheets/html/bl0562.html
Keynote, www.keynote.co.uk
Mintel, http://reports.mintel.com/

References

Bourne, M., Franco-Santos, M., Pavlov, A., Lucianetti, L., Martinez, V., & Mura, M. (2008). *The Impact of Investors in People on People Management Practices and Firm Performance, Centre for Business Performance.* Cranfield School of Management, Cranfield.

BSI. (1987). *Quality Vocabulary: Part 1, International Terms: BS44778.* British Standards Institute, London.

Clarke, F. (1992). Quality and service in the public sector. *Public Finance and Accountancy,* 23(10), 23–25.

Cowling, M. (2008). *Does IIP Add Value to Businesses?* Institute of Employment Studies, Brighton.

Deming, W. E. (1986). *Out of the Crisis,* The Press Syndicate, Cambridge.

Gratton, C., & Taylor, P. (1988). *Economics of Leisure Services Management.* Longman, Harlow.

Israeli, A. A., Lee, S. A., & Karpinski, A. C. (2017). Investigating the dynamics and the content of customers' social media reporting after a restaurant service failure. *Journal of Hospitality Marketing & Management*, 26(6), 606–626. doi:10.1080/19368623.2017.1281193

Juran, J. M. (1988). *Juran on Planning for Quality*. Collier Macmillan, London.

Mosscrop, P., & Stores, A. (1990). *Total Quality Management in Leisure: A Guide for Directors and Managers*. Collinson Grant Consultants, Manchester.

Ramchandani, G., & Taylor, P. (2011). Quality management awards and sports facilities' performance. *Local Government Studies*, 37(1), 121–143.

Silber, I., Israeli, A., Bustin, A., & Zvi, O. (2009). Recovery strategies for service failures: The case of restaurants. *Journal of Hospitality Marketing & Management*, 18(7), 730–740. doi:10.1080/19368620903170273

Van Hoecke, J., De Knop, P., & Schoukens, H. (2009). A decade of quality and performance management in Flemish organised sport. *International Journal of Sports Management and Marketing*, 6(3), 308–329.

Wilson, R., & Joyce, J. (2010). *Finance for Sport and Leisure Managers: An Introduction*, 2nd edition. Routledge, London.

Chapter 17

Financial Management in Sport and Leisure

DOI: 10.4324/9780367823610-17

Summary

Today's sport and leisure management students and employees need to understand the financial side of the industry to offer the most cost-effective solutions to complex problems and an increasingly volatile market. Consequently, this chapter introduces the key financial principles and procedures that are used to plan, make effective decisions, and control a sport and leisure organisation. It acknowledges that sport and leisure organisations are often not financially driven or even based in the private sector. However, the importance of financial management transcends boundaries and places responsibility to operate within mandatory requirements and good practice on all organisations. Finally, within this chapter, a framework is provided to appraise the financial health of an organisation to assess and guide its future financial viability.

17.1 Introduction

It is important before we start that we establish some ground rules. Put simply, finance is *not* just about numbers, and you *do not* have to be a skilled mathematician to understand a set of financial statements. Instead, you need to understand the guiding rules and principles that help compile and structure a set of accounts. As students or managers who work within the sport and leisure industry, it is important that you appreciate the importance of financial management and responsibility and can communicate key financial information to both internal and external stakeholders. The sport and leisure industries are big businesses. The global sports market reached a value of nearly $388.3 billion in 2020, having increased at a compound annual growth rate (CAGR) of 3.4% since 2015 (Sports Global Market Report, 2021). The market did decline slightly from 2019 due to factors relating to the COVID-19 pandemic such as lockdowns, social distancing norms imposed by various countries, and economic slowdown across countries, but the market is expected to recover in the future. Indeed, the sports market is expected to reach $599.9 billion by 2025, and $826.0 billion by 2030 (Sports Global Market Report, 2021).

The commodification and professionalisation of sport and leisure has led to vast sums of money being invested at all levels. At the very top of the industry this has led to sports teams being valued as some of the highest brands on the planet. The Dallas Cowboys (an American NFL team) topped the list in 2021 with a value of $5.7 billion. Owing to these factors, sport and leisure has established itself as a mechanism for creating personal meaning, cultural identity (the purchase of a replica football shirt, for example), and a lucrative career path for many people all over the world. The amount of money to be earned through working in sport means that it is no longer seen as a frivolous career choice.

Unfortunately, however, sport and leisure has lagged other business sectors from a financial management point of view. For the most part sport marketing, planning, and strategy have dominated sport business management education and led to a growing maturity in such areas. Financial management has often been overlooked, anecdotally because individuals claim to have some sort of fear with numbers. There are still many sport managers and graduates with sport management degrees who struggle to even understand the basics of an income statement or balance sheet, let alone have the confidence to make informed judgements on the financial health of an organisation. However, as Wilson (2011) points out, all organisations, ranging from multi-million-pound operations through to small, local, voluntary sport clubs, need to produce a set of financial statements every year. Therefore, if organisations are obliged to comply, the chances are that should managers wish to be successful in the industry, they too will have to understand, communicate, and use financial information.

17.2 Key Terminology

Essentially there are two types of accounts: financial and management. Depending on the nature of a user's information needs, the type of accounts used will be quite different. When looking backwards, it is normal to examine financial accounts, as they are prepared for external use and are based on historical information. They are also required by law and must be presented in a specified manner. A set of financial accounts illustrates the past financial position and financial performance of an organisation at a specific date.

> **Key Term**
>
> **Financial accounting** – the term used to describe the system for recording historical financial transactions and presenting this information in summary form.

However, should managers wish to be more proactive and examine future trends and issues, they will need to examine more forward-looking (future) accounting information. Such information will not be found in financial accounts, hence there are management accounts, i.e. accounts that look forward and are based on providing information for managers to help with the planning, decision-making, and control of their organisations. Unlike financial accounts, management accounts are not a statutory requirement. It is important that managers understand the distinction between the two types of accounts, as they dictate where one should look for information. These two types of accounts also structure the remainder of this chapter. First, we examine financial accounting information, before moving on to management accounts towards the end of this chapter.

> **Key Term**
>
> **Management accounting** – the term used to describe more forward-looking financial data for planning, decision-making, and control purposes.

Managers should appreciate that financial and management accounts work together hand in hand. Even though the law stipulates that financial accounts should be constructed within the parameters set out by the International Accounting Standards (IAS), no manager in their right mind would record financial transactions and hope for the best. Instead, they will plan their operations, consider the implications of their decisions, and control their organisation in such a way to achieve their organisation's objectives. To plan and make effective decisions, a manager will have to adopt the principles of good management accounting, for example budgeting, break-even analysis, and costing – some of which will be explored towards the end of this chapter. Consequently, a rounded understanding of the two types of accounting practice is an essential skill for the successful manager.

Before we continue, it is worth outlining more key terminology that you may encounter when moving through the financial accounting sections.

Key Terms

Income statement or profit and loss account – a summary of financial performance based on income and expenditure over a period of time.

Balance sheet – a snapshot of a company's financial position at a specific point in time.

Cash flow – an analysis of funds flowing in and out of a business over a period of time.

Assets – those things of value that a company owns, e.g. buildings, equipment, vehicles.

Debtor – an individual or organisation who owes the company money or service, e.g. someone to whom you have lent money.

Liabilities – think of liabilities as the opposite of assets, that is amounts that a business owes to others.

Creditor – an alternative word for 'liabilities'.

Depreciation – the loss in value of assets over time, e.g. a treadmill in a gym will be worth less after a year than it was when initially purchased.

17.3 The Importance of Financial Management

The concept behind financial management is not the simplistic idea that you need to manage profit, but more importantly how to monitor, evaluate, and control the income and expenditure of an organisation. It is vital for sport and leisure managers to understand the changing values of the three-sector provision model (as covered in Part II) and recognise that many sport services are provided to achieve social objectives, which operate at a loss and require some form of subsidy to operate. This does not mean, however, that proper financial controls are not important. It is vital that sport and leisure managers understand the costs of the products and services that they offer to operate as effective business entities to generate profits or to ensure that taxpayers' money is used efficiently and effectively.

Many organisations will borrow to fund their expansion plans. In fact, borrowing is part and parcel of everyday life if organisations wish to remain competitive. However, borrowing is normally based on the simple assumption that the organisation's future returns will be sufficient to cover the borrowing and any associated business. Problems, however, often occur when organisations fail to meet their financial obligations. Consequently, an organisation's ability to pay its debts as they fall due is usually the difference between financial success and failure. If managers are to make effective plans and decisions, they need to control their organisation's finances. Borrowing is not necessarily a bad thing, nor for that matter is debt – the main issue is being able to service the debt. This is a problem that Bury Football Club found out the hard way in 2019 (see Case Study 17.1).

Finance, Football, and Bury FC

Bury Football Club was established in 1885. It was a founding member of the Lancashire League in 1889 before being elected to the Football League in 1894. The Club won the FA Cup in 1900 and 1903 and enjoyed a rich history in English Football. However, in August 2019 it was expelled from the Football League following administration and the revelation of financial issues that had mismanagement at their core. These issues became insurmountable, although there had been warning signs for years prior to the collapse. So how did Bury found itself in this position? The Club, after all, had a proud footballing history, including two FA Cup titles and a record for goals scored in four divisions of the English Football League.

The 134-year-old club found itself in a financially precarious position as far back as 2001, when problems linked to the collapse of ITV Digital took Bury into administration and close to collapse. The day was saved by supporters who stepped in and raised enough money for the Club to survive. However, more problems followed in 2012 when the Club had a transfer embargo placed on it after getting into financial difficulties linked to poor attendances and hence reduced income.

In December 2018, Steve Dale bought Bury for £1 from previous owner Stewart Day, who had owned the Club since 2013. He paid an outstanding tax bill to avoid a winding-up order, but a mortgage on Bury's ground at Gigg Lane had been taken out during Mr Day's tenure and, back in May, loans were said to be rapidly accumulating interest – having risen to £3.7 million.

Bury's existing debts were exacerbated by spending unsustainable amounts on player transfers and salaries, with some players reportedly earning £8,000 to £10,000 a week to maintain the team's footing after they were promoted to League One in 2019.

Putting it bluntly, the Club spent considerably more than it was earning and more than it could afford.

When larger clubs are demoted or have 'parachute payments' to spend on players, smaller clubs struggle to keep up with their rivals' spending to maintain their own league position let alone do enough to be promoted. If revenues don't arrive and the Club can't sign new sponsorship deals or fill out match-day crowds, clubs end up in financial distress.

With Bury we saw a club with historical financial problems get further and further into debt while trying to keep up with its rivals. Although the buck stops with the board, the blame can't all be laid at the directors' door.

Sadly, Bury FC's plight seems to be the tip of the iceberg, with around 20% of English Football League clubs currently living a hand-to-mouth existence. Bolton Wanderers were only two weeks away from going the same way as Bury in 2019. In 2021, the Fan-Led Review of Football called for greater regulation and stronger governance to force clubs to become self-sustainable. In finance terms, if they cannot pay their debts as they fall due, then should they really be operating as a business?

There is also a wider financial and economic issue here with Bury. No club means that other businesses suffer as a result, such as local business owners in the town who rely on the spending of supporters. Businesses will struggle without the trade brought in on match days. Pubs, bars, clubs, and restaurants can survive the quiet months of the summer because in the past they've known they can count on match-day incomes. The plight of Bury FC will affect other businesses in other sectors. Such is the extent that football and sport and leisure are deeply embedded in our culture.

There are two main issues here to do with financial management. The first is that managers need to assess the market they are operating within, as this will offer some direction as to how do deal with cost. In Bury's case, overspending on players' wages in a league that does not generate the revenue to match the expenditure was not a financially viable strategy. The second issue is to do with debt. Clearly Bury had operated with a high level of debt relative to the value of the company. However, it was not the concept of debt, nor the concept of borrowing, that led to the Club's downfall. The issue was that it could not service its debt and that wealthy owners prepared to underwrite unsustainable losses from their own resources are few and far between.

(Supporting information adapted from Wilson *et al.*, 2019 www.prospectmagazine. co.uk/politics/bury-fc-news-stadium-debt-football-elegy.)

Discussion Questions

What were the most significant issues that caused the financial decline of Bury FC? What other football clubs, or sport and leisure businesses, have faced similar issues?

17.4 The Users of Financial Information

Financial information will be useful to a wide variety of stakeholders. These will often span several sectors, and each will have slightly different needs for the information. For example, Joel and Avram Glazer (the co-chairmen of Manchester United FC) will want to know how much profit the company has made, to ensure that they can make the necessary interest payments on the loans that they took out to finance the takeover of the Club in 2005. Sheffield City Council will want to know how much subsidy it needs to provide to keep their leisure services running across the city. The Chair of the Cheltenham Swimming and Water Polo Club will want to ensure that enough money is being received through subscriptions and funding to cover their running costs.

Generally, information relating to the finance of an organisation is of interest to its owners, managers, trade contacts (for example suppliers), providers of finance (for example banks), employees, and customers. All these groups of people need to be sure that the organisation is strong, can pay its bills, make a profit if it is commercial, and remain in business. An indicative list of users and their areas of interest is illustrated in Table 17.1.

Discussion Question

Who are the most important audiences for financial information (1) in a private commercial sport and leisure organisation; (2) in a local authority sport and leisure service; and (3) in a voluntary sport and leisure club? Explain why you have made your choices.

Table 17.1 **Users of Financial Information and Their Information Needs**

User groups	Areas of interest
Owners of a company	Owners will want to know how well the management of the organisation is doing on a day-to-day basis and how much profit they can take from the organisation for their own use.
Managers	Managers require financial information so that they can make plans for the organisation and see how effective their decisions have been.
Trade contacts (i.e. suppliers)	Suppliers and other trade contacts need to know whether they are going to be paid on time by the organisation.
Providers of finance (i.e. banks, etc.)	Banks and other lenders of finance need to ensure that any loans and interest payments are going to be made on time before they lend money and during the repayment period.
Her Majesty's Revenue and Customs (UK), Internal Revenue Service (USA), or the Australian Taxation Office, etc.	The tax authorities need information about the profits of the organisation so that they can work out how much tax the organisation owes. They also need details for VAT and employees' income tax.
Employees	Organisations' employees often wish to know whether their jobs are safe and that they are going to be paid on time.
Customers	It is normal for customers to know whether goods/services purchased are going to be delivered/provided. They may also be interested in investing in the company and therefore will want to know whether it is a good prospect.

17.5 Statutory Requirements for Sport and Leisure

Effective management of an organisation, whether it is in the sport and leisure industry or not, takes more than just an understanding of financial management, as it requires individuals to put financial tools to use. Understanding the financial recording and reporting system and being able to apply it enables quick and easy assessment of an organisation's financial health. This is essential for all managers, regardless of the size, style, or type of the organisation, as they must produce a set of financial statements which include a balance sheet and income statement (previously termed a profit and loss account). In short, the balance sheet is simply a list of all assets owned by an organisation and all liabilities owed by an organisation at a specific point in time. It will often be referred to as a 'snapshot' of the financial position of an organisation and is usually stated at the end of a financial year. The income statement, on the other hand, illustrates financial performance by outlining the profits (or losses) recognised over a period of time, usually from the start to the end of a financial year. Profit, or loss, is calculated by deducting expenditure from income.

Any limited company will produce an income statement for the period of one year. However, it is not uncommon for managers to construct interim income statements that are linked to budgets on a quarterly or even monthly basis – further illustrating the link between financial accounting and management accounting, which will be explored in detail later. Organisations that are 'not-for-profit', such as charities and many clubs or societies, will produce a similar statement called an income and expenditure account, which details any *surplus* or *deficit*, which are alternative terms for the more commonly used *profit* or *loss*.

While financial statements might never satisfy all the needs of the user groups, it is worth confirming that financial statements are a statutory requirement and that every organisation, be it in the public, private, or voluntary sector, must produce them. Companies listed on any international stock exchange, e.g. FTSE (UK), NASDAQ (USA), or the ASX (Australia), must go one step further and are obliged to publish their statements and send copies to shareholders.

17.6 The Financial Statements

The objective of financial accounts is to provide useful information for users regardless of who they are. Consequently, the information contained within the set of accounts is concerned with the resources employed and how they are used. This means that the accounts help to communicate the financial performance and position of an organisation. Financial performance and position are communicated by the following three reports, which are typically produced by trained accountants.

1 **The statement of financial performance, or income statement,** which reports on the revenues earned, the expenses incurred, and the resulting profit or loss achieved;
2 **The statement of financial position, or balance sheet,** which illustrates the current levels of assets and liabilities, which in turn reveals the 'net worth' or capital of a business;
3 **The cash flow statement,** which provides details of how much cash an organisation has and how it has used its cash to buy assets or pay off creditors.

Each of these three statements needs to be understood by sport and leisure managers to ensure that they can contribute effectively to the management of an organisation. Consequently, it is worth having a detailed look at the main statements so that you can see the general layout of the accounts and understand the key figures and their implications for the prospects of the organisation. To make this information more consistent and accessible, we use Plymouth Argyle Football Club Limited's annual accounts for the year ended 30 June 2021 (see Case Study 17.2). We use Plymouth as an example of a football club that is run sustainability (as opposed to the Bury FC case study earlier in this chapter) and to highlight the nuances involved with finances in professional sport.

Plymouth Argyle FC in 2021: An Introduction

Plymouth Argyle Football Club is a professional football club based in the city of Plymouth, Devon, England. As of the 2021–2022 season, the team are competing in League One, the third tier of English football. They have played at Home Park, known as the 'Theatre of Greens', since 1901. In 2021, the Club faced one of their most unpredictable periods in modern history, with almost a whole season of League One football played behind closed doors (because of the COVID-19 pandemic). This deprived the Club of one of the most important sources of revenue for a football club – match-day income. The Club had nevertheless continued to make progress towards its public aim of becoming a sustainable championship-level club. Despite a season shrouded in uncertainty, they were able to consolidate their status in League One, with a continuing focus on developing first-team players in their academy. A combination of generous backing from supporters, sponsors, and other stakeholders, coupled with a cautious and mitigating approach from the Board of Directors and senior management, ensured that the Club was able to deliver a profit of £376,043 during the year under review (2021).

Source: Adapted from Plymouth Argyle Football Club Limited Annual Reports 2021

17.6.1 The Income Statement: A Measurement of Financial Performance

One of the first things to note about the income statement is that it is referred to by a variety of terms. Although its new name is the *income statement*, it was previously known as the *profit and loss account* or, in the not-for-profit sector, the *income and expenditure account*.

The income statement indicates the historical financial performance, or profitability, of an organisation. Having already established that most organisations exist to make a profit, or at least break even, the income statement provides some of the most important financial information. Put simply, the measurement of profit first requires the organisation to calculate the revenue generated. Subsequently, the organisation's expenses are added together before this total expenditure is deducted from the revenue to establish whether a profit or a loss has been made (Wilson, 2011).

Revenue, income, or turnover as it is alternatively known, will typically be divided into both operating and non-operating items, i.e. what revenue the organisation has generated from all the day-to-day activities (operating revenues) and what revenue has been generated by exceptional items, funds or grants, etc. (non-operating revenues). In general, revenues in the sport and leisure sector have expanded dramatically over the last few years, but for the average not-for-profit sports club, revenue relies squarely on membership fees, gate receipts, fundraising activities, sponsors, and hospitality.

While revenues are relatively simple to break down, expenses should be treated more prudently. Unfortunately, the IAS allows two methods for the presentation of expenses: by function or by nature. Essentially this means that organisations can choose

PLYMOUTH ARGYLE FOOTBALL CLUB LIMITED
STATEMENT OF COMPREHENSIVE INCOME FOR THE YEAR ENDED 30 JUNE 2021

	Note	2021 £	2020 £
Turnover	4	**5,673,566**	6,968,148
Cost of sales		**(6,418,292)**	(6,840,142)
GROSS PROFIT/(LOSS)		**(744,726)**	128,006
Administrative expenses		**(3,021,640)**	(2,418,235)
Other operating income	5	**4,096,818**	1,633,959
OPERATING PROFIT/(LOSS)	6	**330,452**	(656,320)
Interest payable and similar expenses	10	**–**	(24,434)
PROFIT/(LOSS) BEFORE TAX		**330,452**	(680,754)
Tax on profit/(loss)	11	**45,582**	6,678
PROFIT/(LOSS) FOR THE FINANCIAL YEAR		**376,034**	(674,076)

Figure 17.1 Plymouth Argyle Football Club income statement 2021.

the method which most appropriately represents the elements of the organisation's performance. However, to ensure that one organisation can be confidently compared to another, the standard explicitly states that information on the nature of the expense, including depreciation and staff costs, should be disclosed. To illustrate these points it is worth examining the income statement for Plymouth Argyle Football Club Limited in Figure 17.1.

Figure 17.1 illustrates the usual 'by function' format as outlined by the IAS. The key components of turnover (i.e. turnover from trading), gross profit (i.e. profit before any expenses have been calculated), the profit/(loss) from operations and the profit/(loss) for the year are emboldened for ease of reading. The statement itself details that the profit before interest and tax was modest at £376,000 (first column, halfway down). The Club themselves also state some caution in this figure and the wider impact of the pandemic. The financial risk of divisional sporting performance and their reliance on their owner to fund the Club remains a real threat. This is where football clubs are unusual businesses. Most don't operate to make a profit; it is more about being 'comfortable' with the loss you are making. It must also be said that many sport organisations (including charities and amateur associations and even some National Governing Bodies!) operate in a similar way. Sport might be big business, but that doesn't always mean big profits! Further information will be available in the notes to the accounts should we wish to see further explanation of the data for Plymouth Argyle. For example, upon further analysis of the income statement we can see that the Club were boosted by a grant from the English Premier League (the top tier in English football) and by insurance claims receivable that cover business interruption and lost revenue due to the pandemic. This is a really important point in relation to financial sustainability, as Plymouth was one of a few organisations that took out insurance policies against this kind of event. To that end, whilst the cost of insurance was an expense in the first instance, it meant that the Club could recoup some of the lost revenue through the insurance claim. This, in turn, protected their revenue position somewhat during the pandemic.

17.6.1.1 Interpreting the Income Statement

When users examine a set of financial reports, they will often only examine some of the 'key' information. For example, in Figure 17.1 we might look at the turnover of nearly £5.7 million (down from nearly £7 million in 2020) and leave with the message that the company is not performing well. However, this would not tell the full story, as we know that the pandemic hit football clubs (and sport) hard and playing matches behind closed doors was always going to impact revenue. In many ways, the Club did well to generate any profit at all in 2021. What is important here is to not just take these figures in isolation. Managers need to consider all the moving financial parts to create a more holistic approach to financial performance measurement. While a thorough financial health appraisal is beyond the scope of this chapter, it is worth considering the other useful parts of the income statement before moving on to examine the balance sheet.

When we dig deeper and analyse Plymouth Argyle in more detail for the years covering 2020 and 2021, the figures make intuitive sense. In fact, it is part of the company make-up. To this end, one might accept that this business is always destined to run at a loss (or minimal profit), given its business operations and current structure. Remember, this way of operating is not unusual in sport and leisure.

This analysis discussed demonstrates how managers can become more rounded in their understanding and appreciation of finance. However, we are not finished there. We now need to consider the financial position of the organisation, which we can find in the balance sheet.

17.6.2 The Balance Sheet: A Measurement of Financial Position

The balance sheet provides details of an organisation's financial position by highlighting the value of assets owned by the organisation, the value of its liabilities (i.e. money owed to others), and the net value of the organisation or its capital, which is the difference between assets and liabilities. To underpin the idea of financial position, it is always worth remembering that Assets – Liabilities = Capital, or what you have, less what you owe, is what you have left.

By definition, the balance sheet should balance, hence the equation just outlined. Consequently, it is only ever accurate on the day on which it is produced, as the value of assets and liabilities will change constantly. For this reason the balance sheet is often referred to as being a snapshot or static picture of an organisation. Although this picture is reasonably accurate on the day on which it was taken, it will quickly become dated, and this presents a weakness in its worth to managers.

Normally the balance sheet will split its assets and liabilities up into Fixed and Current Assets and Current and Non-Current Liabilities. Before we examine a balance sheet, you need to familiarise yourself with the meaning of these key terms.

> ### Key Terms
>
> **Assets** – items or resources that have a value to the organisation and things that are used by the organisation and for the organisation. Normally assets are classified as fixed or current. The basic difference is that a fixed asset is something that the organisation intends to keep and use for some time, whereas a current asset is held for the organisation to convert into cash during trading. Some good examples here are the organisation's premises and motor vehicles, which are fixed assets, and stock and cash, which are current assets.
>
> **Liabilities** – amounts owed by the organisation to other people or organisations. Normally liabilities are classified as either payable within one year (current liabilities) or payable after one year (non-current liabilities). Some good examples here are bank overdrafts and supplier accounts, which are current liabilities, and bank loans, which tend to be non-current liabilities.

It is usual for a balance sheet to include a set of notes to the accounts, much like those on the income statement. The key issues that need to be considered are the values of the organisation's total assets, total liabilities, and capital. To illustrate these points, Figure 17.2 presents the balance sheet for Plymouth Argyle Football Club Limited.

17.6.2.1 Interpreting the Balance Sheet

The balance sheet for Plymouth Argyle indicates that the organisation has £15.5 million worth of equity denoted by the figure at the very bottom of the balance sheet. This can be used to determine the overall value of the business, and Plymouth's revenue figure of £5–7 million in the last two years shows a healthy equity position.

Additionally, we can use the balance sheet to establish how in control of itself the organisation is or whether creditors really control things. Figure 17.2 shows that Plymouth Argyle has current liabilities of just under £4 million and long-term liabilities of around £210,000. Again, on first glance, this appears positive against the revenue and equity position of the club.

We also need to consider the assets of the Club, though, and the balance sheet allows us to do that. This is important should any creditors (liabilities) ask for their money back, as the Club will need assets to cover it. Here, again, Plymouth appear in a good place financially. They have £7.6 million worth of current assets to cover £4 million of current liabilities (back to the Accounting Equation!). Additionally, around £6.7 million of these current assets is cash, so Plymouth would be able to get their hands on cash quickly if they need to pay some bills.

Additionally, the Club has over £12 million of fixed assets (this will be the stadium, training ground, and any land that the Club owns). Overall, when applying the Accounting Equation and subtracting liabilities from assets, this leaves us with the net asset (equity) position of £15.5 million. Typically, professional sport and leisure organisations will run things very tight so that they can just about cover any liabilities that are outstanding. In the case of Plymouth Argyle, the balance sheet position is positive in 2021 despite the challenges faced by the COVID-19 pandemic.

PLYMOUTH ARGYLE FOOTBALL CLUB LIMITED REGISTERED NUMBER:07796376
STATEMENT OF FINANCIAL POSTION AS AT 30 JUNE 2021

	Note	2021 £	2020 £
Fixed assets			
Intangible assets	12	328,885	603,216
Tangible assets	13	11,737,559	12,084,190
		12,066,444	12,687,406
Current assets			
Stocks	14	216,014	354,757
Debtors: amounts falling due within one year	15	654,110	910,992
Cash at bank and in hand		6,752,103	3,729,288
		7,622,227	4,995,037
Creditors: amounts falling due within one year	16	(3,970,895)	(5,865,049)
Net current assets (liabilities)		3,651,332	(870,012)
Total assets less current liabilities		15,717,776	11,817,394
Creditors: amounts falling due alter more than one year	17	(209,286)	(184,938)
Net assets		15,508,490	11,632,456
Capital and reserves			
Called up share capital	20	21,219,301	17,719,301
Share premium account	21	1,030,409	1,030,409
Profit and loss account	21	(6,741,220)	(7,117,254)
		15,508,490	11,632,456

Figure 17.2 Plymouth Argyle Football Club limited balance sheet 2021.

17.6.3 The Cash Flow Statement

One of the simplest ways to monitor financial performance is to ensure that an organisation remains solvent (e.g. does it have enough cash to pay its bills). If for any reason the demands of creditors could not be met, the assets of an organisation would be sold with the aim of meeting those outstanding debts. Monitoring the cash position of a company is traditionally done through budgets and cash flow statements. Without cash an organisation cannot continue to trade, regardless of its profit. Although the income statement helps us to establish an organisation's financial performance, it does not give us any idea about any problems that it may have with the flow of cash. This can be important for creditors to an organisation, as they will want to see that the organisation has sufficient cash to pay its bills on time. It is also important to managers, so that they know what cash they have available to purchase materials or to provide their services.

Cash flow statements, therefore, aim to illustrate all movements of cash under three main headings: operating activities, investing activities, and financing activities. The purpose of this is to obtain a picture of the flow of cash in and out of an organisation. The cash flow statement for Plymouth Argyle Football Club Limited is illustrated in Figure 17.3. Such transactions listed in the cash flow statement are there to represent the following: day-to-day spending (operating activities), including things like wages and salaries (cash out) or membership income (cash in); the purchase (cash out) and sale (cash in) of assets (investing activity); and the procurement of capital and borrowing of funds (financing activities), including activities such as loans (cash in) and repayment of loans (cash out).

The cash flow for Plymouth Argyle in 2021 shows closing cash at £6.7 million, up from £3.7 million in 2021. Upon further inspection, we can see that a large part of the difference is due to a new issue of ordinary shares totalling £3.5 million. This figure is linked back to the overall strategic report of the company outlined at the beginning of this case study. Over the course of the year the owner has injected £3.5 million into the club to provide security against a worst-case outcome. This was initially delivered in the form of a loan, and very shortly afterwards converted into share equity. The result is that the club has cash reserves greater than those held in previous years, which explains the rise in cash in 2021. However, the owner also stated that this will be his final cash injection into the club meaning that they will have to manage their cash (and equity) position carefully in the years to come.

> **Discussion Question**
>
> Is profit the same as cash? Which is a better measure to outline financial performance and business risk?

17.7 The Value of Management Accounts

At the very beginning of this chapter you were introduced to the two main types of accounting information: historical (financial) accounts, which include the three financial statements; and management accounts, which provide more forward-looking information. It is, however, important that the two types are recognised as two sides of the same coin and effective managers will be able to use both types in harmony.

Management accounting involves managers being forward looking and proactive, as the information that is generated can be used for planning, decision-making, and control

PLYMOUTH ARGYLE FOOTBALL CLUB LIMITED
STATEMENT OF CASH FLOWS FOR THE YEAR ENDED 30 JUNE 2021

	2021	2020
Cash flows from operating activities	£	£
Profit/(loss) for the financial year	376,034	(674,076)
Adjustments for:		
Amortisation of intangible assets	484,331	444,663
Depreciation of tangible assets	712,582	301,179
Interest paid	–	24,434
Taxation charge	(45,582)	(6,678)
Decrease in stocks	138,743	41,298
Decrease in debtors	266,573	116,394
Increase/(decrease) in creditors	1,665,483	(1,345,708)
Net cash generated from operating activities	3,598,164	(1,098,494)
Cash flows from investing activities		
Purchase of intangible fixed assets	(210,000)	(90,000)
Purchase of tangible fixed assets	(397,651)	(5,065,617)
Net cash from investing activities	(607,651)	(5,155,617)
Cash flows from financing activities		
Issue of ordinary shares	3,500,000	1,500,000
Other new loans	–	4,309,800
Repayment of other loans	(3,467,698)	–
Interest paid	–	(24,434)
Net cash used in financing activities	32,302	5,785,366
Net increase/(decrease) in cash and cash equivalents	3,022,815	(468,745)
Cash and cash equivalents at beginning of year	3,729,288	4,198,033
Cash and cash equivalents at the end of year	6,752,103	3,729,288
Cash and cash equivalents at the end of year comprise:		
Cash at bank and in hand	6,752,103	3,729,288
	6,752,103	3,729,288

Figure 17.3 Plymouth Argyle Football Club limited cash flow statement 2021.

purposes. The information will also be generated and presented in a way that suits the needs of the organisation that it is prepared for, rather than as financial accounts, where the information provided must satisfy the needs of numerous users and is presented in a standard form. Finally, it is important to understand that management accounting information is principally concerned with the efficient and effective use of resources. So, it is vital that to make meaningful decisions, based on effective plans, as a manager you will need to use management accounting information.

While the breadth of management accounting information is beyond the scope of this chapter, we will consider one of its principal functions – budgeting – which provides managers with the information required to plan, make effective decisions, and control the performance of the organisation.

17.8 Planning and Budgeting

To support the planning, decision-making, and control process, it is essential for managers to estimate the costs and expenses involved in implementing plans. They also need to ensure that a range of additional resources are available to support both strategic and operational planning. Understanding and applying conventional budgeting techniques can be the first step in managing finance effectively in an organisation. The purpose of introducing planning and budgeting is quite simple. Every organisation that has designs on being successful, whatever its organisational goals, will require some sort of plan so that managers and employees work towards the same outcome.

In sport and leisure these outcomes can be quite different. In the private sector, health and fitness centres will want to make as much profit from their members as they can, whilst simultaneously providing a high-quality service. In the public sector, local authorities will want to provide sport and leisure services that meet the needs of their communities in a cost-effective way. In the voluntary sector, small sports clubs will want to generate sufficient revenue from their members to survive and maintain their facilities. Once these plans have been agreed, managers should monitor and control activities by comparing what happens in practice relative to what was planned to happen. This is the first link between financial and management accounts. If managers can control the annual costs of their organisation, then they can manage the organisation's cash flow and ultimately help control activities to generate profits or cover costs. Providing plans are controlled, any significant deviation can be addressed, as managers can take action to get the organisation back on course to achieve its objectives.

So, back to budgets. A budget is essentially a plan of action that is expressed in financial terms. Often budgets will be prepared in summary form, but they could quite easily be expressed with plenty of detail. Unlike the income statement, for example, the type of budget and the level of detail contained within it can vary a great deal between organisations, and as such they are not a statutory requirement. Ideally a budget should cover all activities of an organisation and should involve all its personnel in its preparation. A common misconception with the preparation of a budget is that it should be done by an accountant and not the full team. If this occurs, an organisation will not be seen as inclusive by its staff and budgets are less likely to be 'owned' by those responsible to achieving them. Ultimately, a budget should be realistic and ensure that goals and aspirations are met; it will facilitate other management functions such as planning, coordination, motivation, communication, and control.

Management budgets often require numerous iterations to develop as an organisation moves through a growth curve. At the most basic of levels, however, they will list the expected income and expenditure for a project, planned activity, or general business. If expenditure exceeds income, the budget will need to be re-examined and consideration given to a cheaper alternative, to reduce costs. Budgets are often imperfect in their construction and will require constant monitoring and refinement.

17.8.1 The Budgeting Process

Budgeting will play a central role in keeping an organisation's finances on track and should ensure that debts are paid as they fall due. The budgeting process will include costing, estimating income, and the allocation of financial resources so that the budget is realistic. Normally a budget will be based on the following information:

- The financial history of the organisation;
- The general economic climate;
- Income and expenditure that is reasonably expected to be generated with the resources available; and
- Data from competitors.

In advance of the trading year, good managers will spend time developing their budget, using all the information outlined here, and comparing it to the general organisational objectives. Budgeting effectively forces managers to think ahead and to implement any corrective action required or explain any variance from the original projected costs. The budget should cover a defined period, and a significant part of the actual budget can be used to provide information for the construction of the income statement. The two primary types of budgeting that will be explored during the remainder of this chapter are continuation budgeting and zero-based budgeting. An illustration of the budgeting process can be seen in Figure 17.4.

Organisational objectives are commonly monitored using performance measurement tools that are principally focused on financial budgeting and financial measurement. All three sectors of the sport and leisure industry can apply these measurement tools to enhance their operational effectiveness and ultimately their financial health.

17.8.2 Budgetary Control

In business the meaning of control is quite straightforward: Is what happens to an organisation supposed to happen? Providing that you agree and understand that a budget is simply an organisation's objectives expressed in financial terms, we can take this simple definition forward and you can begin to exercise more control over day-to-day operations. For any plan to be achieved, it must be both monitored and controlled to ensure that the organisation is on target to achieve its goals. If it is not on the right course, corrective action can be taken. If the implementation of the budget is not controlled, it is likely that the organisation will not meet its objectives. By providing a mechanism for translating an organisation's strategic plan into realistic financial objectives, staff in the organisation can see where they and the organisation are going. However, to control the budgets, managers must allocate responsibility for monitoring actual costs and revenues to ensure that any problems are identified in a timely manner.

17.8.3 Continuation Budgets

In the sport and leisure industry the most frequently used method of budgeting is continuation budgeting, especially for voluntary sector clubs and public sector leisure services. Essentially,

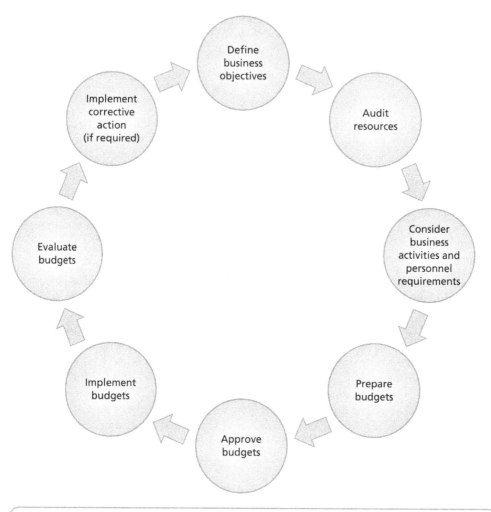

this type of budgeting refers to the notion that an organisation will not change its objectives significantly from one trading period to the next. Such an assumption does not encourage an organisation to grow, as it will not challenge organisational goals and aspirations. It is, however, a very easy method of budgeting to apply and is used frequently in sport and leisure. On the positive side, if the organisation is already working efficiently and making a profit or achieving other objectives, one could argue that continuation budgeting is a sensible and cost-effective way of controlling the financial side of an organisation.

Within the continuation budgeting framework there are two types of budgets: incremental and decremental. Incremental budgets will assume that the organisation will grow in line with inflation. Consequently, all a manager will have to do is obtain the budget from the previous year and multiply everything by the rate of inflation to generate the new period's figures. Decremental budgeting, on the other hand, assumes that there will be a standstill within the organisation or a reduction in funding, so the budget will either roll over as it is or will provide reductions in specific areas. A hypothetical example of an incremental, continuation budget is illustrated in Table 17.2.

Table 17.2 Hypothetical Income and Expenditure Budget for a Residential Sports Camp

Expenditure				
Description	Units	Costs	Original budget, 2020	Projected budget, 2021
Facility hire	1	£6,000	£6,000	£6,180
ACCOMMODATION AND CATERING				
Residential campers B&B	130	£60	£7,800	£8,034
Residential staff	10	£60	£600	£618
STAFFING				
Coaches' salaries	12	£250	£3,000	£3,090
Assistant coaches' salaries	8	£100	£800	£824
Physio	1	£500	£500	£515
CRB checks	25	£36	£900	£927
EQUIPMENT				
Physio equipment			£200	£206
Radio hire			£300	£309
Van hire			£500	£515
MEDIA EQUIPMENT				
Media equipment			£150	£155
MARKETING AND PROMOTION/PRINTING				
Merchandise	100	£7	£700	£721
Promotional material	1	£1,058	£1,058	£1,090
Certificates design and printing	1	£1,000	£1,000	£1,030
Trophies			£-	£-
Prizes	1	£400	£400	£412
Staff uniforms	25	£30	£750	£773
Contingency 5%	1	£4,000	£4,000	£4,119
Total expenditure			**£28,658**	**£29,518**

(Continued)

Table 17.2 (Continued)

Expenditure				
Description	*Units*	*Costs*	*Original budget, 2020*	*Projected budget, 2021*
Income				
Description	*Units*	*Fees*	*Total income*	
Residential campers	130	£295	£38,350	£39,501
Merchandise	100	£20	£2,000	£2,060
Total income			**£40,350**	**£41,561**
Surplus/deficit			**£11,692**	**£12,043**

> **Discussion Question**
>
> What are the benefits and drawbacks of continuation budgets?

17.8.4 Zero-Based Budgets

Zero-based budgeting (ZBB) was developed initially to address some of the criticisms levelled at traditional budgeting techniques such as continuation budgeting. Continuation budgets sometimes do not present a manager with a challenge and do not encourage growth. ZBB takes an altogether different stance by applying a cost/benefit approach to creating a budget for an organisation. Ostensibly, ZBB requires a manager to challenge every single item of expenditure based upon the benefits that it is likely to generate.

The typical way of applying this technique is to begin with a blank sheet of paper and start at zero – hence a zero-based approach! For example, the expenditure for an entire department commences at zero, and the activities that form part of that department's function are clearly evaluated to determine whether they bring an appropriate level of benefit and therefore whether they are necessary. Given that resources are finite for all organisations, this method of budgeting allows managers to prioritise expenditure according to those inputs which bring about the greatest benefit. In sport and leisure, such budgeting techniques are more popular in the not-for-profit sector, as output is often intangible. ZBB can be applied easily when using these simple questions:

1 What is the purpose of this expenditure?
2 On what exactly will this expenditure be made?
3 What are the quantifiable benefits of this expenditure?
4 What are the alternatives to this proposed expenditure?
5 What would be the outcome of cutting this expenditure completely?

ZBB enables managers to identify and remove operations that are inefficient and can encourage the avoidance of wasteful expenditure by asking crucial questions. However, it can mean that the emphasis is on short-term returns instead of long-term benefits because the former are more easily measured. Furthermore, it presupposes that commitments for expenditure are made at the time of preparing the budget so, for example, expenditures that are not supported by the ZBB can be stopped. Moreover, cost/benefit analysis is often problematic, takes time, and requires the manager to have a detailed understanding of the organisation.

Discussion Question

What are the benefits and drawbacks of zero-based budgeting?

Table 17.3 Hypothetical Variance Analysis on Income and Expenditure Budget for a Residential Sports Camp

Description	Budget	Actual	Variance	Direction	Note
Facility Hire	£6,000	£6,200	£200	U	1
ACCOMMODATION AND CATERING					
Residential campers B&B	£7,800	£8,000	£200	U	2
Residential staff	£600	£600	£–	F	
STAFFING					
Coaches' salaries	£3,000	£3,000	£–	F	3
Assistant coaches' salaries	£800	£1,050	£250	U	
Physio	£500	£500	£–	F	
CRB checks	£900	£900	£–	F	
EQUIPMENT					
Physio equipment	£200	£200	£–	F	4
Radio hire	£300	£300	£–	F	
Van hire	£500	£500	£–	F	
MEDIA EQUIPMENT					
Media equipment	£150	£150	£–	F	5

(Continued)

Table 17.3 (Continued)

Description	Budget	Actual	Variance	Direction	Note
MARKETING AND PROMOTION/ PRINTING					
Merchandise	£700	£800	£100	U	6
Promotional material	£1,058	£1,058	£–	F	
Certificates design and printing	£1,000	£1,000	£–	F	
Trophies	£–			F	
Prizes	£400	£400	£–	F	
Staff uniforms	£750	£750	£–	F	
	£–				
Contingency 5%	£4,000	£4,000	£–	F	
TOTAL EXPENDITURE	£28,658	£29,408	£750	U	7
INCOME					
Description	Total Income				
Residential campers	£38,350	£38,700	£350	F	8
Merchandise	£2,000	£2,000	£–	F	
TOTAL INCOME	£40,350	£40,700	£350	F	
SURPLUS	£11,692	£11,292	£400	U	9

17.8.5 Analysing Budgets

This chapter is about financial management, so having appraised the financial statements and outlined the key components of planning and budgeting, it is important that you understand how to analyse budgets. The ultimate purpose of budgeting (and management accounting more generally) is to assist managers in the planning, decision-making, and control of an organisation. To achieve this aim, it is necessary to have a framework which can provide periodic comparisons of actual performance with planned (or budgeted) performance. Table 17.3 illustrates in simple terms how this can be achieved. Essentially, here we are concerned with the variance between actual and planned performance and, providing you have produced your budget on a spreadsheet, this variance is easy to measure by deducting planned from actual performance. Once this is completed, it is possible to note the outcome – i.e. either favourable or unfavourable – and explain the reason behind the variance. Table 17.3 uses the income and expenditure budget from Table 17.2 and applies these concepts.

To: Camp Director
From: Management Accountant

Re: Actual v. Budgeted Notes for Residential

Note 1:   Facility Hire

Facility hire was budgeted as £6,000. However, due to the increase in camp numbers an additional space was needed at the facility to store the equipment required. This was initially priced at £500 but was later discounted, due to next year's booking, to £200. The increase in facility hire has been covered by the increase in camp numbers (see note 8).

Figure 17.5 A qualitative explanation of variance.

In the example there are five columns. The 'Budget' column refers to the approved budget for the financial period. The 'Actual' column provides details of the entries that have been made to the organisation's accounting system, which will be used to construct the financial statements and are often different from the budgeted figures. 'Variance' refers to the difference between the actual and budgeted performance as outlined earlier, while the 'Direction' column provides details as to whether the variance has a positive (favourable) or negative (unfavourable) effect on the financial performance. Finally, 'Note' is a cross-reference to a written explanation of a variance (see an example in Figure 17.5). The numbers in isolation do not necessarily tell the full story, so it is always worth providing a qualitative version of events.

Any member of staff reading the management accountant's report should be able to establish clearly why reported variances have occurred and should be able to cross-reference them against any other relevant information. In the example in Table 17.3, action may be required as the increase in expenditure is not covered by the increase in income, leaving £400 less surplus at the end of the camp, which may or may not be acceptable. Before you move on to this chapter conclusions, take note of the key management accounting terminology.

Key Terms

Budget – the business or overall plan of an organisation expressed in financial terms.
Cash budget – an analysis of how the cash available to an organisation is expected to change over a given period of time.
Continuation budget – budgets compiled based on no change in policies or priorities.
Variance – the difference between actual performance and planned performance.
Zero-based budgeting – a method of budgeting which starts with the priorities of an organisation and allocates resources to the priorities according to their rank order of importance.

Why is it important to compare budgets with actual performance, and how frequently should a manager do this?

17.9 Performance Analysis

The budgeting process enables managers to set targets, while the control process allows for performance to be monitored and any necessary corrective action to be taken. The final step, however, within the management accounting framework for this chapter is a performance analysis. This will assist managers in making a successful transition into the next financial period, by enhancing their skills and moving the organisation forward.

In any management function it is essential that some sort of evaluation is considered. Without it, an organisation cannot review its performance and set budgets for the following year, while the users of financial information are not provided with sufficient detail to answer their information needs. Sport and leisure organisations in the private commercial sector will want to see that more profit has been made from one period to the next; public sector organisations will want to see active communities; and voluntary and not-for-profit organisations will want to provide services to their members in a solvent manner.

Providing an analysis of the main financial statements and an organisation's budget will help managers prove their worth to an employer, as demonstrating effective financial management skills will help an organisation move forward. Arguably it might be more important to demonstrate these skills if an organisation is performing badly, as it will need to steer its way out of trouble. Although this chapter has only provided a framework for appraising the financial health of an organisation, it assumes a series of skills that the average sport or leisure manager does not yet possess, especially in the public and not-for-profit sectors.

17.10 Conclusions

The purpose of this chapter is to demonstrate the importance of financial management within a sport and leisure context. While any detailed analysis is beyond the scope of this chapter, provision is made to equip managers with the necessary skills to communicate, in basic terms, the financial health of an organisation. The cyclical process of planning, decision-making, and control, coupled with the analytical techniques that can be applied to both financial and management accounting information, should enhance the toolbox of skills that any sport or leisure manager possesses. The importance of this process should not be underestimated in both for-profit and not-for-profit organisations, regardless of their size or stature.

The main objective of all organisations should be to operate within their own resources so that they can continue trading. The tools identified in this chapter, including budgeting, should help this process. Furthermore, using financial and management accounting information as two sides of the same coin – which is rarely acknowledged – will help provide managers with the discipline and confidence to plan, make effective decisions, and exercise financial control.

The income statement, balance sheet, and cash flow statement equip managers with information that can determine the financial performance and position of an organisation and demonstrate the difference between profit and the typically scarce resource of cash. The statements also illustrate how an organisation is structured in terms of its assets and liabilities, so that effective investment, borrowing, and service decisions can be made. In addition, it can be determined whether business should be conducted with certain organisations and whether you or your competitors can pay debts as they fall due.

It is not possible within one single chapter to cover all the financial health ratios and budgetary techniques. However, you should have grasped the idea that financial management is important enough to be considered an integral part of any organisation. Other skills are required to come up with a marketing campaign or a training and development plan, but only those who understand finance can establish whether they are financially viable, worthwhile, or even necessary in the first place. The best way to ensure that you develop the full range of financial management skills is to achieve a thorough understanding of the theoretical concepts involved and some tangible experience of finance in practice.

Practical Tasks

1   Identify the key figures that are discussed for Arena Racing Company in the income statement, balance sheet, and cash flow statement. Once you are happy that you can understand where these figures can be found, use the income statement, balance sheet, and cash flow statement for a sport and leisure organisation of your choice to answer the following questions:

(a) What is the organisation's financial performance?
(b) What is the organisation's financial position?

2   Construct a budget for yourself for a typical calendar month. You could use an existing bank statement to provide you with the necessary information. Provide details of income and expenditure, and calculate your financial performance during the month. Once you have produced this budget, try to reconstruct it using the principles of zero-based budgeting. Consider all streams of income and expenditure, and establish whether you are financially viable. Remember to ask yourself all the questions associated with this method of budgeting. For example, is a gym membership required? What is the cost of not paying for car insurance?

Structured Guide to Further Reading

For guidance on recording and reporting financial information and for more detail on performing a financial health analysis:
Wilson, R. (2011). *Managing Sport Finance*. Routledge, London.

For more information on general sport funding especially for not-for-profit organisations:
Stewart, B. (2007). *Sport Funding and Finance*. Butterworth Heinemann, London.

Useful Websites

For free annual reports from organisations in the sport and leisure industry:
Companies House Government Website www.gov.uk/get-information-about-a-company

References

Sports Global Market Report. (2021). *COVID-19 Impact and Recovery to 2030*. The Business Research Company, London.

Wilson, R., Plumley, D., & Mosley, P. (2019). Bury FC's demise reminds us football isn't just about football—It's a whole culture. Retrieved from www.prospectmagazine.co.uk/politics/bury-fc-news-stadium-debt-football-elegy

Chapter 18

Enterprise and Entrepreneurship in Sport and Leisure

In This Chapter

- What are enterprise and entrepreneurship?
- How can enterprising individuals be identified?
- How can the current business position be identified?
- What strategies are needed to stimulate innovation and change?
- What are the key elements of a business plan?
- How can risk be reduced?

DOI: 10.4324/9780367823610-18

Summary

Enterprise involves creating new business development, whilst it is achieved by entrepreneurial skills. Enterprise and entrepreneurship involve much of what is termed 'best practice' in management. They are to be found in all sectors of the economy and are not confined to individual, new ventures in the commercial sector. Enterprise also occurs in existing organisations, and in the non-profit sectors too – termed *social enterprise*. Innovation and change are at the heart of enterprise.

To analyse enterprise and entrepreneurship requires many of the skills and techniques introduced in previous chapters. The principal new material in this chapter relates to what qualities an entrepreneur demonstrates, commercial and governmental sources of finance for enterprise, business and financial planning, and managing risk. But this chapter is also a synthesis of previously covered material and as such it makes repeated cross-references to previous chapters. The core of this chapter is organised according to three stages of business development: assessing the current position; deciding the strategies for change; and then planning how to achieve the desired change.

18.1 Introduction

Enterprise encapsulates the essence of good organisational leadership and decision-making. It is traditionally discussed in the context of new ventures and commercial businesses, but it is more general than that, embracing innovations in existing sport and leisure organisations and in the public and voluntary sectors. It is not confined to the successes of a few self-made, inspirational individuals such as Richard Branson (Virgin) or Steve Jobs (Apple), but it is also achieved by countless managers who seek to innovate and improve their organisations' activities. Analysing the principal ingredients of successful entrepreneurship serves as a summary of best practices in management which are referred to elsewhere, particularly Part 4. In enterprise, the name of the game is innovation, so the best practices reviewed in this chapter necessarily service change in organisations.

This chapter begins by summarising the characteristics of entrepreneurs, the key individuals driving new developments. It then examines three stages of enterprise:

1   Positioning of a business – i.e. where it is now;
2   Strategies for the business – i.e. where you want it to go;
3   Business planning – how it will get to where you want it to go.

(Barrow *et al.*, 2006)

The principles and techniques reviewed are relevant to new independent ventures, and strategies and business planning are essential elements in the start-up phase in the life cycle of a business. However, this chapter adopts the more general and common concept of enterprise as innovation within existing organisations, as well as the more specific development of entirely new organisations.

Some definitions are necessary at the outset. Put at their simplest, **enterprise** is the development of a new initiative/venture/project, whilst **entrepreneurship** is a set of skills and techniques which facilitate enterprise. This chapter concentrates more on entrepreneurship. Two other concepts are important to introduce. First, **intrapreneurship** is a term used to describe corporate entrepreneurship, i.e. a new initiative within an existing organisation, rather than a new independent venture. Much enterprise in sport and leisure is created by intrapreneurship, the creation of a new service in an existing organisation, e.g. the introduction of personal trainers in fitness centres. **Social entrepreneurship** represents entrepreneurship in the voluntary and public sectors, as opposed to the traditional commercial sector entrepreneur. **Social enterprises** are businesses operating for a social purpose, often with charitable status – an example, the Trinity Sailing Trust, is featured in Case Study 18.2. The Office of the Third Sector in the UK estimates that there are around 100,000 social enterprises in the UK, contributing £60 billion to UK output.

Entrepreneurs are risk-takers, because for new ventures they typically must raise substantial funds to realise their dream. However, whereas many small firms are the realisation of enterprise by entrepreneurs, not all small firms demonstrate entrepreneurship. In hospitality, for example, there are many bed and breakfast establishments and cafés which are small, steady-state businesses which do not demonstrate innovation or change. These are not examples of entrepreneurship, although they might have been when they were first set up.

The innovations which are the subjects of entrepreneurship are of various types (Wickham, 2006), all of which exploit an opportunity to do something differently and better. They include:

- New products, services, and brands;
- New production or service delivery techniques;
- New distribution methods;
- New ways of informing customers;
- New ways of managing relationships within an organisation.

One of the most significant demonstrations of new services in the travel and tourism market in recent decades is budget airlines. Southwest Airlines in Texas introduced the simple but devastatingly effective innovation of cutting costs to reduce prices for customers. Other companies worldwide have successfully followed this business model, including Ryan Air, Easy Jet, and Jet 2. Such airlines have reduced costs by such means as using smaller airports and eliminating travel agents, tickets, and free in-flight meals.

Another compelling example of enterprise is the case study of Brawn GP (Case Study 18.1), a combination of new product and brand, together with new finance, brought about by extreme circumstance. It demonstrates that entrepreneurship can be inspirational, especially when it emerges from such a negative stimulus.

18.2 Enterprising Individuals

Enterprise is a function of entrepreneurship, and individuals are at the heart of entrepreneurship. Hisrich *et al.* (2005) identify three sets of skills required in entrepreneurs – technical (including communication and technology), business management (including planning, marketing, and finance), and personal (including risk-taking, innovation, and leadership). Wickham (2006) and Kuratko and Hodgetts (2007) concentrate on the personal attributes of entrepreneurs (see Table 18.1). It's easy to get the impression from such a list that entrepreneurs are extraordinary individuals, and in many ways they are. However, whilst many

Table 18.1 **Attributes of Entrepreneurs**

Attributes	Notes
Hardworking	Entrepreneurs typically (but not always) work long hours.
Self-starting, proactive	They do not wait for instructions but are leaders in identifying and progressing tasks, taking personal responsibility for progress.
Has vision and sets personal goals	They are visionary, with a strategic orientation – just as objectives are important for organisations, so clear and demanding goals are important to entrepreneurs, against which to measure progress.
Resilient, determined	Failures are part of the process of learning, and a good entrepreneur is not afraid to fail and is willing to learn from mistakes.
Efficacy	Entrepreneurs get things done – they have a strong desire to compete and succeed.
Confident, positive, and risk-taking	Entrepreneurs are typically confident, not only of themselves but also of their proposed innovations. They are therefore used to risk-taking and managing risk.
Realistic	Entrepreneurs seek practical solutions and do not gamble but take calculated risks.
Receptive to new ideas	Confidence does not mean refusal to learn from others – entrepreneurs should recognise their limitations and seek appropriate advice.
Assertive and motivational	These are essentially communications attributes – being able to carry important others with the idea – which translate into leadership skills.
Information seeking	An enquiring mind is important to ensure that developments are as well informed as possible.
Eager to learn, problem solving	Entrepreneurs are aware of potential improvements, and a learning attitude helps to achieve them. Even business failures are experiences from which to learn and improve with the next venture.
Resourceful, versatile	Entrepreneurs adapt to different circumstances and respond positively and practically to change.
Attuned to opportunity	This means both seeking appropriate opportunities and seizing them.
Receptive to change	Change is the very nature of entrepreneurship, and a willingness to embrace and promote change is essential.

Attributes	Notes
Committed to others	A recognition that you cannot do it all yourself but will necessarily rely on good people around you.
Comfortable with power	Power can, of course, corrupt, but it is also a part of the outcomes for a successful entrepreneur. Power is one of the facilitators for continued development.

Sources: Adapted from Wickham (2006), Kuratko and Hodgetts (2007).

people work hard, seek information, are problem solving, receptive to change, and committed to others, entrepreneurs add to these qualities some less common attributes, such as being risk-taking, self-starting, and opportunistic, having vision, and not being afraid to fail.

CASE STUDY 18.1

Brawn GP

With three weeks to go until the beginning of the 2009 Formula One season, Honda pulled out of the sport. In a classic twist on the old saying 'Necessity is the mother of invention', the team principal, Ross Brawn, organised a buy-out of the team and rebranded it as Brawn GP. Thus began one of the most successful examples of enterprise in recent sport history.

Whilst the financing of the deal was not disclosed, reports suggested that Honda and Bernie Ecclestone (the sport's commercial rights holder) contributed to it – the former substantially less than their budget for the 2008 season. In addition, Bridgestone and Ray-Ban remained as sponsors, and they were joined in the spring of 2009 by sponsorship from Virgin, MIG Investments, and Henri Lloyd. Despite this essential funding from sponsorship, one of the innovations that Brawn had to make was to radically cut costs, including significant cuts to the pay of the two principal drivers, Jenson Button and Rubens Barrichello, as well as not running a spare car and reducing the support team at GP races to 55, compared with 100 the previous season.

Brawn also instigated two important technical changes, among others. First, he changed the engines to Mercedes-Benz and, second, his were two of the few cars utilising KERS, a system of providing a periodic boost to the engine's power through kinetic energy recovery. Although there is a perennial argument about how important the car and the driver are to winning, there is little argument that the car must be right. Brawn GP's technical achievements in such a short time were outstanding.

The immediate and most publicised successes of this enterprising rejuvenation of a defunct racing team were that in 2009 Brawn GP won the World Constructors' Championship, and Jenson Button won the World Drivers' Championship. Not so well publicised, but equally important for the business future of the company, was that at the end of 2009 Brawn GP was bought out by Daimler and an investment fund, Aabar, which together took a 75.1% stake. The new name for the company is Mercedes Grand Prix – the first time Mercedes has had a team in the sport since 1955. Ross Brawn and his chief executive Nick Fry retained a 24.9% stake in the company, so they have achieved significant financial rewards for the risks taken at the beginning of 2009.

> Following this acquisition, Mercedes has become one of the most successful teams in Formula One history, achieving consecutive Drivers' and Constructors' Championships from 2014 to 2020 with Lewis Hamilton taking six of those seven titles as the team's main driver.

A powerful personal vision is one of the defining characteristics of entrepreneurs; it is a management skill which is particularly relevant to the identification of where the business needs to go and how to get there. A personal vision can be a driving force for an entrepreneur, just as a vision statement can be important as a signpost for an organisation. Vision helps to define project objectives and is important for both the leadership of a development and the motivation of the team involved. Creativity is an important element of vision, and entrepreneurs are often creative not only about their core idea but also about the ways to achieve it, including financing.

Discussion Question

Are Wickham's attributes of entrepreneurs things that they are born with, or can they be developed, e.g. through education and training?

There is a debate in the literature on entrepreneurship about whether entrepreneurial attributes are things entrepreneurs are born with or things that are the product of, or developed by, social processes, including education. This is the same 'nature v. nurture' or 'genetics v. environment' debate which occurs in several fields. However, it is very difficult to measure the extent of such attributes as those in Table 18.1, let alone identify the effect of possible causal factors on them; so the debate is likely to continue. As well as personal attributes, Morrison *et al.* (1999) summarise the environmental or social influences on entrepreneurship. These include the availability of appropriate role models, career experience, deprived social upbringing, family background and position, the inheritance of entrepreneurial tradition, educational attainment, negative or positive peer influence, social marginality, and discomfort with large bureaucratic organisations. Some of these are also difficult to measure and scientifically associate with entrepreneurial behaviour. Like many aspects of the 'nature v. nurture' debate, it is likely that both sets of major influences, genetic and environmental, are important in determining an individual entrepreneur's behaviour.

Entrepreneurship is more than having a good idea; it requires sound planning and risk-taking to see the idea through. Coming up with the idea is the essence of creativity; making the idea work is termed 'innovation'. As Jennings (2009) suggests, creativity is a fundamental driving force for individual entrepreneurship, but in combination with logical analysis. He gives the McDonald's concept, developed by Ray Kroc, as a good example of this combination – a simple and flexible idea at the heart of a global franchising system.

Kuratko and Hodgetts (2007) and Jennings (2009) distinguish left-brain activity, which promotes rational, linear, logical analysis, from right-brain activity, which stimulates greater challenge to custom and routine, through intuition and imagination, and looks for better ways of doing things. Creative thinking is more the domain of right-brain activity, but logical analysis is the product of left-brain activity and is needed to develop creativity into a sustainable enterprise, i.e. innovation. A formal version of creative thinking, typically in a group setting, is 'brainstorming', whereby random ideas, not limited by any boundaries, are invited in relation to a particular problem or issue.

Entrepreneurs also have to cope with what Kuratko and Hodgetts (2007) call the 'dark side' of entrepreneurship. This entails coping not just with a variety of risks, to finances, family, career, and their own confidence, but also with the negatives associated with stress. Stress can be summarised as the gap between expectations and outcomes, and entrepreneurs are particularly exposed to stress because they can be prone to what is termed 'role overload', i.e. taking on too much, with multiple tasks and the excessive responsibility often associated with 'control freaks'.

Where do enterprising ideas come from? Bragg and Bragg (2005) suggest that nearly half of new business ideas are stimulated by the existing work environment; just over one-quarter of ideas come from secondary sources, such as trade journals or venture capital firms; 15% of ideas come from the desire to improve an existing technology, product, or service; whilst 10% of ideas are stimulated by a vision of an opportunity. Hisrich et al. (2005) emphasise the importance of existing or potential customers as sources for new ideas. They can be consulted formally, through such methods as focus groups and brainstorming, for example, or informally through listening to their complaints and needs.

So creativity, innovation, and entrepreneurship are important to, but not just the province of, individuals starting up new enterprises. Individuals working in an existing organisation are not handicapped in their creativity, because their working environment and particularly existing customers can be a strong motivator for new ideas. What is needed, though, is that the individual can identify associated business opportunities and drive the idea through the start-up phase of business development. It is also important that the organisation where the intrapreneur works facilitates the creation of new ideas and is receptive to evaluating, testing, and developing these ideas.

Discussion Question

For a sport and leisure organisation that you know well (e.g. a club you belong to or a professional team that you support) think of an enterprising idea for changing what it does or how it does it. This could concern, for example, the service or product it provides or the markets that it distributes to.

18.3 Evaluating the Current Business Position

Unless the enterprise is a completely new venture, an essential first stage in promoting the development of an innovation is to understand the current business position of an organisation. This evaluation will necessarily stimulate ideas for improvement. It involves many issues covered in previous chapters, including:

- Mission and core objectives;
- SWOT and PEST;
- Finances;
- People, structures, and systems.

A key concept in evaluating the current business position is organisational or strategic 'fit', i.e. the extent to which the organisation's activities fit the business environment. Morrison *et al.* (1999) suggest that the required 'fit' is three ways – between the individual entrepreneur or intrapreneur, the organisation, and the environment. Strategic fit is particularly important because the business environment can change so rapidly – obvious examples being the growth of e-commerce, or legislation such as a smoking ban in public places.

Benchmarking is also important to identify an organisation's position relative to best practice (see Chapter 16). Such benchmarking can involve comparative data, or comparisons of structures and processes. Barrow *et al.* (2006) identify seven best-practice characteristics of organisations against which an organisation should compare itself:

1. **Outward looking** – monitoring the organisation's understanding of customers, competitors, market, technology, and relevant legislation;
2. **Vision** – clarity of purpose which is shared by everyone in the organisation;
3. **Culture** – pride and identification of employees with the organisation;
4. **Empowerment** – sense of ownership of problems within the organisation; staff proactive in taking actions;
5. **Flexible structures** – i.e. adapting to requirements; typically smaller and flatter structures, with possible outsourcing of certain tasks;
6. **Teamwork** – creating a corporate identity by rotating job roles, cross-department meetings, etc. to enhance an understanding of the collective function;
7. **Reward and recognition** – identifying what matters in performance and giving credit for it.

Discussion Question

Is it always necessary to compare oneself with the best to come up with ideas for changes in an organisation, or are examples of failure just as inspiring of creativity?

18.4 Strategies for Improving the Business

Once it is clearly established what shape the current organisation is in and what the current business position is in relation to its external environment, there is a secure basis for plotting the future direction of the organisation and specific new enterprises within it. This requires several strategic decisions, particularly about marketing and financing. Similarly, for new enterprises, once a creative entrepreneurial idea starts to take shape, a strategy puts the idea into a business framework.

Two marketing tools which will help have already been introduced in Chapter 14 – the Boston Matrix and the Ansoff Matrix. The former analyses the product portfolio of existing organisations and raises important implications for changing a business. To what extent is it possible, for example, to use the money generated by 'cash cows' (with high market share and low market growth) to invest in 'stars' (with high market growth as well as high market share)? How quickly is it possible to disinvest in 'dogs' (which have low market share and low market growth)? How much risk should be taken on by continued investment in 'question marks' (with low market share and high market growth)? These questions need active answers, otherwise inertia will hold back change and entrepreneurship because the resources devoted to 'cash cows' and 'dogs' will constrain the potential of 'stars' and 'question marks'.

The Ansoff Matrix is a useful tool for deciding in which forms growth and development are going to be attempted – again for an existing organisation. The options range from the low-risk market penetration (existing products to existing markets) to the high-risk diversification (new products to new markets). They are not alternatives, but a decision is required about the appropriate combination of products in the growth portfolio of an organisation. Many public sector sport organisations, for example, are led by short-term funding into high-growth activities, only to realise that when the funding finishes the enterprise is unsustainable. Key factors influencing the growth decision are rewards and risks. A high-risk growth strategy has potentially high returns, but it is risky! Lower-risk market penetration, on the other hand, typically offers lower prospects for growth, although it can provide reliable cash with which to invest in higher-risk ventures.

Strategic options appraisal helps to identify the best prospects for change and new enterprise in an organisation. It requires consideration of several factors, in addition to those highlighted by both the Boston and Ansoff Matrices. These factors include:

- Organisational objectives;
- Critical success factors (according to customers);
- Growth potential;
- Cash potential;
- Risk;
- Financing requirements.

Any options appraisal lends itself to quantitative analysis. For example, each option for development, such as expansion into a new market or development of a new service in existing markets, can be scored according to important factors such as those listed. The factors might even be weighted to reflect their importance to the strategic direction of an organisation, according to key stakeholders. The result will be a quantitative ranking of different options to help guide the strategic decisions of the organisation.

When considering the competitive strategy for entry into a market, attention needs to be given to the key elements of business success. According to Porter (2004) there are five competitive forces which combine to determine the success of commercial organisations, and indeed the ability of an industry to sustain commercial success, particularly by new organisations. These are as follows:

1 **The entry of new competitors** – conditioned by barriers to entry into markets, which include the existence of economies of scale required to start efficient production (including initial capital funding requirements); absolute cost advantages; the degree of brand loyalty within the market, possibly created by significant advertising expenditure; access to distribution channels; and legal barriers imposed by patents, licenses, or the government. In the restaurant business, for example, entry is relatively easy because there are low barriers to entry, including weak brand loyalty, and relatively small initial capital funding requirements.

2 **The threat of substitutes** – not just immediate substitutes. In sport and leisure generally there is a wide range of alternative ways for a consumer to spend their time and money. The relative prices of substitutes are important, as is the consumer's likelihood of buying substitutes (conditioned, for example, by the degree of brand loyalty). The fitness club industry is relatively competitive, for example, because of the range of alternative means of maintaining health and fitness, as well as low brand loyalty and considerable choice of clubs (in most urban areas in developed countries).

3 **The bargaining power of buyers** – retail or wholesale. Influences on this include brand loyalty, sensitivity to price changes, product differentiation (i.e. key differences in products),

and buyer concentration (the fewer there are, the more power they have). In most sport and leisure industries, for example, the buyers are individual people or small groups, so their bargaining power is weak. Furthermore, they are typically but not always relatively insensitive to price changes. Such factors give greater scope for success in the business.

4   **The bargaining power of suppliers** – influences on this include important differences in inputs such as labour and materials, and the ability to substitute inputs; supplier concentration (the fewer suppliers there are, the more power they have); and the possibility of taking over suppliers (i.e. backward integration). An example of the bargaining power of suppliers is trade unions, particularly in the public sector. The success of commercial contract companies and trusts in the business of managing public sports and leisure facilities in the UK, for example, is partly because over time their labour contracts have not been so conditioned by national agreements with public sector trade unions.

5   **The intensity of competition between rival firms** – entering a highly competitive market will reduce profit margins and leave the enterprise open to the tactics of competitors, such as price discount wars, substantial competitive advertising, or even a takeover. Tourism and hospitality companies, for example, have historically shown a high intensity of competition between rival firms, leading to not only price wars and considerable takeover activity, but also a high rate of business failure, even for the largest of firms.

Morrison *et al.* (1999) identify several strategic options in terms of the organisational form with which to take an enterprise forward. As well as the conventional forms of an independent organisation, or a new section in an existing organisation, these include the following forms:

1   **Franchising** – particularly important in service industries where the customer has to come to the product. With franchising, the original concept is rolled out to a wider market by attracting the motivation and finance of other individual entrepreneurs, thereby achieving growth but spreading the risk. It is particularly prevalent in the fast-food business and relates closely to two of Porter's principles: It enables a company to reduce both barriers to entry and competition by attracting and assisting franchisees to enter the company rather than set up rival companies; and the scale of the operation increases the company's bargaining power with suppliers.

2   **Takeovers** – these provide opportunities for existing organisations to move into other businesses that are felt to be strategically compatible. This can reduce competition if the firm being taken over is in a similar business or reduce the bargaining power of suppliers if the firm being taken over is a supplier. Also, being taken over is a means by which successful entrepreneurs can capitalise on their success and finance other ventures.

3   **Buy-outs** – where a particular operation within an existing organisation splinters off as a new, independent enterprise. A clear example of this is commercial contract management companies which run public sport and leisure facilities in the UK. Many originated as discrete business units within local authorities, after compulsory competitive tendering was introduced in the late 1980s. The more entrepreneurial of these business units then bought the business out from the local authority, thus becoming commercial enterprises. This demonstrates weak barriers to entry because such organisations can develop a critical mass of expertise and experience before the buy-out.

4   **Strategic alliances and joint ventures** – a means of securing economies of scale and facilitating new developments while sharing the risks. Strategic alliances are quite common among airlines and hotel groups, because of obvious synergies in their operations and markets. The Oneworld Alliance, for example, is a global alliance between 13 airlines.

Whatever strategies for change are devised, Johnson *et al.* (2008) emphasise the need for evaluation of their appropriateness and timing. They identify three basic aspects of strategy evaluation:

1 **Suitability** – i.e. the extent to which strategy addresses key issues regarding positioning of the organisation/development;
2 **Feasibility** – i.e. whether or not the new development will work in practice and deliver the strategy; whether it has the right resources – human, financial, and operational;
3 **Acceptability** – i.e. whether the strategy will deliver the expected performance outcomes for key stakeholders, particularly funders, and possibly planners and relevant government agencies.

Discussion Question

If a Premier League football club from England had a strategic intention to increase its fan base in the USA, how would you assess the suitability, feasibility, and acceptability of this strategy?

18.4.1 Financing Commercial Enterprise

An essential factor in the development of enterprise is financing. For a commercial business, the two main options are internal and external financing. Internal financing, through profits and working capital in an existing organisation, or from savings for a new venture, is typically more limited but should nevertheless not be ignored. Increased profits, for example through greater cost control or the realisation of cash from 'cash cows', may contribute significantly to the financing of new enterprises. External financing takes two principal forms for commercial businesses: debt and equity. The ratio of debt to the net worth of the organisation (principally equity) is a key ratio – gearing – and a normal expectation of banks is that for small and medium-sized enterprises it should be 1:1 (Barrow *et al.*, 2006). A higher gearing, e.g. 2:1, gives a greater return on share capital for a given profit but exposes the enterprise to a higher risk of not meeting interest payments on the debt if profits fall. Appropriate gearing depends on the nature of risk for the business – with high business risk (e.g. with diversification) a high gearing is not wise, because whatever happens the interest on debt has to be paid.

Banks are generally the usual source of debt financing, but there are also specialist lenders for people starting up new enterprises, including charity organisations such as the Prince's Trust (for young people) or the Heritage Lottery Fund in the UK.

Governments often supplement banks with other arrangements to facilitate debt financing. In the UK, for example, the Enterprise Finance Guarantee (previously known as the Small Firms Loan Guarantee Scheme) is a government-organised scheme to help the financing of business plans for small and medium-sized enterprises. It provides lenders with a government guarantee for 75% of the lenders' exposure on individual loans. UK businesses with an annual turnover of up to £41 million are eligible to apply, but the banks take a commercial decision on whether to lend. The European Investment Bank also has an arrangement with high street banks for low-cost, longer-term loans to small and medium-sized enterprises. The loans can be for a variety of purposes, including the purchase of physical assets, increasing working capital, or research and development.

Equity is finance raised from external investors, typically in return for a share in the business. Two major sources of equity are venture capital and business angels. Venture capitalists are companies which can organise a total funding package for a fast-growing business, for a few years. They expect a high return and take an important stake in the business. Business angels are wealthy individuals, rather than companies, and they are typically entrepreneurs themselves. They use their own capital to finance new developments and, unlike in other forms of business finance, they like to get involved, using their experience and skills to provide business advice as well as finance. Their return is a share of the new business. The television programme *Dragons' Den* has a panel of business angels deciding which ideas to back with finance and advice. In addition, in the UK the government is active in facilitating equity finance (see Useful Websites), particularly through its Capital for Enterprise Fund, which can provide businesses with longer-term funding when traditional sources have been unsuccessful, and an Enterprise Investment Scheme, which helps smaller companies raise finance by providing tax relief to investors who buy shares in them.

> ### Discussion Question
>
> In seeking funding for a new enterprise, consider the advantages and disadvantages of asking a bank manager rather than one of the *Dragons' Den* investors (i.e. a business angel).

18.4.2 Financing Social Enterprise

For non-profit organisations, debt and equity are not the normal means of financing new developments. Instead, fundraising can be vital in the voluntary sector, whilst a range of government grants are often available in the short term for specific initiatives in both the public and voluntary sectors.

The Office for Civil Society coordinates central government funding opportunities for the voluntary sector in the UK. This includes policy relating to young people, volunteers, charities, social enterprises, and public service mutuals. A recent example of this in action is the £7.5 million funding to tackle loneliness during winter in 2020, when the UK and the wider world was in the midst of the COVID-19 pandemic.

18.5 Business Planning

For any new enterprise, especially in the commercial sector, it is important to have a detailed and persuasive business plan. This is not only the consolidation of all relevant considerations relating to the enterprise but also an important tool for communicating with others, especially potential funders. Furthermore, the business plan is a tool for future and continuing operational business management, as the enterprise matures beyond the start-up phase. A business plan comprises of such elements as the following:

- A clear and compelling mission, vision, and objectives;
- An understanding of the business's environment and positioning – exploiting organisational fit, using PEST and benchmarking;
- A strategy – developing the product portfolio, using methods such as the Boston Matrix and Ansoff Matrix;

- **An operations plan** – location, facilities, plant and equipment, suppliers;
- **A financial plan** – enhancing the financial position, identifying a budget, appraising capital investment, securing appropriate finances;
- **A marketing plan** – exploiting critical success factors, seeking to improve the SWOT, utilising the marketing mix, and forecasting sales with due regard to daily and weekly peak and off-peak fluctuations and longer term seasonal variations;
- **A people plan** – enhancing leadership; building around the personal capacity of the leader; recruiting and retaining key staff; developing an organisational culture; planning the numbers of staff and their required skills and development; designing effective structures, systems, communications, and incentives;
- **Risk assessment** – planning contingencies, managing risk.

CASE STUDY 18.2

Peter Cruddas Foundation (Formerly the Trinity Sailing Trust): An Example of Public Funding of Social Enterprise

Peter Cruddas Foundation (Formerly the Trinity Sailing Trust), a charity established in 1999, is based in Devon in England and has two main objectives: to assist the personal development of disadvantaged and disabled young people through offshore sailing on traditional vessels; and to restore and preserve its vessels as important examples of maritime heritage. A team of administrators and ships' crews are backed by a network of other helpers, including volunteers, trustees, and patrons. The result is that over 500 disadvantaged young people a year are given opportunities to develop through 'sail training', via contracts through which the Trinity Sailing Trust is paid to provide such training. As with many such programmes run through social enterprises, sport and physical activity are the catalyst to motivate young people, change their attitudes and expectations, and encourage them to take steps that may change the course of their lives.

The Trust has received the support and endorsement of many statutory, government, and youth organisations, but it has also engaged in extensive fundraising activities, including the Three Ships Appeal, through which approximately half its expenditure is covered. However, the considerable efforts required to pay for operating costs mean that there is little left for business development.

The government-sponsored programme Futurebuilders invested £20,000 in the Trust to undertake a feasibility study into acquiring and restoring a fourth sailing vessel, through which it can expand its business by fulfilling more public service contracts for the personal development of disadvantaged young people. Subsequently, a further £63,000 was invested for the refurbishment of the fourth vessel and to boost the Trust's capacity to undertake more business.

The Trinity Sailing Trust is an excellent example of capital funding for an extension of business for a social enterprise. The funding satisfied a one-off, capacity building requirement, which means that it is more likely to lead to a sustainable increase in business than a short-term revenue expenditure grant to cover operating costs – less than 10% of the Futurebuilders funding was for operational expenditure.

Not untypically, it was necessary to fund a feasibility study and business plan before the capital funding was released. Social enterprises often do not have the resources to develop business plans independently, so an increasingly important direction for government advice and funding is to help create these plans and make sure that the development of social enterprise is on a sound footing.

Sources: www.futurebuilders-england.org.uk/ and www.trinitysailingtrust.org/

Discussion Question

Discuss the conflict between needing to be concise in a business plan and needing to put such a lot of detail into it. Which parts do you think need more detail and which less detail?

Most of these elements have been covered in previous chapters (particularly Chapters 13, 14, and 17) in relation to existing businesses. They are about first ensuring that the objectives, mission, and vision are clear and persuasive; that the market environment and, for existing businesses, the nature of the current business are understood; and that a strategy for 'realising the dream' has been decided. Then the overall strategy has to be disaggregated into a series of separate functional strategies – marketing, finance, human resources, and production. These strategies paint a broad picture of direction – e.g. key market segments, sources of finance, organisational structure, quality of product, etc. – and justify it with respect to the business environment and the chosen objectives.

The core of the business plan is specifying operational details, i.e. operational plans for each functional department. These require detailed operational objectives and outlines of the physical and human capital, systems, and processes used to achieve the objectives. Techniques to help stitch the detailed plans together, in terms of the tasks to be completed, their sequencing, and the times it takes to complete them, include the following:

- Critical path analysis;
- Programme evaluation and review technique (PERT);
- Network diagrams;
- Gannt charts.

(For details of these techniques, please refer to project management texts.)

Business plans are about managing change in terms of introducing a new business venture in an existing organisation or starting up a new independent enterprise. They are proactive rather than reactive, and they promote desired and well-thought-through change, rather than the crisis-motivated change that all too often strikes in organisations. Business plans for new developments are designed to improve outcomes, and often the change in outcomes takes time to achieve – months, even years. Barrow *et al.* (2006) refer to a U-shaped curve after change is implemented, with productivity immediately falling as staff adjust to major changes, then rising hopefully to a higher level than the pre-change situation, when staff are comfortable with the new development. The initial result of significant changes in the structures or processes of existing organisations is almost always negative, as people take time to adjust, and resistance takes time to be broken down. Only after such adjustment is it likely that positive change is achieved.

In existing organisations, change must be for a purpose, not change for change's sake. Arguably the sector with the greatest inclination for the latter is the public sector because the identity of the politicians in charge alters so frequently. There is no clearer example of this than Sport England, which has had to endure endless structural changes over more than 20 years as new political masters have enforced new reviews. When change is for change's sake, the result is often to lose key staff rather than gain and motivate key staff, and the implications for outcomes are not good. Whereas change is a fact of business life, some stability also has its benefits. Barrow *et al.* (2006) suggest that both internal (push) and external (pull) factors are required to stimulate change in an organisation.

> ### Discussion Questions
>
> Discuss likely internal and external reasons to change what is done in a specific sport or leisure organisation that you are familiar with, e.g. a local or sports club, leisure centre, theatre, or museum. Is the external market changing? Is the internal organisational structure suited to change? Is the physical infrastructure flexible enough to accommodate change?

18.5.1 Financial Plans

The financial 'bottom line' is critically important to a business plan for a new venture, particularly for the funding organisation. Financial forecasts, or budgets, are assembled by six stages:

1 **Forecast sales revenue** – this derives from the marketing plan, requiring forecasted sales volumes at planned prices;
2 **Identify the required capital spending** – and demonstrate through capital investment appraisal the return that will be achieved;
3 **Identify operating costs** – i.e. especially labour, a vital resource and for sport and leisure services typically the principal operating cost (see Chapter 13), plus annual premises costs, materials, marketing, support services, etc.;
4 **Derive an income statement** – identifying the main income and expenditure flows (see Chapter 17);
5 **Draw up a balance sheet** – showing assets and liabilities (see Chapter 17);
6 **Check cash flow requirements** – showing the movement of cash in the organisation (see Chapter 17).

(Stutely, 2002)

An important technique to employ in arriving at these budgets is sensitivity analysis. This involves varying the assumptions made on key factors and reworking the forecasts. Sensitivity analysis demonstrates how sensitive the bottom line is to changes in key variables, such as the demand for the products at the anticipated prices, the extent of competition, the time for capital investments to become operational, the quantity and quality of required staff, or the interest payments due on debts. Sensitivity analysis is often simplified as a 'worst case scenario' and 'best case scenario' but, however it is conducted, it is important to recognise that any forecast is built on assumptions which may be wrong.

One specific set of techniques usually has an important function in financial planning – capital investment appraisal. Because physical capital assets have a relatively long lifetime, it is important to assess whether investment in such assets, as part of new enterprise, generates sufficient return over their lifetime. The best techniques for assessing new capital expenditure are discounting techniques, because they take account of the changing value of money over time (because of inflation and the alternative return that can be made over time). Two discounting techniques are Net Present Value and Internal Rate of Return – here is not the place to detail the mathematics of these techniques, but accounting textbooks will provide details. Many organisations still use non-discounting techniques such as pay-back. This basically requires calculation of the time it will take for an investment to pay back its initial capital costs. Three to five years is a typical period over which a commercial firm would expect capital costs to be paid back. For small-scale capital investment, such as a new piece of equipment, the expected pay-back period might be as short as a year. For very large-scale investments, the expected pay-back may be ten years or more.

Whatever investment appraisal method is used, it relies critically on an accurate identification of both capital costs and the resulting increase in revenues from the new enterprise. Costs are perceived as the more accurate to estimate, but many projects suffer from cost escalation. A notorious example in the UK is Wembley Stadium in London, which was originally budgeted at £326 million but eventually cost £827 million to construct. Revenues can be even more unpredictable, because of unforeseen changes in the external business environment. Yet again, sensitivity analysis is a wise procedure in conducting investment appraisal, e.g. to identify how long pay-back will take to achieve during adverse trading conditions.

18.5.2 Planning for and Managing Risks

The consideration of sensitivity analysis is an example of a process of identifying risks to the business plan and building scenarios and plans to deal with them. The following examples of sources of risk are adapted from Stutely (2002):

- Increasing competition, especially from new market entrants;
- Changing market/reduced sales, e.g. the recent recession;
- Product/service quality problems, e.g. cleanliness in sports facilities;
- Resource constraints, e.g. skill shortages and gaps, particularly in high labour cost locations such as London;
- Unused service capacity at off-peak times, e.g. sports centres, museums;
- Insufficient investment, e.g. lack of car parking at urban locations;
- IT system problems, e.g. inadequate real-time management information;
- Internal politics and relationships, e.g. between key stakeholders;
- Unproductive staff;
- Cash flow problems;
- Increasing interest rates;
- Changes in currency exchange rates.

One way to reduce risks from competition is to seek to protect the intellectual property rights of the new development with legal protection, such as patents or copyright. From the initial idea to the creation of a new business venture, entrepreneurs invest a lot of their intellect into their enterprise, and legal protection is one way to ensure that this advantage can be exploited fully by the entrepreneur. There are different arrangements in different countries to protect intellectual property, and some global agreements. They ensure that for a specified time, entrepreneurs can exploit their idea without direct competition, unless, of course, the idea is licensed or franchised for others to exploit. The main forms of intellectual property rights include:

- **Patents** – registered with the government and can cover product design or production processes;
- **Trademarks** – also registered and typically apply to words or logos that represent a brand, e.g. Apple, Virgin, and Microsoft;
- **Copyright** – not registered but applies to the creation of a new and original work such as a book, a film, a work of art, or a piece of music.

Apart from legal ways of reducing competitive risks to a business, Elliott (2004) identifies the steps necessary to manage risk more generally:

1   Identify hazards and threats.
2   Assess the likely impact of hazards on business activity.
3   Assess the probability of risks and decide priorities.
4   Consider alternative options, including prevention and control measures, insurance, or modifying plans to avoid specific risks.

Acknowledging risks and planning for them is half the battle with new ventures – and much easier than ad hoc crisis management. If the risks can be quantified in terms of possible changes in sales, resources, costs, etc., then techniques such as those used in business planning can be replicated with different numbers to identify possible alternative outcomes. It is then necessary to plan remedial actions in the eventuality of risks becoming reality. If sales of gym memberships fall in a recession, for example, what impact are reduced membership fees going to have on the number of members and on sales revenue? What cost reductions are possible in the short term to compensate for a fall in sales revenue? Planning exercises such as these are necessary to identify contingencies, i.e. rehearsing for the unexpected. As important as planning for risk, though, is monitoring performance to identify emerging risks as soon as possible when they occur.

Discussion Question

How might a sport and leisure organisation, which is reliant on membership subscriptions, reduce the risk of members deserting the organisation and going to competitors?

18.5.3 Practicalities

A business plan should be as short as possible and is typically less than 50 pages long. This is primarily because of the communication function – those you want to win over are unlikely to have the time to plough through hundreds of pages of detail. However, a difficult compromise to achieve is between necessary detail and being concise. A business plan needs to tell a coherent story and not be an endless collection of bullet point lists.

Stutely (2002) recommends that the principal features of the business plan should be relayed three times, for effective communication:

1   Tell them what you are going to tell them – i.e. the executive summary.
2   Tell it to them – the main body of the plan.
3   Tell them what you just told them – the conclusion.

The shorter messages, particularly at the beginning, are as important as the long one in the middle. Barrow *et al.* (2006) suggest that the executive summary is the single most important part of the plan. Many different types of people will need to be persuaded by the business plan, and some will only be interested in the executive summary. Indeed, the concept of the 'elevator pitch' – where you have one minute to persuade an influential person of your business idea – has a sound logic. The essence of the business plan must grab the intended target quickly – this is the concept behind the television programme *Dragons' Den*. If the executive summary fails to attract attention, then the detailed body of the plan is already handicapped.

The targets for a business plan are many and varied. If the plan concerns a new development for an existing organisation, targets will include senior managers in the organisation, internal competitors for development funds, and people who just like to ask awkward questions. If it concerns a development which needs external funding, then the business plan needs to convince either commercial financiers such as venture capitalists or business angels, or possibly government-sponsored sources of finance – either way the plan needs to shine in a very competitive environment. Whoever the intended targets of the business plan are, they will all be looking for different things. Some will concentrate on the bottom line and evaluate its feasibility. Others will concentrate on whether the leadership and management potential is there to carry the development through. In an existing organisation another concern will be with the internal synergy of the proposed development. The business plan must anticipate a variety of questions and answer them all.

> ### Discussion Question
>
> In promoting a new idea, how is your argument likely to vary between convincing your line manager and convincing a potential funder of the idea?

Kuratko and Hodgetts (2007), Hisrich *et al.* (2005), and Stutely (2002) identify several reasons why business plans fail. These include the following:

- Objectives are unrealistic or not measurable.
- The entrepreneur shows a lack of commitment to the enterprise.
- The entrepreneur has no experience in the planned business.
- The entrepreneur does not accurately anticipate potential threats to or weaknesses in the business case.
- There is poor evidence of customer need or what the market is.
- There are presentational weaknesses, e.g. too scruffy.
- The text is too long or too short.
- There is insufficient sensitivity analysis.
- The financial forecasts are unreasonably optimistic.

Stutely also suggests that a reason for failure is if the plan is produced by professional consultants, not the entrepreneur, because it should be the entrepreneur who drives the business plan. However, the use of consultants can be important to compensate for technical weaknesses in the entrepreneur's skill set. Also, in the third sector of voluntary and charitable organisations it is often necessary to seek professional help at the feasibility stage. The earlier case study of the Trinity Sailing Trust (Case Study 18.2) is a good example of initial funding for professional business planning followed by investment funds for the capital expenditure required.

On a more positive note, Barrow *et al.* (2006) suggest that business plans that succeed include the following:

- **Evidence of market orientation** – i.e. an awareness of the market context for the development, the relevant market segments for the product;
- **Evidence of customer acceptance** – i.e. the results of market research and market testing;
- **Exclusive rights** – through patents, copyright, or trademark protection, etc., which reduce risk and competition;
- **Believable forecasts** – based on appropriate precedents and using facts rather than hope;
- **Due diligence** – i.e. demonstrating that the track record and competencies of key people are up to the task.

18.6 Enterprise Failures

It might seem odd to include a section on business failure in a chapter on enterprise, but the fact is that around 60% of new businesses fail in the first three years (in the UK in 2019). Failure rates are worse for specific parts of the sport and leisure industry; for example, UHY Hacker Young (2007) reported that hospitality and catering businesses were three times more likely to fail than the average business. Therefore, it is important to identify the major reasons for new business failures and, as good entrepreneurs do, learn what might be done to avoid them. Whilst evidence relating to business failures typically applies to all businesses – not just new ones, and not just sport and leisure – nevertheless there is no reason to believe that new sport and leisure business failures will be different.

According to Morrison *et al.* (1999), management deficiencies and financial shortcomings are common factors in business failures. Some of the research reviewed by Morrison *et al.* (1999) examines the concept of 'management deficiencies' more closely and suggests that it is attitudes and actions that are at fault, rather than technical managerial skills. In particular, the evidence points to two more detailed reasons for business failures: reliance on intuition and emotion in decision-making, rather than planning; and inflexibility when things start to go wrong. Another contributory factor appears to be managerial inexperience, but that is why failure is an important part of the learning process for many entrepreneurs – it is an unforgettable experience!

Morrison *et al.* (1999) point out one other factor in business failure that might be particularly appropriate in sport and leisure – when a hobby becomes a business. It has become a cliché over time that many professional football clubs run by successful businessmen from other industries are not successful businesses. Similarly, many restaurants and small gyms have been started as a result of taking a serious hobby (e.g. cooking, sport) into a business enterprise. Whilst these entrepreneurs will have tremendous enthusiasm, this might prejudice a sound business plan. Alongside this, failures are also almost always attributable to cash flow problems and not valuing and understanding relevant data.

18.7 Conclusions

Given that enterprise represents the heart of good management, it is fitting to end this chapter and this book with reference to Barrow *et al.* (2006), who provide 12 golden rules for dynamic and successful businesses. These are:

1 **Invest in employees** – a critical resource, particularly in sport and leisure services.
2 **Have a business plan and follow it** – a plan is useless unless it is used as a blueprint.

3 **Demonstrate financial discipline** – finance is another critical resource, particularly the monitoring and controlling of cash flow.

4 **Keep passionate about the business** – i.e. commitment to the business by its leaders.

5 **Monitor performance** – i.e. accountability to the business plan by all employees.

6 **Communicate performance internally** – to generate continued commitment and unity of purpose.

7 **Know the competition** – to avoid nasty surprises.

8 **Work smarter, not longer** – i.e. it is the quality of decisions that counts, not the hours of work.

9 **Get online** – e-commerce is of increasing importance to most businesses.

10 **'Stick to the knitting'** – i.e. for existing organisations the core business is selling existing products to existing markets.

11 **Be financially flexible** – don't rely on one funding source but have a range.

12 **Think globally** – particularly for supply sources.

Although these 12 golden rules are clearly oriented to commercial businesses, many are also relevant to successful organisations in the public and voluntary sectors. It is important to remember that such advice applies as much to existing operations as it does to new ventures. Change is inevitable, particularly in the dynamic environment that sport and leisure management is conducted in – standing still is not an option. All sport and leisure managers can benefit from being entrepreneurial, helping themselves and their organisations to thrive in an industry which is becoming increasingly important in people's lives.

Practical Tasks

1 Think of a new idea for an existing sport or leisure organisation that you are familiar with. It could be a new product, a new service, taking a variant of a different service to a new type of client (e.g. young people, or older people), or delivering the service in a different way. Then think about the market for the new idea and what kind of marketing mix would attract this market; how much it would cost to set up and operate; where the money to achieve this would come from; and what skills are needed to implement the idea. Finally, design a one-minute 'elevator pitch' to sell your idea to an influential person, i.e. a relevant manager or a significant funder.

2 For a new piece of equipment, e.g. a pool table, research how much it would cost to buy, install, and run at an appropriate site (e.g. club or pub); estimate how busy it is likely to be at whatever price you decide to charge for it; and calculate how long it would take to pay back its capital cost. Is it worth investing in?

Structured Guide to Further Reading

For an overview of entrepreneurship:

Barrow, C., Brown, R., & Clarke, L. (2006). *The Successful Entrepreneur's Guidebook.* Kogan Page, London and Philadelphia.

For an overview of business planning:
Stutely, R. (2002). *The Definitive Business Plan*, 2nd edition. Pearson Education, Harlow.

For examples in hotels and restaurants:
Morrison, A., Rimmington, M., & Williams, C. (1999). *Entrepreneurship in the Hospitality, Tourism and Leisure Industries*. Elsevier Butterworth-Heinemann, Oxford.

Useful Websites

For the Department of Business Innovation and Skills:
www.bis.gov.uk/policies/enterprise-and-business-support

For Business Link, an advisory service for enterprise:
www.businesslink.gov.uk

For the Prince's Trust:
www.princes-trust.org.uk

References

Bragg, A., & Bragg, M. (2005). *Developing New Business Ideas*. FT Prentice Hall, Harlow.

Elliott, D. (2004). Risk management in sport. In J. Beech, & S. Chadwick (Eds.), *The Business of Sport Management*. Pearson Education Ltd., Harlow.

Hisrich, R. D., Peters, M. P., & Shepherd, D. A. (2005). *Entrepreneurship*, 6th edition. McGraw-Hill Irwin, New York.

Jennings, P. L. (2009). *Identifying Business Opportunities, Course Notes for Enterprise Development and Business Planning*. School of Management, University of Sheffield, Sheffield.

Johnson, G., Scholes, K., & Whittington, M. (2008). *Exploring Corporate Strategy*, 8th edition. Pearson Education, Harlow.

Kuratko, D. F., & Hodgetts, R. M. (2007). *Entrepreneurship: Theory, Process, Practice*. Thomson South-Western, Mason, OH.

Porter, M. E. (2004). *Competitive Advantage*. The Free Press, New York.

UHY Hacker Young. (2007). *Restaurants Three Times More Likely to Go Bust than Other Businesses*. Press Release, UHY Hacker Young, London.

Wickham, P. A. (2006). *Strategic Entrepreneurship*, 4th edition. Pearson Education, Harlow.

Chapter 19

Law and Leisure Management

By Matt Beecham

In This Chapter

- Why does a sport and leisure manager need to know about law?
- What elements of the law are particularly relevant to sport and leisure managers?
- What is negligence, and how can a manager avoid it?
- How is a sport and leisure manager subject to legal liability?
- How is working with children affected by the law?
- What employment law should a sport and leisure manager be aware of?
- What does good risk management entail?

DOI: 10.4324/9780367823610-19

Summary

This chapter concentrates on key legal areas of responsibility for sport and leisure managers. One of the most important is the avoidance of negligence, which means recognising a duty of care to all customers, volunteers, etc. who visit an organisation and ensuring that there is no breach of duty. Other key legal issues are occupier's liability and vicarious liability, the first of which involves a common duty of care to all visitors, whilst the second concerns liability for employees' actions.

Working with children is an area of law for which there has been considerable change in recent years, culminating in new legislation for anyone working with children and vulnerable adults in the UK – requiring registration with an Independent Safeguarding Authority. There are also specific precedents for the way in which liability in school sport is identified.

A brief overview of some important legal considerations for potential employers of staff is presented. Finally, this chapter closes with consideration of risk management, i.e. ensuring that negligence is prevented and liability is acknowledged in an organisation's systems, particularly in the recruitment and training of staff. A key element of risk management is risk assessment, which involves straightforward procedures to identify risks and take measures to minimise them.

19.1 Introduction

This chapter serves as an introduction to key legal issues that may affect or impact upon people working in the sport and leisure industries. Inevitably for such a broad discipline, this chapter only provides an insight into selected areas, and if readers want further information there are references provided to signpost where that additional information may be found. Many of these references are to cases – case law is very important for setting precedents.

By its very nature, the law is different in different countries, so this chapter concentrates on the way the law operates in England and Wales, for consistency (Fafinski & Finch, 2007; Elliott & Quinn, 2007). However, many of the principles demonstrated will be valid in other countries' legal systems – but they will be enacted by different legislation, different processes, and the legal details will be different. England and Wales operate a common law system, which means that the law can be created through parliament by the passing of legislation or by the creation of precedent by the courts via case law. You will note that throughout this chapter reference is made to both laws created by legislation as well as law developed through the courts.

To locate the case law and legislation cited in this chapter, it is necessary to become familiar with searching the major legal databases. There is a vast quantity of legal material (case reports, journal articles, statutes, etc.) available online. However, most of these are only available to organisations and libraries that pay the appropriate subscription fee. It is highly likely that most universities will have access to at least some of these databases, and you should contact librarians for more details and instructions on how to use these databases. There are three main commercial databases – these are Westlaw, LexisNexis, and Lawtel. For ease of use, Westlaw is probably the most user-friendly. It has a clear, stripped-down, Google-like interface with a whole battery of features available beyond the initial search. It also enables the user to search using a variety of terminology and in a variety of different ways.

19.2 Negligence

It is a fact of life that when people participate in sports and leisure activities, they will sometimes suffer injuries. Sometimes these injuries may be viewed as 'just one of those things'. However, there will be other times when an organisation or an individual may be at least partially responsible for the injuries received and the injured party may therefore wish to pursue an action to claim compensation from those responsible. It is through negligence that such an action is most likely to be pursued.

There appears to be a perception amongst many that the threat of negligence liability is removing much of the risk in society, and that a compensation culture has grown up (Williams, 2005). This perception has developed to such an extent that legislation was enacted in the UK (the Compensation Act, 2006) aimed specifically at protecting those such as sport organisations that provide socially useful activities. In particular, the legislation now asks the courts to specifically look at whether the steps that an organisation may have to take to protect itself from liability may in fact discourage them from providing a particular activity. The provision of school trips and outdoor pursuits courses are particularly relevant, where teachers or recreation providers may be under threat of being sued for accidents which happen whilst participants are taking part in activities such as hiking, canoeing, caving, orienteering, rock-climbing, etc.

Due to the enactment of the Compensation Act, 2006, arguably there is now a reduced threat of being successfully sued, which will be a welcome boon for all involved in the sport and leisure industry. When considering negligence, however, a manager must remember that the basic requirement is for providers and customers to act reasonably. The requirement is not to make an activity 100% safe by eliminating all risk but rather to do what is reasonable to enable people to remain safe. Part of this equation is that the greater the risk of something going wrong, or the graver the consequences for someone should an identifiable risk occur, then the greater the precautions must be to prevent this risk from happening.

Negligence has a wide range of applications, and these include helping to regulate the behaviour and actions of both individuals and organisations in a sport and recreational context. For an injured party to succeed in gaining compensation through a claim in negligence, they must satisfy the court that their injury was caused, at least in part, by the actions of another. They must demonstrate that this party failed to take reasonable care for their safety and that this lack of reasonable care caused or contributed to the injury suffered. The injury suffered may be physical (to person or property), psychological, or financial. In order to win an action in negligence, the claimant (the person who has suffered the injury) must prove the following:

- That the defendant, (the other party), owed the claimant a duty of care.
- That this duty of care was breached.
- That this breach of duty caused or contributed to the injury or loss suffered.

It is important to note that the claimant does not have to demonstrate these beyond reasonable doubt, as the prosecution would have to in a criminal trial. In a legal action in negligence, the requirement on the claimant is to show that *on the balance of probabilities* (i.e. 51%) the defendant was negligent for their actions. This is a far easier standard to overcome than the criminal one. The following sections break a claim in negligence down into its constituent parts to explain the operation of this area of law in a sport and leisure context.

19.2.1 Duty of Care

To establish a claim in negligence the claimant must first show that the defendant owed them a duty of care. A duty of care can be said to be a legal duty to ensure the safety and wellbeing of others. In the famous English tort law case of *Donoghue v Stevenson [1932]*, Lord Atkin formulated a general principle called the 'neighbour principle' to govern when a duty of care would exist in law. Your neighbour being 'persons who are closely and directly affected by my act that I ought reasonably to have them in contemplation as being so affected when I am directing my mind to the acts or omissions which are called in question'. In other words, individuals must take reasonable care in their actions or lack of action so not to cause harm whether physically, psychologically, and financially to those proximate to them. For example, a provider of sport and leisure facilities will almost certainly always owe their customers a duty of care. They will always have a responsibility to make sure that they consider their customers when going about their business.

There are many different relationships in sport and leisure where a duty of care is clearly owed by one party to another, for example (Hartley, 2009):

- Participant to participant;
- Teacher to pupil;
- Event organiser to spectator;
- Private club member to club member;
- Sports governing body to participant;
- Team doctor to sports participant;
- Official to participant;
- Adventure tourism tour operator to tourist;
- Manufacturer of a sport product to a consumer;
- Employer to police on duty at an event;
- Adult to adult on a skiing holiday;
- Occupiers of a sports centre to lawful visitors (even trespassers);
- Hypnotist/theatre/club to audience volunteers;
- Teenagers to other teenagers in informal leisure/recreation.

In almost all relationships in a sports and leisure context, a duty of care will be owed – one party will need to have the other party in consideration when going about their business. So, for example, a tourism operator will have to make sure they do all that is reasonable to maintain the safety of their operations for the tourist. The owner and/or manager of a leisure centre will need to ensure that the centre is reasonably safe for those coming to use the centre, for whatever purpose, (not just the sports facilities, but even the cafeteria would need to be reasonably safe for its customers). It must also be the case that such premises are reasonably safe for employees of the centre to do their jobs.

It is in breach of duty that the courts will assess whether a party has behaved reasonably or taken reasonable steps to maintain safety.

19.2.2 Breach of Duty

Once a duty of care has been established, it must then be proved whether this duty has been breached or not (Deakin *et al.*, 2007). In a sport and leisure context the obligation is to do all that is reasonable to maintain the safety of the participant or spectator. However, the circumstances as to what amounts to 'reasonable conduct' are of fundamental importance. As has been said in an Australian case, the circumstances involved in chariot racing are far different from those involved in a water-skiing. In other words, the nature of chariot racing means that it may take 'more careless' behaviour to breach duty.

To put this in a modern context, the nature and inherent danger in an activity such as rugby union means that mere careless behaviour may not breach duty – something more akin to reckless behaviour may be necessary before breach of duty is established. Alternatively, the circumstances in an activity such as bowls or badminton may be that if one party is careless and this carelessness injures another party, then this is sufficient to breach duty. One could argue that the threshold for the court finding a breach of duty has occurred is lower in non-contact sports than it would be for contact sports. The crucial factor here is the circumstances – a vital issue. What are the circumstances of the event? What are the inherent dangers of the event? What might the weather conditions be? What are the abilities of the participants? What about the presence or otherwise of protective equipment? These issues and many others will play a role in assessing whether behaviour has been reasonable and therefore there has been no breach of duty, or whether it has been unreasonable and therefore there has been a breach of duty.

The case *Caldwell v Maguire & Fitzgerald* (2001) is perhaps the leading and most authoritative case on assessing breach of duty within a sport and leisure context and contains an explanation of how to assess whether there has been a breach of duty of care in a sports and recreation setting.

CASE STUDY 19.1

Caldwell v Maguire & Fitzgerald [2001] EWCA Civ 1054

This case is probably the most significant sports participant negligence case in the UK. It was heard in the Court of Appeal, and its significance lies in the time the Court took to examine the standard of care owed by one participant to another. Before *Caldwell*, the examination of the standard owed had been rather vague and uncertain. The case involved an injury inflicted on a jockey when he was thrown from his mount when it was squeezed for position by two other horses. In the event, both defendants were held not to be liable for the injuries received by the claimant Peter Caldwell. In explaining its reasoning, the Court of Appeal tried to clarify the whole position of negligence in sport. The Court approved five major points, which are:

(1) Each Contestant in a lawful sporting contest (and in particular a race) owes a duty of care to each and all other contestants.
(2) That duty is to exercise in the course of the contest all care that is objectively reasonable in the prevailing circumstances for the avoidance of infliction of injury to such fellow contestants.
(3) The prevailing circumstances are all such properly attendant upon the contest and include its object, the demands inevitably made upon its contestants, its inherent dangers (if any), its rules, conventions and customs, and the standards, skills and judgment reasonably to be expected of a contestant. Thus in the particular case of a horse race

the prevailing circumstances will include the contestant's obligation to ride a horse over a given course competing with the remaining contestants for the best possible placing, if not for a win. Such must further include the Rules of Racing and the standards, skills and judgment of a professional jockey, all as expected by fellow contestants.

(4) Given the nature of such prevailing circumstances the threshold for liability is in practice inevitably high; the proof of a breach of duty will not flow from proof of no more than an error of judgment or from mere proof of a momentary lapse in skill (and thus care) respectively when subject to the stresses of a race. Such are no more than incidents inherent in the nature of the sport.

(5) In practice it may therefore be difficult to prove any such breach of duty absent proof of conduct that in point of fact amounts to reckless disregard for the fellow contestant's safety. I emphasise the distinction between the expression of legal principle and the practicalities of the evidential burden' (*Caldwell v Maguire & Fitzgerald*, 2001, para 11).

The first two propositions make it clear that sports participants owe one another a duty of care and that this duty is to behave in a reasonable manner taking account of the circumstances which you are in. In other words, the level of behaviour expected may be different in, for example, a competitive game of rugby than that expected in a different activity. It is the circumstances which dictate the level of care required. The third proposition tries to introduce some of the kinds of circumstances which may be important in assessing whether a breach of duty has occurred. It raises issues such as the inherent dangers of the sporting activity and the level of skill of the participants. This is not by any means an exhaustive list; there is room for consideration of many different variables or circumstances. The fourth proposition then goes on to attempt to reassure those who worry that the threat of legal liability is dissuading some people from taking part in sport. It states very clearly that a finding of liability does not come easily and that it may only be quite serious behaviour that would lead to a finding of negligence. The final proposition attempts to reconcile an academic debate that has endured since another case in 1963, by stressing that the approach taken by the courts in sports negligence remains harmonious with other walks of life, in that breach of duty will occur where there is *unreasonable* behaviour. However, depending on the circumstances, *careless* behaviour might not be *unreasonable*, and in fact it may not be until behaviour becomes *reckless* that the behaviour is deemed to be *unreasonable* and therefore negligent.

(Also see Useful Websites.)

Discussion Question

What kinds of circumstances may be important in assessing whether there has been a breach of the duty of care in a situation where a player is injured by a tackle in a game of football?

It is perhaps pertinent for those involved in sport and leisure activities that the Court of Appeal in a 2004 case equated children's horseplay (i.e. boisterous fooling around) with organised sport, stressing that the only real difference between horseplay and organised sport is that in the former there are no formal rules. The implications of the decision of the Court of Appeal to equate horseplay by and large with organised sport is that sports negligence principles should be applied across a whole range of activities, wherever there is consensual recreational activity. This means that depending on the circumstances of the activity, *reckless* behaviour rather than ordinary *careless* behaviour may be required to breach that duty of care.

A sporting governing body must have adequate safety measures in place to make sure that participants are protected from reasonably foreseeable risks. In *Watson v British Boxing Board of Control* (2001), the boxer Michael Watson successfully sued the British Boxing Board of Control (BBBC) for injuries he received whilst fighting Chris Eubank for the world title. He was able to establish that the safety measures they had in place were insufficient to protect him from his foreseeable injuries. He suffered a brain haemorrhage after he was knocked out late in the fight.

It was the inadequacy of the immediate aftercare of Michael Watson which was the subject of the negligence action, rather than the events leading up to the knockout. Watson accepted the risks of boxing; therefore, Eubank bore no responsibility for causing Watson's injuries. What he did not accept, however, was that the safety procedures the BBBC had in place to deal with injuries such as those that Watson suffered (which were clearly foreseeable) would not be fit for purpose. Although an ambulance had been called in the immediate aftermath of the contest, by the time it had arrived, severe physical injury has been sustained. Watson's argument was that the BBBC owed fighters a duty of care to provide immediate ringside medical assistance following any injuries sustained by the participants. Following this judgement, it is now commonplace to find medical ringside assistance at all boxing bouts.

Parties only need do what is reasonable to guard against injury. However, it is also the case that the graver the consequences of any injury that may be suffered, the more that must be done to eliminate the risk. It is not necessary that every single risk must be eliminated. In *Bolton v Stone* (1951) a pedestrian was struck by a cricket ball which had been hit out of the ground during a local match. The injured party sued for the injuries she suffered. In the case the Court was told that a ball had only been hit out of the ground in this manner six times in the last 30 years, and due to the infrequency of this happening, it would be unreasonable to ask the defendants to guard against this very small risk. Therefore, it was held that there was no breach of duty, as the injury suffered was not due to a reasonably foreseeable risk which the defendants would be expected to guard against.

If event providers and facility owners/managers are to ensure that they remain on the right side of liability, then it is important that they conform to appropriate recognised safety standards. Such considerations were important in two significant cases heard some 30 years apart. In the first, *Simms v Leigh Rugby Football Club* (1969), a player was injured in a tackle and alleged that his injury was caused by a collision with a perimeter wall that was constructed around the rugby pitch. The Rugby Football League by-laws stated that any perimeter wall must be at least seven feet away from the touchline. This wall was seven foot three inches away and so exceeded the standard expected by the governing body. The Court dismissed the claim.

In the second case, *Wattleworth v Goodwood* (2004), detailed in the following case study, a racing driver died during a race, following a collision with a safety wall constructed of tyres and an earth bank.

CASE STUDY 19.2

Wattleworth v Goodwood (2004)

The interest in this case lies in the fact that an action was brought by the widow of the victim against three different parties – against the circuit itself (Goodwood), against the national governing body (the MSA), and against the international governing body for motorsport (the FIA). The claimant alleged that her husband's death had been caused by the negligent construction of the safety barrier. Goodwood Circuit agreed that as occupiers they owed a duty of care under the 1957 Occupiers Liability Act but claimed that they had discharged that duty by taking all reasonable steps to ensure that the track was reasonably safe by following all advice given to them by both the MSA and FIA.

It was quite clear from the judgment that there had been detailed analysis and several inspections of the safety provisions of the track by both Goodwood and the MSA, and to a lesser extent the FIA. For these reasons, Goodwood did indeed discharge its duty of care, and so no liability was held against them. The MSA denied that they owed a duty of care, because the event in which Mr Wattleworth was killed was not an official MSA event for which they would have issued a licence. However, the Court held that they clearly had assumed a responsibility and that their role as national governing body went far beyond merely issuing licences to circuits. They provided detailed safety advice and worked closely with the circuits to make sure all appropriate safety features were in place, providing guidance and expertise. It was thus fair, just, and reasonable to impose a duty of care upon them. However, the construction of the safety feature was reasonable, and they had taken reasonable care in inspecting it and approving it. Therefore there was no breach of duty. The Court acknowledged the experience and expertise of the MSA inspector and noted that at all times his priority was to keep risks to a minimum. The action against the FIA also failed. It was held that because of the remote nature of the organisation and the fact that the FIA took no direct responsibility for safety at national events (this they delegated to national sporting authorities), they owed no duty of care towards Mr Wattleworth. The conclusion of the Court was that the accident was caused by a momentary lapse in judgment by Mr Wattleworth. His car had gone a few feet offline at the fateful moment, causing him to collide with the safety barrier which unfortunately caused his death. There was no negligence on the part of any of those involved in the organisation of the event. They had done all that was reasonable to look after his safety.

However, it is important to recognise that just because a particular practice or standard is approved by a governing body does not necessarily mean that it will stand up to legal scrutiny. Ultimately, as seen in *Watson v BBBC*, it may well be the case that liability will be held either against the governing body and/or the event organiser, even though that party may be adhering to the governing body guidelines.

The responsibilities and duties of stadium owners and occupiers in the UK have been further defined by legislation concerning Occupiers Liability. The following section will look briefly at this legislation and its impact.

19.3 Occupiers Liability

An issue of real importance for those organising sport and leisure events or providing facilities for such events is that of their potential liability. The Occupiers Liability Acts of 1957 and 1984 are of particular pertinence in this area. The Act of 1984 refers to unlawful visitors (typically trespassers) to the premises, whilst the 1957 Act refers to lawful visitors, and as such, encompasses all participants, officials, coaches/instructors, and obviously any spectators who may be present.

An occupier owes a common duty of care to any lawful visitor to their premises. Typically, the occupier will be the owners of the premises or the managers of the premises. Usually the occupier will be defined as the person or business 'in control' of the premises. The duty owed by the occupier is to ensure that the premises are reasonably safe for the purposes for which the visitor has been invited. For any visitors to a premises there of course remains the possibility of an action in negligence in the event of them suffering an injury. However, where it is the state of the premises that has caused the accident, the statutory duty laid down by the Occupiers Liability Act 1957 means that an action against an occupier has far more chance of success and is therefore far more likely than under ordinary negligence principles reviewed earlier.

If the premises are unsafe for the purposes for which someone is invited, then it is incumbent upon the occupier to either make the premises safe or to ensure that the visitor can remain safe whilst on the premises. In *Cunningham & Others v Reading Football Club Ltd* (1991), police officers were injured when football hooligans from the away team broke pieces of concrete from the ground and used them as missiles, causing injury to the police officers attending the game. The court held that Reading FC should have been aware that violence was highly likely given the violent reputation of the Bristol City supporters. Further, even though the deliberate actions of the hooligans directly caused the injuries suffered, the club had failed to ensure that the ground was reasonably safe, and they had exacerbated that by allowing hooligans access to the defective area. A solution may have been for the club to restrict access to the area of the ground which had the defective concrete. This decision, however, is rare and must be read within the context of the facts. The reputation of the Bristol City supporters, Reading's knowledge of previous incidents, the awful condition of the stadium, and the lack of action from Reading to address this all combined to allow the court to find that Reading had fallen well below the standard of care expected under the Occupiers' Liability Act 1957.

It is not the premises themselves that necessarily need to be made safe. The focus is on making sure that the visitor is safe for the purpose for which they are/were invited. So, for example, a warning notice may enable someone to remain safe. However, it is particularly important to note that a warning notice must make it clear what the danger is and how to avoid it, rather than merely be an attempt to evade liability.

Furthermore, any warning must consider individual characteristics of visitors, so more care will be needed where the visitor is a child or someone who is visually impaired (Harpwood, 2009). Occupiers may also be able to discharge their duty if all appropriate safety checks and recommendations have been undertaken and these are sufficient to ensure that the visitor is safe. In the *Wattleworth* and *Simms* cases referred to earlier, the courts dismissed claims because the governing bodies' relevant technical recommendations had been followed. The more recent decision of *Sutton v Syston RFC* (2011) is a particularly useful illustration of the importance of carrying out appropriate safety checks to ensure that visitors will remain as safe as possible when visiting and using the premises. In the *Sutton* case, the claimant, a 16-year-old rugby player, was involved in a tag rugby match. About 30 minutes into the match, the claimant received the ball and dived for the touchline to score a try. Unfortunately, hidden in the grass was part of a plastic cricket boundary marker which gashed him causing a permanent knee injury. The Rugby Football Union (RFU) guidelines provided a checklist for foreign objects when carrying out a pitch inspection including objects such as 'glass, concrete, large stones, and dog waste'. The guidelines then went on to outline how such inspections should be carried out by outlining that before a game or training session, a pitch should be walked over 'at a reasonable walking pace' by a coach, match organiser, someone on their behalf, or by multiple persons inspecting pre-agreed areas. During the initial hearing, the judge rejected the club's argument that a quick inspection walk over the pitch was sufficient to discharge the club's duty of care. However, on appeal, the Court of Appeal was unsure that the stub could have been discovered and that it was not the club's responsibility to inspect every blade of grass. However, they did note that the club would have a duty to check the touchdown areas of the pitch more closely. However, on the facts, the grass was lush and thick, and even with a more careful inspection, the plastic peg would have been unlikely to have been found. Therefore, the claimant's claim failed.

Many people are also surprised to learn that trespassers are owed a duty of care (albeit a more limited one) by occupiers (persistent trespassers can sometimes attain the status of lawful 'visitors'). The duty, though, only covers personal injury and not damage to property. The duty owed is to take such care as is reasonable in the circumstances, to see that the trespasser does not suffer injury due to any danger identified. Warnings again may suffice to prevent a finding of liability. A case that illustrates these issues very well is *Ratcliff v McConnell* (1999) – see the case study.

CASE STUDY 19.3

Ratcliff v McConnell (1999)

This case involved an action brought by a student who broke into the college swimming pool with two friends after they had been drinking (although the student was not drunk). They climbed over a locked gate; there were two notices saying that the pool was closed and warning against taking glasses and bottles into the pool area at the pool entrance, another 'substantial' warning at the shallow end and another at the deep end stating, 'Deep end shallow dive'. There was also a motion-activated security light (albeit one which did not throw out a great deal of light). The student dived in and hit his head, causing him permanent tetraplegia.

The High Court found for the claimant (subject to 40% contributory negligence on his part), holding that the college were aware the pool was used regularly by its students during prohibited hours, that new students were not specifically warned against use, that no information was made available about specific opening hours, that there was no general prohibition against diving, and that the college did not take such care as is reasonable in the circumstances to, for example, warn of the dangers or to discourage people from encountering the risk.

On appeal, the High Court judgement was quite strongly criticised. They found that the student had dived deeper than he had intended, and that alcohol may have played a part in this misjudgement. Moreover, they found (contrary to the High Court) that there was no evidence of persistent misuse of the pool by students at the college. Further, again contrary to the High Court, it was found that the student had been told that out of hours use of the pool was prohibited and that warnings were posted. In analysing the case in relation to the Occupiers Liability Act, 1984, it was held that the college (the occupier) had done all that was reasonable in the circumstances in relation to this trespasser. The dangers in a swimming pool were two-fold – that of drowning or having an accident as the student had done. Both were obvious dangers to someone of his age and maturity. Furthermore, both dangers were common to all swimming pools, and the defendants had done all that could reasonably be asked of them to guard against this risk. The Court of Appeal summed up the position thus:

> 'The question is whether the defendants should have offered other protection to the plaintiff from a risk which he should have been fully aware of, and indeed was aware of'.

The Court of Appeal answered this question in the negative, leaving the plaintiff (i.e. the claimant, in this case the student) without any compensation at all. It is clear from the case that each will be decided on its own facts. Issues which may be important in deciding if a duty is owed and has been breached may be things such as the age of the claimants, their mental capacity, or indeed the nature of the danger and the resources of the occupier.

19.4 Vicarious Liability

If an employee commits a tort (a civil wrong, e.g. a negligent act) whilst acting during the course of their employment, then the employer is said to be vicariously liable for the tort committed. The practical implications of this are that it will be the employer (or their insurer) who will be responsible for paying the compensation to the claimant, if it can be demonstrated that the defendant is:

- An employee (who may for example be a lifeguard at a leisure centre or a fitness trainer at a gymnasium); and
- The tort (such as negligence) was committed during the course of their employment.

If the person in question is an employee and has a contract of employment, then the first point is relatively simple to answer; however, if the person is, for example, an independent contractor, this question becomes more problematic. The test as to whether someone is an employee for the purposes of vicarious liability is a difficult one to assess and is subject to tests laid down by the courts in previous case law and hinges on the facts of each case. It may well be that where a degree of 'control' is exercised by the employer over the activities of the defendant, then this will be critical in assessing vicarious liability. For example, in *Hawley v Luminar Leisure plc*, it was held that despite a group of doormen being employees of a security services company, the nightclub owner where they operated was vicariously liable for their acts, as he exercised clear control as to how they did their job.

Once it has been established that the defendant is an employee, the second hurdle to clear is to establish that the act which caused the injury was caused during the course of employment. It is difficult to find clear principles which are applicable to all cases. However, if the employee is providing some benefit to the employer, or the position of the employee enabled them to perform the action complained of, then it is likely to be interpreted as acting in the course of their employment.

Even if the employee is doing an act which is forbidden by the employer, if that act is bringing some benefit to the employer, or if the status of their employment has enabled them to carry out that task, then it is likely that they will have been acting in the course of their employment. For example, in *Limpus v London General Omnibus Co* (1862), the company were held vicariously liable following a race between two drivers which injured the claimant, who was the driver of the other bus. Although drivers racing their buses was expressly forbidden by the company, the drivers were employed to drive, and racing was merely an unauthorised method of doing what they were employed to do. In contrast, in *Beard v London General Omnibus* (1900) a bus conductor caused injury whilst moving his bus. The company were held not to be vicariously liable as the conductor was acting outside the course of his employment – he was employed to conduct, not to drive.

An employer may also be held liable for the deliberate acts (rather than negligent acts) of the employee, even if these acts are prohibited by the employer or against the law, if their employment placed them in a position which facilitated these acts, or the employer derives some benefit from the act. This was established crucially in the case *Lister v Hesley Hall*

(2002), which involved children sexually abused by the warden at their boarding home. The House of Lords concluded that it was his employment status that had enabled the warden to commit his acts and that those acts were therefore closely connected with his employment status, and thus it was fair, just, and reasonable to hold his employers liable for the actions of the warden. This was later applied in *Gravil v Carroll & Anor* (2008) where it was held that the part-time employers of a rugby union player were held vicariously liable and therefore had to pay the compensation for an off-the-ball punch that the player threw during a match, which caused his opponent a severe eye injury requiring substantial reconstructive surgery.

What these cases demonstrate is that employers/managers must always take care when employing staff, supervising staff, and training staff to ensure that they do not leave themselves open to compensation claims due to the principle of vicarious liability. The clearest way for an employer to protect themselves from potentially being held to be vicariously liable for the negligent acts of their employees is to ensure that their employees do not commit such acts in the first place. An employer may guard against their employee committing such acts by closer monitoring and training, or by regular staff assessments and appraisals. Such precautions may take place prior to staff taking up employment by closer checks and safeguards during recruitment. An employer must also, of course, always make sure that their systems of working are safe and furthermore that they always encourage and promote safe and best practice. It is important to remember that the fundamental requirement is once again that of reasonableness. There is no guarantee of safety and safe practice, and as long as an employer is doing all that is reasonable to ensure that their staff behave reasonably, then they should not find themselves on the wrong side of a legal claim in this area.

19.5 Working with Children

A large part of work within the sport and leisure industry involves children, and this necessarily involves its own challenges. To this end, a series of guides to the UK legal framework has been produced by the Department for Education – see Useful Websites. The documents are addressed seemingly to all organisations and individuals that may have a role in promoting the welfare and looking after the safety of children, which includes many sport and leisure organisations.

Under the Children's Act 1989, a person with care of a child in the UK must do all that is reasonable in the circumstances for the purpose of safeguarding or promoting the welfare of the child. All organisations that have a responsibility towards children must have in place proper procedures and measures to ensure the protection of the children under their care. Safeguarding children is defined in Working Together to Safeguard Children (see Useful Websites) as: 'protecting children from maltreatment, preventing impairment of children's health or development, ensuring that children are growing up in circumstances consistent with the provision of safe and effective care, and taking action to enable all children to have the best outcomes'.

To work with children in the UK it is a legal requirement to obtain a Disclosure and Barring Service certification (more commonly referred to as a DBS check). Prior to DBS checks, the Protection of Children Act (PoCA) 1999 introduced the PoCA List, whereby the Secretary of State had to record a list of the names of individuals considered unsuitable to work with children – this placed an obligation upon all qualifying organisations working with children to refer the names of individuals who may be unsuitable for possible inclusion on that list. The consequence of this was that criminal records checks had to be made for all potential employees who may have contact with children. If any potential employee or current employee appeared on the list, then they could not be employed in that position by the provider. It was an offence under the Act to employ someone in a childcare capacity (or any other 'regulated' capacity) whose name appeared on the list.

This list worked in tandem with *list 99* (Information held under the Education Act 2002), which dealt with individuals barred from working in schools and education settings in England and Wales. These were replaced by the Vetting and Barring Scheme, which was a recommendation of the inquiry into the Soham murders (a particularly harrowing crime in 2002 in which a school caretaker murdered two ten-year-old girls who had attended the school where he worked). This subsequently brought the POCA list, *list 99*, and a Protection of Vulnerable Adults list under the administration of the Independent Safeguarding Authority (ISA). The rationalisation of the lists and bringing them under the supervision of one umbrella organisation was a key constituent of the Safeguarding Vulnerable Groups Act 2006, which was passed as a consequence of the Soham murders.

The Vetting and Barring Scheme was eventually replaced by the Disclosure and Barring Service (DBS), which helps employers with recruitment to ensure that potential employees are safe. There are currently four levels of DBS check, which include a basic check, standard check, enhanced check, and enhanced check with barred list(s) (see Useful Websites). Once a DBS check has taken place, there is no official expiry date for that check. However, the check is only accurate at the time the check was carried out. Some local authorities recommend that a DBS check is renewed every three years, however, there is no standard practice for this.

Safeguarding children in a sport and leisure setting has come into the spotlight over the past few years due to high profile cases and media exposure. In November 2016, a number of former professional footballers talked publicly about being abused by former coaches and scouts in the 1970s, 1980s, and 1990s. The highest profile of these was allegations against former Crewe Alexandra and Manchester City coach, Barry Bennell. A number of former players under his care came forward and alleged that Bennell sexually abused them while they were under his care. This led to charges being brought against Bennell who then stood trial in January 2018 charged with several offences of abuse, including serious sexual abuse, involving 12 victims aged between 8 and 15 years. Following a five-week trial, Bennell was found guilty of 50 offences and sentenced to 31 years' imprisonment.

The Bennell case illustrates the importance of the Disclosure and Barring Service in protecting children from encountering people who may have motives to harm a child's physical or mental wellbeing.

19.6 Negligence Liability in School Sports

There have been several cases when school pupils have sued their teachers for injuries that they have received whilst taking part in recreational activities in school. The implications of these cases for the schools are of course that, as the employers of the teachers, they are likely to be held to be vicariously liable, and these cases may also have important considerations for sports and recreation centre managers who may employ coaches to work with children (or adults) and who will have the same kind of legal relationship with their charges that schoolteachers have. It is therefore in the best interests of the schools (and leisure centres) to recruit, train, and supervise their staff appropriately to try and minimise the chances of injuries in the first place.

A significant case, by way of illustration, involved an injury to a boy who had been playing rugby union (*Mountford v Newlands School*, 2007). The 14-year-old boy sued the referee/selector and school for injuries inflicted by an overage player participating in an age group rugby match. The school was held liable even though the English Schools Rugby Football Union rules did not prohibit boys playing outside their age group. Furthermore, the tackle that caused the injury was not a foul tackle, nor did the older boy's additional size contribute to the injury.

It seems that if the selector/referee had given the rules and the older boy's suitability to play due consideration and concluded that he was suitable to play, or if he had conducted an appropriate risk assessment, then there may have been no finding of liability. The fact that the selector/referee failed to consider the possible consequences of allowing an older boy to play was vital to the case (Heywood & Charlish, 2007).

The implications of this case for junior sport are potentially far-reaching. Whilst it is impossible to say just how many students play 'down' in lower age groups in school sports, it is undoubtedly the case that it happens and often for very good reasons. It may be the case that without an over-age student playing, an institution may not be able to raise a team, making the over-age player a necessity. Therefore, an unfortunate consequence of this case may be a reduction in participation rates in junior level sports.

In 2013, the Supreme Court gave clarity on the circumstances in which a school or local education authority can become liable for the negligent actions of an independent contractor. The case of *Woodland v Essex County Council (2013)* concerned a 10-year-old pupil of a school under the control of Essex County Council. Swimming lessons were being provided to the school by an independent contractor who provided a swimming teacher and a lifeguard. During a swimming lesson which took place within school hours, the appellant had managed to get into difficulties swimming and suffered a serious brain injury as a result. The case centred on whether the education authority had a 'non-delegable duty of care' towards pupils. In other words, that the council was unable, under any circumstances, to delegate their duty of care towards pupils to a third party who in this instance was the independent contractor. The Supreme Court held that the council assumed a duty to ensure the swimming lessons were conducted and supervised carefully and that such lessons are integral to a child's overall education. Therefore, due to it being an integral part to the teaching and supervisory function of the education authority, it fell within its non-delegable duties. As such, it follows that if the independent contractor is found to be negligent then that negligence extends to the local education authority meaning that in the case of *Woodland*, Essex County Council were held to be liable for the pupils' injuries.

Other problems may arise with staff or coaches taking part in activities with children. Liability may arise, for example, if a tackle is performed which causes injury to a child. A teacher or coach must take reasonable care when performing or demonstrating tackles and, crucially, must be particularly mindful of the disparity in age, size, and physical maturity between them as adults and the pupils/children.

Sometimes, young people need protecting from themselves, particularly if staff are aware of any issues which may make an activity unsuitable for any particular child. This was illustrated in *Moore v Hampshire CC (1982)*, where a 12-year-old girl who had congenital hip problems was allowed by her teacher to do PE, despite being forbidden from taking part in such physical activities. The teacher knew this but still allowed the girl to take part. The result was that the girl broke her ankle, and the school was held liable for the teacher's negligence in allowing her to participate. Again, the implications of this for coaches and teachers are that they must know their pupils or students and, if there are any known reasons that may place restrictions on participation in certain activities, the employers of the teachers or coaches must ensure that their staff comply with these restrictions or face the consequences

Liability is not just relevant to recognised sports. For example, in *A (a minor) v Leeds CC (1999)*, two girls collided with one another whilst taking part in a warm-up activity organised by the teacher during a PE lesson. Again, the school was held vicariously liable for the failure of the teacher to properly organise the warm-up activity. However, it should be stressed once again that schools and others in a supervisory position only need take reasonable precautions when dealing with children and young people.

The courts do not wish to minutely scrutinise all aspects of different activities which may be enjoyed. For example, in *Babbings v Kirklees MC (2004)*, a Year 4 schoolgirl was injured whilst in a mixed PE class with Year 3 children. The injury was caused when she was attempting a routine manoeuvre which involved jumping from a springboard to a high bar and holding onto the bar, then dropping from it and landing on her feet. Unfortunately, she suffered a fracture of her right arm and sued the school, alleging negligence on the part of the experienced teacher. The Court found in favour of the school, making it clear that it would be unreasonable to expect classes to be absolutely free from any risk and further that any move towards complete risk aversion would do PE no favours at all. This was echoed in the more recent Court of Appeal decision in *Hammersley-Gonsalves v Redcar and Cleveland Borough Council (2012)*, where a child suffered facial injuries after being struck by a golf club by a fellow pupil. The teacher with supervision responsibilities was at the back of the 22 boys who was taking part in the activity and did not see the incident take place. It was accepted by the Court that even the most observant teacher would not be expected to see the action of 22 boys no matter where they positioned themselves.

This is obviously refreshing news for educators and providers of sport and leisure services, reiterating that the legal duty is to take reasonable care for the safety of your 'neighbour'. Such measures will ensure that those involved in the sports and leisure industries do not find themselves being held liable for all injuries suffered by participants in activities which they have organised. However, the more recent *Woodland* decision is of more importance to local authorities who throughout the past ten years have increasingly outsourced services to third-party providers. The Supreme Court ruling has meant that education authorities should carry out, at the very least, a risk analysis to consider whether the outsourcing (to save cost) is worth the potential extension of their non-delegable duty of care.

19.7 Employment Law Issues

It is likely that any person involved in sport and leisure management will at some stage be involved either in hiring staff or having to part company with staff. Therefore, this section will deal briefly with some of the legal issues which may result from this.

It is important to remember that any contract of employment contains both express terms (terms written clearly into the contract) and implied terms. The latter are terms that are not written down but nevertheless are part of the contract and may include, for example, the duty to safeguard the health and safety of employees and the duty that, if provided, a reference will be written with reasonable care and skill. An employee has an implied contractual duty, for example, to adapt to new working conditions and to always exercise reasonable care and skill whilst carrying out their job. These terms are binding on both employer and employee.

19.7.1 The Employment Process

In the UK, within two months of the commencement of employment, an employer must provide written particulars of that employment to the employee (Employment Rights Act, 1996). Failure to do so will lead to an award of between two- and four-weeks wages in any case of unfair dismissal, redundancy, or discrimination (Employment Act, 2002)

19.7.2 Discrimination

It is unlawful for an employer in the UK to discriminate on the grounds of sex, race, disability, age, sexual orientation, religious belief, or on the basis of whether the worker is full time, part time, or on a fixed-term contract (Equality Act, 2010). Such discrimination laws typically apply from the job advert stage before employment is commenced, and any employer found guilty of discrimination on one of those grounds would be liable to pay a hefty sum in compensation. Discrimination may be direct (for example not employing someone simply because of their gender) or indirect (for example setting a condition of employment that means that more men than women or vice versa are likely to qualify) – by harassment and victimisation.

Discrimination laws however do not prohibit an employer from specifying gender or race requirements needed for a job due to the nature or genuine occupational requirements of that job. Similarly, an act of indirect discrimination may be lawful if the condition that is imposed is proportionate to a legitimate aim. So for example in the case *Panesar v Nestle Ltd* (1980), it was lawful to prohibit workers to have beards and long hair for Health and Safety and hygiene reasons, even though this was discriminatory against members of the Sikh religion who could not comply with this rule. It is important that any indirectly discriminating measure must amount to the minimum possible restriction necessary to achieve the aim, and no more. An employer also has a duty not to discriminate on the grounds of disability and must make reasonable adjustments to their workplace to ensure that individuals with a disability are not discriminated against. This duty extends to organisations that provide access to the public, such as shops, leisure centres, etc. and means that reasonable adjustments to premises must be made to ensure equality of access for those with disabilities.

19.7.3 Termination of Contract

Two types of employment termination are subject to legal proceedings and therefore to be avoided by managers – wrongful dismissal and unfair dismissal. Wrongful dismissal occurs where employment is terminated contrary to the terms of the contract. It typically occurs where an employee has suffered unjustified, quick dismissal. If an employer follows the relevant notice period, then they will defeat a claim for wrongful dismissal. Also, if an employer can show that the employee was guilty of a fundamental breach of the contract of employment (such as gross misconduct), they will be able to dismiss an employee without providing a notice period.

In order to pursue a claim for unfair dismissal in the UK, an employee must typically have been employed in the job for at least one year. The legislation (Employment Rights Act, 1996) provides for potentially fair reasons for dismissing an employee, such as their qualifications, their conduct, redundancy, or reaching the default retirement age. It also provides details of reasons for dismissal that would automatically be judged as unfair. These include dismissal due to pregnancy or illness, dismissal due to trade union membership, to unfair selection for redundancy, and where an employee makes a protected public interest disclosure – i.e. a whistle-blower. This list is not exhaustive and is considered so serious that the usual one-year employment qualification period to bring a claim for unfair dismissal is not applied.

In the event of a disciplinary process in the UK, it is important that the parties follow guidelines produced by the Advisory, Conciliation, and Arbitration Service (ACAS) – see Useful Websites – which although not law are nevertheless recommended, and if these are not followed it may lead to a higher award of compensation. The guidelines include the following principles:

- Raise issues quickly and promptly and ensure no unreasonable delays;
- The employer must carry out a reasonable investigation to ascertain the facts;

- The employer should afford the employee the opportunity to respond to concerns before any decision is taken;
- The employee should be allowed to be accompanied to any hearing by a trade union representative or work colleague;
- The right of appeal should be offered.

The onus is always on the employer to demonstrate that they have acted fairly and reasonably in dismissing the employee, so for instance if others have committed the same offence, have they been dismissed? If an employer breaches a fundamental of the contract that causes the employee to resign, then that employee may also bring a claim for Unfair Constructive Dismissal. This is designed to prevent the employer from seeking a way around the legislation by not dismissing the employee. Such reasons may include unilaterally reducing pay, failing to investigate allegations of sexual harassment, engaging in harassment, or applying a disciplinary sanction out of all proportion to the offence. Where an employee has been unfairly dismissed or unfairly constructively dismissed then there are three possible remedies:

1 Reinstatement in the same job;
2 Re-engagement in a comparable position in terms of salary, seniority, etc.;
3 Compensation – factors looked at to calculate the compensation will include the age of the employee, length of service, and salary. Additional factors which may be included in any award might be possible overtime losses, pension losses, or losses accrued by the employee seeking alternative employment.

19.8 Risk Management – Health and Safety

Anyone involved in providing trips away, particularly with young people, will be familiar with the need for a risk assessment. It is important that any risks are identified and then managed if necessary. The statutory framework relating to risk management and Health and Safety at work in the UK is for the most part covered by *The Management of Health and Safety at Work Regulations* (MHSW) 1999 and the *Health and Safety at Work etc Act, 1974.* The MHSW 1999, section 3 states:

'(1) Every employer shall make a suitable and sufficient assessment of –

(a) the risks to the health and safety of his employees to which they are exposed whilst they are at work; and

(b) the risks to the health and safety of persons not in his employment arising out of or in connection with the conduct by him of his undertaking. . . .

(2) Every self-employed person shall make a suitable and sufficient assessment of –

(a) the risks to his own health and safety to which he is exposed whilst he is at work; and

(b) the risks to the health and safety of persons not in his employment arising out of or in connection with the conduct by him of his undertaking.'

It is therefore necessary for all employers and self-employed individuals to carry out a formal risk assessment covering both their employees and others who may be affected by what they do. The regulations pay specific attention to the position of young people within the workplace – particularly relevant for those working in the sport and leisure industry. The regulations make it very clear that an employer must not employ a young person unless a review or assessment of relevant material has been made. Particular account should be taken of:

'(a) the inexperience, lack of awareness of risks and immaturity of young persons;
(b) the fitting-out and layout of the workplace and the workstation;
(c) the nature, degree and duration of exposure to physical, biological and chemical agents;
(d) the form, range, and use of work equipment and the way in which it is handled;
(e) the organisation of processes and activities;
(f) the extent of the health and safety training provided or to be provided to young persons; and
(g) risks from agents, processes and work listed in the Annex to Council Directive 94/33/EC[8] on the protection of young people at work.'

19.8.1 Health and Safety at Work, etc. Act, 1974

The *Health and Safety at Work, etc. Act,* 1974 lays out broad principles rather than specific requirements for both employers and employees in the UK. The most relevant sections of the Act are detailed in the text that follows.

Section 1 – Preliminary. This section stresses the duty of employers to ensure the broad provisions that the health and safety of all people are protected from risks connected with the activities of people at work and further, that dangerous substances are kept and used in a controlled manner. Section 1(1) of the Act specifically states:

'(1) The provisions of this Part shall have effect with a view to –
(a) securing the health, safety and welfare of persons at work;
(b) protecting persons other than persons at work against risks to health or safety arising out of or in connection with the activities of persons at work;
(c) controlling the keeping and use of explosive or highly flammable or otherwise dangerous substances, and generally preventing the unlawful acquisition, possession and use of such substances; and
(d) controlling the emission into the atmosphere of noxious or offensive substances from premises of any class prescribed for the purposes of this paragraph.'

Section 2 – General duties of employers to their employees. This section looks at the general duties of both the employer to ensure as far as is reasonably practicable the health, safety, and welfare of all employees, paying particular reference to the provision and maintenance of systems of work, the provision of training and supervision, and that a reasonably safe work environment is maintained. The section then goes on to detail the necessity to maintain and revise procedures as appropriate, to bring these updates to the notice of the workforce, and to consult with trade unions or other employee representatives when making and maintaining arrangements to ensure health and safety at work.

Section 3 – General duties of employers and self-employed to persons other than their employees. Again there is a generic duty, as far as is reasonably practicable for employers and the self-employed, to ensure that persons other than employees (such as visitors and/or customers) are not exposed to risks to their health and safety. Further, both employers and the self-employed should furnish persons (other than their employees) with the information about how the business is conducted which might affect their health or safety.

Section 4 – General duties of persons concerned with premises to persons other than their employees. This section places a duty upon employers to ensure that their premises and equipment within those premises are as safe as is reasonably practicable.

The Act also deals with the duty imposed upon employees whilst at their place of work. It includes:

Section 7 – General duties of employees at work.

'It shall be the duty of every employee while at work –

(a) to take reasonable care for the health and safety of himself and of other persons who may be affected by his acts or omissions at work; and

(b) as regards any duty or requirement imposed on his employer or any other person by or under any of the relevant statutory provisions, to cooperate with him so far as is necessary to enable that duty or requirement to be performed or complied with.'

Whilst the broad provisions of the Act may appear quite daunting, it is worth reiterating that the starting point for any risk management policy is that organisations must do all that is 'reasonably practicable' to protect people from risk. It is a legal requirement that employers look at any risks that may arise in the workplace and then control them by installing 'sensible health and safety measures'. It is not necessary to eliminate all risks, and for those in the sport and leisure industry this is particularly important as many activities linked to the industry by their nature carry risk; and if all such risk was to be eliminated then the nature of the activity would be destroyed. For example, a walking trip may be perfectly safe to engage in during the summer months but may become dangerous depending upon location and weather conditions during the winter. Similarly whilst a kayaking trip across a small lake may be perfectly safe, a proper risk assessment may not come to the same conclusion about a similar trip across a much bigger lake or on coastal waters.

It is not the purpose of this section of this chapter to produce a scaremongering catalogue of various disasters that have befallen sections of the sport and leisure industry in this area. Rather, it is to point the reader in the direction of sound sensible advice in interpretation of the Act. With a little effort, this can help produce reasonable policies which will fulfil the legal and moral requirements placed on organisations to maintain safety for all at work whilst at the same time retaining the central character of their business and the activities their business provides. Whilst all leisure providers have a duty to provide an appropriate risk assessment, it is worth pointing out that a failure to provide such an assessment will not by itself indicate a breach of duty on the part of a provider. In *Poppleton v Trustees of Portsmouth Youth Activities* (2008), the claimant failed to establish liability against an activity centre which provided indoor low-level climbing facilities. The claimant (an inexperienced climber) leapt from one wall and attempted to grab a buttress on another wall. He failed and fell awkwardly onto the matting below, breaking his neck and suffering permanent tetraplegia. Despite the fact that the defendants had failed to carry out a risk assessment, had provided no supervision, and had not given the claimant any explanation of the risks, it was held that there was no breach of duty. The risk of injury from such a fall was an obvious and inherent risk from the activity. The Court stated:

'The risk of possibly severe injury from an awkward fall was obvious and did not sustain a duty in the appellants to warn Mr Poppleton, (the claimant), of it.'

This is a very reassuring decision (not least given the failure to carry out a risk assessment) for all activity providers worried about the threat of legal liability. What this case and two subsequent cases, *Parker v Tui Ltd*, 2009 and *Uren v Corporate leisure (UK) Ltd & Ministry of Defence* (2010), emphasise is that there is risk involved in many activities and that it would be unjust, where an obvious or inherent risk manifests itself, to impose an overly burdensome legal duty upon activity providers; individuals must take care of their own behaviour.

19.8.2 Risk Assessment Guidance

The United Kingdom Health and Safety Executive (HSE) produce numerous very helpful leaflets detailing advice to organisations carrying out risk assessments (see Useful Websites). A central part of good risk management is effective risk assessment, defined thus by the HSE:

> A risk assessment is simply a careful examination of what, in your work, could cause harm to people, so that you can weigh up whether you have taken enough precautions or should do more to prevent harm. Workers and others have a right to be protected from harm caused by a failure to take reasonable control measures.

Whilst there are many ways of conducting risk assessments, the HSE very helpfully have produced a guide to conducting such assessments. It would be sensible for anyone working in the sport and leisure industry in the UK to follow the guidance laid down. The HSE identifies five distinct steps in the process. These are:

1 **Identify the hazards.** Simply by walking around the workplace it is possible to identify what may reasonably be expected to cause harm. Consultation with employees will further enhance this identification. Other practical methods may involve contacting the HSE and any relevant trade association.
2 **Decide who might be harmed and how.** It is important to recognise that particular groups of people (such as expectant mothers, members of the public, people with disabilities, and new workers) may have particular needs with regard to some risks. Similarly, people in the workplace outside of normal office hours such as cleaners, contractors, or shift workers may have particular needs that need dealing with.
3 **Evaluate the risk and decide on precaution.** The legal requirement is to do all that is 'reasonably practicable' to deal with a risk. It is not to eliminate all possible risks. The most sensible action to take is to try and comply with standard industry practice, paying particular attention to procedures followed, equipment used, warnings provided, and welfare facilities provided. Again it is important to discuss issues with staff and involve them in any proposals or procedures you intend putting in place.
4 **Record your findings and implement them.** If an organisation has less than five employees, then there is no legal obligation to record findings. However, if any employer is serious about following good practice, then this is really something they should do. The HSE have examples of good practice that can be downloaded, but essentially an employer must be able to demonstrate five things:

   a. That a proper check was made;
   b. That the employer enquired as to who may be affected;
   c. That obvious hazards had been dealt with and the number of people who might be affected by such hazards was taken into account (the more people who may be affected and the greater the consequences of the hazard, the greater the obligation to deal with it);

d. That reasonable precautions have been taken and any risk remaining is low-level;
e. That staff (or their representatives) have been properly involved in the process.

5 **Review your assessment and update if necessary.** It is recommended that a formal review takes place annually but that informally there is constant monitoring to ensure that any new staff, procedures, or practices are fully embedded into the risk assessment procedure. The HSE conclude on this matter that:

'During the year, if there is a significant change, don't wait: check your risk assessment and where necessary amend it. If possible, it is best to think about the risk assessment when you're planning your change – that way you leave yourself more flexibility.'

6 **There should be a proper system of monitoring and updating.** It is far preferable to set a date in the calendar for a formal update rather than wait until an incident requires attention. Whilst formal updates are important, remaining watchful and listening to employees plays a vital role in the process.

The HSE provide a clear summary of the overall responsibilities of both the employer and the employee when dealing with these matters (see Useful Websites) and information on who to contact if problems arise in this area. If the guidelines produced by the HSE are followed, then there should be no need at all for sport and leisure providers to have any fear of legal liability stemming from an accident in their business. Sound risk assessments and coherent risk management policies play a vital part in the industry. Through such means, good practice is encouraged, which in turn ensures that findings of liability in the event of accidents are unlikely. More importantly, they enable people to enjoy the benefits of all that the industry has to offer whilst being able to experience the ordinary risks of an activity but not being vulnerable to unreasonable risk.

19.9 Conclusion

How the law relates to sport and leisure is a vast area, and this chapter has just touched the tip of an iceberg. It has concentrated on some of the most significant issues. The recurring theme through much of the detail covered in this chapter is that if providers behave reasonably, then they are unlikely to find themselves on the wrong side of the law. The emphasis for anyone involved in these industries should not be merely to ensure that their behaviour, policies, and practices are designed so that they do not find themselves being held liable for injuries suffered by another. Rather, they should ensure that safety is designed into all that they do, so that unnecessary danger is prevented or alleviated. This will, of course, have the effect of ensuring that they are not legally liable, but the emphasis remains on safety for the user rather than merely preventing liability.

If such an approach remains the focus for all involved in the area of sport, leisure, and recreation, this will enable people to remain safe, whilst at the same time providers will not be inhibited. The appropriate level of risk will be managed and, crucially, maintained if the nature of the activity demands it. The courts are not in the grip of a 'compensation culture' or 'Health and Safety mania'. The issues raised in relation to such concerns are necessarily one part of a much wider picture the courts must take in any case that comes before them. This can perhaps best be summed up by Lord Hoffman, who as long ago as 2003 commented:

It is of course understandable that organisations like the Royal Society for the Prevention of Accidents should favour policies which require people to be prevented from taking risks. Their function is to prevent accidents and that is one way of doing so.

But they do not have to consider the cost, not only in money but also in deprivation of liberty, which such restrictions entail. The courts will naturally respect the technical expertise of such organisations in drawing attention to what can be done to prevent accidents. But the balance between risk on the one hand and individual autonomy on the other is not a matter of expert opinion. It is a judgment which the courts must make and which in England reflects the individualist values of the common law.

(*Tomlinson v Congleton Borough Council*, 2003 at para 47)

Practical Tasks

1 Read the Australian case found at:
www.lexisnexis.com.au/aus/academic/text_updater/luntz_hambly/186_alr_145.pdf
What safety measures would need to be taken in England in a similar situation to prevent legal liability in the event of an injury to a spectator, a participant, and a trespasser?
2 For a single trip for a club that you know (e.g. to an away match, to an event, to a concert) conduct a risk assessment, with reference to the HSE guidelines. When it is completed, think of an accident that may happen to one of the club's members during this trip and evaluate the legal implications of this accident.

References

Deakin S., Johnston A., & Markesinis, B. (2007). *Markesinis and Deakin's Tort Law*, 6th edition. Oxford University Press.
Elliott, C., & Quinn, F. (2007). *English Legal System*, 8th edition. Pearson.
Fafinski, S., & Finch, E. (2007). *Legal Skills*. Oxford University Press.
Harpwood, V. (2009). *Modern Tort Law*, 7th edition. Routledge Cavendish, Oxon.
Hartley, H. (2009). *Sport, Physical Recreation and the Law*. Routledge.
Heywood, R., & Charlish, P. (2007). Schoolmaster tackled hard over rugby incident. *Tort Law Review*, 15.
Williams, K. (2005). State of fear: Britain's 'compensation culture' reviewed. *Legal Studies*, 25(3).

Cases

General negligence principles: Donoghue v Stevenson (1932) AC 562

Vicarious Liability

Beard v London General Omnibus Co (1900) 2 QB 530
Gravil v Carroll & Anor (2008) EWCA CIV 689
Limpus v London General Omnibus Co (1862) 1 H & C 526
Lister v Hesley Hall (2002) AC 215

Sports/Recreation Specific Negligence

Caldwell v MaGuire & Fitzgerald (2001) EWCA Civ 1054
Parker v Tui Ltd [2009] EWCA Civ 1261
Poppleton v Trustees of Portsmouth Youth Activities [2008] EWCA Civ 646
Sutton v Syston Rugby Football Club Ltd (2011) EWCA Civ 1182
Uren v Corporate leisure (UK) Ltd & Ministry of Defence [2010] EWHC 46 (QB)
Watson v British Boxing Board of Control (2001) Q.B. 1134

School Sport Negligence

Babbings v Kirklees Metropolitan Council (2004) EWCA Civ 1431
Hammersley-Gonsalves v Redcar and Cleveland Borough Council (2012) EWCA Civ 1135
Mountford v Newlands School (2007]) EWCA Civ 21
A (a minor) v Leeds CC (1999) CLY 3977
Moore v Hampshire CC (1982) 80 LGR 481
Woodland v Essex County Council (2013) UKSC 66

Occupiers Liability

Bolton v Stone (1951) A.C. 850 HL
Cunningham & Others v Reading Football Club Ltd, The Times, 22 March 1991 (HC)
Ratcliff v McConnell (1999) 1 WLR 670
Simms v Leigh Rugby Football Club Ltd (1969) 2 All ER 923
Tomlinson v Congleton Borough Council (2003) UKHL 47
Wattleworth v Goodwood Road Racing Company Ltd (2004) EWHC 140

Discrimination

Panesar v Nestle Ltd (1980) ICR 144

Legislation

Children's Act 1989
Compensation Act 2006
Employment Act 2002
Employment Rights Act 1996
Equality Act 2010
Health and Safety at Work, etc. Act 1974
The Management of Health and Safety at Work Regulations 1999
Occupiers Liability Act 1957
Occupiers Liability Act 1984
Protection of Children Act 1999
Safeguarding Vulnerable Groups Act 2006

Chapter 20

The Importance and Management of Events

By Guy Masterman

In This Chapter

- Why are events important?
- Who are the key stakeholders for events?
- What are the short-term and long-term objectives for events?
- What are the different stages of the event-planning process?
- What are the requirements for the successful planning of an event?

Figure 20.1 A school's football event in Newcastle, UK, organized by university students as part of their event management course. It is more than just a game that is on show here.

Summary

The extent to which events impact on and affect peoples' lives is something that is not easily measured; but throughout history, events have been readily recorded as marks in time and as catalysts for great changes in society. At the other end of the scale, it is difficult to imagine a week going by without an event that an individual relates to and takes note of. Events of all scales are important throughout societies. In analysis they can be seen to be tools for the achievement of sociocultural, economic, environmental, and political objectives. They are also used to develop participation and competition in sport, art, music, dance, business, and politics. In other words they touch all aspects of society, and thus an event can be an agenda for the achievement of as wide an influence as is imaginable. The world's top events are now so important they are much sought after and bid for.

A successful approach to planning an event is a logical, staged process that works from objectives at the outset, to evaluation of results, followed by feedback at the end. However, it is continuous evaluation throughout the process via an iterative approach that will lead to success. If the objectives are used to devise a concept and strategies, there can be evaluation at every stage to ensure that planning can be aligned and realigned to what is intended and that opportunities can be exploited as they occur.

20.1 Introduction

An event can be a lot more than 'just a game' and, whatever its size, it can be of great importance to its community. This chapter will explain why and how this is the case. It is important to start with one key message, and this is that events are fun. They are fun to watch, take part in, and organise. Event management is not for everyone, but for those that aspire to it, the thrill of seeing a 'sold out' sign, the running-order working to time, and planning that provides solutions to complex problems means more than being in the spotlight on the stage or field of play. Event management is a 'behind the scenes' role, and planning and then implementing an event that meets its objectives can be both a vocation and a one-off experience that can be thoroughly enjoyable.

This chapter will provide an overview of the job of organising events by considering how to plan and then implement them, whatever their size or location. First, though, it is important to set the scene and consider why events are important, what they are, and what they can achieve.

20.2 What Are Events?

In the literature there are several differences in the definitions and terms used to identify events. A definition describes an event as a thing that takes place, a public or social occasion, or as a contest; it is also a planned and organized occasion (Collins dictionary, 2020). Event management literature uses a wider range of terms. An event is transient, has a fixed duration, and is unique (Getz, 1997). It can also be planned or unplanned. One of the most famous examples of an unplanned event is an inter-trench football match between enemies who temporarily halted fighting in the First World War. There was very little preparation beforehand, and yet in retrospect we can still analyse this happening as an event. When it comes to event management, though, we are clearly concerned with those events that are planned. Some refer to these as 'special events' (Allen *et al.*, 2005; Getz, 1997; Goldblatt, 1997).

Unfortunately, there is insufficient consistency when it comes to the use of terms such as *major*, *mega*, or *hallmark* events. For some, the Olympic Games is a 'hallmark' event (Goldblatt, 1997; Hall, 1992). For others it is a 'mega' event, while hallmark events are recurrent in a particular city, e.g. the Wimbledon tennis championships occur every year in London (Getz, 1997; Allen *et al.*, 2005). Some refer to hallmark events as sizeable, with wide-ranging target audiences, considerable media interest, including broadcasters, regional and perhaps national government stakeholders, commercial sector partners, and superior technical competencies and human resources (Getz, 1997; Westerbeek *et al.*, 2006). On the other hand, mega events might be sizeable, with a 'dramatic character, mass appeal and international significance' (Roche, 2000). A more recent take on this would be to also use the size of social media an event inspires.

The term *sizeable* also offers some confusion. For an indoor concert, an audience of 5,000 might seem small if it is a venue like Wembley Arena, where the capacity is 12,500, while 1,000 participants at a harvest festival in a local village might be deemed very welcome by that community. Less than 70,000 for a Manchester United home game would be a commercial concern as the Old Trafford 'Theatre of Dreams' holds over 76,000 and is regularly sold out. So, establishing some kind of audience and/or participant number as a threshold is not wholly adequate for definition purposes (Emery, 2002).

The model offered by Jago and Shaw (1998) does go some way to providing a relationship between major, hallmark, and mega events. It at least includes all these terms in a structure that alludes to size and scale. See Figure 20.2 for several examples of major and minor events, mega and hallmark events.

Further classifications of events can identify those events that cut across all aspects of society – culture, sport, politics, and business – and of course may be indoor or outdoor, in purpose-built or temporary venues, predominantly participatory or spectator-led, and competitive or recreational. For example:

- **Cultural events** – art exhibitions; stage plays; pop, rock, classical, and operatic concerts; dance displays; food and drink shows; film festivals;
- **Sports events** – single or multi-sport events in schools and clubs; regional, national, and international competitions; local, regional, and national programmes for sport participation development; frequent league and infrequent cup competition; E-sports:
- **Political events** – local and national party rallies, conferences, and conventions; marches and demonstrations; inaugurations and ceremonies;
- **Business events** – expos; networking symposiums; conferences; trade exhibitions; conventions; media and press launches; product launches, experiential marketing events, and demonstrations; tourism expositions.

Local events have always been important. While there are those mega, hallmark, and major events that many people are aware of, it is local events that arguably have most effect on peoples' lives. They have appeal because they are fun, entertaining, possibly adventurous, and glamorous. They can involve and integrate diverse communities, increase awareness, and promote all kinds of organizations and their objectives. Some attract 'A' list performers and others the more locally famous 'C' list, but they can also display the talents of beginners and local expertise. Consequently they are an important part of leisure and recreation programmes, and as such an increasing importance is being placed on their organization and the development of skills and competence in event management at this level.

20.3 The Importance of Events

Historically, events have played an important role in the development of society, and in many cases key individuals have, sometimes against all odds, created something of significance from the smallest of beginnings. People have always celebrated or marked special occasions such as birthdays, deaths, anniversaries, moons, solstices, and seasons; and through folklore some of the festivals, ceremonies, competitions, and exhibitions we celebrate today were derived hundreds, even thousands, of years ago. In this way, events have been derivatives of society that have evolved into society-shaping agents.

In Ancient Greece events were of such importance that there were truces from war to accommodate them, and as recently as the First World War a game of football was able to temporarily halt warfare between enemies. It is reported that on Christmas Day in 1914 an inter-trench football match was contested and, while reports are varied, this feat has now become legend (Bancroft-Hinchley, 2000).

Religions have played a big role in the creation of the events that are now a traditional part of many societies, and in some cases, they have become so widely encompassing that they have become integrated with a wider culture that incorporates art, music, and sport. The

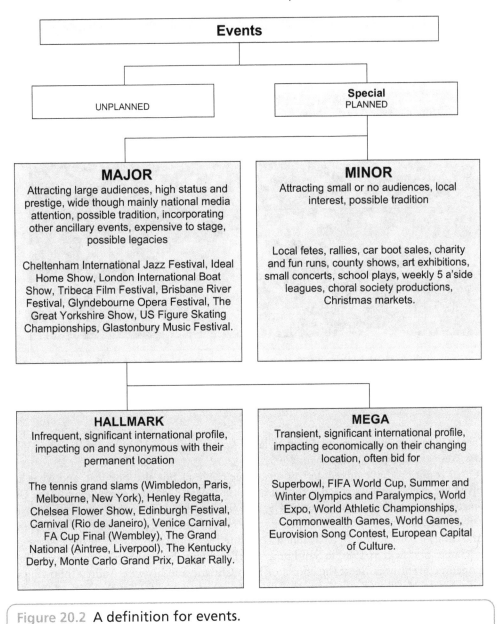

Figure 20.2 **A definition for events.**
Source: Adapted from Jago and Shaw (1998)

Olympics today are a celebration of sport but also dance, music, and art. The Ancient Jews celebrated 82 sacred days, of which 59 were holidays from work, and to organise special events they appointed event managers with the title of Director of the Feast (Smith, 1831). More recently other church groups have played a role in developing sport. For example, basketball was originally a recreational game created at a New England School for Christian Workers by James Naismith in 1891 (Naismith Basketball Hall of Fame, 2020), and in the UK some of the earliest football clubs and teams were formed out of church groups. The Parish of St Domingo's Church in Liverpool founded a team that went on to become Everton

Figure 20.3 A sheep shearing demonstration attracts a small audience as part of the larger programme of the Great Yorkshire Show, Harrogate, UK.

FC in 1879 and, in Birmingham, Aston Villa FC was founded in 1874 by the Parish of Villa Cross Wesleyan Chapel (Masterman, 2009).

Other traditions have mixed derivations, some religious but also political, and what has evolved are events that are deeply rooted in culture: May Day and Hogmanay in the UK, Homecoming and Thanksgiving in the US, and Independence Days throughout the world. Many individuals have risked all in their pursuit for their beliefs, and some have used events as the catalyst for success. Tom Waddell is credited with having conceived the idea of the Gay Games first held in 1982 in San Francisco. The Glyndebourne Festival is a world leading operatic event because of the efforts of John Christie and his wife Audrey following its opening in 1934. The Glastonbury Festival is an internationally famous rock music event dreamed up by Michael Eavis, started in 1970 on his own land. These varied examples demonstrate that society has been influenced by individuals and their creation and implementation of events. Previous editions of this book rightly refer to such events as 'landmarks of history'.

Contemporary events touch all our lives. Events are both derivatives of as well as shapers of society. All scales of events are influenced politically, if only because there is a fundamental requirement to conform to laws and regulations for health and safety, employment, fiscal reporting, and licensing. There are also political events such as rallies, congresses and, of course, marches. The opinion polls for prime ministers have been seen to increase at the time of successful events, such as in France in 1998 during the FIFA World Cup. Equally, if politicians get it wrong, the reverse can happen, and the Millennium Dome in London and its construction delays, the mismanagement of the 2000 New Year celebrations and its initial lack of positive legacy were a negative for the UK government at the time. More recently the scandals associated with several Olympics, for example doping at Sochi 2014 and bribery around construction contracts for Rio 2016, arguably resound still more because they are in the Olympic window. On a positive note, the Black Lives Matter movement that caught momentum in 2020 was launched and progressed via sportsmen and women at their events.

The development of technology and events are interrelated. The development of materials for sports equipment such as rackets and balls, digital timing, and sophisticated call centre operations for ticket selling are all intrinsically involved in the growth and development of sport events (Masterman, 2014). In 2008, technology was a contentious intervention for South African double-amputee sprinter Oscar Pistorius when he was not allowed to use his carbon fibre prosthetics in races as they were deemed to be technically giving him an illegal advantage by the International Association of Athletics Federations (Robinson, 2008). Pyrotechnics almost appear to be standard at many events, and fireworks, once used as enhancements for events, are now the focus of some. The Boston Harbor 4 July fireworks celebrations in the US are a spectacle that enthrals thousands of residents as well as visitors. Television, as an informer and broadcaster of events, also plays an ever-increasing role, as do the internet and mobile and wireless communications. The explosion and relentless development of social media platforms provides event managers with a plethora of communication opportunities, as well as the issues that can also come from those. These media not only provide wide, sometimes global audiences, they are also available 24 hours a day as promotion tools and sales outlets, and as such enhance events while also providing important communications for society at large.

The development of the arts, music, dance, and sport relies on the showcases that events supply. The more people who watch events, the greater the opportunity for spectating and participation to increase. Events that invite participation, such as club open days, coaching workshops, summer schools, and taster sessions, are direct approaches intent on widening participation. Events are therefore potentially significant development tools. However, it is important to recognise that for development to be sustainable there need to be strategies in place that follow up on initial participation. An 'open day' approach, for example, can lead to a number of people turning up to play a sport, try out theatre, appreciate art, or play an instrument, but these events will need to be supported by strategies that ensure that these fresh recruits stay interested in the longer term. Nevertheless, events are important to society as developers of new ways to 'get involved'.

CASE STUDY 20.1

Collaborative Initiatives, the case of +Art

The +Art organization has supported collaborations between artists and communities since 2004. With its beginnings in New York, +Art has created opportunities via education and public art projects. It works with High Line with outdoor installations, for example, and many schools with introductory workshops, as well as lectures and panel discussions for senior citizens and war veterans. To date it has produced more than 40 public art projects and around six education programmes every year.

Source: Moreart (2020)

20.4 Event Owners, Promoters, and Managers

The requirement for excellence in events management is increasing, from audiences and participants as well as organisers. While larger events are organised by promoters, governing bodies, and combinations of agencies that may be well-trained and experienced, local events are controlled by leisure managers, facility, and venue managers and often many volunteers, who may well be organising an event that lies outside their usual remit. The +Art organization featured in Case Study 20.1, for example, is wholly reliant on volunteering.

Event owners are not always the organisers of their own events. Event management organizations, agencies, and promoters can be brought in to run one-off events. Events can also be an integral part of a larger programme, where there may be any number of event organizations staging constituent events that may or may not require close collaboration. This happens a lot in sport, where there are local, regional, and then national phases to competitions, particularly at school and club level. A typical format is to progress from local to regional to national rounds of competition. St Bede's College Under-12 football team, from Manchester, UK for example, progressed through district, county, and regional competition to become English Schools Football Association 9-a-side small school champions in the 2018–2019 season. At the international level, the Association of Tennis Professionals (ATP Tour) and European PGA (golf) operate their tours in a similar way, whereby their year-long programmes consist of different events in cities throughout the world.

Generally, each event has a different promoter, although there are some well-established and sizeable organizations such as IMG Events that have bid for and won the right to promote several tennis and golf events on the respective tours. On the other hand, there are many independent promoters that prefer to keep their stable of events small, such as Ion Tiriac and partners, the organisers of the Madrid Open. While a rock band can also take in many cities, music tours generally consist of daily concerts over an intensive period of a month or two. Ed Sheeran had the highest grossing tour in 2018 (US$ 429 million), taking in 99 shows all over the world, including Gothenburg, Munich, and Zurich in Europe, and Tokyo, Cape Town, and Jakarta (NME, 2020). On the other hand, theatre tours are more usually organised by one promoter/organization and involve longer stays at each venue. For example, the West End show *The Lion King* toured regional theatres throughout the UK in 2019, and the UK TV phenomenon, Britain's Got Talent, has been touring UK arenas since it started in 2008.

Event owners can also be promoters. The Great Run Company owns and organizes the Great North Run, the world-famous half marathon in the northeast of England; it has also rolled out a whole series of 'Great Runs' across the UK as well organizing similar events abroad. Manchester, Glasgow, and Belfast City Councils in the UK have event departments that own and manage events as well as spending considerable time actively attracting other owners and promoters to their cities. The Great Run Company, for example, has worked closely with Manchester City Council in staging an annual 'Great Run' in the city for over a decade; in 2009 it also laid a special 60-metre track on Deansgate, the main shopping street in the city, for a televised race that featured world 100-metres record-holder Usain Bolt.

Governments, regional or local municipal authorities, educational institutions, clubs, and commercial promoters can all independently own and/or stage events. If these are sports events, they will generally be required to run them according to prescribed rules, which might also require a more complex process of applying for official sanction from a governing body. Events can also involve more sophisticated management arrangements. Host cities, supported by collaborative organising groups made up of several partners and stakeholders, can bid to run an event by applying to event rights owners. Sheffield City Council's Event Unit has staged nearly 1,000 events since its inception in 1991, following its hosting of the

World Student Games, for example, including many that it has had to bid for with several different partners.

Many major international events are bid for by organising groups that may consist of the city authority, regional development agencies, national governing bodies, commercial supporters, and national government. These events can have significant impact and in the main are sports related. In Australia and the USA the model is based on State departments. Sport and Recreation Victoria, for example, is driven by a keen strategy that sees Melbourne regularly hosting the Australian F1 Grand Prix, International Air Show, and the Australian Open (tennis), and it has also bid for and hosted the 2006 Commonwealth Games and 2003 Rugby World Cup matches. The State of Utah, having hosted the 2002 Winter Olympics in Salt Lake City, had a state-driven strategy and now lists itself as the 'State of Sport '(Utah Sports Commission, 2020; Masterman, 2014). The growing importance of major events of all types is being increasingly recognised by municipal authorities, and this is highlighted by the emergence of city and state departments such as these.

On a smaller scale, all schools, colleges, and universities organise sports events for intra-mural as well as inter-institution competition, but they also organize exhibitions and con-ferences with a focus on showing off student and staff talent. Hence, they are organizers of exhibitions for art, fashion and design, music concerts, plays, and conferences for knowledge transfer. These events can be credit-bearing in support of educational programmes, but they can also be staged to attract research income, business, and students. They can be to show parents what is being learned.

Other institutions and organizations have also recognised the importance of having event-led strategies. Fast-moving consumer goods manufacturers have seen how events can increase product awareness and sales. For example, several drinks companies have associated them-selves with or owned events, such as Coca-Cola and its Music Festival; Pepsi's lifestyle show, Extravaganza; Red Bull's Air Race; and Guinness' Wittness music festival.

Whatever the size of the event, the volunteers can be critical. The use of 100,000 volun-teers is becoming the norm for a Summer Olympics, with the organisers of the 2012 London Olympics seeking as many as Beijing did in 2008. However, the input from volunteers in the organization of many local events is no less critical. Certainly in sport it is the volunteers who run the clubs, leagues, and associations that ensure that players can take part. It is esti-mated that around 21% of adults volunteered in sport in England in 2018–2019 (Statista, 2020). However, this is also true of other recreations and their provision of events. Local arts, music, and drama societies provide entertainment for their communities with exhibi-tions, concerts, plays, and pantomimes throughout the UK, with sometimes only a handful of members multi-tasking to ensure successful events.

20.5 The Purpose of Events

The key to minimising negative impacts and achieving potential positive impacts is in the effective planning of the event (Masterman, 2014). To plan an event, therefore, an event manager needs to work towards specified objectives. The following criteria form a broad set of purposes for staging events, many of which are interrelated.

20.5.1 Socio-Cultural Objectives

Events can be culturally and socially beneficial. First, they can be fun to attend, participate in and organize, and in this sense, they will meet various individual personal needs. Because they are fun and can satisfactorily meet a number of values held by individuals, they can be readily undertaken, and they are useful tools for society to use as conduits for social inclusion, cohesion, and compliance. So events can bring those of different religion, race, age, and sexual persuasion together. They can also be used to integrate these various sectors for a more harmonious society.

Equally, events are also perceived to provide opportunities for those members of society who might step outside the law and as such are seen to provide them with more acceptable activities. Harlem, in New York, is known for its efforts in this vein, with a number of sports clubs founded. Events such as the Rucker Basketball Tournament, for example, founded by Holcombe Rucker in 1950, were created to inspire Harlem youths and provide them with 'discipline, dedication and teamwork' (Williams & Rivers, 2006). The courts at Rucker Park have helped countless numbers of Harlem youths by bringing in some of the greatest names in US basketball, for example Julius Erving, Kareem Abdul-Jabbar, Kobe Bryant, LeBron James, and Allen Iverson. Boxing has also played a substantial role in Harlem, and in 2009 the Aero Space Gym put on a Focus Mitt Boxing Championship featuring boxing champions and celebrities to aid East Harlem School to provide more opportunities for its pupils (NY 1, 2009).

Figure 20.4 The Rio 2016 Olympic zone at the port was a whole area dedicated to an Olympic influenced cultural experience. Provided free of charge with no sport, it was an area for music, art, and eating and where the sponsors could showcase their involvement and provide entertainment.

The period leading up to an event as well as the event itself can be used to effectively widen the effect of such socio-cultural strategies. In general the International Olympic Committee (IOC) recognises the importance of widening the Olympics and its sports focus so that it can impact right across society. For example, it regards a cultural programme as an 'essential element of the celebration of the Olympic Games', and therefore it is a requirement of a host city to provide one (Masterman, 2014). Salt Lake City, for example, provided an arts festival that included 60 performances, 10 major exhibitions, and 50 community projects, again supported by Coca-Cola (Masterman, 2014; Salt Lake City, 2002). In Rio, the 2016 Olympics was able to inspire and generate street art so that artists and spectators could benefit.

20.5.2 Political Objectives

Events of all sizes can be used politically. First, events can be used at a macro level, whereby party-political objectives can be achieved. Also at a macro level there are examples of events that have been used to extol the benefits and values of certain political ideals. The gaining of worldwide recognition via 'mega event politics', and in particular via measurable economic gain via tourism and inward investment, has long been a political strategy (Hall, 2001; Preuss, 2004). Barcelona is a much-cited example of a city that used its 1992 Olympics to benefit over the long term. It is claimed that the city's main objective was to develop a profile for the city and the Catalan region that might compete with the Spanish capital, Madrid (Roche, 2000). Beijing also used its 2008 'Peoples Olympics' as a means of informing the world about Chinese culture, as did Sochi in opening up its Russian doors to the world in 2016. There are other more controversial examples of nations attempting to develop national and cultural identity via political manipulation focused on the Olympics. In particular, Soviet and East German approaches in their use of sport as a political tool in the mid-twentieth century have been well documented.

Cultural events can also be used for diplomatic objectives. Orchestras, for example, have been the focus of 'soft diplomacy' for some time (see Case Study 20.2).

CASE STUDY 20.2

The Diplomatic Use of the Arts

The use of music, artists, and orchestras for political gain is not new; for example, it is more than 50 years since a Western orchestra, the New York Philharmonic, was taken to the former Soviet Union. While it might not be that clear, there is no doubt that a touring orchestra can be used in a 'soft' diplomatic approach where hard-line international political relations are not as subtle or successful. The appeal is that orchestras and other artists are harmless, and their art is their passport to a country even when relations are aggressive. Art forms such as orchestras can be very useful tools for diplomacy. An artistic tour can be seen as a sign that there is still room for a better relationship on a political front.

There have been some quite sophisticated examples. The Royal Ballet has performed in Beijing's National Centre for the Performing Arts, adjacent to Tiananmen Square. The invitation to China, where dance culture is quite different, and to a particular area of the city that was perceived in the West to be steeped in controversial human rights issues, was meaningful. The tour was unlikely to have had an immediate effect on relations, but as a part of a long-term strategy it was seen as an important step. On the other hand, the message was clearer from the West-Eastern Divan Orchestra, which featured both Arab and Israeli musicians.

The beauty of this kind of implementation is that it can be mutually acceptable because both sides want it to happen. Cuba, for example, invited both the New York Philharmonic Orchestra and the Royal Ballet to perform in the capital, Havana, in 2009.

This was a significant move, virtually unprecedented since Cuba became a Communist state in 1959. It is perceived that in offering this invitation, Cuba indicated its desire to develop positive relations with both the USA and the UK. The invitation might have been refused, of course, but in this case President Obama lifted the 40-year-old embargo on Cuba to allow the visit of the orchestra. The visit of the Royal Ballet to Cuba was the first by such a company since the Bolshoi Ballet visited from the Eastern Bloc almost 30 years previously (Carroll, 2009).

The objective is not always to smooth the political waters; it might also be a more hostile threat that can be imposed. The Ossetian-born conductor Valery Gergiev, a good friend of Russian President Vladimir Putin, was carefully selected to take a Russian orchestra to South Ossetia in 2008 at a time when the region was troublesome for the Russian government. While this was a selection that showed a willingness to work together, the choice of music was also significant – it included Shostakovich's 7th Symphony, a composition that relates the story of the siege of Leningrad.

Sources: Carroll (2009); Higgins (2009)

Discussion Question

To what extent can or should events be apolitical? Discuss this in relation to one or more events you are familiar with.

20.5.3 Development Objectives

An event is a showcase and can be used to widen awareness of the arts, music, sport, dance, a political idea, or a commercial product, with the intention of widening participation and/or increased support and interest. The latter may be to increase numbers of fans and followers generally, and numbers of paying spectators or members specifically. The 'come play an instrument' approach is a simple concept, and the Peoples Music School, Chicago, founded in 1976 by Rita Sino, is a master of it. The school gives opportunities to young people of all financial backgrounds by providing free tuition and puts on its own Street Festival. 'Come try art' is also a simple but effective idea and can involve adults and children alike. In Brisbane, Australia, drawing workshops are staged in the street by city agencies, with the objective of getting people to participate in art.

While all sports events can be used to promote the sports involved, newly created events can also be used for specific purposes. Following the lead of London and the founding of its Youth Games in the 1980s, there are now county Youth Games throughout England that are designed to get non-playing youngsters into sport as well as promote competition for those who are already participating (see Case Study 20.3).

The North Yorkshire Youth Games

The North Yorkshire Youth Games, run by North Yorkshire Sport (NYS), an Active Partnership, formerly a County Sports Partnership, has been an annual event since 2000. While the culmination is one day in August for teams and young sportsmen and women of all school ages, the event is something that stretches over the entire year. Teams represent the eight local community sports networks in the county of North Yorkshire in boccia, kurling, rugby league and union, swimming, orienteering, cross-country, athletics, cheerleading, football, hockey, kwik cricket, netball, tennis, and gymnastics. To reach the finals at the Games, teams compete in leagues and knock-out competitions throughout the year within their districts.

The aim of the Games is to develop and sustain participation and competition in sport. Many of the sports' governing bodies are involved via their regional offices in the administration and coaching that is required to improve performance and also to enthuse young athletes into sport. The key, though, is for this enthusiasm to be sustainable and for these athletes to carry on in sport after the Games. Of course, there is the ongoing opportunity to compete for as long as the young people are at school and therefore in as many Games as that allows, but the critical factor is ensuring that they participate after they are eligible, in other words in out of school hours and once they have reached school leaving age. The dropout from sport at this latter stage of the life cycle is of particular concern for Sport England.

NYS as a partnership consists of not only the local district councils but also the various school sports partnerships in the region and the national governing bodies with regional representation. This allows NYS to hold dialogue and build programmes with schools and sports clubs. It operates the Games to encompass both school and club teams in order to build the links so that the bridge for sport participation between schools and clubs can be created.

In addition to hosting 1,500 young people at the Games and the many more that compete throughout the year, NYS also supports this activity with other government-sponsored programmes that provide investment to impact the lives of young people.

20.5.4 Economic Objectives

Commercial firms from the manufacturing and service sectors are not the only organizations that might derive revenue from an event. Cause-related events are designed to deliver funds for charities, and promoters of music, dance, and sports events are typically intent on realising a profit. Event owners, whether they have development objectives or not, may also seek a profit so that funding may be raised to add to their overall development effort. Small as well as large events can be designed for economic objectives, and while events can be used as loss leaders at the outset, the ultimate aim for all event managers is at least to break even. Most will seek a surplus, driven by a budget, whether the surplus is to be used for commercial or non-profit purposes.

How might the North Yorkshire Youth Games be commercially developed?

While an event is a budget-driven project, there is a further area of economic gain to be considered. For major, hallmark, and mega events there is the critical importance of a wider economic impact. A negative impact on the economy can result in a legacy that taxpayers have to bear. The cost of the 1976 Montreal Olympics and Sheffield's 1991 World Student Games, for example, have both been heavy and long-term financial burdens on those two cities. However, there can be a positive outcome via the attraction of inward investment prior to an event, event tourism during an event, and then the 'image' gained from the event can be leveraged to attract business after the event is over (Preuss, 2004).

For example, Barcelona attracted sufficient inward investment to regenerate its waterfront with infrastructure for its 1992 Olympics and has since further utilised the initial benefit in the long-term for what is now a well-recognised positive legacy. The original Olympic Zone is now a thriving resort area consisting of a marina, retail outlets, and residential housing in what was once a rundown area. The city also claims to have increased its meetings, incentives, congresses, and exhibitions (MICE) business as a result of its staging of the event. Prior to the Games, in 1990, there were 100,000 congress attendees, which grew to over 200,000 after the Games in 1996.

While sports events are prominent media topics when it comes to reviewing economic legacies, there are other examples of cities gaining economic impacts from hosting cultural events. For example, the Eurovision Song Contest and the European Capital of Culture have been sought and used as economic catalysts. In 2014 Copenhagen's Eurovision hosting is estimated at generating over £13 million, 39,000 visitors, and 87,000 overnight stays in local hotels. Liverpool, as European Capital of Culture in 2008, used its event to help boost tourism numbers between 2002 and 2006 by 16% and tourist expenditure by 24% (RBS, 2020; Liverpool, 2009a, 2009b). World Expo is a major event that has been sought for economic impact, and Shanghai was intent on using its hosting of Expo 2010 not only to create new infrastructure and develop business but also to create links between its two key areas, which sit on opposite sides of the river: Puxi, the home of the famous skyscraper skyline, and Pudong, the more popular tourist area (Wasserstrom, 2009). Shanghai is widely seen as being a success in attracting a then-record 73 million visitors.

An issue with economic impact studies of events is that they are invariably communicated as positive legacy. However, while cities perceive there to be a possibility of developing their economies because of hosting major events, this is not universally accepted among academics. The scepticism derives from our lack of capacity to measure such benefits over the long-term and then be assured that the impacts are undoubtedly as a result of staging an event (Jones, 2005). Milan's Expo in 2015 was considered to be a flop for example, and several Eurovision hostings have only managed to break even at best. However, with all events there is the almost unmeasurable impact of destination awareness to also consider; if this could be accurately evaluated, then a more rounded analysis of impact would result.

20.5.5 Environmental Objectives

Major events are recognized as having the potential to be catalysts for 'greening' regeneration and development projects. The Department of Environmental Affairs and Tourism in

South Africa, for example, appointed the Environmental Evaluation Unit and Steadfast Greening to provide greening guidelines for large sporting events in 2009. In particular, the guidelines focused on the 2010 FIFA World Cup but also considered the greening of other sporting events (EEU, 2009). Such initiatives are widely acknowledged as being initiated by the precedent set at the Sydney Olympic Games in 2000, where standards that addressed waste management and recycling as key contemporary issues for event managers were instigated (Allen *et al.*, 2005). Since then 'green' Games have been a controlled requirement for the IOC. For the Games in 2004, for example, Athens addressed waste management, water quality, and air pollution and, for 2008, Beijing went to some effort with afforestation, air pollution prevention, recycling, and water installation in particular (Masterman, 2014). In 2016 Rio promised to host the most sustainable Olympics ever, and it certainly faced some significant challenges, in particular the city's water pollution. While there is some controversy in the outcome, the IOC (2020) does claim a successful environmental legacy with improved sanitation, river courses, waste treatment approaches, and nil landfill since 2012.

All events, whatever their size or location, have the potential and now responsibility to be greener. Even users of temporary venues for music concerts need to adopt good practice when it comes to waste disposal, sanitary utility provision, and the handing back of the site to owners in a state at least as good as before. Waste disposal is a constant activity for most events throughout their duration, and in many cases, it is a job that is outsourced.

An environmental issue that will prevail within the event industry is that of carbon footprint evaluation. Clearly many of the events used as examples in this chapter involve a lot of travel, worldwide tours, and international events that attract the world's best performers, while tourists from around the globe require significant air travel. The dilemma here is that while technology such as television and internet broadcasting has allowed audiences to see events they cannot attend, all events are nevertheless successful because they are 'live' and the experience of attending an event is the main product on offer. There will no doubt be continuing reluctance from event organizers to detract from that offer. Despite some examples of innovation and success in online events during COVID-19 lockdown, the live experience is what makes events special.

20.5.6 Regeneration Objectives

There are benefits that can be gained by incorporating regeneration projects into event planning and the use of events as catalysts for the achievement of municipal objectives. An event that necessitates the development and utilisation of land that would have otherwise been redundant can then leave physical legacies for future social, cultural, and economic benefit, and for some cities this can help justify the initial event staging costs. This capacity is generally limited to major events and mainly mega sports events: for example the 2000 Olympic Games and the regeneration of the Homebush area of Sydney; the 2002 Commonwealth Games and the regeneration of the Eastlands area of Manchester; and East London's transformation in connection with the 2012 Olympics. The transformation of urban space via event-led strategies is a form of 'urban boosterism' whereby events are an attractive municipal proposition because they are perceived as stimulants to urban economic redevelopment (Andranovich *et al.*, 2001; Hiller, 2000).

20.5.7 Physical Build or Renewal Objectives

This is a contentious area of objectives, not because events cannot be catalysts for new facilities, but because many facilities that have been built as a result of hosting events have turned out to have negative legacies or be 'white elephants' because of underutilisation. In particular, these are sports- and Olympics-related. Stadium Australia, for example, remains a financial challenge to date, and the main Olympic site created for the 2004 Games in Athens is now almost completely unused and derelict. The key issue is planning – it is entirely possible to plan for and achieve physical legacies out of the planning of major events, and Manchester has shown this to be the case in relation to the facilities it built for its Commonwealth Games, which have been in continuous use since 2002 (Masterman, 2014).

Essex and Chalkley (2003) suggest that over time there have been three types of Olympic host city – those that have sought to keep the scale of transformation to a minimum (Los Angeles 1984, Salt Lake City 2002); those that have produced substantial sports facilities but little in the way of wider urban provision (Munich 1972, Moscow 1980, Calgary 1988); and those that have produced sports and/or major urban infrastructure (Grenoble 1968, Sapporo 1972, Seoul 1988, Atlanta 1996, Sydney 2000, Athens 2004). Add to the latter Beijing 2008, London 2012, Sochi 2014, and Rio 2016. Noticeably these were not in three distinct periods through time; there are cities that were early developers of infrastructure, as well as later and very recent examples of more frugal approaches.

There is an important link to be made between the new facilities that are built for major events and the other physical infrastructures that are put in to support them, in particular structural 'hard factors' such as housing, telecommunications, and transportation (Preuss, 2004). For example, in building facilities in disused and outer-city areas, there arises the need to provide adequate transportation, if only for the event itself. Clearly this requires further investment – for example AU$ 80 million for Sydney's 2000 Olympics (Holloway, 2001) – and its future use becomes reliant upon the long-term success of the facility it serves.

In contrast, events do not in general provide a great stimulus for legacies in the form of accommodation, hotels, and room increases, etc. There are few examples in the industry of new build, refurbishment, and even renovation of hotels, simply because the increases in event tourism are not proven as sustainable (Essex & Chalkley, 2003; Hughes, 1993). However, the mountain cluster that was created for the Sochi 2014 Winter Olympics with a whole street, indeed a small town of hotels and support infrastructure, serves three snow resorts. While it is dependent on tourism rather than future events, it is indeed an event legacy. To date, this is a developing area that appears to be successful.

There are two types of post-event usage – sports, leisure, and recreational use by the local community and/or the staging of other future events. The 1992 Barcelona Olympics were a part of a wider long-term city strategy for modernisation and provide an example of both types of after-use. The strategy 'Barcelona 2000' was implemented in the mid-1980s and included six new sports stadia, an Olympic Village on the waterfront, a new airport, and communication towers. Two distinct organizations were created to manage the legacies, one to attract and run major events and the other for public sports participation. This strategy helped to 'popularise the Olympic event, to develop public-private sector partnerships in the post-event management of facilities and also to promote the after-use of the facilities by the mass public' (Roche, 2000).

> ### Discussion Question
>
> What objectives do you think are important in order to gain local political and commercial support for a new event in your community?

The Event Planning Process

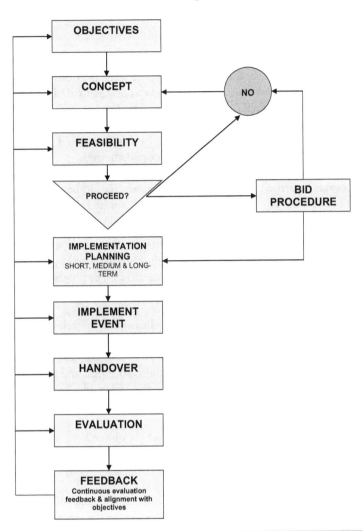

Figure 20.5 **The event planning process.**
Source: Masterman (2014)

20.6 The Event Planning Process

In order to achieve any combination of the objectives considered earlier, whatever the scale or nature of the event, an event manager needs to underg an event planning process. The remainder of this chapter is devoted to explaining this process, which encompasses both short-term requirements for the implementation of the event, and the long-term objectives regarding the legacies of the event (Masterman, 2014). Figure 20.5 contains a model of this planning process.

The event planning process model consists of up to ten different stages. As can be seen from Figure 20.2, each stage may be revisited iteratively, so that realignment with objectives can be undertaken if required. A description of each stage in the process now follows (adapted from Masterman, 2014).

20.6.1 Objectives

The first stage in the planning of any event is to determine its purpose – the previous discussion provides several options. The Great North Run, for example, was originally designed to widen participation in running in northeast England. The Tribeca Film Festival was created by Robert De Niro with the City of New York to further promote the city as an international centre for filmmaking. Manchester aimed to use its 2002 Commonwealth Games as a catalyst for the regeneration of derelict areas and to increase employment opportunities.

The setting of specific and measurable objectives provides direction for the planning, execution, and evaluation of the event. In order to do this, all stakeholders should be identified and consulted so that their requirements can be considered and incorporated, if necessary, into the planning of the event. Stakeholders in events can be any of the following:

- **Customers** – individual and corporate ticket buyers, participants or competitors, advertisers, corporate package buyers (e.g. franchised spaces), sponsors, merchandise buyers.
- **Suppliers** – the organizations that are used to supply equipment, services, or goods in connection with the event, for example equipment, legal advice, food and beverages, transportation, security, and emergency services.
- **Partners** – many sports events are not possible without the sanction of the relevant regional, national, and international governing body. Other partners may well be local, regional, or national governments or their agencies. Separate event management organizations may well combine forces to put on an event, as may clubs, societies, and associations. Sponsors are often referred to as partners both in their title rights and because of the longevity and/or closeness of the relationship, as too are media organizations that purchase event rights.
- **Investors** – some of these partners may also be investors in that they have a vested interest as a result of providing funding either financially or via in-kind services. Municipal or agency investment may require non-financial returns such as sporting, cultural, or social development.
- **Staff** – permanent staff, short-term event hired personnel, sub-contracted staff, and volunteers.
- **External influencers** – these include the event publics that are important for the success of the event and therefore influence any decision-making, even if they are not directly connected to the event in any of these terms. For example, the local community in which the event is delivered, pressure groups, local and national governments, individual politicians, and the media.

Following stakeholder analysis and any consultation, the key questions for those managing the event are:

- Why is the event to be held?
- What is to be achieved?
- Who is to benefit and how?

If the event is to be managed by an appointed agency, then it is important to consider any briefs that have been received for the event from the event owners, as these will form the basis of the objectives. Often it is the brief that forms the invitation to pitch for the right to manage the event, and so it forms the earliest of guidelines for the planning that follows.

Once the objectives have been formulated, they then become the basis for the design of the event which follows at the next stage. These objectives are essentially built in as mechanisms to align subsequent planning. At all stages of the process, there should be regular evaluation to see if planning is still on track. If planning has gone awry, or indeed new opportunities may be possible, then realignment is possible. Alignment can be achieved with the identification of performance indicators and targets that are tied to the objectives, both for the short- and long-term.

For all scales of event, the planning process identifies its own integrated indicators, i.e. through the setting of deadlines for the achievement of budgeted levels of income, appropriate cashflows, prescribed levels of media coverage, or the signing of appropriate contracts with suppliers and partners. It is also important to incorporate mechanisms to allow for the exploitation of any new opportunities for improving the project during implementation.

20.6.2 Concept

Once the objectives have been determined, the event can be designed. The design or event concept is guided by clear and measurable objectives. The Beijing Olympics adopted an approach that utilised new and existing facilities all over the city, including on its outskirts and further afield by partnering with other cities such as Shanghai and Quingdao. London's Millennium Dome year-long 'show' in 2000 set out to provide a snapshot of as wide a picture of the world as possible and did that by creating zones that showcased technology in particular, but also fun elements like the circus.

Having undertaken a stakeholder analysis, it is possible to identify the decision-makers for the planning that follows. The key questions asked at this stage are:

- What is the event?
- What does it look like?
- Who are its target audiences and customers?

Using environmental analysis tools, including competition analysis, will ensure that the concept can be fully developed to achieve the objectives. Consideration of the following should also be undertaken:

- The scale of the event;
- How it will operate;
- When it will be staged;
- Where it will be staged – locations and venues;
- What facilities and equipment will be required;
- Who the key partners are – local or national government, governing bodies, event owners, and promoters and charities.

At this stage, consideration should also be given to what kind of show will be put on. All events are entertainment and can be expensive to stage, so it is necessary to determine what will be the base requirement and what the possibilities are for enhanced provision. The location and venue may be supplied with some of the requirements already intact, while sponsors may supply other enhancements such as ancillary entertainments, decorations, and special effects. The quality of the performance is critical, and so the level of performer is also a consideration at this stage. The items that may be costly and which it may be tempting to ignore in order to keep costs under control may also be the factors that are essential if customer satisfaction is to be achieved. For example, waste disposal, clean toilets, accessible parking, and pleasant and informative stewarding may all be costs, but they may also be factors that can affect competitive advantage.

After-use is also an important consideration at this stage. Whatever the scale of the event, facilities, equipment, and venues may need to be handed on or back to their owners; alternatively, divestment may be an option. There will be cost and effort involved, and so it is critical that this be considered and planned so that handover can be executed effectively at the right time, even though at this stage this might appear to be a long way off.

Discussion Question

What event concept would you develop for your local town to meet the following objectives?

- Integrate all sections and age groups in the community.
- Involve local groups, associations, or societies.
- Encourage local retail and business interest.
- Utilise local outdoor facilities and spaces.
- Develop regional interest and awareness of the town and its assets.

20.6.3 Feasibility

This stage of the planning process is concerned with deciding if and how the concept can run. As long as this is approached with flexibility, the concept can be revisited until feasibility is ensured.

The concept needs to be tested. This might require a dress rehearsal, or a run-through of key aspects. For major events this may involve the delivery of one or more events that are used as learning curves. Beijing, for example, as was required by the IOC, put on a number of high-profile events prior to 2008 and in the Olympic venues, including international tae-kwondo, swimming, diving, and water polo championships (Beijing, 2008 (2008)). London 2012 ran a whole years of test events.

There needs to be a thorough audit of how financially robust the concept is at this stage. Whatever the scale of event, a cost/benefit evaluation needs to be undertaken in order that the budget can be set. This will enable organizers to forecast cash flows, which will help form appropriate performance indicators. By determining costs prior to any decisions to proceed, organizers can ensure that unnecessary costs can be kept to a minimum and that there will be no surprises. It may be a peculiarity of the UK, but both Manchester and London's Olympic bid books for 2000 and 2012 respectively contained unresolved tax issues. London 2012 did not know whether the government required VAT payments to be made throughout its planning period.

Further consideration at this stage should be given to the feasibility of long-term after-use, or the need for handover of legacies at the end of the event. To identify costs and a firm budget, the following questions need to be answered:

- Who is responsible for the delivery of the objectives (short- or long-term) and the timings that are involved?
- What resources are required, from where, and when – financial, personnel, facilities, equipment, marketing, services?
- If there is a bidding process, what criteria are to be met and at what cost – can this be written off, or is a return on the investment required, even from a losing bid?

- What is required for event implementation, execution, and evaluation, and when?
- Are there any intended legacies, how will they be handed over, and to whom – are there any requirements for the long-term after-use of facilities that need to be addressed at this stage?

Whatever the scale of the event, a Master Plan is required. This might be a manually derived and maintained schedule, and for many small events this will be handwritten or produced at home. However, the more complex the event, the greater the requirement for each individual aspect of planning to be planned so that they create the Master Plan, which comprises:

- Facilities;
- Staff and personnel;
- Administration, documentation, and finance;
- Sales and marketing;
- Equipment;
- Presentation and media;
- Support services;
- Health and safety.

For large events, the Master Plan is more complex; for example, for Beijing 2008 it consisted of the following departments, each of which provided a separate contributary plan, coordinated by a Project Management Department (Masterman, 2014; Beijing, 2008 (2008)):

- International relations – liaison with the IOC and national Olympic committees;
- Sports – organization of all competitions;
- Media and communications;
- Construction and environment;
- Marketing – sponsorship and licensing;
- Technology – office and event communications;
- Legal affairs – contracts and legal counsel;
- Games services – housing, transportation, registration, and spectator services;
- Audit and supervision – overseeing of funding and staff performance;
- Human resources – recruitment, training, and management of staff;
- Finance – budget management;
- Cultural services – festival management;
- Security;
- Media relations – press centre operations;
- Venue management;
- Logistics – materials and services for the Games;
- Paralympic Games – liaison with the IPC;
- Transportation;
- Torch relay;
- Accreditation – for athletes, officials, and dignitaries;
- Ceremonies;
- Villages – accommodation operations;
- Volunteering – recruitment, training, and management;
- Ticketing – ticket sales and distribution.

20.6.4 Proceed

If the event is feasible, the decision on whether to proceed or not can be made. If the event is deemed infeasible, there is an opportunity to revisit the objectives and the concept to determine a way forward. If this can be achieved, the decision to go ahead can be made; but if not, there is also the option to abort the event.

20.6.5 Bidding

For some larger-scale events there is a bidding process to undergo. For example, many major international sports events are bid for. This is also now an approach that rights owners from the arts have adopted in strategies to take their events to cities around the world. The 2007 International Indian Film Festival Awards, for example, were hosted by Bradford in the UK. The city beat New York and Melbourne to be the host, and its subsequent successful staging of this event led to it being declared by UNESCO the world's first City of Film in 2009. Clearly a bid can be expensive, and as there can only be one winner there are a number of losers with sunk costs. Therefore the decision to proceed to bid and the costs that will be incurred should be a consideration at the feasibility stage of the planning process.

With bidding costs high, it is becoming more common for cities to look carefully at the objectives that might be achieved just by bidding – in other words, gaining a return on the bidding investment, even if the bid fails. For example, it is not unreasonable to say that Havana, Cuba, submitted its bid for the 2012 Olympics with a low probability of winning. Even though its bid was rejected in the early rounds of the process, it might be assumed that there were diplomatic, possibly even trade, benefits to be realised from bidding.

20.6.6 Implementation Planning

The next stage is the planning for the implementation of the event. This is when both short- and long-term strategies are developed to achieve the objectives set. For the delivery of the event itself, the short-term operational strategies need to cover a number of key areas, each of which may be organized into a unit and coordinated by a dedicated team. Every event is unique, but what follows is a general indication of what might be planned for.

The skills of those involved, whether they are full time or volunteers, are clearly varied, and for major events specialists in administration, finance, marketing and public relations, support services, catering, sponsorship, facility, and media management may well be employed. Skilled event directors can adapt themselves to run all kinds of events and as such can also become much sought after. However, for those events with lower profiles there will be smaller management teams, and in many cases the personnel involved will have to be multi-skilled.

If there are long-term objectives, it is important that long-term strategies are also implemented at this stage. For these events, expertise in economic generation, urban regeneration, town planning, city marketing, cultural and sport development, and environmental sustainability may be required.

Both the short- and long-term strategies that are required to deliver the event need to be included in the development of a critical path. Their alignment with event objectives is again an important element in an approach that requires continuous evaluation. Readdressing the budget requirements and assessing performance indicators throughout this stage will help to ensure event planning stays on course.

20.6.6.1 Critical Path

An event is a complex project and as such requires project management skills. A successful event manager will adopt a process that looks to identify and then break down all the tasks that are involved in staging the event and place them into a time plan that maximizes effectiveness and efficiency. A critical path is such a time plan, with the sequencing and pre-requisites for each key task clearly identified. There are several areas and types of tasks that are critical for every event, and these must be identified in advance, together with the time-lines required to complete them. This approach provides a backbone for event implementation planning and a calendar with deadlines for all tasks.

The chart can become overcrowded and extremely complex, and to identify any clashing schedules, tasks need to be prioritised. Analysis can be used to determine a critical path, identifying deadlines by which tasks absolutely must be achieved. This analysis shows how many tasks will impact upon others and limit effectiveness. An event manager can then identify the consequences of not achieving each task and identify who will coordinate each one. The objective remains the same: an effective and efficient set of tasks performed in the right sequence. To initiate this process, the following general areas of work should be considered:

- **Programme** – coordination of the schedules, the running order of each component, main stage and ancillary activities, liaison with acts, players and performers, choreography, rehearsal, show entertainment;
- **Staff** – management and accreditation of full-time and volunteer personnel, human resource issues, training, welfare, and payments;
- **Administration and services** – financial and resource management, legal agreements and contracting, venue bookings and arrangements, facility and equipment coordination, recruitment and coordination of sub-contractors and suppliers, licenses, security, transportation, accommodation;
- **Marketing** – product, prices, distribution, and promotion management;
- **Commercial** – sponsor recruitment and relationship management, franchised space, licensing and merchandising, advertising, retail sales, ticket sales;
- **Technical** – coordination of the purchase, hire, supply and return of equipment, provision of effective and legal health and safety, creation and execution of audio-visual effects and communications, environmental sustainability, sanitation;
- **Catering** – management of retail, hospitality, and staff catering;
- **Media** – press and broadcaster relationship management;
- **Public relations** – government liaison, governing body liaison, stakeholder development, and enhancement.

20.6.7 Event Implementation

Once plans have been made, they can be executed, so this stage of the process is a separate one. However, it is neither essential nor practical to assume that all planning can be done prior to all the implementation that has to be undertaken. Some decisions can be made and implemented before others, provided that the impacts they have on each other have been fully considered. There is also a degree of flexibility required in all planning, especially the longer the time period, in order to allow for opportunities that were initially unforeseen. For example, the organisers of the 2012 London Olympics had to address a global recession since they won their bid and the effect that had on construction and purchasing costs as well as reduced interest in sponsorship.

If the planning for implementation has been in accordance with the objectives set, a successful event may be achieved. The reality, of course, is that events will always throw up opportunities and issues both during planning and during the event itself, and so these will need to be addressed. There is significantly more time and capacity to do this if the planning has been as comprehensive as possible. The unforeseen can be addressed if the foreseen is well planned for. This was indeed pertinent in 2020 with COVID-19 lockdown in place; all event organizations in full planning flow had to readdress their schedules and, in most cases, postpone or cancel their events. Many innovatory approaches followed, and in many ways event managers have gained.

20.6.8 Handover

The event is not completed for another three stages yet. This stage begins with the shutdown of the event and concludes with the handing back of facilities and equipment to the owners. An example is parkland, seating, and staging following a jazz concert at Kenwood in London. Other examples include forestation after the conclusion of an orienteering event on farmers' land, and the Intercontinental Hotel in Beijing following its use as a media centre for the 2008 Olympics. There is also the handover of any legacies that are to be managed in the long-term, such as new facilities to new owners. This might be newly developed staging, seating, and backstage facilities provided so that the arts might be staged in the long-term at ancient venues such as the Acropolis in Athens (theatre), the amphitheatre at Verona (opera), or the new Globe in London (Shakespeare).

Shutdown involves returning the site to its original state or to a state that has been agreed with the incoming management. This might involve cleaning up as well as clearing out, and a strategy has to be in place so that this is as efficient and effective as possible, not least because this is a costly time that has no income return. This is therefore a stage of the process that should already have been planned. For some events this might also be a long period and particularly costly. The Sydney Olympic Park was not handed over for a year following the closing of the 2000 Olympics, and the City of Manchester Stadium also took a year to reconfigure before it was handed over to lessees Manchester City FC following the 2002 Commonwealth Games. The handing over of the responsibility for evaluating the legacy over the long-term was also a consideration for both these events (Adby, 2002; Bernstein, 2002).

20.6.9 Evaluation

There is general agreement that evaluation is performed in the short-term after an event, but there is less consideration of long-term evaluations. Subjective as opposed to objective evaluation of an event after it has ended, in the short-term, is common. However, measurement against the objectives set is a practice that is often seen as time-consuming and costly. Assessing the impact of an event in the long-term is not a widespread practice for similar reasons. It may also be a case of the responsibility for this task being unassigned. This is prevalent at the highest levels with the IOC itself – only committing to a comprehensive approach to short-term evaluation in 2002 via its Transfer of Knowledge programme. Even now the IOC is less conclusive about how it should encourage long-term evaluation in its host cities.

As a minimum, a formal overall evaluation report is always required that at least covers the process up to the close of the event. It is this that will enable the managers of the next event to easily decide how the new event should be delivered (Felli, 2002). However, evaluation is not just necessary at the end of the process, as has already been discussed. Continuous alignment with objectives, whatever the scale of the event, is a requirement throughout the planning process.

20.6.10 Feedback

The final stage of the process is one that ensures that everything that can be learned from planning is fed into the next event. So the evaluation of whether it achieved some or all of its objectives, strategies, tactics, and tools can be used to guide future decision-making. Processes are therefore required to ensure that evaluation reports and formal discussions are used and that any changes to planning and new developments for planning are made possible.

20.7 Conclusions

Given the increasingly recognized importance of events, there is a call for greater advances in the field of event management. Practitioners can now be trained and educated in many aspects of event management, and there is still burgeoning academic support in research and theory. However, there are few standards, and professionalism varies. Event evaluation, for example, is not consistent either in application or in commonly accepted tools. Similarly, approaches to planning vary greatly.

It is, though, still early days for a subject that did not have a university degree until the mid-1990s, and there are successful events to be found throughout the world that continue to beat expectations. These successes, as well as failures, are gradually feeding into the field, informing us of better ways to use and manage events.

Practical Tasks

1 Select an event of your choice from your neighbourhood that has only local interest. Analyse who the stakeholders are and determine what objectives this event seeks to achieve.

2 For a small, local event such as a sports tournament or a festival in a park, devise a first draft of a critical path which identifies the key tasks to deliver the event and the minimum timescale necessary to achieve them.

3 For past events that you know well, from personal experience or from media reports, identify key problems and discuss whether better continuous evaluation might have prevented these from happening.

References

Adby, R. (2002). Interview with the director general. Olympic Co-Ordination Authority, Sydney 2000 by email questionnaire on 9 July 2002.

Allen, J., O'Toole, W., McDonnell, I., & Harris, R. (2005). *Festival and Special Event Management*, 3rd edition. John Wiley & Sons, Queensland.

Andranovich, G., Burbank, M., & Heying, C. (2001). Olympic cities: Lessons learned from mega-event politics. *Journal of Urban Affairs*, 23(2), 113–131. Urban Affairs Association.

Bancroft-Hinchley, T. (2000). Football match between first world war enemies on Christmas Day 1914 really took place. Retrieved from www.english.pravda.ru/sport/2001/01/01/1795 (accessed 22 May 2003).

Beijing. 2008 (2008). Retrieved from www.beijing2008.cn (accessed 11 February 2008).

Bernstein, H. (2002). Interview with the chief executive of manchester city council. Chief Executive Office, Manchester Town Hall, 28 June, 2002.

Carroll, R. (2009). Obama administration grants exemption from 40-year embargo. *The Guardian*, 14 July. The Guardian Group, Manchester.

Collins dictionary. (2020). Retrieved from www.collinsdictionary.com/dictionary/english/event (accessed 25 August 2020).

EEU. (2009). Retrieved fromwww.eeu.uct.ac.za (accessed 4 August 2009).

Emery, P. (2002). Bidding to host a major sports event: The local organising perspective. *The International Journal of Public Sector Management*, 15(4), 316–335.

Essex, S., & Chalkley, B. (2003). *Urban Transformation from Hosting the Olympic Games*. University lecture on the Olympics. Centre d'Estudis Olimpics, Univesitat Autonoma de Barcelona. Retrieved from www.olympicstudies.uab.es/lectures (accessed 19 March 2005).

Felli, G. (2002). Transfer of knowledge (TOK). Paper: Architecture and international sporting events: Future planning and development. International Conference, Lausanne, June 2002. IOC, Documents of the Museum, Lausanne.

Getz, D. (1997). *Event Management and Tourism*. Cognizant, New York.

Goldblatt, J. (1997). *Special Events: Best Practices in Modern Event Management*. John Wiley & Sons, New York.

Hall, C. M. (1992). *Hallmark Tourist Events – Impacts, Management and Planning*. Bellhaven Press, London.

Hall, C. M. (2001). *Imaging, Tourism and Sports Event Fever. Sport in the City: The Role of Sport in Economic and Social Regeneration* (C. Gratton & I. Henry, Eds.). Routledge, London.

Higgins, C. (2009). Striking a conciliatory note. *The Guardian*, 14 July. The Guardian Group, Manchester.

Hiller, H. (2000). Mega-events, urban boosterism and growth strategies: An analysis of the objectives and legitimations of the Cape Town 2004 Olympic bid. *International Journal of Urban and Regional Research*, 24(2), 439–458.

Holloway, G. (2001). After the party, Sydney's Olympic blues. Retrieved from www.europ.cnn.com.2001 (accessed 13 March 2002).

Hughes, L. (1993). Olympic tourism and urban regeneration. *Festival Management and Event Tourism*, 1, 157–162.

IOC. (2020). Retrieved from www.olympic.org/news/olympic-games-rio-2016-environmental-legacy (accessed 25 August 2020).

Jago, L., & Shaw, R. (1998). Special events: A conceptual and differential framework. *Festival Management & Event Tourism*, 5(1–2), 21–32.

Jones, C. (2005). The potential economic return to stadia and major sporting events or a month on the lips, a lifetime on the hips? Conference paper at The Regional Studies Association, The Regeneration Games, 14 December, 2005, Goonerville.

Liverpool. 2008 (2009a). Retrieved from www.econstudy.net (accessed 4 August 2009).

Liverpool. 2008 (2009b). Retrieved from www.liverpoolcapitalofculture2008.co.uk (accessed 4 August 2009).

Masterman, G. (2009). *Strategic Sports Event Management: Olympic Edition*, 2nd edition. Elsevier, Butterworth-Heinemann, Oxford.

Masterman, G. (2014). *Strategic Sports Event Management*, 3rd edition. Routledge, Oxford.

Moreart. (2020). Retrieved from www.moreart.org/mission-history/ (accessed 25 August 2020).

Naismith Basketball Hall of Fame. (2020). Retrieved from www.hoophall/about/about-hall (accessed 25 August 2020).

NME. (2020). Retrieved from www.nme.com/news/music/these-are-the-highest-grossing-tours-of-2018–2417386 (accessed 25 August 2020).

NY 1. (2009). Retrieved from www.ny1.com/content/ny1_livinh/99171/boxing-benefit-helps-out-harlem-school (accessed 4 August 2009).

Preuss, H. (2004). *The Economics of Staging the Olympics: A Comparison of the Games 1972–2008*. Edward Elgar Publishing, Cheltenham.

RBS. (2020). Retrieved from www.rbs.com/rbs/news/2016/05/the-cost-of-winning-the-eurovision-song-contest.html (accessed 25 August 2020).

Robinson, J. (2008). Amputee ineligible for Olympic events. *New York Times*, 14 January 2008. Retrieved from www.nytimes.com/2008 (accessed 29 January 2008).

Roche, M. (2000). *Mega-events and Modernity: Olympics and Expos in the Growth of Global Culture*. Routledge, London.

Salt Lake City. (2002). Retrieved from www.saltlake2002.com (accessed 24 April 2002).

Smith, H. (1831). *Festivals, Games and Amusements: Ancient and Modern*. Colborn and Bentley, London.

Statista. (2020). Retrieved from www.statista.com/statistics/420045/sport-volunteers-uk-england (accessed 25 August 2020).

Utah Sports Commission. (2020). Retrieved from www.utahsportscommission.com (accessed 25 August 2020).

Wasserstrom, J. (2009). Retrieved from www.csmonitor.com (accessed 4 August 2009).

Westerbeek, H., Smith, A., Turner, P., Green, C., & van Leeuwen, L. (2006). *Managing Sport Facilities and Major Events*. Routledge, London.

Williams, L., & Rivers, V. (2006). *Forever Harlem*. Sports Publishing LLC, New York.

Chapter 21

Management Consulting in the Sport and Leisure Industry

By Rob Bailey

In This Chapter

- What is management consulting?
- What is the key terminology of the management consulting industry?
- What is the size and structure of the UK management consulting industry?
- What roles do management consultants play?
- What is the management consulting process?
- What skills do management consultants need?
- What career opportunities are there within sport and leisure sector management consulting?

DOI: 10.4324/9780367823610-21

Summary

Management consultants provide independent, external advice to help improve the performance of their clients' organisations. These clients come from across the private, public, not-for-profit, voluntary, and charity sectors. The management consulting industry has grown rapidly in the UK, especially during the last 20 years. The Management Consultancies Association estimated that revenues for the industry were £12.5 billion in 2020.

Consequently, this chapter provides an overview of this dynamic and diverse industry, particularly where management consultants work on behalf of sport and leisure sector clients. Management consulting is a fast-moving and constantly changing industry, reflecting the wider business environments within which the clients operate, and the many commercial, market, competitor, operational, financial, and other challenges, and opportunities they face. To make a positive impact for their clients, good consultants should develop and revise their services regularly to remain relevant and warrant the (often large) fees paid for their services. The number and type of consultants and consultancies that complete sport and leisure sector work is vast, ranging from individual management consultants and small consultancy companies to the larger, multi-national consultancies such as KPMG, Deloitte, PwC, EY, Accenture, McKinsey & Company, Boston Consulting Group, IBM Consulting, Bearing Point, and Bain & Co., to name but a few. This chapter concludes with a discussion of the sport and leisure sector management consulting career opportunities that exist for any reader to pursue.

21.1 Introduction

Management consultants are external advisors who provide independent, specialised expertise and support to clients in exchange for a fee. Consultants assist clients across all business functions, including strategy, finance and accounting, sales and marketing, operations, information technology, human resources, and research and development. There are many reasons why clients seek external assistance from consultants, ranging from problem solving to exploiting and maximising opportunities. In many cases, the objective is to help improve the performance of the client organisation. Depending on the nature of the organisation, the way 'performance' is measured varies. By way of example, this includes financial performance measures such as income, operating profit, and return on investment, in the case of a profit-orientated businesses such as a private health and fitness club, hotel, or theme park, to other performance measures associated with social, community, educational, health, and wellbeing objectives – in addition to financial measures – which would be more relevant to a not-for-profit organisation (e.g. a sporting National Governing Body or the Community Foundation of a professional football club).

Not all organisations use, or even need, management consultants (e.g. because they might have the necessary skills and experience within their organisation). However, consultants are active throughout the UK economy, including within the sport and leisure sector and its constituent parts such as professional sport, community sport and physical activity, commercial leisure and entertainment, events, hotels and resorts, bars, restaurants and other hospitality establishments, arts and culture, visitor attractions, travel, and tourism. Examples of consultancy projects and their clients are as follows:

- Assessing the market and financial feasibility of a proposed new community sport and leisure centre on behalf of a local council;
- Developing a marketing strategy to help a professional rugby union club generate more profitable income on non-match days through activities such as conferences and events;
- Preparing a business plan to help a professional cricket club raise finance to fund the redevelopment of its stadium;
- Creating a talent retention plan for an international hotel chain;
- The creation and implementation of a new customer booking system on behalf of a private health and fitness chain.

These are only a few examples of projects and clients but give a flavour of the diversity of consultancy work.

Management consulting has a certain mystique despite being embedded within many sectors. A perception of management consultancy was once (and might still exist in some quarters) about highly experienced industry experts being parachuted into failing organisations to help them turnaround their commercial fortunes. There is an adage that a management consultant is someone who borrows your watch to tell you the time and then keeps your watch. In other words, the consultant gets paid for telling the client something they already know. There will always be demand for experienced management consultants, and the quality of the consultancy work will vary, with some consultants making more of a positive impact on client organisations than others. However, broad-brush views such as these are not representative of the current management consulting industry. A cursory look at available UK management consulting industry statistics provides an indication of the importance of consultants across many industries and sectors. The Management Consultancies Association (which is the UK's representative body for management consultancies) estimated that total UK consultancy revenues exceeded £12 billion for the first time in 2020, even with the COVID-19 global pandemic. Management consulting is big business!

21.2 Overview of the Management Consulting Industry

Management consulting is an advisory activity built on the relationship between a client and a consultant. Management consultants are regarded as experts who draw on a professional knowledge base to help their clients solve various types of problems which they may be experiencing or assist with exploiting a commercial or other opportunity. Consultants are often in demand with clients when the service the consultant offers is beyond the experience or capabilities of the client organisation, such as that organisation not having the required subject matter or technical expertise within its ranks.

Whilst this is a useful starting point to our understanding of management consultancy, the industry is more complex. As noted by Srinivasan (2014), the industry is fragmented, with some very large multi-national consultancies to many smaller consultancies, including individual consultants. The industry is also unregulated, unlike other professional services such as accountancy and law. Finally, there are a huge variety of services provided by consultants, many of which are constantly evolving. Given this diversity, it is tricky to define 'management consulting'. Attempts have been made. A useful definition is provided by the Management Consultancies Association (2021). On their website, they define management consulting as 'the practice of creating value for organisations through improved performance, achieved by providing objective advice and implementing business solutions'. This definition includes important aspects which relate to consulting in practice, as follows:

- Consultants should try to create value for their clients. After all, the client will expect a 'return' for their fees, which can be substantial in the case of the larger consultancy projects and programmes.
- The consultant's advice should be practical and deliverable. Clients do not want a nice looking, chunky report that sits and gets dusty on a shelf for years. They require solutions that will help improve their performance, now and in the future.
- The advice should be objective, which involves consultants giving impartial advice based on reliable and valid evidence. 'Know-it-all' consultants rarely last long, as clients have increasingly high expectations and demands of the quality of advice they receive.

Clients come from the private, public, not-for-profit, voluntary, and charity sectors. Each sector has specific market, organisational, financial, and other challenges and opportunities which influence their requirements for management consultancy services, whether it be to help them start-up, grow, or survive.

Management consultants get paid fees for their services. There are different types of fee arrangements between clients and their consultants. These vary according to the type of assignment, including its complexity and the length of time the consultant is involved, as well as other factors such as the budget the client has available to fund the fees. Common fee arrangements include the following, although in some instances a consultant might work for a combination of these arrangements:

- **Time and materials fees**. This is where the client agrees to pay a set daily or hourly rate, plus project expenses such as travel. Consultants invoice their clients for this rate based on the time worked (e.g. £600 per day for ten days of work results in an invoice for £6,000). If the consultancy is VAT registered, VAT will be added to their invoice. This arrangement involves the consultant invoicing the client on a regular basis for the period their advice is provided. A risk to the client here is that consultancy fees can increase quickly over a short period (e.g. if the consultant spends more time on the project than the client expected). This means that the client will need to carefully monitor the time being spent by the consultant on the project.
- **Fixed fees**. Under this arrangement, a fixed fee is agreed before the start of the work between the client and consultant for a specific output (e.g. a feasibility study report). The consultant invoices for this fee regardless of how much time it took to complete the work. From the client's perspective, a benefit of this approach is that they know precisely how much they are going to pay for the services of the consultant. This minimises the risk of unexpected fees. From the point of view of the consultant, it is important to plan effectively to ensure they can complete the work within the fixed fee.
- **Risk and reward fees** (sometimes called 'performance-based fees'). This involves the client and consultant sharing the risk and reward of a large project or programme. The client might pay a small, fixed fee, but then additional fees are based on how successful the consultant's involvement has been (i.e. a performance-related element to the fees). For example, the consultant could be appointed by a local authority to advise on the transformation of their leisure and sport service so that it can deliver a high-quality service (e.g. leisure centres, sport development, and public parks), but at a lower cost of delivery, due to a reduction in the available budget within the Council. The fees could be based on a percentage of identified cost (efficiency) savings created by the consultant's work. The benefits of this arrangement to the client include the consultant being incentivised to find cost savings and improve the efficiency of the service, and – if not – they will not get paid.

This reduces the need for the local authority to dip into precious financial reserves for consultancy fees or divert revenue from other Council budgets, which could be large in the case of challenging and complex transformation programmes.

- **Retainer fees.** Here, the client pays a regular fixed amount to retain the services of the consultant. This fee arrangement ensures the consultant is available when the client needs their services. This option would be appropriate where there is demand for a particular consultant's expertise and a client wants ready access to this as and when they require it.

In some cases, consultants will work for clients free of charge (often termed 'pro bono'). This type of work might be undertaken for clients from the voluntary and charity sectors who have projects that will make a positive social or community impact. Many of the larger consultancies have Corporate Social Responsibility programmes which focus on helping local communities. Independent consultants might also undertake pro-bono work for a cause that is close to their heart.

Key terms

Client – a person or organisation that pays fees for the services of a management consultant. Clients 'appoint' or 'commission' consultants, often through the agreement of a consultancy contract (which confirms the terms and conditions of the consultancy assignment, including the scope or work, fees, and timescales).

Fees – the remuneration paid by clients for the services provided by management consultants.

Independent or individual consultant – someone who works as a management consultant. They are sometimes called freelancers.

Management consultancy – the organisation that employs management consultants. Sometimes called 'consultancy firms'.

Management consultant – an individual or organisation that offers consultancy services to clients. Within the larger consultancies, there are different roles, ranging from junior consultants (e.g. researchers and analysts), up to consultants, managers, senior managers, directors, and partners. The job titles vary from consultancy to consultancy, but there is often a hierarchy.

Project – a task that has a clearly defined start and end point (e.g. the completion of a business plan for a client).

Programme – a group of interrelated projects managed in a coordinated manner to generate benefits that would not be available if the projects were managed on an individual, project-by-project basis (e.g. the implementation of a new Customer Relationship Management system across a multi-national company).

Services (sometimes referred to as 'service lines' by consultancies) – the work offered by consultants to assist clients.

Tender – a formal invitation to bid for consultancy work, which is prepared and issued by the client. The purpose of tendering is for the client to get the best value for money by selecting the most appropriate consultant for their project based on factors such as the consultant's experience and fees. Tenders can be issued by private, public, and other clients. There are strict rules and regulations associated with public sector tenders, as discussed in more detail later in this chapter.

21.3 Size of the UK Management Consulting Industry

The UK has one of the largest and most active management consulting industries in the world. Based on estimates provided by the Management Consultancies Association, Figure 21.1 illustrates how industry revenues have increased from £7 billion in 2011 to £12.5 billion in 2020, representing a growth of 79% of this period. At the time of writing, the Management Consultancies Association suggests that there will be continued growth in 2021, as many organisations implement plans that were put on hold because of COVID-19, as well as reflecting the general growth in the UK economy as it recovers from the pandemic.

UK management consulting revenues have grown quickly over the past few years. Figure 21.2 shows that the growth in consulting revenues outpaced the growth of the UK economy, as measured by gross domestic product (GDP). Research undertaken by the European Federation of Management Consultancies Associations (2020) found that the fastest growing segment of the consulting industry over recent years has been information technology (including digital transformation), as many organisations look to improve their business processes and activities through improved technology. Other fast-growing areas of consultancy have been sales and marketing, finance, strategy, and operations. The COVID-19 pandemic did not stop the growth of the industry, as it seems that many organisations turned to consultants to help them through the challenges posed by the pandemic. For example, although

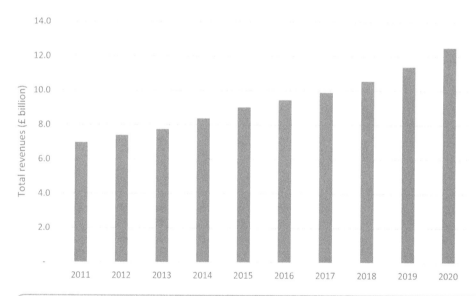

Figure 21.1 Total UK management consulting industry revenues, 2011 to 2020.

Note: The annual Management Consultancies Association estimates are based on the revenues generated by its members and non-members.

Source: Information published on the Management Consultancies Association's website

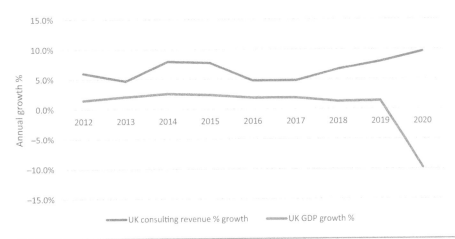

Figure 21.2 **UK management consulting industry annual revenue growth versus UK gross domestic product annual growth, 2012 to 2020.**

Source: Author-generated based on information from the Management Consultancies Association and Office for National Statistics (2021)

UK GDP decreased by 9.8% between 2019 and 2020, management consultancy revenues grew by 9.6%.

Demand for management consultancy services has therefore remained strong, even during the turbulent economy of recent years. This has created challenges for clients from across the sport and leisure sector. For example, many organisations have had to deal with increased competitive rivalry due to consumers having less disposable income and being more selective of their spending on discretionary activities such as leisure (Deloitte, 2019). The public sector has experienced budget cuts over the past decade or so (as part of the government's austerity programme), which has resulted in reduced expenditure by local authorities across all their services. As local authorities in England and Wales must legally provide services such as education, children, and adult social care, planning and housing, road maintenance, waste collection, and library services (termed 'statutory services'), this has put severe pressure on other (non-statutory) activities such as sport and leisure. The legal contexts for local authorities are different in Scotland and Northern Ireland. Regardless, many councils have had to make tough financial decisions over recent years. This has led to smaller sport and leisure service budgets in many areas, which has created challenges around how to keep delivering this important service with less financial and other resources.

The challenging economic environment has also resulted in many sporting and leisure not-for-profit organisations and charities having to work with reduced budgets because of competition for grants and reductions in sources of finance such as donations and sponsorship.

Even against this volatile economic backdrop (which has been compounded by COVID-19 since early 2020), demand for consulting services from the private, public, and voluntary sectors has been strong over recent years. Many organisations have sought external assistance to help them identify and implement cost savings, investment opportunities to grow revenues, new management and operating arrangements, business transformation programmes, and new information technology systems.

21.4 The Structure of the UK Management Consulting Industry

The UK management consulting industry is fragmented. There are many types and sizes of management consultancies, reflecting the variety of work undertaken and the diverse client base. Whilst some consultants work for themselves, others are employed by consultancy companies and firms. According to the Management Consultancies Association, there were 80,000 people employed within the management consulting industry in 2019, of which 75,200 were consultants and 4,800 were support staff. These employees worked within different types of management consultancy, such as the following:

- **Consultancies that are part of a larger accountancy or other professional services firm** – These include the 'Big 4' accountancies which have large, financially focused consultancy teams, namely PwC, Deloitte, EY, and KPMG. These firms are referred to as the Big 4 because they are global and generate the largest revenues from their various accounting and other services they provide, including consultancy. In the UK, this category also includes the smaller accountancy firms such as BDO, Grant Thornton, and RSM, all of which have consultancy teams. These firms have consultants who will complete sport and leisure sector work. Also included in this category are other professional service firms which provide consultancy services to the sport and leisure sector within their portfolios, such as chartered surveyors, property advisors, cost consultants, project managers, planning advisors, and architects. Examples of these include Colliers, Knight Frank, Savills, Avison Young, CBRE, Gardiner & Theobald, Faithful and Gould, Lichfields, Arup, and AECOM, although there are many more.
- **'Pure' management consultancies** – These are management consultancies that only provide consultancy services. They will work with clients from all sectors and often have a specialism around a particular business function, such as strategy (e.g. McKinsey & Company, Bain & Company, and Boston Consulting Group), human resources (e.g. Korn Ferry, GameShift, and Mercer), or information technology (e.g. Atos Consulting). However, there are some pure management consultancies that offer services across different functions (e.g. Accenture and Baringa Partners). This category also includes many of the independent consultants and smaller consultancies which have a particular functional and/or sector specialism (e.g. a management consultant that specialises in providing financial and commercial services to clients from the sport and leisure sector).
- **Consultancies that are part of information technology companies** – These consultants help organisations implement and maximise information technology, which can involve systems' analysis, design, implementation, cost effectiveness, and administration/management (e.g. Fujitsu and IBM Consulting).

Each year, the *Financial Times* completes a survey of the leading UK management consultancies based on recommendations from clients and peers. Based on this research, management consultancies are ranked by sector and services provided. Whilst the *Financial Times* does not focus specifically on the sport and leisure sector, possibly because it only makes up a relatively small amount of total management consulting industry revenues, the survey is a useful source of information for both clients, and those looking to start their careers within the industry. The 2021 rankings can be found via the *Financial Times* website (www.ft.com).

Based on research undertaken by Source Global Research (consulting.uk, 2018), one-fifth of UK consulting revenues are generated by independent consultants such as freelancers. The benefits cited by clients for appointing independent consultants – over bigger consultancy firms – include flexibility, price, quality, and ease/speed of contracting. Conversely, the larger consultancies can be attractive to clients for more complex consultancy projects and programmes, where they have greater resources, a broader range of available expertise, and their brand names give credibility and comfort (e.g. financial consulting, regulatory/compliance work, and business transformation).

21.5 Roles Played by Management Consultants

The scale of revenue-growth within the UK management consulting industry indicates the continued demand for consultancy services. The key question is, 'Why do clients need management consultants?' There is no simple answer, as clients commission consultants for various reasons, as discussed previously. Wickham and Wilcock (2020) provide a useful summary of the various roles that consultants offer to clients, as follows:

- **Providing specialist expertise** – Organisations rarely have all the necessary skills and experience to be able to perform the various activities they need to be successful. This means they sometimes must seek external advice and support in specialist areas such as strategy, finance and accounting, sales and marketing, operations, human resources, information and technology, and risk management.
- **Providing a new perspective** – Consultants can help clients by challenging existing behaviour and decision-making within the organisation and helping to solve problems by bringing in experience gained from working on other consultancy projects (i.e. offering a fresh industry-wide approach or alternative perspective to the problem).
- **Providing support for internal arguments** – If there is disagreement over a particular course of action within the organisation, a consultant can provide objective and impartial advice (i.e. an external perspective on a business problem that the board of a company has been debating over).
- **Providing support for gaining a critical resource** – Consultants can help organisations attract resources to support growth, including loans from banks; investment from venture capitalists and other investors; grants from the public sector; people with particular skills and knowledge; and specialist materials, equipment, or services (e.g. new information technology).
- **Facilitating organisational change** – All organisations undergo change (e.g. a change in strategic focus of the business, changing the structure of the business, or changing the operating practices). This can sometimes be faced with resistance from staff, even when it is in the best interests of the company. Consultants can help manage this change by providing external advice and support. This area of consultancy is called 'change management'.

Consultants perform these roles throughout all functions of organisations. The European Federation of Management Consultancies Associations summarise the different types of services offered in relation to key business functions, as shown in Table 21.1. Additionally, the split by business function of the UK's total £11.4 billion consulting fees in 2019 is shown. This illustrates how 'technology' was the biggest segment, followed by 'people and change', 'strategy', and 'operations'. Table 21.1 by no means includes the complete range of consultancy services but illustrates the types of services offered to support the business functions of organisations across all sectors, including sport and leisure.

Table 21.1 A Classification of Management Consulting Services and UK Fee Income, 2019

Business function	% of total UK consulting fee income (2019)	Reason for consultant's involvement	Examples of consulting services
Technology	34%	Helping organisations understand their technology requirements.	Services to assist organisations in evaluating their information technology and digital strategies with the objective of aligning technology with business processes. These services include strategic support for decisions related to the planning and implementation of new technologies for business applications, including Information Technology Network and Security and Data Centre architecture.
People and change	17%	Helping clients attract, retain, and develop talent, which is extremely important within competitive employment sectors, including sport and leisure.	Services to help organisations in dealing with the effects that change has on the human element of the organisation (e.g. Change Management), which also includes Human Resources Consulting, targeting the improvement of the 'people' element of an organisation through Human Resource strategies, performance measurement, benefits, compensation and retirement schemes, talent development programmes, and executive coaching.

Strategy	13%	Working with clients to develop strategy, either at a corporate level or business unit level.

Clients of all types have various reasons for developing a new strategy. This might include growing its products and services within its existing markets, expanding into new markets, developing new products or services, and creating a more efficient and effective operating model (e.g. reorganisation of the company's structure). | Services to support organisations in analysing and redefining their strategies, improving their business operations, and optimising their corporate and business planning, business modelling, market analysis and strategy development.

It also includes governance of major organisation redesigns, including company-wide transformation and restructuring programmes and strategic advisory in major financial transactions (e.g. mergers and acquisitions). |
| Operations | 13% | By way of example, sports' equipment manufacturing industry clients might require assistance across all parts of operations' management, including manufacturing, purchasing, logistics, and customer relationship management. | Services related to the integration of business solutions through Business Process Re-engineering, customer/supplier relationship management, turnaround/cost reduction, purchasing and supply chain management, including manufacturing, research and development, product development, and logistics. |

(Continued)

Table 21.1 (Continued)

Business function	% of total UK consulting fee income (2019)	Reason for consultant's involvement	Examples of consulting services
Finance	11% (This relates to fees from both finance consulting and risk management consulting.)	Clients may require assistance to improve the efficiency of their finance function, cash management, revenue growth whilst controlling costs, corporate transactions, and investment decisions.	Services to support organisations in analysing and redefining their financial decision-making, planning, budgeting, and performance management. For example, feasibility analysis, business planning, capital investment advice, corporate finance, corporate transaction services (such as corporate valuations, due diligence, and post-merger integration), tax advice, financial regulatory assistance, real estate advisory, and forensic and litigation advice.
Risk management		Helping clients ensure their organisation manages financial, operational and others risks, as well as complying with relevant financial and other regulations.	Services to improve the capabilities in identifying, measuring, and managing organisational risks ('enterprise risk management'). Services to ensure compliance with relevant regulations, including data protection and cyber security.

Sales and marketing	2%	Advising on the development of a marketing strategy and the implementation of this strategy. Organisations can benefit from external assistance to better understand customer needs and behaviours, competitors, and distribution channels.	Services to evaluate and redesign sales and marketing activities in terms of customer insight (including market research), relationship management, sales and channel management, product portfolio management and branding, and digital marketing.
Other services	10%		All other types of services, of which there are many (e.g. economic, social, and environmental impact studies, and other specialist services).
TOTAL	100%		

Source: Author's adaptation of the European Federation of Management Consultancies Associations' classification of consultancy services. The UK revenue shares are based on figures from the Management Consultancies Association, which were quoted in the European Federation of Management Consultancies Associations' Survey of European Management Consulting, 2020.

There is little published academic or industry research that specifically focuses on the size and significance of management consulting within the UK's sport and leisure sector. The sector is often included within other categories researched by the likes of the UK's Management Consultancies Association and the European Federation of Management Consultancies Associations, including 'retail and leisure' (which includes commercial leisure such as bars, restaurants, and cinemas, but merged with the retail sector), and 'government and the public sector' (which includes local authority sport, leisure, culture, and tourism sector consultancy work). At the time of writing, the author is not aware of any estimate of the specific value of sport and leisure consulting in the UK. However, it is evident that consultants are active across the sport and leisure sector, with many consultancies specialising in providing advice to this sector. The Big 4 (PwC, Deloitte, EY, and KPMG), certain other accountancies (e.g. BDO, Grant Thornton, and PKF), and other professional services firms have sport, leisure, hospitality, entertainment, and/or tourism sector specialists within their consultancy teams. In addition, there are many highly experienced individual consultants and consultancies across the UK that specialise in the sport and leisure sector and its sub-sectors, such as community sport and leisure, commercial leisure, arts and culture, hotels, hospitality, entertainment, conferences, travel, and tourism, to name but a few areas of specialism.

21.6 The Management Consulting Process

Management consulting activities can be considered in terms of a process. Although each consultancy has their own approach to finding and delivering work (sometimes with their own terminology), there are common stages. There are often four main stages of the consulting process, namely finding the work, winning the work, doing the work, and reviewing the work. Within each stage, there are various important tasks. The tasks will vary from one consultancy project to the next (as each project will have specific objectives, client requirements, deadlines, and outputs). However, the following gives an indication of the types of tasks which are typical within each stage:

- **Finding the work** – The first stage is to develop services that the consultants think specific clients will find valuable and be prepared to pay for. For example, the services could be focused on one of the business functions outlined in Table 21.1 (i.e. technology, people and change, strategy, operations, finance, risk management, or sales and marketing). Consultants promote these services through their websites, social media, networking, and writing articles and industry reports ('thought leadership'), as well as looking to build relationships and rapport with target clients. An objective of this stage is to identify consulting projects and other fee-earning opportunities. In terms of public sector clients, this includes formal Invitation to Tenders, which are published on public sector tender websites, so that the tenders are widely available for consultants who might be interested in tendering. Regarding the private sector, opportunities can be identified through getting to know and building trust with potential clients to get an insight into their business problems and opportunities for which they might seek external help, as private sector consultancy opportunities are rarely advertised publicly.
- **Winning the work** – This is often the most challenging stage, as the consultancy market is extremely competitive, including within the sport and leisure sector. The tasks within this stage will vary depending on whether the client is from the private, public, or another sector and the complexity of the work. For example, it can be simpler and more straightforward for a private sector client (such as a professional football club or private health

club) to appoint a consultant than it is for a public sector client (e.g. local authority or National Government Department). This is because the public sector is dealing with tax-payers' money, so there are rigid rules and regulations associated with how they purchase external services such as management consultancy. It is common for a potential client to request a Fee Proposal from the consultant. This document will confirm the consultant's understanding of the client's requirements, the proposed scope of work, the deliverables (outputs) which the client will receive such as a report, information on the fees, and the team that will complete the work for the client. This gives the client a detailed under-standing of what they will be paying for. It is also likely that the consultant will present their proposal to the clients, which also gives the client the opportunity to ask questions. Often there can be a period of discussion and negotiation around aspects of the proposal, including the scope of work and fees. If the consultant is successful, and is formally ap-pointed, a contract is often signed between the client and consultant. They will then move to the next stage of actually 'doing the work'. However, if the consultant is unsuccessful, it is good practice to request feedback from the client, as this should help improve their proposals in the future.

- **Doing the work** – This is when the consultant completes the work for which they are being paid fees. The specific research, analysis, and other tasks will vary according to the client's objectives, scope of work, deadlines, and outputs for the assignment (an example of these is provided in the case study at the end of this chapter). However, there are some tasks that can be useful for the successful completion of consultancy projects. These in-clude the following:

  - *Preparation of a Project Initiation Document* (sometimes called the 'Project Char-ter') – This document confirms all aspects of the consultancy project prior to com-mencement. It includes confirmation of the project's objectives and scope of work, the research strategy, the team that will complete the work, the deliverables which will be produced such as a report, the timescales, and project risks (and how these will be mitigated/managed should they occur). It will also outline 'ground rules', includ-ing how the consultancy team will communicate with the client in terms of regular progress updates, project meetings, workshops, and presentations. Once the Project Initiation Document has been reviewed and approved by the client, the consultants will start the work.

  - *Utilising relevant project management tools and techniques to ensure the efficient and effective completion of the project.* These might include a project plan (which breaks down the consultancy project into different tasks/actions and identifies the responsi-bilities of each team member to complete these), Gantt Chart (which provide a visual representation of the different project tasks and the timescales/deadlines for these), project meetings and workshops, and time management systems. Time management systems are particularly important within larger consultancies to ensure consultants are being productive (i.e. utilised on client work) and are focused on fee-earning work. Each project often has a budget and associated utilisation targets for each consultant. This helps the consultancy monitor the financial performance of different types of work.

  - *Completing the research and analysis tasks to inform the completion of the project, including providing the evidence-base for the report.* This stage involves analysing the problem or opportunity being examined and then completing the necessary research and analysis. The specific tasks will vary from project to project, as they will relate to the nature and purpose of the project. The evidence base for projects can come from primary and secondary research. There are various analytical tools and techniques that can then be used. Commonly used examples include operational and financial reviews, internal audits, internal and external benchmarking, SWOT Analysis, PESTLE Analysis, Porter's Five Forces, Balanced Scorecard, Boston Consulting Group Matrix, Ansoff Matrix, scenario analysis, options appraisals, statistical and financial modelling, data analytics, and risk analysis. These are only some of the tools and techniques employed by consultants. There are many more. In some cases, consultancies have their own proprietary tools and techniques which they have developed and use. The research and analysis completed should be relevant and produce reliable and valid information upon which the report's conclusions and recommendations are based.

- *Many consulting projects require the completion of a written report*, which is often presented formally to the client upon completion of the work. In many instances, clients will want to see a draft version of the report so they can review and feedback comments for consideration by the consultants for inclusion in the final version of the document.

- **Reviewing the work** – Once the project has been completed, it is good practice to evaluate the success of the project by formally requesting feedback from the client. After all, the success of a consultancy project should be based on how satisfied the client is. Such post-project dialogue shows the client that the consultant values their relationship. It also helps pave the way for potential follow-on work by the consultant, assuming the client was happy. Such feedback should also help improve the services for other clients. Not all consultancy work is successful (there can be unhappy clients!), so understanding the reasons for this is extremely useful for both the client and consultant, as it should help both parties in the future. If the client was happy with the work, they might provide an endorsement which the consultant can use as part of their promotional activities for future work.

Figure 21.3 provides a summary of the main stages of a typical management consulting process, from finding the work through to its completion.

21.7 Public Sector Clients in the Sport and Leisure Sector

Government and the wider public sector are a major buyer of consultancy services. The public sector is diverse. In brief, the public sector includes central government (both at the UK level and within each of the nations which make up the UK), local authorities, and the many agencies and other bodies which support central and local government. The specific roles central and local government play within sport and leisure was discussed in Chapter 5.

In 2018, the public sector accounted for 22% of consultancy revenues in the UK, spending £2.3 billion on fees (European Federation of Management Consultancies Associations, 2019). Whilst sport and leisure-related consulting comprises a relatively small percentage of these total fees, the public sector is an active market for consultants, as sport, leisure, arts, culture, heritage, and tourism are important sectors for various parts of the public sector (given the positive community, social, economic, and other impacts generated). Local authorities are an important client base for many consultants, as they have a large scope of leisure and related services ranging from the provision of indoor and outdoor sport and leisure facilities and activities, tourism services, entertainment, and other community services (e.g. play centres, community halls, and urban farms).

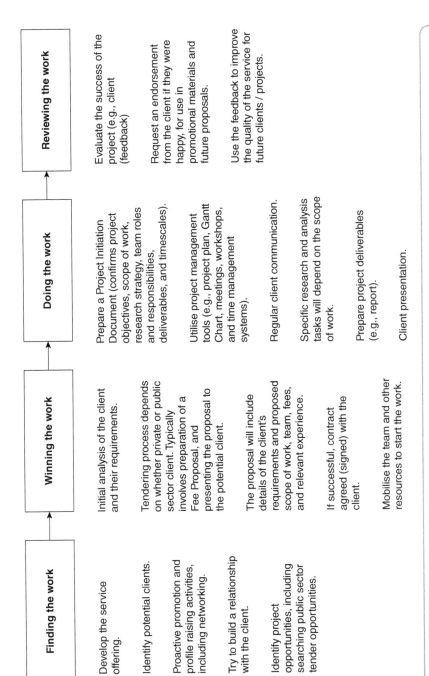

Finding the work

Develop the service offering.

Identify potential clients.

Proactive promotion and profile raising activities, including networking.

Try to build a relationship with the client.

Identify project opportunities, including searching public sector tender opportunities.

Winning the work

Initial analysis of the client and their requirements.

Tendering process depends on whether private or public sector client. Typically involves preparation of a Fee Proposal, and presenting the proposal to the potential client.

The proposal will include details of the client's requirements and proposed scope of work, team, fees, and relevant experience.

If successful, contract agreed (signed) with the client.

Mobilise the team and other resources to start the work.

Doing the work

Prepare a Project Initiation Document (confirms project objectives, scope of work, research strategy, team roles and responsibilities, deliverables, and timescales).

Utilise project management tools (e.g., project plan, Gantt Chart, meetings, workshops, and time management systems).

Regular client communication.

Specific research and analysis tasks will depend on the scope of work.

Prepare project deliverables (e.g., report).

Client presentation.

Reviewing the work

Evaluate the success of the project (e.g., client feedback)

Request an endorsement from the client if they were happy, for use in promotional materials and future proposals.

Use the feedback to improve the quality of the service for future clients / projects.

Examples of the tasks during each stage

Figure 21.3 An example of the management consulting process.

Because it is such a large market for management consultants, it is necessary to examine, albeit briefly, public sector procurement. For those readers with a burning desire to know more about public sector procurement, there are many useful information sources, including the websites of UK government, and the Local Government Association.

Procurement is the process of acquiring services, goods, and works, which includes the services of management consultants (Local Government Association, 2019). The world of public sector procurement is complex. It is a highly regulated area, as public sector organisations are dealing with taxpayers' money. Public sector bodies have a responsibility to ensure the best value for money for the taxpayer, as well as optimising the social value from the consultant's involvement (i.e. maximising the benefits of the consultancy project for local communities, economy, and the environment, where possible). Public sector clients cannot therefore just appoint management consultants. These bodies must adhere to various rules to ensure fairness and transparency in the way that the tender process is conducted.

Some charities must also adhere to public sector procurement rules. This includes charities that receive substantial funding from public sector bodies such as central government or local authorities (i.e. more than 50% of their funding from these sources) or have more than half of their Trustee Board appointed by such public sector bodies. Other charities have more flexibility with regard the procurement of consulting services, although they will still seek value for money.

Local authorities often publish Invitation to Tenders for sport and leisure consultancy work. Invitation to tenders from local authorities (and other public sector organisations) usually include defined requirements of the consultant's tender (proposal). When looking to work for local authorities and other public sector bodies, consultants must prepare a tender, and often have to compete for projects against other consultants. This competition can be intense. It is common for multiple tenders to be received for consultancy projects, even if these projects have a relatively low fee. Consultancies can incur significant costs when tendering and end up unsuccessful. Because of this, consultants often carefully analyse ('qualify') tender opportunities before deciding whether to bid or not, by asking themselves various questions which will help determine whether they have a reasonable chance of being successful with their tender or not (e.g. How well do we know the client? Have we worked for the client previously? If so, was our previous work successful? Do we have relevant experience? Are other consultancies better placed to win this project than us?).

The tenders received are evaluated by the client against various criteria, including the price (fees) and quality (e.g. how well the consultant addresses the requirements of the client's Brief and the relevant experience of the team). Sometimes, the local authority will short-list the highest scoring tenders and invite the consultancies in to present their proposals and answer various questions from the client team. After this, the successful consultant will be identified and appointed.

For the largest contracts, UK public sector procurement rules were heavily influenced by the European Union. Tenders over a certain value threshold had to be advertised on the Official Journal of the European Union (OJEU). However, Brexit has changed this. As of 1st January 2021, the UK government put its own procurement rules in place, which replace the European Union's regulations. These changes include the creation of a new e-notification service called 'Find a Tender', where the largest tenders must be advertised rather than OJEU. The existing tender portals from across the UK will remain in place (e.g. Public Contracts Scotland, Sell2Wales, and eTendersNI). There are other changes which aim to make it easier for smaller consultancies to bid for public sector work.

Even with these changes in the way the public sector will procure management consultants, there will continue to be strict rules and regulations because of the principles of best value, fairness, and transparency. This means that consultants will still be competing for work, the process will be long and sometimes arduous, and there is a risk that after expending significant time and resources, they might be unsuccessful. On the other hand, the attraction of public sector consultancy contracts is huge, particularly given the scale of their expenditure on consultancy services each year, and with public sector bodies continuing to be an important provider of sport and leisure services across the UK, and the likelihood that this will generate demand for the services of management consultants in the future.

21.8 The Skills Required by Management Consultants

With the wide range of clients and consultancy services, there is no single set of skills required to be a management consultant. As noted by Newton (2019), communication is a core skill of management consultants, as the way consultants talk, present, and write is key to their success. The range of skills can be categorised in terms of personal and interpersonal skills, and technical and analytical skills. The technical and analytical skills required will vary by the type of consultancy. For example, KPMG require consultants that are proficient with numbers and have financial acumen, as much of their work involves providing financial-related advice, whereas a technology consultant will require a different set of analytical skills. Table 21.2 illustrates some of the skills required.

21.9 Career Opportunities with Management Consulting?

There are various reasons for considering a career in management consultancy. According to Inside Careers (2018), these reasons include the diversity of the projects, ongoing training opportunities, competitive salaries, promotion prospects, as well as other reasons such as the opportunity to work in different countries. Because of this, it is often competitive to get a job within the management consulting industry, particularly if you wish to work within a particular sector such as sport and leisure where the number of industry-specific consultancies is limited, as many of the teams are small.

There are various routes to start a career in management consultancy. When considering management consulting as a career, it is important to consider the focus, size, culture, and working style of the different consultancies, as each will be different. In addition to advertised job opportunities, particularly experienced professionals can often get 'head hunted' to join consultancies.

For a student looking to enter the management consulting industry, there are two main routes, as follows:

- A large, global consultancy might offer a broader range of opportunities in terms of projects, team size, and location. The biggest consultancy firms have hundreds, if not thousands, of consultants across multiple offices, and offer many services to different sectors. Many of these consultancies have graduate schemes to recruit and train junior consultants. A few examples of consultancies with graduate schemes during 2020 and 2021 are KPMG, Deloitte, PwC, EY, Grant Thornton, BDO, McKinsey and Company, Boston Consulting Group, Bain and Company, Kearney, PA Consulting, and Capgemini. The entry requirements for graduate programmes typically involves a first-class or upper-second

Table 21.2 Examples of Management Consulting Skills

Type of skill	Examples of specific skills
Personal and interpersonal skills	● Communication ● Problem identification and solving skills ● Confidence and ability to build client relationships ● Ability to work successfully individually and in teams ● Effective listening skills ● Flexibility to be able to work on multiple projects at the same time ● Time management, as meeting a deadline is critical to the success of consultancy projects (This can mean regular reprioritisation of tasks to meet client deadlines, especially when working for more than one client at the same time, which is common.) ● Enthusiasm and energy, as the projects can be complex and challenging ● Professionalism, as clients expect a high quality of service and output for their fees ● Emotional intelligence and empathy (e.g. recognising and reflecting on the client's perspective but remaining objective) ● Resilience, as it is important to keep on going even when things do not go as expected (e.g. if a client brings forward the deadline for report due to an unforeseen issue within their organisation)
Technical and analytical skills	These will depend on the type of consulting work, but could include: ● Ability to get to analyse and get to grips with client issues quickly ● Proficiency with qualitative and quantitative data collection and analysis methods ● Knowledge and application of various strategic and other analysis and planning tools and techniques ● Project management ● Interviewing (e.g. consultations to gather data) ● Numeracy and proficiency with the analysis of financial, economic, and other statistics ● Reporting writing ● Preparing high-impact presentation documents

degree, or a postgraduate qualification such as a Master of Business Administration. Whilst many consultancies do not have specific requirements for the academic discipline studied, some prefer graduates from related subjects such as mathematics, economics, finance, accounting, business, and management in the case of strategy and finance-related graduate schemes, or technology-based subjects in relation to information technology consultancies. In addition to work experience, high-quality graduate programmes will offer graduates the opportunity to gain professional qualifications in accountancy, marketing, or project management. The competition for these graduate programmes can be intense and the application process challenging, often involving interviews, numerical tests, and other individual and group assessment tasks.

- The many smaller, niche consultancies (often with less than 20 employees) can offer different opportunities, such as a chance to work on particular types of work within a specific sector. Being part of a smaller organisation means that there can be opportunities to undertake a broader range of tasks on projects. These consultancies may not offer formal graduate schemes, but they do regularly advertise for new consultants across all levels – including junior research consultants and analysts – as well potentially responding to speculative approaches, if they are looking to recruit.

If you are currently a student and think that management consulting might be a career option, you could dip your toe in the world of consultancy during your course. It is possible for business, management, and other students – on undergraduate and postgraduate courses – to gain experience of management consulting through internships, work placements, and work-based projects that form part of their degree. The benefits of this approach are that (1) it gives the student experience of consulting, to see whether it appeals to them or not, and (2) it is a way of 'opening the door' to consultancies (possibly without being paid!), so they can assess the student's performance. If the student does well (e.g. works hard and becomes useful, or even indispensable), the consultancy may well offer employment upon graduation.

A quick search of the internet will identify the many management consultancies that specialise in providing services to the sport and leisure sector in the UK, and the various segments including community sport, professional sport, arts and culture, hotels, hospitality, and tourism.

21.10 The Future of the UK Management Consulting Industry

At the time of writing, the UK has entered 2021 in a 'post-Brexit world' whilst continuing to face the economic challenges caused by COVID-19. As shown over recent years, economic disruption has created demand for the services provided by management consultants from across the private, public, not-for-profit, voluntary, and charity sectors. No one is saying that management consultants are the 'magic wand' for the success of all organisations, but they have been shown to help many of their clients.

How the UK management consulting industry will develop over the next few years is difficult to predict, not least because of the uncertainty facing the future growth of the UK's economy (you only have to have a quick look at the different GDP growth forecasts for the next few years to see this!) and what this means for the sport and leisure sector and its component parts. However, it is safe to say that whilst organisations need help solving their problems or exploiting opportunities, there will be a role for management consultants.

A Sport and Leisure Sector Consulting Project

The case study provides an example of a sport and leisure sector consulting project completed on behalf of a local authority client.

Title of the project

A market and financial feasibility study on proposals for a new community leisure centre.

The client

A large city council in the North of England.

Fees

Fixed fees of less than £25,000 excluding VAT.

How the consultant was selected

The Council advertised the Invitation to Tender on their e-tendering system in 2021. The Council received six tenders from interested consultancies, which were evaluated against criteria such as price and quality of the tenders. After short-listing, three consultancies were invited to present their proposals to the Council and answer questions about their tenders.

The preferred consultancy was then appointed, and a contract signed between the Council and the consultancy. As soon as the contract was signed, the consultant started their work.

The Council's requirements for this consulting project

The Council owned a site near the city centre, which they wanted to develop a new, state-of-the-art community leisure centre that will meet the needs of residents now and in the future.

An over-riding objective of the Council was for the new leisure centre to both maximise usage and participation and generate sufficient income so that it operates without any subsidy from the Council (i.e. at least break even at operating profit level). This was a challenging objective, but necessary as the Council was under severe financial pressures, with a reducing budget for its sport and leisure service.

The specific issues the Council wanted to be addressed by the consultants were as follows:

- Is the site appropriate for a leisure centre such as this?
- What facilities and activities should the new leisure centre have, including both community facilities, as well as more commercial activities which could generate profitable income?
- How much could this leisure centre cost to build, and how could these costs be funded?

- What is the optimum programming and pricing?
- What is the likely Profit and Loss statement for the new leisure centre?
- What are the most appropriate optimum management and operating arrangements (e.g. directly operated by the Council or managed by a third-party leisure operator on behalf of the Council)?
- What are the main commercial and financial risks which will need to be considered, and what impact could these have on financial performance should they occur?
- What other issues will the Council need to consider if it was to progress with the development of this leisure centre?

21.10.1 The Work Undertaken by the Consultant to Meet the Council's Requirements

In order to address the client's issues, a comprehensive, evidence-based approach was developed by the consultant that included (1) an evaluation of the potential site (e.g. size, layout, accessibility, and visibility); (2) review of available research, analysis, and intelligence (e.g. including research undertaken to investigate community leisure needs and the current pricing, programming, and performance of other Council-owned leisure centres); (3) consultations with local stakeholders and National Governing Bodies to get their views on the potential for the project and explore possible funding options; (4) assessment of the current and anticipated future supply of public, private, and charity sector leisure provision across the city to identify market opportunities; (5) identification of gaps in provision now and in the future which could be exploited by the new leisure centre using catchment area analysis tools including those produced by commercial suppliers (to understand the profile and leisure buying behaviour of local residents) and a review of national leisure trends; (6) assessment of 'comparable' leisure centres from across the UK in order to identify key characteristics and potential implications for this project (e.g. facility mix, capital costs and funding sources, management and operating arrangements, pricing and programming, and commercial performance); (7) appraisal of the different facility mix and operating options to identify the preferred option for this project; (8) completion of a financial appraisal that comprises capital cost estimates and possible funding sources, and a projection of possible Profit and Loss performance; (9) analysis of the financial and commercial risks associated with the project, and the ways these could be managed/mitigated should they occur; and (10) assessment of other relevant issues and the implications they could have on this project (e.g. environmental, transport, planning, design, and delivery issues).

21.10.2 The Deliverable

The output of this project was a report that detailed the findings, conclusions, and recommendations. This report was presented to the client team.

21.10.3 Timescales for the Completion of This Project

This project took three months to complete from the date of being formally appointed.

21.10.4 Completion of the Contract

Upon successful completion of the work, the consultant issued their invoice, which was paid within 30 days.

Structured Guide to Further Reading

Deloitte. (2019). *Experience is Everything – the UK Leisure Consumer*. Deloitte, London.
European Federation of Management Consultancies Associations. (2019). *Survey of European Management Consultancy, 2018–19*. FEACO, Brussels, Belgium.
European Federation of Management Consultancies Associations. (2020). *Survey of European Management Consultancy, 2019–20*. FEACO, Brussels, Belgium.
Inside Careers. (2018). *The Official Graduate Career Guide to Management Consultancy, 2017 to 2018*. Inside Careers, London.
Local Government Association. (2019). *A Councillor's Guide to Procurement*. Local Government Association, London.
Newton, R. (2019). *The Management Consultant – Mastering the Art of Consultancy*, 2nd edition. FT Publishing, London.
Srinivasan, R. (2014). The management consulting industry – Growth of consulting services in India. *IIMB Management Review*, 26, 257–270.
Wickham, L., & Wilcock, J. (2020). *Business and Management Consulting: Delivering an Effective Project*, 6th edition. Pearson, London.

Useful Websites

'Consulting.uk' is an excellent online source of UK and global management consulting information, including research published by research organisations such as the Management Consultancies Association, and Source Global Research. The website's address is: www.consultancy.uk

The *Financial Times* survey of the leading UK management consultancies is a good source of information for both clients and those looking to start their careers within the industry. The 2020 rankings can be found via the *Financial Times'* website (www.ft.com).

The Management Consultancies Association is the UK's representative body for management consultancy firms. Their website is a valuable source for information on the size and structure of management consulting industry. Their website address is: www.mca.org.uk/

Reference

Office for National Statistics. (2021). *www.ons.gov.uk*. Office for National Statistics, London, UK.

Practical Tasks

1 Search the internet to identify five UK-based management consultancies that specialise in the sport and leisure sector. What services do these consultancies offer? Who are their target clients for these services? How do they promote their services to their target clients?

2   Search the internet to find an example of a published consultancy report for a UK local authority client. What was the purpose of this report (its aims and objectives)? What research and analysis did the consultancy complete to address the aims and objectives? What were the conclusions and recommendations? Did these conclusions and recommendations meet the client's requirements?

3   In what ways do you think the UK management consultancy industry will grow and evolve over the next five years? Which consulting specialisms do you think will be most popular with clients, and why do you think that?

Index

Printed in the USA
CPSIA information can be obtained
at www.ICGtesting.com
LVHW022248270824
789488LV00005B/38